MW01054823

ROADS TO THE TEMPLE

LEON ARON

Roads to
the Temple

TRUTH, MEMORY, IDEAS, AND IDEALS IN THE MAKING

OF THE RUSSIAN REVOLUTION, 1987–1991

Yale UNIVERSITY PRESS

NEW HAVEN AND LONDON

Published with assistance from the foundation established in memory of Philip Hamilton McMillan of the Class of 1894, Yale College.

Copyright © 2012 by Leon Aron.
All rights reserved.
This book may not be reproduced, in whole or in part, including illustrations, in any form (beyond that copying permitted by Sections 107 and 108 of the U.S. Copyright Law and except by reviewers for the public press), without written permission from the publishers.

Yale University Press books may be purchased in quantity for educational, business, or promotional use. For information, please e-mail sales.press@yale.edu (U.S. office) or sales@yaleup.co.uk (U.K. office).

Set in Scala type by Westchester Book Group.
Printed in the United States of America.

Library of Congress Cataloging-in-Publication Data

Aron, Leon Rabinovich.
   Roads to the temple : truth, memory, ideas, and ideals in the making of the Russian revolution, 1987–1991 / Leon Aron.
   pages ;   cm
   Includes bibliographical references and index.
   ISBN 978-0-300-11844-5 (cloth : alkaline paper)   1. Soviet Union—History—1985–1991.
2. Glasnost.   3. Social action—Soviet Union.   4. Social change—Soviet Union.
5. Values—Soviet Union.   6. Soviet Union—Moral conditions.   7. Collective memory—
Soviet Union.   8. Soviet Union—Intellectual life—1970–1991.   I. Title.
   DK286.A76 2012
   947.0854—dc23

                                                                                    2011047918

A catalogue record for this book is available from the British Library.

This paper meets the requirements of ANSI/NISO Z39.48-1992 (Permanence of Paper).

10   9   8   7   6   5   4   3   2   1

For Carol, Andrea, Dani, and Alexandra
For Mother and Father

The invocation to historians to suppress even that minimal degree of moral or psychological insight and evaluation which is necessarily involved in viewing human beings as creatures with purposes and motives . . . seems to me to spring from a confusion of the aims and methods of the humane studies with those of natural science. . . . It becomes the business of historians to investigate who wanted what, and when, and where, in what way; how many men avoided or pursued this or that goal and with what intensity; and, further, to ask under what circumstances such wants or fears have proved effective, and to what extent, and with what consequences.

—Isaiah Berlin, *Four Essays on Liberty*

I shall begin by depicting them as they were in the heyday of the Revolution; when love of equality and the urge to freedom went hand in hand; when they wished to set up not merely a true democratic government but free institutions, not only to do away with privileges but also to make good and stabilize the rights of man, the individual. . . . That [was an] age of fervid enthusiasm, of proud and generous aspirations, whose memory, despite its extravagances, men will forever cherish: a phase of history that for many years to come will trouble the sleep of all who seek to demoralize the nation and reduce it to a servile state.

—Alexis de Tocqueville, *The Old Regime and the French Revolution*

CONTENTS

ACKNOWLEDGMENTS   ix

INTRODUCTION   1

PART ONE: REVOLUTIONS, IDEAS, AND THE END OF THE
SOVIET UNION

1 The "Mystery" of the Soviet Collapse and the Theory of
Revolutions   11

2 For Truth and Goodness: The Credos of Glasnost   36

PART TWO: КТО МЫ? WHO ARE WE?

3 Inside the "Deafened Zone"   63

4 In Search of History   71

5 "The Innocent, the Slandered, the Exterminated"   76

6 The Peasant Hecatomb   99

7 The Unraveling of the Legitimizing Myths, I: Food, Housing,
Medical Care, the "Golden Childhood," and the Standard of
Living   112

8 The Unraveling of the Legitimizing Myths, II: Progress, the
   "State of Workers and Peasants," Equality, "Freedom from
   Exploitation," Novocherkassk 131

9 The Unraveling of the Legitimizing Myths, III: The Great
   Patriotic War 151

10 The "Immoral" Economy 172

11 The "Disintegration of Souls": *Homo Sovieticus* 187

PART THREE: *КТО ВИНОВАТ?* WHO IS TO BLAME?

12 The House That Stalin Built: The Master State and Its Political
    Economy 199

13 "De-individualization," the "Original Sin," and the
    Nationalization of Conscience 210

PART FOUR: *ЧТО ДЕЛАТЬ?* WHAT IS TO BE DONE?

14 Stalin, Memory, Repentance, Atonement 223

15 The "Spirit of Freedom" and the Power of *Nyet* 236

16 The Freedom Canon: Mandelstam, Dombrovsky, Solzhenitsyn,
    Platonov, Grossman 255

17 In Man's Image, I: "Privatizing" the State and Economy 270

18 In Man's Image, II: The Empire, the "Garrison State," and the
    World 287

Epilogue 296

GLASNOST'S SIGNPOSTS: THE THEMES AND THE TEXTS 307
GLASNOST'S TROUBADOURS 321
NOTES 331
BIBLIOGRAPHY 427
INDEX 467

ACKNOWLEDGMENTS

SEVERAL LONG CONVERSATIONS with Christopher DeMuth, president of the American Enterprise Institute—who, in addition to his many other amazingly numerous and deep gifts, has the tastes and insights of a superb literary editor—shaped the initial design of this book and gave me the confidence to take it on.

Succeeding Chris as AEI's president in the last two years of the book's writing, Arthur Brooks preserved the scholarly autonomy and integrity, on which AEI is founded and without which this book, as well as many others, would not have seen the light of day. When Arthur spoke about the "moral imperative of liberty" in his superb Bradley Lecture in May 2010, he cast the essence of the book in terms that inspired me mightily at the time when I needed every ounce of energy for the final push. No matter what the final judgment on the book is, just to have attempted to describe this "moral imperative" as the book's heroes experienced it will forever give me pride and satisfaction.

David Gerson, the institute's executive vice president, saw to it that I had everything necessary for the research, and the staff support he provided was, as usual, efficient, flawless, and graceful. Vice President for Foreign Policy and Defense Studies Danielle Pletka appreciated the pressures of book writing and rejoiced as it reached completion.

My principal intellectual debt is to Bernard Bailyn's *The Ideological Origins of the American Revolution*. Bailyn's boldness in staking out the claim for the centrality of ideas in revolution and his skill in teasing patterns out of disparate texts are a model for a historian of ideas. Even on the third or fourth reading, Simon Schama's *Citizens* and Robert Darnton's *The Literary Underground of the Old Regime* were infectious in their zeal for unearthing and following the pathways of subversive ideas with elegance and wit. Isaiah Berlin's "archaeology of ideas," as always, has been an inspiration.

One of the finest American writers and critics, Cynthia Ozick, was a dear friend-at-a-distance; her own work and kind, handwritten notes inspired me to make this book as good as I possibly could.

I am grateful to Dr. Roy Lennox for our delightful phone chats and New York dinners during the past six years. For almost two decades his friendship and his generous support of my work has been a source of pride and has encouraged me to reach higher.

I also hope that, together with other products of the Russian Studies Department, Charlie Ryan finds this book good enough to justify his own generosity.

Dr. Derek Leebaert urged me to start a new book when I was still recovering from the previous one, and then found the time in his unimaginably busy schedule as a corporate executive, author, Georgetown professor, and entrepreneur to read most of the chapters. His comments were detailed, generous, and marvelously energizing. Derek's friendship and collegiality were vital at every perilous juncture.

Over five years, Nick Eberstadt's warmth, his instant understanding of the many involved subjects I was grappling with, his wonderful sense of humor, and the unfailing trust in my abilities to carry out a fairly ambitious design made our lunches a delight and a source of badly needed good cheer. Nick's comments on the first tentative drafts of chapter 1 were helpful and stimulating.

Vance Serchuk, who was very keen on my writing a "cultural history" of the latest Russian Revolution, shouldered initial research and gave me the benefit of his customary acuity. George Breslauer, Masha Lipman, Vladimir Mau, and Nikolai Petro commented on the outline of the book, and their enthusiasm strengthened my belief in the need for this work. Harley Balzer, Tim Frye, Fred Kagan, Blair Ruble, Doug Seay, and Lilia Shevtsova read the first two chapters and gave me very helpful comments. David Remnick's generous reaction to a draft of chapter 2 was most heartening, as was Jonathan Sanders's long response to the introduction. Short-lived though they turned out to be, the lunch sessions of the "writers' support group" that Mauro Di Lorenzo and I attempted to organize were most enjoyable and stimulating.

An old and dear friend, Mikhail Reznikov, made me an invaluable gift of two volumes containing every issue of *Moskovskie novosti* from 1988 and 1989—a veritable two-part Bible of glasnost. Misha also educated me on the anatomy and the cooking of *okorok* and *vetchina* (Russian hams), making the passage about the 1987 dreams of good and accessible food all the more authentic. My thanks also to Cita and Irwin Stelzer for their endless encouragement and to Cita Stelzer for introducing me to the magnificent essays and poetry of Zbigniew Herbert, with which this book ends.

Anders Åslund's and Vladimir Mau's reaction to a chapter that condensed to less than four thousand words glasnost's enormous oeuvre on the Soviet economy in the second half of the 1980s (in the knowledge of which they have few, if any, equals) made me believe that I was generally on the mark. I am grateful to Richard Tempest for helping me in my search for the best English translations of a word from Anna Akhmatova's *Requiem* and of one from Alexander Solzhenitsyn's *In the First Circle*.

I was very fortunate in having Jadwiga Rogoza, all the way from Warsaw, as a graduate research associate at AEI (and the reader of *Sovietskaya kul'tura*) and in having Assya Dosseva as my part-time research assistant. The interns Nikki Gorbanova (*Literatrurnaya gazeta*), Neal Kumar (*Kommunist*), Diana Iskelov (*Komsomol'skaya pravda*), and Diora Ziyaeva (*Moskovskie novosti*) bore the brunt of primary research. Their work was ably carried on by Angelica Anishi, Iliya Bourtman (*Argumenty i fakty*), Milana Veyner (*Sovetskaya kul'tura*), Amanda Nelson-Duac, Alexandra Prokhorova, Boris Rivkin, Kevin Thomas, Dan Doty, and Valentina Lukin. They were a remarkable group of young women and men, and the multiplicity of their origins—Azerbaijan, Bulgaria, Nigeria, Poland, Russia, Ukraine, the United States, and Uzbekistan— somehow was always marvelously inspiring.

Four superb research assistants—smart, conscientious, creative, hardworking—became full-fledged co-conspirators: Vance Serchuk, Igor

Khrestin, Kara Flook, and Kevin Rothrock. Their thoughtfulness, research excellence, and diplomatic skills have helped me enormously to juggle book writing and researching, writing, and publishing a quarterly essay (Russian Outlook), as well as essays and op-eds for "outside" publication; organizing events, including major international conferences and the regular U.S.-Russia Working Group luncheon seminars; discharging collegial obligations on panels and in book and grant reviews; giving interviews; and participating in all manner of private briefings and meeting.

In addition, Igor read several years' worth of *Moskovskie novosti,* and *Komsomol'skaya pravda.* Kara read and commented on several first chapters. In the last year of writing, Kevin Rothrock proofread some of the longest and most complicated final chapters. In addition, his questions and suggestions in the margins have clarified much in the text and made it so much more readable. Gina Lentine, who interned in Russian Studies during the last year and half of writing, was simply wonderful in the persistence and speed with which she located and copied material from Russian newspapers, magazines, and books at the Library of Congress for last-minute references and quote verifications.

It has fallen to Dan Vajdic to conclude the effort of this outstanding group with his own excellent effort. Working with me through the last phases of the project, Dan proved invaluable in assisting me with the editing of the manuscript and reading proofs. In that last job, he and I were very lucky to have the assistance of Samantha Costello, our superb intern.

In addition to the acute pleasure of speaking and hearing the Moscow Russian, the long, tri-weekly phone conversations with my mother, Dr. Ella Rabinovich, gave the inestimable benefit of a wise and infinitely supportive and loving friend.

My wife, Carol, has proofread the galley and improved it in so many ways. So has my daughter Andrea, who read and corrected during her Christmas break from college. My daughter Dani has made things much more manageable by helping to tame the PDF format. In their very presence, Carol, Andrea, and Dani were the greatest comfort a man wish for. Among other innumerable forfeitures its writing caused, this book kept me away from them every single Sunday morning, from eight to noon, for four years. A total of 832 hours. May God help me to organize the rest of my life to make up for this loss.

Introduction

IN THE FINAL SCENE OF Tengiz Abuladze's 1987 film *Pokayanie*
(Repentance)—a magnificent anti-Stalinist saga that heralded glasnost and became one of its key artistic achievements and most popular
symbols*—an older woman asks a passerby which street leads to the

---

* Its mass release coinciding with the January 1987 Plenum of the Central
Committee, at which Gorbachev inaugurated the policies of glasnost and
"democratization," *Pokoyanie* was seen by 700,000 people in the first ten days
and by 2.6 million in the first one and a half months. (Stephen Wheatcroft,
"Unleashing the Energy of History, Mentioning the Unmentionable and
Reconstructing Soviet Historical Awareness: Moscow 1987," *Australian Slavic
and Eastern European Studies*, no. 1, 1987: 101.)

   With its striking visual metaphors, *Pokoyanie* was a recurrent reference in
liberal media in 1987–88, and the "road to the temple" turned into a veritable
trope of glasnost. For instance, Igor Klyamkin titled his seminal November 1987
essay in *Novy mir*, "Which street leads to the temple?" (Kakaya ulitsa vedyot k
khramu?). The radical *Moskovksie novosti* weekly marked the fifth anniversary of
Mikhail Gorbachev's coming to power with a cover story "Five years on the road
to the temple" ("Pyat' let po doroge k khramu," April 22, 1990).

   For *Pokoyanie* in public debate, see, for example, L. Ayzerman, "Trevozhit'sya
i dumat' (To worry and to think), *Novy mir* 10, October 1987: 180–93; Lev Anninskiy, "Monolog byvshego stalintsa" (A monologue of a former Stalinist), in Kh.
Kobo, ed., *Osmyslit' kul't Stalina* (To comprehend Stalin's cult), Moscow:
Progress, 1989: 56–57; Boleslav Vol'ter, "Prozrenie idyot slishkom medlenno"

1

temple or the church (*khram*). "Not this one," she is told. "What's the use of a street," the woman then asks quietly but with conviction, "if it does not lead to the temple?"

All great revolutions begin with the search for streets, or roads, to the "temple"—a kingdom of dignity, justice, goodness, fairness, equality, freedom, brotherhood. These ideals, and ideas about how to reach them, frame revolutions, give the upheavals direction, and shape their course. Russia's latest revolution, too, began with the search for these roads, and its self-liberating quest for a better state and society is one of the most inspiring stories of our times.

Rarely, if ever, in its 1,000-year history was Russia as honest with herself as in the years between 1987 and 1991. The national scrutiny was intellectually dazzling and almost incredibly bold. A long-atheistic nation battered by terror, numbed by fear and cynicism, was forced to confront the matters of ultimate concern that inspired religious revivals and all great modern revolutions: goodness and evil, truth and falsehoods, virtue and sin, liberty and slavery, justice and tyranny. Who are we? glasnost demanded to know. Do we live honorable, dignified, moral lives, fully responsible for ourselves, our compatriots, and our country? And if not, what should we do to lead such lives? What is our real, unvarnished history? Have we been governed well? What are just, equitable relations between man and state? Is virtue possible without liberty, and could there be a just and sustainable polity and state without virtue?

Within a few years, this national soul-searching led to the rethinking of some of the most fundamental aspects of the country's existence: one-party dictatorship and state ownership of economy; the country's relations with the outside world; the legitimacy of the Soviet Union's control over east-central Europe and of Moscow's control over the constituent republics. The onrush of new ideas and ideals engendered the thirst for

(The regaining of the sight proceeds too slowly), in *Moskovskie novosti*, November 6, 1988: 2; Svyatoslav Fyodorov, "Chtoby nikogda ne povtorilos'!" (So as not to let it happen again!) *Ogonyok* 8, 1987, an insert between pp. 5 and 6. For fine detailed reviews of the film, see Boris Vasiliev, "Prozrenie" (The recovery of sight), *Sovetskiy ekran* 6, March 1987: 4–5, and N. Zorkaya, "Dorogoy, kotoraya vedyot k khramu" (By the road that leads to the temple), *Iskusstvo kino* 5, 1987: 33–53.

freedom of speech and press, free elections, human rights, private property, and civil society independent from the state. Judging by public opinion surveys and, more important, the votes cast by millions of Russians in increasingly free elections between 1989 and 1991, this must have been one of the shortest successful national intellectual and moral reorientations in modern history.

Sparked in the way virtually all modern revolutions have started—by a kind of intellectual and moral pause, uncertainty and hesitancy at the top followed by an attempt at liberalization or "modernization" "from above"*—this remarkably peaceful upheaval became a revolution "from below" with wholesale rejection of ruling elite at the ballot box in 1989 and 1990, the demonstrations of the hundreds of thousands in 1990 and 1991, the election of Boris Yeltsin as president of Russia in June 1991, and the mass resistance across Russia to a short-lived hard-line coup two months later. In another four months, Russia had not only a new, de facto multi-party political system but a new economic order and a new state on the map. A victorious revolution it certainly was, its power attested to by the fact that the million-strong old ruling class (the *nomenklatura*)—political, economic, military, and secret police—was not able, or willing, to save the ancien régime.

Russia's "roads to the temple" have turned out to be much longer than was hoped (and seemed possible) at the time. Yet there could be little doubt about the changes the ideas wrought, the genuineness of the quest for virtue and dignity, the commitment of those who undertook

---

* See, for example, Bernard Bailyn, "How England Became Modern: A Revolutionary View" (*New York Review of Books*, November 19, 2009: 44–46). Reviewing Steve Pincus's definitive *1688: The First Modern Revolution* (New York: Yale University Press, 2009), Bailyn wrote that, having surveyed the entire current literature on the subject of origins and structures of revolutions (Arnedt, Huntington, Lefebvre, Soboul, Malia, Tilly, Skocpol, and Goldstone, most of whom, along with the subject matter, will be revisited in the next chapter), Pincus concludes that "revolutions happen not when old regimes collapse because they are incapable of adjusting to changed circumstances, or when alienated conspirators overturn traditional states, or when structural disorders explode but only when the old regime commits itself to modernization. . . . They occur only after regimes have determined, *for whatever reasons*, to initiate ambitious modernization programs." (Emphasis added to alert the reader, again, to what follows in the next chapter.)

it, and the passion of the thousands who led and the millions who followed.

In the process, glasnost established a gold standard for Russian political prose that had not been seen for almost a century and which will not likely be seen again soon. If essayistic brilliance be considered a hallmark of all great modern revolutions, from British to American to French (as I think it ought to be), then the latest Russian upheaval certainly qualifies. Anyone doubting Russia's ability to speak honestly and beautifully to itself and about itself should reread what was published between 1987 and 1991.

It was in order to recapture and thus preserve at least some of the extraordinary voices that inspired and shaped the latest Russian revolution and to make them speak as directly as possible to readers twenty years later that this book was written.

Embodied in articles, essays, and books, these voices were pearls without a string. I found them scattered thickly throughout 8,000 pages of Russian originals: newspapers, magazines, and books. For three long years, those who are thanked in the Acknowledgments (but can never be thanked enough) brought me copies of thousands of articles and essays after looking through every issue of newspapers and magazines as well as monthly literary journals between 1987 and 1991. These periodicals were known as the "flagships of glasnost": *Argumenty i fakty, Izvestia, Komsomol'skaya pravda, Literaturnaya gazeta, Moskovskie novosti, Novoe vremya, Novy mir, Ogonyok, Oktyabr', Kommunist, Sovetskaya kul'tura,* and *Znamya.*[1] Many others, including *Pravda,* the *Vek XX i Mir* and *Stolitsa* weeklies, and the *Druzhba narodov* monthly journal, were read selectively.

This being Russia (where, as one of glasnost's best-known essayists put it, "literature [is] a principal national means of self-discovery"),[2] no research of the kind I had in mind could have left out the finest of the novels, stories, or poems published at the time. From what we know about readers' reaction, the role of these books in the search for truth and moral betterment was hardly diminished (indeed, was likely to be enhanced) by the fact that they were "fiction." They were central to the moral and intellectual history I have attempted here and, as such, have been accorded pride of place. Often after decades in hiding and banishment, these voices, too, deepened and strengthened the spiritual revolution: Anna Akhmatova, Alexander Bek, Mikhail Bulgakov, Yuri Dombrovsky, Vladimir Dudintsev, Vasiliy Grossman, Daniil Granin, Andrei Platonov, Anatoly Pristavkin, Anatoly Rybakov, and Varlam Shalamov. Along with the pleasure that the essays and articles gave me, reading or rereading these works was the most enjoyable part of my work, its more-than-just reward.[3]

Following the example of Bernard Bailyn, whose book about the ideas that inspired the American Revolution was a model for this effort, my research was largely limited to revolutionary (that is, liberal) ideas, leaving aside the arguments of perestroika's and glasnost's opponents, both on the left and on the right. This book, thus, is far from a full intellectual history of the Russian revolution—an enterprise whose execution would fill many more volumes and which other historians, especially those critical of my design, are most heartily invited to undertake. As Bailyn wrote, "There were of course articulate and outspoken opponents of the Revolution, and at times I referred to their ideas; but the future lay not with them but with the leaders of the Revolutionary movement, and it is their thought at each stage of the developing rebellion that I attempted to present."[4]

The book has been designed accordingly. In the first chapter I lay out my reasons for doubting that the fall of the Soviet Union could ever be fully explained without an analysis of the "nonmaterial" factors: values, ideas, and ideals. Satisfied that this indeed was the case, I devote the rest of chapter 1 to the role of ideas in revolutions and then return to a profound shift in values during 1987–91 uncovered by public opinion research. The rest of the book is an attempt to provide an explanation for this shift (and thus, to a large extent, the revolution itself), using articles, essays, and books to record an unfolding moral and intellectual transformation.

Both thematically and chronologically the book's tripartite structure mirrors glasnost's progression. Thus chapter 2 records the sudden revelations of what Andrei Sakharov called the "moral degradation" of the society and explores the determination of glasnost's most celebrated authors to restore dignity and citizenship by unleashing a "spiritual revolution" as a prelude to a political one. Part II ("Who Are We?") begins with a description and analysis of the outpouring of memories of the Stalinist terror (chapters 5 and 6). Then, following glasnost's shift from past to

present, I reconstruct the suddenly uncensored and unflinching por-
trayal of the country's real condition and the swift demolition of the legitimizing mythology of the Soviet state (food, medical care, "golden
childhood," poverty, equality, the "state of workers and peasants"), with
the emerging true story of world war further undermining the regime's
legitimacy. The picture of the irrational and morally destructive economic system (chapter 10, "The 'Immoral' Economy") that daily corrupted and demoralized Soviet working men and women (chapter 11
"The 'Disintegration of Souls': *Homo Sovieticus*") delves further into
glasnost's exploration of moral devastation that the state inflicted on
the people of Soviet Russia.

Part III ("Who Is to Blame?") records glasnost's moving beyond the
definition of Stalinism as "an aberration" ("alluvium" on the healthy
body of Soviet socialism in Gorbachev's famous phrase) to viewing it, and
the Soviet totalitarianism in general, as a product of the state's economic
monopoly and the "nationalization of conscience," that is, the imposition
and enforcement of "official" morality.

Finally, part IV ("What Is to Be Done?") examines and analyzes suggestions for arrangements that would forever preclude the recurrence of
a Stalinist dictatorship and secure a path to a "moral society": a national
repentance and atonement for Stalinism; the recovery of the usable past
of resistance to Stalinism and the affirmation of free will; a shift of economic and political power from state to society through democracy and
private property, which was by then deemed democracy's most reliable
foundation; independent courts, uncensored media, and a multi-party
system as a means to sustain such a dignified political, social, and economic order; and the refashioning of the country's foreign and defense
policies in accordance with a new moral guidelines. The rejection of the
empire and the "garrison state," described in chapter 18, followed logically.

In the conclusion I suggest how the record presented in this book
helps to explain the origin and course of the latest Russian revolution
and speculate about the reasons why this course has, thus far, proved so
uneven and contradictory.

In the end, the string has proved far too short for all the pearls, of
course: around 700 original Russian articles, essays, and books, refer-
enced and listed in the bibliography, are but a small part of the riches

uncovered, leaving it to other, undoubtedly more skillful scholarly jewelers to set more of glasnost's gems to a far more elegant advantage.

Whatever this book turns out to be—an "intellectual," "cultural," or moral history—the highest aspiration I have for it is what an eighteenth-century French historian called a history "of human spirit, or at least a history in which the human spirit appears from the highest point of view."[5]

PART ONE REVOLUTIONS, IDEAS, AND THE END OF THE SOVIET UNION

The "Mystery" of the Soviet Collapse and the Theory of Revolutions

EVERY REVOLUTION IS A surprise. Still, the latest Russian Revolution (1987–91)[1] must be counted among the greatest surprises. Of course, many had talked and written about the "system's" *eventual* transformation or demise, yet no Western expert, scholar, official, or politician—or, judging by their memoirs, the future revolutionaries themselves— foresaw the collapse of the one-party dictatorship, of the state-owned economy, and of the Kremlin's control over its domestic and Eastern European empires by 1991.[2] When Mikhail Gorbachev became general secretary in March 1985, no contemporaries saw an impending revolutionary crisis. While they disagreed about the size and depth of the Soviet system's problems, no one felt them to be life-threatening any time soon.

Whence such strangely universal shortsightedness? The failure of Western experts to anticipate the Soviet Union's collapse may in part be attributed to the "revisionism" and anti-anti-communism that tended to exaggerate the Soviet regime's stability and legitimacy. Yet others who could hardly be considered "soft on communism" were just as puzzled by its demise. George Kennan, one of the architects of U.S. strategy in the cold war, wrote that in reviewing the entire "history of international affairs in the modern era," he found it "hard to think of any event more strange and startling, and at first glance inexplicable, than the sudden and total disintegration and disappearance . . . of the great power known successively as the Russian Empire and then the Soviet Union."[3] Richard Pipes, perhaps the leading anti-revisionist historian of Russia, called the revolution "unexpected."[4] The author of *The Soviet Tragedy*, Martin Malia, thought the "suddenness and completeness of the Soviet system's collapse to be "the greatest surprise of the end of the twentieth century."[5] François Furet concluded his rather gleeful postmortem on "the idea of communism in the twentieth century" by stating that "the manner in which first the Soviet Union and then its empire fell apart remains mysterious."[6] A collection of essays about the Soviet Union's demise in a special 1993 issue of the conservative *National Interest* was titled "The Strange Death of Soviet Communism."[7]

After being duly noted, this collective lapse in judgment could have been safely consigned to a mental file containing the memories of other oddities and caprices of the social sciences and then safely forgotten. Yet even today, twenty-five years after Mikhail Gorbachev unknowingly started the revolution by promulgating glasnost and democratization in January 1987, the foundation of the consensus in what was then known as the "Sovietological community" seems just as solid. It rested on conclusions reached by the standard method of placing available knowledge in the context of the regime's history. Both that knowledge and that history bespoke continuation, or, at most, a long decline.

Indeed, in 1985 the Soviet Union possessed many of the same natural and human resources as it had ten years before. There was no devastation from a natural disaster or epidemics. To be sure, the standard of living was much lower than in most of Eastern Europe, let alone the West. Shortages, food rationing, long lines in stores, and acute poverty (especially among the elderly and those living in the countryside) were endemic. But things had been much worse. Food shortages and de facto food rationing, for instance, had been in place in most provinces since the early 1930s, and while resented by some, they were accepted as normal by the generation that came of age during or immediately after World War II—or most Russian adults. The Soviet Union had known far greater calamities and had coped without sacrificing an iota of the state's grip on society and economy, much less surrendering them.

In any case, as Cuba, North Korea, or Iraq under Saddam Hussein (not to mention the Soviet Union under Stalin and China under Mao)[8] has amply shown, in totalitarian regimes the connection between popular deprivation and policy change is tenuous at best and usually results not in liberalizing reforms but in heavier repression. It was in the wake of the poor economic performance and brief bread shortages of 1963–64 that liberalizing but erratic Nikita Khrushchev was replaced by a conservative regime that remained in power for the next twenty years. Greater "discipline" was the thrust of Yuri Andropov's brief (1982–84) reign, which elsewhere I have called a "police renaissance."[9]

No key parameter of economic performance prior to 1985 pointed to a rapidly advancing disaster. In 1981–85 the growth of the country's GDP, although slowing down compared with the 1960s and 1970s, averaged 1.9 percent a year.[10] The same lackadaisical but hardly catastrophic pattern continued through 1989.[11] Budget deficits, which since the French Revolution have been considered among the prominent portents of a revolutionary crisis, equaled less than 2 percent of the GDP in 1985. Although growing rapidly, it remained under 9 percent through 1989—a size most economists would find manageable.[12]

The sharp drop in oil prices, from $66 a barrel in 1980 to $20 a barrel in 1986[13] (in 2000 prices) certainly was a heavy blow to Soviet finances. Still, adjusted for inflation oil was more expensive on world markets in 1985 than in 1972 and only one-third lower than throughout the 1970s.[14] Similarly, at $29 billion in 1985, the external debt was decidedly not life-threatening, and the debt service was to remain "within a reasonable limit" in relation to the hard-currency export earnings until 1989.[15] All in all, the financial crisis did not become "acute" until 1988 and could still be "averted" as late as summer 1990.[16] Meanwhile, the incomes of the Soviet population increased by more than 2 percent in 1985,[17] and inflation-adjusted wages continued to rise (albeit with their purchasing power increasingly eroded by shortages of goods) in the next five years through 1990 at over 7 percent on average.[18]

Thus, the subsequently much belabored "stagnation" was obvious and worrisome, but as an astute commentator wrote recalling the Soviet Union before the revolution, "chronic ailments, after all, are not necessarily fatal."[19] In the end, even the leading students of the economic causes of the latest Russian revolution (which fully corresponded to the classic definition of a sudden and irreversible overthrow of political and economic systems) admit that in 1985–87 the situation "was not at all dramatic."[20]

What could have been will forever remain a mystery. Yet it is quite plausible that while raising questions about the system's long-term viability, the obviously deteriorating economic performance was hardly a harbinger of inevitable doom. The Soviet economy could have "continued to stagnate" for a very long time.[21] It is undeniable, however, as Peter Rutland puts it, that the "real [economic] breakdown" began only after 1988 and was as much "a product of political processes as their cause."[22]

From the regime's point of view, the political situation was even less troublesome than the economic slowdown. After twenty years of relentless repression, virtually all the prominent dissidents were imprisoned, exiled, as Andrei Sakharov had been since 1980, or forced to emigrate, or had died in camps and jails.

Far more menacing were the widespread sentiments of national liberation, the aspirations for a greater autonomy or outright independence from Moscow, especially in the Baltics, western Ukraine, and Georgia. The centrifugal pressures mounted and eventually were certain to result in fissures in the long run.[23] Yet the long run is a long time. In the meantime, the terror had been successful in decimating the ranks of the "nationalists," who were meted out especially brutal and lengthy prison terms, often tantamount to death sentences.

With the state of the Soviet economy and politics falling short of supplying a satisfactory explanation of a pre-revolutionary crisis, the other traditional cause does not fill the gap either: the Soviet Union in the mid-1980s was hardly crumbling under external pressure. On the contrary, the previous decade was correctly judged to "amount to the realization of all major Soviet military and diplomatic desiderata."[24]

Of course, Afghanistan increasingly looked like a long war, but for a 5-million-man armed force the losses there were negligible. The bloody, drawn-out anti-guerilla war in the reconquered Lithuania and western Ukraine after 1945, not to mention the casualties in World War II, sustained well-founded hopes for an eventual victory in Afghanistan through the sheer weight of the mammoth military preponderance unrestrained by domestic or international public opinion.[25] Although, as we shall see, the enormous financial burden of the empire and the defense expenditures were to become major issues in the post-1987 debates, the cost of the Afghan war itself was hardly crushing: estimated at $4–5 billion in 1985–86, it was less than 1 percent of the Soviet GDP.[26]

The "Reagan Doctrine" of resisting and, if possible, reversing the advent of the Soviet Union's client regimes in the Third World put considerable pressure on the perimeter of the empire: in Afghanistan, Angola, Nicaragua, or Ethiopia. Yet the Soviet difficulties there, too, were far from fatal and could have been alleviated, if not undone, with the inevitable turn in U.S. public opinion, domestic politics, and, especially, the occupancy of the White House.

As a precursor to a potentially very costly competition, the Strategic Defense Initiative (SDI) was crucial—but not as a sign of a pending military defeat. Like the vociferous opponents of the program in the West (above all, in the United States), the Kremlin knew very well that effective deployment of space-based defenses was decades away. The obvious lag in high defense technologies was disconcerting, and the enormous costs of catching up to the United States did seem to matter—but only *after* the revolution was under way and the leadership began to pay attention to domestic public opinion and the standard of living, which the SDI contest was likely to beggar further.

The 1980 peaceful anti-communist uprising of the Polish workers had been a very disturbing development, which underscored the precariousness of the Soviet Union's east-central European empire. But occasional tentativeness is not the same as defeat. Suppressed by the Polish military regime and contained by martial law, by 1985 the Solidarity revolution looked exhausted. The Soviet Union seemed to have adjusted well to undertaking bloody "pacifications" in its Eastern European empire every twelve years—Hungary 1956, Czechoslovakia 1968, Poland 1980—without much regard for world opinion.

Overall, in 1985–87, the Soviet Union was at the height of its world power and influence, anchored in the strategic nuclear parity with the United States. So strong was the conviction in the permanence of the Soviet power in general and its occupation of East Germany in particular that the West German elites and public alike were determined to "march through" the Soviet and East German "institutions" for generations, in hope of cajoling and bribing Berlin and its Moscow masters into incremental changes and rapprochement. Following the West's lead, Eastern European elites seemed prepared to tolerate Soviet domination and occupation indefinitely, and some of its leading dissidents aspired only to make "Mittel Europa," a "bridge" between the Soviet-owned East and the democratic West. "We tend to forget, "Adam Ulam would note later, "that in 1985, no government of a major state appeared to be as firmly in power, its policies as clearly set in their course, as that of the USSR."[27]

Thus the "mystery" of the Soviet collapse was not, for the most part, a product of negligence, incompetence, or ideological biases of individual Sovietologists. Yet instead of relief, exoneration brings with it a still larger difficulty: the key traditional areas of inquiry—economy, foreign policy and defense, and domestic politics—fail to point to, or even hint at, the possibility that the vast and vastly powerful imperial state, which looked (and, apparently, was) solid enough to last many more years, would fall apart so stunningly swiftly and completely only a few years later. The only conclusion possible is not that the search for the causes of the revolution was not diligent enough, but that it was restricted to the wrong places.

At the time (as today) the reigning paradigm for anticipating and analyzing large-scale social upheavals—the method that several generations of social scientists, including experts on the Soviet Union, who came predominantly from the ranks of historians and political scientists, had come to accept and deploy routinely—was structuralism.

The approach is rooted in Marx's "historical materialism," whose causal scheme is centered around the "forces of production" (the economic system), which constitute the "basis" of any social and political organization. In their constant development, the "forces of production" come into conflict with the increasingly obsolete and constraining "relations of production" ("superstructure"), or the political and social arrangement of a society. There ensues a revolution led by the "classes" whose locations in the economic system make them especially desirous of change. The constraining political, cultural, and social "superstructure" is cast aside and with it the impediment to economic progress, which, one day, was to bring about a classless communist society without exploitation and political conflict.[28]

Modifying and updating the Marxian theory, most structuralists among the students of revolutions reject Marx's philosophy of history, in which class wars and revolutions are stages toward the inevitable triumph of classless communism. Following Max Weber,[29] they also emphasize the relative autonomy of state, state institutions, and state bureaucracies as collective political actors—in contrast to Marx's view of them as nothing more than the "committees" for carrying out the agenda of the economically dominant class. Thus the causes of "social" (or what used to be known as "great") revolutions are traced to the states' inability—because of the "macro-structural" domestic economic, demographic, or political constraints, or unfavorable international environment—to effect the necessary economic, social, or political reforms. The result is a breakdown in state organizations, especially in their administrative, military, and coercive capabilities.

This is not an occasion to review the immense literature of structuralism in any detail. Of relevance to us here is that all the "meta-factors" of the structuralist analysis—whether economic, political, institutional, or demographic—are invariably "material" and "objective."[30] They are independent of (or "exogenous to") people and people's ideas. In the words of Theda Skocpol, who is perhaps the leading structuralist theorist of revolutions today, "revolutions are not made; they come": it is "objective relations and conflicts" among "groups and nations" that explain revolutions, not "the interests, outlooks, or ideologies."[31]

With apologies to Skocpol, Barrington Moore, Charles Tilly, Jack Goldstone, and other expounders of structuralism (each of whom calls attention to different elements of pre-revolutionary situations),[32] let us note only that structuralist explanations can be very helpful in identifying long-term tendencies, tectonic shifts, as it were, in economy, institutions, politics, demography, or international environment as causes of revolution. Yet nothing in history is automatic or inevitable. Something having happened—and, in retrospect, having had very good reasons for happening—does not mean that it was inevitable and, moreover, should have happened only in the way it did. To use Charles Tilly's frequently made distinction, a "revolutionary situation" is different from a "revolutionary outcome."[33] Throughout history, only a tiny fraction of political or economic crises have become revolutions.

If a revolutionary process is represented by a line on which letters from, say, *a* to *d* mark the stages of the revolution from first stirrings to the triumph, the structuralist approach may be very helpful in uncovering what happened on the *c*-to-*d* stretch, from a clear crisis to a revolution. But it is clearly deficient in illuminating what happens between *a* and *c,* especially in explaining why structures that were present in ancien régimes for decades before suddenly became risk-enhancing factors.[34]

The latest Russian revolution is no exception. There were plenty of structural reasons *why* the Soviet Union should have collapsed as it did, yet they fail to explain fully *how* it happened. How, that is, between 1985 and 1989, in the absence of a sharp worsening in the economic, political, demographic, and other structural conditions, did the state and the economic systems it owned—ridden as they were with large and visible faults, failures and deficiencies yet appearing viable and lasting both to the overwhelming majority of its citizens, their leaders, and outside experts—suddenly begin to be seen as shameful, illegitimate, and intolerable by enough men and women among the politically active minority, which everywhere and at all times makes revolutions, to become doomed?[35]

In explaining the Soviet collapse we have no choice but to stray outside the universe of the "objective" factors and take into consideration the enormous and enormously subversive influence of ideas—what William Sewell called the "metaphysical" aspects of social upheavals and the "autonomous power of ideology."[36]

Perhaps the most celebrated "archeologist of ideas," whose almost entire oeuvre seems to have been intended for illumination, in a language of remarkable elegance and clarity, of the connection between what people thought and the great changes they wrought in the ways they lived and governed themselves, Sir Isaiah Berlin felt that understanding the upheavals of modern times was impossible without realizing that

> these great movements began with ideas in people's heads: ideas about what relations between men have been, are, might be and should be. . . . Such ideas are substance of ethics. . . . These beliefs about how life should be lived, what men and women should be and do, are objects of moral inquiry. . . . If we are to understand the . . . world in which we live (and unless we try to understand it, we cannot expect to be able to act rationally in it or on it), we cannot confine our attention to the great impersonal forces, natural and man-made, which act upon us. The goals and motives that guide human action must be looked at in the light of all that we know and understand;

their roots and growth, their essence and above all their
validity, must be critically examined with every intellectual
resource that we have.[37]

The proponents of the "idea-centric" approach to explaining revolutions start with the premise that revolutions, like all political movements, "originate in the minds of men."[38] It is "ideas and actors," rather
than "structures" (or some "broad sweep of history"), that are the primary engines of revolutions."[39]

In a passage the implications of which are not often fully appreciated
despite its being often quoted, Tocqueville places people's subjective assessment of their situation at the center of a pre-revolutionary crisis:

> It is not always that when things are going from bad to worse
> that revolutions break out. On the contrary, it oftener happens
> when a people . . . suddenly finds the government relaxing
> its pressures. . . . Thus, the most perilous moment for a bad
> government is one when it seems to mend its ways. . . . Patiently
> endured so long as it seemed beyond redress, a grievance comes
> to appear intolerable once the possibility of removing it crosses
> men's minds.[40]

Revolutions may be preceded by the easing of political repression,
brought about by explicitly "intentionalist" acts of the liberalizing ruler
or the ruling elite,[41] and, Tocqueville further notes, the genesis of a revolution may coincide with at least temporary improvement in economic
well-being as well. (There was, for instance, the "steady increase of
wealth" under Louis XVI, and in none of the decades immediately following the revolution did France's "national prosperity make such rapid
forward strides as in the two preceding it.")[42] Yet far from "tranquilizing"
the population, the steadily increasing prosperity everywhere "promoted
the spirit of unrest," and it was precisely those parts of France where the
improvement in the standard of living was most pronounced that were
to become the "chief centers" of the revolutionary movement.[43] Revolutions, thus, may be conceived at least as much in hope as in despair. As
Tocqueville famously puts it: "For the mere fact that certain abuses have
been remedied draws attention to the others and they appear more gall-
ing; people may suffer less, but their sensibility is exacerbated."[44]

What "exacerbates" these "sensibilities" and how has been the business of the students of the "metaphysical" roots of modern revolutions. While the effects of "objective" (structural) factors may be latent in the first stages of a revolution, ideas, ideals, and values shape the upheavals' progression from beginning to end.

The initial phases of such social and political transformations everywhere have been attended by the "swarm of ideas," "an extraordinarily energetic ideological period," and "an immense and unprecedented" ideological debate.[45] As to precise modes of the interaction of the "ideal" and the "structural" in the early stages of revolutions, these venues are too specific to the events to lend themselves to generalizations. Instead, we can say with Crane Brinton

> that in our pre-revolutionary societies the kind of discontents, the specific difficulties about economic, social, and political conditions on which hard-boiled moderns focus are invariably accompanied by a great deal of writing and talking about ideals, about a better world, about some very abstract forces tending to bring about that better world. It is, indeed, the expression of ideas, rather than particular ideas—which may vary enormously in different revolutions—that makes the uniformity. We find that ideas are always a part of the pre-revolutionary situation, and we are quite content to let it go at that. No ideas, no revolution.[46]

When ideas begin to provide "alternatives to the current view," to challenge the "categories" in which people think,[47] pre-revolutionary situations (which may last for years, if not decades) become revolutionary crises (which move at a dizzying speed). The content of new ideas shifts from increasingly harsh condemnations of the old order to sketching the principles of a new and better one. They start to coalesce into "new theories of how the world works, [into] new creeds," novel concepts of the "nature of good society" and, more generally, of "good and evil, truth and falsity, justice and injustice."[48] Contention and confrontation over symbols—culture, ideology, beliefs—are the essence of social revolutions.[49] For a brilliant moment "everything"—the economy, society, and, of course, politics—"yields" in people's minds to this ideological struggle.[50]

The result is the beginning of the transformation of the entire "value systems" of a society, the laying down of the "metaphysical principles of the new order."[51] Ideas acquire an "autonomous role" and unleash a powerful, hitherto nonexistent dynamic.[52] All manner of radical and unanticipated outcomes become possible—be they the overwhelming desire for liberty arising out of the struggle for independence in the American Revolution or the sudden, all-conquering egalitarian impulse of the French one.[53]

With alternative "societal values" seen as "a key" to successful revolutions,[54] their creators and purveyors—the writer, the journalist, the teacher, the artist, the preacher[55]—become indispensable. As Tocqueville observed, they "put into the minds of men the seeds of those novelties that were to become the institutions of the new order" and "help to create that general awareness of dissatisfaction, that solidified public opinion which . . . creates effective demand for revolutionary change."[56] Suddenly, "the entire political education" of the nation becomes the "work of its men of letters."[57]

Modern revolutions are invariably preceded by such a "transfer of allegiance" by the intelligentsia ("cultural elites").[58] Brinton thought withdrawal of their support for the ancien régime to be "in some respects the most reliable symptom [of a social revolution] we are likely to meet."[59] With the state's resistance suddenly drained of conviction and fervor and at best "half-hearted and inefficient"—be it the proclamations against the sale of "Seditious and Puritan books" under James I or the censorship under Louis XVI—the "dangerous writings" in pamphlets, newspapers, books (or plays like Beaumarshais's *Marriage of Figaro*) multiply exponentially, to a "hail."[60]

In what Brinton called an "ideological revolution," the relentless and increasingly bold critique of the ancien régime is now combined with the advocacy of alternative societal values, rendering the present political system "inconsonant" with the rapidly changing "basic values" of the politically active minority.[61] The old order's ideological foundations unravel. Power loses its "moorings."[62]

With the "decomposition" of *moeurs*, Tocqueville writes, "a class ostensibly at the head of society" for many years becomes "an officer corps without soldiers and thus could be overthrown in a single night."[63] "The contempt into which the governing class swiftly falls," he continues, is so "general and profound" that it "paralyzes" the resistance to a revolution of those who have the greatest "objective" (economic, social, political) interest in preserving the status quo.[64] "Weariness and doubt" infect the ruling class and render it severely handicapped in the business of defending the status quo.[65]

The rulers attempt to alter policies not so much to meet the "objective" challenges as to bring at least some aspects of their rule in accordance with these new ideological imperatives. In this sense, too, all great revolutions begin "from above." The "suicide" of the elites and the regime, or at least their self-incapacitation, is among the "uniformities" of these cataclysms:

> The old ruling class—or, rather many individuals of the ruling
> class—come to distrust themselves, or lose faith in the tradi-
> tions and habits of their class, grow intellectual, humanitarian,
> or go over to the attacking groups. . . . The ruling class becomes
> politically inept.[66]

Anyone familiar even with the basic outline of the latest Russian revolution will immediately be struck by how apposite these observations are to what transpired between 1987 and 1991. Two themes in the "metaphysical" explanations resonate especially strongly: the obviously "intentionalist" ("voluntarist") impulse at the revolution's inception and the explicitly "ideological," value-bound character of the concerns by which that impulse was informed.

The Soviet liberalization (of which abolition of censorship and, thus, glasnost was the central element) was started by one man, and his reasons for launching it extended well beyond the necessity to correct the economy or make the international environment more benign: by all available evidence, faced with the same "objective" state of affairs no other top contender for the supreme Soviet leadership would have embarked, in 1985, on an even remotely comparable project. The core of Gorbachev's enterprise was undeniably "idealistic" and "subjective."[67]

Of course, much like many Western historians and political scientists, Gorbachev and his few initial allies had been brought up in the Marxist tradition (albeit of a much cruder, Stalinesque kind) and lacked the conceptual categories (and, one suspects, often even a vocabulary)[68] to give coherence to their "non-material" concerns. Yet while economic betterment was their banner, there is little doubt that Gorbachev and his supporters set out to right, firstly, moral rather than economic wrongs.

On closer inspection, many of the publicly expressed concerns about economic problems often seemed no more than a foil for the anguish over the spiritual decline and the corrosive effects of the Stalinist past. It was the beginning of a desperate search for answers to the grand questions with which every great revolution starts: What is a good, dignified life? What constitutes a just social and economic order? What is a decent and legitimate state? What ought such a state's relationship with a civil society be?

"A new moral atmosphere is taking shape in the country," Gorbachev told the Central Committee at the January 1987 meeting, where he declared glasnost and democratization to be the foundation of perestroika. "A reappraisal of values and their creative rethinking is underway."[69] Later, recalling his feeling that "we couldn't go on like that any longer, and we had to change life radically, break away from the past malpractices," he called it his "*moral* position."[70]

The same "position" shines through the memoirs of Gorbachev's first prime minister, Nikolai Ryzhkov, for whom, too, the "moral [*nravstennoe*] state of the [Soviet] society" in 1985 was its "most terrifying" feature:

> [By 1985] the stuffiness in the country has reached maximum: after that only death. Nothing was done with any care. . . . [We] stole from ourselves, took and gave bribes, lied in the reports, in newspapers, from high podiums, wallowed in our lies, hung medals on one another. And all of this—from top to bottom and from bottom to top.[71]

Another member of Gorbachev's very small original coterie of liberalizers, Foreign Minister Eduard Shevardnadze, was just as pained to see "the faith" in the regime being undermined by ubiquitous lawlessness and corruption.[72] "Rot and disintegration were particularly horrifying," Shevardnadze later wrote, "when contrasted with the rampant exploitation of Communist and patriotic phraseology."[73] He recalls telling Gorbachev in winter 1984–85: "Everything is rotten. It has to be changed."[74]

Unlike Khrushchev's effort between 1954 and 1964, perestroika almost from the very beginning was about "symbolic politics." Khrushchev knew firsthand how precariously positioned was the edifice of the house that Stalin built on terror and lies. Gorbachev and his group appeared to believe that what was right was also politically manageable. Democratization, Gorbachev declared, was "not a slogan but the essence of perestroika."[75] Many years later he told interviewers:

> The Soviet model was defeated not only on the economic and social levels; it was defeated on a cultural level. Our society, our people, the most educated, the most intellectual, rejected that model on the cultural level because it does not respect the man, oppresses him spiritually and politically. . . . That is why the most important for us [was] everything connected with freedom."[76]

There is hardly a better example of the primacy of the moral component in Gorbachev's initial reforming crusade than the anti-alcohol campaign, undertaken and sustained in the face of extremely adverse (and mounting) political and economic consequences. In 1985 the state's annual income from the sale of alcoholic beverages constituted between 12 and 14 percent of total budget revenues.[77] In 1990 Gorbachev would disclose that alongside oil revenues, vodka sustained the Soviet Union's treasury between 1970 and 1985.[78] "The country was drinking itself into the ground," Ryzhkov remembered. "[People] drank everywhere. Before work. After work. In the *obkoms* [regional party committees] and in the *raykoms* [district party committees]. At the construction sites and on the shop floor. In offices and in the apartments. Everywhere."[79]

Between 1985 and 1988, the restriction on the production, sale, and consumption of alcoholic beverages cost the Soviet treasury 67 billion rubles in lost revenue[80]—an equivalent of almost 9 percent of the 1985 GNP, 17 percent of that year's revenue, and nearly four times the sum spent on healthcare.[81] Yet when Ryzhkov objected to the campaign's excesses he was overruled by other members of the Gorbachev "team" because, as they put it, he was "concerned about economy instead of morality" and the "morals of the nation must be rescued by any means available."[82]

That within three years reforms gave rise to a revolution was due largely to another "idealistic" and personal factor: Gorbachev's aversion to violence and, hence, his stubborn refusal to resort to mass coercion when the scale and depth of change began to outstrip his original intent. This abiding abhorrence of repression was a cornerstone of the ideal that inspired Gorbachev's quest: a humane, "democratic," one-party socialism with a so-called mixed economy of some private enterprise and a dominant state presence. Gorbachev's ideal (which he pursued so devotedly and to which, as far as one could see, he remained faithful to the very end) was a mythical but fervently believed-in rendering of the Soviet Union during the New Economic Policy (NEP), initiated by Lenin in 1921 and ended by Stalin in 1929.[83] To deploy Stalinist repression even to "preserve the system" would have meant making "a lie of [Gorbachev's] whole inner life."[84] (A witness recalls Gorbachev saying in the late 1980s: "We are told that we should pound the fist on the table," and the general secretary clenched his hand in fist to "show how it is done." "Generally speaking," continued Gorbachev, "it could be done. But one does not feel like it.")[85]

When he returned to the Soviet Union in 1983 after ten years as the ambassador to Canada, Alexander Yakovlev's recollection of what he saw was much the same as Gorbachev's, Ryzhkov's, and Shevardnadze's:

> The moment was at hand when people would say, "Enough!
> We cannot live like this any longer. Everything must be done in
> a new way. We must reconsider our concepts, approaches, our
> views of past and our future." . . . There has come an under-
> standing that it is simply impossible to live as we lived before—
> intolerably, humiliatingly.[86]

Yakovlev makes it clear that both for him and for Gorbachev democratization was the most urgent objective of perestroika. In describing later what happened between 1985 and 1991, Yakovlev, who took charge of the "ideology" in 1985, uses "reformation" more often than "revolution." It was first and foremost a moral and spiritual transformation, an "attempt to . . . end the amorality of the regime."[87]

In a secret memorandum that he handed Gorbachev in December 1985, a few months after becoming a secretary of the Central Committee,

Yakovlev wrote: "The main issue today is not only economy. This is only the material side of the process. The heart of the matter is in the political system . . . and its relation to man."[88] Hence, the "main principles of perestroika": democracy (understood, first and foremost, as a freedom of choice in multi-candidate elections); glasnost (freedom of speech and press); independence of courts and judges; a law on human rights, which must include the inviolability of the individual, his property, and his personal communications as well as freedom of demonstration, meetings, religion, and travel, and the ability to sue any official or official organization in court.[89]

In a speech that persuaded the Congress of People's Deputies in December 1989 to repudiate the 1939 Soviet-German treaty (which included the secret protocols that divided Poland and gave the Soviet Union free hand to seize Estonia, Latvia, and Lithuania), Yakovlev said: "The theory of relativity, comrades, is a great step in the understanding of the universe. But there can be no relativity in morality. . . . We have to understand that the lawlessness is horrifying not only in its direct effects but also because it creates situations when amorality and opportunism start to be considered the norm. Thus any evaluation we make [of the pact], Comrade Deputies, will not be only political, but moral as well."[90]

In 1990, when it seemed that the revolution would be extinguished any day by the cold, hunger, or a military coup, Yakovlev wrote:

> We have something that is irreversible. It lies in the impalpable
> yet real sphere of spirit. The society will never be the same, for
> there has been a qualitative breakthrough in consciousness.
> Irreversible is the deliverance from the myths, stereotypes,
> self-deception, and self-satisfaction, which have poisoned our
> brains and our feelings for decades. Irreversible is the realiza-
> tion that life fashioned by conformism leads only to the quag-
> mire of lagging behind in history. Irreversible is the gradual
> return of common human ideals and values, the realization of
> their moral imperative: freedom of an individual, conscience,
> decency, kindness, charity. Irreversible is the awakening of the
> thirst for active life, for the freedom of exploration. . . . Man is
> made strong by spirit, and people's history is moved by spirit.

The spiritual birth of perestroika is painful. But without it renewal of the society is hopeless. This birth has taken place and what perestroika has already accomplished will enter history as one of the moral and intellectual feats of mankind.[91]

Yet the Russian revolution's place in what is known as the "social history of ideas"[92] has been secured mostly by what happened *outside* the Kremlin. Although the per capita income of the Soviet people had doubled between 1965 and 1980, "dissatisfaction grew," a leading Soviet economist noted in 1989, and so did "mistrust" of the system.[93] The "Tocquevillian paradox," which established an ambiguous causal link between the material well-being and social discontent, was on display again. A leading Soviet journalist and later a passionate herald of glasnost, Alexander Bovin, wrote in 1988 that the ideals of perestroika had "ripened" amid people's increasing "irritation" with corruption, brazen thievery, lies, and the obstacles in the way of honest work.[94] While not yet rebelling, a witness testifies, many had "simply stopped believing."[95]

Anticipations of "substantive changes were in the air," another witness recalled, and they forged "an appreciable constituency" for radical reforms.[96] Indeed, the expectations that greeted the coming to power of "a new, dynamic leader," Gorbachev, were so strong, and growing, that they shaped policies of the regime which would not (or could not) dare defy them. Ideas became a "structural factor" in the unfolding revolution.[97]

The "credibility" of the official ideology, which, in Yakovlev's words, held the entire Soviet political and economic system together "like the hoops of steel,"[98] was quickly weakening—and waning with it were the "mental constructs," which sustained the one-party rule.[99] New perceptions contributed to a change in attitudes toward the regime and to "a shift in values."[100] Gradually, the legitimacy of the political arrangements began to be questioned. In what, following W. I. Thomas's insight, the great American sociologist Robert Merton called "Thomas theorem"— "if men define situations as real, they are real in their consequence"[101]— the "objective" deterioration of Soviet economy became relevant only *after* and *because of* a fundamental shift in the ways in which the regime's performance was perceived and criteria by which it was evaluated.

By March 1989, there were 60,000 "informal" (private and independent) groups and clubs in the Soviet Union.[102] "There are no longer the dark masses which could be ruled easily, whose minds could be controlled," a prominent Russian sociologist wrote of these newly minted citizens. "There are thinking people."[103]

In 1989–91, in one election after another, millions of Russians rejected the conservative Party leaders and chose those who publicly espoused first reformist and then revolutionary agendas.[104] Every consecutive vote—in spring 1989 (the Congress of People's Deputies of the USSR), in spring 1990 (the Congresses of People's Deputies of the Republics), and in June 1991 (the presidency of Russia)—demonstrated "an inexorable decline" in the popularity of Gorbachev's [moderate] supporters and the increase in the influence of "the politicians who called themselves radicals."[105] In the election to local Soviets in March 1990, pro-reform "democrats" won in fifty Russian cities, including the three largest: Moscow, Leningrad, Sverdlovsk. In Moscow the voters gave them fifty-seven out of sixty-five seats in the City Council.[106]

Disenchantment with the prospects for "socialist modernization" is said to have made millions of people increasingly "receptive" to the "non-socialist alternative" and attracted to the "liberal-democratic ideology and values of the Western civilization" to fulfill their hopes.[107] The political leadership, noted a Russian historian, passed from Gorbachev to Yeltsin, who was campaigning "under an anti-communist, pro-Western liberal banner."[108] Almost at the same time, Yeltsin's radical allies Gavriil Popov in Moscow and Anatoly Sobchak in Leningrad were elected mayors of the "dual capitals." As if "to underscore the repudiation of socialism," the Leningraders voted to change the city's name to St. Petersburg.[109] As a Russian historian puts it, the "liberal-democratic and simultaneously anti-communist revolution" occurred in Russia "mostly via electoral ballots."[110]

When the fate of the revolution hung in the balance, huge but remarkably peaceful mass demonstrations in Moscow and, on a smaller scale, in many other cities, as well as the two national strikes of miners in 1989 and 1991, came to its rescue.[111] The revolution culminated in August 1991 in the rallies and strikes throughout Russia in support of Gorbachev and Yeltsin and against the communist coup. The demonstrations took place in almost all of Russia's largest cities.[112] An estimated

200,000 marched in Moscow and St. Petersburg, and 50,000 held an around-the-clock vigil at the besieged seat of the Russian Federation's government, the "White House."[113]

Years later, the first elected mayor of Moscow, Gavriil Popov, wrote of these men and women:

> But the main and decisive factor in the victorious revolution were people themselves. Thousands, hundreds of thousands of citizens participated in the revolution. Young and old, men and women, workers and students, Russians and representatives of our other peoples. They voted in the elections. They, time and again, went into the streets. Taking risks for themselves, their families, their loved ones. On workdays and on weekends. In sunlight and in rain. They did not shoot. Or break windows. Or storm the buildings. Or burn cars. And in this opposition won those who, to use Tolstoy's expression, were stronger in spirit.[114]

Writing to a Soviet magazine in 1987, a Russian reader called what he saw around him a "radical break [*perelom*] in consciousness."[115] We know that he was right because Russia's was the only great revolution whose course has been charted in public opinion polls almost from the beginning. This record affords the students of revolutionary ideas a unique opportunity to trace and measure the spread and the effect of the new ideas and values in "real time," as it were, rather than to reconstruct them ex post facto. "For the first time in history, we can study a social revolution from within," a leading Soviet pollster Yuri Levada told an interviewer in 1989. "Because at the time of the American and French and other great revolutions, there were no sociologists out polling. But we [are]. . . . This is *very* interesting."[116]

In 1989–91 Russian pollsters joined Tocqueville's "men of letters"—journalists and essayists—as the nation's "teachers." They were also political seismologists, detecting the shifts of the tectonic plates of the national consensus and announcing their findings to the mesmerized nation, which lived from one weekly cultural and political earthquake to the next. This self-discovery, this sudden ability to learn what one's fellow citizens really thought after seven decades of enforced muteness and deafness was so exhilarating and so central to the entire enterprise of democratization that in early 1988 sociology (understood primarily as the study of public opinion), was proclaimed "one of the most democratic sciences."[117]

In 1989 and 1990, surveys of the Soviet population began to detect the first fissures of what would become an astonishingly swift and deep erosion of the ideological foundation of the ancien régime. Men and women began first to doubt, then revise, and finally discard the former certainties: the one-party rule and the suppression of dissenting views; the state monopoly over mass media and economy;[118] the control over Eastern Europe; and, by 1991, the legitimacy of Moscow's rule over other republics of the Union. Gradually replacing these seemingly bedrock certainties were visions of different, just, equitable, and effective political and economic organization, in which everyone would be entitled to free expression and political representation, and where the state's total control of people's livelihoods would be increasingly supplanted by individual responsibility for one's welfare.

After four generations under a one-party dictatorship (and with independent parties still illegal), the first representative national public opinion survey in November–December 1989 found overwhelming support for competitive elections and the legalization of parties other than the Communist Party of the Soviet Union (CPSU).[119] The fetish of unanimity (*edinodushie*) as a cornerstone of a political order and the notion of dissent as treason were being discarded in favor of freedom of speech, plurality of opinions, and tolerance.[120] Russians were welcoming "political views that are fundamentally different from the [views] of the majority."[121] Over two-thirds of them disagreed with the view that society should not put up with such views, while nine in ten felt that it was necessary for everyone to "express themselves freely."[122] Almost one-third of the sample preferred a free society to an orderly one.[123]

Russians evinced no universal longing for a "strong hand," attributed to them by an age-long stereotype. Of those surveyed in 1989, half thought that "under no circumstances" should all the power be given to one person.[124] Among the deputies in the Soviet Union's new parliament (Congress of People's Deputies) elected from the Russian Federation and in Russia's own new legislature (the Congress of People's Deputies of the RSFSR), the majority of industrial workers were just as committed as their colleagues from the intelligentsia to amending the

Soviet constitution in order to eliminate the Party's "leading role," sub-ordinate the Party to the state, and prohibit Party membership for judges and prosecutors.[125]

Among other portents of a rapidly changing political culture was what a Western pollster called "rights consciousness."[126] By an over-whelming majority, residents of the Russian Federation, surveyed in 1990, agreed that everyone was entitled to "the same legal rights and protections" regardless of their political beliefs.[127] (In their emphatic as-sertion of more than a dozen basic political and human rights—among them, freedom of speech, association and conscience, equality before the law, the rights to privacy and to travel abroad—the residents of the Moscow region were found to be "uncannily" like the citizens of twelve Western European nations.)[128]

Although not as quickly or sharply as in the case of political and civic rights and liberties, the Soviet people began to question other "core com-ponents of socialist ideology": the correctness of the country's economic system, the distribution of incomes, and "beliefs about the role of the state," especially the extent of the state's responsibility for the well-being of individuals.[129] By the end of 1989, an overwhelming majority thought that the state should provide the opportunity for everyone "to earn as much as they can," and almost half of the national sample believed that "people should look out for themselves for success in life."[130]

Early in 1990 over half of the respondents in a Russian region agreed that "a healthy economy" was more likely if "the government allows indi-viduals to do as they wish."[131] Six months later an all-Russian poll found 56 percent supporting a rapid or gradual transition to a market econ-omy.[132] Another year passed, and the share of the pro-market respon-dents among the citizens of the Russian Republic (RSFSR) increased to 64 percent.[133] By January 1992, majorities of Russians expressed prefer-ences for virtually all the key features of market economy about which they were asked: income inequality, private ownership of enterprises, the sale of enterprises to private owners, or private ownership of agricul-tural land.[134]

As in other revolutions, many of the politically active were growing impatient with the pace of change. By 1989 a national sample was split approximately in half between those who supported "decisive and rapid changes" and the proponents of a "slow and cautious" approach.[135] A year later, over two-thirds of the Moscow region sample disagreed with the proposition that the political reform is "moving too rapidly."[136]

Again as in all such upheavals, the younger, better educated, and urban among the respondents were considerably more susceptible to ideological revolution than men and women who were older, less educated, and rural.[137] Age was especially relevant, with "striking differences" among age groups' attitudes toward democratization.[138] Younger Soviets in general and Russians in particular were also more supportive of private ownership of industry and of the right to demonstrate or strike, and more tolerant of dissent.[139]

In 1989, 60 percent of the Soviet citizens believed that the Party had "led the country along a wrong path."[140] Nine months later, the Center for the Study of Public Opinion found a "crisis of socialist ideology." The "moral code" that "cemented" the Soviet order was "falling apart" and there was no "renewed socialist idea" that could replace it.[141] By then, depending on the wording of the question, the "socialist choice" was supported by between 10 and 20 percent of the Soviet people. This segment had diminished rapidly in the previous two years and consisted largely of "older people," while the "overwhelming majority" of the younger generations were found to be "turning away from socialism."[142] (Between October 1988 and October 1989, 4 million young men and women ended their membership in the Communist Union of Youth, the Komsomol.)[143]

If in February 1989 a majority of Russians favored a "socialist way of the development of the USSR, in May 1991, 56 percent agreed that "communism has brought Russia nothing but poverty, lines [in stores], and mass repressions."[144] By summer 1991, in the words of a Russian historian, "the passive part of the population" looked on with indifference at the agony of the regime, while "the active were inspired by completely different ideas."[145]

The collapse of the Soviet regime in August–September 1991 coincided with what a leading student of Russian post-Soviet political history called an "unprecedentedly sharp" change in the Russian people's attitudes.[146] In September 1991, 73 percent of the respondents thought that "our entire political system must be radically transformed."[147] Continuing the trend that started a year before, solid majorities were now in

favor of some key features of liberal capitalism: openness to the outside world (74 percent), a multi-party political system (69 percent), and
a market economy (63 percent).[148] Among the events that gladdened
them the most in 1991, more Russians mentioned the demise of the
CPSU than any other development. The next most popular occurrence,
cited by one-fifth of the sample, was "the abandonment of communist
ideals."[149]

From 1988 to 1990, surveys also signaled the crumbling of the erstwhile
certainties about outside threats faced by the Soviet state, the defense
against these threats, and the preservation of the Soviet domination in
Eastern and Central Europe.[150] By early 1990, the belief in the besieged
state that had been central to legitimizing Soviet foreign and domestic
policies for so long was no more. Almost three-fourths of residents in
the European part of the Soviet Union were largely unconcerned about
dangers from outside the Soviet borders.[151] Breaking yet another ideological taboo, Russians began to question spending on defense, for which
until then no sacrifice had been too great.[152]

The "widespread commitment to pacifist views"[153] started to corrode
beliefs about another cornerstone in the ideological base (and the key to
the Soviet Union's superpower status): the country's nuclear arsenal. By
1990 over two-thirds of the interviewed opposed the continuation of
nuclear testing in general, about the same proportion thought the Soviet
Union should stop testing contingent on U.S. behavior, and two-fifths
endorsed a *unilateral* Soviet ban.[154]

By the time the democratic and national liberation revolutions swept
the Soviet Union's east-central European empire in 1989–90, the values
transformation at home had eroded the support for preserving the Warsaw Pact by all means possible. Immediately following the anti-communist
revolutions in Eastern Europe, in January 1990, two-thirds of Muscovites thought that the Soviet Union should not oppose an east-central
European country's withdrawal from the Warsaw Pact (fewer than one in
four thought it should).[155] Three-quarters of the sample in Russia, Ukraine,
and Lithuania either "completely approved" or "more approved than dis-
approved" of the changes in the region.[156] A narrow majority felt that a
unified Germany posed no threat.[157] Asked at the end of 1990 what made

them happy that year, a plurality of the respondents in a national poll mentioned "reduction in armaments [and] the withdrawal of [Soviet] troops from Eastern Europe."[158]

Even the state that the Russians had forged and dominated for so long was no longer sacrosanct. Although slightly more than half of the Russians surveyed in February 1991 still wished for "a unitary and undivided Soviet Union" and believed that republics ought to try to forge a new union, only one-third of the respondents thought that the Soviet Union must be maintained by all means available, and half were of the opinion that those who wanted to leave the Soviet Union should be allowed to do so.[159] (One-fourth of the sample felt that Russia *itself* should leave the union, in effect discarding all the imperial conquests of almost three centuries.)[160] Less than a year later, in January 1992, a 43 percent plurality was either in favor of Russia's membership in the Commonwealth of Independent States, a loose confederation forged after the Soviet Union dissolved, or for a completely "independent Russia."[161]

Like every great revolution, Russia's was a complex affair, engendered, driven, and shaped by multiple impulses. A stagnant economy; the growing disjoint between the existing political institutions and the needs of an educated and urbanized middle class; the pressures and expenses associated with the cold war, which was about to enter an utterly novel, computerized, and space-based phase—all are indispensable pieces of the explanation.

Yet it is just as obvious that they tell only part of the story, which can be fully explored only when the "ideal" ("metaphysical") causes are taken into account. As we know of no reliable public opinion data from the Soviet Union dealing with the essence of the country's political and economic systems prior to 1985, it is impossible, of course, to say whether glasnost was responsible for the appearance of new ideas and values or if they had been espoused before by a significant segment of the population and the new freedom helped disseminate and radicalize them. If the experience of other great revolutions applies, both developments most likely unfolded in parallel and reinforced each other. Yet it is undeniable that what happened first to the Russian intelligentsia and a few years later to the millions of their compatriots must constitute one of history's most startling instances of the impact of newly articulated values and ideals on perceptions, then attitudes, and, finally, political and economic choices.[162]

It is in the investigation of the sources, the channels, and, most important, the content of glasnost's most notable creations that the explanation of the "mystery" of the Soviet Union's collapse ought to be sought. The answer is in the thousands of pages of books, articles, and essays, that shaped the national metamorphosis. Into them we are about to plunge.

CHAPTER TWO

For Truth and Goodness

THE CREDOS OF GLASNOST

The main problem today is the problem of a new structure of values.
—Alexander M. Yakovlev, "Otverzhenie i utverzhdenie" (Rejection
and affirmation), *Ogonyok* 43, 1988: 14

The key is the reordering of the system of spiritual and moral
values, the understanding of what man lives for, of what his calling
is. Today, the entire economic development of the country is up
against the moral essence of man. Nothing can be changed
significantly for the better in the economy if we ourselves do not
change for the better.
—Mikhail Antonov, "Tak chto zhe s nami proiskhodit?" (What
really is happening to us?), *Oktyabr'*, August 1987: 54, 56

We want to change the economy, we are taking on the renewal
of the society, but until we have a clean conscience—we will not
succeed in any area.
—E. S. Kochetkov, letter to the editor, *Znamya*, August 1988: 228

As we enjoy this generally joyful state of convalescence we should
not forget about the essence of the moment. It seems simple and
obvious: truth, only truth, and nothing but the truth.
—Konstantin Smirnov, "Moment istiny i istina momenta" (The
moment of truth and the truth of the moment), *Ogonyok* 36, 1988: 24

It is like this, and only like this, that such a thing happens. At first
only a few realize the necessity of the renewal of ideas, and the
majority does not hear them and even are afraid to touch them, as
though they were lepers. But gradually the crushed and eviscerated
ideas of democracy and liberty begin to gather momentum. They
become an opaque consciousness of the majority, while remaining a
firm understanding of a few. And then, when this new understanding
is announced out loud, sounded out on the radio and in newspapers,
many people, first resisting it, embrace this new consciousness.
—Vladimir Lakshin, "Narod i lyudi: O romane Vasiliya Grossmana"
(People and men: About Vasily Grossman's novel), *Izvestiya,*
June 25, 1988: 3

EVERY GREAT MODERN revolution began, in essence, with a search
for dignity. The latest Russian revolution started as a rebellion against
the indignity of lies—"ubiquitous and all-consuming"[1] lies that had become the "norm of life."[2]* As the fear of punishment for publicly challeng-
ing the lies (or for refusing to be complicit in their production) began to
recede, the first, tenuous advances of truth were felt by witnesses in very
direct, physical ways. They were compared to a mighty river that broke a
dam, leaving behind the formerly confining "rusted armature" and all
manner of "junk and muck."[3] The sudden ability to impart and receive
truth was like a flow of oxygen to the survivors trapped in a collapsed mine,
or like being cured of leprosy.[4]

The "life-giving liquid of glasnost† and freedom of speech slacked
the enslaved society's thirst for truth,"[5] recalled Alexander Yakovlev, the

---

* Unless otherwise specified, throughout the book, all translations from Russian
  are by the author.
† The term "glasnost" was part of the Russian political discourse at least as far
  back as 1841, when Russia's first great liberal reformer, Count Mikhail Speransky,
  listed "glasnost" among the recommendations for the "governing of Siberia"
  in an article not published until two years after his death. (Mikhail Speransky,
  "Obozrenie glavnykh osnovaniy mestnogo samoupravleniya Sibiri. Napechat-
  ano po Vysochayshemu poveleniyu" [An overview of the main arguments
  for the local self-rule of Siberia. Published at the Highest order (of the tsar)],
  St. Petersburg, 1841: 8, as quoted in S. G. Svatikov, "Rossiya i Sibir'" [Russia and
  Siberia], 91. The author is most grateful to Dr. Jonathan Sanders for providing a

Politburo member second only to Mikhail Gorbachev in his responsibility for launching and sustaining the liberalization.* The "first gulps of freedom," Yakovlev continued, "the ability to speak freely, to think freely without the fear of denunciations or camps . . . exhilarated" and "intoxicated."[6] The society began to "learn the truth about itself," rejoiced the literary critic Igor Vinogradov, and this process was becoming uncontrollable![7]

Newspaper and magazine articles "stunned" the readers, a leading essayist recorded at the time.[8] The mailboxes from which Russians retrieved their newspapers and magazines became daily purveyors of miracles. In their armchairs, on couches, or on the Metro, millions of people read about subjects that as recently as three years before would have qualified as a crime under Article 190 of the Criminal Code of the Russian Federation: "spreading of the obviously false fabrications besmirching the Soviet political system."[9]

"We would not dare think that which we write today," a prominent playwright noted in the fall of 1986.[10] In a popular Moscow joke of those days, a delirious man calls his friend on the phone to make sure he had read an article in the latest issue of the weekly *Moskovskie novosti* (Moscow news). "I haven't yet," was the reply. "But what's in it?" "Are you crazy?!" the caller answers (assuming, as did everyone, that his phone was tapped). "I cannot possibly discuss this over the phone!"

In a July 1987 speech, Yakovlev called glasnost "our communal return to truth,"[11] and the result was compared by the editor of a premier liberal weekly to a "spiritual earthquake."[12] The "acute thirst for truth" became the most pronounced national trait, a "civic and political credo of millions."[13] Foreign observers saw a country transfixed by truth, undergoing an "exorcism" and "catharsis."[14] Truth—about anything and everything: the country's economy and politics, how people really lived and what they really thought, leaders past and present, the world outside the still-sealed borders—became "almost the main word in the vocabulary" of the nation, the "symbol and the slogan" of change.[15]

---

copy of Svatikov's article. The book or journal in which Svatikov's article was published, however, could not be found.)

* For more on this remarkable man, see Leon Aron, "The 'Mystery' of the Soviet Collapse," *Journal of Democracy* 17 (2), April 2006.

Even for those who were directly involved in the almost daily expansion of truth's reach—writers, journalists, essayists—so swift and dazzling were the advances that at times they, too, had to remind themselves of the enormity of this "breakthrough to freedom":

> The spiritual life of our society is changing right in front of
> us. . . . Truth that used to be hidden behind seven locks and seals
> has been let out of its prison and has become our interlocutor.
> Even those who . . . for a long time kept truth gagged are now
> forced to listen to it. . . . And it is only in looking back . . . to see
> how far behind we have left the "ice age" one realizes how sharp
> have been the shifts in our life and in our conscience, what
> blinkers we are shedding, and what powerful machinery for the
> suppression of living and free thought we are dismantling.[16]

All the conduits of truth were passionately sought after. Lines to newspaper kiosks—sometimes "huge crowds" around the block—formed at six in the morning and the daily allotments were often sold out in two hours.[17] One of these readers called this daily ritual "morning newspaper rallies."[18] Newspapers and magazines with articles by the most celebrated essayists of glasnost—Nikolay Shmelyov, Anatoly Strelyaniy, Yuri Chernichenko, Gennady Lisichkin, Lyudmila Popkova, Vasiliy Selyunin, and Gennady Khanin—were reported "disappearing" from the library stacks.[19] Magazine essays were retyped or photocopied and read till "there were holes" in the pages.[20] And yet, a journalist asked, "has our thirst for the full truth been satisfied, our thirst for—finally!—calling all the unpleasant things by their own names—and aloud? No, we are only acquiring a taste for it."[21]

The readership of the most daring newspapers and magazines grew by numbers that now seem fantastic. Between 1986 and 1989 subscriptions to the weekly *Argumenti i fakty* (Arguments and facts)—formerly an execrable aide to Party propagandists and now purveyor of hard-hitting commentary and formerly secret facts and figures about all aspects of life in the Soviet Union—increased tenfold to 20,458,000.[22]* Subscriptions to another liberal weekly, *Literaturnaya gazeta*, doubled to 6,627,700; to *Izvestia*, by over 40 percent to 10,138,000; and to *Komsomol'skaya pravda*,

---

* A year later, the weekly's subscription reached 32,959,000 ("K chitatelyam" [To the readers], an editorial, *Argumenti i fakty*, January 6–12, 1990: 1).

by nearly 20 percent (from the second largest subscription base in the country of 14,466,000).*

Another former propaganda sheet, the flagship of glasnost, *Moskovskie novosti* (which had been distributed largely abroad in half a dozen languages), doubled its Russian edition in 1987 to 250,000, with further increases in print runs banned by the Party's Central Committee.[23] The newspaper was sold out in minutes every Wednesday morning, with lines forming from 5:00 a.m. It was then passed hand-to-hand throughout the country. Informal meetings and political debates were held daily outside of the paper's editorial offices on Pushkin Square in the center of Moscow.[24]

The circulation of the other most audacious periodical, the illustrated weekly *Ogonyok*—until 1986 a "devastatingly platitudinous" magazine— increased from a few hundred thousand copies to 3.5 million.[25] The magazine's "A Word from the Reader" column, where letters were published without changes, became what rightly was called "the first national forum of open political and social debate available to Soviet citizens."[26] *Ogonyok* received 15,372 readers' letters in 1986; the next year, 49,619; and 112,842 in 1988.[27] "For the first time in my life (and I am seventy years old), I have given a bribe," one of these letters read. "Do you know what for? For a subscription to *Ogonyok*. How much? Fifty rubles above the listed price. And my pension is only eighty rubles a month. I am forced to act dishonestly because I can't live without the magazine."[28]

After leading literary magazines (known as "the thick" ones) adopted a liberal "agenda"[29] and started to publish some of the finest of the formerly forbidden Russian writers (and soon added revolutionary essayists) they, too, began rapidly to acquire new subscribers.† Led by the

---

* The leader in the overall number of subscribers, the conservative daily *Trud* grew only by 9 percent, and *Pravda*'s subscription declined slightly. At the peak of the newspaper and magazine "boom" (1988–89) subscription to the leading conservative publications began to fall: *Pravda* lost 183,000 readers, and *Sovetskaya Rossiya*, 392,000 (*Izvestiya TsK KPSS*, no. 1, 1981: 139).

† Discussing the "magazine boom" in an interview published in January 1988, two leading public opinion experts attributed the upsurge in the subscriptions to the acclaim of the publications of the poets Nikolay Gumilyov, Vladislav Khodasevich, Anna Akhmatova (*Requiem*), Osip Mandel'shtam, Boris

newly appointed editors, between 1986 and 1989 *Novy mir* (New world) and *Znamya* (Banner) grew more than fourfold; *Oktyabr'* (October), by

Pasternak, Alexander Tvardovsky (*Po pravu pamyati,* or "By memory's right"), Marina Tsvetaeva, and Vladimir Vysotksiy; and the writers Mikhail Bulgakov, Vladimir Nabokov (his poetry would be published later), Alexander Bek (*Novoe naznachenie* [A new appointment]), Vladimir Dudintsev, Daniil Granin (*Zubr* [Bison]), Andrey Platonov (*Chevengur*), and Varlam Shalamov. According to the authors' surveys of readers and librarians, Anatoly Rybakov's novel *Deti Arbata* was the most popular work of 1987. (Lev Gudkov and Boris Dubin, "Chto my chitaem" [What we read], interviewed by Mikhail Gurevich, *Literaturnoe obozrenie* 1, 1988: 93–94. The titles next to the authors' names are from L. Ayzerman, "Trevozhit'sya i dumat" [To worry and to think], *Novy mir,* October 1987: 182–83, and Natal'ya Ivanova, "Perekhod cherez boloto" [Crossing a quagmire], *Ogonyok* 25, 1988: 14. Among the magazine "hits" of the first half of 1988, Ivanova singles out the translations of Aldous Huxley's *Brave New World* and of Orwell's *Animal Farm* and Evgeny Zamyatin's 1920 anti-utopia *My* [We].)

For a good discussion of mostly the same publications, as well as the politics of the editorial appointments, by Western observers, see Geofrey A Hosking, "At Last an Exorcism" in the *Times Literary Supplement,* October 9–15, 1987: 1111, and Riitta H. Pitman. "*Perestroika* and Soviet Cultural Politics: The Case of the Major Literary Journals," *Soviet Studies* 42, no. 1, January 1990: 111–32. Hosking rightly adds Anatoliy Pristavkin's *Nochevala tuchka zolotayar* (Where a little golden cloud spent a night) to the list. Pitman also includes Vasily Grossman's *Zhizn' i sud'ba* and Boris Pasternak's *Doktor Zhivago,* both published in early 1988 in *Znamya* and *Novy mir.*

Among the authors of the most influential essays, Gudkov and Dubin list Grigoriy Khanin, Vasiliy Selyunin, Ludmila Popkova, Yuri Chernichenko, Yuri Afanasiev, Gavriil Popov, and Anatoly Strelyaniy. Nikolay Shmelyov's 1987 essay "Avansy i dolgi" (Advances and debts) was singled out as the most popular at the time. A year later, compiling a list of "perestroika's leaders, its 'brain trust,'" of those who "personify" perestroika, an *Ogonyok* media analyst added Ales' Adamovich, Fedor Burlatsky, Yuri Karyakin, Otto Latsis, Andrei Nuykin, Andrei Sakharov, Svyatoslav Fyodorov, and Natan Eidelman. Along with the writers in Gudkov's and Dubinin's article, essays and articles by all these authors will be cited in the chapters that follow. (Lidiya Pol'skaya, "Televizion-naya provintsiya" [A television province], *Ogonyok* 10, 1989: 22.)

Many of the magazines without a revolutionary agenda also expanded subscriptions and print runs between 1981 and 1987, but the readership of the most popular conservative magazines, *Molodya Gvardiya* (The young guard) and *Nash sovermennik* (Our contemporary) reportedly shrank by 26 percent and 34 percent, or by 230,000 and 113,000 (Gudkov and Dubin, 96).

nearly three times, and the previously obscure *Druzhba narodov* (Peoples' friendship) by over 900 percent.[30]*

As usual, the intelligentsia spearheaded the magazine readership boom.[31] "Intellectuals here are completely caught up in the process of keeping up with all the journals and newspapers," an American journalist reported from Moscow in June 1988.[32] Indeed, according to the responses to questionnaires distributed among the patrons of the Soviet Union's main Lenin Library in early 1989, between one-third and one-half of them had read at least some of the key texts of Russia's recovered literary canon (the "new old books," as they came to be known), published in the "thick" magazines at most a few months before: Andrei Platonov's *Kotlovan* (The foundation pit), Mikhail Bulgakov's *Sobach'e serdtse* (Dog's heart), Vassiliy Grossman's *Zhizn' i sud'ba* (Life and fate), and Boris Pasternak's *Doktor Zhivago*.[33]

Yet the intelligentsia alone could not have accounted for the resonance that the reclaimed truth elicited throughout the country. "Dear editors!" a woman wrote *Novy mir* in January 1987:

> This is the first time in my life that I write about my reaction
> to the printed word. I have never been especially interested in
> politics: like most women, I simply don't have much time for
> it. . . . With the arrival of M. S. Gorbachev and the suddenly
> appearing freedom of the press I began to read newspapers
> (mostly *Literaturnaya* [*gazeta*]), began, as many so-called
> ordinary folks, to evaluate and reevaluate the situation in
> the country far deeper than I ever have done before. . . . So
> one cannot avoid this conclusion: how urgent [must be] the
> necessity of solving all these problems [before the country] if
> even I, a rank-and-file Soviet person, a woman, have felt the
> truthfulness and correctness of this entirely new approach to
> our life?[34]

---

* Like Gudkov and Dubin, a leading Russian liberal literary critic (and a new member of *Znamya*'s editorial board), Vladimir Lakshin, attributed this phenomenal growth to the publication of *Deti Arbata*. (Vladimir Lakshin, "Gresti vyshe" [Aim higher], *Moskovskie novosti*, December 20, 1987: 4.) Rybakov's novel had waited its turn for twenty years, having first been slated for publication by *Novy mir* in 1966.

The latest articles caused heated discussion on buses and trams.[35] Debating clubs sprang up in colleges, scientific institutes, high schools, and factories. One such society, the "N. I. Bukharin Club"—named after a top Communist theoretician, Lenin's comrade-in-arms, who opposed Stalin's "collectivization" in the late 1920s and was shot after a show trial— was organized at a giant Kama Automobile Plant (KamAZ) in Naberzhenye Chelny on the Volga. "At my first meeting I must confess I was flabbergasted," a KamAZ metalworker told visitors from Moscow in September 1988. "Glasnost is great but one must know where to stop. And then I thought: who is to determine how far one can go [in a discussion] and by which criteria can they measure [freedom of speech]. I simply was unused to a free exchange of opinions. Now I see freedom of thought as something natural."[36] A fellow club member added: "When I think back to what I was two years ago, the difference is enormous. I have realized that I had no idea what social sciences are: what I knew instead was no more than political superstition; I had no position of my own."[37]

It is almost certain that eight months later the Bukharin Club members were among the tens of millions who watched every minute of the ninety-five hours of live broadcast[38] of the inaugural session of the Congress of People's Deputies—the first uncensored public political debate in the country's legislature in seventy-two years. During three weeks in May and June of 1989, the country almost came to a standstill— "enraptured," as a leading national daily put it, by the "euphoria from the degree of glasnost."[39]

The Congress was followed, on television or radio, by an estimated 70–90 percent of adults in the country's largest cities.[40] Everyone who could sat in front of a television set, wrote one of the most popular of the glasnost essayists, Igor Klyamkin, because something "utterly unimaginable in its openness, frankness, and the heat of political passions" unfolded in front of them.[41] Transistor radios hung from the push bars of baby carriages as the mothers listened to the proceedings.[42] Economic production fell by an estimated one-fifth compared to the same time the year before.[43]*

---

* During those "weeks of wonder," as leading Soviet sociologist and pollster, Yuri Levada, called them, when the entire country, "as if under a spell, sat in front of television sets," they heard things that "only a year before" one could not imagine seeing in a newspaper. If someone had shown him a year before what

Interviewed a day after the Congress adjourned, one of the deputies, Russia's most respected liberal thinker, former dissident leader, and Nobel Peace Prize winner, Andrei Sakharov, suggested that the main effect of the gathering was "the awakening of the political sense of the millions of people."[44] The Congress proved, Sakharov continued, that "the people are not at all passive. They simply had no outlet for their [political] effort. And when such an outlet emerged, emerging with it was real political action. Its significance will become clearer as time passes."[45]

They were learning to speak their mind, "to say what we think, what we really feel," wrote the *Izvestia* columnist and television commentator Alexander Bovin, whose hefty bulk, enormous Balzacian head and mane, and luxurious moustache were familiar to millions of Soviet viewers:

> It has proved to be a difficult science. . . . The screaming
> muteness was not a dreadful dream, but a dreadful reality. The
> decades of triumphant lies, empty speeches, spiritual paralysis
> doomed truth to become awkward, barely coherent. And now
> we are learning to tell truth. . . . About ourselves, about our
> future and our past. We are learning to evaluate the scenarios
> of the future, as it is being made today. The problem of truth is
> not just a personal problem of each of us. It is a problem of
> conscience, morality, self-respect.[46]

Among the first discoveries of this "difficult science" was that after seven decades of the symbiosis of censorship and terror, one of the tallest obstacles to a better future was self-deception (*samoobman*). When "totalitarianism began to destroy souls,* creativity was replaced by myth-making [*mifotvorchestvo*]."[47] Other nations had experienced self-deception,

---

he saw, wrote the editor in chief of *Moskovskie novosti,* Egor Yakovlev, he would have thought that the show was part of an elaborate ruse. (Yuri Levada, "Poezd speshit i opazdyvaet" [The train hurries up and is being late], *Sovetskaya kul'tura,* October 14, 1989: 2; Egor Yakovlev, "S'ezd i politicheskaya reforma" [The Congress and the political reform], *Moskovskie novosti,* June 18, 1989: 3.)

* "Spirituality" is another way to translate *dukhovnost',* which was one of the most popular terms in the early conversations of glasnost and which connotes the nobler, loftier, creative, and moral side of human existence. I feel that "souls" fits better here.

Klyamkin commented: "We have had self-deception squared. Which is why we produced liars of the kind that the world had not seen before. It looks like only now we begin to understand how huge our self-deception was, what a dangerous illness it is."[48]

At the root of this "tragic" self-delusion[49] were ideological dogmas, grotesquely divorced from life yet unchallenged for generations. Born of the "thick fog of fear and demagoguery," myths had taken the place of reality.[50] They had shaped the political, social, and moral vocabularies. They informed actions. Never before "in the history of humanity had anyone been as enslaved by myths as our people," wrote political philosopher Alexander Tsypko.[51] From top to bottom, everyone "prayed to the old idols," like the pagans who continued to worship the old gods long after Prince Vladimir, the baptizer of Kievan Rus, threw their images in the Dnieper. This "blindness of non-freedom" was like a "cataract" on the eyes of the entire people.[52]

Could it be otherwise, when the economy is "deformed" and the political system is "inhumane"?[53] How can people's conscience remain "normal"?[54] It was from the need to reconcile the "normal logic" with the "general pathology" of Soviet life that scores of ideological myths had sprung up "to help the Soviet man to believe that he lived well and was the happiest man in the world."[55]

No one could help the country, "not even God," until the myths were discarded—and with them, the "chronic non-understanding of ourselves [khronicheskoe samoneponimanie]."[56] The choice was stark: "Will the society again be entangled in the net of myths, fettering free will and free action and spawning illusory hopes—or will free spirit and free mind of a self-conscious man, a man capable of finding his place in the world without the soothing idolatry, prevail?"[57]

De-mythologization (demifologizatsiya) was seen as central to Russia's "difficult return to civilization."[58]* "Curing ourselves" of self-deception

---

* The demolition of some of the key legitimizing myths about the Soviet Union's history, society, and economy will be discussed in the next part of this book. For a useful account of the linguistic "assault of demystification" and of how the "various myths" about Soviet socialism were "overturned" and "deconstructed" in the Soviet media (and, in turn, "abetted the deconstruction of Soviet social system"), see Nancy Ries's book about the "perestroika folklore": *Russian Talk: Culture and Conversation during Perestroika* (Ithaca: Cornell University Press, 1997).

meant nothing less than "becoming a different people."[59] It meant the "rejection not only of the military-communist violence but also of the military-communist illusions . . . and the military-communist blind faith."[60]

Troubling as it was, the national self-delusion was only one aspect of what Sakharov called the "moral degradation of the society."[61] The decade of Khrushchev's on-and-off liberalizing "thaw" (1954–64) aside, the "moral quagmire"[62] was the "truly terrifying result" of the four and a half decades of Stalinism and the corrupt "soft" totalitarianism of the Brezhnev era, with its numbing mixture of "deception and self-deception" and "sterile" public discourse.[63]

The break with "the elemental notions of good and evil" was now believed to be such that the "civilized world had not seen before."[64] Fear—whether during Stalin's "Great Terror" of 1937 or during the Brezhnev years, "horrible in the banality" of their evil—had corroded and eaten through the people's souls "worse than acid," wrote one of the Soviet Union's most popular film actors Georgiy Zhzhyonov.[65] People "suffocated" from the inability not just to say what they thought but even to think freely.[66]

In a letter to *Komsomol'skaya Pravda,* a reader decried the "ghastly and tragic . . . loss of morality by a huge number of people living within the borders of the USSR."[67] Symptoms of moral debility were in plain sight: apathy and hypocrisy, cynicism, servility, and snitching.[68] The suffocating "miasma of bare-faced and ceaseless public lies and demagoguery";[69] the powerlessness before the "bureaucratic omnipotence";[70] the blinding, "dense fumes of fear and demagoguery";[71] the widening void between their lives and the deafening propaganda slogans—these key features of Soviet totalitarianism had engendered what the writer Anatoly Pristavkin called "an almost new biological type" of man: "a man without responsibility," who had unlearned how to act or even to think without "a command from above."[72] "*Homo* supine," Pristavkin labeled it, "*homo* indifferent," and "*homo* initiative-less [*bezynitsiativniy*]."[73]

To one of the founders of Soviet sociology and one its brightest stars, Vladimir Shubkin, what happened to the Russian people in the previous seven decades was not just a "demographic and genetic catastrophe,"[74] wrought by the loss of millions to terror, war, and starvation. The greatest calamity was "the liquidation of a social man" and his replacement by a "biological" one:

All independence [from state] social life was banned. For it is impossible, of course, to call "social" a life of the obligatory boredom of all kinds of demonstrations and meetings, the shame of the compulsory and completely controlled one-candidate "elections," the mechanical unanimity of voting, in which regularly and reliably hands go up. . . . Most people were doomed to purely biological existence. For multitudes, the unimaginable difficulties and privations in procuring the most elementary needs for food, clothing, and shelter displaced every thought of rights and civil dignity. The biological man became the hero of that time.[75]

An urgent redress was essential, vital. A 1987 article— "What is really happening to us?"—declared that the people must be "saved": not from external dangers but "most of all from themselves, from the consequences of those demoralizing processes that kill the noblest human qualities."[76]

Saved how? By making the nascent liberalization fateful, irreversible— not a "thaw" but a climate change. And what would guarantee this irreversibility (*neobratimost'*)? Above all, the appearance of the "free, unshackled [*raskreposhchyonnyi*] man, immune to the recurrences of spiritual slavery."[77] We must understand, finally, an *Ogonyok* editorial declared in February 1989, that only the "man" incapable of being a police informer, of betraying, and of lies, no matter in whose or what name, can save us from the reemergence of a totalitarian state.[78]

The circuitous nature of this reasoning—to save the people one had to save perestroika as a spiritual "revolution" and perestroika could be saved only if it was capable of changing man "from within"—did not seem to trouble anyone. Those who thought out loud about these matters seemed to assume that the country's salvation through perestroika and the extrication of its people from the spiritual morass were tightly— perhaps, inextricably—interwoven, and left it at that.

What mattered was reclaiming the people to citizenship from "serfdom" and "slavery." "Enough!" declared Boris Vasiliev, the author of a popular novella about World War II, which was made into an equally well-received film. "Enough lies, enough servility, enough cowardice. Let's remember, finally, that we are all citizens. Proud citizens of a proud nation!"[79]

With glasnost and "democratization," declared by Mikhail Gorbachev in January 1987, barely half a year old, Alexander Yakovlev dwelt on the moral foundation of the political revolution he had helped start and sustain. Achievements founded on the "violation of the principles of honesty and morality" could be neither deep nor lasting, he told Party activists in Kaluga in the summer of 1987.[80] In a break with the official dogma, he declared the primacy of the "spiritual" over "material": political and economic accomplishments, no matter how dazzling, he asserted, were "temporary." Only "man and his values [were] eternal."[81] Home and family. Freedom and duty. Honesty, decency, and fairness. The love of peace, humanism, and generosity. Courage, loyalty, and self-sacrifice. Work and creativity. Intelligence and talent.[82]

For Yakovlev, the return to these values after the decades of their subjugation to the state was vital. There could be no revolutionary changes without "profound moral improvements." Democracy and morality were inseparable. Indeed, in the long run, the "essence of the reforms" was to Yakovlev in the "restoration of morality [nravestennost'] everywhere and in all instances."[83] Morality, he concluded, had acquired "political meaning."[84] Forging a moral man and a citizen out of Homo sovieticus—the popular shibboleth for someone who bore no responsibility for himself or his country, a scared and aggressive conformist, a sullen and shoddy executor of the masters' orders—was now seen as an imperative, a sine qua non of the political revolution.

No matter what they would write about in these five years—food shortages or World War II, industry or culture, the standard of living or medicine, Stalinism or Marxism, democracy or market economy—the finest of the glasnost essayists were moral philosophers, who believed that a "new structure of values" was the "key issue" of what they firmly believed was an unfolding revolution, not a mere "change of decorations."[85] They were moralists—passionate and impatient, speaking the language of absolutes. The "betterment of the moral condition" of society was their goal.[86] No, not enough: the "reorientation of conscience" or even a "different morality"![87]

This was a tall order. Shubkin described a "sad reality": people "debased, insulted, deceived" and only now, timidly, "beginning to guess that they could be citizens."[88] And yet, he concluded, there was no other way out of the crisis but through a "moral renaissance."[89] Shubkin, called the mission "moral education": the "awakening" of people's conscience.[90]

Such, indeed, seemed to be the consensus. To Sakharov, the "regeneration" of Soviet society was "possible only on a [new] moral [*nravstvennoy*] foundation."[91] Glasnost, he wrote, was also first and foremost a means to create "a new moral climate in the country," in which "corrupting lies, silence and hypocrisy" would be "forever banished" and "man . . . [would] feel free."[92] Mikhail Gorbachev saw the goal of "democratization" in fashioning a new "moral atmosphere."[93] A leading economist counted "revolutionary changes in human spirit" as "the first condition" of societal "self-renewal."[94] To a preeminent legal scholar, "our peaceful revolution could succeed only as a highly moral process."[95]

In a fine book about vast and fateful breakdowns in societal mores (*The Great Disruption*) political philosopher Francis Fukuyama has called such attempts at national moral healing "renorming." The "Great Disruption," Fukuyama argued, will not correct itself automatically. People will have to recognize that their communal lives have deteriorated, that they have to work to "renorm" their society "through discussion, argument, cultural argument, and even culture wars."[96]

By 1988, such "renorming" of Soviet Russia was the key item on the revolution's agenda. "We are on the verge of a spiritual revolution . . . which will require from us an utmost effort and true creativity," wrote Igor Klyamkin. "It looks like only now we are beginning to understand what profound and difficult spiritual renewal we will have to live through."[97]

The need to anticipate—and inspire!—this moral revolution prompted the pro-reform opinion leaders to shift the uses of truth. By the middle of 1988, there was already a change from cathartic exultation over the erosion of censorship to a better focused, more disciplined, and more instrumental deployment of truth both as a diagnostic tool to assess the damage done to the country in the previous seven decades and as a device of moral repair. Speaking honestly to the people about what had happened to them and their country was now an indispensable means of "strengthening values and moral notions."[98]

The only path to a free, prosperous, and dignified Russia lay through a scrutiny, by millions of Russians, of the country's past and present. For the glasnost troubadours there was no higher, more vital mission than to "assist" this revolutionary "processes of self-comprehension [*samosoz-nanie*]."[99] There could be no moral recovery without unflinching self-discovery. Above all, perestroika needed a most sober, most merciless burning out (*vyzhiganie*) of any self-delusion.[100] What people concealed and what they feared was the same, concluded a young essayist.[101] If hiding truth was a sign of fear, revealing it was to remove the dread.[102] A road to a Russia in which a free individual flourishes ran "only . . . through completely honest self-learning [*samopoznanie*] and self-awareness [*samosoznanie*]."[103]* One of Russia's finest poets, Fyodor Tyutchev, was brought to bear on the matter: "For society, as well as for an individual, self-knowledge is the first condition of any progress."[104]

Tell the truth and shame the devil—the devil of self-delusion, betrayals, and self-abasement! Those who wished for perestroika to succeed may have found their motto uttered by Shakespeare's Hotspur.[105] Without truth, a reader wrote to *Znamya*, "we will never acquire dignity and believe in the sincerity of perestroika."† If we now, today, don't openly

---

* "The Party and the people need the entire truth," Gorbachev said at the time, "the truth in things large and small. Only the truth rears people with a developed sense of civic duty, while lies and semi-truth corrupt consciousness, deform individuals . . ." (as quoted in Vasily Selyunin and Grigory Khanin, "Lukavaya tsifra" [The cunning figure], *Novy mir* 2, February 1987: 200).

† Indeed, in its first two years, glasnost was considered not just a condition or a key "institution" of perestroika but its "guarantor" and an "expression" of a new, "different view of an individual," of new and different "relations between people." In one of the first public opinion polls, conducted by *Argumenty i fakty* in early 1988, a very strong plurality (31 percent compared with 13 percent for the next most popular definition) defined democracy as the "freedom to express one's opinion" ("to say what you think without the fear of consequences"). Conversely, the absence of glasnost was not simply lack of information but a "symbol of non-democratic social relations," an equivalent of "lawlessness and arbitrariness." When "people are silent, autocracy and petty tyranny reign"; the country without glasnost means "stagnation and death of the society." (N. K. Kozyrev, a letter to *Ogonyok*, in Christopher Cerf and Marina Albee, eds., *Small Fires: Letters from the Soviet People to Ogonyok Magazine, 1987–1990*, New York: Summit Books, 1990: 87; Yuri Burtin, "Vozmozhnost' vozrazit'" [The possibility of voicing an objection], in Yuri Afanasiev, ed., *Inogo ne dano* [There is no other way], Moscow: Progress, 1988: 479; O. Maslova, "Kak my predstavlyaem sebe demokratiyu i glasnost?" [How do we view democracy and glasnost?],

"tell the truth," she insisted, "we will deserve nothing but contempt from other nations."[106]

Having lied to itself for so long, the country must undergo "penance" (*epitim'ya*) by truth.[107] Every institution—political, economic, social—must be subjected to "trial by truth and conscience."[108] To be afraid to tell the truth, "the whole truth," when the country found itself "on the brink of catastrophe" was "immoral."[109]

A merciless national introspection of astounding breadth and intensity ensued—the most important element of the mammoth and desperate effort to forge a more honorable, virtuous man, state, and society. What those who prodded the nation to embark on in this painful trek of self-discovery saw along the way and what they thought should be done about it will fill the subsequent chapters of this book.

Before we turn to them, however, a word is in order about those whose sensibilities and concerns so powerfully shaped the ideas and ideals of the gathering revolution: the troubadours of glasnost and perestroika, the "morally passionate malcontents,"[110] or, in Dr. Johnson's phrase, "teachers of truth."[111]

There were hundreds of them: writers, essayists, journalists, the makers of documentaries, scholars. They published and broadcast everywhere from *Izvestia* and national television to the myriad local newspapers and local radio and television stations. They were as different as the audiences they served, as the landscapes, climes, and the time zones of their enormous land.

Yet there was consistency in the biographies of some of the most famous and influential of them. Whether in their forties, fifties, or sixties, they proudly counted themselves among the *shestidesyatniki,* or the people of the 1960s: those who came of political age and got a taste of the truth about Stalin in Khrushchev's 1956 speech to the Twentieth Party Congress and again in the anti-Stalinist campaign of 1961–63. The hatred of Stalinism was at the center of their "political culture," and everything they

Argumenty i fakty, February 20–26, 1988: 4; Alexander Bovin, "Perestroika . . ." in Afanasiev, ed., *Inogo ne dano,* 550; Grigoriy Baklanov, "Vystuplenie na plenume pravleneniya soyuza pisateley," speech at the Plenum of the Presidium of the Writers' Union, April 27–28, 1987, *Literaturnaya gazeta,* May 6, 1987: 2.)

wrote was informed by the ardent belief that "in any honest and thinking person Stalinism could not but call forth the fiercest rejection, protest, countervail [*protivostoyanie*] the desire to change this anti-human system."[112] And so it was they who, in the words of Alexander Yakovlev, "tore off the rusted locks of bolshevism and let truth out of an iron cage."[113]*

As often happens in revolutions, the ferocity of this assault stemmed from the guilty conscience of the revolutionary apostates: the need to atone for their acquiescence to (and, in many cases, complicity in) the policies of a regime they now declared immoral, especially its "ban on truth" and "the organized oblivion" during the previous quarter century.[114] It was their chance—so precious, so unexpected!—to redeem their lives, to make amends for "one's silence, toadying, and worship of false idols."[115]

Some of glasnost's biggest stars were correctly labeled "functionaries of Staraya Ploshchad'" (Old Square), where the Central Committee's building stood.[116] Others had worked in research institutes that served the Central Committee or helped mightily to spread its "line" in leading national newspapers and magazines, on television, in books or university auditoria: Yuri Afanasiev and Alexander Bovin, Fyodor Burlatsky and Yuri Chernichenko, Len Karpinsky and Yuri Koryakin, Ivan Laptev, Gennady Lisichkin, Otto Latzis and Alexander Pumpyansky, Vasiliy Selyunin and Nikolai Shmelyov, Egor Yakovlev, and, of course, Alexander Yakovlev himself.[117]†

---

* Among other stars, whose names were mentioned with remarkable consistency, are Ales' Adamovich, Yuri Burtin, Andrey Nuykin, Vladmir Shubkin, Gavriil Popov, and Anatoly Strelyaniy. (See, for example, Lev Gudkov and Boris Dubin, "Literaturnaya kul'tura: protsess i ratsion" [The literary culture: the process and the rationing], *Druzhba narodov* 2, February 1988: 179; Yuri Chernichenko, "Zemlya, ekologiya, perestroika" [Land, ecology, perestroika], *Literaturnaya gazeta*, January 29, 1989: 3; and Tatyana Ivanova, "Kto chem riskuet" [Who risks what], *Ogonyok* 24, 1988: 10.)

† For instance, Shmelyov was a Central Committee lecturer and, for a time, Khrushchev's son-in-law; Burlatsky, before becoming editor of *Literaturnaya gazeta*, was a former senior Central Committee aide and *Pravda* columnist; Bovin, who had been Yuriy Andropov's aide, was an *Izvestia* columnist and television commentator; Lisichkin was another *Pravda* columnist; Egor Yakovlev was an ex–editorial board member of *Pravda*, as were Len Karpinskiy (who had also been a secretary of the Komsomol's Central Committee) and Yuri Karyakin;

They considered themselves "irradiated in the explosion" of Khrushchev's de-Stalinization.[118] But they later realized, having "shaken and tilted the idol," that explosion failed to bring it down. Now that, as one of them declared, "the children of the 20th Congress have come to power in our country,"[119] the time had come to make up for the wasted time of "veils" and "subterfuges."[120] *"Dobit' Stalina!"*—"Finish off Stalin!"— became their first battlecry.[121]

Glasnost began, literally, with the 1986 anti-Stalinism allegory, the film *Pokoyanie,* or "Repentance," mentioned in the introduction. Its release was forced through the Politburo by Alexander Yakovlev after heated debates.[122] For the next year and a half, the expanding freedom of the press was virtually synonymous with the publications of anti-Stalinist works in the "thick" literary magazines by their *shestidesyatniki* editors: Rybakov's novel *Deti Arbata* (The children of Arbat), Tvardovsky's poem "Po pravu pamyati" (In memory's name), and, of course and most important, Vasily Grossman's *Zhizn' i sud'ba* (Life and fate). They were soon followed by George Orwell's *1984;* Varlam Shalamov's *Kolymskie rasskazy* (The Kolyma tales), the literary account of the worst of the Soviet extermination camps; Vladmir Dudintzev's *Belye odezhdy* about the Lysenko pogrom of Soviet genetics in the 1940s; and Anatoly Pristavkin's *Nochevala tuchka zolotaya* (A golden cloud slept here), with its harrowing description of Soviet orphanages and of deserted Caucasus villages after the murderous deportation of the Chechens in 1944.

Yet, as Macaulay noted, "in revolutions men live fast,"[123] and the intellectual odyssey of astounding pace and daring soon brought the "teachers of truth" to the understanding that, for all his "sensational" courage, Khrushchev never had confronted the "cardinal question": What needed to be done for these "nightmares, this terror, this genocide" never to be repeated?[124]

It is this quest that they now were determined to pursue with vengeance and to the end. Like the seminarian Khoma Brut, who confronted evil spirits in Gogol's gothic horror tale *Viy,* they gathered all their courage to gaze upward, to step outside the chalked circle of the previously

---

the dean of the History and Archives Institute, Yuriy Afanasiev, had been the head of the Young Pioneer Organization (Chernichenko, "Trava . . . ," 600–601).

permissible.[125] If before they had been lucky to be able to criticize exceptions to the rules, now they were taking on the rules themselves.[126]

The stakes were enormous. The initial diagnosis of "deep illness" and "degradation" was upgraded to a "deep, comprehensive crisis."[127] The two preceding decades (the "shameful bacchanalia of Brezhnevism") brought the country "on the verge of national catastrophe," a nationwide, "universal Chernobyl" (after the 1986 tragic accident at a Soviet nuclear plant): "economic and political, social and national, ideological and moral."[128] This was "the last boundary," beyond which lay an "abyss."[129] If the revolution was defeated, the motherland would continue to slide, inexorably, toward being "an underdeveloped country, especially in science and technology, bristling with the fence of megaton nuclear missiles."[130]

Now the "train of the country's history" suddenly began to move.[131] History was being "resumed" (vozobnovlena).[132] Yet for the teachers of truth the tragedy of Khrushchev's aborted "thaw"—and the memory of their fathers, mothers, and older brothers murdered or tormented by Stalin—was in their bones. The "teachers of truth" were haunted by a sense of the fragility of the miracle Mikhail Gorbachev had worked. "Gifted" to them by Gorbachev, this chance would never present itself again, and history would not forgive them if they missed it.[133] "Not to be late!"—Kak by ne opazdat'!—was their main concern, their obsession:[134] the country's, and their, "dignity, pride, and honor" would be either restored and preserved[135]—or lost forever.[136]

In the discharge of this monumental, self-appointed mission there could be no retreat. Khrushchev's failure to drive a stake through the heart of Stalin's "cult" became their "lesson for life," and "Never again!" (Nikogda bol'she!), their banner.[137] "Could we stop now" and let the illness again be driven inward and "the violation of basic human rights continue?" asked the Lenin Prize winner in literature Chingiz Aytmatov. "This must not happen. N-E-V-E-R!"[138]

The Fatherland is in danger, Academician Dmitry Likhachev, the former Gulag prisoner and a leading historian of Russian literature, told the First Congress of People's Deputies. "And its fate is in your hands."[139]

The "teachers of truth" remind one of men and women whose moral crusade precipitated an upheaval over a century before in a country that had been Soviet Russia's perennial model and a bugaboo—the United States. Like American abolitionists, the leaders of glasnost were driven by an unshakable belief in a "moral . . . revolution" that could "terminate only in the success on the side of freedom."[140] Like them, Russian liberators began as a handful of voices for emancipation. They thought of themselves as "heating coils [kipyatil'shiki] in public opinion's cauldron,"[141] and, like the abolitionists, their "capacity to arouse outrage," too, has proved "disproportionate" to their numbers.[142]

At least for the first two years of perestroika, they were moral crusaders more than political revolutionaries. The chains they set out to break "shackled not only legs but the mind and the will." All around them they saw "a slave in every man" or a smug, conceited authoritarian, "a triumphant boor."[143] Until the dignity in the mastery of one's life was restored, any talk of the "guarantees" against tyranny's return was senseless.[144]

This was an intensely personal mission. "Sooner or later," one of them wrote, "there comes a moment when people who have not lost their conscience save their people, their society, their Motherland."[145] This was *their* "turning point," *their* "moral revolution—such a monstrous, tragic, lucky" occurrence![146] *They* were the guarantors of the irreversibility of this "radical, revolutionary change."[147] Not to wait for the revolution to help me, but to help it myself! The decisive factor is "*my* responsibility, *my* courage, *my* bravery."[148] Like the abolitionists, they were not interested in reform. They wanted conversion.[149]*

In the question from *Pokoyanie*—What is the use of a street or a road if it does not lead to a temple?—the writer Boris Vasiliev heard the people's rebuke and a plea: "When will you, the intelligentsia, restore the road to the temple of people's dignity, morality, happiness?"[150] Rising to this call, the troubadours of glasnost contemplated no less than "a new vision of the world," prepared to show "an example of the uncompromising, selfless search for truth."[151] They contemplated, in the words of the *Novy mir* editor Sergei Zalygin, "reattaching" their country to the "all-human" values from which it had been "separated by the iron curtain."[152]

---

* "Every day of perestroika," wrote the *Moskovskie novosti* columnist Vitaly Tret'yakov, "means souls saved by it" ("Spasyonnye perestroikoy" [Saved by perestroika], *Moskovskie novosti*, January 1, 1989: 3).

They were uncompromising, passionate, and wishful, and their plans were grandiose and fateful. Yet they were not blind to the enormous impediments that stood in the way. "Squeezing out" one's inner "slave," drop by drop, in Chekhov's famous words, was a long and painful chore.[153] Just as only weeds grow without cultivation, so only aggressiveness and intolerance could be generated spontaneously. The ability to think like a free man will come only after difficult effort.[154]

They suspected that it would be a very long time before the country recovered from the moral "paralysis," before the "cataracts" encrusted in the decades of lies fell off people's eyes and their truth became "the people's truth."[155] Parting with the myths would be painful and would discomfit many.[156] Freedom required effort. Freedom was responsibility and the lack of certainty.[157] To learn to "inhale in the air of liberty and to appreciate its enormous gifts," they knew, were very difficult skills to master.[158]

People had to be jolted out of complacency to overcome their natural resistance to the "bitter truth."[159] Tocsins of sorrow had to be sounded. A truth that did not "injure someone's conscience"—a convenient, carefully measured (*dozirovannaya*) truth—was of no use to them now.[160] Only the one that "blows up our comfort to pieces" would do.[161]

Like the prince in *Romeo and Juliet,* the "teachers of truth" volunteered to be the "generals of woes": the lead mourners for the millions killed by terror, starved and worked to death in camps, wasted in the wars fought with incompetence and utter disdain for soldiers' lives. Responsibility for themselves and their country began "with pain, with the feeling of guilt, and personal guilt at that, for everything that is happening around us."[162] Moral accountability and personal culpability were the key prerequisites of national revival. (Marx, still a demigod, was quoted on the necessity "for people to be appalled at themselves to breathe courage into them.")[163]

The Russian abolitionists were inspired by the glorious national tradition. For Russia's belles lettres was "a teacher's [*uchitel'skaya*] literature," as Zalygin put it.[164] It taught morality. It was the priest, the prosecutor, the sociologist. It "judged the society by the laws of ethics and common sense."[165] Russia, he continued, had not had a Kant or a Hegel; instead "we had Pushkin, Dostoevsky, Tolstoy."[166]

It was this kind of "moralizing" literature they sought to revive or resurrect. They were convinced that there had never been (and may never again be) another such enchanting time for Russian literary endeavors.[167] The writer was to be "a doctor performing a lifesaving surgery" of truth on a gravely ill country, his prose, like "a knife's blade," curing with truth, whether Varlam Shalamov in *Kolyma Tales,* Yuri Dombrovsky in *The Department of Useless Things,* or Vasily Grossman in *Life and Fate.*[168] The "cry of liberation" was again heard "escaping from the literature's breast."[169] This was to be not (God forbid!) a "cultural revolution," but "a revolution by culture"—a culture of "cleansing," "purification," "laver," among other meanings of the versatile Russian word *ochishchenie.*[170] If truth was a necessary condition of the collapse of totalitarianism, an *Oktyabr'* essay contended, "de-mythologization" was one of the ways in which literature could participate in this process."[171]

Where others saw and carped at the inconsistencies and hesitance of the often contradictory economic and political reforms, the "teachers of truth" welcomed and celebrated perestroika as the "purification of the moral atmosphere, the forging of a new moral climate, the liberation of thought."[172] Like Vitaly Korotich, editor of *Ogonyok,* they believed that although "brought up on lies," people were now "refusing to accept these lies as the basis for their lives," for they were realizing that "the right to truth is equal to the right to life."[173] Tired of lies, people wanted "truth at any cost"—and they themselves were "becoming more trusting, braver, purer."[174] One of glasnost's finest essayists, Yuri Chernichenko, saw "millions learning to spell *M-y n-e r-a-b-y: W-e a-r-e n-o-t s-l-a-v-e-s!*"[175] "Spiritual liberation" and "moral revolution" were believed to be gathering speed in the "rebirth" of people's dignity, their overcoming of the "slavish psychology."[176]

With Andrei Sakharov the troubadours of glasnost were convinced that despite the "tragic deformation of our people because of the terror, and the many years of living in lies and hypocrisy . . . morality is always alive in people."[177] This "moral force" was capable of growth—if only given a chance to develop.[178]

They seemed confident that Russia would emerge from this merciless self-examination as if from a Russian *banya* (sauna): bleary-eyed and with red stripes left by the birch twigs with which sauna-goers lash themselves or one another—but, at long last, clean, light, sober, serious, and ready for hard and honest work. Yes, so many huge tasks lay ahead, but people were "liberating themselves from fear, submissiveness, a life with their eyes closed," they were "shedding their skin," they were re-defining "the foundations of our morality."[179]

The "teachers of truth" saw the evidence of this transformation in the hundreds of thousands of letters that poured into the editorial offices of their magazines: 10,000 a week for *Argumenty i fakty;*[180] 200,000 a year, by 1990, for *Ogonyok,*[181] as people "discovered the freedom to dis-cuss the actions of those who had brought tragedy upon their country and used this freedom to the fullest."[182]

They were daily encouraged by their compatriots' understanding and gratitude. "Thank you for all you do for the country," a reader wrote the *Znamya* magazine. "For who will defend us if not writers–social commentators [*pisateli-publitsisty*]. I know that you sacrifice your creative work for the sacred cause of the Revival."[183] In a questionnaire, *Mos-kovskie novosti* asked readers to respond to before they voted for the Con-gress of People's Deputies in March 1989, the most popular category of an "ideal" candidate for a deputy was "a journalist-essayist, a writer, and a scholar, whose work reflects the most important problems of our times."[184]

As early as April 1987 one of glasnost's authors was remarkably pre-scient in anticipating the manner in which this support for the moral revolution-by-truth and its leaders was to unfold:

> What they tolerated only yesterday has become intolerable
> today. . . . In a society where the unexpressed unhappiness was
> accumulated for so long, the word becomes a detonator. A
> publicly uttered thought acquires a magic force. Everyone, it
> seems, knew the truth, but silently, each to himself. And even
> if they actually spoke truth—first looking around and lowering
> their voice, always—nothing changed. It is hard to gather
> courage for individual protest when you see that what causes
> anger in you others bear with seeming equanimity. But as soon
> as the conspiracy of silence around a social evil is broken, public
> opinion crystallizes rapidly. What a man yesterday considered
> his personal problem, a misfortune, or injustice is suddenly

instilled with social dimensions and is thought of as a social phenomenon. Demands to change the current state of things, to renew the economic and political life begin to be voiced [at] full-throat. Impatience is about. And beware, all, if it does not find an outlet.[185]

PART TWO *КТО МЫ?* WHO ARE WE?

Who are we?
—Sergey Zalygin, "God Solzhenitsyna" (The year of Solzhenitsyn), *Novy mir* 1, January 1990: 234

Where are we? Who are we? What do we want?
—Gennady Lisichkin, "Myfy i real'nost'" (Myths and reality), in Kh. Kobo, ed., *Osmyslit' kul't Stalina* (To comprehend Stalin's cult), Moscow: Progress, 1989: 247

Something always prevents us from giving an honest and merciless answer to the questions: who are we and where are we today?
—Viktor Krivorotov, "Russkiy put'" (The Russian path), *Znamya* 9, September 1990: 186

The curtain has risen—and we have seen ourselves.
—Mikhail Gefter, "Andrei Dmitrievich Sakharov: In memoriam," *Znamya* 1, January 1990: 5

We are advancing toward truth. The ability daily to distinguish it from lies is urgently needed.
—Vitaly Korotich, "Idyom k pravde" (Advancing toward truth), *Ogonyok*, no. 47, 1988: 6

Glasnost has brought our society to a decisive and curative self-cleansing. How many blank (or to be more precise black) spots have we cleared out, how many abscesses lanced in these years. Democratization and glasnost have made us upright, opened our eyes to the reality, albeit not very joyful.

—Evgeny Ambartsumov, "Sotsializm ili Stalinizm" (Socialism or Stalinism), *Sovetskaya kul'tura*, September 19, 1989: 2

There is no joy in writing about all this—a face is seized with a spasm. But one must.
—Vasily Selyunin, "Istoki" (The sources), *Novy mir*, May 1988: 178

CHAPTER THREE

Inside the "Deafened Zone"

They [the authorities] don't trust us. Why is that? Don't we have brains? Are we unreliable? Don't we deserve trust?
—M. Shur, letter to *Ogonyok*, 1989, in *Small Fires: Letters from the Soviet People to Ogonyok Magazine, 1987–1990*, ed. Christopher Cerf and Marina Albee, 84

We did not know the country in which we live.
—Mikhail Gorbachev, *Perestroika: New Thinking for Our Country and the World*, 7–8

"WHO ARE WE?" PROVED A very difficult question. The road to self-discovery, now deemed vital to the country's revival—indeed, her survival—was found to be full of vast gaps.

The doling out of information, deciding what the people should and should not know, was now found to be one of the Soviet regime's congenital features. The readers of *Moskovskie novosti* learned that pre-publication censorship was officially introduced in December 1921 and that half a year later the Council of People's Commissars created the infamous Glavlit, a body originally tasked with compiling the lists of forbidden books and later with censoring every book and every magazine.[1]

The "secrecy mania," now judged to be "incompatible with a civilized society,"[2] had been upheld by censorship, whose scale and "ferocity" far exceeded the "records" set by tsarist Russia.[3] Forbidden subjects, the lists of which reportedly filled "volumes,"[4] included crimes and suicides; the real value of the ruble against other currencies; drug addiction, alcoholism, and industrial accidents; how clean the water and the air really were; and how much grain the Soviet Union imported and at what price.[5] Just try to learn anything about the previous year's inflation, an economist cried out, or the cost of the space program, or the size of the national debt, the budget of ministries or even the budget of your own city![6] Goskomstat, the country's main statistical body was helpless: as its deputy director admitted in 1988, most data remained "closed," that is, kept from the statisticians by the ministries and administrations in whose purview they fell.[7]

But the true picture of the Soviet people's world was obscured not only—and perhaps not even so much—by the concealment of specific facts but by the hourly construction and maintenance of a "parallel," "brilliant" reality. Anything that might challenge it was consigned to a "conscious, premeditated, well-organized oblivion."[8]

> Forget! Forget! A silent order
> To drown in oblivion
> The throbbing pain . . .
> Forget, they demand or "request" softly.
> Not to remember: the memory placed under seals.
> Lest a freed word
> Confuse the uninitiated somehow.[9]

These lines, by one of Russia's most beloved poets, Alexander Tvardovsky, are from the poem *Po pravu pamyati* (In memory's name), which had been banned for eighteen years and was first published in 1988.[10]

Control of the past was central to this effort. The similarities between the forging and upholding of the official version of the past in the USSR and those in Orwell's *1984*, which had just been published for the first time in the Soviet Union—along with such totalitarian dystopias ("anti-utopias") as Evgeny Zamyatin's *My* (We) and Aldous Huxley's

Brave New World—quickly became a commonplace.* Vasily Grossman's masterpiece *Life and Fate* was quoted to attest to practices remarkably like those of Orwell's fictional Ministry of Truth: "a new past" was created by the Soviet state, which "refashioned, according to its own specifications, the past movement of cavalry and reappointed heroes of the events that had occurred."[11] For the state "had enough power to re-play what had already happened and forever completely change . . . the already read speeches [and] the position of figures on the already taken photographs."[12]

Reviewing a high school textbook in *Izvestia,* a writer, scholar, and former schoolteacher found it aimed at leaving "nothing to upset the rosy picture of an "uninterrupted march" of the country's glorious history: not the "monstrous distortions of the collectivization," or the hunger of the 1930s, or the banning of cybernetics and genetics in the 1940s.[13] As recently as fall 1986 an article by a prominent historian, who "tried to prove the necessity of truth in history," was turned down by an influential magazine whose editor thought the piece too daring.[14]

We "don't know millions of facts" of the country's history, complained a scholar and glasnost essayist: out of 1,300,000 "special access" files, only 700,000 were "scheduled to be opened" to the public. And that is in just one nonspecialized state archive—what about the others?!"[15] (A commission, created in 1988, was to "think about" the transfer of books from the closed archives accessible only with all manner of clearances to "regular" libraries.[16])

The permitted version of the country's history (the "new past") was populated by what a historian called "invisible" men and women.[17] A department head of the Central Committee's Academy of Social Sciences

---

* Recalling, in addition to *1984, We,* and *Brave New World,* Vladimir Nabokov's *Priglashenie na kazn'* (An invitation to a beheading), and Kafka's *Castle,* literary critics called for a "dispassionate analysis" of how this "anti-utopian" future could come "so close to the truth"; how, that is, these grim auguries are echoed so unmistakably in Varlam Shalamov's *Kolyma Tales,* Andrei Platonov's *Chevengur,* Yuri Dombrovsky's *Fakul'tet nenuzhnykh veshchey* (The department of useless things), and Vasily Grossman's *Zhizn' i sud'ba* (Life and fate). (P. Gal'tseva and I. Rodnyanskaya, "Pomekha—chelovek" [Man is the problem], *Novy mir* 12, December 1988: 217, and Natal'ya Ivanova, "Proshchanie s utopiey" [A farewell to utopia], *Literaturnaya gazeta,* July 18, 1990: 4.)

now bemoaned the decades during which not a word written by the key authors of the non-Bolshevik Left or the prominent "bourgeois liberals" of the February 1917 revolution had been allowed for publication. Among the "invisible" were the Mensheviks Pavel Aksel'rod and Lenin's formerly close friend Yuli Martov; the leader of the Constitutional Democrats (the Kadets) Pavel Milyukov; and the historian and philosopher Petr Struve, as well as the leaders of the October Revolution and the first decade of Soviet Russia murdered by Stalin: Grigory Zinov'ev, Georgy Pyatakov, Karl Radek, and Nikolai Bukharin.[18] The most maligned of these muted ghosts was Stalin's nemesis and near-obsession, Leon Trotsky, the man second only to Lenin in his role in the October Revolution and the commander of the victorious Red Army in the civil war. "No less than two generations have not been allowed to see a line of his writings," a reader complained in a letter to *Ogonyok*.[19]

Non-persons and non-events were not confined to the Stalin era. In October 1962, when "our people were led to the edge of the nuclear precipice" during the U.S.-Soviet confrontation over the installation of the Soviet nuclear-tipped missiles in Cuba, they were not allowed to know what was happening.[20] The dean of Soviet foreign reporters, *Izvestia*'s Stanislav Kondrashov, called this "the grim apotheosis of secrecy."[21] He blamed the same truth phobia for the torment of the parents of eighteen-year-olds killed in Afghanistan: they were ordered not to open the zinc coffins and to inter them in secret, with no mention on the headstones of where the boys died.[22]

Entire cities were deprived of history. After it was renamed "Ustinov" in December 1984 to honor the deceased Politburo member and minister of defense, every trace of the old name of Izhevsk (the capital of the autonomous republic of Udmurtiya) was excised from official documents and banned in mass media. In the domestic passports of all born in Izhevsk, the place of birth was changed to Ustinov. As late as spring 1987, the Secretariat of the regional Komsomol (Communist Youth) Committee forbade the local newspaper to publish readers' letters about the matter.[23]

One did not have to be a Menshevik, Kadet, or Trotskyite to have one's name forever banished from libraries and bookstores. These were constantly "sanitized" to rid them of volumes, most of them utterly apolitical, by authors who emigrated or were declared "dissidents." The

"Aggregate list" (*Svodnyi spisok*) of the "books subject to removal from libraries" in just one year (1973) contained 100 titles.[24]

In a typical case of a prolific author who had emigrated—a prominent professor of jurisprudence at Leningrad State University—Glavlit decreed the removal of all his "scholarly works" from the libraries and "the bookselling network." In addition to his textbooks for future Soviet lawyers, the now-banished "works" included such titles as *Legal Reference Book for Population* and the brochure "Morality and Law in the Struggle for Communism"—altogether thirty-one titles.[25]

Everything about and by Jews was subject to an especially exacting scrutiny. A mention of "Caanan" in a 1925 poem by an obscure author resulted in the abrupt end, in 1981, to one of the finest series of Russian literary history: *Yearbook of the Manuscript Section of the Pushkin House* published by the Institute of Russian Literature of the USSR Academy of Science.[26] (The publication was resumed in 1993.) Glavlit interfered in the writing of the endless saga *The Ulyanov Family* (Sem'ya Ul'yanovykh), about Lenin's origins and upbringing, by the much-decorated and thoroughly loyal Soviet writer Marietta Shaginyan after the Central Historical Archive had given her a photocopy of a baptismal certificate of one of Lenin's grandfathers, Abel Blank, a Jew. The archive researchers who found and released the certificate were fired; the document itself was moved to a secret section of the archive; and Shaginyan was ordered never to mention the fact in her book.[27]

In the early 1960s, a fine movie, *Komissar*, about a Jewish *schtetl* at the time of the civil war, was shot by the leading Soviet director Alexander Askol'dov. Based on a short story by Vasily Grossman and featuring two of the most popular Soviet actors, Rolan Bykov and Nonna Mordyukova, *Komissar* was instantly banned. All prints of the film were ordered to be destroyed, and Askol'dov was forever prohibited from directing.[28] (One miraculously saved copy enabled the film's release in 1988—twenty-six years after it was shot.)

This same "struggle against Zionism" led to the removal from libraries of all the books by the early Zionist leaders (Theodore Herzl and Vladimir Zhabotinsky among them) and Jewish thinkers (Martin Buber), as well as the Jewish magazines and books sympathetic to the Jewish people's plight in tsarist Russia and to their national aspirations. (They were last allowed for publication in the Soviet Union in the 1920s.) The banned publications included such titles as *The Jewish Question in the Communist Movement* (1926), and "Truth about Jews" (a 1928 brochure that branded anti-Semitism as a "shameful fact" and a "vestige of the past").[29]

The most vivid and refined part of any nation's conversation about itself and its most effective means of self-knowledge, art was watched especially carefully for any deviation from the official "brilliant reality."* Literature, which Alexander Solzhenitsyn called "a living memory of a nation" in his Nobel lecture (written in 1970 and first published in his motherland nineteen years later),[30] had been subject to an especially thorough, systematic, and merciless search for deviations.

In addition to Vasily Grossman's *Zhizn' i sud'ba* (Life and fate, 1962),[31] the roster of recovered masterpieces included Boris Pasternak's *Doktor Zhiavago* (1957), whose author was awarded the Nobel Prize in 1958;[32] Alexander Solzhenitsyn's *Rakovyi korpus* (The cancer ward), *V Kruge pervom* (In the first circle), both completed in 1968, and *Arkhipelag Gulag* (1973); Evgeny Zamyatin's *My* (We, 1920);[33] Andrei Platonov's *Kotlovan* (1929–30) and *Chevengur* (1926–29);[34] and Anna Akhmatov's *Requiem* (1935–40). Not a word by Vladimir Nabokov or by his close friend and fellow émigré, one of Russia's greatest twentieth-century poets, Vladislav Khodasevich, had reached at least three generations of Soviet readers. They were sentenced, in the words of a literary critic, to "universal, multi-year ideological imprisonment."[35]

Not published since the 1920s or the early 1930s had been the finest Russian poet of the twentieth century, Osip Mandel'shtam, who most likely died of starvation and dementia in a prison camp in 1938–39, and writer Boris Pil'nyak, who was never heard of after his arrest in 1937. The works of Isaak Babel, executed in the Lybyanka basement in 1940, were republished in the "thaw" of the 1950s and never reprinted since.[36]

Lionel Trilling's "dark and bloody crossroads where literature and politics meet" were now shown to have been part of the Soviet cultural topography for seven decades.[37] The finest Russian literature of the Soviet era was said to be not an ivory tower but a tower of the bones of the per-

---

* Literature, Lionel Trilling observed, "takes the fullest and most precise account of variousness, possibility, complexity and difficulty"—anathema, all, to the "brilliant reality." (*Liberal Imagination,* New York: Doubleday, 1953: 10.)

ished authors.[38] This war on Russian literature was declared a "spiritual genocide, which had lasted for decades, a crime against talent, intelligence, and the conscience of one's own people."[39] In the place of destroyed art, the "state literature"[40] had been designed not just for a faithful service to the "general line" of the Party but for a "blind" devotion to it.[41] The official reigning literary doctrine, "Socialist realism," was now classified as a "cultural emanation of totalitarianism."[42]

A country of almost universal literacy, Soviet Russia was a pre-literary society in anything having to do with real politics. It lived on tales and gossip, periodically swept by wild rumors.* If people dared talk frankly about affairs of state, the conversations—it was now admitted—were mostly confined to hushed late-night talks in the kitchens, whispers while walking dogs, or campfire chats.[43]

Even on such decidedly nonpublic occasions, one had to be very careful: even private, oral communications contradicting the official version of life were a crime. Article 190 (Section 1) of the Criminal Code of the Russian Soviet Federative Socialist Republic listed "systematic spreading . . . of falsehoods besmirching Soviet state and social order." The punishment was several years in camp or jail. For the recalcitrant, there was Article 70: "propaganda and agitation with the intent of undermining" the Soviet state.[44]†

The articles' casualties were not confined to "dissidents" and *samizdat* readers from the intelligentsia. In 1984, a truck driver, frustrated by what he thought was an unjust court verdict and determined to seek a review, wrote letters to Soviet institutions and, having received no answer, to the country's leaders. He was convicted and sentenced to a year and a half of jail for "spreading orally, as well as producing in a written form and

---

* "Rumors," or *Slukhi*, was the title of one of the most popular songs by Russia's favorite bard, Vladimir Vystosky, who died in 1980. Despite the efforts of his friends and admirers, including the poet Andrei Vozenesensky, "not a line" of Vysotsky's had been published until glasnost. (Andrei Vozenesensky, "My byli toshchiee, i uzhe togda nichego ne boyalis'" [We were thin as rails but already then not afraid of anything], *Ogonyok* 9, 1987: 28.)
† Article 190 was repealed on April 8, 1989.

spreading, obviously false concoctions besmirching the soviet state and social order."[45]

Those charged with being every nation's voice, eyes, and ears—the journalists—now confessed to having been afflicted with "servility" (*kholuystvo*) so deeply that it had become second nature.[46] Even now, after several years of perestroika, it required a mental effort to stop oneself from lying to one's readers.[47] The Russian intellectual and moral revolution was to fill the void in a society "without even the most elementary knowledge of itself."[48]

The "decades of triumphant lies," which only a few dared dispute, made the nightmare of the "screaming muteness" (*krichashchaya nemota*) a "daily reality."[49] Imprisoned in this "deafened zone," the nation had lost a "spiritual cohesion" and "ceased to be a single people."[50] Although they seemingly spoke the same language, Solzhenitsyn wrote, one's fellow countrymen had become "more difficult to understand than the Martians."[51] Osip Mandel'shtam's lines from over half a century before still rang true: "We live without feeling the country's soil under our feet. / What we say is not heard beyond a few paces from us."[52]

CHAPTER FOUR

In Search of History

Our common misfortune is that we have been deprived of the
opportunity really to know our history.
—A. Drobko, letter to *Komsomol'skaya Pravda,* December 28,
1990: 2

For a long time we have been separated from our history. . . .
Perhaps no other nation has known this type of war on the history
of one's own people. Our historical sense has been methodically
murdered. We are used to an invented history, to the stereotypes of
shameless lies.
—Boris Vasiliev, "Lyubi Rossiyu v nepogodu . . ." (Love Russia in
bad weather), *Izvestia,* January 16, 1989: 3

This was deception the likes of which history had not seen.
—Igor Klyamkin, "Pochemu trudno govorit' pravdu" (Why it is so
difficult to speak truth), *Novy mir* 2, February 1989: 226

Why poke at the past? Learned folk explain: it is our enemies who
drag us into a debate about the past in order to distract. O, the
enemies are cunning, no question about that. Only how are we to
learn from history, if we again start covering its lines with fingers:
this you can read, but this is a no-no? . . . A people that forgets its
history is doomed to repeat it.

—Vasily Selyunin, "Istoki" (The sources), *Novy mir,* May 1988:
163, 178

GLASNOST'S FIRST UNCENSORED glance was backward. In 1987
and 1988, relearning Soviet history became a national pastime and passion. Millions seemed to be burning with curiosity about their country's
true past, which, they strongly suspected, was quite different from what
they, their parents, grandparents, and now their children were taught.
Never before had the truth about the past been searched for and recovered on such a scale, wrote the literary critic Arkady Sakhnin.[1] Everyone
understands, he continued, that progress would be impossible without
an "exhaustive" analysis of this truth—"and the entire country is now
preoccupied with this analysis."[2] The circulation of the newspapers
and magazines, where historians—with vastly different degrees of
competence—claimed inordinately large spaces for almost daily revelations, doubled and quadrupled.

"I never cease to be amazed at how little I know of my own [country's]
history," a reader wrote *Ogonyok* in January 1988.[3] "There is not a country
in the world whose history has been as falsified as ours," concluded Yuri
Afanasiev, the rector of the Moscow Institute of History and Archives.[4]
In the high school textbook of the history of the Soviet Union, Afanasiev
could not find "a single unfalsified page. The entire textbook is a lie."[5]
The standard version of the Soviet era of Russia's history was found to
be so "monstrously distorted," as national daily *Izvestia* put it, that the
national high school examination in history, required for graduation,
was abolished in June 1988.[6] The exam was restored the next year, but
the old textbooks remained banished while new ones were being readied
for the ninth and tenth grades (the junior and senior years).[7]

As a motivation for further exploration, sheer curiosity was first
supplemented, and then gradually replaced, by other considerations.
Without truthful history, there could be no lasting remaking of the country's political foundation and therefore no dignified citizenship and no
genuine self-rule. The "mythologization" of the past, wrote the leading
essayist Len Karpinsky, makes possible falsification of the present and,
thus, "mystification" of the future.[8] Conversely, averred Natan Eidelman, a writer and biographer of Russia's first great historian, Nikolai

Karamzin, an "emancipated past" afforded invaluable insight into "today and tomorrow."[9]

A reborn Russia could not start its "new history"[10] without recovering and absorbing a full and fully candid old one. Writing the first honest high school history textbook was declared a goal of national significance, earning the author of the proposal, veteran teacher V. Svirsky, half a page in the country's main daily after *Pravda, Izvestia,* in July 1987.[11] The absence of a truthful history was not just a hiatus in knowledge, he contended, but at once a result of and a powerful contribution to "our age-long tradition of blaming everyone and everything for our mistakes and setbacks—cold winters, draughts, the intrigues of world imperialism—all, except ourselves."[12] In addition to engendering arrogance and negligence, doctored history spawned "moral irresponsibility."[13] Bitter historical truth was hard but a sugar-coated one was "immoral."[14] Real patriotism, Svirsky continued, was inseparable from knowing and speaking the truth, while "patriotism founded on semi-truth is not patriotism but its lazy, complacent imitation."[15] He quoted one of Russia's first "dissidents," Petr Chaadaev, pronounced mad by Nicholas I in 1836 and confined to house arrest: "I could not love the fatherland with my eyes shut and my mouth clenched. . . . The time of blind attachments is gone, and today we owe our fatherland, first and foremost, truth."[16]

The urgency of this "honest labor of self-discovery"[17] stemmed from the same central conviction that informed so much in the glasnost oeuvre: a moral state was impossible without moral citizens, and only those unafraid to speak the truth about the past could be trusted to say, and act on, the truth about the present and future—and thus guarantee the irreversibility of the democratization.[18] An "unexamined past" was tantamount to an inability to begin a new, better life.[19]

So close and vital was the connection between honesty about the past and hopes for a better tomorrow that candor was now seen as "a litmus test of our seriousness about the future," argued one of Gorbachev's principal economic advisors, Abel Aganbegyan.[20] A reader's letter to a leading liberal "thick" journal, *Znamya,* quoted from Tvardovsky's poem-testament *Po pravu playmate* (In memory's name): "He who zealously hides the past /Is hardly friendly with the future."[21] Another reader asked: "I look at my daughters and think anxiously: in what sort of society will they live? Will it be truthful, brave, democratic, or won't it be?

And could they grow up to be full-fledged citizens of their Motherland, if they will not know and understand their history?"[22]

There was only one cure for self-deception, which had already been diagnosed as a "main illness":[23] to relearn "how it all began" by going to the roots of the "terrifying nightmare" from which the country only now began to awaken.[24] Historical memory was the most reliable means of "de-mythologization," a powerful enemy of all dictators and of the illusions they foist on people.[25]

Could it be that the country's misfortunes, including, of course, the horrors of Stalinism, were in large measure caused by the fact that "we have not learned to respect truth, the truth of our history, its lessons?" asked the political philosopher Alexander Tsypko. If so,

> "beginning our new history with the 'rehabilitation' of truth, we must travel this road to the very end. We can no longer evade truth, engage in myth-creation. We must trust truth. We need the truth . . . about our history. Only [truth] could guarantee us from the return of Stalinism."[26]

A people could deal with its history in two ways, Igor Klyamkin wrote: by denying it—"crossing it out" and thus "separating from it"—or by "overcoming" it.[27] Until now, he continued, "we mostly crossed out and separated."[28] The severance of connection to one's own history, the attempts to take the past away from the people was a moral disaster.[29] Only when the Soviet people "knew the entire, whole truth about our past," contended literary critic Igor Vinogradov, would the country be ready for a "spiritual cleansing"—and only then would it feel a "true, deep need" for it.[30] The "giant voids" in the national historical memory were suspected to be somehow connected to the "giant voids" in the country's "moral framework."[31] We must know our history—all of it, to the last hidden bit, wrote the poet Evgeny Evtushenko. Otherwise, the blank spots in history may become black spots on the national conscience.[32]

One must be "horrified to become brave enough" to condemn and forever break with the past where most of one's life—and that of one's nation—was spent, a military historian wrote *Moskovskie novosti*.[33] One should look into an abyss, no matter how terrifying, in order not to fall into it again.[34] Was it not more dignified to reconcile oneself to the truth, no matter how hideous, "thus calming one's souls and making oneself ready for labor and hardships to come?" asked Alexander Tsypko.[35]

Chekhov was enlisted, by way of Trofimov in act 2 of *The Cherry Orchard*: "We philosophize, complain of ennui, and drink vodka. But isn't this abundantly clear that to begin living—really living in the present—we must first redeem our past and be done with it? And we can redeem it only by pain and only by an extraordinary and constant labor."[36]

But the heaviest artillery in support of unadulterated memory came from Tolstoy's article about sadistic punishments of soldiers in the reign of Nicholas I:

> We are saying: why remember? . . . Why remember the past? It
> is no longer here, isn't it? Why should we remember it? . . .
> Why disturb the people? . . . What do you mean: why remember?
> If I were gravely ill and I were cured, I will always remember [the
> deliverance] with joy. Only then will I not want to remember,
> when I am still ill, in the same way or even more seriously, and
> I wish to deceive myself.[37]

The playwright Mikhail Shatrov, who quoted Tolstoy, could have added another stunning quote from the same article:

> Why annoy people, why remember that which has passed?
> Passed? What has passed? How could it have passed—that
> which we not only have not started to eradicate and heal but
> even are afraid to call by its name? How could a brutal illness be
> cured only by our saying that it is gone? And it is not going
> away and will not and cannot go away until we admit that we
> are ill. In order to cure an illness one must first admit that one
> has it. And it is precisely what we are not doing. And not only
> not doing, but we aim all our efforts at not seeing it, not calling
> it by its name. And consequently, it is not going away but only
> mutates, only penetrates deeper into our flesh, our blood, our
> bones, our marrow.[38]

CHAPTER FIVE

"The Innocent, the Slandered, the Exterminated"

In the black years of *ezhovshchina* I spent seventeen months in the prison lines.* One day someone recognized me. Then, a woman with blue lips who stood behind me woke up from the trance into which we all fell and whispered in my ear (everyone whispered there): "And this, can you describe this?" And I said: "Yes, I can." And then something like a smile glimmered on what once had been her face.

—Anna Akhmatova, "Vmesto predisloviya" (Instead of introduction), *Requiem, Oktyabr'*, March 1987: 131

---

* Along with hundreds of thousands of mothers and wives, Akhmatova was at the time trying to learn the fate of her son, Lev Gumilyov, who was arrested when Nikolai Ezhov was the NKVD chief from September 1936 to November 1938 (hence, *ezhovshchina*, or the Ezhov era). The writer Lidya Chukovskaya described the ordeal of the mother of another arrested son, a talented young engineer, charged with "participation in a terrorist act," in a short novel *Sof'ya Petrovna* (Moscow: Moskovsky Rabochiy, 1988). In another autobiographical short novel, *Spusk pod vodu* (A descent underwater), published in the same book, Chukovskaya recalled a woman, whose nursing baby died while she stood in line to learn about her arrested husband. Afraid of losing her place in line, the woman continued to wait, holding the dead baby in her arms (p. 198).

When was it happening to us?
In which year, which Spring? . . .
When? When? When? When?
Oh, years with no end!
Oh, days with no news or rumors:
One empty, another emptier still,
And a third like a black pond,
In which even toads cannot live.
And this is where my tale will start:
As we lay sprawling by the wall,
And guns of the entire country
Were aimed at us.
—Yuri Dombrovsky, the epigraph to *Fakul'tet nenuzhnikh veshchei*
(The department of unneeded things)

Maybe, as they say, we should look in Magadan or the Urals for the graves of our loved ones—the innocent found guilty, the slandered, the exterminated? Where to go, where to go? Whom to beg? Before whom to bow to learn the entire truth, to the end?
—Mariya Stepanovna Dranga, letter to *Znamya*, August 1987: 235

I imagine the Memorial like this: a gray, granite wall, very long—almost endless—and in it, contours of human faces. Women, children, men. Thousands, tens of thousands of faces! And no last names, no dates. Just the faces, in whose stone eyes is forever frozen the question "What for?"
—Vladimir Kolesnik, a worker, letter to *Znamya*, August 1987: 235

Chukovskaya herself spent months in prison lines after her husband, the theoretical physicist Matvey Bronshteyn, was taken away in 1937. He was shot a year later. But "after killing him, they continued to lie to me for many long years," she wrote in *Spusk pod vodu*. After spending days and weeks in the same lines with Akhmatova, she was told: "There are no foundations for a review of the case. When he serves out his sentence, he will write you himself. Maybe he's alive, maybe dead. How would I know? We are not the ZAGS [the acronym for State Registry of Civil Conditions, that is births, deaths, and marriages]. They don't notify us of deaths. Go to ZAGS citizen" (p. 160).

ANYONE OPENING A MAJOR Russian newspaper or magazine in 1987 or 1988 was instantly surrounded by names, faces, voices—the ghosts of thwarted lives of one's compatriots: slandered, arrested, tormented, shot, starved, or worked to death.* The martyrology that included every stage of descent into Stalin's hell suddenly acquired texture, sounds, smells: from the offices, where fates were decided by the compilers of proscription lists, to the arrests, "investigation" and torture, the sentencing, and the executions by bullet or camp. "History began to speak!" (*Istoriya zagovorila!*) proclaimed a reviewer of a slew of documentaries released in 1987–88: those who seemed to be doomed to eternal silence spoke.[1]

Who were they and how many? The first of the many shocks was the shattering of what might be called the Twentieth Congress myth. Until then, what Khrushchev said in his "secret speech" about Stalin's crimes at the congress in 1956 had been the "official version," and thus the only allowed narrative.[2] In it, the "great terror" occurred in 1937–38 and consumed the flower of the Soviet state: its marshals and generals, Party and government leaders, the masters and founders of the intelligence apparatus and secret police, and the creative intelligentsia, especially writers. These victims numbered perhaps thousands, tens of thousands at the most.

Yet just in Kuropaty near Minsk, one of the many secret mass execution sites uncovered by volunteers between 1987 and 1989, people were shot *daily* from 1937 to 1941:[3] 510 mass graves, an average of 200 bodies in each—at least 102,000 in total.[4] Another estimated 120,000 were buried in unmarked graves around the village of Bykovnya outside Kiev.[5] (One of Bykovnya's last intakes was a column of Red Army officers and men who broke through the German encirclement and were shot by the NKVD [the secret police] three weeks before Kiev fell to the Nazis in September 1941.)[6] In the Zolotya Gora (Gold Mountain) gold-

---

* *Ogonyok* was correct to note in 1988: "The information about the atrocities [*zlodeyaniya*] of Stalinsim is coming to us from the pages of newspapers and magazines, from the television screens. The press and the creative associations [of writers, journalists, cinematographers] have taken on themselves the educational task of telling people about mutilated lives, about discoveries not completed and manuscripts that were forbidden—about Stalinism's crimes against the people." ("Afisha nedeli" or "The playbill of the week," *Ogonyok* 46, 1988: 31.)

mine near Chelyabinsk in the southern Urals, 150,000 lay in unmarked mass graves.[7] There were not enough top Party and government functionaries—the terror's main victims in the Twentieth Congress version—to fill just the ravines and mines in Kuropaty, Bykovnya, and Zolotya Gora.

In the November 27, 1988, issue of *Moskovskie novosti* (and two months later in *Argumenty i fakty*) the Marxist historian and former dissident Roy Medvedev for the first time in the Soviet press estimated the number of the "repressed" (the euphemism still used then for arrested, imprisoned, or shot) *prior* to 1937: 17–18 million, of which "no less than" 10 million perished.[8] Even among the 5–7 million arrested in 1937–38, only 1 million were Party members,[9] much less Party nobility.

The sociologist Vladimir Shubkin put the number of those executed or killed by hunger and overwork in camps during Stalin's dictatorship (from about 1929 to Stalin's death in 1953) at 12 million.[10] Extrapolating from the average population growth of 2–3 million a year in the mid-1920s, before the "collectivization" and the worst of the terror, economists now estimated that even with the official number of World War II casualties (20 million) subtracted, in 1989 the Soviet Union was "missing" 40 million people—killed by bullet or hunger, or unborn to the killed.[11]

A popular Belarusian writer Ales' Adamovich revealed that in his native village of Glusha every third worker in a small glass-making factory was arrested and never came back: eighty-five in all.[12] A twenty-four-year-old "loading worker" in a Blagoveshchensk forestry trade depot in the Far East was charged in 1938 with "giving consent to participate in a counter-revolutionary, sabotage terrorist organization." At the trial, which lasted from 2:00 to 2:15 in the afternoon, he was found guilty as charged and sentenced to death. He was shot later the same day.[13] In 1941, an illiterate peasant woman from a tiny Siberian village, a mother of seven by the name of Matryona Chuchalova, was accused of "counterrevolutionary propaganda": a fellow collective farmer had reported that while weeding millet Matryona said something about praying openly for the Germans to win (or, in Matryona's version, that there be peace with Germany again). She was sentenced to six years in the camps and never heard of again.[14] A "simple worker" from a village on the Svir' River in the Leningrad province was called to the regional department of the NKVD and never came back. "Mother was left with five children," his daughter wrote *Znamya* magazine:

I was the oldest, ten, and the youngest, twins, were one year
old. Also living with us was *babushka,* my father's mother, who
was eighty-six. We were left with no means of existence. To
feed the family mother took a job, walking three kilometers
one way. I was left to be the mistress of the house. Soon, one of
the twins died. Then, Grandma.[15]

For tens of thousands of readers, the list of "simple people" consumed by the terror continued in the thoughts of Krymov from Vasily
Grossman's recovered and widely popular *Life and Fate.* Waiting to be
interrogated in the Lubyanka prison, the veteran Bolshevik and the former division commissar remembers the soldiers in whose almost certain
death he was complicit after "acting on" the reports he had received from
"political workers":

The Red Army soldier Ryaboshtan wears a cross on his chest,
calls communists "godless." How long did Ryaboshtan last in
the penal [*shtrafnoy*] battalion? . . . The Red Army soldier
Markevich said: "All communists are thieves, when the time
comes we will raise them on our bayonets and the people will
be free." The military court sentenced Markevich to the firing
squad.[16]

The state-sponsored oblivion now yielded the April 7, 1935, decree of the
Council of People's Commissars, which lowered the legal age of defen-
dants to twelve years. Children were to be tried as adults and "subject to
the entire range of sentencing."[17] A secret memorandum of explanation
sent out to courts and prosecutors on April 20, 1935, confirmed that the
"entire range" of sentencing to be applied to children included "the ultimate measure of punishment," that is, execution by shooting.[18]

There was a sixteen-year-old schoolboy from Erevan, sentenced to
twenty years for plotting to assassinate the Armenian Party boss.[19]* Another boy, Fedya Shchapov, only son of a widow from an Altai village,

---

* The first secretary of the Armenian Communist Party, Agasi Khandzhyan,
  was reported by Shalamov in the same story to have been shot and killed by
  Lavrenty Beria in Beria's office. As usual, Shalamov's history was correct: in a
  definitive study of Stalin's "henchmen" Donald Rayfield confirms the circum-

was sentenced to ten years for slaughtering the family's only sheep. (Slaughtering livestock was prohibited, no matter how starved the owners were.)[20] Both boys died in their first year in a camp.[21] In *Gulag Archipelago,* published by *Novy mir* in the second half of 1989, Solzhenitsyn wrote how badly he wanted to meet the prosecutors who sent twelve-year-olds to camps: to feel their ears, to touch their noses to see if they were human.[22]

In a sequel to one of the most popular books of the glasnost period, Anatoly Rybakov's *Deti Arbata* (The children of Arbat), the NKVD chief Ezhov told the future star "defendant" of the first show trial, Lenin's former Politburo deputy Lev Kamenev, that one of his co-defendants had confessed to plotting with Kamenev's son Yuri to assassinate Stalin. "But . . . But . . . ," a stunned Kamenev mumbled. "Yura is still a pioneer."[*] "Do you know the decree of . . . April 7, 1935?" Ezhov replied and read the decree. "See now?" Ezhov continued, "And your son is older than twelve. For plotting an attempt on Comrade Stalin's life he is sure to receive an appropriate, that is, ultimate, measure of punishment." "Scoundrel! Scum!" Kamenev cries out. Ezhov phones an order to arrest the boy and leaves without looking at the father.[23][†]

As usual, Rybakov's facts were impeccable. Yuri Kamenev was shot in January 1938 at the age of sixteen. The sentence of the Military Collegium (panel of judges) of January 30, 1938, read: "Kamenev, who was under mental influence of his father, the enemy of the people L. B. Kamenev, has learned the terrorist guidelines of the anti-Soviet, Trotskyite organization; being aggrieved at the repression applied to his father as

---

stances of Khandzhyan's (Khanjian's) death. (Donald Rayfield, *Stalin and His Henchmen,* New York: Random House, 2004: 350.)

[*] Modeled on the Boy and Girl Scouts, the Young Pioneers was a state organization, membership in which was obligatory for all children up to the age of fourteen. Yura is the diminutive of Yuri.

[†] In the same book, another sixteen-year-old boy, the mentally ill son of veteran Bolsheviks, the husband and wife Kondratievs, was allegedly overheard crying out "Down with Stalin!" and was sentenced to death for "a call to a terrorist act." His mother pleaded with a close friend and one of Stalin's confidants, Klement Voroshilov, to spare the boy: he could not even pronounce the words correctly, never cried out, and mostly mumbled something quietly to himself. Yet even Voroshilov could not help. (*Strakh,* 156.)

the enemy of the people. . . . Yuri Kamenev told other [high school] students of his terrorist intentions with respect to the leaders of the VKP (b) [the All-Union Communist Party (Bolsheviks)] and the Soviet state."[24]

For the children of the "enemies of the people," their parents' sentence was theirs too: if they survived the hunger, the beatings, and the daily humiliations of NKVD prison-like "special orphanages" (*spetsdetdom* or *detopriyomnik*), their mothers' and fathers' "crimes" haunted them all their lives. "And seared by that brand from birth / Were children of the enemy's blood," Tvardovsky wrote in *In Memory's Name* (*Po pravu pamyati*),[25] published sixteen years after his death.

Babies and younger children were doomed to grow up not knowing their parents. The eight-month-old son of Marshal Vasily Blyukher (who had withstood weeks of torture, refused to confess, and was reportedly shot by Beria) is said to have "disappeared without a trace."[26] (Blyukher's wife was sentenced to eight years in the camps, and the older children were sent to *detopriyomniks*.)[27]

A former inmate in a Leningrad prison in 1950 remembered a nursing mother who left behind her six-month-old baby when she was arrested. She had wrapped the baby in a blanket to take with her but was told that she would be back in a few hours. The blanket "envelope" with the baby was left lying on the bed. The woman was sobbing uncontrollably, and her cellmates banged on the door and kept calling for a doctor.[28]

In March 1941, a former German actress, Karola Neer-Genschke, who had moved to the Soviet Union with her communist husband, Anatoly Bekker,* wrote from prison to inquire about her son who was two when she was arrested:

To the director of orphanage L. Konika:
 I, the undersigned, am the mother of a German boy, Bekker Georgy Anatolievich, born in 1934 in Moscow and who is in your orphanage. Because I have had no news of him in 1–1.5 years, I ask you to answer the following questions: How is my son developing physically and mentally? In what state of health

---

* The husband had been arrested first and was believed to have been executed.

is he? What is his weight and how tall is he? What does he do?
Is he already learning to read and write? You understand with
what impatience I am awaiting the moment when I can write
him directly. When is he starting school? Does he know about
his mother?

I would be most grateful if you would send me his most
recent photograph. Is he musical? Does he draw? If yes, please
send me his drawing, which he drew!

I await with great impatience your response. I thank you
with all my heart for all the good that you can do for my
beloved child.

Genschke, Karolina N.

10.III.1941, Oryol, Post-box office 15.

Please forgive the shortcomings in the letter, I don't know the
Russian language well.[29]

A few months later Karola Neer-Genschke disappeared, presumed
shot by the NKVD along with the other inmates of the Oryol prison
shortly before the city fell to the invading Nazis. Anatoly Bekker first
learned about his parents when he was thirty-four.[30]

In a handful of cases, usually after Lavrenty Beria replaced Ezhov as
the chief of the secret police in November 1938, some of the suddenly
released parents managed to find their children. When, after an "unimaginable effort," a mother located her daughter in a *detdom,* the girl
was silent, with not even the faintest smile for her mother. Only on the
train back home, she whispered: "Mommy, why can't I feel happy?"[31]

No matter what the arrested confessed or did not confess to under torture, the "results" of the "investigation" usually appeared to have little
bearing on their sentence. It was all but predetermined by the original
charge at the time of the arrest. "Personal innocence is a relic of the
Middle Ages," the former NKVD general Katzenelenbogen declared in
Life and Fate. The ex-chief of a giant labor camp above the Arctic Circle,
he tells his fellow inmate Krymov: "Tolstoy declared that no one was
guilty. We, the Chekists have advanced the highest thesis: 'No one is innocent. He is guilty for whom an arrest order has been made out. And
an arrest order could be made out for anyone.'"[32] His advice to Krymov

was to "help" the *sledovatel* (a combination of prosecutor, investigator, and interrogator) and in this way to avoid the "one-hundred-hour conveyer" interrogations (when the interrogators, leaving at the end of the day, passed the victim on to the next officer). And what for? Katzenelenbogen asked. In the end, the Special Commission (*osoboe soveshchanie*) would rubber-stamp the investigator-interrogator's charge and "slap on an 'appropriate' sentence anyway."[33]*

Like Rybakov, Grossman was scrupulous in his details. "If they really needed to get something out of you, they did get it," a former inmate told *Moskovskie novosti*. "Or they killed you."[34]† He lived to tell his tale, having

---

* In Yuri Dombrovsky's *Fakul'tet nenuzhnykh veshchey* (The department of unnecessary things), a veteran prisoner of the Gulag explains the Osoboe Soveshchanie (OSO) to a new cellmate: "There are no judges, no articles of the Criminal Code, no witnesses. . . . Instead of the articles of the Criminal Code, there are acronyms: ASA (anti-Soviet agitation), ASD (anti-Soviet activity), or KRA (counterrevolutionary agitation), KRD (counterrevolutionary activity), KRTD (counterrevolutionary Trotskyite activity), and PSh (suspicion of espionage)." The last two acronyms were most lethal. "You might as well hang yourself. They will not let you live, even if you are not executed right away." The identities of the three members of the OSO who handed down sentences of eight, ten, fifteen, twenty, twenty-five years in the camps and, of course, executions, were kept secret. When, usually in "nonpolitical" cases, prosecutors-investigators-interrogators could not convince even the Soviet court of the guilt of the arrested, they sent the "materials" to the OSO, where, as a top prosecutor from Moscow admits in a speech to provincial colleagues, "your findings are accepted and signed off on without reading. There are no reviews and no amnesties. Those whom you [thus] convict are convicted forever!" The OSO existed from 1934 to 1953. (Dombrovsky, *Fakul'tet*, 330–34, 468.)

† In Lydia Chukovskaya's novel about a mother whose son was arrested and sentenced to ten years in "faraway" (*dal'nie*) (that is, the most lethal) camps, the doomed young man, formerly a brilliant engineer at one of the largest plants in the country, writes: "Dearest Mommy! . . . My sentence is based on the testimony of Sashka Yartsev—remember, there was this boy in my class? Sashka has testified that he involved me in a terrorist organization. And I, too, had to confess. But this is not true, we did not have any terrorist organization. Mommy, the investigator Ershov beat me and trampled me and I don't hear very well in one ear. I have written many requests but all received no reply. Write yourself, as an old mother, and provide the facts in your letter. You are aware, of course, that I did not even see Sashka since we graduated from high school, he studied at a different college. And we were not even friends in

survived the interrogations and the sentence of twenty-five years in the camps with the stipulation "to be used only in hard, underground labor [with] medical assistance prohibited." But a young woman, a North Ossetian teacher, Fatimat Angaeva, in the late 1930s, did not. After eight days and nights of continuous interrogation she died while being hung by her braids on a spike in the wall.[35] At the time, her tormentor and executioner, the *sledovatel'* Vladimir Boyarskiy (whom the young investigative journalist of *Moskvoskie novosti*, Evgeniya Al'bats, found and interviewed in 1988) bragged to Moscow about the "Stakhanovite methods" he used "to uncover a counterrevolutionary organization in the North-Ossetian Komsomol organization." Of the 103 people Boyarskiy arrested, 51 were shot and most of the rest died in camps.[36]

In many cases, even the almost inevitable "confession," beaten out of the arrested, was deemed unnecessary. In Kuropaty, the things found at the site—the remnants of wallets, shopping bags, clothes, and shoes—testified to many of the victims not having spent any time in prison. They were taken to the shooting grounds directly from their homes.[37]

In *Fakul'tet nenuzhnykh veshchey* (The department of unnecessary things), finished in 1975 and published in the Soviet Union in 1989, eleven years after the author's death,[38] Yuri Dombrovsky cited a cover note sent by Ezhov to Stalin with a list of names: "Attached for your approval are four lists of those to be tried by the Military Tribunal: List Number One (generals); List Number Two (former military functionaries); List Number Three (former NKVD functionaries); List Number Four (wives of the enemies of the people). I ask for the authorization to convict all to the first category." By then, Stalin had already received (and signed) hundreds of such lists, each containing thousands of names. "First category" meant execution.[39]

As usual in the Soviet Union, once adopted at the top, the practice was replicated at every level of administration. In the notes that his widow sent to *Moskovskie novosti*, a former head of the "criminal," that is, not secret, police of the Ivanovo province, 380 kilometers (236 miles) northeast of the Soviet capital Moscow, remembered the "troika" tribunal receiving a "quota of 1,500" from Moscow. That meant "the right to

school. He must have been beaten also. I kiss you warmly. Dear Mommy, please do this soon, because one cannot last here long" (*Sof'ya Petrovna*, 97–98).

shoot 1,500 people without investigation or trial."[40] The troika members were handed the lists of people with nothing but a name, surname, date of birth, and an alleged crime. Against each name, in red pencil, the head of the local NKVD put a capital R, the first letter of *rasstrel,* or execution by firing squad. The other two "troika" members, the heads of the local Party and the regional Soviet's executive committee, usually signed "post-factum," with no dissent.[41] In one case, an entire family was shot: a railroad worker, his wife, sons, and daughters. "They all were Japanese spies," the head of the NKVD explained to the author of the memoir.[42]

Arrest as sentence, without even a pretense of personal wrongdoing, was the punishment of those guilty of belonging to an "alien class" or a "traitor people." After the Politburo member and the Leningrad Party boss Sergey Kirov was assassinated by a lone gunman in December 1934, an estimated 1 million former noblemen, *dvoryane,* were arrested and expelled from Leningrad, Moscow, and some other large cities.[43] Among them was a great-grandson of Russia's greatest poet, Alexander Pushkin. "Well," a procurator, whose job was to uphold the law, told a Pushkin expert who had the temerity to complain, "wasn't Pushkin a nobleman, a *dvoryanin?*"[44]

There were no personal "cases" for "tens of thousands" of the "repatriates"—former Soviet citizens who had been forced laborers or concentration camp inmates in Germany. An endless procession of steamboats unloaded them in 1945–46 in the Far Eastern port of Magadan for work in some of the deadliest labor camps. Their official designation was "off-the-records" (*bezuchoytniki*). For some of them the sentence read: "Six years for verification" (*Na shest' let dlya proverki*)—in the camps, where six months was an almost certain death sentence.[45]

Nor was there individual "investigation" or sentencing of those arrested in 1939–40 and deported from the occupied parts of Poland and Rumania (referred to as "Western Ukraine," "Western Belorussia," "Bessarabia," "Northern Bukovina") as well as Latvia, Estonia, Lithuania, deeded to the Soviet Union under the 1939 Molotov-Ribbentrop Pact— or in 1944–45, when these lands were reconquered ("liberated").* The

---

* Much like the kulak families before them, the Estonian exiles in 1949 were
  loaded onto cattle cars. Each such car, made to transport at the most eight

number of victims was now estimated to be at least 2 million in 1939–40 and 2–3 million in 1944–45.[46] (How many died en route, in exile, in camps? Two hundred thousand? Three? Half a million?)

Those deported on a July night in 1949 from a small town in the formerly Rumanian Bessarabia (now part of the "Soviet Socialist Republic of Moldavia") were given an hour and a half to gather their belongings before they were loaded on trucks and then trains to take them to Siberia: peasants and veterinarians; those who had been in the anti-Antonescu underground* and fought the Nazis; socialists and members of peasant parties alike.[47] At two in the morning precisely, those who were to arrest them (soldiers, local communists, and village "activists," led by NKVD officers) opened sealed envelopes with the names and went door-to-door. They stood guard as the doomed—men, their wives, and children, clinging to their mothers—wailed, or sat motionless, petrified by grief, or said farewells to neighbors, or patted for the last time their cows and dogs. Everyone, including the civilian members of arresting parties, was paralyzed by fear and shame, overpowered, lost, submerged in the all powerful "alien will."[48] Only one woman, quickly silenced by her husband, attempts a protest: "Boss," she says to the director of the local high school, a Party member sent there from the Urals. "What for, boss? . . .

---

horses or thirty-two soldiers, was filled with fifty prisoners. Nothing was done to prepare the cars for a long winter trek. There was not even a hole in the floor, and the old bucket to be used as a toilet was filled right away. After a day and a half without water or food, an infant died. At a long stop at a Siberian station, people ran toward the sealed cars, knocked on the walls, tried to pass on food or warm things. "All in vain," recalls a witness, "the soldiers hit them with rifle butts, leaving those on the inside to grow numb from cold and hunger." (Alexander Nikishin, "Ne naverdi!" [Do no harm!], *Ogonyok* 28, 1989: 5.)

In March 1944 the head of the NKVD's transportation department advised the NKVD's deputy chief, Kobulov, that "in light of the fact that 40–50 percent of the special contingent were children, the densification [*uplotnenie*] of the number of people in each car to 45 was quite reasonable." In addition, "the abolition of the baggage cars in the special trains has allowed us to lessen the numbers of cars by a significant amount." (Nikolai Bugay, "V bessrochnuyu ssylku" [Into indefinite exile], *Moskovskie novosti*, October 14, 1990: 11.)

* Ion Antonescu, the prime minister and dictator of Rumania and a Nazi Germany ally, 1940–44.

Where is the court, where is the trial? There is always a trial. Why is there no trial?"[49]

The Crimean Tatars were also awakened at two in the morning—the hour must have been established by the GPU/NKVD science as the time of their prey's greatest vulnerability—on May 18, 1944. By then, throughout the entire Crimean peninsula, their villages had been surrounded by the NKVD troops.[50] Stunned into "half-craziness," women, children, and the elderly were given ten minutes to get into the waiting trucks and were driven to the railway stations where the trains of cattle cars were waiting. They were forbidden to take warm clothes or food.[51] At the time all the able-bodied men were fighting the Nazis in the Red Army. When they returned home, they were sent to join the rest of the exiled.

The Tatars were destined for the cotton fields of Uzbekistan. The Uzbek NKVD reported that 151,424 arrived. There was no mention of how many had died of hunger, disease, or thirst along the way. (The guards shot at those who tried to run out to get water at the stations.) Although not formally arrested, the exiled could not leave the "special settlements" and were to work in the fields for as long as they were ordered. They envied the "real" prisoners, who at least were fed.[52] Of the 400,000 "specially resettled" (spetspereselentsy) "traitor peoples" in Uzbekistan—there were also the Balkars from the Caucasus, the Kurds from around the Black Sea, and the Meskhetian Turks (Meskhetians) from Georgia—an estimated 130,000 died in the "cotton Gulag."[53]

A Crimean Tatar woman who had fought in the anti-Nazi underground was arrested "with my entire people" and then spent nine years of "hard labor" in a Vorkuta camp above the Arctic Circle ("in mines, tundra, despair"), wrote Ogonyok from Samarkand in Uzbekistan. She lived alone, "with no relatives or children."[54] She wanted to see if the magazine could help her increase by even a little bit her meager pension of sixty-three rubles a month—after "forty years of labor, including my participation in the struggle against the German occupation."[55]

Altogether, according to the NKVD archives, in 1946 there were 2,463,940 "specially resettled" peoples in the places of their "perennial exile" (bessrochnaya ssylka).[56] Among the largest "ethnic contingents" were the Volga Germans (August 1941), the Kalmyks (October 1943, "26,359 families or 93,139 people," as per the NKVD's count), the Karachai (November 1943, "14,774 families or 68,938 people"), and the Chechens and the Ingush (February 1944, "459,486 people"). Among the "specially resettled," the NKVD counted 829,084 women and 979,182 children under sixteen years of age.[57] As many as a million, mostly children and the elderly, may have died in the first few years of exposure, starvation, and disease.[58]

There were no trials, and no sentences were read to the 4,404 Polish officers who were unloaded from the trains in Smolensk or at a small railway station in Gnezdovo, near the village of Katyn in April or May (the month was uncertain) 1940. Their 6,287 comrades were shot in the same month in the Kalinin province, and 3,896 were sent to die in Khar'kov.[59] Another 544 men, whose place of execution was not known in 1990–91, brought the total number reported, in 1940, to the NKVD headquarters in Moscow to 15,131. All had voluntary surrendered to the advancing Soviet troops in September 1939.[60]

The massacred Poles were mentioned for the first time in *Komsomol'skaya pravda* in January 1990. A year later they reappeared in the meticulous compilation of archival documents in *Novy mir.*[61*] Preserved in the NKVD (by then KGB) archives were requests and inquiries that the doomed Polish majors, colonels, and generals addressed to their Soviet jailers between the fall of 1939 and April 1940: Why are we not sent home? How long are we going to be "interned"? Why are you holding military doctors and pharmacists, who should be sent to a "neutral state" as per the Geneva Convention?[62]

According to the driver of one of many trucks that took the Polish officers to the Katyn forest, they were unloaded directly into a ravine of "about 100 meters long and 2–3 meters deep."[63] They were shot point-blank and, in some cases, "finished off with a bayonet." The bodies were arranged in "neat piles" and covered with soil.[64]

---

* In between, *Moskovskie novosti* published several articles about the Katyn executions in addition to those cited in this chapter. Among them: "Katyn. Trudnyi put' k istine" (Katyn: A difficult path to the truth; April 22, 1990: 4); "I eshcho raz o Katyni" (Once more about Katyn) by Natal'ya Lebedeva (May 6, 1990: 6), and "Stranitsy katn'skoy tragedii" (The pages of the Katyn tragedy; May 13, 1990: 11) by Igor Nekrasov and Gennady Zhavoronkov, the latter article based on a roundtable discussion with Polish and Soviet historians.

There were also letters from the officers' wives. (Their addresses had been given to the NKVD by the soon-to-be-executed prisoners, who believed they were going to be united with their families. Instead, their wives, children, and elderly parents in the Soviet occupation zone in Poland were arrested, loaded in cattle cars, and sent to Siberia and Kazakhstan—around 110,100 people, in over 100 "special trains" [*eshlony*].)* Where is my husband? the women wrote. Why are my letters returned with a note that the camp has been closed and my husband was "deported to an unknown destination"? Please help me find him as I am here in Kazakhstan with two small children and in "hard material conditions!"[65]

In halting and misspelled Russian, a Polish girl, Krysya Mikutskaya, wrote Stalin in May 1940:

> Our dear beloved father Stalin! I nau lie sick and I am very
> missing my Dady, who I did not see almost nine monts. And I
> thought to me that only You Great Stalin can return him. He
> was engineer and for the war he was called to the army service
> and he was taken as prisoner. He nau in Kozel'sk in Smolensk
> province. We from Pinsk were moved to the Kazakhstan Repub-
> lic to the district of Aryk-Balyk, kolkhoz Imantov. We have no
> relatives here. My mother is little and wik. Send us our father, I
> ask with my all hart.

When Krysya wrote this letter, her father, the engineer Eugeniush Mikutskiy (in the Russian transcription of a Polish name) had already been shot at Katyn.[66]

The last minutes of the executed, the ways in which they were killed, too, were being wrested from oblivion. Those buried in Bykovnya were shot at night in the Kiev Lukyanovo prison, in the office of the "commandant for the special cases," who personally executed between 130 and 150 people every night in the years 1936–41.[67] Every morning, five or

---

* There were "usually" fifty-six cars in each "special train." (Nikolai Bugay, "V bessrochnuyu ssylku" [Into indefinite exile], *Moskovskie novosti*, October 14, 1990: 11.)

six trucks, filled with bodies and covered with tarp, stopped on their way to Bykovnya in the yard of the October Revolution Palace of Culture. A dwarfish porter would throw a cart wheel on the tarp to keep it from flapping.[68]

In Smolensk, according to the eyewitness testimony of a former NKVD yard-sweeper (*dvornik*) and watchman, Petr Klimov, a prisoner was told that he or she was being transferred to Moscow, stripped, and taken to the basement of the NKVD building on Dzerzhinsky Street.[69] There prisoners were forced down on the floor, their heads placed on the edge of a manhole over a sewer, and shot in the temple or in the back of the head. In the evening the bodies were loaded on trucks ("thirty to forty bodies per truck"), driven to the Koz'i Gory forest outside the city, dumped into ravines, and covered with soil. The diggers lived right there, on the site.[70]

"They shot every day," Klimov remembered. At first the truck drivers carried the bodies out from the basement on stretchers, but then a conveyer belt was installed to deliver the executed directly to the trucks.[71] Klimov was paid an extra five rubles to wash the blood off the trucks.[72] Most of the executions took place in the years 1933–39.

In Kuropaty, too, the holes in the skulls, exhumed from the carefully hidden graves, were consistent with shots fired point-blank into the back of the head. Sometimes, according to witnesses from nearby villages, the victims were lined up along the edge of the ditch, their hands tied and mouths gagged, and the executioners aimed more powerful rifles at the side of the head of those on either end of the row, attempting to kill at least two people with one bullet. "They were saving the ammo," a witness explained, and also "showing their professionalism."[73]

Executions in the Katyn forest started as early as 1935, long before the Poles were murdered there. Children from a nearby village used to wait until the trucks left and then dug up the pits, which were "barely" covered with earth, to pull off clothes and, especially, boots ("some of them were even of box-calf skin, *khromovye*, issued only to top military officers!").[74] Sometimes the children found the pits "breathing." "Meaning, they did not manage to kill everyone to the end. Because they were in a hurry. The ravines were deep. They'd put a layer of earth on top of a layer and then quickly line up the next row [of people to execute]."[75]

A former guard of a Far Eastern camp talked readily to a fellow patient in a "special" (that is, accessible only to the privileged) heart clinic in Moscow about his additional duties as an executioner:

—After a shift we used to stop by the guards' house to pick up rifles, down a glass of vodka, and get the lists [of names]. [Then we] went to the cells calling out the names and then putting the people in the open trucks: face to face, six of them, four of us.

—Did they know where you were taking them? Were they read the sentence?

—No, no sentences, nothing. Only: "Get out, straight ahead, get on the truck!"

—And how did they behave in the truck on the way?

—Well, men, those usually were silent. Women began to cry, they were saying: "Oy, what are you doing, we have not done anything, comrades, what are you doing"—and some such. . . . After riding about 12 kilometers, in the hills, we got them off the truck.

—So now you read them the sentence?

—What was there to read? We shouted: Get out, form a row! And there is a ditch, freshly dug, right in front of them.

—And did they say anything?

—Some said nothing. Others begin to shout that they were perishing for no reason and so on, women mostly cried and huddled up together.

—Did you have a doctor with you?

—Why would we need a doctor? We shoot, if any one is moving, we finish them off—and back on the truck. And the work brigade was already standing on the side.

—What kind of brigade?

—We had a special work team made of convicted criminals. Their job was to fill up the graves. So we drive off and they throw the bodies into the ditch, fill it up, and dig up another ditch for tomorrow. Done—and back to the camp. This counted toward their work quota. They were fed pretty good and it was a plum job—nothing like felling trees.

—And you?

—We would get back to the camp, hand in the rifles, and drink as much
vodka as we want. Others, they drank a lot at the state's expense, but
I would down my one glass, have something hot to eat, and go to the
barrack to sleep.[76]

Executions continued in camps. In the Soviet Union's first "special designation" (*osobogo naznacheniya*) extermination camp, set up on the So-
lovetskie Islands in the White Sea in 1923, some of the doomed were tied
to a log and pushed down "a long and steep staircase." Half a minute
later, witnesses remembered, a "shapeless bloody mass" reached the foot
of the steps.[77] In the summer, the condemned were tied naked to poles
and left to be eaten by the swarms of mosquitoes. This was called "to
stand up for the mosquito" (*postavit' na komara*).[78]

Mass executions, however, started later, in 1937 and 1938, when
the "hurricane of mass, mindless shooting" swept the camps in the
"North and the West."[79] In the Dal'story administration of the Gulag
in northeastern Siberia, "tens of thousands" of prisoners were executed around the clock, with tractor motors revved to mute the shots.[80]
The names of the executed were read to the rest of the inmates twice a
day, at the morning and evening lineups, as orchestras played marches.[81]
Many of the intended victims had died in the holding cells, while waiting to be executed. So crowded were these cells that corpses stood
among the still living.[82] Others were taken right out of the tents in
which they slept, manacled, gagged, read the sentence of the "troika,"
and taken to a room where they were shot in the back of the head as
soon as they stepped over the threshold.[83] Those too weak to walk were
dragged.[84]

Individual murders were part of the camp routine. A prisoner carrying a log with another inmate accidentally overstepped a line that marked
boundaries of the *zona* and was shot by a guard, who was commended
and given a two-week vacation.[85] Another *zek* (the camp for "prisoner")
was torn apart by the guard dogs when he stepped out of the morning
lineup to catch a letter from his wife after the piece of paper had slipped
out of his hand and floated in the wind.[86]

In addition to the bullet, sudden death could also come from routine negligence and cruelty. In one such instance, three hundred women prisoners, who were building an airfield in Saransk, about 400 miles east of Moscow, lived in a ditch, two meters deep and covered with a straw roof. When a fire started, the inmates were ordered to stay in the ditch. Six women eventually managed to crawl out. One of them, who wrote in *Ogonyok,* was saved by a "political [prisoner]," a former doctor, who cut out her burns with a razor.[87]

Yet most camp inmates died not of bullets or fires but of daily, hourly mortification. Some of them, too, now had names, chroniclers, and mourners. Survivors described the main instruments of their lethal degradation: work, hunger, and cold. Whether prospecting for gold, felling trees, or draining swamps, political prisoners (the "fifty-eighths")* were assigned the hardest, and for many deadly, jobs. Alongside them, in coal pits or goldmines, professional criminals (the *blatnye*) and others convicted for "nonpolitical" offenses (the *bytoviki*) used jackhammers ("pneumatic hammers"), but the "fifty-eighths" were given a pickaxe (*kaylo*), a shovel, and a steel bar (*lom*). Broken off pieces of coal or gold containing ore (the "sand") were loaded by two or three *zeks* on wooden barrows (*tachki*) for a "barrower" to take, running, up a long wooden ramp. When the "barrower" returned, an already filled *tachka* awaited. And thus went the entire twelve- or fourteen-hour workday, under the watchful eyes of the all-powerful foreman (*brigadir*), the guard, and often the head of the work site (*prorab*).[88] If spotted, unauthorized rest was punished by beating or by the charge of "sabotage," which almost always meant execution.

Beatings did not have to have a cause. The prisoners, especially the gravely weakened *dokhodyagi,* too feeble to hit back or even to evade blows, were routinely kicked, punched, and slapped not only by the guards or the all-powerful *brigadirs* but also by other prisoners: barrack

---

* That is, convicted under the innumerable sections, subsections, and subsubsections of the hugely long Article 58 of the Criminal Code for one of the innumerable "political" offenses, from terrorism, espionage, and "anti-Soviet agitation" to "besmirching the leaders" in jokes.

monitors (*denval'nye's*), the privileged hangers-on in the kitchen, and the *blatnye*.[89] Some, felled by the blows, never got up.[90]

Counting the time to and from the work site, the morning roll call (*razvod*), and the "meals," the workday often left no more than four to six hours for sleep.[91] Men fell asleep the moment they stopped moving. Some managed to sleep while standing or walking.[92] The camp doctor, or paramedic (*fel'dsher*), himself a prisoner, was forbidden to certify as sick more than 2 percent of the camp prisoners. Virtually all "excused from work" were veteran criminals, who threatened to kill the medic if he refused to certify them.[93] For those who were not excused, three "refusals" to work meant execution.[94]

The typical ration was the tepid, slightly greasy water of a "soup" (*balanda*) and bread, or "soup" and herring. Those who fulfilled the previous day's work *norma* (the quota) were entitled to between 400 grams and 500 grams of bread, given in the morning for the entire workday. For those who did not, the *payka* was reduced to 300 grams of bread without the *balanda,* then to 200, then to 100, then to nothing.[95]

The bread was sticky and soggy and full of chaff because most of the "real" ingredients—flour, butter, sugar—were stolen for the table of the camp masters. No matter. It was eaten slowly, one tiny piece after another, not chewed but "sucked on" like candy, like sugar. To drink water while eating the bread was a sacrilege. Only after the last crumb was finished, did *zeks* turn to the "tea": lukewarm water colored with a burnt crust of bread.[96] After only a few months in the camp, they all were said to have the same dream in their sleep: brick-like loaves of rye bread soaring in the sky, "like angels."[97]

Herring was the *zeks'* sole source of protein: half a small fish every other day. On the "herring morning" in the Kolyma camps, the doors of the huge barrack opened and from the four rows of plank beds (*nary*), from floor to ceiling, "two thousand eyes" were glued to the trays with head or tail halves (the two were never mixed on a given day). Like bread, herring was not to be rudely eaten but gently savored, morsel by morsel, scale by scale, one tiny bone at a time. After snatching his piece and tenderly stroking it, a prisoner did not eat. He licked and licked, and the tiny tail or head gradually melted in his fingers.

Then he began to chew the bones—gently, carefully—until they, too, disappeared.[98]*

> The hunger was insatiable, and nothing could compare to the feeling of hunger, a gnawing hunger—the constant condition of a camp prisoner, if he is "political" (a "fifty-eight"). This hunger has not been sung yet. The gathering of dirty dishes, the licking of the bowls, the bread crumbs licked off one's palm—all of this was good only qualitatively, as a momentary pleasure. It is impossible to satisfy this hunger. Many years will have to pass before the prisoner unlearns the constant readiness to eat. No matter how much was eaten—in half an hour, an hour, one is hungry again.[99]

So wrote Varlam Tikhonovich Shalamov, a great Russian writer and the author of the beautiful and unbearable *Kolyma Tales*. He miraculously survived seventeen years in the camps, fourteen of them in Kolyma, the ninth circle of the Gulag.[100] He called his fiction a "lived-through document, with no distortions." "Each story of mine," he wrote, "has an absolute authenticity [*dostovernost*'] an absolute documentary-like quality."[101]

Camp inmates were also killed by scurvy, dysentery (the crazed *dokhodyagi* ate whatever they could find wherever they could find it, including garbage dumps covered with flies), and pellagra, which caused incessant bloody diarrhea and made skin flake and slough off all over the body.[102] The quickest killer was "alimentary dystrophy," which, within a few weeks, reduced a tall, corpulent, healthy man in his thirties or forties to forty kilos (eighty-eight pounds).[103]

---

* In another Shalamov story, autobiographical like the rest of his fiction, on the way to the dreaded office of the camp *sledovatel*', a prisoner sees a slice of frozen turnip skin in the snow. It is a stunning find, unimaginable good luck, a gift from heaven. He chews it, slowly, and feels the long-forgotten smell of earth, of live vegetables, of home. In a minute, he can be shot, but he is blissfully happy the rest of the way. (*Iz Kolymskikh passkazov*, "Pocherk" [Handwriting], 14.) On another such occasion, the narrator pounces on a bite of cheese left by the *sledovatel*': "I rushed to swallow it, to have it before I died." (*Novya proza*, 62.)

In northern camps, the cold was the third—after the work and hunger—accessory to mass murder. There were not enough felt boots (*valenki*), mittens, and cotton wool quilted jackets (*telogreyki*) for the prisoners who built the Kotlas-Vorkuta railroad above the Arctic Circle. The camp administration had calculated that without warm clothes, wearing only what they wore at the time of arrest, prisoners would last two weeks. And that is how the work was planned: after two weeks of work, they were sent "to rot to death" in the camp, their places taken by fresh prisoners.[104]

In Kolyma, bound by the Arctic Ocean, East Siberian Sea, and the Sea of Okhotsk, the prisoners were not taken out to work only when the temperature fell below −56°C (−68.8° Fahrenheit) and spit froze before reaching the ground. In 1940, the "working temperature" was raised to −52°C (−61.6° Fahrenheit).[105] Even in the summer the water on the floor of the Kolyma goldmines was icy and seeped over and through prisoners' *chuni*, rubber galoshes worn on bare feet.[106] Their frostbitten toes oozed puss and blood.[107]

In winter, barracks became "ice chests," and those on the lower tiers of the *nary* spent half the night huddling around the small and barely heated stove. Those up top slept better but there, too, their hair froze to the pillow by the morning.[108] *Telogreyki* jackets served as blankets, and *burki* (boots stitched from cotton wool, *vata*, with soles attached with rope) were pillows.[109]

An OSO ("special trial commission") stipulation of "the sentence to be served in Kolyma" was "a synonym for execution."[110] From 1937 on, "all limitations for disability or age" were eliminated in sentencing: "the legless and sixty-year-olds" and those with tuberculosis and heart conditions were sent to the Kolyma goldmines.[111] There, even a healthy young man usually became an emaciated, dying *dokhodyaga* in two weeks to a month.[112] With the exception of the *brigadir* and his deputy, usually not one of the *brigada* prisoners, who began the "gold season" on May 15, lasted to its end on September 15. *Brigadas* were replaced entirely several times in the four months.[113]

In more lenient camps, death could be slower or faster, depending on who at that time was the chief (*nachal'nik*) of the camp, of the mine, or of the regional Gulag administration.[114] A change of guards (*razvod*) walked through the barrack in the morning, a survivor recalled, and "here they [the dead] are, lying on the *nary*. So they put a cross on the heel with chalk. Then drag them off, load on trucks, and drive them to the cemetery. Every day, early in the morning."[115] ("The learned, they died first," a former prisoner told Russian documentary makers.)[116]

The barrack monitor, *dneval'nyi*, rejoiced when someone died after the *razvod* but before the evening meal: the daily ration of the deceased would be his for the entire day![117]

CHAPTER SIX

The Peasant Hecatomb

There are summer cottages where our village once was. Not a trace is left of us. No, there is one: four white lilac bushes planted by my father. And nothing else. As if we never have existed. This is hard and sad, and no one can console. All relatives have been killed— and for what? What sort of crops does the society hope to get from such a field of sorrow?

—From a letter by Natal'ya Kirilovna Mochalova, an arrested and exiled "kulak daughter," *Komsomol'skaya pravda,* January 25, 1989: 2

Every now and then, there welled up in [Stalin] a dreadful feeling: not just today's enemies were vanquishing him. He imagined that, behind Hitler's tanks, in smoke and dust, marched those whom he thought he had forever punished, quieted, calmed down. They poured from the tundra, they were blowing apart the permafrost that sealed their graves and tearing the barbed wire. Loaded with the resurrected, the trains of cattle cars were streaming from Kolyma, from the Komi Republic. Peasant women, children rose from earth with ghastly, mournful, emaciated faces, more and more of them, and were searching for him with their indifferent, sad eyes.

—Vasily Grossman, *Zhizn' i sud'ba* (Life and fate): 485

And nothing is left. Where is that life, that horrible suffering? Is it
possible that nothing is left? That no one will answer for all of
this? And it will all be forgotten without a trace?
—Vasily Grossman, *Vsyo techyot* (Forever flowing): 82

THE RECOVERED HISTORY soon began to touch on what was likely
the Soviet state's darkest and best-kept secret: arrests, exile, penal servitude, and famine that tormented and killed millions of peasants between
1929 and 1933. Even in the anti-Stalinist zeal and daring of his "secret
speech" at the Twentieth Congress and the height of de-Stalinization of
1961–63 Nikita Khrushchev would not even hint at what the top Party
historians in September 1988 called "the most horrible crime of Stalin
and his henchmen"[1] and a literary critic decried as "a planned extermination of the peasants through monstrous repressions" and "a total war
on the people."[2]*

Unlike the former Gulag prisoners, no collectivization victims came
forward with their tales in the late 1980s. Instead, they were to be told by
their children and grandchildren, historians, and a handful of writers
who touched on the peasant hecatomb in their books, some of which had
waited a quarter century for publication.

They were harder to count than the conventionally "repressed." Most
kulak families (the well-to-do peasants now mourned as the "most energetic," "hardworking," and "self-sufficient" in the countryside)[3] were
herded onto special trains, driven for days, often with little food or water,
and unloaded in the swamps of the European north, the Ural mines, or
the Siberian taiga to build "special settlements" (*spetsposeleniya*). This was
their "exile."[4] (Many heads of these households had been arrested, and
some shot, as "anti-kolkhoz" and "anti-Soviet" "activists" before their

---

* When in the 1970s the so-called village writers (the *dereven'shchiki*) were allowed
  to describe and mourn the "devastation" and "exhaustion" of the Russian
  countryside, "not a word" was permitted about what or who had disfigured the
  village so, when, and how—and nothing "could break through this ban." (Igor
  Zolotusskiy, "Krushenie abstraktsiy" [The downfall of abstractions], *Novy mir*,
  January 1989: 240.)

families were exiled.)[5] Other "de-kulakized" villagers were forced out of their houses, robbed of every possession, and sent—penniless and ostracized—to faraway corners of their own district or province. Some managed to run away to the cities or industrial construction sites in the hope of finding work and feeding their families.

In the first Soviet public discussion of the casualties of the collectivization and the famine, leading Party archivists and historians disclosed in *Pravda* that "no fewer than" 481,000 families were sent into a "far exile" in 1930–32; between 400,000 and 450,000 families were left dispossessed in their provinces; and 200,000–250,000 escaped to cities and factories.[6] Russian peasant families at the time rarely had fewer than five or six members, and families of ten to twelve were closer to the norm.[7] Indeed, in the ever-changing definitions of the kulaks, which the collectivization was to "liquidate as a class," larger families were incriminating evidence of wealth and "socially alien" status.[8] Since entire families were punished—to the last man, boy, girl, pregnant woman, infant, infirm grandmother, the paralyzed, and the mentally ill[9]— the total of 1,081,000 to 1,181,000 families from these estimates should be multiplied accordingly. By Medvedev's count, there were at least 10 million victims.[10] This was also the number Stalin mentioned to Churchill in Moscow in August 1942 as the peasants he, Stalin, had to "struggle with."[11]

How many of the exiles perished no one could tell.[12] As with the "traitor people" a decade later, it was assumed that most of those who died en route and in the first few years were among the oldest and the youngest.[13] Thus the "murder of hundreds of thousands of peasant children," with which the political philosopher Alexander Tsypko charged Stalinism, might be a plausible guess.[14]

Those who died in the 1932–33 famine—said to be the "greatest demographic catastrophe to hit European peasantry since the Middle Ages"[15]—were even harder to count. Medvedev estimated 6–7 million, mostly in Ukraine and Kazakhstan, the North Caucasus and the Volga basin (*Povolzh'e*).[16] The economist Pavel Voschshanov put the number of dead at between 3 and 7 million.[17] In 1988, the prominent Kazakh writer Olzhas Suleymenov told a Party conference that out of 6 million of his compatriots before "collectivization," only 3 million survived.[18] Official

Soviet historians had no number to offer, promising only "a great research effort."[19]

As described in the glasnost publications, the peasant holocaust began with the January 11, 1930, *Pravda* editorial that called for "declaring a war to the death on the kulak and, in the end, sweeping him off the face of the earth."[20] Two and a half weeks later a Politburo commission chaired by Vyacheslav Molotov established region-by-region minimal quotas (*raz-verstki*) of families to be arrested and exiled: for instance, 210,000 families from the key grain-producing areas of North Caucasus, Ukraine, Lower and Middle Volga, and Kazakhstan; 32,000 in the provinces of Leningrad, Moscow, and Nizhni Novgorod.[21] Within each region, local authorities were to subdivide the "plan" numbers among the districts and then the villages.[22] For the functionaries at every level, failure to fulfill the quotas meant at least dismissal and expulsion from the Party, more often arrest, and sometimes execution.

Fear of falling short of the assigned quota and the ambition to "over-fulfill" unleashed a bacchanalia of bloodlust, treachery, and routinized bureaucratic cruelty. Virtually every functionary, no matter how petty and often with no formal authority, including "kolkhoz activists," could declare a man a "kulak" and thus doom him and his family.[23]* Standing on a village street, a sixty-one-year-old man from the Arkhangelsk province said of an "activist" walking by that his fur coat had belonged to an exiled "kulak." For these words he was sentenced to "ten years of camps with no right to correspondence" (which usually meant execution). His nine children were immediately arrested and exiled. In 1989 they still did not know where, when, or how their father died.[24]

"Either you send me your daughter or tomorrow we will deal with you as a kulak [*budem kulachit*]!" a "kulak son" remembered another "activist" telling his father. The father threw a chair at the man and was

---

* Three years later, in an "instruction" for the Party organizations, Stalin and Molotov would admit: "Kolkhoz chairmen arrest and so do the members of the kolkhoz board [*pravlenie*]. The village soviet [*sel'sovet*] chairmen arrest and so do the secretaries of the party cells [*yacheyki*]. District and province functionaries arrest. Everyone arrests—those who just feel like it and who have no right whatsoever to arrest." (Danilov and Teptsov, op. cit.)

arrested the next day for "terror against village activists." Two days later, his family, too, was arrested and herded by the police to a city with other "enemies of the people." The daughter could not be found. The mother cried and pleaded with the guards to let her look for the girl: "Please let me go and find her. I am leaving you the other children. I will be back!" In response one of the police threatened her with a rifle. Half a year later, already in exile in Kazakhstan, the girl's family learned that the mother had hanged herself.[25]

"In our small village twenty kilometers from Kurgan [in the south Urals] six families were 'de-kulakized' [*raskulacheny*], thrown out of their houses in winter 1929," Natal'ya Kirilovna Mochalova wrote in *Komsomol'skaya pravda* in January 1989:

> Everyone—out [of the house]: the children, the elderly, the sick.
> All—out on the street. And those who tried to help, to let us in
> their houses were immediately called into *sel'sovet* [village
> Soviet]: "What? You are helping the kulak scum?!" But what
> kind of kulaks were we? We had neither a mill nor a big farm.
> Only six children.[26]

The Soviet peasants' Road to Calvary: glancing furtively back where there was the cabbage soup, *shchi*, still warm in the oven; smoke rising from the chimney; milk still cooling in the cellar; the precious horse or a cow abandoned in the barn; the beloved dog in the yard. Women were afraid to wail, so sobbed quietly.[27] And the question, like that which "stuck in the brain" of a Belarusian peasant, the hero of Vasil' Bykov's novella, like a "red-hot nail": "People, why are you doing this to me? What bad have I done to you? . . . Why has all of this come down on me so hard? Have I sinned before God or people? Have I killed anyone, robbed, committed violence? Come to your senses, people!"[28]*

---

* Declared a kulak because of a thresher, which he had "bought on credit" and allowed the rest of the village to use "for whatever fee they could afford," Khvyodor Rovba was arrested and sent with his wife and six-year-old daughter to the Komi Republic in the Northeast. After his wife and daughter died within two to three years, he ran away, managed to reach his native village, was recognized, hunted down by a posse of militiamen, border guards, and local activists, and drowned in a swamp. (Vasil' Bykov, *Oblava* [Man-hunt] *Novy mir,* January 1990: 87–140.)

"I remember very well that cold winter day (I was seven then), when two guards and two carts came for us," wrote a man from the village of Sukhoe-Solotino in the Kursk province. "We were all loaded on the carts in what we were wearing and taken to the town of Oboyan, fifty kilometers [thirty miles] from the village. Counting mother, there were seven of us (my youngest brother was three then, my oldest sister, eleven). . . . Along the way people threw things on the carts for us—either an old jacket or an old blanket—and mother would cover us from the cold. In Oboyan, late at night, we were put in a church, where already there were a lot of 'enemies of the people.' "[29]

The "kulak scum" waited sometimes for days under the open sky for trains (they were not allowed inside train stations) of cattle cars to take them where they would live "under the strictest administrative oversight" next to their work sites: the mines of the Urals, the peat bogs in the swamps and forests of the north, or the boulders and trenches of the future White Sea–Baltic Sea Canal.[30]

The cars were so crowded that the exiles took turns sleeping on the floor. At some train stations they were given a bucket of *balanda* and two hundred grams (less than half a pound) of bread for each prisoner.[31] The journey could last for as long as a month.[32] Each car was given a metal bucket for a toilet. In vain did women cry and beg the guards to allow them to empty the bucket more often "because the children were suffocating."[33] "No one counted" the dead; the corpses were thrown off the train.[34]

"We were brought to the Ural Mountains," a kulak daughter remembered. "Next: walk, forty kilometers [twenty-five miles]. My father, on his bad legs, carried the little ones in his arms. Papa was assigned to work in the mines, mama on a construction site. There they perished. And so did all my brothers and sisters. I was sent to a *detdom*."[35]

Those who survived the trek lived in dugouts (*zemlyanki*) or huts made from the trees they felled, working day and night after they were ordered off the trains. The holes in between the logs were plugged with moss.[36] For the luckier there were barracks, with one family per room, no matter how many children they had. In the summer, cockroaches took over; "there was no escaping them."[37] The children were so hungry that they often did not feel the bites.[38] In the winter, corpses were stacked outside the barracks. They would be burnt in spring.[39]

Where "exiles from intelligentsia" could be found, there were so-called schools, which the kulak children were ordered to attend and where they were taught to sing "happy songs about Stalin and our happy childhood."[40] In a "special settlement" village in the Medevezhgorsk district on Lake Onega, close to the border with Finland, all children over fourteen worked alongside the adults, trimming trees into logs during the day. At night they went to school. Most of the children suffered from night blindness because of poor nutrition (especially the lack of vegetables, milk, and eggs), and often could not find their houses. They tripped over stumps and tree branches and fell. So parents went out every evening and

> cried out their children's names at the top of their lungs—all the while not straying too far from their homes, because many of them, too, couldn't see anything. And so, orienting ourselves by our family's voices, we could get home. Whoever did not have someone to call him or her would wander around the camp village for a long time until someone would hear their cry and take them home.[41]

For adult "kulaks" the exile was "eternal," that is, lifelong. Those under eighteen years of age at the time of arrest were later allowed to leave, but not to settle in cities.

"De-kulakized" and "collectivized," the Soviet countryside was to validate by a bumper harvest the brilliance of Stalin's thesis of the immeasurable superiority of collective agriculture—and to provide grain for export with which to earn hard currency for the machines needed for the unfolding "industrialization." Yet by spring 1932 it became clear that the village, paralyzed with fear and barely recovered from the hungry winter of 1931–32, could not be farther from performing the feat. No sooner had the winter wheat and rye (ozimye, which are sown in the fall) come to ear than peasants began to sneak around the kolkhoz fields "snipping" with scissors a few ears here and there to grind into flour or make gruel. They were mostly women desperate to feed their children.[42] On August 7, 1932, a decree drafted by Stalin himself stipulated "the highest measure of social defense: firing squad and the confiscation of all belongings" for "theft of kolkhoz property." Under "extenuating circumstances," capital punishment could be commuted to a prison camp sentence of no less than ten years. Amnesty for those convicted of this crime was prohibited.[43]

The decree became known as "the law on five ears of wheat" (*zakon o pyati koloskakh*): such was the minimal amount of "stolen property" needed to convict.[44] Counted as "theft" were kernels eaten or tucked in pockets while collecting grain off the kolkhoz fields after the harvest, including those found in mice's burrows.[45] In only five months, between August 1932 and January 1933, 54,645 people were convicted under the "five ears" statute; 2,110 of them were sentenced to death.[46]

As harvest time neared in the fall of 1932, the Central Committee "commissions," headed by top Soviet functionaries, were dispatched to the key grain-producing provinces to ensure the "triumph of collectivized agriculture" by extracting record deliveries. The Soviet Union's largest breadbaskets—northern Ukraine, southern ("black earth") Russia, the Volga basin, the Cossack-populated North Caucasus (the Stavropol and Krasnodar provinces), and northern Kazakhstan—were singled out for especially harsh and unyielding quotas. The North Caucasus and Ukraine were to be prodded by some of Stalin's most trusted lieutenants: Lazar Kaganovich and Anastas Mikoyan were to deal with the Cossacks, and Vyacheslav Molotov with the Ukrainians.

Villages, larger settlements, and entire rural districts that were found "sabotaging the grain deliveries plan" were entered on the "blackboard," which effectively spelled "a death sentence."[47] Declared "saboteurs," "kulak-sympathizers," and "mutants" (*pererozhdentsy*), the Party and village authorities of the "blackboarded" areas were arrested, sentenced to "five or better yet ten years," as Stalin put it, and often executed, with the names of the condemned published in local newspapers.[48]

The areas guilty of "sabotage" were to have no grain left: neither for sowing nor for people or livestock.[49] Armed militia and activists searched for grain everywhere: piercing floor boards and barnyards with bayonets, digging up cellars and kitchen gardens.[50] The raiders often took away anything that could be eaten: potatoes and meat, cows and horses, chickens and geese, baked bread and other food.[51] (One of the most impassioned essayists of glasnost, a young teacher, Ludmila Saraskina, heard from her father that "almost his entire family"—parents and eleven brothers and sisters— starved to death after their cow and horse had been taken away.)[52]

Trade cooperatives and kiosks were ordered closed, and the "black-boarded" regions were surrounded by Red Army or NKVD troops to prevent anyone from leaving.[53] "What are we going to feed our children?" peasants from the village of Novoe Zubrilovo in the Saratov province begged the functionary in charge of the grain-requisition raid. "The Soviet power gave you land. Feed them with the soil," he replied.[54] Following the November 4, 1932, resolution of the Central Committee, fifteen Cossack large villages, *stanitsy*, were "left without food.[55] (With an average population of 15,000 in each *stanitsa*, "can you imagine that Hiroshima?" asked leading agricultural economist and essayist Yuri Chernichenko.)

Everyone in the proscribed *stanitsy* was arrested and sent north into a "far exile": children and adults, poor peasants and "middle peasants" (*serednyaki*), who together were to constitute the backbone of collectivized agriculture, communists, teachers, and veterinarians. The very names of the *stanitsy*, which for centuries had supplied Russia with her best cavalry and became synonymous with Russian military valor, disappeared from the Soviet maps: Poltavskaya, Umanskaya, Vogushevskaya, Urupskaya, Medvedovskaya. Repopulated by discharged soldiers and their families, "Poltavskaya" became Krasnoarmeysk, or "Red Army City," and Urupskaya was renamed "Sovietskaya," or "Soviet."[56]

There was armed resistance, first, then full-blown peasant uprisings, especially among the Cossacks.[57] Border Guard troops of the political police (OGPU), led by Mikhail Frinovsky, executed "tens of thousands" of peasants and arrested hundreds of thousands more.[58] When the pilots of an air force squadron refused to bomb and strafe the Cossack villages, the unit was immediately dissolved and every second man executed.[59] Briefing the Politburo on the suppression of the rebellions in spring 1933, Frinovksy reported that "hundreds of bodies" of Red Army soldiers, killed by the rebels, were floating down the rivers in the North Caucasus.[60]

Throughout the fall of 1932, horse-drawn carts with the requisitioned grain creaked along country roads day and night, and a thick dust hung like a fog.[61] There were not enough elevators to store or railcars to move it, or enough tarp to protect from rain the rivers, then lakes, then seas of grain. Wheat and rye were shoveled off the carts onto the ground, where it became wet and rotted, under around-the-clock guard.[62]

"Most disgraceful things (*bezobraziya*) are happening in the Meshchovsky district," peasants from the Smolensk province wrote Stalin:

> What is done to the bread [grain] is harrowing. . . . Cows, pigs, people walk on it. When the bread is taken from the *muzhiks,* we are told that it is for the Red Army, the workers, but instead it is ground into dirt. No storage places, no receptacles or containers of any kind—in short, nothing has been prepared for the thousands of cart trains [*obozy*] with grain. . . . Thousands of poods* of grain are rotting. Many peasants have given it all, to the last grain, and right before their eyes, livestock is walking on the bread and there is not a piece of bread left at home. Is the complete ruination and impoverishment of peasant households in the interest of the Revolution?[63]

With the grain gone, hunger began to descend on the countryside. Unlike city- and town-dwellers, peasants were not entitled to ration coupons. Bread could be bought in the provincial centers or kiosks at larger railroad stations, but these were surrounded by troops to keep the peasants away.[64] By January 1933, all the livestock had been eaten in the areas most devastated by the grain requisitions: northern Ukraine, southern parts of the Kursk and Voronezh "black earth" provinces of Russia, the Kuybyshev and Ulyanovsk provinces along the Volga, the North Caucasus, and northern Kazakhstan.[†]

Potatoes, too, were gone, then potato peals in garbage piles. Acorns were ground and baked.[65] Clover was dried and crushed into "flour," mixed with buckwheat chaff, and eaten with "a nettle gruel."[66] Buds and linden leaves, orache (*lebeda*), and burdocks (*lopukhi*) were eaten. So were dogs and cats; mice and frogs and worms.[67] Hoofs and horns from dead horses and cows were also ground into meal. Sheep skins were cut into strips and boiled.[68]

---

[*] One pood is sixteen kilos or thirty-five pounds.

[†] Slaughtered by their owners or dying from hunger and lack of care alongside them in 1929–33 were 17.7 million horses, over 25 million cows and oxen, more than 10 million pigs, and 71 million sheep and goats. (Yuri Chernichenko, "Trava iz-pod stoga" [Grass from under a haystack], in Yuri Afanasiev, ed. *Inogo ne dano* [There is no other way], Moscow: Progress, 1988: 610.)

With bloated stomachs, on spindly legs, and heads that seemed enormous, "like cannonballs" on their thin, crane-like necks, peasant children were like walking skeletons tightly wrapped in a "transparent yellow gauze" of skin, under which one could see every little bone.[69] (Some of the children who survived the famine of 1932–33 could not walk at five years of age. In Vyatka's province in European Russia's northeast, they were called *siduny,* the "sitting ones." But they crawled very fast when they saw grain, grasping handfuls and stuffing them into their mouths.)[70]

While they still could walk, some peasants would go to railway tracks, where they knelt and cried "Bread! Bread!" at passing trains.[71] Many lifted up their disfigured children for the passengers to see. At first, scraps of food were thrown out of the train windows. Soon, armed guards were posted on the trains passing through the starving regions. They drew the curtains in the cars and kept the passengers away from the tightly shut windows.[72]

The starving moved slower and slower, as if in a daze, stopping and holding onto walls of village houses. After a while they could only crawl. No one had the strength to bury the dead, and corpses lay in the streets or in houses: entire families, on the floors, in beds, at the table.[73] In his brilliant *Vsyo techyot* (Forever flowing)—a meditation on Stalinism and barely "fictionalized" eyewitness accounts of some of its worst crimes— Vasily Grossman writes of the settlers that were brought to repopulate the devastated villages. Women and children were ordered to stay on the outskirts and men were given pitchforks and told to drag out the dead from the houses. Corpses fell apart and the stench was unbearable. Body parts were buried in the fields.[74]

As in the horrific post–civil war famine of 1921, cannibalism was back. First, it was bodies in fresh graves, then live prey.[75] Children were especially vulnerable. Yuri Chernichenko, who grew up in the Kuban' region, remembers never being left home alone: his mother was afraid that he would be stolen and eaten.[76]

Chernichenko's father was an agronomist for a state-run "Machine-Tractor Station" and, as a state employee, received a food ration that saved the family. A swollen woman—likely not older that Yuri's young mother but looking like an old granny, *babushka*—would come to the Chernichenkos and say: "After you wash the dishes, don't pour out the water. I'll drink it." Yuri wanted her to tell him stories and fairy tales, but she only "sighed about her babies who died."[77]

"My uncle, now deceased, told me how [as a boy] he shuffled off [*poplyolsya*]—yes, shuffled off, for he could no longer walk normally—to see his friend," remembered a doctor from Murmansk. "When he entered the yard, he saw him lying on the ground near the well. His mother was cutting up his body with an ax and putting the pieces in the bucket because, I think, she wanted to keep them fresh in the cold water in the well."[78]

A man from the Saratov province, who served in the Red Army in 1933, remembered a letter that a fellow soldier, a Kirill Shilov, received from his mother in a village:

How is your service? she wrote. I take it at least you have enough bread. And here, Praskov'ya is eating her own children. She ate one daughter and when they searched for the other, they found a pot full of meat on the stove. Well, his commander learned about the letter and reported to the commissar. Shilov was called to the Special Department and sent to jail for spreading anti-Soviet lies. But an official query they sent to the village council [*sel'sovet*] confirmed everything. They let him out of jail but warned him to keep quiet.[79]

In 1934, a Gulag prisoner (an actor, arrested in 1929 and sentenced to ten years in the camps for "participation in a student organization") met women from Ukraine at the Kem' camp in the White Sea–Baltic Sea Canal complex. Suddenly, one of them, from the village of Romankovka in the Zaporozh'e province in Ukraine, began to cry hysterically. "She ate her little one," another woman said. "Yes, I have!" the first woman cried out defiantly. "Everyone was eating and so was I. If I hadn't, I, too, would have died. This way maybe I can have another baby someday, can have more children."[80]

"One in ten thousand" starving managed to evade the many checkpoints on the roads and reach the cities.[81] By then most were too weak to walk. In Kiev they crawled among people, who went about their business and pretended not to notice them or those already dead on the pavement, since officially there was no famine anywhere.[82] Early every morning, long, horse-drawn wagons, *bityugi*, rode the streets, collecting those who had died the night before. Grossman wrote of one such carriage, loaded mostly with dead children, although some were still stirring. Asked about these, the driver waved his hand: those too would quiet down by the time he got to the cemetery.[83]

The Soviet Union exported to Western Europe nearly 2 million tons of grain in 1932 and 1 million tons in 1933.[84] Not one distillery in Ukraine, where vodka was made from grain, stopped production.[85]

CHAPTER SEVEN

The Unraveling of the Legitimizing Myths, I

FOOD, HOUSING, MEDICAL CARE, THE "GOLDEN
CHILDHOOD," AND THE STANDARD OF LIVING

Quite a few people are unwilling to part with the myths. . . . Many
others are beginning to ask question after question. We must have
a conversation of utmost honesty. We cannot postpone it any
longer.
—Alexei Kiva, "Krizis 'zhanra'" (The crisis of the "genre"), *Novy
mir,* March 1990: 208

Today we face a decisive choice: will our society again be entangled
in a web of myths, which paralyze free will and free action and
encourage illusory hopes, or choose free will and free intellect of a
self-aware individual, capable of orienting himself in the world
without the comfort of idolization? Without understanding that
the king is naked, it is impossible to affirm universal human
values; the smashing of idols clears the path to ideals.
—Anatoly Bocharov, "Mchatsya mify, b'yutsya mify" (Myths are
whirling, myths are stirring), *Oktyabr',* January 1990: 183, 191

Of course, not everyone is capable of withstanding such a powerful
onrush of almighty truth. A soul could easily break down. But
would the concealment of the whole truth or its replacement with
new lies be better? What kind of ideals are these, if their preservation requires the concealment of truth from the people?!

—Alexander Tsypko, "Khoroshi li nashi printsipy? (How good are our principles?), *Novy mir,* April 1990: 202

The apocalypse of Chernobyl has stunned us. But it was not the nuclear reactors that blew up in Chernobyl; it was professional and social illusions. Because of the low life expectancy, the high children's mortality, the shortage or the absence of modern drugs, equipment, specialists; because of the revolting hospitals, where the elderly after a stroke lie on boards in corridors for hours and where no one comes to look at them; because half of the harvested fruits and vegetables rots away before reaching the consumer's table; because of accidents, traumas, unfiltered streams of waste, the production of goods that no one needs, the barbaric waste of energy, metal, wood; because we don't know how to work, to teach, to save, to cure—because of all of this, do we perhaps, quietly and almost imperceptibly, have a Chernobyl exploding every month? Or every week?
—Leonid Batkin, "Vozobnovlenie istorii" (The resumption of history), in Yuri Afanasiev, ed., *Inogo ne dano* (There is no other way), Moscow: Progress, 1988: 177

ANY LASTING POLITY espouses and propagates essential beliefs by which it lives. They do not have to be literally true; indeed, they seldom are. This, however, does not matter so long as these beliefs, or myths, are accepted as reality by enough people. To cite, again, Merton's "Thomas theorem": "If men define situations as real, they are real in their consequences."[1] The key "consequence," in this case, is the trust in the basic moral soundness of a polity's foundation, which, in turn, invests it with legitimacy.

The Soviet Union, too, had spawned a powerful mythology that legitimized political, economic, and social arrangements. Sustained and renewed daily by unchallenged propaganda and protected from scrutiny by censorship and a ban on travel for all but a tiny elite minority, and defended by prompt and severe sanctions for open allegiance to an alternative version of the Soviet past and present, the Soviet mythology proved durable and often inspiring. Building a "new society" required enormous sacrifices, but the progress was stunning and the country was the envy of the entire world—such, in essence, was the official meta-narrative.

Within a few years, most devastatingly between 1987 and 1989, virtually every constituent myth of this tale was shattered by uncensored truths. Striking with deadly and increasingly overwhelming force, glasnost hollowed the myths out, leaving behind empty and shriveled shells. Each new revelation opened a gap in the moral foundation of the regime, making it unworthy of the allegiance of millions whom it was revealed to have treated so unfairly.

"A crisis of trust" (*krizis doveriya*) was the title affixed by an astute *Pravda* editor to the June 1988 survey of readers' letters, each a story about dreadful human condition: from healthcare to housing to food.[2] Two years later, the deputy editor of *Moskovskie novosti* would write, "Life is snatching away the last trump cards from the propaganda hand of 'achievements of developed socialism.'"[3] For a society that in a large measure defined itself as a vanquisher of the "ills of capitalism"—poverty, hunger, homelessness, healthcare one had to pay for and thus unavailable to the "masses," and childhoods disfigured by all these horrors— this was a very dangerous development.

Of course, millions of Russians had suffered, in various degrees, from these maladies, or saw others who did, or heard about them from friends and relatives. Yet, judging by the letters they sent to newspapers and magazines and by what they told reporters, it was the suddenly bared systemic nature of these ills that they found outrageous. The state had failed not only them, their village, or their town; it had let down an entire great country.

Of these failures, the shortages and low quality of food were among the starkest. Of course, those standing in lines for hours to buy their monthly allotment of sausage may have grumbled for years, even decades. Yet heralded by *Moskovskie novosti* across the eleven time zones with an article titled "Ration cards in peacetime is a shame!" the shortages instantly became a national political issue.[4] While there were lines for most of the produce, the shortage of meat in this largely northern country of meat lovers was especially insulting. Moscow and Leningrad aside, in most cities and towns meat was sold—and only to those who had valid ration coupons—twice a year: around May Day and before the revolution's anniversary on November 7. In the country's third largest industrial city,

Sverdlovsk, the allotment was one kilo per person on each occasion.[5] The rest of the time, meat was available only as sausage—increasingly the butt of jokes because it was so vile. Pale yellow *talony* (ration coupons), distributed monthly by appointed tenants, entitled each family to 800 grams (less than two pounds) of sausage (and 400 grams of butter) a month.[6*]

One day in the summer of 1987, a leading Soviet economist and advisor to Mikhail Gorbachev, Academician Abel Aganbegyan, began to describe to an *Ogonyok* reporter a "normal" meat counter of his dreams: "different kinds of sausage, Frankfurters [*sosiski*], hams [*vetchina*], smoked or salted pork rumps and thighs on a bone [*okoroka*], a wide assortment of beef, fowl." The journalist interrupted the scholar: "I am having a hard time imagining this."[7]

Those who wanted real meat (or a better sausage) could get it only one way: by going to Moscow. The "sausage trains" and their passengers' quest were featured in a long *Ogonyok* story, complete with photographs of weary women with bags and sacks over their shoulders as they walked along a train station platform. "And the trains roll in to Moscow—long, twelve-car trains," the caption read. "They roll in from Kaluga, Ryazan', Dmitrov, Serpukhov, Zvenigorod. They come in every day, and their passengers are preoccupied with only one question: 'Where can we buy sausage?' "[8†] When a contributor to an elite Soviet journal wrote of the reasons for her country's "inferiority complex," along with the "lack of

---

* The same amounts—800 grams of sausage per person per month and 400 grams of butter—could be bought with ration coupons in Kirov in central Russia. (Alexander Bekker, "Myaso na vyvoz" [Meat for export], *Moskovskie novosti*, July 10, 1988: 13.) In the steelmaking city of Cherepovets, in the northwest, the meat substitutes amounted to only half a kilo of sausage a month. (Letter from V. V. Gurevich, in Christopher Cerf and Marina Albee, eds., *Small Fires: Letters from the Soviet People to Ogonyok Magazine, 1987–1990*, New York: Summit Books, 1990: 50.)

† People take vacations and days off, reported a *Pravda* correspondent, and then stand in endless lines, listening to insults like, "Here they are, the hicks [*derevnya*], to eat us out of our supplies," and then "storm" the buses and trains to get back home. "What else is there to do?" said a female worker from a machine tool plant in Ryazan. "You kill yourself for a day, but you supply yourself and your neighbor [with food]. And then it's your neighbor's turn to bring you the stuff. And that's how we live." (A. Chernyak, "Edoki po

freedom" and "low living standards," she listed "sausage for which people travel to Moscow."[9]

Things were much worse in the countryside, which sent all that it produced "to the center." Village grocery stores often were literally empty.[10] To eat meat at least every now and then, a schoolteacher from one of Russia's most fertile regions, Stavropol, had to raise her own livestock. But, she complained in a letter to *Pravda*, there was no feed for animals in stores, and the local *sovkhoz* would not sell grain to "outsiders" unless they worked in its fields at harvest time. The letter writer had faithfully complied for years until the summer of 1989, when she could not help harvest because she had just given birth. Left with nothing to feed her animals she had no prospect of a lasting meat supply. "Is it right to force into a field a woman with a month-old baby?" she asked. "Wouldn't it be kinder to take her circumstances into consideration and sell her a sack of grain?"[11]

If the reforms could not be instrumental to the "banishment of hunger," if the regime failed to feed "all our 300 million people," perestroika was doomed, wrote leading glasnost economic essayist Yuri Chernichenko.[12] Yet as the demands of the striking miners of Kuzbass, one of the country's largest coalfields in southwestern Siberia, showed, this was a very tall order. To settle the strike in the summer of 1989, the government agreed to deliver to Kuzbass "ten thousand tons of sugar, over six thousand tons of meat, five millions cans of dairy products, and one thousand tons of tea."[13]

The myth of affordable, comfortable, and abundant housing, too, was under attack. It was indeed cheap but not terribly comfortable and, most damagingly, in such short supply that tens of millions spent their entire lives without ever stepping into an apartment of their own. Housing was found to be "rationed" at least as stingily as food.[14]

Fourteen million families—between 15 and 17 percent of the country's population, or 40–50 million people—were estimated to be without an apartment of their own. They lived in workers' dormitories (*obshchezhitiya*) or "communal apartments" (*kommunalka*): one room per family,

statistike i v zhizni" [The food consumers in statistics and in real life] *Pravda*, September 1, 1988: 3.)

with shared bathroom and kitchen.[15] The Soviet "sanitary norm" (established in 1922 and unchanged since)[16] required at least 9 square meters (under 100 square feet) of living space per person. Over a third of the population (100 million people) lived in smaller spaces.[17] Hundreds of thousands of families were on waiting lists for an apartment or for a larger apartment.[18]*

A letter to the editor of *Pravda* described a family of six, including children, that for fourteen years lived in a room of 13 square meters (140 square feet)—"like pigs."[19] Another family of six, that of an Afghan war veteran, had 14 square meters, and was on a waiting list behind 108 World War II veterans—in 1987.[20] Three more children—and their father, a theater director and professor at an Institute of Culture and Arts, and their mother, a teacher—were growing up in a room of 9 square meters in their in-laws' "small three-room" apartment, which, in addition to the in-laws, also housed the father's eighty-four-year-old grandmother and his alcoholic brother.[21] "Yes, I know there are problems in the country with housing," the children's mother ended her letter to *Ogonyok* in September 1989, "that we are not the only ones living like this, but how am I going to explain that to my children who are growing up so fast, who need a place to sleep, someplace to crawl and develop. Dear Comrades, I am asking you, I am begging you: help us! Save our family!"[22]

"We, Leningraders born and bred, live in a house unsuitable for living and condemned in 1966," read a comment on a questionnaire published in *Literaturnaya gazeta* in February 1989. "The bathroom is shared by four families, and so is the kitchen, which is 5.5 square meters [59 square feet]. There is mold on the walls and water under the floorboards. I am constantly sick, and my children will grow up [to be] invalids. Our house is forgotten by God and people."[23]

After five decades in a communal apartment, which he called "jail," with his family in an 18.5-square-meter room, a man told public opinion

---

* In the largest Russian cities, 344,800 families and individuals were on the waiting lists: in Moscow, 282,900 in Leningrad, 111,600 in Novosibirsk, and 130,600 in Sverdlovsk. (V. Tolstov, "Kak obespecheny zhil'yom krupneyshie goroda strany" [How well are the largest cities of the country provided with housing], *Izvestia*, September 4, 1988: 2.)

pollsters that he could no longer dream of "our bright future." Instead, he was tormented in his sleep by the visions of "nightmarish, smelly slums [*trushchoby*]." We have no home to call ours, he said. How can we raise our children?[24]

Soviet housing was divided between facilities "with amenities" (*blagoustroennoe*) and those without (*neblagoustroennoe*). For renters in the latter category, eight or even six square meters per person would have seemed a paradise if only there were toilets, running water, and heat. It certainly would have been for Zoya Terent'eva, seventy-two years old, and her neighbors in the city of Yaroslavl, home to the country's largest tire-making plant. Every morning, she descended five flights of stairs with a small milk can, *bidonchik*, for water, as her apartment had none.[25] A woman from the same district, a mother of three, complained of having water, cold, "only on holidays."[26] In an apartment building nearby, inhabitants considered putting latrines in the middle of the courtyard as they had no water to flush the toilets.[27]

Still, these were far from the worst cases. An elderly invalid from Siberia wrote *Pravda* about living in a tiny abandoned bathhouse (*ban'ka*), "rotting and damp," and dreaming of the "heat and light" of a pigsty.[28] There was a family of six with a nursing baby, in one room, with frequent power shortages and gas outages.[29] Or a dozen or so families in a *barak* (a long, one-story hut made of thin wooden boards) which had been declared to be "in emergency condition" twenty-five years earlier, though not one family had been relocated. They had no "amenities" (*udobstva*) except for water, which was shut off occasionally. Their "settlement"(*posyolok*) was next to a city dump and surrounded by oil refineries.[30] When a family in another dilapidated hut, also declared "beyond repair," petitioned for an improvement in their "living conditions," they were told that in their region one-fifth of the population lived like them and that "many" lived in condemned (*podlezhashchie snosu*) buildings.[31]

Yet another family with a young child lived in a one-room dugout (*zemlyanka*). "We heat the stove up before going to bed at night, but in the morning our hair freezes down to the pillow," the sobbing wife and mother told a *Komsomol'skaya pravda* reporter. Upon visiting the abode, a commission from the executive committee of the local soviet concluded that "the family lives in what at the time of the inspection were satisfactory conditions."[32]

Asked at the end of 1988 to rate the most important problems in the country, 44 percent of Muscovites singled out "the supply of food products" and 38 percent mentioned housing—but a full half of those polled named healthcare.[33] Previously secret statistics warranted this concern. According to the economist Aganbegyan, the Soviet Union's healthcare expenditures in 1987 were about 3–4 percent of the country's GDP: not only the "lowest" share among the "developed countries" but around seventy-fifth among 126 countries worldwide.[34] Two billion rubles a year (3.2 billion dollars by the widely inflated official exchange rate) were spent annually on medical technology, whereas that perennial yardstick of national progress, at once the main foe and the material ideal, the United States, spent 35 billion dollars.[35] The "medical technology saturation" (osnashchyonnost' meditsinskoy tekhnikoy) of an "average hospital bed" was between 10 and 15 percent of the U.S. level.[36]

As with other key myths, the heaviest damage was inflicted by the details. Thirty-five percent of healthcare facilities (1.2 million hospital beds) were said by the minister of healthcare to be without hot water (in rural areas, 65 percent of hospitals lacked hot water); every sixth hospital had no running water at all; 30 percent lacked indoor toilets.[37] In the Altai region in southwest Siberia, with a population of over 2.5 million, 88 percent of rural hospitals were in "decrepit" (vetkhie) buildings without running water and indoor toilets.[38] In the summer of 1988, there was a shortage of 1,000 operating tables and 5,000 surgical lamps.[39]

In addition to their salaries "hovering around the poverty line,"[40] the acute shortage of nurses and nurse's aides was explained also by the lack of mechanization: a mop, a bucket, and a stretcher are "all we have," a physician from Khar'kov wrote Pravda.[41] Kitchen staff carried breakfast, lunch, and dinner into wards in buckets as well.[42]

In Volgograd, a city of 1 million, hospitals were reported to be short of gowns and of such disinfectants as chloramines and hydrogen peroxide.[43] The number of scalpels made in the country was less than 62 percent of the amount needed.[44] In January 1988, a Ministry of Healthcare commission found the "most common" rubber gloves to be "few and of low quality."[45] "I am scared to come up to the operating table," a surgeon in Barnaul, the capital of the Altai region and a city of over 600,000, told the First Congress of People's Deputies in June 1989. "I am scared for the patient because we lack the most basic stuff."[46]

A leading Soviet pharmacologist called the scarcity of drugs "catastrophic."[47] The technology at many of the country's pharmaceutical enterprises, he added, was "decades behind" the modern level.[48] Prime Minister Nikolai Ryzhkov disclosed in summer 1989 that Soviet industry produced only 45 percent of the medications the country needed.[49] On closer examination by journalists and experts, this figure was even more frightful: only 60 percent of the demand for cardiovascular drugs was met; 450 drugs were in short supply in the country as a whole, and within the Russian Soviet Socialist Federative Republic, 657 were not available in sufficient numbers.[50] At a nationally televised session of the First Congress of People's Deputies, a physician called for an emergency hard-currency appropriation to buy at least "fifteen, twenty, thirty drugs without which we cannot live": insulin and its derivatives, and hormonal and cardiovascular medicines. She appealed to the directors of enterprises with access to hard currency (valyuta) among the deputies and those watching on television: please donate some of these funds to help buy these drugs abroad![51]

In 1988, the Soviet Union was thirty-second in the world in life expectancy.[52] For men, life expectancy dropped from sixty-six to sixty-two years between the mid 1960s and late 1970s, regaining (as it turned out, only briefly) two years in 1987 because of the soon discontinued anti-alcohol campaign.[53]

Myocardial infarctions (heart attacks) caused by the blockage of a coronary artery killed on average 1.8 million Soviet citizens (mostly men) every year,[54] yet coronary artery bypass graft surgeries (aortokoronarnoe shuntirovanie) were a rarity. In France, with a population almost five times smaller, 22,000 such operations were annually performed, reported Minister of Healthcare Chazov—100,000 people should have been operated on and saved in the Soviet Union each year. Instead, Chazov fulminated, 870 were.[55]

In February 1989 another shortage temporarily overshadowed others: that of single-use (odnorazovye) syringes, needles, and catheters. Their absence was blamed for the spread of a still rare and exotic illness,

AIDS, in a pediatric ward of the Infectious Diseases Hospital in the city of Elista, the capital of the Kalmyk Autonomous Republic in southeast Russia near the Volga delta. Twenty-seven children, most of them infants, and six mothers were discovered to have contracted the illness in the hospital.[56] Three months later, 23 children were found infected with AIDS in the city of Volgograd, over 225 kilometers north of Elista. One of them died a few days after he was diagnosed.

A government commission attributed the outbreak to the recycling of syringes and needles for intravenous injections and catheterizations: no disposable units were available, and the multiple-use instruments were not properly sterilized between injections.[57] Of the 3 billion single-use syringes needed in 1989, the Soviet Union manufactured only between 50 million and 150 million.[58] In the meantime, rushed from Moscow to Volgograd were 250,000 disposable syringes, 5,000 blood transfusion systems, and 10,000 surgical gloves.[59]

Within a year, four Volgograd children died of AIDS, and seventy-seven others (although initially diagnosed with other illnesses) died after stays in the same wards. In May 1990, a *Komsomol'skaya pravda* correspondent reported from Volgograd (a major industrial center with a population of 1 million) that infamous Pediatric Hospital No. 7 still "simply lacked many single-use instruments and systems," and 5,000 disposable syringes delivered earlier could not be used for the want of needles, thus "tempting" nurses to reuse the regular syringes. In many cases, disposable needles "did not fit" catheters: the former were Soviet-made, the latter imported.[60] "The city," the reporter continued, "is suffocating without the most important drugs for strengthening the immune system, such as immunoglobulin and interferon . . . without the basics to save its children."[61] Volgograd emergency medical teams (*Skoraya pomoshch*) were allotted five disposable syringes per shift, while there could be three times as many emergency calls.[62]

By then there was an almost expected tragic symbolism in the fact that children became the country's first publicly identified victims of AIDS. For even alongside other revelations about the healthcare system, the truth about pediatrics and obstetrics was dreadful. The distress was all the greater because the allegedly infinite care for the well-being of the children had been so central to the legitimizing mythology. "The most privileged class," they were called. "To the children—only the best!" ran a notorious slogan.[63] "Our golden childhood / Grows brighter every day," exulted a song, which everyone learned in kindergarten or grade school. "Under a lucky star / We live in our native land."*

The "golden childhood" myth had already been badly damaged by the news that half of the country's schools had no central heat, running water, or indoor toilets.[64] A quarter of all Soviet students had to study in two shifts and "some" in three, with some classes as large as forty-two students.[65] An inevitable comparison with the United States was made to dramatize the issue: "they" spent 12 percent of the national income on education; "we," only 7 percent—and the "incomes" were "very, very different."[66]

There were stories about "working children," as young as ten years of age, working twelve-hour days ("even at night") in the fields[67]† and about 35,000 labor accidents involving children under fourteen in 1986.[68] Overall, fifty of every thousand Soviet schoolchildren below the age of fourteen incurred traumas and "not infrequently" died.[69] Reporters went to orphanages (*internaty*) and brought back harrowing stories of destitution, exploitation, and abuse, especially heartbreaking in the cases of the "retarded," many of whom were criminally misdiagnosed, and neglected healthy children.‡

---

*   Детство наше золотое
     Все светлее с каждым днем,
     Под счастливою звездою
     Мы живем в краю родном. ("Nash kray" [Our land], D. Kabalevskiy [music] and A. Prishelets [lyrics], 1955)

†   In fall 1988, schoolchildren picking cotton in Uzbekistan and Turkmenistan were seen "many times" by the members of the non-government environmental "expedition." Children worked eight-hour days under the "burning sun" in fields treated with defoliants. There was very little food, and the water from the irrigation canals was "unsuitable for drinking." (V. Perevedenstev, Ph.D., letter to *Ogonyok* 4, 1989: 3.)

‡   An orphanage in the Kalinin region, 150 kilometers north of Moscow, was housed in a "semi-collapsed" (*polurazrushennyi*) pre-1917 landlord's manor (*usad'ba*), "dank and cold." There was no hot water, and children sawed wood and collected coal in order to "wash in warmth at least once a week" in a bathhouse as there were no bathrooms. The children also repaired ceilings, which in one room had collapsed completely. The staff was half the required

Still, few newspaper readers were likely prepared for the truth about the country's obstetrics and pediatrics. According to the minister of health, in 1988 infant mortality in the Soviet Union was higher than in forty-nine countries, behind Barbados and Mauritius.[70]* The incidence of infant deaths (under one year old) was two and a half times higher than in Great Britain, West Germany, or the United States.[71] Of the sixty "items of equipment" necessary for modern obstetrics, the Soviet Union manufactured six, complained a leading obstetrician, and there was little

---

size because of low salaries: a night orderly (*nyanechka*) was paid 98 rubles a month; a teacher, responsible for twenty-five to thirty children all day long, 138 rubles. (Natal'ya Davydova, "Dolgi nashi" [Our debts], *Moskovskie novosti*, September 10, 1989: 5.)

Diagnosed as "chronic psychologically abnormal invalids" (*psikhokhroniki*), the "working children" of an orphanage in the Kursk region, 450 kilometers south of Moscow, started their shift at a nearby dairy farm by removing manure, and washing and milking the cows. They then had breakfast (without washing their hands as "soap has not been issued for a long time") and went back to the farm. No one knew what happened to the money the children earned, but in a special store for the staff there was milk and meat—an in-kind payment the children also received for their work at the farm. The "back-breaking" (*neposil'nyi*) labor gradually turned children into "obedient and torpid slaves," a *Komsomol'skaya pravda* correspondent concluded. "In orphanages today we are seeing a deliberate lowering of children's intellect, the extinguishment of human spirit from their consciousness. . . . May fate keep you from ever stepping over the threshold of this house." (T. Vishnevskaya, "Raby—nemy" [The slaves are mute], *Komsomol'skaya pravda*, January 9, 1990: 2.)

Quite a few of *Moskovskie novosti* and *Komsomol'skaya pravda* readers were likely to compare these accounts with the searing portrait of a 1944 orphanage in Anatoly Pristavkin's beautifully written autobiographical novel *Nochevala tuchka zolotaya* (A little golden cloud spent a night), published to huge acclaim in the March and April 1987 issues of *Znamya*. Although the children were no longer dying from starvation, life in orphanages forty-five years later was not as unrecognizable as one might have hoped.

* Even these grim statistics likely understated the problem. According to Professor V. I. Kulakov, the leading Soviet obstetrician and director of the All-Union Center for the Health and Safety of Mother and Child, only children born weighing 1,000 grams or more counted as a live birth in the Soviet Union (those under that weight were considered miscarriages and thus excluded from the infant mortality statistics), whereas the World Health Organization counted infants weighing as little as 500 grams as live births. (V. I. Kulakov, "Rebyonok bez prismotra?" (An unattended child?), *Pravda*, August 10, 1987: 4.)

hard currency (*invaluta*) left for the "impoverished" obstetrics after other state "agencies" and institutions received their share.[72]

"Thousands" of babies were lost every year because of the lack of ultrasound diagnostic equipment. "Not a single Soviet-made [ultrasound] machine in thirty years! In the entire era of space exploration!" Professor V. I. Kulakov, the director of the All-Union Center for the Health and Safety of Mother and Child, cried out to an interviewer.[73]* There were no single-use gowns and surgical boots (*bakhily*) for doctors, he went on, or single-use wraps for newborns, while "badly laundered" wraps could lead to infections.[74] A woman from the Altai region wrote in the most popular Soviet women's magazine, *Rabotnitsa* (A working woman) of drawing a maternity nurse's attention to a small abscess on her newborn's face. "We don't have *zelyonka* [a common bright green mild topical antiseptic]. If you can get it, apply yourself," the nurse answered.[75]

Earning some of the lowest salaries in the Soviet Union, nurse's aides (*sanitarki*) were as scarce in pediatric wards as they were in regular hospitals, and their duties were increasingly performed by the little patients' mothers. "Everyone knows," wrote a *Komsomol'skaya pravda* reporter, that "mothers wash the floors, change the bedpans, do the laundry, take out garbage—they are real peons of our free healthcare."[76] Fourteen of these mothers, who had brought their children to the regional pediatric hospital in Khabarovsk in the Far East, wrote to *Ogonyok* in October 1988:

> What conditions our children are being treated in! It is impossible fully to describe the shabbiness of the hospital building, the peeling plaster in the wards (*palaty*), the rotted floors with giant holes for rats,† mice, and cockroaches, . . . the rusted-

---

* By October 1987, the Center had been under construction for fifteen years. Intended as a showcase for maternity hospitals throughout the country, the partially built facility suffered from nonfunctioning air-conditioning thermostats, "interruptions" in the hot water supply, and elevator breakdowns. ("Poterpite, zhenshina!" (Hang in there, woman!), letters to *Rabotnitsa*, February 1989: 23.)

† In 1988, one of Russia's most popular poets, Andrei Voznesensky, published a short poem titled "V roddome" ("In a maternity hospital"), which read, in part: A rat in a maternity hospital has eaten through a baby's cheek!

through plumbing which oozes sewage, the overcrowded wards, with fifteen to eighteen children in them. There are mothers among us who have brought their children here for ten years, but they see no changes for the better. You think the ministries of the USSR and the RSFSR [the Russian Republic] don't know about this? They do! During this hospital's lifetime so many different [government] commissions have come and gone that if at least some good had come from all of them, not just a [new] hospital but a whole new city could have been built![77]

In late 1988 and early 1989, "thousands" of former maternity hospital (*roddoma*) patients wrote *Rabotnitsa* in response to a letter about one woman's birthing experience, titled "A Nightmare?"[78] One of the letters described a Moscow hospital that was filled to double its capacity, with women giving birth on chairs and lying on gurneys "for days" afterward. Because of the chronic shortages of the *sanitarki*, no one was surprised at the sight of maternity nurses (*akusherki*) washing floors and then, "dropping the mop, [running] to deliver," as a Moscow nurse put it.* Just as common, apparently, was seeing a nurse running "throughout the entire hospital" (and a Moscow hospital at that!) in search of a stethoscope, "one for all," to listen to a baby's heart.[79]

Women about to give birth were left alone in their tiny cubicles (*bokses*). No visitors were allowed, while nurses, as one of them wrote, had no

---

We ourselves are rats, droning on all the time
All about things exalted.
A rat in a maternity ward
Has eaten through a baby's cheek!
We save people on ice floes,
We send projects to Mars,
a rat in a maternity hospital
has eaten through a baby's cheek. (*Literaturnaya gazeta*, October 5, 1988: 6)
* "Do our nurses even have an opportunity to work normally?" asked an *Izvestia* reporter. "It is no secret that for her miserly salary one nurse does the job of two or three nurses. Besides, in many hospitals nurses do the work of nurse's aides—something that the rules of sterilization categorically prohibit yet that some existing instructions permit." (S. Tutorskaya, "Potryasenie" [Shock], *Izvestia*, March 7, 1989: 3.)

time to "come up, to talk, to encourage," much as they would like to: they had to deliver meals, clear and wash the dishes, clean up the birthing rooms after use, administer medicine, and take patients' blood pressure—all by only three nurses per shift.[80] In the Bryansk regional maternity hospital, women themselves washed floors ("instead of gymnastics").[81] One woman remembered turning on the light in the middle of the night and "screaming in horror: the floor and the walls were covered with cockroaches."[82]

Perhaps in no other instance was the distance between the myth and reality as dramatic as in the case of poverty—something that could not have possibly happened in the "first socialist state." "Millions of ordinary people are doomed to a semi-hungry condition," a reader complained to a major national newspaper: librarians, secretaries, museum workers, kindergarten teachers.[83]

When the term "poverty line" (*cherta bednosti*) appeared for the first time in the Soviet press in 1989, it was said to apply to 43 million Soviet citizens (15 percent of the 1988 population) who lived in families with incomes of less than 75 rubles per person per month."[84] Another quarter of Soviet families were revealed to spend every kopeck of a salary on bare necessities, unable to save anything at all, and one in ten had to borrow from friends and family every month to make ends meet.[85]* Only one in eight Soviet citizens had a savings account.[86]

A year later, non-governmental experts concluded that those with a monthly income of 100 rubles or less lived in poverty—81 million people (28 percent of the population).[87] Fifty million more (18 percent) earned

---

* In the essay "Marginaly" ("The marginal people," *Znamya*, October 1989), Evgeny Starikov cites similar numbers from a study by the research "group" headed by Academician Tatiana Zaslavskaya: 8.8 percent of the people could not survive on their salaries, month-to-month, and 24 percent had money only for bare necessities (p. 153). In their answers to the questionnaire published in *Literaturnaya gazeta* in early 1989, 27 percent of the respondents indicated that they had only enough money for bare necessities, and 29 percent reported that their salaries were not enough to last from the first to the last of the month, forcing them "constantly" to borrow from relatives and friends. (A. Golov, A. Grazhdankin, L. Gudkov, B. Dubinin, N. Zorkaya, Yu. Levada, A. Levinson, L. Sedov, "Chto my dumaem" [What we think], *Literaturnaya gazeta*, March 29, 1989: 12.)

between 100 rubles and 125 rubles a month, which was now considered "next to the poverty threshold."[88] Thus, 131 million people, or 46 percent of Soviet citizens, were now defined as poor.*

A fifty-year-old worker from Moscow told sociologists that "in his entire life" he could not buy his children a bicycle, "never mind anything else."[89] Earning 200 rubles a month (a high salary in 1989), a worker with a family of four to five people could not "save a single ruble for a rainy day," according to a reader's letter in *Komsomol'skaya pravda*. "We live only day-by-day. We have no thoughts of a future."[90] In a country where, in 1988, the average per capita monthly income was 125 rubles,[91] a "wardrobe" of the most necessary things for a seven-year-old girl (a coat, tights, boots, shirts—provided, of course, these things could be found in stores at all) cost 420 rubles.[92]† I would like to ask

---

* In January 1992, when Russia became an independent country after the disintegration of the Soviet Union, 49 million Russians (34 percent) had incomes below the "minimal subsistence level." By 1995 this number would decline to 25 percent. ("Main Socioeconomic Indicators of Living Standard of Population," Goskomstat [Federal State Statistics Service], available at www.gks .ru/free_doc/2006/ruso6e/07–01.htm, accessed on July 10, 2007; and "Chislen-nost' naseleniya s denezhnymi dokhodami nizhe velichiny prozhitochnogo minimuma" [The size of the population with the monetary income below minimal subsistence], Goskomstat, available at www.gks.ru/free_doc/2006/ bo6_13/06–25.htm, accessed on July 10, 2007.)

† In a letter to *Pravda* in December 1989, a woman complained that her daughter had worn [the same] fur-lined boots for [the last] three years, "but finally we threw them out this past spring. . . . Since then, two or three times every week, we have gone from store to store but found nothing. I myself sew and knit and clothe my entire family. But I cannot make shoes. For the first time in four years I bought myself shoes in a consignment [*komissionniy*] store. Until then I'd worn cloth shoes and got myself sick with a chronic illness. We don't live in the south, you know!" (T. Aglyamova, "Bosye po nasledstvu?" [Hereditarily barefoot?], *Pravda*, December 19, 1989: 2.)

On a considerably higher rung of the Soviet social hierarchy, portrayed in a roman à clef by the leading essayist, economist, and economic historian Nikolai Shmelev, a crying wife tells her husband: "Poverty. . . . Look at what I am wearing. . . . Do you know how many times I had these shoes repaired. And my husband is a *docent* [the equivalent of an associate professor] and I am hardly the most insignificant person. . . . [I am] a senior editor at a prestigious journal." (Nikolai Shmelev, *Paskhov dom* (The Pashkov house), *Znamya*, March 1987: 107.)

our sociologists, a woman told public opinion pollsters, how can a family live on 50 rubles per person?[93]* In fact, Soviet sociologists did answer her, indirectly: according to their calculations, in order to satisfy their "normal needs," the parents in a family with two children had to earn no less than 400 rubles each[94]—an astronomically high income.

Even on a relatively large salary of 140 rubles a month, a single mother and a skilled printer could not have avoided penury without her parents' assistance. She spent 90 rubles every month on food ("fish, butter, potatoes, cereal [groats], and eggs"), while winter boots cost 120 rubles, and a television set and a refrigerator (Soviet apartments were rented without refrigerators) cost state several hundred rubles each.[95] She could buy all these items (and a small area rug and a folding "chair-bed" for her son) only with her parents' help.[96] (A monthly state allowance for a single mother was 20 rubles a month.)[97]

Like her, two young physicians with a young child, could not have afforded their refrigerator, television, and even clothes without their parents' largess: the rent they paid for a room in someone else's apartment (there was "little hope" for an apartment of their own), food, and childcare left very little for anything else.[98]

But it was among the elderly and the handicapped that the poverty was found to be as striking as it was ubiquitous. "Shamefully low" were the pensions of the "overwhelming majority" of the retirees, Andrei Sakharov wrote in a 1988 article, his first published in the Soviet Union.[99] "How can we not be horrified by the pensioners' condition?" a reader asked in a letter to *Ogonyok*.[100] Indeed, a third of retirees in the cities and more than eight in ten (84.7 percent) in the countryside received pensions of less

---

* After working for thirty years as a railroad electrician, a fifty-two-year-old man had to retire for health reasons. His pension was 41 rubles "and 71 kopecks"; his wife's salary, 90 rubles; the pension of his mother-in-law, who lived with them, was 31 rubles; and his son, who was a student, received a stipend of 30 rubles. "This is less than 50 rubles per person," the man wrote *Pravda*. "How can we live?!" ("Semeyniy byudzhet: dokhod i raskhod" [Family budget: income and expenses], *Pravda*, May 19, 1989: 5.)

than 60 rubles a month[101]—and were really "living from hand to mouth" (*bedstvuyut*), a leading expert told *Sovetskaya kul'tura* in June 1988.[102]*

"What is your pension?" a leading documentary filmmaker Stanislav Govorukhin asked an elderly woman in a northeastern Russia village near the Urals. "Twenty-six rubles," she answered. "And what does this cover?" "What do you think? Bread. I grow my own potatoes."[103]

An eighty-three-year-old woman from a village in central Russia wrote *Pravda* that she had worked in the *kolkhoz* all her life, and even at seventy-five went out into the fields. Her husband was killed in World War II (the "Great Patriotic War"), and she was left with three children. Her two boys did not survive and the daughter became an invalid. "I never asked for any help while I still could work. I receive a pension of 40 rubles and 5 rubles for my husband. But now my health is shaky. I asked the chairman of the village soviet for some wood for my stove. 'Go away, go to a home for the elderly,' he told me. 'We have lots of the likes of you.'" She "did not remember" how she got home, so upset she was. She cried for a week afterward.[104]

In another kolkhoz a man and his wife (both sixty-three years old) received no pension at all: because of frequent illnesses their individual "service term" (*rabochiy stazh*) was two years short of the twenty-five-year minimum. "Dear Comrades!" the man wrote *Izvestia*, "Please understand me correctly. If we had children, with whose help we could have lived out our old age, I would not have bothered you." He was asking for "no more than 20 rubles, for bread" as a "laborer with an incomplete work term." The local authorities had turned him down.[105]

Although the number and incomes of physically and mentally handicapped people was still secret (or perhaps simply not known), in letters and articles their lot looked worse than that of rural pensioners. "Invalids-from-birth" under sixteen years of age received pensions of 20 rubles a

---

* "We, pensioners, live just like beggars" (*prosto nishchenstvuem*), a woman wrote *Sovetskaya kul'tura* in summer 1989. "I have worked as a typist all my life. Now I am a pensioner and very ill. My [monthly] pension is 72 rubles. Of these, I spend 13 rubles on rent and 15 rubles on medications. Can one live on 44 rubles?" (As quoted in Nikolai Petrakov, "Dokhody i raskhody" [Incomes and expenses], interview with *Sovetskaya kul'tura*, July 6, 1989: 6.)

month, which was increased to 30 rubles on January 1, 1987.[106] Still, in 1989, a twenty-year-old handicapped man was reported to receive 26 rubles in monthly assistance.[107] An invalid single mother received "31 rubles and 48 kopeks" to support herself and her child.[108]

"Oh, this enormous rich country," the filmmaker Govorukhin wrote. "All these forests, rivers, furs and fish, almost 70 percent of the world's black soil, the colossal mineral wealth—oil, gas, rare metals, gold. And poverty—a depressing, debasing poverty."[109]

CHAPTER EIGHT

The Unraveling of the Legitimizing Myths, II

PROGRESS, THE "STATE OF WORKERS AND
PEASANTS," EQUALITY, "FREEDOM FROM
EXPLOITATION," NOVOCHERKASSK

It is said that victors are not to be judged. Yet a comparison of
results with the price paid for them is mandatory in economics.
Only when we figure this out will we understand what it was in
reality: victory or defeat?
—Vasily Selyunin, "Istoki" (The sources), *Novy mir*, May 1988: 176

And what have we found after we awoke from self-deception? . . .
We have found something like an underdeveloped superpower,
which was losing the ability for development.
—Ales' Adamovich, speech at the First Congress of People's
Deputies, *Izvestia*, May 29, 1989: 2

What were millions of people dying for—from backbreaking
labor, hunger, and diseases—in villages and the camps for
"special settlers"? What were the peasant uprisings cruelly
supressed by the NKVD troops? In the name of what strategic
goals were the village laborers "de-kulakized" and forced into
kolkhozes? Where is it, that highest goal, which is supposed to
justify the destruction of the village, which amounted to a
national tragedy?
—Vladimir Popov and Nikolai Shmelyov, "Na razvilke dorog" (At a
crossroad), in Kh. Kobo, ed., *Osmyslit' kul't Stalina* (To comprehend
Stalin's cult), Moscow: Progress, 1989: 297

Socialism is where the working people live better. It is free labor. It is prosperity. It is access to culture and healthcare. It is guaranteed human rights. We, on the other hand, are still trying to define socialism mechanically: one ruling party, a single ideology, state property, and a planned economy. For fifty years we have lived with these mechanisms—and what's the result?
—Fyodor Burlatsky, "Sud'ba reformatorov strany" (The fate of our country's reformers), *Literaturnaya gazeta*, June 27, 1990: 1

It is a myth that there is no exploitation of man by man [in the Soviet Union]. We do have exploitation! The exploitation of those who work well by those who work badly; of workers by administrators and bureaucrats; and of all laborers—by the state.
—Rayr Simonyan and Anatoly Druzenko "Kuda my idyom?" (Where are we going?), *Ogonyok* 37, 1989: 3

The interests of which class were defended by the leaders of the Khrushchev era, when they gave the orders to shoot the workers in Novocherkassk in 1962? . . . Whose interests guided all those raikom, gorkom, obkom party functionaries and other apparatchiks, when they were bumped to the top of the line to receive luxurious apartments? When they built more and more dachas, hunting lodges, sanatoriums, and rest homes, constructed palaces for their headquarters at a time when many working families were huddled in barracks, tiny apartments without amenities, lived in settlements next to steelmaking, chemical, and other large enterprises and breathed their poisonous air.
—Alexei Kiva, "Krizis 'zhanra'" (The crisis of the "genre"), *Novy mir*, March 1990: 214–15

I am very upset with my country. It has humiliated me, it has made me inferior and defective. . . . I love my country, as one loves his mother, no matter who she is. We, this mother and I, travel abroad, look around, and I am upset at her for making me, intelligent and talented, look like an idiot. . . . I am very upset with my mother, who has made me lazy, uncultured, unbelieving, cynical, and shabby. And so my Motherland and I, we walk around the world, like two

beggars from the sixteenth century, from the era of constant and devastating wars.
—Mikhail Zhvanetsky, a popular humorist, "V Yaponiyu i nazad, k sebe" (To Japan and back home), *Izvestia*, September 8, 1989: 5

RECAST BY MARXISM as the ultimate validation of a superior "mode of production," Hegel's fetish for historical progress had been a key legitimizing component of the Soviet canon. With state ownership of the economy as its "base," and a one-party dictatorship as its political "superstructure," the progress under the "Soviet power," allegedly portrayed as unprecedented in its rate and reach, was to justify any and all sacrifices that attended its march.

First to fall was "the enduring myth" that Stalinist industrialization and collectivization had resulted in the world's highest rates of industrial and agricultural growth.[1] To begin, the Soviet economists discovered, the country's economy had not, as touted, expanded ninetyfold since 1928 but, still very solidly but hardly fantastically, six- or sevenfold.[2] The economy, moreover, grew five to six times more rapidly during the New Economic Policy (NEP) years of 1921–27, *before* its complete nationalization followed by the alleged "industrialization" breakthrough of the official myth.[3] Indeed, it was precisely then, during the first "heroic five-year plan" *(pyatiletka)* —the time of hunger, suffering, and death for millions of Soviet people—that the rates of growth were the lowest, while the expenditure of material resources per unit of output, the highest.[4] Overall, between 1928 and 1985, the rate of resource "inputs" always outpaced economic growth and the return on investment steadily declined.[5]

Comparing the rates of economic growth during the NEP and after the establishment of what was now labeled the "command-and-administer system," attended by "mad profligacy," leading economists were now convinced that the Soviet Union could have built twice as many plants, factories, and electrical power stations without "robbing" the peasants to pay for industrialization.[6] The village, too, would have continued to feed the country at least as well as it had done under the NEP without the "horrific casualties" of the collectivization and without dooming the countryside to almost a quarter of a century of life "on the verge of death from starvation" between 1929 and 1953.[7]

"We can never escape the tragic fact that the price [the country paid] was in no way commensurate with the results," wrote prominent economists and economic historians Vladimir Popov and Nikolai Shmelyov. "We speak not only of millions of people who died for nothing. We speak of things that might not be as emotionally charged but not less horrible: about the destroyed forces of production, wasted resources, the time irretrievably lost, the millions of lives spent entirely to pay in sweat and blood for the ambitions of Stalin and his semi-literate and immoral henchmen, who usurped power."[8] Furthermore, compared to the countries with which pre-revolutionary Russia was on par or close to in economic development in 1914, the Soviet Union in 1990, "with some rarest exceptions," lagged behind "in every area of human endeavor."[9]

In 1987, half of all Soviet workers and peasants were engaged in manual labor—a rate that was 30–35 percent above the norm in other industrialized nations and higher even than in the Soviet Union thirty years before.[10] Almost 9.5 million people worked in "hazardous industrial production" (*vrednoe proizvodstvo*), and 30 percent of them were women.[11] Two-hundred-seventy-five thousand women were also "engaged" in "hard physical labor."[12] According to the deputy chairman of the State Committee on Statistics (Goscomstat), there were 690,000 labor accidents in 1987, 14,600 of them fatal.[13]*

Another price exacted by the "extensive" mode of industrialization was a massive environmental crisis. In the summer of 1988, according to the chairman of the State Committee on Environmental Protection, 50 million Soviet citizens in 102 cities were exposed to a "concentration of harmful elements in the air [that was] was ten times or more" above the healthy norm."[14] Or, as the Soviet Union's top environmental expert put it a year later, one-fifth of the country's population lived in "environmental disaster areas," and another 35–40 percent "under environmentally unfavorable conditions."[15]

---

* A labor safety expert argued that if those who died annually from the illnesses contracted at work were counted, there were around 200,000 casualties every year. (Vladimir Volin, "Okhrana ot bezopasnosti" [Protection from security], *Moskovskie novosti*, August 27, 1989: 10.)

Academician Sakharov must have startled the Soviet reader in 1988 when he wrote that most scientific and technological ideas came to the Soviet Union from the West—often years or decades later.[16] By Prime Minister Ryzhkov's own confession, it was a devastating blow for him to learn, in 1985, that the country he had thought to be the world's leading industrial power "imported everything: from grain and pantyhose, to industrial machinery and equipment."[17] Half of the chemical industry relied on imported equipment, Ryzhkov continued, as did 80 percent of light industry and food production. Of the USSR's total imports, machinery and equipment constituted as much as 40 percent![18] A country that in 1913 exported 9 million tons of wheat was now among the world's largest grain importers, buying tens of millions of tons every year.[19] Every third loaf of bread and every second pack of noodles (*makarony*) in the Soviet Union was made from imported grain.[20]

Yet even these mammoth imports, paid for mostly with oil, gas, and gold, could not make up for all the instances of backwardness and deficiency. One of Moscow's largest fabric mills, the Pavolvskiy posad, was housed in a 1910 building and used looms made "at the beginning of the century."[21] For a kolkhoz chairman from the Stavropol region it was "a punishment" to use the Soviet-made plows, with which it was impossible to turn up soil evenly, resulting in "huge losses" in yields.[22] In his village, a prominent writer Vasily Belov told the First Congress of People's Deputies in June 1989, peasants mowed grass the same way they did in the twelfth century.[23] When the miners of the Kuzbass coal basin in southwest Siberia went on strike in the summer of 1989, their demands included towels, cotton-padded jackets (*telogreyki*), and 800 grams of soap for post-shift washing up.[24*]

"Do you have computers?" the filmmaker Govorukhin asked in the fall of 1989 at a police station in Perm, a city of 1 million on the European

---

* In another key mining region, Donetsk, the administration refused to provide the after-shift soap, suggesting that the miners bring their own. When it turned out that there was a dire shortage of soap in the miners' homes, the authorities calculated the "norm" to be distributed: 18 grams (0.64 ounces). "So we were wondering," the miners wrote *Izvestia*: "should we grate the 18 grams off a bar or just weigh the soap bubbles?" ("18 grammov myl'nykh puzyrey" [18 grams of soap bubbles], a letter by miners from the Kiselev mine, the city of Torez, *Izvestia*, April 15, 1989: 2.)

side of the Ural Mountains. "We don't have enough typewriters—and you ask about computers!" a detective answered.[25] In another city with a population over 1 million—Kuibyshev (now Samara), in southeast Russia, the largest industrial center in the Middle Volga region—60 percent of street police officers (*uchastkovye militsionery*) did not have telephones in their apartments.[26]

Still, the cops were somewhat better off than the regular folk. In the Russian Federal Soviet Socialist Republic only one family in five had a telephone.[27] In the Soviet Union as a whole, there were phones in just 30 percent of urban "dwellings" and in 10 percent of rural ones.[28] Communication between villages was maintained by a tractor or a horse.[29] There were nearly 14.9 million unsatisfied individual requests for telephones, over a million of them from invalids.[30] By December 1987, one textile worker from a city in the Moscow province had been waiting for a phone for twenty-two years.[31]

Some of the bitterest truths emerged when for the first time the Soviet Union was honestly compared to other countries. Tens of millions of ordinary men and women—who, despite the daily travails, firmly believed that they lived better than most people—suddenly learned that they were poor. The Soviet Union turned out to rank seventy-seventh globally in per capita consumption.[32] The country was fifty-eighth in per capita car ownership—the rate 3–4 times lower than Hungary and Czechoslovakia, ten times lower than West Germany.[33] India was said to have more paved roads.[34]

Salaries turned out to be orders of magnitude lower than in the "developed countries."* Worse yet, the Soviet people were revealed to be worse off not just in absolute but in relative terms as well. Not only was the purchasing power of the ruble below that of the dollar in the United States (a country to "catch up to and surpass," in Nikita Khrushchev's famous propaganda slogan)—it was inferior both to the pre-revolutionary, pre–World War I ruble of 1913 and to the ruble of the last years of the

* "The average salary here is around 200 rubles," the editor of *Literaturnaya gazeta* fulminated in summer 1990. "But in the USA, Britain, Japan, etc.—1,500 dollars. This is a simple fact. And no ideological sophistry can deny it." (Fedor Burlatsky, "Sud'ba reformatorov strany" [The fate of our country's reformers], *Literaturnaya gazeta*, June 27, 1990: 1.)

NEP. A senior scholar at the elite Institute [for the study of the] USA and Canada calculated that an average Soviet worker had to labor 10–12 times longer to buy meat, 3 times longer for milk, 7 times for butter, 10–15 times for eggs, 18–25 times for bananas and oranges (neither usually found, anyway, except in Moscow), and 2–8 times for bread.[35] In terms of the labor equivalent, a kilo of meat cost 1.5 times more in the Soviet Union of the 1980s than in 1927 or in Russia in 1913: three hours of work now, two hours then. In 1985, the same scholar calculated, the urban population of the Soviet Union consumed, per capita, almost 50 percent less meat than did city dwellers in Russia in 1913.[36] (In 1985, the per capital meat consumption in the Soviet Union was half that of the United States.)[37]

To pay for what the Soviet nutritionists called the "ideal monthly ration" (the availability of these products aside), the average Soviet family of four, with both adults working and earning 380 rubles a month, would have to spend 59 percent of its income on food, compared to 15 percent for an average American household.[38*] If, instead of the "rational norms," an average Soviet household had to pay for the quantity and quality of products consumed in the United States, food would have cost 180 percent of the monthly income.[39]

An average Soviet worker indeed paid far less for his tiny apartment (if he was lucky enough to have one) than his American counterpart. Yet, as the same scholar, Alexander Zaychenko, pointed out, when the space and conveniences are taken into consideration, a square meter in an apartment was 41 percent more expensive in the Soviet Union than in the United States: an average Soviet urban worker had to labor 1.23 hours to pay for it; his or her American counterpart, 0.87 hour).[40] The total housing space "with amenities" was 6–7 times larger in the United States, and there was about as much per capita living space in the Soviet Union in the 1980s as in St. Petersburg in 1913.[41]

Finally, when it came to both clothes and "durable" goods, the ratio of prices to salaries was 10–20 times higher in the USSR than in the United States.[42] In general, retail prices for goods and services (especially food) in the Soviet Union were said to be "among the highest in the world."[43]

---

* The share of monthly food expenditures in an average family's income was 20 percent in Japan, 23 percent in Greece, 25 percent in France, 45 percent in Spain, and 21 percent for Western Europe as a whole. (Zaychenko, "SShA . . . ," 17.)

Probably even more painful was the revelation that in the country that prided itself on being the most progressive and sophisticated spiritually, the "consumption" of culture, too, lagged behind many other countries and its cultural institutions were supported far less generously. The Soviet Union placed twenty-ninth in the world in the number of its museums—and last, per 100,000 people, among the seven European members of the Council for Mutual Economic Assistance (Comecon), the Soviet-dominated economic organization of socialist states.[44]* Proportionate to the population size, the Soviet Union also ranked last among other European socialist countries in attendance at concerts of classical music and art exhibitions.[45]

The Soviet Union's status as the "country that read most in the world" (*samaya chitayushchaya strana mira*) proved but another myth. Per 1 million inhabitants, the Soviet Union published only 25 percent more book titles than Russia did in 1913—and only half as many as the United States and Japan; a third the number of the Federal Republic of Germany, Great Britain, the Netherlands, and Spain; and one-fourth of what was printed in the Scandinavian countries.[46] According to the Soviet public opinion and publishing experts, the share of children's books in the USSR's overall production was found to be lower than "practically in any other large book-publishing country."[47] The Soviet Union was forty-seventh in the world in per capita production of paper,[48] and the consumption of paper for writing and publishing was less than half that of Hungary and East Germany, and one-sixth of Great Britain's. Canada produced almost eight times as much paper; Sweden, the United States, and Finland made almost twelve times more.[49] The budget of the Library of Congress was fifteen times that of the Lenin Library in Moscow.[50] According to another Soviet researcher, 34 percent of men and women between the ages of eighteen and twenty-four attended a college or a university in the United States; in the Soviet Union, 15 percent.[51]

The miners' strike in the summer of 1989 occasioned the Soviet press's first truthful and sustained foray into the sanctum sanctorum of the

* Known by the Russian acronym SEV (or the Council of Mutual Economic Assistance), the council included Bulgaria, Czechoslovakia, East Germany, Hungary, Poland, and Rumania.

founding mythology: the "state of workers and peasants." How, really, do they fare in "their" state, its alleged masters?

In the heart of the striking Kuzbass region, a reporter visits an armature plant, where the steel "skeletons" of concrete slabs are made. The plant's workers are heavyset, prematurely aged women in faded tank tops (*mayki*) and wide trousers (*sharovary*). They are striking because the administration fired the shop's steward (*master uchastka*), "a young girl," who helped the workers to write a complaint about salary underpayment: "They spit on a working person!" the women shout. "They wanted to cheat us, to con us out of our money." The young woman-steward is sobbing: "All I did was to write a complaint for them. Because they are illiterate."

The plant is a "brick box," with all the windows broken. On the floor is a pile of steel rods from which the women "knit" armature. One of them has worked here twenty-four years, two others, nineteen. "So we tie this iron. Now it's OK, but in the winter . . . There is no heat, there is no bathroom. If someone brings a jar of boiling water, that's half a cup for each of us." Next to them, male workers weld the rods together. Classified as "hazardous," their work entitles the men to retire early—but not the women, who, as they put it, "breathe the same air." That is what their complaint was about.[52]

Because of the shortage of potable water in Kuzbass, the taps were turned off and on according to a "timetable" (*grafik*) in the "majority" of towns and settlements of the region, but there still was not enough pressure to reach the upper floors of apartment houses.[53] "Will we have housing with running water?" the striking miners of Kuzbass demanded to know in July 1989.[54]

In another key coal-mining area in northeastern Ukraine, 20 percent of the residences lacked running water, 26 percent were "not connected" to any sewage system, 28 percent did not have central heat, and 63 lacked hot water.[55] InKuzbass tens of thousands of families were "de facto" without their own apartments, stuck for decades in buildings formally condemned as being "in a state of emergency" (*avariynoe sostoyanie*), living with no amenities at all and in "anti-sanitary" conditions, which included street garbage dumps.[56]

The revealed squalor was all the more difficult to tolerate because of the collapse of another myth: that all citizens are equal in the "state of workers and peasants." For millions the notion of fairness in the distribution of national wealth—in good times and in bad—was a social contract central to the legitimacy of the regime and made daily travails easier to bear.[57] Yet quickly established and almost daily reaffirmed by newspapers and magazines were privileges not rooted in the "objective criteria" of earned wages or professional qualifications. Instead, they were tied "exclusively" to a person's position in the political hierarchy.[58]

The "system" was revealed to be enormously wide, meticulously detailed, and rigidly enforced. For the blessed chosen, it spelled not only a fine gradation in the quantity and quality of food in their monthly "parcels" (*payki*), but what an *Ogonyok* reporter called differences in the "degrees of comfort" of their spacious apartments, the "nuances" of the menus in the "special" dining rooms, and the makes of the chauffeured cars that drove them to work (and took their wives and daughters shopping in "special" stores).[59]

Kindergartens, too, were different: some were "like palaces," with pools and playrooms, where children were fed caviar and taken to the countryside in the summer "for fresh air"; in others, children played, ate, and slept in one room.[60] Maternity hospitals, too, were poles apart, the elite ones brimming with "absolute hygiene" and "extra-attentive" nurses.[61] And of course clinics and hospitals were distinct: staffed and supplied by the fabled "Fourth Directorate," a government branch in charge of the separate, exclusive healthcare network.[62]

The disparity in food availability and quality was particularly stark. In one central Russian province (*Pravda* would not identify it by name), the staffers of the apparatus of the *obkom* (the regional party committee) and *oblispolkom* (the executive committee of the regional soviet) and their families consumed between 56 percent and 100 percent of all the "delicacies" allotted to the region—while they constituted 0.04 percent of the population.[63] A woman from the ancient Russian city of Ryazan, 196 kilometers (122 miles) southeast of Moscow, informed the readers of *Ogonyok* that she could not get "a gram of butter for two to three weeks" until a shopping trip to Moscow. At the same time, almost 400 tons of caviar, over 6,000 cans of crab, a ton and a half of smoked and dry-cured sturgeon, and half a ton of oven-baked ham (*buzhenina*) were sold in the two country-house settlements belonging to the Ryazan *obkom* and *oblispolkom*.[64]

"We don't want to go down into the mines hungry!" a reporter heard striking Kuzbass miners shout in the central square of the city of Prokop'evsk.[65] When the strike committee took over food supplies, a miner elected to be in charge of trade went off to examine a "closed" food depot. "I am forty-one," he told a reporter later. "The way I reckon, two-third of my life is gone. But many of the foodstuffs we found there I not only have not seen before—I did not even know they existed. But they were there, for someone . . ."[66]

"If a 'Big Boss' stood in line for two or three hours to see a doctor at a regular district clinic, and the doctor then treated him in five minutes," a reader wrote *Ogonyok* in the fall of 1987; "if he had to wait for two or three years for dentures; if he lay in a hospital hallway for a while, and they didn't have the medication he needed; [and] if his wife started wearing the kinds of boots they sell in ordinary stores . . . *then* we could really expect some changes!"[67]

People were beginning to suspect, wrote leading essayist Andrei Nuykin, that it was not they or *their* grandchildren who were to benefit from their sacrifices "on the altar of the common cause of building communism."[68] By July 1988, 44 percent of those polled by *Moskovskie novosti* felt that theirs was an "unjust society."[69] One of the first commissions created by the Supreme Soviet, elected by the First Congress of the People's Deputies, was a "Commission on Benefits and Privileges."

Inequalities in the availability of housing, healthcare, and food rankled the most. In the same *Moskovskie novosti* poll, 67 percent of the respondents thought it "unjust" that the elite were given "apartment houses of a superior design in prestigious areas"; 60 percent deplored hospitals and clinics "solely to service the leadership"; and 84 percent resented the "acquisition of goods from stores and canteens [*bufety*], closed to others."[70] The disparity in "access to quality goods and services" led the economist Zaychenko to describe the country's "social pyramid" as "very tall and sharply pointed," with the top 2 percent "rich," 11 percent in the "middle," and 87 percent "poor."[71]

As it emerged from essays and articles by economists and historians, the "state of workers and peasants" was also an "exploiter" in a classic Marxist sense—and of a kind that could teach "capitalist states" a lesson or two in exploitation. Not only were the salaries of Soviet workers but a

fraction of what "Western" workers earned, their earnings also constituted a much smaller share of the national economy: the total wages
(*fond zarplaty*) ranged from 28 percent to 42 percent of the country's
GDP, compared to 60–70 percent in the West. (For the United States,
the USSR's eternal benchmark, the figure was 61 percent in 1985.)[72]*

Nor did the Soviet state return a great deal in the way of "public
funds" (*obshchestvennye fondy*), similar to welfare expenditures in the
West: 20 percent of USSR's GDP compared to 29 percent in the United
States.[73]† Personal consumption was said to constitute 41 percent of the
economy in 1987, compared to 60–70 percent in the "capitalist countries" (and 66 percent in the U.S.). The closest to the Soviet Union in
that regard were Gabon (46 percent) and Congo (54 percent).[74]

Thus, in Marxist terms, the Soviet state extracted from its workers far
more "surplus value" and left much less for their "needs" (what Marx in
Capital also called the "necessary labor") than did the capitalist West.[75] The
Soviet state's policy was now condemned as "the directive planning of a
beggarly standard of living" and "the mechanism of penury reproduction"
(*mekhanizm vosproizvodsva bednosti*).[76]

Proving Marxism remarkably prescient with respect to the first socialist state, economic exploitation was said to go hand in hand with political repression. In January 1989, *Moskovskie novosti* readers identified
the "bureaucratic system of rule" and "defenselessness before the arbitrariness of the functionary (*chinovnik*)" among the "most acute" problems facing the country.[77] "Socialist people's power has been supplanted
by the power of a narrow circle of individuals, representing the top of the

---

* As a share of the country's industrial production, workers' wages were the
  largest in the last year of the NEP, at 58 percent. They plunged to 33 percent in
  1950 and rose to 38 percent in 1987. (Alexander Zaychenko, "Kak delit' pirog"
  [How to divide the pie], *Moskovskie novosti*, June 11, 1989: 12.)

† In absolute terms, the numbers, as Vasily Selyunin put it, were "simply
  incomparable" even by the widely inflated official rate of exchange of $1.65 for 1
  ruble: 38 billion rubles vs. $179 billion for education, 20 billion rubles and $175
  billion for healthcare; and 61 billion rubles and $458 billion for social security
  and pensions. ("Chyornye dyry ekonimki" [The black holes of the economy],
  Novy mir, October 1989: 157.) In the Soviet Embassy in Washington in 1989,
  $100 was exchanged for 320 "certificate" rubles that entitled the bearer to shop
  in the exclusive "Beryozka" shops. (Yuri Chernichenko, "O khlebe nasushchnom" [Of our daily bread], *Komsomol'skaya pravda*, March 12, 1989: 2.)

bureaucracy," read the resolution adopted by the workers' committees of Kuzbass in November 1989.[78] A political scientist described the Soviet political system as "the dominance of a ruling administrative hierarchy, all-powerful and unelected by people."[79]

In this "party-police state," as a retired major general of the KGB called it, there was not a "single sphere of life" where the secret police did not have its agents: from the Academy of Sciences to the Holy Synod of the Russian Orthodox Church, from athletes to musicians and literary critics.[80] There were said to be more secret domestic police in the Soviet Union than on the entire continents of Europe, North America, and Asia (excluding Communist China).[81]

The consolidation of the present political and economic system was now revealed to be attended with repression against workers. The heightened exploitation met no resistance after the trade unions lost the last vestiges of their independence and became yet another agency of state control in the early 1930s.[82] By 1940 industrial workers were arrested, tried, and sent to camps if they attempted to change their employment without authorization or were a few minutes late for work.[83] Teenagers in trades schools (*proftekhuchilishcha*) were arrested, tried, and sent to "colonies" (labor camps for minors) if they attempted to quit.[84]

The peasants, again, suffered the most. Rendered dispossessed and powerless by the collectivization, their condition was almost routinely described by economists, historians, and journalists as "serfdom" (*krepostnichestvo*) and they as "serfs" (*krepostnye*).[85] For over thirty years, from 1932 to the early to mid 1960s, they were denied internal passports, which were necessary to travel inside the country. A peasant needed permission from his village soviet to go to the provincial capital, let alone any cities beyond.[86] Until 1953 they were paid not in money but instead, if they were lucky, in produce.[87] For instance, in 1950 in the black soil province of Kursk, a peasant's entire pay for a "workday" (*trudoden'*) was 200–300 grams of bread.[88]

Set by the state purchasing monopoly, the prices for grain, meat, and milk were not always enough to cover even the kolkhozes' costs of getting the produce to the nearest train station.[89] (The state, for instance, "bought" grain from kolkhozes at 80 kopecks for a *tsentner,* or 100 kilos.)[90]

Writing to *Moskovskie novosti,* a reader recalled seeing in Russian and Ukrainian villages in 1949–53 "a most horrible poverty of people who had no passports and who received almost nothing in return for their labor."[91] "The bread in our village was baked with sawdust, with clover leaves—and when potatoes were added, that was a holiday," Vasily Selyunin wrote of his post-collectivization childhood. "The worst thing was to go to the outhouse afterwards: the undigested sawdust and grass scratched the anus and drew blood."[92]*

Unlike the workers in the cities, the kolkhoz peasants were not entitled to food rations. Yuri Chernichenko remembered his classmate in 1946, a "kolkhoz boy," Kolya, who did not receive a "bread card" and came to school solely for the tiny piece of bread that was given for breakfast. The reason, Chernichenko knew even then, was that "we were born free [vol'nye] while Kolya Kryuchkov was a serf [krepostnoy]."[93]

Peasants survived only by what they managed to grow on their tiny plots after working all day on the kolkhoz without pay, just like their ancestors under barshchina (the corvee in Western feudalism).[94] Still, the "state's serfs"[95] were also obligated to pay state taxes in kind on whatever their parcels of land yielded. In addition, each household in the starving postwar Russian villages was to deliver 40–60 kilos of meat a year, 100–280 liters of milk, and several dozen eggs.[96] "And what a large agricultural tax [sel'khoznalog] we had to pay!" read a letter to Znamya magazine. "The most urgent thing was to pay off the state. We had to buy meat, milk, and eggs and then hand them over."[97] Potatoes and hides also have been mentioned among the tax-in-kind items.[98] In addition, "every apple tree" was taxed and there was a 10-ruble tax on each black current bush.[99]

"After father came home from the [Great Patriotic] war, he was sick for a long time," remembered a Komsomol'skaya pravda essayist.

> He was still bedridden when a functionary came in to demand the taxes. Everything was taxed: animals, chickens, apple trees, bushes, and, of course, the kitchen garden. We had nothing to pay with. There was nothing to eat. Only the cow had been saving us. "If you don't pay tomorrow," the functionary warned

* "The 'clean' black bread, without potatoes and acorns, people ate like a cake, only on holidays," a character in Vasily Grossman's Forever Flowing remembered of her days as a kolkhoz chairman. "I once brought white bread to a sister in the village, and children were afraid to eat it—they had never seen one before" (p. 61).

sternly, "watch out, you know what will happen." Even I, a boy, knew what would "happen." They will make an inventory and then take everything away [*opishut*]. What to do? At dawn Mom and I started off with the cow—to sell her at the market. She, our last hope and provider. Mom was leading the cow by the rope and cried while we walked all the ten kilometers. I walked behind, slapping the cow with a twig, and cried also from the injustice of it all—we were all going to die from hunger! . . . That evening, back from the market, mother was taken ill. She kept looking at me, my baby brother in a cradle, and my two sisters and sighed: "What will happen now to us? How can we live?"[100]

In 1989, the editor of *Oktyabr'*, a leading liberal "thick" magazine, reviewed the results of the collectivization, that great "breaking point" (*velikiy perelom*) of the official history: a countryside with no roads and drowned in impassable mud; thousands of disappeared villages, with tens of thousands of homesteads in them; millions of hectares of "written-off" (condemned) land, overgrown with trees and weeds.[101] Economists added: the labor productivity equal to one-fifth to one-fourth of the American farmer; average grain yields per hectare less than one-third that of Western Europe and the U.S., less than half the milk per cow.[102]

A much-decorated kolkhoz chairman lamented the absence of gas, running water, and indoor toilets in the Russian countryside.[103] "We pump natural gas to Europe," he fulminated, "but we have not a single gas burner in our villages, even those next to those pipelines!"[104] By the 1970s most of the Russian countryside had electricity but the peasants still lugged water from wells, and washed up in a metal laundry tub (*koryto*).[105] At four in the morning, dairymaids still walked in the dark to the farm in tall rubber boots because the mud reached up to their knees. They still used pitchforks to spear and carry "on their bellies" heaps of nauseatingly foul-smelling fermented silage (*silos*). And their children still walked four kilometers to the nearest school.[106]

Yet as always, the deepest and most enduring damage was deemed that to people's souls. The continuing "bureaucratic serfdom," read a letter to *Znamya* in August 1989, "has brought our peasantry to such a condition that it no longer even has a notion of the free, creative labor of the tiller of the land."[107]

One of the most graphic counter-narratives to the "state of workers and peasants" myth was the story of the Novocherkassk massacre, first outlined by Alexander Solzhenitsyn in *The Gulag Archipelago* almost two decades before and suppressed along with the rest of the book. The newspaper accounts of the Novocherkassk tragedy heralded a breakthrough even by the already spectacular standards of truth-finding. First, because the shooting of the unarmed workers happened *after* Stalin's death and at the height of Khrushchev's "de-Stalinization," in the same year when the existence of the Gulag was first publicly acknowledged in the publication of Solzhenitsyn's *One Day in the Life of Ivan Denisovich*. Second, the victims were not the customary targets of state-sponsored murder—the peasants, intelligentsia, top leaders, military officers, the Old Bolsheviks—but ordinary industrial workers, members of the master ("hegemonic") class of the official propaganda, the ostensible mainstay of the "Soviet power." Finally, unlike the purges of the 1930s, many of those who carried out the orders to shoot were still alive—as were hundreds for whom their bullets were meant.

Journalists dug relentlessly, each publication seeking to "restore the truth" because such "lessons must be diligently learned," as the first article, published on the twenty-seventh anniversary of the massacre, June 2, 1989, declared.[108] Another long essay appeared three weeks later, and two more came out in 1990 and 1991. Guided by letters from witnesses, the reporters expanded the investigation, looking for a secret mass grave and trying to identify each victim by name.

The first lines of the tragic plot were drawn in January 1962, when the state began to cut payments (*rastsenki*) for specific industrial operations at all Soviet plants and factories until they were reduced by 30–35 percent.[109] By May the measure had affected every shop of the giant Novocherkassk Electric Locomotive Construction Plant (Russian acronym NEVZ) in the city of 120,000 in the Rostov province about 900 kilometers (560 miles) south of Moscow. Then on June 1, the government announced a sharp rise in the price of meat and butter.

Right away, the workers in the steel mill shop lay down their tools. Shouting angrily, they went outside, where they saw the plant's director.

How will we make ends meet now, the workers demanded to know. "Don't worry," the director answered. "You'll do just fine. Not enough money for meat and sausage? Well, then, you'll have to eat pies with liverwurst then [*pirozhki s liverom*]."[110]

By most accounts, these words were the "spark" that started the protest.[111] The plant's whistle was sounded, signaling a general strike. Workers tore down a gigantic portrait of Khrushchev from the plant's façade, smashed smaller ones in the administrative offices, and threw them into a bonfire. Placards sprang up: "Give us meat and butter!" "We need apartments!" (Like millions of Soviet workers, many NEVZ families were "tormented" by living in barracks or rented single rooms in houses or apartments for 35–50 rubles a month—a "huge" part of their budget.)[112] In one photograph taken from clandestine surveillance by the secret police, a poster read: "Meat, butter, salary raise!"[113] Climbing onto trucks, workers spoke, one after another. The rally continued into the night.

Early the next morning some of the more vocal strikers were arrested.[114] Still, under red flags and portraits of Lenin, between seven and eight thousand workers marched ten to twelve kilometers from the plant to the City Party Committee (*gorkom*) headquarters in the center of Novocherkassk.[115] (On a surveillance photo from the archives of the Office of the Prosecutor General of the Armed Forces, the column was fifteen people across, with no end in sight.)[116] By then, surrounded "on all sides" by tanks and troops at the nearby headquarters of the local military garrison, two members of the Party's highest body, the Presidium, Anastas Mikoyan and Frol Kozlov, were giving orders.[117]

Soon, the square in front of the empty *gorkom* (its staffers had "run away") was filled with workers. "How can we live?" people shouted. "There is nothing to eat!"[118] Soldiers and tanks began to advance on the crowd. Suddenly there came a salvo from Kalashnikovs, then another. People started to run, carrying the wounded. Many, likely war veterans, dropped to the ground and crawled. Dead bodies covered the square.[119] According to the former first deputy commander of the North Caucasus Military District, General Matvey Shaposhnikov, at least twenty-two to twenty-four people were killed and thirty wounded.[120] The exact numbers may never be known.

The bodies were never returned to their families. In summer 1990, twenty-eight years later, the burial place remained unknown—still a state

secret. One of the bodies was that of a fifteen-year-old boy, Gena Terletsky. He was killed by a stray bullet while peeking through a crack in
the stockade around the police headquarters, where protesters gathered
to demand the release of those arrested in the morning. A year later his
mother was called into the headquarters and asked if she knew where
her son's body was. "I will [know] if you tell me," the mother answered.
She was given a death certificate and sent away. Almost three decades
later, she was still afraid to talk about her son.[121] (The family of a local
hairdresser, killed while working in her salon, never saw her body either.)[122]

The mother of another boy killed remembered going to the police,
who sent her to the city soviet. "My boy was killed," she recalled telling
one of the Soviet's secretaries. "At least give me his body. And he told
me: no one has shot at anyone and no one has been killed. Then a young
man came and took me away and held his hand over my mouth."[123]

A policeman from a neighboring town had to sign an "acknowledgment" (raspiska) on June 4, 1962, "pledging to carry out a government
task and keep it a state secret." If "I violate this oath," the "acknowledgment" went on, "I will be subjected to the punishment of the highest
measure, an execution."[124] (Most likely, the "task" was the transportation
and the burial of the bodies.)[125] In January 1991, a police officer, who
was said to have participated in the interment of those killed on June 2,
was whisked away by "the local authorities" on the day he was to be
interviewed by Russian documentary filmmakers.[126]

Back in school the day after the shooting, a Novocherkassk fifth-
grader was told that "yesterday enemies of the people and spies attempted a provocation."[127] A student at an engineering college, who
discussed the events with his neighbors, was castigated at a Party meeting, expelled from the Komsomol, and denied the graduation diploma,
and for a long time he could not find a job. When, in June 1989, he spoke
about the massacre, it was the second time in twenty-seven years.[128]

The blood in the square in front of the gorkom was first washed off
with fire truck hoses, then with a street-washing machine fitted with
long brushes, and finally covered with a thick layer of new asphalt.

Two months later, in August 1962, at a special session of the Supreme
Court of the RSFSR, fourteen alleged "organizers" of the "provocation"

were tried in Novocherkassk. Seven were sentenced to death and quickly shot.[129] The main evidence against them was secret-surveillance photographs, apparently taken continuously by plainclothes KGB operatives on June 1 and 2. (The originals of those photos mysteriously disappeared in 1990 from the eight volumes of the "Novocherkassk Case," kept in the Office of the Prosecutor General of the Armed Forces. Fortunately, copies had been made shortly before the disappearence and reproduced in the newspaper accounts.) Each culprit was marked by a cross. A caption under one of the photographs read: "Expressed dissatisfaction with the policies of the Party." Another: "Conducted himself extremely insolently. Shouted that he would kill anyone who would not give him meat and butter." And this, under a photo of a woman near the gorkom building: "Expressed dissatisfaction. Hardcore inciter [podstrekatel]."

The oldest among those executed in August 1962 were fifty-five and thirty-nine years old. The two youngest were twenty-five. By April 1991, six of them were completely "rehabilitated" (cleared by a court of any wrongdoing). One was found guilty of "hooliganism," which carried a maximum sentence of three years.[130]

One of the executed, a worker by the name of Andrei Karkach from the neighboring electrode plant, was charged with welcoming the NEVZ delegation that came to ask the plant's workers to join the strike. Additionally he was accused of "slandering the material situation of the laboring people."[131] His sentence also stipulated the "confiscation of all personal property." Thirty years later, reporters were led by his wife and daughter to this "confiscated property": an abandoned, dilapidated shack which used to be the family's house.[132]

The rest of the "organizers" received lengthy prison terms. One, Petr Siuda, was sentenced to twelve years for speaking at the June 1 rally at the NEVZ, asking the chief engineer a "provocative question," and suggesting that the workers march on the gorkom to present their demands.[133] Another defendant, according to his lawyer, was "still a boy" and out of curiosity pushed his way to the front of the crowd, where he was photographed. There was no other evidence of his guilt. He was sentenced to ten years.[134]

On June 2, 1990, the first commemorative meeting and a "civil funeral service" was held in Novocherkassk. Reporting it, a journalist from Moscow was hopeful that soon the killed would be buried "properly, like human beings," and that there would be a memorial on the square where they died.[135]*

Meanwhile, readers' letters about more shootings of striking or protesting workers poured in: "a long and troubling sequence."[136] A *Komsomol'skaya pravda* reporter estimated that there could have been as many as "forty novocherkassks" after Stalin's death.[137] Who better, another journalist asked in the summer of 1990, but the first freely elected Supreme Soviet to "take on itself the bitter mission of analyzing this sad list of the crimes against the people?" In doing so, he added, we will help ensure that no more such lists will ever have to be compiled.[138]

---

* A large stone with an Orthodox cross and inscription, "June 2, 1962," was placed in the square in front of the gorkom on May 31, 1991. Twenty-six bodies were interred in the city cemetery. On June 11, 1996, President Boris Yeltsin came to Novocherkassk to announce that he had signed a decree fully "rehabilitating" all those prosecuted in 1962.

CHAPTER NINE

The Unraveling of the Legitimizing Myths, III

THE GREAT PATRIOTIC WAR

Somehow, we have managed to invent another war. I, a frontline
soldier, have had nothing to do with what was written about that
war. I fought in an entirely different war.
—Viktor Astaf'ev, speech at a conference, "The urgent questions of
historical scholarship and literature," Moscow, April 27–28, 1988
(*Literaturnaya gazeta*, May 18, 1988: 4)

NO OTHER TALE in the official canon bound the people and the regime
tighter than the tragedy and heroism of the Great Patriotic War, which
started with the German invasion of the Soviet Union on June 22, 1941.
For over forty years the official myth had been simple and dependable.
Confronted with the prospect of imminent Nazi invasion and betrayed by
France and Great Britain (which, while pretending to conduct negotiations with the Soviet Union on an anti-German alliance, all the time con-
nived to "push Hitler East," into the war with the Soviet Union) the Soviet
government had no choice but to contrive to buy itself some "breathing
space" (*peredyshka*) by concluding, in August 1939, the Treaty of Non-
Aggression (the "Molotov-Ribbentrop Pact") with Germany.

The artful maneuver worked. The German onslaught was postponed
by almost two years, allowing the Soviet Union mightily to strengthen its
defenses; greatly increase, modernize, and train its armed forces; and

stockpile materiel and supplies. Then, after initial setbacks in 1941, caused by the utter surprise of the German onslaught and the aggressor's over-whelming advantages in men, weapons, tanks, and airplanes, the Red Army proceeded inexorably, methodically, and adroitly to vanquish the enemy, liberating the world of the "brown plague." The sacrifices were huge but absolutely necessary to secure the victory, which the Soviet Union achieved largely on its own, thanks to the genius of its wartime leaders and the skill and bravery of Soviet officers and soldiers, with little help from its reluctant "allies."[1]

With the exception of the soldiers' astounding valor and self-sacrifice, every component of this myth came under assault by the glasnost myth-slayers in 1987–89. Henceforth, the tale would be instilled with a pro-found ambiguity, which stemmed from the regime's enormous and inexpiable complicity in the deaths and suffering of millions of its citi-zens, soldiers, and civilians.

In this new version of the war's history, the rapprochement with Ger-many began well before mid-August 1939—and looked far more genuine than the allegedly forced expedient of the official mythology. As Foreign Minister Vyacheslav Molotov proclaimed in his toast to Stalin on the night of August 23–24, after the Treaty of Non-Aggression was signed, it was Stalin's speech at the Eighteenth Party Congress on March 10, 1939—the speech "so well understood in Germany," Molotov was pleased to add—that became a "turning point" in the relations between the Soviet Union and Germany.[2]* Two months later, Molotov's predecessor in the Foreign Ministry and a firm proponent of an anti-Hitler coalition with Western democracies,[3] Maxim Litvinov, was dismissed and virtually the entire Foreign Ministry's top personnel arrested and shot.†

---

* Fascism is not an issue, Stalin told the Congress. For instance, fascism in Italy did not prevent the Soviet Union from having "the best possible" relations with that country. (Vasily Kulish, "U poroga voyny" [On the war's threshold], interview with *Komsomol'skaya pravda*, August 24, 1988: 3.)
† Stalin was said to direct Molotov to "purge the ministry of Jews." "Thank God for these words!" Molotov recalled. "Jews formed an absolute majority in the leadership and among the ambassadors. It wasn't good." (Albert Resis, "The Fall of Litivinov," *Europe-Asia Studies* 52 [1], January 2000: 35.) Born Meir-Enoch Wallach-Finkelstein, Litvinov was referred to by the German radio as "Litvinov-Finkelstein." "The eminent Jew," Churchill would later write, "the target of

It was, furthermore, a "distortion" to insist, a prominent Soviet historian concluded, that France and Britain did not change their "appeasement" following Germany's occupation of Czechoslovakia in March 1939.[4] On the contrary, the Western powers' diplomatic activity clearly pointed to an earnest desire for an anti-Germany coalition. Even Germany's chief "appeaser," British Prime Minister Neville Chamberlain, paid the Soviet Embassy in London an unprecedented visit.[5]

As for the Western powers' "foot-dragging" in the negotiations with Moscow, even with the Western leaders' quite real anti-communism, on which the official Soviet history blamed their perfidious hesitance in the negotiations with Moscow, France and Britain were said to have valid reasons to be extremely wary of an alliance with Stalin's Soviet Union.[6] Why should they have been more trusting of a "repressive dictatorship," a "leftist despotism," hostile to democracy and led by a man who "trampled any semblance of morality underfoot and who resorted to criminal and cruel means in unprecedented repressions to strengthen his authoritarian power?" prominent Soviet historians asked.[7] And why, it was now asked, should the military officers in the French and British delegations have hurried to forge an alliance in the negotiations in which the Soviet side was represented by Marshal Klementi Voroshilov—a man not too bright or literate, with no diplomatic experience whatsoever but utterly loyal to Stalin and deeply complicit in "massacring the flower of the Soviet military" just two years before?[8]

It was the Soviet Union that, according to Russia's "new historians," conducted negotiations with Hitler behind the backs of Western powers, and it was the Soviet Union that broke off the negotiations with Britain and France before concluding its pact with Germany.[9] "Klim, Koba [Stalin] says: close down this hurdy-gurdy [*sharmanka* or useless noise-maker]," read the note that an aide to Voroshilov remembered passing to his boss.[10]

Mores aside, rushing to sign a treaty with Hitler was now judged a huge strategic blunder. Germany needed the pact far more than the

---

German antagonism was flung aside . . . like a broken tool. . . . The Jew Litvinov was gone and Hitler's dominant prejudice placated." (Nora Levin *The Jews in the Soviet Union since 1917: Paradox of Survival,* New York: New York University Press, 1988: 330.)

Soviet Union and was said to be "desperate" to secure it.[11] In this version of history, Hitler was ready to make war either in the east or in the west but he could not, at the time, do both.[12] His top generals, including the army commander, Field Marshal Walter von Brauchitsch, had warned the Führer in no uncertain terms against the invasion of Poland if there remained a possibility of the Soviet Union's getting involved on the side of Britain and France.[13] A war with the Soviet Union immediately after the conquest of Poland would have been "madness."[14] Hence Hitler's command to Ribbentrop to secure the Soviet Union's neutrality "at any cost."[15]

If Moscow's goal was to prevent a war, a far more prudent course to follow would have been to continue negotiations with France and Britain, even while talking to Berlin. One explanation for the urgency of striking a deal with Hitler (and thus allowing Germany to attack on the Western Front) was Stalin's apparent belief that, like World War I, the next world war was a product of "imperialism's contradiction"—and thus would provide another spectacular instance of the correctness of Lenin's 1914 stratagem of "turning an imperialist war into a civil one," which the Bolsheviks implemented in October 1917. For another round of socialist revolutions, history needed a push that would make a war between "imperialist powers" more probable.[16*]

That the Molotov-Ribbentrop Pact signified far more substantive closeness than the official myth allowed was confirmed by the pact's secret protocols, the existence of which the Soviet Union had denied for half a century. Dividing "spheres of influence" between Moscow and Berlin, the protocols gave the Soviet Union free hand to occupy Latvia, Lithuania, Estonia, and Eastern Poland (the latter henceforth to be known in Soviet history textbooks as "Western Ukraine" and "Western Belorussia"). A new Soviet-German border was to run through Poland.[†]

---

* "We are not at all against the imperialist powers getting into a big fight and weakening themselves quite a bit," Stalin told the Comintern's General Secretary Georgi Dimitrov on September 7, 1939. "Hitler . . . is undermining the imperialist system. We can maneuver, stir up one side against the other, so that their fight heats up even more." (Vasily Kulish, "Byl li vybor?" [was there a choice?] *Moskovskie novosti*, September 3, 1989: 12.)

† A photocopy of the Russian-language version of the protocol was published for the first time in the Soviet Union in the Latvian Russian-language newspaper *Sovetskaya molodezh* on July 5, 1989. It read:

It was these protocols that, in the opinion of Alexander Yakovlev, turned the *dogovor* (pact or treaty) into a *sgovor*—"collusion" or "conspiracy."[17] Chaired by Yakovlev, the "Commission on the Political and Legal Evaluation of the Soviet-German Non-Aggression Treaty of 1939," elected by the First Congress of People's Deputies in June 1989, could not locate the originals. Instead, it "authenticated" the copies in the Soviet archives, which "left no doubt whatsoever that such a protocol did exist."[18] Reported by Yakovlev in a nationally televised speech on December 24, 1989, this was the first official admission of the protocols' genuineness.

SECRET SUPPLEMENTARY PROTOCOL At the time of the signing of the treaty of non-aggression between Germany and the Union of Soviet Socialist Republics the undersigned plenipotentiary representatives of both sides discussed in strict confidentiality the matter of the division of the spheres of mutual interests in Eastern Europe. This discussion has resulted in the following:

1. In the case of a territorial and political rearrangement of the regions [that are currently] inside the Baltic states (Finland, Estonia, Latvia, Lithuania), the northern border of Lithuania becomes simultaneously the border between the spheres of interests of Germany and the USSR. At the same time, the interests of Lithuania with regard to the Vilna province [of Poland] are recognized by both sides.
2. In the case of a territorial and political rearrangement of the regions [that are currently] inside the State of Poland, the border of the spheres of interests of Germany and the USSR will run approximately along the rivers Narev [Narew], Visla [Vistula or Wisła], and San.
3. Whether the preservation of an independent Polish state is in the mutual interests [of Germany and the Soviet Union], and where the borders of such a state are, will be resolved only in the course of further political development. In any case, both governments will be resolving this issue in a friendly bilateral manner.
4. Regarding the southeast of Europe, the Soviet side underscores the interest of the USSR with respect to Bessarabia. The German side declares its complete political disinterestedness in these regions.
5. This protocol will be kept in strict secret by both sides.

The plenipotentiary of the government of the USSR V. *Molotov* (signature). For the government of Germany *J. Ribbentrop* (signature) (Ol'ga Avdevich, Elena Vlasova, "Sdelka" [A deal], *Sovetskaya molodezh,* July 5, 1989: 3. See also Yu. Fel'shtinskiy and N. Eydelman, "Za nedelyu do nachala vtoroy mirovoy voyny," *Moskovskie novosti,* August 20, 1989: 9.)

(Shortly after Mikhail Gorbachev's resignation in December 1991, the originals of the protocols would be found in the presidential archive.)[19]

A war invalid, badly wounded as a nineteen-year-old marine on the Northwestern Front in 1942, Yakovlev persuaded the Congress to repudiate the pact, after the parliament had refused to denounce it only a few months before. Calling the treaty "morally unworthy, unacceptable, incompatible with socialism,"[20] Yakovlev, as we have seen, added:

> The theory of relativity, comrades, is a great step in the understanding of the Universe. But there can be no relativity in morality. . . . We have to understand that lawlessness is horrifying not only in its direct effects but also because it creates situations when amorality and opportunism start to be considered the norm. Thus any evaluation we make [of the pact,] Comrade Deputies, will be not only political, but moral as well.[21]

In the new retelling, a temporary and limited character of the Soviet-German rapprochement was further belied by the evidence of the Soviet leaders' being genuinely animated by what might be called the "spirit of the protocols." There was, for one, Stalin's toast to Hitler (described by the German note-takers as "unexpected") after the signing of the pact: "I know how strongly the German nation loves its Supreme Leader, which is why I want to drink to his health."[22] The next day, a *Pravda* editorial predicted that the "friendship between the Soviet peoples and Germany, the friendship that has nearly been driven to a dead end by the efforts of the enemies of Germany and the USSR, will now acquire all the necessary conditions for development and flourishing."[23] Stalin himself proclaimed that this friendship, "having been sealed with the blood" of the Soviet and German people, had "every reason to be long and solid."[24]

If it was Polish blood Stalin had in mind, the Soviet-German "cooperation" indeed appeared to have been much solidified by it. Two days after the Red Army invaded Poland on September 17, the Soviet Union and Germany signed a "communiqué" in which the Wehrmacht and the Red Army were proudly assigned the task of "restoring the peace and order disrupted as a result of the disintegration of the Polish state."[25]

Nine days later, another treaty, "On Friendship and Borders," was concluded to formalize the division of Poland in a mutually agreeable fashion.[26]* In a public statement that accompanied the accord, Moscow and Berlin called for an end to the "state of belligerence" between Germany, on the one hand, and France and Britain, which had declared war on Germany after it invaded Poland, on the other. If, however, Paris and London refused to heed this call, they would "bear the responsibility for the continuation of the war, in which case the governments of Germany and the Soviet Union will consult each other on necessary measures."[27]

Meanwhile, according to the new history, the German ambassador in Moscow reported to Berlin that the Soviet government was "doing everything possible to change the population's attitude toward Germany." The Soviet newspapers, he continued, "seemed to have been changed overnight. Not only have the attacks on Germany completely disappeared, but all the accounts of international events are in large measure being based on German reports, and all anti-German literature is being taken out of publication."[28] Speaking to the Supreme Soviet on October 31, 1939, Molotov boasted that "a strike against Poland first by the German army and then by the Red Army was enough to ensure that nothing was left of this ugly spawn [*urodlivoe detishche*] of the Versailles Treaty."[29] As for the "ideology of Hitlerism," the Soviet foreign minister declared that one could "accept it or deny it, but everyone understands that ideology cannot be destroyed by force. Which is why to engage in a "war to destroy Hitlerism, under the cover of the false banner of the struggle for 'democracy' [was] not just senseless but also criminal."[30]

German communist refugees were forcibly "repatriated" to face executions or slow death in concentration camps.[31] Among the refugees

---

* On one of the secret maps appended to the treaty (and reproduced in *Literaturnaya gazeta* around the fiftieth anniversary of the Molotov-Ribbentrop Pact) a black ink line was drawn from the Latvian city of Liepaja in the north down to Budapest to "establish the division of mutual interests in the area of the former Polish state" in accordance with Article 1 of the agreement. In a red pencil in a corner, Ribbentrop set down the date, "28.IX.39," and his signature. Stalin signed in large letters in thick blue pencil across the middle. "Is my signature big enough for you?" he reportedly asked Ribbentrop jokingly. ("Podpis' na karte" [The signature on a map], *Literaturnaya gazeta*, July 5, 1989: 9.)

was Margarete Buber-Neumann, the wife of the German Communist Party leader Heinz Neumann. After he disappeared in the Great Purge in 1937 (his exact fate has never been determined), she was sent to the Vorkuta camps and then, in 1940, handed over to the Gestapo and imprisoned in Ravensbrück.[32]

The Soviet-German rapprochement culminated in Molotov's November 12–13, 1940, visit to Berlin to explore the possibility (and the price) of an even closer alliance. The event's fiftieth anniversary was marked by a *Moskovskie novosti* article, which described how, at a meeting with Hitler on November 13, Stalin's emissary reportedly told the Führer that the Soviet Union's joining of the Tripartite Pact (of Germany, Italy, and Japan) was "absolutely acceptable in principle"—provided Hitler satisfied the Soviet Union's wish list: Finland, Southern Bukovina (then part of Rumania), and most, important, the establishment of Soviet military bases "in the area of" the Bosporus and Dardanelles strait. Hitler would not promise, and Molotov returned to Moscow "empty-handed."[33]

Bought at the exorbitant price of the "Soviet-German alliance"—which popular writer Vladimir Amlinsky called one of the "blackest and most shameful pages of our history," and the historian Chubar'yan proclaimed the epitome of "cynicism and outrageous [*vopiyushchya*] immorality"[34]—in the version of events now advanced by Soviet military historians, the very value of the allegedly brilliantly executed *peredyshka* was shown to be an illusion. Instead, between 1939 and 1941 the Soviet strategic position vis-à-vis an almost certain aggressor significantly worsened.[35]

Plagued by bureaucratic delays and incompetence, the Red Army's "reorganization" and rearmament, begun in 1940, proceeded with great difficulty as the industry failed to keep up with the military's need to for modern weapons and ammunition.[36] In place of a war doctrine, the military continued to be guided by the unshakable belief in socialist revolutions to be sparked by "an imperialist war." These, in turn, would enable the Red Army to engage in "swift victorious operations beyond our borders and with little blood" (*na chuzhoy territorii, maloy krov'yu*).[37] With their proponents among the Soviet top command having perished in the purges, newer models of tanks and airplanes were deployed slowly, if at all. Instead, cavalry was in vogue again, with ninety-two new cavalry divisions planned for deployment in 1942.[38] Automatic weapons were declared "bourgeois" inventions: the Red Army was to rely on the World War I rifle (*tryokhlineyka*) and, better yet, on the bayonet.[39] Trucks and mechanized artillery were spurned in favor of horses as the cheapest and most reliable means of transportation.[40]

By contrast, Germany used the years between 1939 and 1941 to huge advantage. His hands untied in the east, Hitler transferred all but ten of his 136 Divisions to the Western Front against France, Belgium, and the Netherlands, leaving behind sparsely manned units stretching from the Baltic Sea to the Carpathian Mountains.[41] After winning the war in the west, the Wehrmacht returned to the Soviet borders as a larger and better equipped force with invaluable battlefield experience. Compared to 1939–40, the German military almost doubled in size (to 7,234,000), as did the number of its tanks and warplanes.[42]

Millions of tons of grain, oil, nickel, manganese, metal ore, and rubber for tires were shipped to Germany from the Soviet Union in accordance with trade agreements between Moscow and Berlin.[43] According to a leading "revisionist" historian of the Great Patriotic War, Mikhail Simiryaga, Soviet supplies played a major role in the sharp growth of Germany's strategic reserves between 1939 and 1941: an almost eightfold increase in iron ore; the doubling of coal; a fourfold growth in grain; and a twentyfold one in oil.[44] The last freight train crossed the Soviet border on the way to Germany an hour before the German invasion, at three in the morning on June 22.[45]

In the new rendering, yet another key component of the official myth—the "utter surprise" of the German invasion—turned out to be not a surprise at all, or at least it should not have been. Soviet spies, including the legendary Richard Sorge in Japan, continuously sent to Moscow "most detailed information"[46] about Germany's preparations for the assault. The chief of the Soviet General Staff was said to have had a copy of the Barbarossa plan as early as March 20, 1941.[47] Yet such intelligence was dismissed as a "provocations." One after another, five heads of the Chief Intelligence Directorate of the General Staff were arrested and executed.[48]

Instead of heeding these warnings, in spring 1941 Stalin sent Hitler a note about German military activity on the Soviet border. In his reply, Hitler swore by "the honor of the Reichkanzler" that Germany was not planning an attack on the Soviet Union and that the 130 Wermacht divisions, which by then had been amassed on the Soviet border, were there to escape harassment by the British Air Force.[49]

The sagacious and wily Stalin of the myth apparently believed him. The fortifications along the "old" (pre–September 1939) western border of the Soviet Union were dismantled, and the new border was left defenseless. When the head of the Defense Fortifications Directorate of the Red Army Corps of Engineers, Major General Leonty Kotlyar, requested funds to at least keep the abandoned fortifications from falling apart, an irate Stalin ordered their demolition, with all the armor to be stripped and sent east for use at construction sites and all the fortified "pillboxes" (*doty*) to be given to kolkhozes as silos.[50]

In accordance with the doctrine of a victorious march west to spearhead the socialist revolution among the "imperialist nations" weakened by mutual bloodletting, the Soviet Union continued to keep on its unfortified western frontier 30 percent (25,000 freight railcars' worth) of all the ammunition and 50 percent of all fuel and food. All of the supplies and materiel would be destroyed or captured by the Germans in the first few days of the war.[51]

German reconnaissance planes routinely violated Soviet airspace along the western border. Yet not only did Stalin forbid intercepting them (not to mention shooting them down), but when Luftwaffe pilots ran out of fuel, they were welcome to land at Soviet military bases for refueling.[52] Nor was Moscow disturbed by Berlin's sudden interest in locating the graves of German soldiers killed in World War I in what was now the Soviet Union's territory. The request for the "search parties" to look for these graves was apparently readily granted, allowing the Wehrmacht's intelligence officers to roam freely in the rear of the Red Army's Western and Central Command between the Baltic and the Black seas.[53]

On June 14, 1941, eight days before the invasion, the TASS news agency published an "informational statement" (*soobshchenie*), which affirmed that Germany was not preparing an invasion and sternly warned those who "succumbed to the rumors of Germany's hostile intentions."[54] The commanders of the western military districts issued orders allowing officers and their families to leave the bases for the weekend of June 21–22.

It was the Kremlin's tactical and strategic ineptitude and not Germany's "overwhelming preponderance" of the official myth that Soviet researchers now blamed for the disaster of the first months of the war. For Operation Barbarossa, Germany deployed around 3 million men, 48,000 artillery pieces and mortars, 2,800 tanks, and 5,000 planes. Facing them on the western border were the Red Army's 3 million men, and, although still mostly older models, nearly 100,000 artillery pieces and mortars, 12,000 tanks, and nearly 18,000 planes.[55] Yet according to a Soviet military historian, never before in Russia's history did any invader from the west manage to advance as far east—and against the largest Russian army in history, which on June 22, 1941, had a total of 5 million men under arms.[56]

As entire fronts "collapsed" in the first days of the German invasion and "desperate cries" for direction and command were coming to the "center" from "everywhere," Stalin hid at his dacha in Kuntsevo for ten days.[57] (Even among Stalin's myriad unforgivable deeds, these ten days stand out, wrote the popular writer Ales' Adamovich.)[58] The Soviet high command seemed utterly bewildered, overwhelmed, and incompetent. One blunder followed another. Thus on the night of June 22, the armies of the Western Front, which were already riddled through by German panzers and troops, were ordered by Moscow to immediately "counterattack" and take the city of Lyublin, on the "German" side of Poland. As they followed the order, most of these armies were soon surrounded and decimated.[59]

The costliest deficiency was the Soviet high command's inability or unwillingness to organize a deep strategic defense and order a retreat, which could have saved millions of lives.[60] Instead, the supreme commander's headquarters (*Stavka Verkhovnogo Glavnokomanduyushchego*) would continue, in a historian's words, to "throw" millions and millions of troops "under the German locomotive"[61] until the sheer heroism of the rank-and-file soldiers stopped the Wehrmacht less than thirty kilometers from Moscow. By then, according to the military historian, Lieutenant

General Nikolai Pavlenko, Stalin was reportedly ready to plead with Hitler for peace under the most humiliating conditions.*

"We simply did not know how to fight," a veteran and popular writer Viktor Astaf'ev told a conference on "History and Literature" in May 1988. "We ended the war not knowing how to fight. We drowned the enemy in our blood; we buried him under our corpses."[62]

In the absence of any trustworthy official statistics, the assessments ranged from four Red Army soldiers killed for every German[63] to an almost incredible "fourteen of our boys for each German" killed on the Western Front.[64†] (In World War I, the Russian losses were approximately equal to the combined casualties of Germany and the Austro-Hungarian empire on the Eastern Front.)[65]

One of the key causes of such hideous lopsidedness was the Soviet Union's starting the war with a "beheaded" (*obezglavlennyy*) military.[66] Over 80,000 Red Army officers were arrested and executed between 1937 and June 1941.[67] They included over 60 percent of all field and senior officers: 512 of the 767 marshals, generals, and admirals; all the military district commanders and their staffs; all the corps and division

---

* Pavlenko recalled hearing, at Zhukov's dacha in the village of Sosnovka outside Moscow, Marshal Georgy Zhukov's reminisce in the mid-1960s about the early days of the war. About to be appointed commander of the Western Front, he was granted an audience with Stalin and Beria. Suddenly Stalin began talking about how in 1918 Lenin concluded a separate peace with Germany in Brest-Litovsk, taking Russia out of World War I and saving the Soviet regime at the price of enormous territorial losses. With the enemy approaching the country's capital and without sufficient forces to defend it, Stalin felt it might be necessary to follow in Lenin's footsteps and asked Beria to try to "test the waters through his secret channels." According to Zhukov, Stalin reportedly was ready to give up not only the newly acquired Baltic states and Moldavia, but also Belarus and part of Ukraine. (Beria did find a go-between to Berlin, a Bulgarian diplomat by the name of Statenov, but Hitler anticipated a speedy victory and was not interested in negotiations.) (Nikolai Pavlenko, "Tragediya i triumph Krasnoy armii" [The Red Army's tragedy and triumph], *Moskovskie novosti*, May 7, 1989: 9.)

† The author Yuri Geller estimated the Soviet battlefield losses at 22 million men, compared to 1.5 million Germans, and the total loss of Soviet lives at 46 million, or one-quarter of the Soviet Union's population. (Geller, "Nevernoe eho bylogo" [A wrong echo of the past] *Druzhba narodov*, September 1989: 242.)

commanders and their staffs; all the fleet and flotillas commanders; the entire apparatus of the General Staff and of Strategic Intelligence; most professors of the General Staff Academy; over half of all regiment commanders; and many battalion and even company commanders.[68*]

No military defeat in modern times, including that of the Wehrmacht in 1945, resulted in such "monstrous" casualties among the officer corps.[69] As a result, according to a leading Soviet historian of the Great Patriotic War, Professor Vasily Kulish, by summer 1941 only 7 percent of Red Army officers had a higher military education; 37 percent had no military education at all.[70] Many divisions were commanded by majors and even captains; many regiments were led by lieutenants.[71]

The veterans among historians and writers were convinced that, in the words of one of the most famous commanders of the Great Patriotic War, Marshal Alexander Vasilevsky, the extent of the "destruction of the Soviet military cadres" played a significant role in Hitler's decision to invade.[72] "Without [the purge of] 1937," they agreed, "there might not have been 1941"—or it would have been far less devastating.[73] We would never know, wrote veteran and writer Grigory Baklanov, "how many millions of lives could have been saved."[74]

Combined with what an *Ogonyok* editorial called the regime's "grandiose neglect of the ordinary man,"[75] the "criminal unpreparedness"

---

* The first victims of the purge were tried on June 11, 1937, and executed at dawn the next day: Marshals M. Tukhachevsky and I. Yakir, and top military commanders I. Uborevich, R. Eideman, B. Feldman, A. Kork, V. Primakov, and V. Putna. They were shot on Khodynskoe Field in Moscow, and their bodies were thrown into an unmarked ravine and covered with quicklime. (Geller, "Nevernoe ekho," 238.) Among the last to be arrested before the war, in the second or third week of June 1941, were Commander of the Soviet Air Force and Hero of the Soviet Union Lt. General Pavel Rychagov; his predecessor in command and later deputy chief of the General Staff of the Air Force, twice Hero of the Soviet Union Lt. General Yakov Smushkevich; and the Commander of the Far Eastern Front, a Hero of the Soviet Union, and the commander of the successful 1938–39 operation against the Japanese at Lake Khassan and the Khalkhin Gol River in Outer Mongolia, Colonel General Grigory Shtern. (Konstantin Simonov, "Uroki istorii i dolg pisatelya" [Lessons of history and a writer's duty], *Nauka i zhizn'*, June 1987: 45.) All three were accused of plotting against Stalin, tortured horribly in the Lubyanka prison, evacuated to Kubyshev (Samara) when the Germans approached Moscow, and shot on October 28, 1941.

continued to kill Soviet soldiers long after June 1941.[76] Preparing for his battle around the city of Rzhev,* 190 kilometers (about 120 miles) northwest of Moscow, writer and veteran Vycheslav Kondrat'ev remembered being ready to forgive the regime for the terror of the 1930s and even to join the Party if he survived. Instead, he was "shaken by the total unpreparedness and total disregard for the soldiers' lives" he saw the next day.[77] The senseless attack bogged down and his battalion fell back, leaving half of its soldiers dead in the field. "Then I understood," Kondrat'ev continued, "that this war was being conducted and would be conducted with the same cruelty toward our own people with which the collectivization and the decimation of the 'enemies of the people' [in the purges] had been executed: not sparing people's lives in peacetime, Stalin would not spare them in war."[78] Kondrat'ev never joined the Party.

In May 1942 around the Crimean city of Kerch, 176,000 soldiers were killed under the command of Stalin's personal emissary, the head of the Chief Political Directorate of the Red Army, Lev Mekhlis. A commissar with no military education or experience, he was known as the "Bloody Dog" for his role in the Red Army purge in 1937–39. Immediately after arriving in Kerch, he dismissed the commander, General Tolbukhin, for building defense fortifications. Mekhlis forbade digging trenches lest it damage the soldiers' "attacking spirit."[79] In the end, the three Soviet armies around Kerch were "pushed into the sea" by two German tank corps.[80]

Among the most senseless victims of this endless carnage were the hundreds of thousands—perhaps millions—of soldiers in the "people's volunteer corps" (narodnoe opolchenie). Found physically unfit or too old to be drafted even in wartime, yet still volunteering to serve, these heroes were thrown in, untrained and in many cases unarmed, into some of the worst "meatgrinders" (myasorubki) of the war.† Among the most devas-

---

* In January–July 1942, the Red Army lost between 500,000 and 1,000,000 around Rzhev in attacks ordered by Stalin against strongly fortified German positions. These casualties include those killed and captured when an entire Soviet army was encircled and routed.

† "And so he went to war," Solzhenitsyn wrote of one of his characters, an electrical engineer and volunteer, "in his minus-three [diopters prescription] glasses . . . and an empty pistol holster—in the second year of the 'well-

tating of these was the battle of Vyaz'ma, where three Soviet armies were surrounded and wiped out by the Germans in October 1941. Among the fallen were the flower of Moscow intelligentsia—math geniuses and poets, philosophers and musicians, art historians and teachers.* Many, perhaps most, memorials to the Soviet soldiers killed in the war are also monuments to the victims of Stalinism.

Soviet soldiers were tormented by a "psychosis" of mistrust even as they were mowed down by German bullets, bombs, and shells.[81] There was constant spying and the "paranoid verification of identity" by the NKVD and the SMERSH military counterintelligence (from "Smert shpionam!" or "Death to spies!").[82] Executions of suspected "cowards," "panic-mongers," and "deserters" were routine. In a 1990 war documentary, a convicted soldier is forced to dig his own grave.[83] He finishes, climbs out, and for a few seemingly long moments stares into the barrel of his executioner's gun. Then a point-blank shot rings out and the body is shoved into the pit.[84]

Prompted by what he saw in the documentary, a veteran recalled an execution of a soldier from his platoon. The man went missing during the previous night. He said he had lost his way. He was charged with wishing to desert to the enemy. Brought out to be shot, the soldier kept falling in the snow, all the time muttering about his innocence. Lifted, he fell again, apparently believing that he would not be executed lying down.[85]

The so-called blocking units (zagradotryady) were created by Stalin's "Not one step backward!" (Ni shagu nazad!) Order 227 on July 28, 1942. The order prohibited retreat under any circumstances "without the

---

prepared-for war,' there were not enough side-arms for officers." (V kruge pervom [In the First Circle], Moscow: Act, 2006: 211.)

* Outside a village near Moscow, a hero of Solzhenitsyn's novel In the First Circle comes across an obelisk that reads: "Eternal glory to the warriors of the Fourth Division of the people's volunteer corps, who died the death of the brave. . . . From the Ministry of Finance." "Finance? And finance, too!" a "stunned" Innokentiy Volodin ponders. "How many of them have laid down their lives here? And for how many of them was there only one rifle? The Fourth Division of People Volunteer Corps? . . . A division of the unarmed! Poor clerks! And [it was] already the fourth [such volunteer division]! What a monstrosity of a war it was—the 'people's volunteer corps.'" (V kruge pervom, 322.)

authorization of the Command of a Front," and the "blocking detachments" were to be deployed to shoot soldiers at the first instance of hesi-
tation or attempted retreat.[86]* *Zagradotryady* were especially busy during
reconnaissance in force (*razvedka boem*), in which soldiers were ordered
to advance solely to reveal the enemy's machine guns, mortars, and can-
ons as they shot at the attackers.

Reconnaissance in force was part and parcel of all Soviet infantry
units' tactics but it was especially frequent in penal battalions: *strafnye
batal'ony,* or *shtrafbaty* for short. Creatures of Order 227, *shtrafbaty* were to
be staffed with officers and soldiers guilty of "a breach of discipline due to
cowardice or bewilderment." They were to be deployed "in difficult sectors
of the army to give them an opportunity to redeem by blood their crimes
against the Motherland."[87] If a *shtrafnik* was lucky enough to be injured
but not killed, he was transferred back into a regular unit. The practice
became known as the "till the first blood," or *do pervoy krovi,* rule.

The sentencing to a penal battalion was entirely up to an immediate
superior and could not be appealed. Veterans recalled that the punishment could be meted out for any transgression, no matter how minute—
or simply to get rid of someone a commanding officer disliked, including
a potential rival for the affection of a nurse, a radio operator, or any other
female in a unit. (These were known as "a field wife" [*pokhodno-polevaya
zhena* or PPZh].)[88]

Writing in *Literaturnaya gazeta,* a veteran traced the grotesque ease
with which soldiers and officers could be sent to the *shtrafbats* to the ca-
sual cruelty of the regime in peacetime,

> when such horribly long sentences were passed down for a nail
> taken from a factory or an ear of rye from a field. A labor army
> was needed, one which would work for free and could be sent

---

* "Each Army is to form three to five well-armed defensive units (up to 200
persons in each) and deploy them directly behind unstable divisions and
require them in case of panic and scattered withdrawals of elements of the
divisions to shoot immediately any panic-mongers and cowards and thus help
the conscientious soldiers of the division fulfill their duty to the Motherland."
(The Order of the National Commissar for the Defense of the Soviet Union, July
28 1942, Moscow. http://www.stalingrad-info.com/order227.htm. Accessed
March 28, 2010.)

anywhere to do the hardest labor. And that is also what was needed in the war: units with which all the "holes" could be plugged, the high command's mistakes corrected, and the enemy's firepower located at the cost of hundreds and hundreds, sometimes thousands of lives—well, they were convicts, weren't they, their lives were worth nothing and no one will answer for them. And so they threw one *shtrafbat* after another into the worst hellholes.[89]*

How many soldiers were killed in the penal battalions' reconnaissance in force? How many more were slaughtered by the machine guns of the blocking units? How many were executed? A writer and a veteran who posed these questions in early 1990 doubted that "we will ever learn because these casualties were not counted by the Command. Tens of thousands, hundreds of thousands? . . . Poor, hapless Russia. The poor and hapless Russian people that were destined to live through *this*."[90]

By a formerly very secret count, which, too, came to light in the late 1980's, 5,734,528 Soviet soldiers were taken prisoner.[91] In their relentless search for the truth about the Great Patriotic War, Soviet historians and journalists attributed this almost incredibly high number to the murderous insanity of forbidding retreat under any circumstances. "The most important thing was not to give up the current positions!" a researcher concluded after looking at dozens of orders and instructions.[92] German commanders, he continued, were surprised at the sight of Red Army

---

*   A veteran's poem read:
   Reconnaissance in force—nothing is more terrifying.
   Reconnaissance in force—like the world's coming to an end.
   But what can you do, when there is only one road for you,
   No matter how black.

   Only forward, only forward.
   Not one but many machine guns behind us.
   It is called a blocking unit,
   Manned by fat-faced NKVD boys.
   And it is hard to say, whether it was them or the Germans
   We hated the most in that dreadful minute. . . . (Vyacheslav Kondrat'ev, "Parii voyny" [The pariahs of the war], *Literaturnaya gazeta*, January 31, 1990: 8.)

soldiers continuing to fortify the front lines long after the German Panzers passed them deeply in the flanks. "They continue to hold positions
that we are no longer attacking," the chief of staff of the Wehrmacht's
infantry noted in his diary in October 1941.[93] Among the victims of this
"madness" were 665,000 prisoners taken around Kiev in September
1941, when Stalin forbade retreat; another 662,000 in Vyaz'ma two
months later; 207,000 were captured in the Izyum-Khar'kov offensive,
ordered by Stalin in May 1942 over the objections of his generals; and
150,000 under Mekhlis in Kerch, also in May 1942.[94]

Almost one-fifth of these prisoners (1,310,000) died in captivity. Some
were executed for trying to escape, others died from diseases, overwork,
punitive mass executions, and random torture. Most perished from starvation. The Soviet Union had refused to sign the Geneva Convention
with its provision for humane and dignified treatment of prisoners of
war.[95] Stalin also rejected the appeals of the Red Cross, which offered to
mediate the transfer of food from the Soviet Union to its prisoners of
war—an act that the historians now claimed could have saved at least
half of those who starved to death.[96] Instead, the "traitors to the Motherland" were dying in what Alexander Solzhenitsyn—who fought in the
war from the first day until his arrest in East Prussia in February 1945 on
the charges of "anti-Soviet propaganda" and "founding a hostile organization" (the infamous Article 58, Paragraphs 10 and 11, of the Criminal
Code)—called "cannibalistic" camps, where Soviet soldiers ate tree bark
and the corpses of their comrades.[97] In just November–December 1941,
400,000 Soviet prisoners died of starvation in German camps.[98] Of the
235,473 British and American soldiers held prisoner in German camps
throughout the entire war, 8,348 died.[99]

Yet another of Stalin's orders—Number 270 of August 16, 1941*—
was a collective death sentence for all Soviet POWs. Henceforth, having
been taken prisoner was considered a voluntary act, a soldier's choice.
The phrase used in the order was not the customary "to find oneself
prisoner" (popast' v plen) but "to render oneself a prisoner" or to "surrendered to become prisoner" (sdat'sya v plen). "Soldiers who surrendered to
become prisoner," the order read, "are to be exterminated by all means

* Read to the frontline soldiers, neither this order nor Order 227 had been
  published in the Soviet Union until glasnost.

[weapons] on land or from the air." The families of POWs were to be denied "state support" (that is, ration coupons or "food cards"), dooming, in the words of a Soviet historian, "hundreds of thousands" of children and elderly—soldiers' sons, daughters, and elderly parents—to starvation.[100] Officers who "surrendered" were considered "malignant [zlostlnyi] deserters," and their relatives were to be arrested "as families of deserters who violated their oath."[101]

To be taken prisoner was "worse than death," Soviet veterans agreed: "better a bullet in the head."[102] To be missing in action was tantamount to surrendering. "I understand now," a veteran was quoted in a *Moskovskie novosti* article, "why before assault river crossings (*forsirovanie*) soldiers implored one another: 'Brother, if I drown, please tell them that you saw me killed.'"[103]

Branded traitors by Order 270, prisoners of war were never to be trusted again, even those who escaped and were allowed to fight in the Red Army. Many, if not most, were convicted under Article 58 and sent to the Gulag.[104] The eponymous hero of Solzhenitsyn's *One Day in the Life of Ivan Denisovich*, who had escaped from a German camp after his entire army had been surrounded in February 1942, was accused of being an agent sent over by "German intelligence on a mission" (*zadanie*). Neither Ivan Denisovich (who signed the confession, after being beaten "a lot" and because the alternative was a swift execution) nor his interrogator-*sledovatel'* could think of what that "mission" was. So that is how it was listed in Ivan Denisovich's sentence: a "mission."[105]

Two of the fifty Soviet generals taken prisoner in the early months of the war—Pavel Ponedelin and Nikolai Kirillov—miraculously survived the German camps. Liberated by the allies, they were handed over to the Soviet command in April 1945. After five years of "investigation" in the Lefortovo political prison, both men were executed.[106]

In the last months of the war, when over a million former POWs were fighting in the Red Army, Stalin ordered the NKVD and SMERSH, as well as the commanders of the First, Second, Third, and Fourth Ukrainian Fronts and of the First and Second Belarusian Fronts, to set up 100 camps for all "civilians and prisoners of war" who spent any time in captivity. Each camp was to hold 10,000 people.[107] A special directorate "For Prisoners of War Affairs" was created in the Ministry of Internal Affairs.

In 1945–46, the inmates of these camps would constitute the single largest "stream" (*potok*) to the Gulag.[108] Hundreds of cattle cars with bars on the windows carried them east: soldiers and officers who, in the words of the popular writer and veteran Grigory Baklanov, were for the second time "destined to pay for our not having been prepared for the war, for all our defeats."[109] Like many characters in Solzhenitsyn's roman à clef *In the First Circle*, they were convicted for "voluntary surrender" (*dobrovol'naya sdacha v plen*).[110] They would "dig mines, build power stations on rivers, and erect cities, near which they would forever lie in the frozen earth."[111]

A rare survivor of both the German and Soviet camps wrote *Moskovskie novosti* of former POWs transported for weeks in cattle cars across almost the entire Eurasian continent: from Germany to the Soviet Far East. There they were "packed" for a week in a steamer's hold on their way to Magadan on the Pacific coast. Only once during that week were they fed: a big pot with boiling water mixed with flour was lowered on a rope into the hold, where, half-crazed from hunger, the men scooped the scalding brew with their hands. After the steamer docked in Magadan's Nagaevo Bay, the dead were thrown overboard and the living were taken into the forest (*taiga*) to camps.[112]

As late as the 1950s, former prisoners of war were required to come to police stations on appointed dates for registration.[113] To miss the registration was a criminal offense. In May 1988, when the country celebrated the fifty-third anniversary of the victory, a reporter asked the chairman of the All-Union Council of Veterans if the prisoners of war were veterans too. No, they were not, a former commissar answered. "And why are you writing about them? Don't you have enough real soldiers to write about?"[114] Here it was, the reporter thought, the morality of Stalinism, thickly laced with the blood and suffering of millions of soldiers. For thirty-five years, he wrote, we have lived "without the 'Father of the Peoples,'" but we continued, somehow, to "honor his tenets." And where was one to go, before whom should one bow to the ground (*bit' chelom*), on which red Kremlin wall to knock to beg for giving the imprisoned solders back their dignity, restore their good name? How do we squeeze Stalin's slavery from our souls?[115]

What was for the Soviet people the war for national survival, fought with bravery and sacrifice that would never cease to astound, was now seen, as a Soviet philosopher put it, also as a clash of two hideous regimes, marked by an "eerie historic similarity" in their "humiliation of man" and denial of his "liberty, will, dignity, choice."[116] For the four long years of the war, the poet Evtushenko wrote, millions of soldiers and tens of millions of civilians were ground between the two blood-stained mill-stones, "suffocated" in "the clash of two rotten winds."[117]

Almost incomprehensible in its vastness, the Soviet people's tragedy did not end with the end of the death and devastation of the Great Patriotic War. Their calamity persisted, seemingly irredeemable even by the people's enormous sacrifice. A veteran, Boris Vasiliev, famous for one of the finest short novels about the Great Patriotic War, *But Sunrises Are Very Quiet Here* (*A zori zdes' tikhie*),* wrote that in vanquishing the Nazi "reaction" outside the country, "we not only strengthened but also justified political reaction" inside it. "We justified the crimes of Stalin and Stalinism," Vasiliev continued, "the Gulag and executions without trials, the transformation of the peasants into state serfs and of the state apparatus into a new class of exploiters."[118]

This was a "tragic war," Solzhenitsyn had his character say. "We have saved the Motherland—and we lost it again." For Russia now was, finally and hopelessly, "permanent property of the whiskered one [*usach,* or Stalin]." "We have tightened the noose around our neck," his interlocutor agreed. This was the "most miserable war" in Russian history.[119]

Vasily Grossman's verdict on the outcome of the "Stalingrad triumph" captured the result of the entire war: "The silent dispute between the victorious people and the victorious state continued. And the fate of man, his freedom, depended on the outcome of that dispute."[120]

---

* Published in 1969, the novel was about the short life and heroic death of an anti-aircraft platoon of young women somewhere in the Russian northwest in 1942. The 1972 film was just as popular.

CHAPTER TEN

The "Immoral" Economy

We must instill in every aspect of our social life the notion that what is economically ineffective is immoral. It is my deep conviction that the economically ineffective situation of universal shortages is the main reason for thievery, bribery, died-in-the-wool bureaucratization, all manner of secrets, immoral privileges, and bitterness. The economically ineffective, waste-making planning mechanism has engendered the thoughtless pilfering of our national resources, the immoral attitude toward our national treasures.

—Nikolai Shmelyov, *Novye trevogi* (New concerns) *Novy mir*, April 1988: 175

ONE OF THE MOST consequential discoveries made by the glasnost crusaders was the "monstrous," even "surpassing imagination,"[1] waste, neglect, and despoliation in the country's economy. The irrational, "lop-sided" (*skosobochennya*) system was found to work not "for man but, more and more, only for itself."[2] It was called an "insatiable" and "self-consuming" (*samoedskaya*) Moloch, which year after year devoured more resources and labor and produced less.[3]

Of course, every Soviet citizen had seen this Moloch in action. Yet, as with other aspects of the national self-discovery, it was the scope of the generalizations, founded on the no-longer-secret numbers, merciless and irrefutable, that startled. Such was, for instance, the disclosure, in July 1988, that the Soviet Union expended over three times more electricity to produce a ton of copper than did the Federal Republic of Germany, and over twice as much of "reference" (or "equivalent") fuel (*uslovnoe toplivo*) (a universal measure of energy spent, regardless of whether it is coal, or oil, or electricity) as Japan.[4] In addition, the low energy efficiency of consumer electric devices annually cost the Soviet economy 20 billion kilowatt-hours annually—equivalent to the energy generated by a giant power plant.[5]

Among the most shocking aspects of this system was its "anarchy,"[6] despite obsessively meticulous and rigid planning. (Agricultural production alone was guided by 700 parameters for production, accumulation, and distribution; 400 for capital investments; and around 200 for labor, wages, and finance.)[7] This anarchic "self-consumption" and "self-ruination" (*samorazorenie*)[8] was epitomized by huge projects that cost billions of rubles and were now revealed to have been without much, or even any, use or profit and often hugely damaging to the land, air, and water. There were, for instance, the 4,324 kilometers (2,687 miles) of the Baikal-Amur Railway (BAM), on which "there was nothing to transport."[9] The "economic essence" of the ninety recently built hydroelectric power stations was said to be "not much different from the Egyptian pyramids."[10] In the preceding two decades the dams erected to service these stations flooded some 10 million hectares, or 25 million acres, including fine meadows, at a time when the country "desperately needed" cattle fodder to alleviate the chronic shortages of meat.[11]

Started and unfinished industrial construction was another plague. Newspapers were suddenly filled with damning vignettes, including one about the Karaganda metallurgical plant, which, after being planned for twenty years, was now in the eleventh year of construction.[12] Despite solemn pledges to do something about it, the reformist government appeared to be unable to stop the madness: construction had grown by 40 percent, or 30 billion rubles, reaching the "astronomic" amount of 150 billion rubles.[13] (The Soviet Union's GDP in 1989 was estimated at around 900 billion rubles.)[14] All that the new authorities could do was reduce the average length of construction to eight and a half years.[15]

There were three times more buildings in various degrees of completion than could be supplied with materials necessary to finish the jobs.[16]

Jobs were considered completed, production quotas fulfilled, salaries paid, and taxes levied on the total physical volume of production (the *val*) regardless of whether anything was produced, sold, or utilized in any way.[17] A car may fall apart just off the assembly line, complained a leading economics essayist, Anatoly Strelyaniy, but the plan, "subjugated to the mindless *val*," dictated that "the labor that went into its production had to be remunerated by the state."[18] That same plan assigned far greater value to digging foundation pits, pouring concrete into foundations, and erecting walls than to performing the rest of the jobs that would make buildings usable. Accordingly, directed by myriad ministries and "administrations" from the "center" in Moscow, republics, and provinces, construction crews dug the pits, put down foundations, built walls—and moved on to start another site.[19]

Added to the "pyramids" was another pursuit of ancient civilizations: canal-digging. This was performed by the glasnost essayists' bête noir, the Ministry of Water Industry, or the *Minvodkhoz*. For this seemingly unstoppable juggernaut, which employed 2 million people, the "plan" (and medals and bonuses for the "plan's" fulfillment) was calculated in the kilometers of canals dug and the areas "meliorated" (that is, supposedly reclaimed or improved by irrigation). Between 1968 and 1988, the *Minvodkhoz* was said to have spent 130 billion rubles on the "land reclamation" without any increase in harvests in the "reclaimed" soil.[20] For every ruble invested in the "melioration," the return, on average, was 30 kopecks.[21] Just the numbers that were made public (no one doubted that they covered only part of the total) showed that the state had "written off" 3,500,000 hectares (8,650,000 acres) of the "meliorated" lands. In the summer of 1988 the government condemned another million hectares of "drained" or "watered" lands as no longer suitable for agriculture.[22] Yet the annual budget of the ministry, its work now declared "mostly harmful or, at best, useless," continued to amount to between 10 and 12 billion rubles.[23]

Still, the most morally damaging aspect of the Soviet economy was not these spectacular feats of profligacy, but rather the daily acts of negligence and waste at millions of workplaces, in factories and on farms, in fields and orchards. Much of the squandering stemmed from the production quotas in the "plan" dictating that every enterprise and every worker do what was prescribed—and nothing else. A complex industrial economy was subdivided into millions of semi-feudal subplots, rigidly planned by the "center" and separated from others by the administrative moats and stockades, which no one was allowed (or had any incentive) to bridge or overcome.

A Crimean kolkhoz attempted to make an "unplanned product" by milling into flour the grain left after the planned quota was delivered to the state. They made bread with it and sold it in a nearby town. And what gorgeous loaves they were reported to be: tall and golden, the color of "a summer sunset!"[24] Yet almost immediately, the chairman was upbraided by the Ministry of Agriculture and told to "stay within the boundaries of the plan." "We will never count the grain expended on bread toward your quota!" he was told. "You are trying to moonlight, we know."[25] Henceforth the bread sold in the town was again "centrally distributed" and reverted to the color of the loaves everywhere else in the country: "gray, the color of dirty trucks and roofing slates," in the words of a leading essayist Yuri Chernichenko—"the color of [state] monopoly."[26]

Far more than good bread was lost with the excavation of iron ore in open pits. To get to the iron, the bulldozers turned up millions of tons of sand, gravel, clay, and limestone. But there was nothing in the ore-diggers' plan about these "unrelated" products, and they were left unutilized.[27] Similarly, factories were to ship as much of their production speedily and paid fines for holding up freight cars. So when there were "unrelated" goods or raw materials left in the cars from the previous jobs—sometimes "100–200 kilos, sometimes 2–3 tons of valuable products"—they were discarded as trash.[28]

Russia's unique treasure, its forests, were found to be monstrously wasted. Unable to process or transport all the tens of thousands of logs cut down every day in the fulfillment of the "plan" quotas, local logging administrations (lespromkhozy) were worried at least as much about covering up the waste as they were about the production. Precious wood was buried in ravines, dug just for that purpose, or burned in "giant crematoria, which stayed ablaze for years."[29] For kilometers around the logging sites, wood was found lying everywhere: on the ground; protruding in half-rotten stacks of pine out of swamps; lashed together into rafts and piles, clogging small taiga rivers like beaver dams; or arising from Lake Baikal like ghost forests.[30] At just one logging site, in the Republic of Komi in the Russian northwest, 250,000 cubic meters (8.8 million cubic feet) of wood were destroyed every year.[31] Duplicated or exceeded at thousands of other *lespromkhozy,* this despoilment helped explain the perennial shortage of paper in the country with the world's largest forests.[*]

One of the biggest outrages was caused by the disclosure of the loss of millions of tons of fruit and vegetables in a country where in many northern regions—some the size of a European country or two—fresh tomatoes, cauliflower, or grapes were a rarity. For instance, fruit and vegetables that were to be shipped out of the Soviet Socialist Republic of Moldavia perished in the ground, on the trees, or on the vine as the trucks waited in endless lines to be unloaded at the side of railroads. According to a Moldavian writer, the produce was stored "in enormous piles" near railroads, where "everything spoiled" and where corn and sunflower tended to "self-ignite"[32] from heat and gases. Still, overflowing with grapes, tomatoes, corn, and peppers, Moldavian collective farms were not allowed any "freelancing" in attempting to ship their produce north and east on their own.[33] Anything outside the "export plan" had to be consumed inside the republic, where up to half of the harvest was fed to farm animals or perished.[34]

Such fruit and vegetables from Moldavia and other southern republics that did make it to giant holding depots (*bazy*) were far from certain to reach stores and customers. Tons and tons were to rot away, in part because of the primitive conditions of storage but also because those who worked at the depots, "from directors to the rank and file," were not interested in preserving the produce: the more that was legally "written

---

[*] There were other reasons as well. The minister of Wood-Processing and Paper-Making Industries was now permitted to say publicly that the equipment, some of it 60 years old, allowed his workers to turn into paper no more than 12 percent of the cut wood, compared to 60–70 percent in other countries. And so, from 1,000 cubic meters of wood, Canada made 85 tons of paper and carton, Sweden, 129 tons, the U.S., 137 tons, Finland, 164 tons, and the Soviet Union, 27 tons. With 0.8 hectares of forest per capita, the United States produced 143 kilos of paper per inhabitant; the Soviet Union, with 3 hectares, made 22 kilos. (Lev Gudkov and Boris Dubin, "Literaturnaya kul'tura: protsess i ratsion" [The literary culture: the process and the allotment], *Druzhba narodov* 2, February 1988: 173; and N. Zyat'kov, "Laboratoriya perestroika" [The laboratory of perestroika], *Argumenty i fakty,* January 28–February 2, 1990: 7.)

off" within the "spoilage" quota, the more they could take home, sell, or give as bribes by taking away the choicest stuff and sending rotting apples and tomatoes to stores.[35] Such in-kind "bonuses" were winked at by the authorities as compensation for the miserable salaries of the *bazy* workers—as was similar commerce by salesclerks and by those working in the meat- and milk-processing plants.

Every fall, tens of thousands of city dwellers—workers and college students, engineers and surgeons, lawyers and art critics—were dispatched, sometimes for several weeks, to the surrounding kolkhoz fields to dig up potatoes. Still, an estimated 60–70 percent of the potatoes were left in the ground, snowed over, and plowed under and buried the next spring.[36] Altogether, in just three months of 1988, nearly 800,000 tons of unharvested potatoes, fruits, and vegetables "rotted away."[37] Around 20 percent of the annual grain yield was lost every year (left in the fields, spilled by trucks on the way to the elevators, rotted in uncovered heaps under rain and snow)—about the same amount (30 million tons) that the Soviet Union bought abroad in 1987.[38]

Something is always in short supply in the country, two prominent economists and economics historians wrote in May 1988: from children's soap to railroad tickets.[39] Apart from the miracle of reading these words in a Soviet magazine, the fact itself was hardly a surprise to any living Russian: shortages were as natural a part of their gess as breathing. What Vladimir Popov and Nikolai Shmelev wrote afterward was bound to startle, however, because they no longer blamed the *defitsit* on the usual suspects: "single inefficiencies," incompetence of "some bureaucrats," or even obsolete technology or thievery. The "persistency of the deficit," the scholars continued, made one look for some sort of economic "law."[40] And they found it in

> the system of planning that has taken root in our country—the system which in its current form not only does not exclude shortages but in fact inevitably produces them, makes them chronic and impossible to eradicate. Under the current mechanism of planning, the deficit is not an exception but the rule: it is a naturally reproduced phenomenon, an integral part of the economic system.[41]

The epitome of the "economy of chronic shortages"[42] was lines. "Exhausting and senseless," they were estimated to cost the Soviet Union 65 billion man-hours annually—the equivalent of a year's worth of work-time of 31 million people.[43]* The shortages and administrative distribu-

---

* Lines could last for hours or even days (and nights). One of them, for pantyhose, was spotted by the economists and essayists Vladimir Popov and Nikolay Shmelyov in early spring 1987 outside the "Goods for Women" supermarket in Moscow, on the corner of Petrovka and Kuznetsky Most streets, an easy fifteen-minute walk to the Kremlin. The "thick" line ran from the supermarket's door up Petrovka Street for about 50 meters. A policeman with a bullhorn was supervising, periodically asking the women to stay on the sidewalk and not impede the traffic. (Popov and Shmelyov, op. cit., 158.)

A far more complex and fraught, but also quite typical, arrangement was reported by a *Komsomol'skaya pravda* correspondent from the industrial city of Kursk, a provincial capital 450 kilometers (280 miles) south of Moscow in February 1990:

A phone call from a friend threw me into a tizzy.

"I have signed us up for Italian boots," she said. "Come for a roll call [*pereklichka*] at 8 p.m. to the 'House of Footware.'"

Boots! To wear in the fall. On a high heel. From a good leather! Every woman's dream!

. . . Twice before my friend and I had tried to enter long lines. . . . The first one was for a cosmetic set [*nabor*] . . . for 200 rubles. Tempting but, alas, not for our pocketbooks. The other time we hoped to buy cardigans [*dzhempery*]. The crowd went berserk and a wimpy policeman had to hide behind the counter as the big guys in the crowd attempted to take the counter by storm. We heard a woman's cry: "Robbery!" and we left.

This time around, everything promised to be totally different: a presale sign-up is the greatest achievement of Russian thought as far as trade in hard-to-find goods is concerned. One signed up, received and remembered one's number, came to name check—and, presto, one was the happy owner of a thing one had really wanted.

A crowd was milling in the darkness, near the black entrance to the store. I heard several people exclaim: "Where is the list?" Somebody replied: "It is being retyped." The leaders explained the rules:

—We will take attendance now, and then again in the middle of the night.

—Can't we do it in the morning?—I asked timidly.—So that we don't have to endure [lining up at night]?

tion of goods and services resulted also in a "multibillion"-ruble black market.[44] But the worst damage, in the estimation of the glasnost moralists, as usual, was to the souls: those who produced the country's wealth were daily humiliated, "debased" by those appointed to distribute it, from bureaucrats to salesclerks.[45]

What leading economist and Gorbachev advisor Leonid Abalkin in July 1987 called the "chronic shortages of everything"—modern machinery, metal, energy, food, consumer goods—coexisted with absolutely unnecessary work.[46] "Work collectives," even entire industries, were reported to make that for which there was no demand, that which "nobody wants."[47] The "light" (consumer goods) industry manufactured millions of pairs of shoes that even the unspoiled Soviet consumer refused to buy because of their ugliness and discomfort. In fall 1987, there were 2.5

I merited only a condescending look. And I understood: only the strongest deserve to win. The rule was this: one could add another person to the list but roll calls must be attended by everyone in person.

"We are 360th," said the girlfriend.—Behind the Krukovs couple.

Suddenly everyone's attention was drawn to an elderly man in a military-style jacket.

—Comrades!— he said loudly and portentously. Everything will be in perfect order tomorrow. I have personally spoken to the head of the police district, and he promised to send a ten-man detachment to keep order.

—And where is your list?—people asked him suspiciously.

—I don't know, but your list will follow the one that comes after ours.

—And when did you sign up?

—Back in January.

The crowd buzzed alarmingly. Suddenly people formed a line:

—We shall stand here until the store opens!

It was getting colder. The girlfriend and I looked at each other and went home.

That night I dreamed about boots. Black they were, indeed, with a heel, and made of first-rate leather!

Next morning, passing the store on a bus on the way to work, the girlfriend saw a crowd of hundreds of people standing outside shoulder to shoulder. Around noon I walked past the store myself. I saw the fortunate souls tearing their way through the tense crowd, clutching the precious box to their bosoms. I saw two women tearing each other's hair out.

(T. Belaya, "Moya ital'yanskaya mechta . . ." [My Italian dream], Komsomol'skaya pravda, February 13, 1990: 2.)

billion rubles' worth of unsold goods in the depots of the Ministry of Light Industry, a million square meters (almost 11 million square feet) of fabrics among them.[48] Far costlier still was the overproduction (or importation for gold or hard currency) of machine tools: three times more were made or bought than could be used. (The Soviet Union produced more machine tools than the United States, Japan, and West Germany combined.)[49]

Many machines, including some of the most sophisticated, were destined to "rust out" or be "torn apart" for spare parts because there were not enough skilled workers.[50] In a letter to a major newspaper, a "lathes adjuster" from Moscow reported that up to 40 percent of lathes during his shift were idle because there were not enough workers to operate them.[51] The average for the entire economy was 60–63 workers for 100 lathes.[52]

Altogether, there were 700,000 industrial workplaces that could not be filled because of the shortage of skilled labor.[53] By 1989 uninstalled industrial equipment was priced at over 14 billion rubles, and yet, year after year, "new plants were built, for which, everyone knew, no workers could be found."[54]

The mismatch was especially glaring in the countryside. While no more than 470,000 combines (harvesters) were needed, by the second half of the 1980s there were 1 million of them—14–16 times their number in the United States, where per capita yields of grain were two and half times higher (1,313 kilos vs. 490 kilos) than in the Soviet Union.[55] Costing several million rubles each, harvesters were sold to collective farms at less than half price—and still three in ten were turned down because kolkhozes and sovkhozes did not know what to do with the machines they already had.[56] Yet the production of the giant "Don" harvester continued unabated and a huge tractor plant was being built in Elabuga on the Volga.[57]

The Soviet countryside also was flooded with 2.8 million tractors, "hundreds of thousands" of which "had nothing to do" as drivers could be found for only 452,000 tractors and combines[58] In addition, 250,000 tractors were estimated to be broken on any given day.[59] Since their repair often cost more than a new machine sold by the state at a huge discount, thousands of rusting hulks, stripped for parts by rural mechanics, dotted the Russian countryside.[60] Like millions of other produced but never-used items, the superfluous tractors and combines were duly recorded as part of the country's GDP.[61]

By 1989 the cost of the "redundant material items" (that is, things made but not utilized) reached an estimated 470 billion rubles, or about half of the national economy.[62]

Thousands of plants and factories were loss-making along with almost every fourth collective farm (6,500 kolkhozes out of 26,000, often for decades), and up to 90 billion rubles were estimated to be spent every year to subsidize them.[63] The collective farms' debt alone approached 140 billion rubles.[64]

Day after day, the labor of myriad men and women was wasted as well. According to secret sociological surveys conducted in the early 1980s and now made public, "barely one-third" of the Soviet industrial or agricultural workers labored conscientiously, "at full force" (*v polnuyu silu*).[65] "We pay ten people so that they can do the job of five," wrote a top economist.[66] Gorbachev's advisor Abel Aganbegyan estimated that "millions" received wages "not commensurate" with their "labor contributions"—often "for doing nothing at all."[67] True, their salaries were often "miserable," but then many workplaces, too, were a "lazybones' paradise" (*ne bey lezhachego*).[68] When offered a hypothetical opportunity of being able freely to hire, employ, and fire their workers and pay them what they thought they were worth, agricultural managers in the Altai region of Siberia estimated that 15–20 percent of the current workforce would become "superfluous."[69] In the Soviet Union as a whole, up one-fourth of the labor force was said to be "excessive at their current place of work."[70] (In 1987 that meant 35.5 million people.)[71] The "administrative apparatus," which employed between 17 and 18 million people, including 1.5 million personal drivers, was singled out for the bitterest criticism.[72]

Salaries barely, if at all, rewarded productivity, skill, and conscientiousness. In a profitable kolkhoz in the Vladimir province workers earned only 10 rubles a month more than their neighbors in a perennially loss-making collective farm.[73] The administrators, concluded prominent essayist Gennady Lisichkin, seemed to prefer the badly run collective farms and those who "would not or could not" work over those who would and could.[74] The former were consistently "fed" at the expense of the latter.[75]

Again, this was not only, perhaps not even so much, an economic problem as it was a moral one. Those who received subsidies, Lisichkin continued, "quickly became unaccustomed to standing on their own feet," leaning more and more on those "who pulled the wagon."[76] The latter, meanwhile, were said to be "dreaming of equality"—not the equality of earnings but the "equality of labor," in which those who worked harder and produced more would be paid better than those who did not.[77]

Designed for "equality in distribution," wrote economist Larisa Piyasheva, the Soviet economic system, indeed, had "had some remarkable successes": a surgeon earned as much as a supermarket salesclerk, and theft, bribe-taking, parasitism, and dependency became routine.[78] If the current economic system is allowed to continue, wrote essayist Mikhail Antonov, the Soviet people will "degrade completely."[79]

The wasted labor was not a surmise. Several "experiments" in the 1970s—limited in scope and quickly suppressed at the time but now remembered hopefully—had established beyond doubt the outrageous waste of workers' time and the state's money. Conceived and managed by the sovkhoz "bookkeeper-economist" Ivan Khudenko, autonomous work teams (*brigady* and *zven'ya*) in a Kazakhstan sovkhoz were entirely responsible for their part of production, and their salaries, no longer set by the plan, depended on the results of their work. Production costs were reduced by a factor of seven, the profit per worker also grew sevenfold, and earnings were four times what they had been.[80] The venture, whose initiator was arrested for "embezzlement" and died in a labor camp in 1974, was now said to show that Soviet agriculture could increase its output fourfold while employing only 5 million people instead of nearly 28 million.[81]

In another soon-discontinued experiment at a clothes factory in the Black Sea resort of Sochi, two brothers organized an "experimental work team," whose orders were determined not by the plan but by contracts with stores and customers. The factory management was reportedly as "stunned" by the growth in output as they were by the cheapness of production. The team's profits were fifteen times that of the factory's "norm." Asked about their secret, the brothers explained: "There are over a thousand workers at our factory, but the same output could be achieved with fifty."[82] (When, under Gorbachev, such experiments could be carried out with impunity, Belarusian Railways alone laid off 11,000 workers with no adverse effect on its operations.)[83]

At least 200,000 prices were set every year by the State Committee for Prices (the *Goskomtsen*): from iron ore and pulp, to pencils and tomatoes, trousers and television sets. Virtually all food products were sold for what, on average, was half of the production cost.[84] In a country tormented by the shortages of meat, the prices at which the state bought it from the kolkzhozy and sovkhozy were so low that raising cattle brought the producers "nothing but losses" and they would have "gladly slaughtered" all of their herds a long time ago had it not been for the overseers and enforcers from the local party committees.[85] Half of the money the Soviet state raised through its single largest source of internal revenue (the so-called turnover tax, which was levied against the total monetary value of the goods produced) was spent on food subsidies—up to 50 billion rubles a year.[86]

While some of the prices choked incentives by being ridiculously low, others were inflated to make unimaginable luxuries of the normal needs of millions in the highly educated modern workforce. With the average salary in 1986–87 around 100–120 rubles, a pair of "decent" men's shoes cost 50 rubles, a color television, 700 rubles, and a car, 8,000 rubles.[87]

But then whether subsidized or inflated, prices (and money in general) did not mean much because of the shortages of virtually everything of quality. Everyone knew, wrote a prominent commentator on the country's economy, that "our money is not money."[88] A leading economist called the ruble "helpless"; another, Gorbachev's advisor Nikolai Petrakov, a "binky" (*pustyshka*).[89]

Unlike "normal" currencies, the value of the ruble, that is, its convertibility into goods and services, depended on where on the political hierarchy its carrier found himself.[*] As a journalist put it, "one ruble was not equal to another."[90] On the exalted end of the spectrum was the "foreign currency," or *invalyutniy*, ruble, which, in the form of "certificates"

---

[*] After extensive surveys, the Soviet Union's leading labor sociologist and public opinion expert Tatiana Zaslavskaya named the "equal purchasing power of the ruble" among the top conditions of the earnings "according to one's labor." (Tatiana Zaslavskaya, "Chelovecheskiy faktor razvitiya ekonomiki i sotsial'naya spravedlivost'" [The human factor in the development of economy and social justice], *Kommunist* 13, 1986: 69.)

of different colors, allowed the carrier to taste opulence in stores guarded, discretely but constantly, by the secret police: blue jeans, American cigarettes, Coca-Cola, the hard Finnish salami, "servilat," ballpoint pens, or imported toilet bowls. The "ordinary" (or, as they soon began to be called, "wooden") ruble, in which tens of millions were paid their salaries, entitled them to queue, often for hours and with uncertain results, for meat, eggs, milk, or butter or to shop at "farmers' markets" in the cities that had them—an extravagance that only a few could normally afford. When a group of skillful counterfeiters was arrested in Lenin's birthplace of Ulyanovsk, an *Ogonyok* reporter was very keen to learn what kind of denominations they made: twenty-five rubles? fifty? one hundred? No, he was told, the crooks dealt in ration coupons for meat and butter.[91]

In between the open sesame of the "certificates" and the "wooden" rubles was the currency of those who worked at the right places. The manager of a railway station in one of Russia's larger cities was reminded of this ruble's existence when he was offered a job at the district executive committee (*ispolkom*). Of course, the district party secretary told him, the salary would be about the same but "the *ispolkom* ruble is heavier." "How so?" asked the naïve railway man. "Oh, like you don't know . . ." was the answer.[92] "We do indeed!" fulminated the reporter who publicized the incident. A manager or worker of a large enterprise, where there were "advance orders," had "free access to sausage, meat, and butter" and thus could "cash in" his ruble in a way that was "entirely different than, say, a teacher or a medical doctor, who could buy these same victuals without standing in line only at a farmer's market, at exorbitant prices."[93]

Access to anything of quality was determined not so much by money as by closeness to power in its myriad incarnations—or to where such quality goods were made or distributed. As an essayist put it, when someone, for the same money, could not buy something available to a fellow citizen, they were paid not just for their labor but for something else.[94]

People could live strikingly differently while earning the same salaries. Meeting one another, they asked, "What's your salary?" much less frequently than, "Where do you work and what's the supply situation there?"[95] Finding a place where "all was available" through a "special" (that is, closed to others) store, a tailoring shop (*atel'e*), or a "buffet" (cafeteria) with good sausages, fruits, and cheese was a national obsession.[96] Everyone knew very well what damages such practice does to their consciousness, a journalist concluded ruefully.[97] "Money was not the universal equivalent of labor," concluded Academician Yuri Ryzhov. As a result, "labor was not a guarantee of well-being."[98]

With one in two rubles printed between 1971 and 1985 "unsupported" by goods or services,[99] the Soviet Union was a largely a premonetary economy. Barter, or "natural exchange of anything in short supply," was a far more reliable means of obtaining what one needed than money.[100] To receive from other enterprises resources necessary to fulfill "plan" quotas, managers had to engage in all manner of deals and trades in kind, and the "gray" market for goods and services (and the corruption it spawned) was "almost legal."[101]

Such was what another of Gorbachev's economic advisors, Nikolai Petrakov, called "a surreal economy, ten times stranger" than the paintings by Salvador Dali: incentives for hard work came not so much in high salaries but in sausages and good cuts of smoked meats.[102] It was more prestigious to be a butcher than a surgeon.

When the state wanted kolkhozes and sovkhozes to grow more buckwheat, the authorities raised the purchasing prices several times, but the acreage continued to drop since the agricultural managers "reasonably" concluded that the extra money could not buy them anything that they needed.[103] The situation was reversed only when for every 100 kilos of buckwheat, the farms were bartered 100 kilos of mixed fodder (*kombikorm*) or grain fodder (*zernofurazh*) for the cattle.[104]

Industrial enterprises, scientific research institutes, and hospitals grew (or were mightily "encouraged" to grow) vegetables and raised chickens, cattle, and pigs for meat and eggs. In 1987, three in four enterprises under the Ministry of Non-Ferrous Metals had "auxiliary agricultural farms," in which they grew food for workers and raised cattle for beef and milk.[105] (The Presidium of the Supreme Soviet rebuked the ministry for the remaining quarter of enterprises that had neglected this important work). Those who drilled for and pumped oil and gas in the Soviet Union's West Siberian "Eldorado," earning the country "billions of dollars" and themselves often earning astronomic monthly salaries of 800 or even 1,000 rubles—they, too, with some luck, grew their own potatoes, wrote a leading essayist Yuri Chernichenko.[106]* "The feeding of the population is an extracurricular activity of that same population, including of those living next to the Arctic Circle," he continued sardonically. "This is how the planned economy humiliates the people."[107]

Meanwhile, those whose job it was to grow vegetables, tend to cattle, and milk cows bartered their produce for manufactured goods. In an Altai kolkhoz, for instance, the *obrok* (a word from the serfdom era, meaning "rent in kind") for a gasoline chain saw was 150 pounds of meat delivered to the state.[108] The "price" of a coupon that entitled the bearer to buy a carpet was 2,000 liters of milk—again, from the owner's, not the kolkhoz's, cow.[109] In the Altai story, the latter transaction failed because a salesclerk in charge of carpets insisted that the bearer was 500 liters short. "What do you mean short?!" cried out the farmer. "Can't you see?! I have it written right here!" The woman behind the counter yawned and turned away.[110]

* "Never mind the oil or the gas," Chernichenko wrote. "What sort of food can a Siberian [oilman or a gas man] get from them? None. And what feeds him? Taiga. You clear six *sotka*'s [600 square meters, or 0.15 acre], bring sand and peat, buy manure, get seeds—and by September, if you know what you are doing, you'll be eating your own potatoes." (Yuri Chernicheko, "Zhdat' uzhe pozdno" [It is already too late to wait], *Ogonyok* 23, 1989: 4.)

CHAPTER ELEVEN

The "Disintegration of Souls"

HOMO SOVIETICUS

The most terrifying for the people is not the economic
devastation, but the disintegration of souls, the loss of the need
to be better, purer, nobler, to have one's conscience test one's
actions.
—Mikhail Antonov, "Tak chto zhe s nami proiskhodit?" (What
really is happening to us?), *Oktyabr'*, August 1987: 56

The main crime of the Stalinist regime is the forging of a new
kind of man. He was raised in the atmosphere of lies, treachery,
slavish devotion to the leader. He was brought up in a society in
which the meaning of many concepts was shifted and took an
opposite meaning: white became black, honor and nobility were
faults, and informing on neighbors civic duty.
—Stanislav Govorukhin, "Voyna s prestupnost'yu" (The war on
crime), *Sovetskaya kul'tura*, July 29, 1989: 6

What have we turned into? Will normal people understand what
caused us to tremble with fear? And how far [lower] can we go? . . .
One thing is clear: the country is at a dead end. Here is what they
have done to the people: nothing to eat, thievery and depravity are
everywhere, and nobody knows how to fight this, where to look for
a way out.

—Fyodor Abramov, "And people are waiting and waiting for changes: From diaries and working notes" (November 1969, October 1979, November 1981), *Izvestia,* February 3, 1990: 3

For decades the state has conducted a most immoral internal policy—a policy of deception and violence. Today it is people that are bearers of this immorality. There are many of them but they are a consequence of the many years of the immoral totalitarian state. It was cruel—and they have become cruel. It recognized only the cult of brute force and was unscrupulous in the means of dealing with its own citizens—and they also have become unscrupulous.
—Alexander Shindel, "Svidetel'" (A witness), *Znamya,* September 1987: 217

Everything starts here—all our troubles, all our weaknesses. And before we try to change the particulars . . . let's find out at what point in our lives bribery, thievery, lies, humiliation of the powerless, and servility toward the powers that be have become more than just a deviation from the norm.
—Maya Ganina, "Bez obol'shcheniy prezhnikh dney" (Without the delusions of bygone days), *Literaturnaya gazeta,* January 13, 1988: 11

IN THE END, AS WITH ALL other aspects of the national quest for self-knowledge, the ultimate and most urgent concern was not the economy itself but rather what it did to the men and women who worked in it: their ideas, their views of themselves, their conscience—their "souls." Surrounded by waste and negligence, poverty and neglect, arbitrariness and incompetence of all-powerful bureaucracies implementing myriad irrational laws and regulations, men and women were found to have lost, or to be about to lose, much of what was needed to make their country free and prosperous.

The economy in which wasting resources and "lowering quality" was profitable[1] spawned and nourished *Homo Sovieticus,* whose acquaintance we made in chapter 2. Max Weber might have classified him as yet another of his "ideal" types: a sociological or philosophical category, a phenomenon rather than a real person.[2]

Homo Sovieticus became both a symbol of the spiritual crisis and its epitome. Before glasnost, the exiled dissident Alexander Zinoviev had devoted an entire book, published abroad, to the subject.[3] It never reached the Soviet reader, of course, but its subject now could be found in hundreds of newspaper and magazine pages.

Homo Sovieticus had "forgotten" what it meant to be responsible for the results of his labor.[4] The daily ruination of his kolkhoz, or factory, where more was consumed and paid in salaries than produced, did not trouble him. He may be bored out of his mind, "suffocating from idleness," but he would not work hard—and he resented others who did.[5] With "earning" far less important to the betterment of one's living than the ability to "extract" (*dobyvat'*) through connections or by political preferment,[6] the prospect of higher pay for better, harder work appealed to few. "Why would they want to?" a reporter wrote after observing a meeting of kolkhoz employees. "A tractor driver profits from his machine being in disrepair. He'd come, fool around with a bolt for a few minutes, and then go back home, all the while being paid."[7]

Homo Sovieticus was envious of his neighbor who managed to earn more: "better that my cow dies than that my neighbor has two." The squalor of the Soviet village, concluded a leading economic essayist, was "retribution" for over five decades of "violating common sense, violating everything that urges man to a normal, conscientious labor."[8]

"Utterly dependent" on the orders from above, buckling under the weight of the innumerable "forbiddens" (*nel'zyas*), people had grown mistrustful of laws and lawfulness. Filled with the "ardent" desire to escape state-imposed discipline,[9] *Homo Sovieticus* was a habitual, almost unconscious lawbreaker, forced to live by dodging (*lovchit'*): doctoring work records and accounts or "working on the side" (*levachit'*), instead of doing the job for which he was paid.[10] "Treachery" was in the blood of *Homo Sovieticus,* concluded documentary filmmaker Govorukhin, and "mistrust" was always in his eyes.[11] The "type" was said to be forever on the lookout for a chance to "grab his piece," to accept a bribe, to flatter his superiors in the crudest way, and to meet the suffering of others with "absolute indifference."[12]

Not just truck drivers, or salesclerks, or waiters—all of whom had come to embody this modus operandi in the Soviet lore—but "entire work collectives" daily deceived their superiors and violated laws.[13] Lied to constantly, one had to become a skillful and experienced liar oneself in order to cover the shoddiness of one's work. As a result, an engineer's project, a statistician's numbers, or a scientist's expertise could no longer be trusted.[14]

Homo Sovieticus also was an almost compulsive thief, who felt it rightful, even righteous, to steal from his place of work.[15] Pilfering was nothing to be ashamed of, lamented a leading economic essayist, so long as one "filched" (*pryot*) from the state.[16] It was not even called "thievery," and the pilferer was no longer a "thief": a special term was invented for him, *nesun* ("one who carries").[17] Two popular sayings illustrated the general rule: "Tell me where you work and I will tell you what is in your bag when you are going home," and "When you do not steal from the state, you are stealing from your family." In a 1986 national survey almost half of Soviet plants and factories were found to inflate their production numbers, incur illegal expenses, and suffer from systematic theft.[18]

After an especially tough winter of shortages, the head of a regional *obshchepit*, or public caterer, called a meeting of the managers of workers' canteens and pleaded with them not to steal meat to sell privately or give as bribes for twenty days—just for twenty days until the hoped-for shipment was to arrive from some central depot: "When the fowl and the pork come back, you will be able to go back to the old practice, if you cannot operate otherwise. But in this twenty days, please don't: this is my personal request to you."[19]

Homo Sovieticus disliked, often hated, work, any work. Entrepreneurship, daring, inventiveness had been either "destroyed physically" with their bearers or "morally suppressed" long ago.[20] We have lost respect for our work, wrote a leading Russian actor Kirill Lavrov.[21] The universal "lack of the working form" (*rastrenirovannost'*), shoddiness, negligence, and laziness were "a national bane."[22] The *Homo Sovieticus* had all but extirpated the *Homo faber*. The honest, conscientious laborer was looked at as something shameful, or at least as something akin to being "God's fool" (*yurodiviy*).[23] We amaze the world by our incredible carelessness, our inability to work well, wrote political philosopher Alexander Tsypko.[24] The Soviet people had "unlearned" how to work and, for the country to rebound, had to be replaced with, or miraculously turned into, "millions of completely different" workers: the ones who would "respect the creative master in themselves, who would appreciate honest, quality work."[25]

Homo Sovieticus was a net destroyer of value, "making bad things from good materials, turning the worthy into the worthless."[26] A sovkhoz milkmaid refused to feed her hungry cows, who were lowing loudly: "I am paid 370 rubles to get to the farm and to milk," she explained. "And that's enough for me. To add feeding to this—well, why should I?"[27]

Walking alongside a field, two retired military officers and World War II veterans saw a tractor about to plough over a field with unharvested vegetables still in it. The men began to shout to the driver to stop, but to no avail. Then, limping from the wounds and leaning heavily on a walking stick, one of them ran to stand in the tractor's path. Within a meter of the man, the tractor stopped. "Get off the field, Pops, or I will run you over," the young driver shouted. "What are you doing, you son of a bitch?!" responded the veteran. "Don't you see that the field has not been harvested?!" "It's you who thinks that it hasn't," the driver replied, "but it has been reported as harvested and ploughed as well." "All right, I understand that your bosses need to report lies but what about your conscience of a working man? Don't you see that you are destroying the labor of others?" "Are you kidding?" the driver laughed. "Don't you know that we are in the era of universal electrification? Everything is as far as a light bulb for everyone."[28] ("As far as a light bulb," or *do lampochki,* was popular slang for not giving a damn.)

"Where everything is *ours,* nothing is *mine,* nothing for which your heart aches," wrote Anatoly Anan'ev, editor of *Oktyabr'.* So what if the plow is at the wrong depth, upturning and spoiling the fertile top layer of soil? So what if on the way to the elevator grain spills from the truck onto the road? A pood (sixteen kilos) more, a pood less and, besides, tons of grain already rot there, so what's the difference? Such reasoning, Anan'ev concluded, has become part of our conscience, and, for many, their "life's platform."[29]

A search for the roots of the people's "moral degradation,"[30] epitomized by *Homo Sovieticus,* turned up a badly eroded dignity as the trait most responsible for the calamity. Far from being a personal matter, an *Ogonyok* writer averred, dignity was like the air one breathed: it was impossible to deprive one person of it without subtracting from the amount of air available to all.[31] The "diminution of individual dignity" was found responsible for a lowering of the "moral level of the entire society,"[32] for the "abyss of spiritual poverty, oppression, and humiliation" into which the country was said to have descended.[33]

"Suddenly I understood what I lack to be able to call myself a human being," a Moscow University student wrote in *Ogonyok* in April 1988. "I understood that I lacked dignity, that it was very easy to humiliate me."[34] The Soviet people had been "humiliated" by decades of "depressing" living in shabby hostels (*obshchezhitiya*) and communal apartments, noted writer Daniil Granin. By the rudeness of the authorities. By shortages and the endless lines they engendered, for flour and for boots; to be seen by a doctor in a clinic or to place a child in kindergarten; to see any bureaucrat, no matter how small; for an apartment of one's own. "Lines, lines, and lines again—frenzied and hopeless!"[35]

Generations had "choked on wariness, on the constant expectation of deception and trickery," surmised *Literaturnaya gazeta* essayist Maya Ganina.[36] The "gene" of dignity (and the one of duty) had been weakened to the point of disappearance, leaving behind only "sterile fatigue and lazy indifference."[37]

Amid what the writer Yuri Nagibin described as "total disorder [*sploshnoy razval*], do-nothingness [*bezdel'nichestvo*], and lies,"[38] and "enslaved" by the absurdity of the existence over which they had no control whatsoever, as the philosopher Tsypko put it,[39] people sought refuge in alcohol. Already quoted in chapter 1, Prime Minster Nikolai Ryzhkov was right: the country was indeed "drinking itself into the ground."[40] Among the single largest sources of government revenue (vodka contributed 12–13 percent of the Soviet Union's budget),[41] vodka played "a colossal economic role," Nagibin wrote: while destroying the workers physically and mentally, it also paid much of their salaries.[42] Four and a half million alcoholics were registered by the police, but their overall number was estimated at between 18 and 22 million.[43]

The Russian countryside was especially hard-hit. Moving in 1988 from a city to a village in the Gorky (now Nizhny Novgorod) province in central Russia, a worker found a "moral nightmare." After twenty-three years of work, he told public opinion pollsters, I thought I had seen everything, but "I could not have imagined that in the center of the European part of our country, there could be a sovkhoz like ours. Drunkenness has become completely routine."[44] When asked in the first national sociological surveys in 1988 and 1989 to name the "causes of today's problems," drunkenness (grouped with the social ills of corruption, thievery, and speculation) was blamed by more respondents (between 57 and 59 percent) than any other economic, political, or social problem.[45]

Abortions were pandemic. With about 6 percent of world's population, the Soviet Union accounted for almost one-quarter of all recorded abortions: 8 million a year, more than in any other country.[46] (This number did not include "unregistered" abortions, performed in the USSR outside hospitals and estimated to amount to as much as 50–80 percent of the in-hospital ones.)[47] The abortion incidence in the USSR was 6–10 times higher than in developed countries and 2–4 times higher than in the European socialist countries.[48] For every 100 women between the ages of fifteen and twenty, there were 30 abortions performed. Every fifth Soviet woman of childbearing age had an abortion. An estimated one-third of all obstetrics and gynecology beds in the Soviet hospitals were serving women who were undergoing abortions. Around half of the 60,000 gynecologists and obstetricians in the country were estimated to be doing little else except performing abortions.[49]*

Of all the almost uncountable varieties of humiliation that the regime inflicted on the people, fear was the gravest. In Grossman's *Life and Fate,* an inmate in the Lubyanka prison composed and recited a verse:

> What your shell is made of, dear?
> I once asked a turtle. And was told:
> It's of fear, stored and hardened fear—
> There is nothing stronger in this world![50]

Although loosened since Stalin's death, the "shell" of the inbred fear, rigid and oppressive, was still "second nature," "instilled in our brains forever"—the fear of not saying "yes" on time or of not betraying someone fast enough.[51]

---

* With no more than 10 percent of the amount of needed contraception devices available to Soviet women, abortion was the most common means of contraception. (Andrei Popov, op. cit., 19.)

We are afraid of everything and everyone: of a man in a
uniform, of a phone call from the apartment building manag-
ing office [zhek], a character reference, a sudden knock on the
door. . . . We are afraid to speak out at an employees meeting at
work, to run into the boss in the lobby . . . , afraid to ask the
salesclerk to repeat an item's price, [we] grovel before a girl
behind the glass in a government office, [we] beg to accept food
for a patient in a hospital; we are wary even of a Metro employee when we go down the escalator: what if she says something to us.[52]

Daily reminded of the unbridgeable gap between themselves and
"those who rule and decide and of whom one should be very afraid"
(they were above, while you, "worthless" and "subservient," far below),[53]
the people became instilled with a "slave-like psychology," a "slave's world-
view."[54]

The popular poet Robert Rozhdestvensky mourned this state in
early 1989:

And even as our spaceships fly between the stars,
We still are slaves, slaves.
And like a deep stain, this slavery of ours is impossible to clean
off.[55]

This modern slave was said to hate his fellow citizens who were "different."[56] He believed that force solved everything and was certain of his
right to abuse those below him.[57]

Much of this hate and abuse was learned by millions of men drafted
into the Soviet army, where many of the first-year soldiers were subject
to sadistic hazing and daily torment by the second-year *dedy*. "Officers . . .
deliver fresh recruits to the abuse by older soldiers—the abuse bestial in
its cruelty, uncontrollable and unpunishable," commented a public opinion survey respondent from Moscow. "Desertion and suicide are rampant. Young men return home angry, morally and physically disfigured."[58]

When in July 1988 *Komsomol'skaya pravda* published an account
of a soldier who killed his tormentors after eight months of beatings
and sleep deprivation,[59] the newspaper received 14,247 letters from the
readers. Out of every 1,000 letters, 100 mentioned beatings of first-year

soldiers or "other forms of abuse," 19 contained accounts of mutilations, 8 told of desertions, and 6 of severe psychiatric disorders caused by the torment.[60]

The time came "to sound the tocsin" to arrest, by word and deed, the country's slide into the "torpor of backwardness, corruption, thievery and drunkenness,"[61] the editor Anan'ev declared. A letter to *Komsomol'skaya pravda* was blunter still: "We need to build a new society lest the Russians become a nation of slaves."[62]

PART THREE *КТО ВИНОВАТ?* WHO IS TO BLAME?

We are looking for the sources of our misfortunes. We go from the simpler to the increasingly complicated as we try to understand what has happened to us.
—Alexei Kiva, "Krizis 'zhanra'" (The crisis of the "genre"), *Novy mir,* March 1990: 207

To find an answer to this huge "Why?" hanging over his life and fate and the lives and fates of hundreds of thousands of others . . .
—Varlam Shalamov, "Pervyi chekist" (The first Chekist), in Varlam Shalamov, *Proza, stikhi* (Fiction, poetry), *Novy mir,* June 1988: 125

The decisive question for me is: why has all this become possible?
—Lev Anninskiy, "Monolog byvshego stalintsa" (A mono-logue of a former Stalinist), in Yuri Afanasiev, ed., *Inogo ne dano* (There is no other way), 57

And so: Stalinism. What is it, finally? Where did it come from—this nightmare in a country whose revolution was forever to end exploitation, violence, indignity and was to become the beginning of the kingdom of humanism on Earth?
—G. Vodolazov, "Lenin i Stalin. Filosfsko-sotsiologicheskiy kommentariy k povesti V. Grossmana 'Vsyo techyot'" (Lenin and Stalin: A philosophical and sociological commentary on V. Grossman's novella *Forever Flowing*), in Kh. Kobo, ed., *Osmyslit' kul't Stalina* (To comprehend Stalin's cult), Moscow: Progress, 1989: 142

An economic crisis. A crisis of morality. A crisis of an individual. Who is to blame?
—A. Bystrov, "Prostye lyudi" (Ordinary people),
Komsomol'skaya pravda, January 29, 1989: 4

Why have equality, collectivism, and justice, which were constructed to preclude the so-called commercialism [*torgashestvo*], social stratification, individualism, and injustice, led not to the triumph of universal love but to the barrack-type leveling, everyone's de-individualization [*obezlichivanie*] and the escalation of hatred? . . . Why has the desire to elevate ourselves above "commercialism" . . . brought about our sinking into barbarism?"
—Igor Klyamkin, "Pochemu tak trudno govorit' pravdu" (Why it is so difficult to speak truth), *Novy mir,* February, 1989: 238

I think the roots of Stalinism are to be found in the cardinal errors in the development of our society. These are deep causes—and they are not connected to the peculiarities of Stalin's personality.
—Andrei Sakharov, *Komsomol'skaya pravda*, December 16, 1989: 2

To condemn terror and to erect monuments to its opponents and victims is not enough. Monuments may be destroyed, we may forget whom they were to commemorate. Only analysis and understanding are capable of tearing the mystical veil off totalitarian power and giving us, if not a guarantee, than at least a chance that the past will not come back.
—L. Gozman and A. Etkind, "Kul't vlasti: Struktura totalitarnogo soznaniya" (The cult of power: The structure of totalitarian conscience), in Kh. Kobo, ed., *Osmyslit' kul't Stalina* (To think through Stalin's cult), Moscow: Progress, 1989: 337

CHAPTER TWELVE

The House That Stalin Built

THE MASTER STATE AND ITS POLITICAL ECONOMY

> Authoritarianism, totalitarianism, Stalinism became possible in
> our country because all the sources of an individual's well-being,
> all the means of his existence were in the hands of the state.
> —Alexander Yakovlev, speech at Moscow State University, Febru-
> ary 12, 1990, in Alexander Yakovlev, *Muki prochteniya bytiya* (The
> torments of reading life), Moscow: Novosti, 1991: 100

AS THE FOG OF MYTHOLOGY began to yield the true contours of the
Soviet state, its foundation and key structures and functions, the glasnost
investigators became increasingly certain that an omnipotent and omniscient state—the state that "consumed" the society, "devoured," ab-
sorbed," "crushed" it[1]—had become the sole and unchallenged master of
the country and the people. No matter what the label—"administrative-
bureaucratic system," "barrack socialism," "state socialism," "state-
bureaucratic socialism," a "totalitarian, anti-democratic regime," or simply
"totalitarianism"[2]—that essence and its impact on the society were largely
the same.

"The people who created this state thought it was a means to the realization of their ideal," wrote Grossman. "But it turned out that their
dreams, their ideals were the means for [the construction of] a great and
terrible state. From a servant, the state became a dark sovereign. The

state became the master."[3] Even more than autocracy or totalitarianism, the political regime was a "state-aucracy" (*étakratism*).[4]

It had proved incomparably easier to denounce some of Stalin's crimes in 1956 and again in 1961–64, release the Gulag survivors, and even allow the publication of Solzhenitsyn's *One Day in the Life of Ivan Denisovich* than to dismantle the "fetish" of state power itself.[5] Khrushchev's "thaw" had undermined Stalin's "empire of death" but not the system of power on which it relied.[6] It abolished the "cult of personality" but did not—some were saying could not, others, would not—do away with the "cult of the state,"[7] with the "étatist principles"[8] of society's organization. Khrushchev, in effect, had told the Soviet people: until now the state power (*vlast'*) had been bad and from now on it would be good—but the state power *itself* was to remain boundless.[9] He fully preserved the "cult of *vlast'*," which was the "essence" of Stalinism even more than the "cult of personality."[10] In this crucial sense, the Soviet Union was still the house that Stalin built. Khrushchev's "thaw" was seen only as an attempt to weed out the "tops" (*vershki*) of the party-state rule leaving the roots (*koreshki*) intact[11]—and it was the *koreshki* of the regime that the glasnost revolutionaries were after now, Stalinism's systemic roots.[12]

They found Stalin's legacy in the economic, political, ideological, and moral threads that riddled the society.[13] In its every aspect—political, social, civil—the present system had "coalesced and congealed" under Stalin and was connected to its creator "genetically," by "historic blood kinship."[14]

Nowhere did the blood lines run thicker and darker than through the "ruling apparatus"[15]—the "monstrous bureaucratic pyramid"[16] that bore down relentlessly on the people and the country. Unaccountable to anyone or anything in its "administrative-bureaucratic omnipotence," this "ruling oligarchy" of the self-selected *nomenklatura* was the sole owner of the country and its riches.[17] This was a "dictatorship of the bureaucracy": its dominance "total" and its power "unlimited."[18]

The last obstacle to the state's omnipotence, "the last bulwark of the people's independence," was said to have been the 28 million peasant households, each master of its own tiny domain.[19] It is to the "rout" of the peasantry—which also caused the destruction of much of Russia's culture and religion—that glasnost writers traced the establishment of the reign of "complete lawlessness" (*vsedozvolennost'*) and "cruelty."[20]

After 1933, the repression would know no bounds, as the *nomenklatura* was now "ready to commit any crime" in defense of its rule.[21]

A "giant" and "sophisticated" apparatus of terror was deployed by the state to extinguish any independent action, any attempt at the self-organization of the society.[22] The *nomenklatura* viewed anything "it could not 100 percent control" as a dangerous and unforgivable offense against the power they personified.[23] The "suppression of thought" was "total."[24] Violence became the regime's alfa and omega, the "main principle" of governance and its "main tool."[25]

There had been no comparable orgy (*razgul*) of violence in history, contended sociologist Shubkin.[26] "Violence ruled," one of the Soviet Union's most celebrated athletes and the Soviet propaganda's "strongest man on the planet," former world champion weight lifter Yuri Vlasov declared in his speech at the First Congress of People's Deputies in June 1989. "It has become the only legal norm in our society. Violence, fear, intolerance, and cruelty permeated our life, were its main nerve. . . . It still prevents us from straightening our backs."[27]

It was in this victorious party-state founded on violence that Grossman, in *Life and Fate*, saw a key similarity between Stalinism and Nazism. "What is the cause of the animosity [between Stalin's USSR and Nazi Germany]?" the commandent of a Nazi prisoner-of-war camp, Liss, demands to know of his prisoner, division commissar and the old Bolshevik Mostovskoy sometime in the winter of 1943: "I cannot understand this. . . . There is no abyss between us. It is a fantasy. We are different forms of the same substance: the party-state. There are two great revolutionaries on this earth: Stalin and our leader. Their will has given birth to the national socialism of a state. [At the moment] we are your mortal enemies, yes. But our victory is your victory. Do you understand? And if you win, then we at once will perish and will live in your victory. . . . Losing this war, we will win it, we will develop in a different form but in the same essence."[28]*

---

* In another great novel reclaimed by glasnost after a decade and a half of banishment and hiding, Yuri Dombrovsky's *Fakul'tet nenuzhnykh veshchey* (The department of unnecessary things), the soon-to-be-arrested hero dreams of telling Stalin: "O, how scary it will be if either of you, the Führer or you, will win this war. Then the world is doomed. . . . Then man will worship only the fist, will bow only to the knout, and will find peace only in prison. . . . Then

Next to violence, the other pillar of Stalinism and its successor regimes was state ownership of the economy. One of the most disappointing and fraught discoveries was that the "transfer of the economic wealth to the people"—one of the October Revolution's key slogans and for seventy years one of the Soviet regime's main claims to legitimacy—turned out to be a fraud: instead of the people, it was the "undemocratic" state that received custody of the economy. Alongside the Party leadership and the "Marxist-Leninist ideology," state ownership was the "fundamental principle" of "real" Soviet socialism.[29] "Socialization" became "étatization" (*ogosudarstvlenie*): "comprehensive," "maximalist," "unsparing," and "all-pervading."[30]

Educated Marxists all, the glasnost essayists came to see in the Soviet Union a version of what Marx called the "Asian" mode of production: an economic and political arrangement in which the state, instead of being confined to the political "superstructure" (as it was in the "European" mode), not only penetrates deep into the economic "basis" of society but becomes its "decisive element."[31] Political power "merges" with property; the state becomes the owner of the means of production, while the "working masses" are forever "alienated" from them.[32] The worker is but a *vintik* (literally a small screw), in Stalin's infamous simile[33]—and coercion could not but become the central principle of such an "organization of labor."[34]

It was in the "étatization" of the economy that glasnost authors found at least a part of the answer to the question to which everyone seemed to demand an answer: Why in the naturally richest country in the world, blessed with "colossal treasures of land, wood, oil, gas, and metals," whose people were "quite educated," did they lack, in quantity and quality, in "food, housing, clothes, books"?[35]

At first, most explanations were "technical," stemming from the impossibility of controlling a modern economy from a single center. For instance, to prevent waste and theft, the state planners would have had to calculate the "norms of utilization" for raw materials and labor for around

---

intellect, conscience, goodness, humanism—all that was forged for millennia and was considered the goal of human existence—are worth absolutely nothing. And then democracy is just a silly little story about the ugly duckling, who will never become a swan" (pp. 274–75).

25 billion industrial products.[36] (By the mid-1970s, an entire institute under the state's main distribution agency, the Gossnab, managed to perform such calculations only for "several thousand" items.)[37] Shortages (*defitsit*), which, as we have already seen, were declared not "temporary" or "local" failures but a perennial, regularly "reproduced," and "integral" feature of the Soviet economic system, a consequence of the "directive" (command) planning, with its 18 million planners and administrators.[38] This "system" could not but reproduce economic "disproportions": they were "built into the very principle of centralized planning."[39]

The only time a more or less "effective" economy was said to have existed in the Soviet Union—that is, one in which the inputs of raw material and labor were reasonably proportionate to the results—was during the New Economic Policy (NEP) in 1921–28, when small and middle-size private enterprises coexisted with state-owned but autonomous *trusts*. According to the leading economist Nikolai Shmelyov, after these seven to eight years, the tempo of economic growth "went rapidly down."[40] NEP produced by far the fastest-growing Soviet economy on record—across the board, in industry as well as in agriculture, in the rate of output growth as well as that of labor productivity and consumption. By 1928 the country's GDP was 10 percent larger than in 1913, the best year before World War I—a faster growth than that of the United States during the same time.[41] Not only would the Soviet economy never again expand as fast, but the NEP tempo was achieved without rationing, impoverishment, starvation, arrests, labor camps, millions of prisoners, and deaths.[42]

As almost invariably with glasnost exploration, the deeper causes and more devastating effects were soon traced beyond economy and politics to people's values and attitudes. Thus the hope of inculcating the overseer-bureaucrat with the sensibility of a true master, whose care for production's quality and efficiency would be deeply personal turned out to be "as utopian as making a vegetarian wolf."[43] Bereft of a real owner, the economy was said to be, in effect, no one's.[44] When bureaucracy administered the economy on behalf of a state that was at once the monopolistic producer, the sole seller, and the only buyer of the goods and services produced, the country's natural wealth was "free" and, along with the Treasury, defenseless against the plunder in pursuit of mad bureaucratic schemes.[45] Corruption, too, became endemic, "total": no longer an individual vice, it was a product of the "ultra-centralized" economic system, which endowed its functionaries with unlimited power in the "social life," rendering people powerless and supplanting laws with administrative "instructions."[46]

Still less could the state count on the diligence and care of the "laboring masses" in the factory shops or in the fields. Built with "the knout and commands,"[47] the economic system tended to disfavor and eventually destroy the inspired or even minimally conscientious worker. Stalin's "vintiks" could not and would not work diligently and imaginatively because it is "alien" to "man's nature" when "everything is decided for him by someone else" in plans and production norms.[48] Those who contended this much drew on the suddenly popular explanation by the nineteenth-century radical socialist Nikolai Chernyshevsky, who wrote that "it is impossible to train a serf to be energetic in the field of wheat and, at the same time, absolutely powerless in the overseer's office." "How can you expect energy in production from the same man who has been trained not to show it in defending himself against oppression?"[49] How much "energy" could there be in a man, Chernyshevsky asked again, "who is used to the impossibility of defending his lawful rights, a man in whom the feeling of independence and a noble self-regard have been killed?"[50]

This contradiction, which was said to doom the Soviet economy to falling further and further behind the West, was traced back to Peter the Great's "modernization," which served as a model for Stalin. The great nineteenth-century Russian historian Vasily Klyuchevsky was quoted on Peter's wanting "a slave to act self-consciously and freely, while remaining a slave."[51] Peter, Klyuchevsky continued, had founded a political order on everyone's rightless-ness (*bespravie*), which is why in his state, "next to state power and laws, absent was that universally invigorating element: the free individual, the citizen."[52]

Just as Chernyshevsky and Klyuchevsky had predicted, the argument went, it proved impossible for the Soviet state-owning state to make an unfree man operate freely at his workplace. Coercion could not make him a hard worker. It could only make him unlearn how to be one, to cause him to detest labor.[53] Fear can constrain vice but it cannot turn it into goodness.[54] It can make the lazy work, but it cannot turn laziness into industriousness.[55] Instead of representing the "apex of human intelligence," a national economy organized as one big factory, with a single all-powerful "dispatcher service," the state's complete ownership of the economy turned out to be an "economic absurdity" that "enslaved" the economic and spiritual energy of the people.[56] *Homo faber* was eroded also by the centralized allocation of amenities, as the same bureaucrats "took the products of someone else's labor" and redistributed them.[57] Personal diligence—as well as honesty and dignity—becomes "superfluous" or even "burdensome" when the well-being of one's family depends on the "good graces" of a redistributing functionary in charge of "ration coupons for happiness."[58]

As honest work was thus systematically "excluded from the system of human values," the erosion of work ethic "inevitably" "lowered morality" in general.[59] A nation of workers becomes "a nation of beggars and bullies," determined by all means to reach out to and grab the largest pieces of the common pie—until there is nothing from which to make it and no one left to bake it.[60]

This is, then, how our old acquaintance, *Homo Sovieticus* came to be. "Alienated" from the fruits of his labor, of which he was no longer the master, his creativity suppressed by bureaucratic agencies (*vedomstva*) and drowned in endless commands and instructions, the man became a "pseudo-laborer" (*lzhetruzhennik*).[61] When honest and imaginative labor is no longer valued or rewarded by society, the society "inevitably begins to reward indifference and baseness (*podlost*)."[62] The vicious circle closes when the authorities, in turn, conceive and act on the notion of the Soviet man as "a lazy slave" whom only the knout could force to work.[63]

As workers had no one but the state to sell their labor to the state became the "monopolistic owner" of the "most important means of production"— people's time, their efforts, and skills.[64] Deploying, again, the Marxist analytical apparatus and elaborating on the already discussed matter of "exploitation" in the "state of workers and peasants," the observers concluded that the situation amounted to a "new form of exploitation": exploitation by the state.[65] Vasily Selyunin calculated that in the West an average worker spends 60–80 percent of the workday "working for himself" (that is, his labor was "returned" to him as salary and benefits) and the rest of the time, "for society."[66] In the Soviet Union the proportion was reversed, with 60–80 percent of workers' time "not paid for" but "taken for free" by the state.[67] In giving the *nomenklatura* an "undivided and absolute possession of all of the country's riches," the "bureaucratic ownership" produced a master class of "new exploiters."[68] For it mattered little to the worker *who* takes away ("expropriates") the results of his labor (Marx's "added value"): a private individual or a state.[69] One tyranny, that of aristocracy and bourgeoisie, is replaced with another, that of "authoritarian bureaucracy" or "bureaucratic bourgeoisie."[70]

Unlike with the "classic" Marxist bourgeoisie, however, the dominance of this new class was founded not only, and perhaps even not so much, on the appropriation of added value as on the control over its redistribution.[71] Hence, unlike their counterparts in capitalist countries, Soviet workers were *personally* dependent on their employers.[72] All the key amenities were controlled by them or by their comrades in another branch of state bureaucracy and thus could be bestowed or withdrawn at a bureaucrat's whim: an apartment, a telephone, a car, or an occasional "parcel" of quality food. More important still, only employment by the state conferred the key rights of Soviet citizenship: the residence permit and, with it, medical care and school for the worker's children. Not being employed by the state made one a pariah "somewhere beyond the pale."[73] Unemployment meant not just utter impoverishment (since unemployment had been pronounced nonexistent, there were no unemployment benefits) but also, eventually, homelessness and perhaps even criminal charges of "parasitism" and a labor camp.

This was, then, a *political* economy par excellence: bound to the Soviet *polis* by the day-to-day production, directed by the new "exploiting" class of state-employed managers, and sustained by the ownership of the resources and the "appropriation" of the fruits of the workers' labor. Yet this economy's political character stemmed from more than its modus operandi or distribution of added value. Its key objectives, indeed its very raison d'être, were inextricably entwined with the attainment of political objectives central to the perpetuation of the regime. First among these aims was the relentless strengthening and the expansion of the state's sway over society, and it is this goal that drove policies that "contradicted the elementary notions of economic common sense.[74]

It was these *political* goals that explained, finally, not just the glaring (and by now much deplored) deficiencies of the Soviet economy, but what came to be seen as its stark irrationalities: the 3 million "overseers" (administrators) in agriculture; or Minvodkhoz's irrigation schemes that were supposed to pay for themselves in 40–100 years; or the recently adopted "raving-mad" plans to build 90 more hydroelectric stations "in a country that lacked the basic goods and services."[75] In the end, it mattered little how people worked and how they lived so long as they all worked and lived "under the same state's roof."[76] People did not need heavy industry, with its blast furnaces and tank-making plants; they did not need the White Sea–Baltic Sea Canal, or the Arctic mines, or railways above the Polar Circle, or plants "hidden in the taiga," Grossman concluded.[77] The Soviet state did. Its needs and those of the people were "poles apart," never to be reconciled.[78] The "primacy" of politics over economy[79] was absolute.

The Soviet state's wealth was said to have been built not on people's prosperity but on their impoverishment—and this misery, too, was rational in political terms. For the meager salaries and the absence of proper rewards for conscientious labor not only were now seen as a consequence of the "suffocating burden of military expenses" or the enormous, daily waste, but also helped to preserve the powerlessness and penury necessary to secure society's docility, its complete obedience to the state.[80]

In the long run, however, by far the most devastating effect of the state's economic monopoly was found in its incompatibility with civil and political liberties, equality before law, and, in the end, democracy. Not Stalin's "personality cult" but the entire Marxist project, as interpreted by Lenin—the project to which the destruction of private property was essential—was now blamed for "totalitarianism." "With the abolition of private property, the foundation of individual freedom is destroyed: nothing is left to a man but to serve the state on the conditions that the state dictates," wrote Selyunin. The state, in turn, is no longer limited in its actions, and it is entirely up to the state which intermediate institutions of civil society are, or are not, permitted to exist.[81]

The Soviet totalitarian-bureaucratic state was said to have emerged "in the process of the liquidation of private property."[82] Where the "state-bureaucratic" system dominated, democracy is deprived of its economic base, making political liberties "impossible in principle."[83]

Conversely, something of a consensus now held that the "economic underpinnings of democracy" were just as crucial: "parliamentarism" grew out of economic freedom, and there could be no political liberty without economic self-determination that private property confers.[84] Democracy, it was now argued, was the sovereignty of the people, but they could not be sovereign when every person was dependent on the state, which fully controlled his or her income, making each, in effect, "the property of the state."[85] Democracy could not exist where an individual's sovereignty was "totally destroyed"[86] and the state's sovereignty was complete and indivisible.[87]

Among the most conspicuous victims of the state's boundless sovereignty was democracy's key element: equality before the law. Suppose, a leading Soviet jurist explained, a person concludes that he was cheated by a cobbler who either failed to do the job correctly or charged more than was agreed. In a lawful state, the aggrieved customer may go to court. But under the "unbelievable, unthinkable étatization of the society," the cobbler is a state employee, protected by the "thick armor of government agencies."[88] He does not care if the customer is happy: his salary is paid not by his clients but by a Ministry, and it is that Ministry that he needs to please. Where there is no "direct exchange" of goods, services, and fees between private producers and customers, there can be no legality.[89] A lawful state, continued the same legal scholar, is the one in which state power is *limited* by law, not armed by it. Instead, he concluded, the relationship between the Soviet state and the people is more like a "military-fendal system," supported by "an inquisition-like criminal law," which, along with other "bourgeois values," rejected the presumption of innocence.[90]

The state-owned economy was now believed inevitably to generate such a profoundly anti-democratic phenomenon as a single, monopolistic political party, which, in turn, becomes its engine and the glue that holds it together.[91] (If, Vasily Selyunin noted presciently in November 1989, we were to bar the Party from directing the economy, the latter would not be able to function.)[92]

Thus, even the most sincere attempt to preserve political and civil liberties, while nationalizing the economy, would be, the philosopher Butenko argued in *Komsomol'skaya pravda*, like trying to stretch a sheepskin to fit an elephant.[93] Not only did democratic arrangements prove "utterly incompatible" with the "nationalized monopolistic property," but the latter inevitably led to an autocratic, dictatorial power and "despotism."[94] That is why, in seventy years, communist systems were said to have thrown up more "political monsters"—Stalin, Rákosi, Mao, Pol Pot, Hoxha, Ceaușescu—than civilization based on private property had produced in the preceding three centuries.[95]

Thus, in full accord with Marx's description of it, the modern version of the "Asian" economic and political model had resulted in "universal slavery" (*pogolovnoe rabstvo*).[96] Having destroyed "tens of millions," the Soviet totalitarian regime "turned the rest of its subjects into slaves."[97] This slavery had "damaged" people's souls "in a most horrible way," depriving them of dignity, of enterprising initiative, and responsibility, of the love of work — and of the love of liberty.[98]

"De-individualization," the "Original Sin," and the Nationalization of Conscience

How could it turn out this way: that the man, the crown of Creation, has become nothing but a material resource for social experiments, a fertilizer to permeate the soil under the planned universal happiness?
—Vasily Selyunin, *Istoki*, 163

In seventy years, a system has been built that is organically indifferent to the real, existing man, hostile to him.
And not only in the mass repressions, the victims of which are millions, but in daily life, where a person means nothing, has nothing, and cannot obtain even the most basic things without humiliation.
—Alexander Yakovlev, "Ob opasnosti revanshisma. Otkrytoe pis'mo kommunistam" (On the danger of revanchism: An open letter to the communists), August 16, 1991, in *Muki prochteniya bytiya*, 343

The present system arose, entirely, on the principles of suppression of the individual, the powerlessness of each of us, and as a result, our defenselessness.
—Yuri Vlasov, speech at the First Congress of People's Deputies of the USSR, in "S'ezd Narodnykh Deputatov SSSR," transcript, *Izvestia*, June 2, 1989: 4

And how many different aspects, what multitude of horrors does this one word contain: slave! Here is [the root of] the vicious circle, in which we all perish, powerless to break it. Here is the cursed reality that turns into nothing our noblest actions, our most generous instincts. Here is what paralyzes the will in all of us, here is what sullies all our virtues.

—Petr Chaadaev, as quoted in Vladimir Kantor, "Imya rokovoe" (The fateful name), *Voprosy literatury*, March 1988: 71

The unfreedom [*nesvoboda*] triumphed completely from the Pacific Ocean to the Black Sea. It was everywhere and in everything. And everywhere and in everything liberty was murdered. This was a victorious assault, and it could be effected only by spilling so much blood: for liberty is life, and by overcoming it Stalin killed life.

—Vasily Grossman, *Vsyo techyot* (Forever flowing), 103

THE RELENTLESS AND deepening quest for the ultimate causes of the persistently exposed ignominy of the present state of affairs uncovered a novel human condition. It was labeled "de-individualization." The Russian term, *de-individualizatsiya*, appears to have been coined in January 1988 by a well-known Soviet social psychologist, Igor Kon, who described it as a "hypertrophied sense of one's powerlessness" and "social apathy."[1] A year later, a prominent essayist defined "de-individualization of society" as the loss of the right to liberty and autonomy and of the right to define one's own interests. As a result, individual "self-worth" had been lost as well.[2] Dispensing with scholarly terminology, a leading sociologist defined the condition as "the reduction of the man, the individual to the status of an insect whom the state can swat down at any time."[3]

Since the main, overarching postulate of glasnost was that the emergence of the new, transformed, "re-moralized" citizen was the key precondition for new, equitable and dignified, political, economic, and social arrangements, the story of de-individualization—its manifestations, origins, maintenance, and effects—became a central preoccupation of glasnost authors. The most obvious cause of de-individualization was thought to be the daily indignities of Soviet life. The daily struggle to provide for their "elementary biological needs"—where and how to get meat, butter, sugar, shoes, clothes—tired "tens of millions" of people, destroyed their "higher predestination," made them "forget all values" and concentrate on the "primary wants."[4] The inability to buy what one wanted by simply paying for goods and services "with one's labor" (that is, with money) without the "extra efforts" of "ingratiating smiles," personal connections, or bribes amounted to a "denial of economic dignity," which was the "foundation of dignity in general."[5] "Souls were destroyed" by the daily insult of lines[6]— the lines, where in addition to waiting for hours, one could be overcharged, cheated out of what one paid for, and slipped shoddy or spoiled goods.[7] Eighty percent of the queuing time was spent on "food stuffs."[8]

People were "chained to humiliation for life," a reader from Krasnodar wrote *Komsomol'skaya pravda*.[9] They encountered it everywhere: in a store, in a tailor's shop, at a post office.[10] Yet nowhere did they feel more powerless than before the representatives of the state. Even before actually stepping into a state office, one felt "inferiority" and even "guilt" before the state.[11] Daily, hourly, people were again and again found by the glasnost authors to be "separated from their dignity," and "every second" of this "multifaceted and petty" denigration reinforced the sense of the state's omnipotence and their powerlessness.[12] At "every step" they found themselves "face-to-face with the entire enormity of power structures."[13] Life's "defenselessness" against power was endless and enforced by the equally "boundless violence" of an all-mighty state.[14]

A vocabulary of social disapprobation and of criminal culpability had sprung to extirpate and punish individualism. It was branded deviant and equated with "parasitism," alcoholism, and drug addiction.[15] Declining to work for the state was "loafing" and "sponging" (*tuneyad-stvo*); the wish to profit from one's work became "acquisitiveness"; the aspiration to become independent of the state's wardship by having savings of one's own was labeled "money-grabbing" (*nakopitel'stvo*).[16]

Far from being an epiphenomenon or an unintended consequence of political and economic arrangements, de-individualization was found to be essential to the doctrinal foundation of the Soviet state. Indeed, as some suggested, it may have derived from the orthodox interpretation of Marxist canon. As the "masses" ("classes") made history by relentlessly advancing progress through revolutions, the individual was an infinitesimally insignificant "grain of sand."[17] His stubborn, "petty bourgeois" insistence on a better life *now* and *for himself* was an impediment to history's march toward a glorious future for *all*. The will of the majority (naturally, as interpreted and guided by the revolutionary party) "subsumed" that of an individual, it "smashed" his sovereignty and independence.[18] The abolition of private property was merely a "material means" to this "denial of individuality."[19] Like the cult of state, the "cult of the masses" had preceded Stalin's cult, enabled and sustained it.[20]

De-individualization was traced also to Marxist millenarianism—a belief in the coming of the kingdom of peace and justice. A key legitimizing device of the regime, the "deification" of the future overshadowed or even negated quotidian needs of man, his normal, "natural" life.[21] For since "eternal happiness and justice" lay ahead, was it not "ignoble," really, to notice "lies," sacrifices," or even "spiritual impoverishment" along the way?[22]* A mere stepping stone toward the "great goal of the future," the present was thus rendered a "moral desert" in which not only daily hardships and indignities were to be overlooked, but so were the betrayal of friends; universal fear and suspicion; lies; and the "tears of children guilty only of having parents who failed to please the powers that be."[23] The present was not yet "real" life, only a preparation for it—and there, in the beautiful future, everything would be forgotten, written off, forgiven.[24]

---

* Russian social and cultural tradition was thought to help the state-sponsored adulation of the future at the expense of the present. "We think about the future as if beside the present," Gogol was quoted as saying. "Our misfortune [stems] from our looking into the future, not into the present. As soon as we, having looked at the present and noticed that some things in it are sad while others are outright disgusting, . . . we give it all up as hopeless and begin to look intently into the future." Chaadaev, for his part, linked this contempt and neglect of the present to the ease with which the Russian rulers plunge into reforms. If Russia's present deserved no more than "sympathy," then "the people's life can be easily interrupted, and one beautiful morning people can reject their old life and begin to live in a new way." (Alexander Tsypko, "Istoki Stalinisma," [The origins of Stalinism], part 3, *Nauka i zhizn'*, January 1989: 50, 52.)

Whether facilitated by Russian history, revolutionary millenarianism certainly was not an invention of Marxism or Leninism. "There was gradually built up in men's minds an imaginary ideal society," de Tocqueville wrote of the French Revolution, "in which all was simple, uniform, coherent, equitable, and rational in the full sense of the term. It was this vision of the perfect state that fired the imagination of the masses and little by little estranged them from the here-and-now." (*The Old Regime and the French Revolution*, trans. Stuart Gilbert, New York: Anchor Books, 1983: 146.)

It is in this moral mutation that Vasily Grossman finds the answer to a question that generations of Soviet historians asked about the "Old Bolsheviks" and the Old Bolsheviks asked themselves, tormented in prisons or starving to death in camps: Why were they—the makers of the revolution, the heroes of the civil war, the engineers of first Five-Year plans, the selfless and, when necessary, ruthless builders of the socialist state—silent when their comrades were arrested, tortured, executed?[25] No, it was not, could not have been, just fear.[26] It was a willful "liberation from morality."[27]

For those who saw de-individualization as a cardinal feature in the design of the Soviet state, the suppression of personal and political freedoms was the key evidence. Its extinguishment could no longer be traced to Stalin's "cult of personality." Instead, the policy to exterminate (*istrebit'*), to eradicate (*iskorenenit'*) the very "spirit of liberty" was traced to the first months after the October Revolution, when Stalin was but the humble People's Commissar for Nationalities.[28] Like Grossman, those who advocated this view traced the founding of "unfreedom" to the betrayal of the Russian democratic revolution of February 1917.

It was now believed to be the Soviet regime's "original sin" (*pervorodnyi grekh*): the "murder of the Russian democracy" and of liberty born in February 1917. It was fatally wounded in October and finished off a few months later, after the "destruction" of Russia's first democratically elected legislative body, the Constituent Assembly, in January 1918.[29]* To

---

* For the first time, in the vignettes in Solzhenitsyn's *In the First Circle*, hundreds of thousands of *Novy mir* readers witnessed the dissolution of the Constituent Assembly and the dispersal of the demonstration in support of the Assembly on January 5, 1918, in Petrograd (St. Petersburg).

There were lots of students, schoolchildren, clerks, remembered one of the book's characters, Uncle Avenir. They marched under different flags, but mostly under red, social-democratic ones. There were around five thousand of them, and they were somber and sang no songs. "We understood that this was the only day of the only free Russian parliament— whether 500 years in the past or 100 years in the future. They began to shoot at us, from the roofs, from the courtyards, and soon from the sidewalks. . . . We did not respond, there was not a single revolver among all of us. Two or three people carried out the dead and the wounded but the rest continued their walk. . . . At the Liteyny boulevard they were met by the Red Guards. "Disperse!" And they began to shoot in salvos. . . . People began to disperse, some turned around and ran. And they shot us in the back, shot and killed.

seize power, wrote Grossman, "Lenin has sacrificed the most sacred of Russia's possessions—her liberty."[30] He "despised" freedom, Grossman continued, and "a state without freedom"[31] was central to his design.*

In *Life and Fate*, Grossman has an "Old Bolshevik," dying in a makeshift "hospital" of a Gulag camp somewhere above the Artic Circle, asking his former comrade and fellow prisoner to hear his confession:

> I don't want to say it; it is like a torture to say it. . . . But this is my last revolutionary duty and I will do it. . . . We have made a mistake. . . . And no repentance can make up for it. . . . We did not understand liberty. We crushed it. And Marx, too, did not appreciate it: it is the foundation, it is the "basis" of the "basis." Without liberty, there is no proletarian revolution.[32]

"Non-freedom" (*nesvoboda*) remained, as Grossman put it, in the foundation of the building started by Lenin, erected by Stalin, and extended by his successors.[33] Its mortifying weight bore down not just on the intelligentsia—the intellectual, the writer, the scholar. Freedom, concludes the hero of Grossman's *Vsyo techyot*, is not just freedom of speech, of press, of religion. Freedom was the peasant's right to sow what he wanted, or any tradesman's right to make shoes and boots, to bake bread, and to sell to whomever he wanted or not to sell at all. Freedom was the same for the turner or the steelmaker as it was for the artist: live and work as you wish, not as you are ordered.[34]

It is the suppression of this "economic freedom" that was now blamed for the "backwardness, shabbiness, shortages."[35] For "non-freedom"

And how easy it was for them to shoot, these Red Guards—to shoot unarmed civilians, and in the back. Just think about it—this was well before the Civil War started! But the mores were already suitable [for such a war]. (Alexander Solzhenitsyn, *V kruge pervom* [In the first circle], Moscow: Act, 2006: 467–68. See also Alla Latynina, "Solzhenitsyn i my [Solzhenitsyn and we], *Novy mir*, January 1980: 246.)

* "Do you even understand what the free election to the Constituent Assembly meant for Russia?!" Menshevik Chernetsov tells the prominent Bolshevik Mostovskoy in a Nazi prisoner of war camp on the pages of Grossman's *Zhizn' i sud'ba*. "In a country of a thousand years of slavery! In the thousand years Russia was free less than half a year. Your Lenin has not 'inherited' Russian liberty; he murdered it" (p. 228).

cannot be comfortable and plentiful: it can only be "gloomy, grungy, littered with refuse, and gray."[36] In politics, too, the rejection of the "formal, bourgeois" democracy had resulted in the elimination of any democracy as such, and this eradication "turned into fiction" individual rights and liberties.[37] What Grossman's called the "synthesis of socialism with non-freedom"[38] was now thought to have taught humanity a crucial lesson: the "enslavement of the individual" undermine the noblest, most humane ideas by which de-individualism is justified.[39]

The extirpation of "bourgeois liberties" also had resulted in the denial of one's right to one's own opinion. In "lowering civic dignity," this rejection, too, was now held responsible for the disappearance of the citizen and, with him, of civil society.[40] Without an honest and considered personal opinion, there was no individual, poet Evgeny Evtushenko wrote in early 1987—and without an individual, there was no people as a coherent and powerful political and social force.[41] Culture was dying because there could be no culture without personal convictions.[42] There loomed a break with civilization and a return to barbarism.[43]

Perhaps more vigilantly than against any other transgression, the totalitarian state was found to guard against an extension of individual convictions: man's personal responsibility.[44] Defining and acting in one's own interests, not to mention taking responsibility for one's own country, was punished more brutally than other "political" sins.[45] Instead, the state had assumed responsibility for all people, "infantilizing" men and women and turning the country into a nation of children led by the "state-pedagogue."[46] Like a limb that is not used, the personal *I* had begun to "atrophy."[47]

The "super-violence" (*sverkhnasilie*) with which the de-individualization was enforced—murder as the foundation of the state's "daily functioning" and the systematic "lowering of the value of human life all the way down to zero"—paralyzed the human spirit.[48] The glorification of violence "poisoned blood" and disfigured conscience:[49] Over the decades, the universal and seemingly irrational nature of this violence, the inability of a sane human mind to account for it, made millions not just into slaves but slaves "devoted to the system that crushed" them, worshipping, in the words of Orwell, whose books were being published in Russia for the first time, the boot perennially planted on their faces.[50]

Two entwined founding doctrines of the Soviet state were now placed at the root of the ultimate de-individualization. One was the view of progress as the relentless expansion of the state's control over society. The temptation to expropriate the "individual himself" logically followed from the establishment of the state's total ownership of the means of production.[51] Individual values were "confiscated" along with other "private" societal assets.[52] Having usurped the "earthly powers," the state strove to capture the "spiritual" ones as well.[53] The result was the monopoly on the spiritual life of every member of society and thus on the spiritual life of the entire people.[54]

The other principal source of nationalized conscience was the conviction that there were no "eternal ethical principles," no "universal" (literally, "panhuman" or *obshchechelovecheskaya*) morality.[55] Hence the rejection—along with the rest of the "superstructure" of the bourgeois state, "laws and religion," "parliamentarianism and freedom of the press"—of such components of the "millennial moral tradition" as mercy, tolerance, and compassion.[56] Goodness became relative, situational, instrumental—and infinitely malleable. "Our ethics [*nravstvennost'*] is completely subjugated to the cause of the proletariat's struggle," Lenin was quoted again and again as declaring in 1920. "Our morality is defined by the interests of the class struggle. . . . We are saying: morality is that which serves the destruction of the old, exploitative society and the unification of all toiling masses around the proletariat, which is erecting a new society of communists."[57] (Fifty-six years later, at the Party's Twenty-Fifth Congress, General Secretary Leonid Brezhnev confirmed, "In our society everything is moral that serves the interests of the building of communism.")[58]

The "class morality" means that good and evil were defined not by human conscience but by a "directive from above."[59] With virtue but a tool in the "service of the cause of communism"[60] its opposites—wrongdoing, transgression, sin—too, became "relativized." Unlike the Catholic Church, which, even while selling indulgences, did not abolish the very notion of sin, the Stalinist state defined the morality of human action solely in terms of its current utility to the cause. It had become the universal and final absolver: it "accepted and justified everything."[61]

This, then, was the essence of Stalinism, the key to its unimaginably routine savagery: a demoralized intellect; an intelligence no longer rooted in and corrected by "cultural values"; a morality "dissolved in politics."[62] If morality's sole function was to justify the state's actions, if "good and evil, conscience, soul, heart—in short, God" were no more, wrote Vasily Selyunin, then "everything was allowed," and one could march, "knee deep in blood," to the "bright future."[63]

Submitting to and carrying out any order that "served the cause" became the "main virtue" of the "Party's soldiers," while mercy and dignity were dangerous for survival.[64] Any idea that claims to bestow happiness on mankind but places itself above it, pointed out a veteran foreign correspondent of *Izvestia*, Stanislav Kondrashov, inevitably requires "implementers" who would step over "common morality."[65] When political ("class") interests suppress universal human values, when, from the "master," morality becomes a "servant," then an individual's life loses its moral value, wrote *Komsomol'skaya pravda* columnist Inna Rudenko.[66] The value of an individual human life is reduced to zero, nay, to below zero.[67] Stalin had implemented "class morality," but the idea had preceded him and was a key enabler of Stalinism.[68]

"Follow me!" commanded the state, personified by the infallible and eternal leader. "Leave behind your father and mother—and you will find yourself in paradise," Alexander Tvardovsky (whose parents, brothers, and sisters were exiled as kulaks) wrote in his last poem, a meditation on Stalinism:

And we, so proud of our disbelief in God,
In the name of new holiness
demanded sternly the sacrifice:
Cast off your mother and your father . . . *
The task is clear, the cause is sacred,—
Onward, then, straight to the highest goal.

* A character in another literary symbol of glasnost, Vladmir Dudintsev's novel *Belye odezhdy* (The white garments), describes the advertisements in newspapers from 1930, which he just uncovered: "I sever all the ties to my father as with a kulak element"; "I am breaking all the relations with my parents as they sow religious opiate in the consciousness of laboring masses" (p. 70).

Along the way, betray your own brother
And your best friend, in secret.
And don't you burden your soul
With human feelings, trying to spare yourself,
And go ahead, bear false witness
And be a beast in the leader's name.[69]

The state's behavior became the "ethical ideal."[70] Virtue was "prescribed from above."[71] The morality was "blown to smithereens," and the "moral foundation" of the nation was said to have been demolished with a thoroughness that history had not known until then.[72]

The result was a "giant spiritual vacuum."[73] People became "inured to the constant fear, lies, orders, slogans," used to the "smell of blood and steel."[74] They stopped believing in decency and virtue, in honest work, in being able to live without stealing—or in the state that would help instead of cheating and oppressing them.[75]

Most disastrous of all was the obliteration of the very essence of human individuality and the "necessary condition of morality": the capacity for moral judgment and choice.[76] Without them, man was denied the "right to morality" and deprived of the very "need for conscience."[77] The latter was "collectivized"—and thus effectively "abolished," replaced by a nationalized conscience, the conscience of the state.[78]* The state—

---

* While the "cause of communism" justified everything for Levin, Stalin and his
successors acted in the name of the "Party," "state," and "the leader." "Conscience is an abstract notion, an empty one," Anatoly Rybakov imagines Stalin's
thinking to himself in *The Children of Arbat*. "It is nothing but a cover for
dissent. And people who have the so-called conscience are dangerous people."
They are dangerous, Stalin continues, because they consider themselves as
having the right to decide what is moral and what is immoral. And this so-called
conscience, then, allows them to judge the actions of the party and the state and,
thus, HIS actions. This so-called conscience allows them to have their opinions
that are different from HIS. This must be stopped, once and for all. For "HE has
created the idea of a party as a kind of the highest and ultimate authority
[*absolut*], which replaces everything: God, morality, home, family. . . . But if the
party is the ultimate authority, then its leader is the ultimate leader as well. He,
then, is the embodiment of its morality, its ethics. And what he does is ethical
and moral. There can be no other morality, no other ethics." (*Deti Arbata,* book
2, *Strakh* [Fear], 323–24.)

infallible and eternal—shifted the "entire weight of responsibility" on its "iron shoulders," delivering the people from what Goebbels called the "chimera of conscience."[79]*

"Life-giving conscience," Alexander Yakovlev wrote, had been forced underground or gradually "dried up."[80] And a "dying conscience" meant a "dying nation."[81]

---

* "If everything is regarded from the point of view of its utility for a particular social layer, class, or state," literary critic Vladimir Lakshin concluded, "then there is no moral judgment—and no personal moral responsibility." ("Nravstvennost', spravedlivost', gumanizm" [Morality, justice, humanism], *Kommunist* 10, 1989: 41.)

PART FOUR *ЧТО ДЕЛАТЬ?* WHAT IS TO BE DONE?

Both the "top" and the "bottom" of the society have said: enough! we cannot retreat any longer, we want to live like humans. Who and what is to blame for the past is clear. The question is: what should be done in a new way and who would do it?
—Pavel Bunich, "I srazu i postepenno" (Both at once and gradually), *Literaturnaya gazeta,* May 30, 1990: 10

To say "this street does not lead to the temple" is like crossing something out without replacing it with anything. In what rocket and from what place should we start now in order to be certain to reach the temple?
—Igor Klyamkin, "Kakaya ulitsa vedyot k khramu?" (Which street leads to the temple?), *Novy mir,* November 1987: 185

Today we are passionately arguing about ideals real and false, preparing to implement them in our life, to move from words to action.
—Vladimir Novikov, "Vozvrashchenie k zdravomu smyslu" (The return to common sense), *Znamya,* July 1989: 217

And let such myths as are necessary for the spiritual existence of people be born from social knowledge and not the cunning calculations or vain delusions of politicians. And let them be dictated by the trust in human nature and human hopes—not by the promises of a paradise by such and such date but by the answer to the question: what should we live for and how?
—Anatoly Bocharov, "Mchatsya mify, b'yutsya mify" (Myths are whirling, myths are stirring), *Oktyabr',* January 1990: 191

So who does all this depend on? Well, on whom else but all of us? On the explosion-like expansion of our own dignity, our honor, our fastidiousness, if you wish.

—Yuri Karyakin, "Zhdanovskaya zhidkost'" (Zhdanov's liquid), in Yuri N. Afanasiev, ed., *Inogo ne dano* (There is no other way), Moscow: Progress, 1988: 421

CHAPTER FOURTEEN

Stalin, Memory, Repentance, Atonement

Rivers do not flow back.
People do not live twice.
But a just trial may be held a hundred times.
—Yuri Dombrovsky, epigraph to *Fakul'tet nenuzhnykh veshchey*
(The department of unnecessary things), Moscow: Sovetskiy
pisatel', 1989

We saw everything—and we were silent. Silent was our conscience.
—Dmitry Likhachev, "Trevogi sovesti" (Troubles of conscience),
Literaturnaya gazeta, January 1, 1987: 7

To our killed,
to our tortured to death
not even a monument have we managed to erect.
Who are we then,
What sort of people are we then?
Shame.
—Yuri Levitansky, "Iz raznykh desyatiletiy" (From different
decades), *Ogonyok,* no. 26, 1988: 16

National pride without national historical shame for crimes turns
into chauvinism. Historical shame becomes not a destructive but a
constructive force.

—Evgeny Evtushenko, "Sud'ba Platonova" (Platonov's fate),
Sovetskaya kul'tura, August 20, 1988: 5

And if, as we learn about the Gulag from memoirs, we begin to
understand that we have not been asking the right questions, that
the questions themselves must be different—well, then perhaps
we will draw closer to the truth about ourselves and the world in
which we live.
—Andrey Vasilevsky, "Stradanie pamyati" (The anguish of memory), *Oktyabr',* April 1989: 191

Repentance is a difficult moral deed. It demands the decision to
confess precisely to that which one most wishes to conceal or
forget, to call past sins and crimes by their proper names. One
ready to repent takes on himself the guilt of many, considers
himself responsible for the evil that came to reign.
—N. Zorkaya, "Dorogoy, kotoraya vedyot k khramu" (By the road
that leads to the temple), *Iskusstvo kino* 5, 1987: 52

We cannot possibly escape a national repentance; it is coming.
I mean not a one-time ritual but a moral self-cleansing of every
person and the society as a whole.
—Yuri Afanasiev, "Perestroika i istoricheskoe znanie" (Perestroika
and the science of history), *Literaturnaya Rossiya,* June 17, 1988: 3

I imagine a Memorial [to the victims of Stalinism]: a gray, granite
wall, very long—almost endless—and in it contours of human
faces. Women, children, men. Thousands, tens of thousands of
faces! And no names, no dates. Just the faces, in whose eyes of
stone is forever frozen the question: "What for?"
—Vladimir Kolesnik, a "worker," in a letter to *Znamya,* August
1987: 225

A GEOLOGIST COMPLAINED to a visiting Moscow journalist about
working in Kolyma: "Our bulldozer takes off the topsoil and we see lay-
ers of dead bodies. They are so close to the surface and the permafrost
has preserved them just as they were. There is frost on the beards but
other than that they look alive. How can we go through them?"[1]

The geologist's plea echoed a theme that dominated the country's leading liberal journals and newspapers in 1987 and 1988. What to do about Stalin and his legacy became the first instance of national introspection, what *Ogonyok* called "self-cleansing and awakening."[2] Suddenly, there was something of a consensus: without, somehow, "going through" Stalin, without settling scores with him and the regime he forged—now judged the "peak of inhumanity, amorality, contempt for human beings and their dignity"[3]—the fledging revolution would be severely limited, perhaps even subverted, and a new Russia nearly impossible.

In the previous thirty years, Khrushchev's "half-truth" (as if "looking over its shoulder") was followed by two decades of "the strangling of the truth."[4] Although the instrument was said to be not a noose but "a soft pillow," the result was the same: the regime had "flawlessly" calculated that if the subject was not taught in school and people were not reminded of it daily, it would be very quickly forgotten by a vast majority of the people.[5] Stalin's body was still in the Kremlin wall, the country's most hallowed burial ground.

"Going through" Stalin meant, first, "erasing the sacrilege" of the unmarked mass graves in which millions lay.[6] Not to know, to ask "How many people died in camps? How many of them were women and children? Where do their bodies lie today? Who buried them?"—to ask and to receive no answer was "immoral."[7]

Recovering the names of the "de-kulakized" peasants was seen as a particularly urgent moral obligation because the scale and viciousness of the crime, on the one hand, and the thoroughness of the state-organized oblivion, on the other, were remarkable even by the standards of Stalinism. In a nationally televised speech on August 20, 1990—the first and, thus far, only address by a Soviet or Russian leader on the subject of the repression from the 1920s to the 1980s and on the moral imperative of atonement—Alexander Yakovlev deplored the "unprecedented, summary violence" against "tillers of land." "History," he added, "had not known such a concentrated hatred toward mankind."[8]

But the national act of acknowledgment and commemoration had to be more than a tribute to the dead, no matter how noble and urgently needed. In parting, decisively, not just with Stalin but with the system he forged, recovered memory was to serve as a "guarantee," a hedge against the recurrence of totalitarianism. Only a perpetual, living, and constantly renewed memory of the mass murder—"in all its details and with all the interlocking networks of the causes and mechanisms"—could become a reliable barrier against the "restoration of the criminal regime."[9] The truth about the magnitude of the oppression would serve as a kind of "shock therapy": forcing people to look into the abyss in order to prevent them from allowing the country to be taken down that road again.[10] Without such a "therapy," the society's "moral health" would be impossible to restore.[11]

The nightmarish tale had to be retold not only as a credible and complete history, but as a moral parable to be read anew by every man and woman, every boy and girl for generations and centuries—the tale of "lies, of the repugnant sophistication of operations, the cynicism of those who arrested and tortured."[12] Memoirs of survivors, which school-teachers would read to their students, would become a moral equivalent of "inoculations against cholera, smallpox or plague," insisted an *Ogon-yok* columnist:

> Let them shudder, let them dissolve in tears, let them be
> horrified—the shudder will be cleansing, the horror healing.
> They must know what Stalinism does to man, they must [learn
> to] be vigilant in order to see it under any masks, in order to
> battle it, not sparing themselves. Because it brings death,
> physical and moral, to the country, its citizens and their
> children and grandchildren.[13]

Progress was no longer considered possible without overcoming the key "nonmaterial" vestiges of Stalinism: fear, servility (*rabolepie*), and, most important, its profound immorality.[14] "We are all victims of Stalinism," *Ogonyok* insisted, "even if we were not in the [Gulag] camps. Only by freeing ourselves from it, can we change the moral climate."[15] Unatoned and unredeemed, Stalinism was like an open, "bleeding wound," an "abscess" (*naryv*) that needed to be lanced before it burst and poisoned the entire body.[16] A "moral cleansing" (*nravstvennoe ochishchenie*) was required.[17] Confronting Stalinism was a matter of the "spiritual health of the country," of its "spiritual hygiene."[18]

Just as state-induced amnesia was now seen as a pillar of totalitarianism, memory was a medicine that would help restore the souls eroded, corrupted, and disfigured by Stalinism. Memory was used to assist mightily in relearning "humanity's vocabulary": charity, mercy, compassion.[19]

Most of all, the commemoration was counted on to extirpate fear—the "freezing, paralyzing fear"[20] bred into generations of Soviet people. Getting rid of the dread was central to forging men and women who understood that those who do not protect others from lawlessness themselves become its victims.[21] A new Russia was impossible without those who, hearing a loud knock on the door in the middle of the night, would not "freeze with horror" but would only wonder who had the gall to bother them at this hour.[22*] It was such men and women—masters of their own life and therefore responsible stewards of their country's destiny, who "think freely, speak boldly and decide independently"—who were to become the ultimate "internal guarantee" of the irreversibility of the changes.[23]

The creation of such moral impediments to Stalinism was bound to be "painstaking and slow."[24] It required more than the recollection of every martyr of Stalinism. It necessitated turning from victims to victimizers, perpetrators, and, even more important, to the tens of millions of their accessories-after-the-fact.

For Stalinism was not only the Russian people's greatest tragedy but also their enormous guilt:

> It is the guilt of us all—those who lived in that tragic time and those who did not, because the guilt of our fathers and grandfathers, who lived then, . . . their children and grandchildren.

---

* If the victims of famine and "de-kulakization" were not remembered among the "martyrs of Stalinism," wrote Yuri Chernichenko, if their names were not inscribed on "monuments" in every village where they had been arrested, the roots of fear would forever remain in the soil of rural Russia. The "harrowing years" would stay the souls of the people as an "oppressive weight, shackling their initiative, causing uncertainty and mistrust of life," and impeding the return of the "children and grandchildren" of those who were forced off the land. (Yuri Chernichenko, "Zemlya, ekologiya, perestroika" [Land, ecology, perestroika], *Literaturnaya gazeta*, January 29, 1989: 3; and Anatoly Anan'ev, "Po techeniyu ili naperkor" [Going with the flow or against it], *Oktyabr'*, October 1989: 5–6.)

And ours it will stay until we redeem it today by our
repentance—for them and in their name because it is our
inheritance. . . . Guilty were those who organized and inspired
the crimes; and those who committed them; and those who
knew of them, remaining silent witnesses, and those who did
not or would not know, because ignorance did not exclude
them from the death-strewn existence. . . . This is everyone's
guilt—different in kind but guilt all the same.[25]

For the perpetrators—the compilers of the lethal lists, the interrogators, the jailers, the murderers in prisons or camps, from the mid-1920s
to what Yakovlev called "the time of the dissidents"[26]—there were to be
"trials of conscience." People must know their names, each and every
one of them, just like those of their victims, so that society could judge
them by moral if not legal criteria—the criteria that the country "needed
so badly" to restore and act upon.[27] "Today we live not only among heroes and martyrs," editorialized *Ogonyok*. "We also live among scoundrels,
the scum. We must know them and execute them—by our contempt, for
generations to come."[28*]

For millions of men and women, whose souls were poisoned by supporting, cooperating, or merely coexisting with the criminal regime—by
their silence, by their raised hands at meetings and rallies, by their pretending not to notice the starving, the tormented, the arrested among
neighbors, relatives, friends, compatriots—for them there was "public repentance."[29] The atonement was to be earned by commemorating the
memories of innocent victims;[30] condemning, unconditionally, their
murderers;[31] and, most of all, by building a new and just Russia. Recognized in shame and remorse, shuddered and wailed over, the horrors of

---

* Others were far from certain that just moral judgment was sufficient. Former
executioners and torturers were enjoying themselves, wrote the poet Anatoly
Zhigulin, who survived the blackest of the camps in Vorkuta, Kolyma, and
Tayshet. "Until they are punished," Zhigulin continued, "we will not
overcome Stalinism. . . . Stalinism's criminals must be put on trial. Even
post-humously." He also insisted on making "propaganda of Stalinism" a
criminal offense. (Anatoly Zhigulin, "Vina! Ona byla, konechno . . ." [The
guilt! Of course it was there . . .], interview with *Moskovskie novosti*, July 31,
1988: 12.)

Stalinism were to be redeemed by the creation of a state and society that would never again allow the country to be ruled by mass murder.

The time "of societal penitence and moral cleansing has come," declared one of Russia's most popular actors, Georgy Zhzhyonov, himself a former inmate of Stalin's camps.[32] What a wonderful, capacious word "repentance" is, wrote Russia's finest eye surgeon, Svyatoslav Fyodorov, whose father, too, perished in Stalin's purges. "How fitting it is for our times! To repent, to tell all without holding anything back in order to begin a better life!"[33]

"To recall everyone by their names!" became a motto of the "All-Union Voluntary Historical and Educational Society" Memorial, set up in August 1988 by *Ogonyok* and the Unions of Cinematographers, Theater Workers, and Architects.[34] Its executive committee ("Public Council") was to organize and supervise a competition for the design of a "Memorial to the Victims of Stalinism" and to launch a nationwide fundraising drive for its construction. A vast archive and a museum filled with objects "gathered throughout the country" was to be built next to the monument.[35]*

In January 1989, 500 delegates from Memorial's chapters throughout the Soviet Union came to Moscow for a national inaugural congress.[36] The society's co-chair, dean of the Institute of History and Archives, Yuri Afanasiev, saw Memorial as "first and foremost a moral movement, a movement of conscience" and its key task as "overcoming the alienation of man from history."[37] We understand, Afanasiev continued, that to regenerate [conscience] in a society as a whole is possible only through regenerating it in every individual. In many languages, the

---

* The page of *Ogonyok* that carried the announcement carried a letter from a reader: "My family, which has been subjected to all the horrors of Stalin's repression, thinks that the monument should be constructed in such a way as to be visible from the rather well-known building [of the KGB headquarters] in the Lubyanka [Square]. The monument should be at the center of it. But a monument to all is faceless. Which is why we suggest, in addition to the monument, a memorial park, where wives, sisters, children, grandchildren could plant a tree in memory of their perished loved ones. And, most certainly, [there must be] a book with the names of all the victims of Stalinism. We must hurry, time is not waiting. This is a responsibility of all the living." (V. Shamborant, *Ogonyok* 37, 1988: 29.)

word "conscience" (*sovest'*) is close to "consciousness" (*soznanie*). We believe that making people "conscious," aware [of Stalinism], is precisely the right path to their conscience, to the feeling of guilt, to repentance.[38]

From the beginning, "recalling all by their names" proved a monstrously difficult task. News of the methodical destruction of the burial sites during the preceding quarter century streamed to newspapers and magazines from all over the country. One such item was about a conference that took place in the office of a Party official in the town of Kolpashev in West Siberia, 225 kilometers (140 miles) from the provincial capital of Tomsk in September 1965. Also present were the head of the Tomsk regional KGB and a "comrade from Moscow." The latter produced a sealed envelope and asked the official to open and read it in their presence.[39] The memorandum informed the local authorities that the mass grave of the executed "enemies of the people," buried along the Ob' River next to the old NKVD building, was in danger of being washed out. "The remains might be exposed and identified by relatives." The memo ended with a "request" to "assist in the destruction of the material evidence."[40]

Following the orders, wells were bored throughout the site with drill rigs borrowed from local geologists. The wells were filled with quicklime (*negashyonaya izvest'*) and water. The cleanup was conducted at night by the local military detachments. (The draftees would be discharged from their two-year service early, "so that they don't talk about the operation to the local population.") Still, the chemical reaction produced a thick white and yellow smoke. The alarmed Kolpashev residents were told that firefighting exercises were under way.[41]

Fourteen years later, in May 1979, the Ob' bared yet another layer of the sand bank and from it protruded "legs, arms, heads."[42] Local boys, who found the remains, would throw skulls in the river or put them on sticks and run with them around town. Soon a battalion of construction troops (*stroybat*) arrived and fenced off the area. The barrier around the site was manned by police around the clock. A barge was called in to help collapse more of the bank, and the remains were "pushed into the Ob.'"[43] Upon the completion of the work, the Tomsk KGB rewarded the barge's pilot with a transistor radio. Some of the "operation" participants— soldiers, river pilots, geologists, and the students of a local vocational school—were given watches, or twenty rubles, and a personal "commendation" by the KGB chief, "comrade Andropov."[44] By November 1990, only boards were "sticking out" from the bank here and there. They were said to be part of the underground passage that used to lead from the NKVD building to the execution site.[45]*

Even the direct descendants of those executed over fifty years before were not allowed to read the "investigation" files. One of them was the son of a professor of mathematics at the Industrial Academy, then the Soviet Union's top finishing school for up-and-coming Party functionaries and plant managers. The father was taken away when the son was four months old.[46] Although his father had been "fully rehabilitated" (that is, his sentence was voided "due to the lack of the crime"), a KGB official informed the man that he was "absolutely forbidden" to see his father's file.[47] If he had "specific questions" about the "case," they might be answered, provided they were submitted in writing.

How could he ask "specific questions?" the son asked. He knew nothing of his father's "case," had no idea what to ask. (He, his mother, and two brothers, ages ten and five, were exiled to Kazakhstan after his father's conviction.) Could someone at least read to him from the file—whatever they found suitable for de-classification? The KGB agreed,

---

* A prominent Russian poet-symbolist and a close friend of the great Sergei Esenin, Nikolai Klyuev, was exiled to Kolpashev after his arrest in 1933 and wrote friends a year later: "The settlement of Kolpashev is a clay knoll, covered with huts, blackened by misfortunes and bad weather. There is nothing to eat: food is either absent or ridiculously expensive. I have no means of supporting myself, and there is nobody to beg from, as everyone is roaming around, like wolves, in search of grub [zhran'ya]. . . . The summer brings rains from the swamps, which stretch around as far as the eye can see, and incessant wind, and in the winter it is [minus] 50 degrees. . . . The population is 80 percent exiles: Chinese, Central Asians, people from the Caucasus, Ukrainians, former officers, students—people from all the corners of our country, all alienated from one another and often hostile, and everyone is searching for grub, which does not exist, since Kolpashev long ago has been picked to the bone. . . . Remember me—a wretched old man, whose appearance makes shudder even the 'special settlers' [spetspereselentsy] long used to the hellish pictures of human grief. I can say only this: 'I would have liked to be the most despised of all creatures rather than an exile in Kolpashev'" (Zapetskiy, "I snova . . ."). Klyuev was executed in 1937. Were his remains, too, swallowed by the quicklime or sunk into the Ob'?

provided there would be no tape-recording. The man scribbled notes as a KGB colonel read from the records.*

When the reading was finished, the son of the murdered professor wanted to take snapshots of the two photographs on the file's front cover (full-face and profile, as usual). They were his father's last images. After an initial refusal ("Only by the order of the Procurator General of the Soviet Union or the Chief Military Procurator!"), a compromise was reached: the file's front page was covered with a thick paper except for a small window through which the photographs could be seen.[48]

The clamor for truth and memory grew louder every day. Professors and students of the Moscow Institute of History and Archives called for the publication of a "White Book" (a compendium of crimes) about "Stalin and his regime" and demanded that the committee in charge be given full access to the archives of the Central Committee, the OGPU-NKVD-KGB, the prosecutors' offices (*prokuratura*), and the personal papers of the victims.[49]

Activists in Krasnoyarks in south-central Siberia (they wanted their historical society to be named "People's fates") were planning to find and interview witnesses of the sinking of barges filled with prisoners in the Yenisei River.[50] Farther east, in Chita, volunteers were trying to set up a museum and a society of former camp prisoners. When they began looking for execution sites and interviewing former NKVD functionaries, the amateur historians were deluged with phone calls and letters, "containing threats and demands to stop the search."[51] They reported "not being scared" and continued the work. A most welcome help was a thousand deutsche marks, sent by several former prisoners,

---

* The author, Grant Gukasov, learned that his father confessed to having been "invited by the director of studies of the Academy to join a counterrevolutionary organization and to engage in sabotage." The latter consisted of "my including in the program a large volume of material which some students could not fully comprehend, while inflating their grades at the examinations, thus creating an illusion of understanding the subject, which subsequently handicapped them in the learning of related subjects." He was sentenced to ten years in the camps and five in exile by the Traveling Military Collegiums of the Supreme Court. "Why 'Military'?" Gukasov asked. "Because," he was told, "the crime concerned the top managers of industry."

now living in West Berlin, who had spent twenty-five years in the Vorkuta camps.[52]

Perhaps the most striking instance of the yearning for a reckoning with Stalinism was the "Week of Conscience" (*Nedelya sovesti*) held in Moscow, from November 19 to 26, 1988, Saturday to Saturday, in the Culture Club of the Electric Lamp Plant in Zhuravlev Square. The cavernous hall, with three tiers of balconies from floor to ceiling, could not accommodate all those wishing to attend. The line stretched around the block for almost a quarter of a mile.[53] People waited for hours in the wet snow and slush of a Moscow November.[54] In the end, more that 33,000 visitors entered the building to "take part, personally, in the revival of truth and justice."[55]

Responding to requests from *Ogonyok,* the event's principal sponsor and organizer,[56] some of the liberal intelligentsia's brightest stars came and spoke: the actors Mikhail Ul'yanov and Yuri Nikulin, the playwright Mikhail Shatrov and the eye surgeon Sanislav Fyodorov, the poet Evgeny Evtushenko, the writer Ales' Adamovich, the essayists Yuri Karyakin, Lev Razgon, and Yuri Chernichenko.[*]

Designs of the monument to the victims, submitted for the first round of the competition, were exhibited next to the Information Center, where a list of 15,000 names of those sentenced to the "highest measure of punishment"—firing squad—was on display.[57†]

At the heart of the exhibit was the Wall of Memory (*Stena pamyati*): 280 photographs and 1,700 documents submitted by relatives of the

---

[*] The "Week of Conscience" was sponsored by the Union of Theater Workers of the Russian Federation (their day at the exhibit was November 19); "creative and social organizations" of Leningrad on November 20; the Union of Composers of the Russian Federation on November 21; the *Yunost'* (Youth) literary magazine on November 22; *Moskovskie novosti* on November 23; *Literaturnaya gazeta* on November 24; the Union of Cinematographers on November 25; and *Ogonyok* on November 26. ("Memorial sovesti" [The memorial of conscience], *Ogonyok* 47, 1988: 7.)

[†] These were the victims "rehabilitated" in only one year, 1955, and only by the Military Collegium (tribunal). (Rehabilitations were conducted by the provincial courts as well.) Altogether, the author of the collection, a student of the Institute of History and Archives, Dmitry Yurasov, compiled a card catalogue containing the names and brief histories of 128,000 victims. (Nemirovskaya, "Nedelya . . ." and Kabakov, "Nedelya . . .")

perished, following a plea for documents in *Ogonyok* three months before.[58] Among the photographs on the brick wall—the martyrs' young
faces were reported to be "so intelligent, kind, radiant"[59]—was one with
a caption: "Basyubin, Vasily Grigorievich, head of the Hydroelectric Administration. Died in a camp. Basyubina, Tatiana Efremovna, surgeon,
arrested. Svetlana Vasilievna Basyubina, daughter, was born in a camp and
lived there."[60] Another message read: "Martem'yanov, Ivan Mikhailovich.
Lived in the village of Blagoveshchenskoe, had nine children. Arrested in
1937. Fate unknown."[61] Another: "Who knew my father, Sergei Alexeevich
Zaytsev?" And next to a photograph of a young couple with a baby: "Who
knew Sergey Ivanovich Makeev? Until May 1937 a printer in Dushanbe,
Tajikistan. May–June, the Lubyanka prison, July–December, 1937, and
later: camps."[62] And written underneath six old photos: "None of my relatives has returned. K. A. Dudinskaya, Gorky."

Next to the Wall of Memory was a map of the Gulag drawn on
bricks—a symbol of thousands of "industrial objects" and entire cities
built by the prisoners —with the location of 162 camps marked in white
paint. Survivors spoke in front of the map: "My number was Щ -270.
Above the Arctic Circle in Inta. It is a city now. We built it."[63] "I was nineteen in 1945 . . . and arrested with my student friends. The youngest of
us was sixteen, a talented mathematician. His sentence was later extended and he was used in the hardest jobs in the camp. He has not lived
to pursue math."[64]

Nearby stood the symbol of Stalin's industrialization and the *zeks'*
key tool, the ubiquitous barrow (*tachka*). People started dropping do-
nations in it and by the end of the exhibit it was filled with 57,000
rubles.[65]* (The average monthly salary at the time was around 100 ru-

---

* In the middle of the "Week of Conscience" on November 23, *Moskovskie novosti*
  printed a special issue of the paper, sold by volunteers, with the revenue going
  to the "Memorial" fund. Among the volunteers were actors of one of Moscow's
  most famous theaters, Vakhtangov; officers in the Political Section of the
  General Staff of the Air Force; scholars from the Institute of Chemical Physics
  of the Academy of Sciences; and the students of the Department of Journalism
  of Moscow State University. For a paper that cost 10 kopeks, people paid a ruble,
  two and half rubles, even 25 rubles. Forty-five additional copies were sold and
  18,500 rubles donated to the "Memorial." (Kabakov, "Nedelya . . .")

bles.) Heaps of fresh flowers covered the lower part of the Memory Wall.

After "decades of fear," was a mere one "week of conscience" too little? asked a *Moskovskie novosti* article. No, the author answered himself, it was so much already: for "now a continuation was possible!"—the continuation of memory, repentance, and moral rebirth.[66]

CHAPTER FIFTEEN

The "Spirit of Freedom" and the Power of *Nyet*

The Kolyma Tales is an attempt to ask and resolve some important
moral questions that simply cannot be resolved in any other
material. . . . [It is about] man's struggle with the machine of the
state, the essence of this struggle, the struggle for oneself, the
struggle inside oneself. Is it possible to influence one's fate even as
it is being ground between the cogs of the state, between the teeth
of evil? . . . Is it possible to be sustained by powers other than
hope?
—Varlam Shalamov, *Proza, stikhi* (Prose, poetry), *Novy mir,* June
1988: 107

What will we say in the Court of the Past and the Future? There is
no blanket exoneration for us. But this we will say: there had never
been a time harder than ours, but we did not let perish what is
human in the human being. . . . We continue to believe that life
and liberty are indivisible, that there is nothing higher than the
human in the human being.
—Vasily Grossman, "O Sistinskoy Madonne" (On the Sistine
Madonna), as quoted in Lazar' Lazarev, " 'Pravda bezuslovnaya and
chestnaya': Vasily Grossman i traditsii russkoy klassiki"
("Truth unconditional and honest": Vasily Grossman and the
traditions of the Russian classical literature), *Literatura,* no. 2, 2002

How must one live in order to remain human under any, even the most extreme, circumstances, in any circle of hell, to remain an autonomous and responsibly acting individual, not to lose dignity and conscience, not to betray and not to backstab, how to survive, passing through fire and water, to hold out, without shifting the burden of one's fate onto the generations that follow—how?
—Lev Voskresensky, "Zdravstvuyte, Ivan Denisovich!" (Hello, Ivan Denisovich!), *Moskovskie novosti*, August 7, 1988: 11

Now that we so belatedly learn about so many tragedies and histories, one becomes at times unbearably ashamed of the people and the history. But, fortunately, there is a positive side to this belatedness. Belatedly but happily we learn that even in the cruelest years there were people who stood up to the mass psychosis.
—Evgeny Evtushenko, "Stalinizm po Platonovu" (Stalinism according to Platonov), in Kh. Kobo, ed., *Osmyslit' kul't Stalina* (To comprehend Stalin's cult), Moscow: Progress, 1989: 198

We have witnessed not just the collapse of the old myth but also the restoration of the truth about the real heroes of the Fatherland, the heroes whose glory has been deliberately obscured or almost entirely erased.
—I. Prelovskaya, "Mif i sud'ba" (Myth and fate), *Izvestia*, July 15, 1989: 3

THE REDISCOVERED PAST was not uniformly shameful—something solely to rue, repent, and redeem. Next to the mighty chorus of condemnation, there gradually emerged and grew stronger the quieter but insistent, crystalline notes of light and heroism. They inspired and gave hope.

Returning in books of fiction that often had waited decades to be published; in memories that could extend beyond whispers; and in documents from which the country's true history was being assembled were the luminous tales of those determined to remain true to their own definitions of good and evil, of the Russian righteous who resolved to remain moral in some of the most extreme conditions by which human soul had ever been tried. In the darkest days of Stalinism they asserted their right to be human: to think, speak, and even act as their conscience bade them. They refused to surrender the ability for moral judgment and thus moral choice. They embodied the "spirit of freedom" (*dukh svobody*), to recall the title and the leitmotif of the first, and still the finest, essay about the then just-published greatest Russian novel of the twentieth century, Vasily Grossman's *Life and Fate*.[1]

Among the most vivid and multitudinous displays of this spirit was the Great Patriotic War of 1941–45. Suddenly, one of the ultimate and noblest of personal responsibilities that fate bestows on man—to come to the rescue of one's Motherland in mortal danger—fell to each and every one of the millions of Soviet soldiers, the former Stalin's *vintiks*. The merciless war-to-the-end conferred on them what Grossman called "natural equality"; it made them "confident and strong."[2] This strength and this confidence brought freedom—the exhilarating, palpable freedom of the trenches, of the brotherhood of those about to die.

The same miracle was reported by other surviving writers and poets, all of them soldiers or war correspondents. In a poem titled "I Was Infantry in a Field with No Place to Hide," the veteran-poet Semyon Gudzenko wrote (in the lines removed by the censors at publication): "O, what freedom I was friends with!"[3]* In besieged Leningrad, poet Olga Berggol'ts recalled,

> In dirt, in darkness, in hunger, in sadness
> where death, like shadow, dragged behind us
> so happy were we at times
> such freedom we breathed
> that our grandchildren would envy us.[4]

How "freely one breathed" in Stalingrad! wrote Grossman,[5] who reported for the *Red Star* from the besieged city from the first days of the battle in summer 1942 until the German surrender in February 1943. Stalingrad had "a soul," he concluded, after watching the Red Army—its regiments often reduced to "dozens of soldiers,"[6] incessantly bombed

---

* Gudzenko chose the collective "infantry" (*pekhota*) over the singular "an infantryman" (*pekhotinets*) in the poem's title to underscore this awesome and exhilarating responsibility of an individual soldier for the outcome of the war and the fate of the Motherland.

and shelled—hour after hour, day after day beating back German troops and tanks. This soul was "freedom."[7] It was freedom, Grossman wrote, that "derailed" Field Marshall Paulus's strategy.[8] It was freedom that was the key to the "miracle of Stalingrad."[9]

The freedom for which they fought and died for was freedom not only from Nazi "slavery" but from the indignity of Stalinism. "What do you want?" a commissar in *Life and Fate* asks Captain Grekov, whose dwindling detachment held out against the daily Nazi attacks in the epicenter of the Stalingrad hell: the ruins of the famous "House Number 6/1." "Freedom," Grekov answers calmly, even "jauntily. "This is what I fight for." "We all want it," the commissar parries. "Don't tell me this," Grekov replies "What do you want with freedom? All you want is to defeat the Germans."

—And you—change the course of Soviet history?
—And you, return everything?
—What everything?
—The universal dragooning [*prinudilovka*].[10]

They all were killed, the defenders of "House 6/1," but did not retreat an inch. They died free men to save their country, where only a few months before they counted for nothing; now, suddenly, they were its full-fledged and proud citizens.[11]

Another Grossman hero was Major Ershov, an underground resistance leader in a Nazi prisoner-of-war camp, who ten years before had been denied entrance to a military academy for refusing to disown his exiled father the kulak. Instead of renouncing them to save his career as so many did, Ershov traveled for days to the place of the exile: a tiny village "between the swamp and the forest's edge." He found only his father: his mother and two young sisters died in the first two years. In the filthy, damp dugout, "reeking of beggar's food and beggar's clothes," his father told the crying Ershov of the fifty-day trip in winter in a cattle car with a hole in the roof; of women carrying children in their arms as they walked for days through the snow; of having been brought to a winter forest and told that this was their place to live.[12]

No sooner had Ershov returned to his detachment than a denunciation (*donos*) of his visit reached his superiors. Then a lieutenant, he was immediately discharged from the Red Army. Notification of his father's death came soon thereafter. Given back his commission on the second day of war, Ershov fought heroically. Like Grekov, Ershov "fought for a free Russian life." For him the victory over Hitler would be also a "victory over those camps where his mother, sisters, and father perished."[13]*

Everything is in their power; all you have is your *nyet*, a veteran prisoner of the Gulag tells the hero of Yuri Dombrovsky's *Department of Unnecessary Things*.[14] But the power of "nyet"—what Isaiah Berlin called the "negative liberty," the liberty of not being coerced into doing something one does not want to do, the liberty of not being "interfered with"[15]— becomes the mainstay of moral freedom when often not a shred of other liberties or dignities remains. "The fate leads the man," Grossman wrote as he followed his characters through the stark moral choices of war, the Gulag and Nazi death camps. "But man is free not to want to go"—even if the price of choice is his life.[16]

In a column of Jews on their way to a gas chamber, a military doctor, Major Sofia Levinton, "resisted the hated power" by not stepping out of the column to answer the repeated, life-offering call of the overseers: "Doctors? Surgeons?" And again: "Doctors? Surgeons?"[17]

In another Nazi camp, a Russian émigré Ikonnikov, too, chooses to die a moral man when he refuses to work at the gas chamber construction site, knowing that the punishment is execution. "Don't say: they are

---

* The fight against Nazism as a wider struggle for freedom apparently was a sentiment shared by heroes in other nations, and the "contest" continued wherever heroic resistance to Nazism was supplanted by resistance to the "native" totalitarianism. When, in 1982, during the martial law rule in Poland, the authorities approached one of the leaders of the Warsaw Ghetto 1942 uprising, Dr. Marek Edelman, with a "request" to help celebrate its fortieth anniversary, he said: "Don't use me to cover your shame. Forty years ago we did not fight merely to survive—we fought for life in dignity and freedom. To celebrate our anniversary here, where enslavement and humiliation are now the lot of the whole society, where words and gestures have become nothing but lies, would betray the spirit of our struggle." (Matt Schudel, " 'No Easy Moments' for a Leader of the Warsaw Ghetto Uprising," *Washington Post*, October 5, 2009: B9.)

guilty who coerce you, you are a slave, you are not guilty because you are not free," Grossman has Ikonnikov declare. "I am free! I am building the *Vernichtungslager* [the gas chamber site]. I am responsible to the people who will be gassed there. I can say 'no'! What power can forbid me to do this, if I find in myself the power not to be afraid of extermination! I will say 'no'!"[18]

In Kolyma, "prisoner Patashnikov"—formerly a healthy thirty-year-old man, who barely had the strength now to climb up to his plank bunk in the barrack at night and whose brain and soul felt "frozen and shrunk"—dreamed only of dying in a hospital and in a real bed, not on a camp "street" or in the barrack, under boots, amid curses, dirt, and "everyone's complete indifference." Yet he refused the only way he could save himself—by becoming an overseer, a brigade head, or someone else in the camp hierarchy—because he had "long ago sworn never to rape other men's will."[19]

On the verge of dying from starvation, cold and overworked in another Siberian camp, Solzhenitsyn's Ivan Denisovich, a peasant and a soldier, would not extend even by a few inches the distance "between himself and death," if the price of an extra bowl of soup or quarter pound of bread was informing on his fellow prisoners to the *kum* (the camp spymaster) or by ingratiating himself with the hated camp powers in any other way. He, too, was "preserving his soul," keeping it from the "blackness of violence," betrayal, and other "filth."[20]

A few were lucky to have died fighting, even killing some of their tormentors and executioners. Brought to Varlam Shalamov's Kolyma with the hundreds of thousands of Soviet soldiers from the Nazi POW camps "to be next in line to become like these still walking corpses," were Major Pugachev and his eleven comrades—veterans, all, "brave and believing only in their weapons" and in "dying free." For months they painstakingly planned their escape and broke out early one morning after killing two guards and seizing rifles and ammo from the camp depot. With pilots among them they headed toward the nearest military airfield to commandeer a plane. Tracked down and surrounded by hundreds of troops, they refused repeated offers to surrender, and each man fought until he was killed or unable to shoot because of wounds. They shot dead twenty-seven of their pursuers, including the head of the camp's guards. About to be captured, Pugachev remembered every one of his comrades by name and "smiled to each of them." Then he put the barrel of a handgun in his mouth and pulled the trigger.[21]

"What is the most precious thing in the world?" reads an entry in a diary of a character in Alexander Solzhenitsyn's *In the First Circle.* "That you will not participate in injustices [*nespravedlivosti*]. They [the perpetrators of injustices] are stronger than you, they were, are and will be—but not abetted by you."[22] Bequeathing a future Russia this priceless gift of a literary culture of resistance to moral slavery, choosing, heroically, personal nonparticipation in evil, Grossman, Solzhenitsyn, and Shalamov constructed most of their characters from men and women they knew or heard about. One of them could have easily been a Russian peasant, Fyodor, arrested in 1937 with all the members of a Siberian commune. (Unlike a kolkhoz, it was a truly voluntary collective farm, inspired by Tolstoy's teaching of nonviolence, self-sufficiency, and rejection of earthly authority.) When they came to arrest him, Fyodor refused to climb on the carriage to be conveyed to a prison. He was shoved inside a mattress case tied to a horse's tail and dragged for many kilometers in the snow. In prison, Fyodor would not walk to interrogations and was dragged by his feet from the third floor, "his head bumping on the steps," while he remained silent.[23]

A former candidate member of the Central Committee and a secretary of a district Party Committee in Moscow, Martimyan Ryutin was expelled from the Party in September 1930 because of his membership in the "rightist opposition," led by the critics of the breakneck "industrialization" and "collectivization," Nikolai Bukharin, Alexei Rykov, and Mikhail Tomsky. Instead of following the "oppositionists'" usual route to "reinstatement"—recantation, repentance, admission of "errors," and oaths of undying devotion to Stalin—Ryutin, together with a few other members of what was known as the "Bukharin little school" (*shkolka Bukharina*), attempted to organize an underground "Union of Marxists-Leninists." He also wrote a scathing 200-page-long critique of Stalinism, which became known as the "Platform of the Ryutin Group."[24]

In June 1932 Ryutin tried to distribute a shorter version of the "Platform": "An Appeal to All Party Members." "The Party and the dictatorship of the proletariat have been brought by the Stalin clique to an unprecedented dead end and a mortal crisis," Ryutin wrote. "In the past five years, Stalin . . . has established a personal dictatorship . . . of the most unbridled personal adventurism and savage personal despotism." The "adventurist" tempo of industrialization and collectivization, Ryutin continued, and "backbreaking" taxes resulted in a "monstrous impoverishment of the masses" and widespread starvation. The "forced" collectivization was a "wholesale robbery" of peasants, which "killed any personal motivation" in agriculture, leaving only "coercion and repression." A famine the next year, 1933, was a very likely possibility, Ryutin warned.[25] He continued:

> The entire country is muzzled. Lawlessness and violence hang over every worker and peasant. Every law is broken! . . . The working class and peasantry are driven to desperation. . . . The soviets are but the shabby appendages of the party apparatus. . . . The trade unions have become an ancillary organ of the pressure on the workers and the punishment of dissidents [inakomyslyash-chie]. In the hands of Stalin and his clique the press has become a monstrous factory of lies, falsifications and terrorism against the masses. . . .

> We must start the work immediately! It is time to end the confusion and fear of repression by that shameless and unprincipled politico, that traitor to the cause of Leninism, and begin a selfless struggle, not waiting for the beginning of the struggle from above but starting it from below. Let us marshal courage against the terror! From comrade to comrade, from group to group, from town to town—spread our slogan: down with the dictatorship of Stalin and his clique, down with the gang of unprincipled politicos and liars![26]*

---

* In a manuscript of the book *Stalin i krizis proletarskoy diktatury* (Stalin and the crisis of the proletarian dictatorship), Ryutin described Stalin's Soviet Union in the early 1930s as a "country that is impoverished, robbed, devastated, naked, and hungry, where labor productivity was undermined, along with the [population's] purchasing power; a country that lost faith in the cause of socialism, terrorized, and angry." (Alexander Borshchagovsky, ed., "Prislushaemsya k golosu Ryutina: Otryvki iz rukopisi tak I ne stavshey knigoy," [Let's listen to Ryutin's voice: Passages from a manuscript that has never become a book], *Moskovskie novosti*, May 27, 1990: 16.)

Ryutin was arrested almost immediately, yet in 1932 Stalin still needed the Politburo's consent to execute a prominent Bolshevik, and the majority voted to spare Ryutin's life.[27] Sentenced to fifteen years, Ryutin was steadily transferred to worse and more remote prisons, until he was thrown into a "strict regime" jail in the Urals, from where he could not even send letters. Returned to Moscow in 1937 (and even allowed to make a phone call to his family), Ryutin was most likely being cast in an important role in one of the show trials. Yet apparently even months of torture could not break him: he did not feature in any of the show trials.[28]

Ryutin was executed, no one knows when or where. His wife, Evdokiya, died in a camp. One of his sons, Vasily, was shot in the Lefortovo prison in Moscow; the other, Vissarion, sent to a camp in Central Asia and killed there. Only the daughter, Lyubov', survived.[29]*

Like Ryutin, a decade and a half later several dozen high school students in Voronezh were horrified by the violence, suffering, and despair around them.[30] After returning from a winter holiday ski trip through the Russian countryside, where they saw people boiling the bark of birch trees for food, they organized an anti-Stalinist "Communist Party of Youth," complete with a program, rules, an emblem, and magazines.[31] Children of top functionaries of the Voronezh oblast among them, they were well aware of the danger of their actions. Arrested, most of them would not name other members, saving dozens of lives: of the fifty-three to sixty-three members, only twenty-three were convicted.[32] Continuing to abide by their "conscience," "honor," and "honesty,"[33] after

---

* A few days before Ryutin was expelled from the Party, a meeting of workers from several plants in Moscow and Podol'sk (the largest city in the Moscow region) adopted and, on September 19, 1930, sent to the chairman of the All-Union Central Executive Committee, Mikhail Kalinin, a resolution as fearless and proud as Ryutin's "Appeal." The workers demanded that Stalin, a "despot" and "usurper," be "immediately removed" and put on trial for "uncounted crimes against proletarian masses." They also called for free elections of the country's leadership, instead of their "self-appointment," and a "change of policy" in a spirit of "real," and not "Stalinist," Leninism. Sent to "crush a viper of counterrevolution," as a headline in a local newspaper proclaimed, the OGPU was quick and thorough: not one participant of the meeting could be found alive in the 1980s. (Oksana Bogdanova, Alexander Stanislavsky, and Evgeny Starostin, "Soprotivelenie" [Resistance], *Ogonyok* 23, 1989: 10–11.)

eleven months of interrogations and torture (under which some of them were driven to madness) most were sentenced by the OSO to ten years at some of the most lethal camps in Vorkuta, Tayshet, and Kolyma.[34] The survivors, among them the group's future chronicler and a prominent poet, Anatoly Zhigulin, were saved from another term—and then another and another, until they were dead—by Stalin's death.

Another tale of moral rectitude in the face of mortal danger, was Vladimir Dudintsev's novel *White Garments* (*Belye odezhdy*), with which glasnost in Russian literature began in January 1987. It chronicled the resistance of Soviet biologists to the violent obscurantism of "Lysenkovism," named after Stalin's pet, the charlatan Trofim Lysenko. Lysenko's "socialist" biology rejected genetics as a "bourgeois pseudo-science" and insisted on the ability of organisms to pass on acquired characteristics. The latter were to be instilled by rigorous "upbringing" and "training" and, in the end, were to produce, among other things, such miracles as "frost-resistant wheat." With genes and chromosomes declared "nonexistent"[35] following the infamous Conference at the Academy of Agricultural Sciences in August 1948, biology textbooks containing these heresies were burned in bonfires in the backyards of academies, institutes, and research centers. The flames of these bonfires, in the words of one of Dudintsev's characters, were of the same "chemical composition" as those of the Inquisition fires five centuries before.[36]

White Garments, a Soviet critic noted, is about that "most difficult moral problem": how to behave "before criminals endowed with state power."[37] Like millions of their compatriots, the book's characters could not choose where and in what time to live but they could choose their "path"—the path of "conscience and intelligence," of "inner freedom," of making the "moral choice between good and evil."[38]

Some in Dudintsev's book chose an open protest, like the head of the Department of Selection and Genetics of an unnamed "institute," Professor Natan Heifitz, who refused to recant. Instead, he told a booing and hissing crowd at the institute's general meeting that they were wandering in the dark, as if "drugged, as if they had inhaled poisonous vapors," trampling the innocent underfoot.[39] Fired on the spot, before he finished speaking, he walked out, calling out "Obscurants!" (*Obskuranty!*) and slamming the door of the auditorium behind him.[40]

246 WHAT IS TO BE DONE?

All of the novel's main characters—Fyodor Dezhkin, Elena Blazhko, and Ivan Strigalyov—remained true to their calling by preserving and practicing true science in the scholarly underground. "I am protecting the cause," says Elena. "If they discover [us], [the Lesenkovites] will destroy everything."[41] Having already earned a Gulag sentence and been saved only by being drafted in the Red Army after the Nazi invasion, Ivan Strigalyov is the most talented of them and the most successful in genetic experiments. He is close to developing a new, more productive sort of potato, so much needed in his starving, postwar country—all the while pretending to follow the "progressive Soviet Lysenko science." "If you want to be a scientist . . . if you have a discovery on your hands . . . and if it is priceless, "Strigalyov explains, "and is threatened by something . . . forget about death. The fear of death is an accomplice and mainstay of evil. [One must] take away from evil its sole power—the ability to deprive one of life and liberty . . . "[42]

As were the heroes of Grossman, Shalamov, and Solzhenitsyn, Dudintsev's characters were inspired by real men and women. Lysenko's main opponent, a genius botanist and plant geneticist, Nikolai Vavilov, was tortured mercilessly during the "investigation" and starved to death in prison in 1943. Arrested and then released, geneticist Vladimir Efroimson continued openly to criticize Lysenko and was rearrested as "a socially dangerous" element.[43] Fired from a professorship in Moscow University and hounded, plant physiologist Dmitry Sabinin preferred suicide to surrender.[44] Geneticist Nikolai Timofeev-Resovsky—the legendary *Zubr* (Bison) of Soviet biology—too, "followed his convictions under any circumstances" because "he was free" in his will and his conscience, as his 1987 biography put it.[45*]

Rearrested and perishing in the Gulag, Ivan Strigalyov stood for the scores of the martyrs of Soviet science: those who followed Vavilov, Efroimson, and Sabinin—some perished in prisons and camps, others were fired,

---

* Timofeev-Resovsky refused to return from a research stint in Germany to a Soviet Union of the triumphant Lysenkovism. Captured by advancing Soviet troops at the end of World War II, he was sent to the Gulag. Dying of starvation, he was revived and was given a laboratory in the Urals, akin to a "sharashka" in Solzhenitsyn's *First Circle*, where, still a prisoner, he continued his research.

ostracized, and penniless. The publication of Dudintsev's novel occasioned the first public recognition of their valor and honor: Astaurov, Barinov, Dubinin, Formozov, Karpechenko, Lebedev, Levitsky, Lobashov, Polyansky, Rapoport, Sukachev, Tolaykov.[46] One day, the author of Timofeev-Resovsky's biography, Daniil Granin, fervently hoped, a "history of their resistance" would be written and they all would feature as heroes in it.[47]

While true heroes, in life as in literature, rebelled openly or resisted elaborately, many more guarded against a complete surrender of dignity by deploying the power of *nyet* in a quieter, less self-conscious— yet just as unyielding—way. Outside or inside the Gulag, they affirmed moral autonomy. Its motto, reported by Solzhenitsyn, Shalamov, and Dombrovsky, among other survivors, was a popular saying among zeks: *Ne ver,' ne boysya, ne prosi:* Don't trust, don't be afraid, don't beg.[48]

Early in his "concentration camp" years, Varlam Shalamov discovered a way to "undermine the slavery": act first and ask for permission later.[49] After washing the floor in the camp's headquarters, Ivan Denisovich, for instance, poured out the bucket of dirty water on the path "where the bosses walked" and where it instantly froze at minus forty degrees Celsius. Yet perhaps the most common tactic in this war on servitude was to claim one's right to say what one thought, at a time when, as one of Yuri Dombrovsky's characters warned another, a truthful word was a crime.[50] Even in the wartime Soviet Union of *Life and Fate*— with informers seemingly behind every wall and around every corner and with the SMERSH executioners hunting for "panic-mongers" and "provocateurs," "mutineers," "spies," and other "traitors"— men and women risked all for as little as a word of truth, thrown in the face of the "fear that prevented humans from being human."[51] Oh, that "magic, clear force of a frank conversation, the force of truth!" Grossman wrote. "What a horrible price people paid for a few brave words uttered without looking over one's shoulder."[52] And yet like so many, a character in *Life and Fate* dreams recklessly, out loud in front of several friends:

> Ah, dear Comrades, can you imagine what this is, the freedom
> of press? When instead of the letters of laborers to the great
> Stalin, or the information about the workers of the United

States "entering the New Year in an atmosphere of despon-
dence and poverty"—when instead of all of this, you know
what you find? Information! Can you imagine such a newspaper? A newspaper that brings information? . . . You'd know
about everything that is happening in the country: about good
harvests and poor harvests; about an accident in a mine; about
disagreements between Molotov and Malenkov; about a strike
and about speeches made by Churchill or [French Prime
Minister] Blum. . . . You know why there is no buckwheat in
stores and how many grams [of flour] a *kolkhoz* member gets
for every workday—know from the newspapers and not from
your housekeeper, whose niece came to Moscow to buy bread.[53]

"Swept up in this crazily unusual talk," all in the room knew what
they risked by not denouncing Madyarov immediately, that very night.
"Oh, what the hell," the hero of the novel, physicist Viktor Shtrum,
thought walking home that night. "At least we have spoken like human
beings, without fear, without hypocrisy."[54]

Others went further still by writing letters, like those sent to the Reception Room (*Priyomnaya*) of the Supreme Soviet. Many "expressed
disagreement with the methods of comrade Stalin"—and prompted
some of the reception room staffers to risk their own lives by hiding or
destroying some of the letters to save those who wrote them.[55]

Yet they could do nothing for others who, at the height of the terror,
wrote directly to their Supreme Soviet deputies and gave their full names
and addresses. One of them—a brother of a thirty-two-year-old architect
and inventor arrested in March 1938, convicted of "suspicion of espionage," and sentenced to eight years in the camps—deplored "careerists
and toadies," who "earned their keep" by arresting "honest people," and
by perpetrating "the horrors of 100 percent collectivization." Are you, the
Supreme Soviet deputies, good only to applaud and shout "hooray" to
Stalin and Yezhov? he demanded to know. "Please pass on this letter
to Stalin," the letter concluded. "Don't be afraid. I am not a madman. I
am a real person, with a family and a son. . . . But my sense of truth is
stronger today than my fear of the ten years of camps."[56]

Do you know what is going on in the camps, Georgy Solovyov asked
in his letter to writer and Supreme Soviet Deputy Alexei Tolstoy in August

1941? Do you know that they are filled mostly with innocent people be-cause of the complete and uncontrolled sway illiterate functionaries bent on self-preservation have over our judicial and investigative system?

> Do you know that the prisoners are kept in nightmarish
> conditions, in the open, without a roof over their heads, like
> animals, practically without food and with almost no medical
> assistance, and because of this they are dying slow and painful
> deaths? . . . Do you know that imprisoned there are thousands
> of talented doctors, engineers, agronomists—specialists for
> whom we have so urgent a need? That among these millions of
> prisoners there are women with nursing babies, that women
> give birth in these inhumane conditions, with no medical
> assistance whatsoever? We need an amnesty for at least 5–6
> million people. Please report this to Stalin . . . and I will
> consider to have done my part in this historic event by drawing
> your attention to this situation.[57]

Along with the brave candid words, friendship with the ostracized was the stuff of this quiet heroism. In early 1953—when the Soviet Union was enveloped in state-sponsored anti-Semitic hysteria and her class-mates vigorously debated whether everyone would be allowed to attend the hanging of the Jewish "doctors-wreckers" (the "murderers in white gowns") in Red Square or only those with special passes or invitations—a Moscow high school student, Natasha Tomilina, regularly visited her friend Natasha Rapoport, the daughter of one of the arrested "doctors-poisoners." Rapoport was afraid to go to school and lived with her mother in the corridor of their apartment, its rooms having been sealed off by the Ministry of State Security (MGB) after the search and arrest of her father.

Always with an apple or a sandwich for Rapaport, whose memoirs were first published in 1988, Natasha Tomilina, until then an A student, suddenly had difficulties in physics or geometry, algebra or chemistry—whatever they were studying in school that day. She took the textbooks out of her briefcase-*portfel'*, and asked her friend to "help." When the "doctors' plot" ended with Stalin's death two months later, Dr. Rapaport was freed with many apologies, and Natasha Rapoport returned to school. She found she had not fallen behind in any subject because of the tutorials her friend had engineered. For her part, Natasha Tomilina continued to insist she was just too lazy to do the homework.[58]

In the quickening onrush of a revolution, the more proximate, post-Stalin purveyors of the "spirit of liberty" received far less attention and appreciation than their Stalin-era counterparts, fictional or "real." Yet emerging from the relatively rare tributes to those who saved their and Russia's honor after Stalin's death was a credo remarkably similar to that of those who resisted Stalinism: moral self-determination; the right to personal, not state-made, notions of right and wrong; and, most of all, freedom as the mainstay of human dignity.

In 1989, a former defense attorney for many "dissidents" of the 1970s and 1980s and herself a member of the Helsinki Group, Sofya Kalistratova, remembered some of her former clients in a short newspaper article. Among them were those who protested against the 1968 invasion of Czechoslovakia by unfurling on Red Square the banner "For your and our freedom" (*Za vashu in nashu svobodu*). They had held it aloft for a few seconds before they were overwhelmed by plainclothes police, beaten, and whisked away to jail: Larisa Bogoraz, Konstantin Babitskiy, Natalya Gorbanevskaya (who came with a nursing baby in a carriage), Vadim Delone, Vladimir Dremlyuga, Viktor Feinberg (whose front teeth were knocked out by the attackers), and Pavel Litvinov.[59]

While the "Red Square Seven" were in jail, camps, mental hospitals, or exile, some of their comrades attempted to assist other political prisoners and their families with disbursements from the Solzhenitsyn Fund, established with the royalties from *Gulag Archipelago*. The fund's first "executor" (*rasporyaditel'*), Alexander Ginzburg, was arrested four times and finally sentenced to eight years in a camp. Those convicted, like Ginsburg, under Articles 190, Section 1 ("dissemination of knowingly false fabrications besmirching the Soviet state and social order"), and 70 ("anti-Soviet propaganda and agitation") of the Criminal Code were "not certain if they would be able to get out of the camp alive": another recently adopted law allowed camp administrators to "prolong indefinitely" inmates sentenced for "violations of the camp regimen."[60] These "violations" included an unfastened button on one's shirt, and three such "violations" meant an automatic retrial and a new sentence.[61]

Still, others came forward to replace Ginzburg as the fund's executor, and, one after another, they, too, were arrested: Tati'ana Khodorovich, then Mal'va Landa, Arina Ginzburg, and Sergei Khodorovich. The last was routinely and "savagely" beaten in the Butyrka prison, where he contracted tuberculosis. Khodorovich was sent to serve a sentence at a camp in Norilsk, the northernmost city of Siberia, above the Arctic Circle.[62] Only death from cancer prevented the arrest of the fund's last executor, Andrei Kistyakovsky.[63] A writer and former "dissident" prisoner, Felix Svetov, told *Komsomol'skaya pravda* in August 1990 that the human rights movement was proof that, despite everything, "the moral force survived among the people."[64]

Along with the mindless cruelty and its cover-up, the 1962 Novocherkassk massacre, too, had its heroes. A worker at the Novocherkassk Electrical Locomotive Construction Plant, Petr Siuda, spoke from a flatbed truck at the June 1 rally. He called on the striking workers to be "disciplined" and "restrained," to draw up a set of demands and march to the city center to present them to the authorities. He was arrested early next morning and two months later sentenced to twelve years in the camps.[65]

Released after serving four and a half years, Siuda devoted his life to a private investigation of the slaughter. His archive—the only known one of the event—was "enormous."[66] In June 1989 reporters from Moscow found him in a tiny room surrounded by piles of documents. The papers filled the shelves of a bookcase, covered the desk and the floor.

Even under Gorbachev, he declined to appeal for a "personal rehabilitation": "Far more important for me is the rehabilitation of all the participants in the strike and restoration of historical justice." Siuda quit the plant in early 1989 to work full time on his archive.[67] (In 1980, he had openly supported Sakharov's protest against the invasion of Afghanistan in a signed letter to Brezhnev. A few days later he was badly beaten by unknown assailants.)

In May 1990, Siuda was found dead on a Novocherkassk street, ostensibly from a "cerebral hemorrhage." The attaché case, in which he carried the key archival materials and with which he never parted, disappeared. Petr Siuda's only epitaph was a 1990 article about the Novocherkassk massacre: "He has devoted his life to the discovery of the truth. He has become a fighter against the regime in which a repetition of Novocherkassk was possible."[68]

Siuda never knew of another man who was working nearby to keep the same memory alive. The First Deputy Commander of the North Caucasus Military District, Hero of the Soviet Union, Lieutenant General of Armored Forces Matvey K. Shaposhnikov was ordered to deploy his tanks against the striking workers of the Electrical Locomotive Construction Plant as they approached the bridge on the Tuzlov River on their way to the city center and to shoot at them "if necessary." Shaposhnikov responded: "I don't see an enemy against whom tanks need to be deployed."[69] Instead, he ordered the troops and the tank crews to empty the magazines of their Kalashnikovs and machine guns.

After the carnage in the square before the Gorkom, he insisted that those who gave the order to shoot be prosecuted. Prevented from speaking publicly, he started writing letters of protest—to the Union of Soviet Writers, to the office of Prosecutor General, to the Central Committee, to the Party Congresses.[70]

"It is extremely important today that workers and intelligentsia understand the essence of the political regime under which we live," Shaposhnikov wrote in the 1960s. "They must understand that we are ruled by the worst form of authoritarianism, supported by a huge bureaucratic and military power. . . . It is vital that people begin to think, instead of blindly believing. . . . Our people have been turned into day-laborers, with no rights.[71]

He was discharged from the armed forces and expelled from the Party. His apartment was searched, and his prosecution under Article 70 was under way. Only the stellar combination of his rank, his being a Great Patriotic War veteran, and the Gold Star of the Hero of the Soviet Union, the country's highest military award, saved him from jail.[72]

In his last letter, to the Twenty-Seventh Party Congress in February 1986, General Shaposhnikov continued to "excoriate myself for not having been able to prevent the tragedy in June 1962."[73] When *Literaturnaya gazeta* reporters met with him in 1989, the eighty-three-year-old general continued to be animated by his cause: "He showed no sign of old age. He forgot nothing. He does not want to forget anything."[74]

What compelled him to act as he had, the reporters wondered. "We think," they concluded, "that it was the hatred of the spiritual slavery, which the system inculcated in people, the taking away all that was human in them."[75]

Glasnost's most celebrated embodiment of this rejection of the "spiritual slavery" was Academician Andrei Sakharov, the "father" of the Soviet hydrogen bomb and thrice Hero of Socialist Labor (the Soviet Union's highest civilian award). From wealth and privilege unimaginable to the average Soviet citizen, he followed his conscience into a life of harassment, vilification, and exile.

His death, after three brief years of freedom—December 1986 to December 1989—afforded a unique occasion for national retrospection and homage. Several hundred thousand people followed his coffin to the cemetery under a thick, wet snow in Moscow on December 17, 1989. He was hailed, first and foremost, not as a political "dissident," however influential, but as the "moral pillar" (nravstvennaya opora) in the "abyss of our spiritual poverty, oppression, and humiliation."[76]

This unlikely hero—tall, slightly stooping, shy, burring—defended his country with thermonuclear (hydrogen) weapons he helped engineer—but also, and perhaps more important, he defended it with his "heightened moral sense" (obstryonnoe nravstennoe chustvo), as Alexander Yakovlev put it in one of the many tributes to Sakharov published in every major national newspaper and magazine.[77] He was one of his country's most devoted patriots, but his "world patriotism" was stronger, and he reaffirmed it by protesting the invasion of Czechoslovakia in 1968 and of Afghanistan in 1979.[78]

Most of all, Sakharov's patriotism was in "raising the dignity" of his country by raising the dignity of its individual citizens.[79] In his 1975 Nobel Peace Prize speech, which was published for the first time shortly after his death fourteen years later, he insisted on the moral necessity of "fighting for each person, against every instance of injustice and violation of human rights."[80] Following this moral imperative, Sakharov managed to "turn the conscience" of his compatriots from a "blind obedience to anyone in power" to the realization of one's own worth: "From thinking of oneself as a tiny cog or a bolt in a gigantic machine that grinds out millions of human fates, to the understanding of the uniqueness of each life. And from a slave who exalts in receiving his food ration for good behavior, to the responsibility of a free man."[81]*

But most of all, it was said to be his example. For he was a "free man"—even when, alone, he was up "against a vast ideological machine," which in the end could kill neither his commitment to truth nor his will to "think freely."[82] Even "shackled," he was "free inside," following only the voice of his conscience, his life a reaffirmation that "freedom was inside each of us."[83]

---

* A *Moskovskie novosti* reporter recalled how stunned he and his colleagues were by Sakharov's response to the paper's request for his "wishes" for the pending Gorbachev-Reagan summit in December 1987. It was not so much the boldness of his suggestions (ignore the Strategic Defense Initiative, withdraw the Soviet troops from Afghanistan), although they were, of course, utterly novel in the Soviet political discourse at the time. It was the tone of the letter: he talked to the General Secretary of the Communist Party of the Soviet Union "like an equal." (Gennady Zhavoronkov, "Zapreshchyonnyi Sakahrov" [The forbidden Sakharov], *Moskovskie novosti*, December 9, 1990: 16).

CHAPTER SIXTEEN

The Freedom Canon

MANDELSTAM, DOMBROVSKY, SOLZHENITSYN,
PLATONOV, GROSSMAN

Only a few geniuses remained free because a genius does not
know any other form of spiritual existence.
—Alexander Shindel', "Svidetel'" (Witness), *Znamya*, September
1987: 208

Writing her *Requiem*, Akhmatova was free amid total slavery. . . . A
slave dreams of freedom, but a free artist simply lives in it.
Freedom is a state of the soul.
—Alexei German, "Sny po zakazu" (Dreams to order), *Moskovskie
novosti*, December 15, 1990: 14

Who in the twentieth century saved the honor of the nation? Were
they not Platonov, Bulgakov, Akhmatova, Solzhenitsyn? Should we
not revere them as we revere the heroes who died on the battlefield, as we revere Andrei Sakharov?
—Igor Zolotusskiy, "Solzhenitsyn: krug pervyi" (Solzhenitsyn: the
first circle), *Moskovskie novosti*, August 26, 1990: 14

WITH NORMAL CHANNELS for dissent and public debate disfigured,
blocked, or severed entirely by authoritarianism for most of its history,
Russian literature always intruded into the political realm. Writers were
at once guides to a morally superior existence and its paragons. Yet rarely

before had there been a time when the lives and work of so many of Russia's finest artists—now recovered by their newly liberated compatriots and giving their revolution much of its conviction and strength—were as tightly entwined and provided so stark an affirmation of their art's core themes as during the crucible of Stalinism and its aftermath. Aesthetic choices became inseparable from moral or even existential ones.

Foremost among these themes was the right to practice their art as they chose, to embrace what Osip Mandelstam, one of Russia's greatest poets, called "moral freedom." He traced this quality to the brilliant writer, historian, and philosopher Petr Chaadaev, who—ostracized, placed under house arrest, and declared insane by Nicholas I—remained defiant to the end.[1]

In fall 1933 Osip Mandelstam wrote a sixteen-line poem about the "Kremlin mountaineer," whose "thick fingers" were like "fat worms" and the whiskers like those of a cockroach. Surrounded by the "rabble of thin-necked" lesser chiefs, he "toyed with the services of half-humans," and executions tasted "sweet as raspberries" to him.[2]

Mandelstam freely circulated the poem, and all who read it had no doubts that he would pay with his life for it. "I am ready for death," he told his close friend Anna Akhmatova, and from that moment until he was arrested half a year later, Mandelstam, in his words, was "preparing himself mentally" to be shot.[3] His *sledovatel'*, indeed, promised a firing squad not only for Mandelstam but also for his "accomplices," that is, the readers of the poem.[4]

This was an "open rebellion,"[5] the poetic equivalent of Ryutin's manifesto. As a commentator suggested, in writing the poem instead of trying to hide from his fate, Mandelstam went out to confront it—he had "chosen it and became its master."[6] He stepped up to the barrier, like a nineteenth-century duelist,[7] like Pushkin or Lermontov—standing on the other side was not D'Anthes or Martynov but a totalitarian state.

His was not sudden heroism born of desperation; it was conviction. A poet should never apologize to anyone, Mandelstam wrote in his early twenties: "This would be unforgivable! For poetry is nothing if not the consciousness of one's righteousness."[8] This "consciousness" was "absolute": Mandelstam was convinced of the "eternal and unshakable" nature of his "righteousness."[9]

No matter what other members of the "creative intelligentsia" did to "adjust," *he* would not be Stalin's "comb-playing" court jester. Impoverished, unpublished for years, without a room he could call his own, he would not let *his* poetry be used to "teach hangmen to chirp."[10]

Amazingly, Mandelstam's life was spared after the "Kremlin mountaineer" poem. He was sentenced to a relatively mild exile in Voronezh, not far from Moscow. An amateur poet in his youth, Stalin seemed to have a soft spot for the trio of Russia's greatest living poets, Mandelstam, Anna Akhmatova, and Boris Pasternak—"masters," as Stalin put it in his famous phone call to Pasternak. When the "Kremlin mountaineer" became a Russian tsar, he seemed to feel that it was his duty to preserve these artists as his reign's patrimony, along with Mother Russia's other crown jewels. He would torment them by arrest of their relatives, husbands, and lovers; doom them to stretches of penury, ostracism, and well-organized outpourings of "people's wrath." But they were not to be killed. "Isolate but preserve," was Stalin's initial verdict on Mandelstam.[11]

The poet was rearrested in May 1938 and sentenced to five years in the camps for "counterrevolutionary activity"—another almost incredibly light sentence amid the carnage of the Great Purge. He was transported to a camp in Vladivostok in October. In his only known letter from there, Mandelstam wrote to his wife that his health was "very weak" and he was "emaciated to the extreme." It probably did not make sense to send food or warm clothes, Mandelstam continued. Yet could she still try? He was "freezing." He died shortly after, sometime in December 1938.[12]* His grave was never found.

Like Grigory Zybin, the hero of his novel *Department of Unnecessary Things*, Yuri Dombrovsky was determined to remain "at peace" with himself and preserve his good name in the eyes of the "sternest of judges"—future generations.[13] In each of his three arrests, there was never a shred of evidence against him—not even the "merest indiscretion, a slip of the tongue."[14] His *sledovatels* knew it and wished only for him not to "interfere" with

---

* In a secondhand account of a Vladivostok camp, Mandelstam appeared to believe that his *payka* (food allotment) was poisoned, and he started stealing bread from other inmates. He was repeatedly and "savagely" beaten and eventually thrown out of the barrack. He lived near garbage piles, eating refuse. "Dirty, with long gray hair and beard, in rags," he became the "camp's scarecrow." (Struve, "O. E. Mandel'shtam," xlix.)

the "investigations." Yet Dombrovsky insisted on "interfering." He refused (again, like Zybin) to admit guilt or "implicate" anyone. ("Who are
you, really?" Zybin counters the interrogator. "Who are your leaders?
What cause do you serve? . . . Plankton, slime on the ocean's surface?
Yes, historically you are just that—slime!")[15]

Dombrovsky was tortured and, as an "incorrigible," sent to serve his
sentences in what he would call "the farthest and blackest corners of the
Gulag": Kolyma, Far East, and the deadly *Ozerlag* in Taishet in Southwest
Siberia.[16] Miraculously surviving starvation and cold, pellagra and beatings,
a death sentence and a prison fire, Dombrovsky was released in 1956 after
almost a quarter of a century in prisons, camps, and exile.[17]

In the "vicious hand-to-hand combat between man and the state"[18]
(as glasnost commentators described the main theme of *The Department
of Unnecessary Things*), Dombrovsky the writer reaffirmed that which
was a "moral imperative above all laws and regulations" for Dombrovsky
the man:[19] one's right to one's own conscience. Conscience, he insisted,
was both the "main tool" and the key measure of a writer's talent: without it, the talent "crumbled."[20] We have nothing, Dombrovsky said, tears
in his eyes, toward the end of his life in the 1970s, "no money, no things,
no place in life, and, essentially, no recognition. We have only conscience
and the dignity it confers."[21]

The torment of oppressed human dignity was worse than physical
torture. It was dignity's key attributes—morality, honor, justice, truth[22]—
that Zybin's NKVD interrogator dismissed as relics from a "department
of unnecessary things"[23]—and it was them that Dombrovsky, like the heroes of his books, spent his life defending.

Toward the end of the novel, one of the characters recalls a Pushkin line: "He despises liberty / and there is no Fatherland for him." So
that's how it is, the man decides. "He who despises liberty, has no use
for the Fatherland. Because a Fatherland without liberty is no better
than a prison."[24]*

Alone in this canon, Alexander Solzhenitsyn was reclaimed by Russia
not after his death but with the publication of his major work in 1989–90.

---

* On at least one occasion Dombrovsky himself was assisted by an anonymous
  seeker after "inner liberty." After he had been released from camp and

He was exceptional (and supremely lucky) also in being able not only to resist the regime but to attack it openly, becoming one of the most feared and revered opposition figures in the Soviet Union of the late 1960s and early 1970s.

As Solzhenitsyn the artist kept writing and hiding the work he never thought he would live to see published (the publication of *One Day in the Life of Ivan Denisovich* and a few stories in 1962–63 was a miracle), Solzhenitsyn the citizen insisted on his right "not to live a lie" (*zhit' ne po lzhi*)[25]—and called on his fellow citizens to do the same. Solzhenitsyn insisted that every social and political institution and every idea for social, political, and economic improvement, no matter how great and lofty they seemed at first blush, be judged by the same ethical standards that are applied to individuals and their actions. Before its alleged utility is to be assessed, the advocates of a doctrine or movement must answer this question: Regardless of its presumed results, was what they proposed noble or base, brave or cowardly, hypocritical, false, cruel, or just and magnanimous?[26]

A World War II veteran, a survivor of cancer and of eight years in the Gulag, Solzhenitsyn believed that in his opposition to the Soviet regime he was guided by a God-given destiny to help close the "horrific gaps" in the Russian people's memory—thus enabling contrition and, with it, moral recovery.[27] His patriotism, Solzhenitsyn wrote, was not "in obsequiously pleasing" his nation but in an "honest assessment of its flaws, its sins and repentance for them."[28] Most of all, it was about remembering those "buried without a coffin, naked except for a tag on a toe."[29]

We will be asked, Solzhenitsyn wrote in his Nobel lecture, written in 1972 and published in Russia seventeen years later: what can literature do against open, shameless violence? "Let us not forget," he answered,

---

exonerated in 1956— in the standard verdict of those days, "due to the absence of the elements of crime" (*za otsutsviem sostava prestupleniya*) —Dombrovsky answered a knock on the door to find a man proffering him a typical Soviet nylon-mesh shopping bag, an *avos'ka*, filled with typewritten pages. This was the manuscript of a book Dombrovsky finished in 1939 just before he was arrested for the second time. "Here's your novel," a man said. "I was ordered to burn it but I've saved it." (Anisimov and Emtsev, "Etot . . . ," 706.)

that violence cannot live by itself: it is always interwoven with a lie. For violence has no cover but a lie, and a lie cannot sustain itself except though violence. Anyone who proclaims violence his method, must choose a lie as his principle. . . . For the regular person, the [necessary] step is not to participate in the lie. Even if it dominates the world—let it not do so through me. Yet a writer, an artist could do more still: he can vanquish the lie! For in its struggle with the lie art has always won and continues to win. . . . For the lie can hold out against all sorts of things in this world—but not against art. And no sooner has the lie been dispersed and violence is seen in all its revolting nakedness than the decrepit violence will fall."[30]

Andrei Platonov was a writer of such utter originality that a random sentence—no, half a sentence—from his story or a novel is enough to establish him, unmistakably, as the author. In his starkly distinct, almost subversive version of the literary Russian, familiar, well-worn words are forced into a syntax so singular, combinations so unexpected, seemingly haphazard and awkward, that they protrude, scratch, and bruise the eye.

What an astute critic called the "destruction of illusory wisdom,"[31] which Platonov's oeuvre accomplishes so thoroughly, begins in Platonov's sentences. They unfold like the onslaught of a ragtag army of a peasant rebellion: anarchic, porous, spurning formations and uniforms, with each soldier dressed in bright rags of his own—and yet somehow holding together, overwhelming and victorious in the end.

After recovering from a "light contusion" of Platonov's prose[32] the reader becomes a full-fledged linguistic co-conspirator, thrilling to the sight of familiar words illuminated by new meanings, and acquiring strange and fascinating facets, subtler and unknown hues.

The son of a "proletarian" and himself a metalworker in his youth, the oldest among eleven children, Platonov was a fervent supporter of the 1917 revolution but by the late 1920s became one of the first major Russian writers to investigate its unenlightened, fanatical idealism married to the relentless, everyday violence. He was an indefatigable observer and record keeper of the irreducible humanity of his compatriots. Like one of his most memorable heroes—the "Doubting" (*Usomnivshiysya*) Makar

Gannushkin—Platonov "started to worry" about the revolution's increasingly unbearable toll on the soul. The "clear voice" of a nameless "proletarian" in the Makar story seemed to be Platonov's guiding artistic impulse: "to us, force is not valuable"; there is always more than enough brute force; "it is the heart that matters."[33]

It was the fate of this collective Russian "heart" amid the "cult of violence," spawned by a consolidating totalitarianism of the late 1920s, and early 1930s, that became the overarching subject of Platonov's novels—a deep, gnawing worry about, as Platonov put it, the "perishing or surviving people of his poor Motherland, so merciless to herself."[34] At a time when brutality reigned unchallenged, every death signaled to Platonov a breach of a "moral law," the coarsening of the soul of the "masses," the "cheapening" of their lives and the "devaluing" of their sacrifices.[35] Lies, too, perverted the goals of the revolution. "Land to the peasants!" a village blacksmith declares angrily in the novel *Chevengur*, recalling one of the revolution's main and most powerful slogans. "And so what happened? They have given us the land but have taken all the grain, to the last. Go ahead and gag yourself on such land."[36]

As an "avalanche" of insanity, of "mass psychosis" descended on the country, Evgeny Evtushenko wrote in one of the first essays on Platonov's recovered work; as this catastrophic landslide "buried under it the formerly fecund fields, villages, churches, the dignity of the Russian worker, and the intelligentsia's habit of free thinking"; and as the people, swept up in this murderous flood, voluntarily or from fear, turned into rocks that "smashed everyone who refused to become stone-like," Platonov stood athwart the deadly stream and, like Makar Gannushkin, "began to doubt."[37]

Stalin reportedly called the "Doubting Makar" story "ambiguous"—at a time, the Critic-in-Chief added, when ambiguity could not be tolerated.[38] Two years later, the *vozhd*'s sentence was stern and final: "scum!" "bastard"! (*svoloch! podonok!*), Stalin was said to have written in the margins of a Platonov novella. By 1930 Platonov was no longer "publishable."[39] With the exception of a 1946 story, immediately condemned by the official critics, no fiction of his was to see the light of day in his lifetime.

Like the other "masters," whose lives Stalin was said to have "managed" personally—Anna Akhmatova, Mikhail Bulgakov, Boris Pasternak, and, until 1938, Osip Mandelstam—Platonov apparently was to be "isolated but preserved."[40] He was never arrested. He was even allowed to become a war correspondent for the Red Army's main newspaper *Red Star*. But his fifteen-year-old son, a schoolboy, was taken away in 1938, served a six-year sentence in lead mines, and was released mortally ill with tuberculosis. Nursing him, Platonov likely contracted the same illness, which in a few years would kill him too.[41]

Unpublished and starving, he did odd menial jobs for the Writers' Union: sweeping the grounds in front of the union's magisterial villa in the center of Moscow and removing snow with a wooden shovel.[42] ("Here's the Writer!" the head of the Writers' Union, Alexander Fadeev, was rumored to have said to a visitor, pointing to Platonov, sweeping the courtyard of the union's luxurious headquarters in downtown Moscow. "And I am shit.") Platonov died in 1952 unmourned and seemingly forgotten.

Platonov's greatest novels, *Chevengur* and *Kotlovan* (The foundation pit), published in Russia almost six decades after they were written, are about "utopia in power":[43] in a "spontaneous commune" of the small provincial Russian town of Chevengur and among the diggers of a giant foundation pit for a building that was to house all the "local proletariat." Chevengur was a proto-totalitarian mini-state, a "model" of still-unconsolidated Stalinism and Nazism, and the roles of the protagonists were fixed with an eerie prescience[44]—as if they were stock characters in a totalitarian Commedia dell'Arte. There is Leader, who thinks deep although not always coherent thoughts; wily Manager, who implements these "cannibalistic" thoughts (not forgetting to snatch choice pieces of plundered property along the way); and Executioner, who shoots anyone without thinking twice.

Anticipating not only the peasant hecatomb in the Soviet Union but also the Holocaust in hundreds of Polish, Ukrainian, and Russian towns and villages a decade later, Platonov portrays a mass killing of "surplus class scum." The "petty bourgeois" inhabitants of Chevengur are forced into the town square to be shot by regular troops. In *The Foundation Pit*, the kulaks are "liquidated" as men, women, and children are crowded on a giant raft and pushed off the shore "into the unknown," crying and calling out to their neighbors and friends.[45]

"What should I do in this life to be needed by myself and others?" the desperate Doubting Makar asks, in a dream, a "learned man," who "stood high on a hill and would not break his silence to answer."[46] For Platonov, salvation came through empathy and work. "The most important thing is to plant souls in people," Platonov wrote in his diary.[47] His art was the means of accomplishing this task, and his life's unbending resolve was to practice it, come what may. "Labor is conscience," Platonov would repeat.[48] "He who has taken up a pen, must write! If we don't write, what then?"[49]

For Platonov, the truth could only be one and whole. It could not be bent or partial, and the betrayal of ideals was "impossible."[50] Even inside a catastrophe, a man can live his life treasuring his "secret, reconquered," inner freedom.[51] That freedom was the sum of all that is "accidental," "unordered," and truly heartfelt in a man's soul.[52] It was this faith, more than anything, that appeared to have helped Platonov believe that the "twilight that hangs over the world and casts its shadow on the human heart is not an eternal darkness, only fog before sunrise."[53]

One is almost certain to be stunned to learn that Vasily Grossman wrote most of *Zhizn' i sud'ba* in the 1950s—some of it when Stalin was still alive.[54] There is not a slightest sign of "internal censorship" in the book. The degree of what a critic called the "concentration of truth, fearlessness, and inner freedom"[55] is striking and likely without parallel in Soviet Russian literature. In a still-totalitarian Soviet Union, barely "thawed" from the paralysis of the Stalinist terror, Grossman's was "the novel of a man who regained his sight, a man who was free."[56]

He continued to behave like a free man after he submitted, in 1960, the finished manuscript to a leading literary journal, *Znamya,* and was told by an editorial board member that his "harmful," even "hostile," novel would not be published in less than "250 years."[57] So terrified were the *Znamya* editors that, posthaste, they forwarded a copy of the manuscript to the "appropriate authorities." The KGB came, searched Grossman's apartment, and took away all sixteen copies of the manuscript along with every page of the drafts and every used sheet of carbon paper.[58] None of these materials were ever seen again. The novel published in the first four 1988 issues of the *Oktyabr'* magazine was put together from two surviving texts: a "clean" copy and a draft, each kept hidden by a different friend for twenty-seven years.[59]

Grossman wrote a letter to First Secretary and Prime Minister Nikita Khrushchev. And that note, too, was unprecedented in the tone of an address by a Russian writer to a Russian ruler. "The current situation is senseless," Grossman insisted. "I am physically free but the book to which I have dedicated my life is in jail—but it is I who wrote it, and I have not repudiated and am not repudiating it. . . . I continue to believe that I have written the truth and that I wrote it loving, empathizing with, and believing in the people. I ask for freedom for my book."[60]

The writer was granted an interview with the Soviet Union's final authority on such matters, the ideology's guardian-in-chief Mikhail Suslov, who confirmed the *Znamya*'s board verdict. (By some accounts it was Suslov who gave *Life and Fate* the 250-year pre-publication sentence.) After Suslov, there could be no appeals.

Grossman never recanted. He died of lung cancer in poverty and obscurity three years later. No book or story of his was allowed to be reprinted in the next twenty years, and his name was forbidden to be mentioned in print.[61]

In 1988, leading Soviet literary critic Vladimir Lakshin compared reading *Life and Fate* to standing in a dense crowd inside an immense, airy temple, whose walls and cupola contain the echoes of hundreds of conversations.[62] (Some twenty years later Harvard's Stephen Greenblatt would call the book a "stupendous twentieth-century heir" to *War and Peace*.)[63] Yet consciously Tolstoyan by design, Grossman's novel had another model as well: Chekhov.[64] In a passionate, unguarded soliloquy delivered by one of his characters, Grossman extols Chekhov — with his "millions of characters" and his attention to each of them —as the first "democrat" among Russian writers. They were unique human beings (*lyudi*) to Chekhov, Grossman continued, every one of them: *lyudi* first—and only then "priests, Russians, shopkeepers, Tatars, workers."[65] Chekhov was the "standardbearer . . . of a real Russian democracy, Russian freedom, and Russian human dignity."[66]

For Grossman, freedom was not so much the sum of legal norms but "an inner independence, freedom of spirit."[67] The preservation of this freedom, this dignity, was the most important, fundamental condition of a properly human existence, and there was no doctrine or public yearning to which this freedom and this dignity could be sacrificed.[68]

"I saw the unflinching force of the idea of public good, born in my country," Grossman wrote in one of the many *War and Peace*–like direct authorial interpolations in *Life and Fate*:

> I saw it first in the universal collectivization. I saw it in [the Great Purge of] 1937. I saw how in the name of an ideal, as beautiful and humane as that of Christianity, people were annihilated. I have seen villages dying of starvation, I have seen peasant children dying in Siberian snow. I have seen trains carrying to Siberia hundreds and thousands of men and women from Moscow and Leningrad, from all the cities of Russia—men and women declared enemies of the great and bright idea of public good. This idea was beautiful and great, and it has mercilessly killed some, disfigured the lives of others, and has torn wives from husbands and children from fathers.[69]

It was in this sacrifice of individual freedom to the state's ideology that Grossman discerned the key parallel between Stalin's Soviet Union and Hitler's Germany—an analogy that even at the height of Khrushchev's "thaw" was "beyond the pale," "mortally dangerous," and among the most terrifying to the *Znamya* editors of the novel's so many heresies.[70]

"We are all brave today, to be sure," the editor of the *Oktyabr'* magazine (and chairman of the "commission on the literary legacy of V. S. Grossman"), Anatoly Anan'ev, told a readers' conference a few months after he published *Life and Fate*. "But who else would have dared to compare the two regimes—Stalin's and Hitler's—three decades ago; compare them along parameters that are so obvious to us now? Stalinism destroyed the most important in man—his dignity."

Another participant at the same conference was struck by the shedding of "ideological stereotypes" in the book:

> How was the [Great Patriotic] war presented to us before [Grossman]? Here are we, there are the Nazis. Here's light, there's darkness; here's truth, there're lies; here's goodness,

there's evil. Grossman was the first to have changed the propor-
tions; [he] approached these two systems not just in their
opposition but in their sinister historical similarity. For as far
as a human being is concerned, the regime that Hitler represented and the one Stalin inculcated intersected in the humiliation of man, his freedom, his will, his dignity, his choice.[71]

To recover and maintain the man's "right to be different, unique, to
live, feel and think in his own, separate way" was for Grossman the defining objective of "human associations."[72] Sometimes, he writes in *Life and
Fate,* "a powerful prejudice" is born and, instead of a means of strengthening human community, "race, party, and state" become the end.[73] "No, no,
no! The sole, true, and eternal objective of the struggle for life is *man*," his
"humble particularity," his "right to this particularity."[74]

This right was granted by freedom. Don't you understand that a man
cannot live without democracy and freedom? émigré-Menshevik Chernetsov implores (in vain) the already mentioned "Old Bolshevik" Mostovskoy, the former division commissar and now a fellow inmate in a
German prisoner-of-war camp.[75] "It seems to me that life could be defined as freedom," insists another character. "Freedom is the main principle of life. It is here that the borderline runs: freedom and slavery, dead
matter and life. The entire evolution of the matter is the movement from
a lower degree of freedom to a higher."[76] And when a man dies, continues one of the authorial digressions, he moves from the world of freedom to that of slavery: "Life is liberty, which is why dying is a gradual
extinguishment of freedom. . . . The consciousness fades away, the fire
of freedom goes out."[77]

Since freedom was life, Grossman believed, totalitarian "non-freedom"
(*nesvoboda*) was doomed, despite the string of smashing, horrible victo-
ries for slavery and tyranny in the twentieth century. The "innate human
desire for freedom is indestructible," Grossman wrote. "It could be suppressed but it cannot be eliminated."[78] The "superviolence of a totalitarian state," he continued, can drive out freedom—but only temporarily, for
"a man would never voluntarily reject freedom. And in this conclusion is
the light of our time, the light of the future."[79] No matter how tall the
buildings of "non-freedom" and how powerful its cannons, reasons the
hero of Grossman's lightly fictionalized meditation on Stalinism, *Forever*

Flowing, "no matter how boundless the power of the state and empires, all this is a fog, which will disappear. Forever extant, developing and alive is the only one true power—the power of freedom. To live, for man—is to be free."[80]

Amid a brilliant academic career, the main character of Grossman's *Life and Fate,* nuclear physicist Viktor Shtrum, whose acquaintance we have made in the preceding chapter, is denounced for defending the "bourgeois" physics of Einstein against the emergent "national" Soviet "science." Although repeatedly warned that refusing to recant promptly and publicly was "akin to a suicide," he would not attend the meeting at his institute where he was to be excoriated and then expected to confess his "deviations" and beg for forgiveness.[81]

His phone silent, his colleagues and friends crossing the street to avoid greeting him or his wife or his teenage daughter, Shtrum expects the "proverbial knock at the door" heralding his arrest or at the very least the order to vacate his apartment and surrender his ration cards in the starving 1943 Moscow. Yet in the middle of it all Shtrum is suddenly filled with an unknown thrill: the freedom to resist, to stand his ground! The "terror" that permeates the life of every Soviet citizen—aware of one's own "pitiful powerlessness" before the boundless and "lethal" power of the state and its "all-annihilating wrath"—seems to have disappeared. In this sudden, exhilarating liberation, Shtrum is no longer afraid to say what he thinks. He stops whispering and speaks loudly to his wife and daughter about the "unbearable" mendacity of the newspapers and of the insult of seeing the "ignoramuses with party membership cards" direct science and culture.[82]

In a few days, the phone rings. It is Stalin. Suddenly "interested in the division of atoms' nuclei," the *vozhd'* is very supportive of Shtrum's work in nuclear theory. The two-minute conversation vaults the ostracized physicist to the very top of the Soviet state's science "conglomerate." He is given his laboratory back; his every request for equipment and personnel is immediately granted. A personal car with a chauffer waits to take him to the institute every morning.

Yet after a few weeks of triumph Shtrum begins to feel "empty." Stranger still, he is nostalgic for the "lightness" that was his when the phone did not ring and colleagues and acquaintances pretended not to see him. Those days, when his head "brimmed with thoughts of truth, freedom, God," seem so happy now.[83] A "piercing" sense of loss envelops Shtrum—the loss of something "strangely wonderful, touching, good," a regret for "something precious" that was forever gone.[84]

One sleepless night Shtrum thinks he has happened on the source of growing despair: he had exchanged his "inner freedom" for a place on the "state's magic carpet," which lifted him higher and higher—and away from himself.[85] He had been so much "freer and stronger" abandoned by everyone, listening to steps on the staircase.[86] He no longer has—and must regain!—the ability to live what he preaches when, lonely and frightened but determined not to retreat, he encourages his sister-in-law to persist in her efforts to find and help her just-arrested ex-husband:

> "Zhenya, my dear, you have done as your conscience has told you. Believe me, doing so is the finest thing that could be given a human being. . . . This is our main misfortune—living not according to our conscience. We say what we don't believe. We feel one thing but do another. . . . But socialism is not [about triumphs in] heavy industry. It is, first of all, the right to one's own conscience. It is awful—to deprive man of his right to conscience. And if a man finds in himself the strength to do as his conscience directs him, he feels such a swelling of joy!"[87]

The Shtrum pages of *Life and Fate* end with the hero's pledge to the memory of his mother, killed by the Nazis in a Ukrainian town, like Grossman's own mother, who was shot along with thousands of Jews in Berdichev on September 15, 1941:[88c*]

---

* "My dearest," Grossman wrote his mother, Ekaterina Savel'evna, on the twentieth anniversary of her murder, "twenty years have passed from the day of your death. I love you, I remember you every day of my life, and the grief has been in my heart for all these twenty years, never leaving. . . . You remain the same, as when you lived—in my heart. . . . And as long as I live—you will live too. And when I die, you will live in the book, which I dedicated to you and whose fate is like your fate." (As quoted in Lazar' Lazarev, "Dukh svobody" [The spirit of freedom], the postscript to Vasily Grossman, *Zhizn' i sud'ba* [Life and fate], Moscow: Knizhnaya palata, 1989: 671.)

Everything in the world is nothing compared to the truth and purity of one little man—not the empire, spread from the Pacific Ocean to the Black Sea, not science. . . . Every day, every hour, year after year, one must fight for one's right to be human, kind, and pure. And there mustn't be pride in this struggle, nor vanity, only humbleness [*smirenie*]. And if black times bring an hour without hope, man should not be afraid of death if he wants to remain human.[89]

CHAPTER SEVENTEEN

In Man's Image, I

"PRIVATIZING" THE STATE AND ECONOMY

A man for the state—or the state for a man? This is the main question.
—Rayr Simonyan and Anatoly Druzenko, "Kuda my idyom?"
(Where are we going?), *Ogonyok,* no. 37, 1989: 3

Let so-called great progressive ideas step aside, let's begin with man [an individual].
—Vasily Grossman, *Zhizn' i sud'ba,* 214

Perhaps our entire revolution today is in this: attention to an individual. To raise the value of each man, his uniqueness — I think this is the most important thing now.
—Oleg Efremov, People's Actor of the USSR, *Argumenty i fakty,* November 14–20, 1987: 7

We must learn to love and respect not the man that will be but the one that is. . . . There is not, nor can there be, any alternative to common human morality, to the ideals of goodness, justice and respect for each individual. There is not, nor can there be, any alternative to the rights and liberties of man.
—Alexander Tsypko, "Khoroshi li nashi printsypy?" (How good are our principles?), *Novy mir,* April, 1990: 202

Perestroika is a natural development toward humanism and democracy. Toward every person's and every people's right to a conscious creator of one's own fate. Toward rationality and responsibility, and toward the moral basis as the center of the personal and social life.
—Alexander Yakovlev, "Rabotat' po sovesti, zhit' chestno" (To work conscientiously, to live honorably), *Pravda*, February 28, 1989: 2

The goal and the responsibility of the citizens and the state are to secure social, economic and civil rights of the individual.
—Andrei Sakharov, "Konstitutsiya Soyuza Sovetskikh Respublik Evropy i Azii" (Constitution of the Union of Soviet Republic of Europe and Asia), December 1989,* in "Konstitutsionnye idei Andreya Sakharova" (Constitutional ideas of Andrei Sakharov), *Oktyabr'*, May 1990: 145–46

LIKE EVERY GREAT MODERN revolution, this one was about reclaiming and extending human dignity, however it was defined by public opinion leaders at the time. Almost from the beginning, those who began the reforms in search of a non-Stalinist socialism "with a human face"—and those who cheered them on so effectively—appeared to resolve to put man (*chelovek*, or individual, human being) at the "forefront" (*na pervyi plan*)[1] of their political, economic, and social agendas.

For Mikhail Gorbachev, the "renewal" of the society was inseparable from "the struggle for the dignity of man, his elevation, his honor."[2] The "ideal" they struggled to attain was a "spiritually autonomous" and "free" man: free to have his own opinions and to follow his conscience.[3] "Understood as a work-in-progress," two historians wrote in *Izvestia*, "socialism is but the sum of reference points, among which people should be free to choose their own Temples and their own roads to these Temples."[4]

---

* According to Elena Bonner, Sakharov's wife, he worked on the draft of the constitution up until an hour before his death on December 14, 1989. (Elena Bonner, "Iz vospominaniy" [From the memoirs], in "Konstitutsionnye idei Andreya Sakharova" [Constitutional ideas of Andrei Sakharov], *Oktyabr'*, May 1990: 165, 168.

Man's freedom, his sovereignty, his right to "social justice" were declared the "highest values of socialism."[5] For the first time in more than
seventy years the individual was to be not the means of the party-state's
aims, but a key objective himself.[6] He was placed squarely "at the center
of the system,"[7] his value proclaimed "sovereign"[8] and "innate."[9]

What political and economic arrangements would be most conducive
to such an arrangement? What would best secure man's "sovereignty, self-
development, and self-realization"?[10] First, there would have to be a completely different type of state: a state that was not afraid of its people but
founded on their free will,[11] a state to which the people's liberty and political self-determination were indispensable. "Socialism cannot be coerced
into existence," wrote a contributor to a 1990 collection of essays. "Slaves
cannot build a free, just society, just like humanism cannot be affirmed by
fire and sword. Great goals can be achieved only by free people."[12]

The political and, even more important, moral sovereignty of each
citizen necessitates what Alexander Yakovlev called a "self-regulating"
society,[13] and a state that such a society would forge should be as responsible to individual citizens as they were to it.[14] The state's interests could
no longer be "above" those of the people.[15]

Soon, however, even such a dramatic redistribution of responsibilities between a formerly all-powerful state and a society, until then completely dominated by the state, was no longer considered just and had to
be redrawn in society's favor. The interests of the individual had to be
given priority over the interests of the state.[16] "The state for the people,
not the people for the state!" was the "central principle" of the electoral
platform of the "voters' bloc" Democratic Russia in January 1990.[17]

Society must not merely be on equal footing with the state but be
elevated high "above" the state and "control" it.[18] The old political order
was declared as dangerous an "absurdity" (*nelepost'*) as a hotel in which
the employees ordered the guests around.[19]

The Soviet power pyramid had to be inverted, vaulting the erstwhile
vanquished over the victor. In this nation of avid chess players, the metaphor of "castling" (*rokirovka*) was used to illustrate the goal: from the executive's controlling the society to a society "unconditionally" in command
of the executive branch.[20] Decision-making must be changed from "top
down" to "bottom up," a reader from the Pskov region wrote *Komsomol'skaya
pravda* in March 1989.[21]

Formerly all-powerful, omniscient, and inscrutable, the state was to be "demystified" (*razmistifitsirovano*) and desacralized.[22] Instead of people serving the state, the state should serve the people, concluded a former cosmonaut and Hero of the Soviet Union Konstantin Feoktistov.[23] People, not the state, were the rightful "subject" of national economy, the owner of the country's wealth, and the state was merely an administrator, a "manager" (*rasporyaditel'*).[24] Just as material amenities were no longer something for which the people should be eternally grateful to the state, so rights and liberties were not granted to them by the executive.[25]

The state could do a great deal, but—and this was now seen as a bitter but indisputable lesson of the twentieth century—it was "extremely dangerous" to allow the state to claim all the power and *all* the property.[26] First, the radical essayists reasoned, the state had been shown to be unable to manage the whole of the economy, culture, and morality, proving that civil society was utterly indispensable for these tasks.[27] Second, and most important, such a claim and such administration resulted in the individual's "total dependence" on the state.[28] Instead, *society* should construct the state and hire its apparatus. These "employees of the people" should have no material privileges or, more important, "psychological" advantages and immunity from the law.[29]

Thus, the country's "central vector" of development should point toward self-rule (*samoupravlenie*): all that people can do themselves—in politics, the economy, and "social" matters—they must do without the interference of the authorities.[30] Self-rule was the only reliable road to a *real* "government by the people" (*narodovlastie*), as opposed to its hollow propaganda equivalent.[31]

To be sustainable, this newly "privatized" social order required a new "psychology" of citizenship. First, it was necessary to discard the notion of the "conflict-less" society. A society without conflicts of interests and political diversity—under an all-knowing and infinitely just state—was a myth. The attempts at such a "paradise on earth" had inevitably led to a "countrywide prison," a giant concentration camp.[32] Just as competition among the producers of goods was the engine of an economy, so the competition for power was the motor of political development and a guarantee against stagnation.[33] The state's role was to reflect and enforce compromises between competing interests.[34] This new "just" state would not "drag" society toward a "common goal"; instead, it would guard—"vigilantly and fiercely"—everyone's equality before the law, the parity of rights and opportunity.[35]

"Learning to live without the leash"[36] of a master state—at once a guardian, taskmaster, and prison warden—required the exercise of a nearly forgotten and almost atrophied moral limb: personal responsibility. "Perestroika is creating a new type of social relations, in which, instead of the leaders taking care of the welfare of an infinitely submissive (vsepokornyi) people, everyone truly becomes the master of one's own fate," philosopher Leonid Gol'din wrote in August 1989. "This means: I am responsible for myself. . . . Instead of equality in poverty and powerlessness [bespravie], perestroika has given everyone a chance for change."[37]

In turn, individual responsibility presupposed the recovery of individual choice; first and foremost, moral choice.[38] Entering a "world of democracy and individual rights" entailed the end of the "mono-" or "total" ideology and required the "de-ideologization" of the state.[39] Morality had to be denationalized: "moral norms and rules" were to become "personal" again.[40] The state would no longer force views and beliefs on anyone, even if they were the views and beliefs of the majority.[41] On the contrary, one of the main tasks of this new species of authority would be precisely to prevent infringements on the freedom of thought and conscience.[42]

"Universal values" (obshchechelovecheskie tsennosti) were to be recovered and acted on.[43] Of course, state policies change, a reader from Voronezh wrote Komsomol'skaya pravda, but there is something "eternal," something separate from the business of state: charity, tolerance, honesty.[44] They were "inner reference points" (vnutrennie orientiry) to live by.[45] Just as the economy could not be revived without "real" money as the universal tender and equivalent of all goods and services, so the "moral sphere" would not revive without the return to its own "convertible currency": dignity and honor.[46] Only recently labeled "bourgeois values" the latter were, instead, a "product of humanity's long history," the "crown of civilization."

Only a "moral democracy" was consistent with an emerging design for a new Russian state—one "based on deep-rooted morality and conscience," Alexander Yakovlev hoped.[47] Our revolution, wrote a leading legal scholar, would succeed only as a "highly moral process."[48] The "joining" of politics and morality was the key postulate of perestroika, agreed the writer Ales' Adamovich.[49]

In this "moral democracy" people would be able to defend their own rights—as well as assist their fellow citizens in protecting theirs. Monitoring the state's human rights performance would no longer be a "dissident" activity, the business of a few heroic, self-sacrificing individuals.[50] Everyone could, and should, participate in the enforcement of individual rights.[51] The "opportunity to object" (vozmozhnost' vozrazit') must be open to everyone. Without such openness, wrote prominent commentator Yuri Burtin, "we cannot live."[52]

Did we not sign the 1975 Helsinki Accords, which included commitments to human rights and liberties? a professor of jurisprudence demanded to know. And did we not confirm these commitments at the follow-up Vienna Conference on Security and Cooperation in Europe in January 1989?[53] If so, we must scrupulously fulfill our obligations and not evade them by hiding behind the fig leaf of "national "sovereignty," as the Soviet Union had done for decades. The "moral dignity" of the country was something more important than its "sovereignty."[54]*

The head of the Soviet delegation at the Vienna conference agreed: securing human rights was a common chore, not the monopoly or privilege of only some nations.[55] "Is it the West that needs the Soviet people to have access to the entire panoply of liberties that are traditionally known as human rights?" Foreign Minister Eduard Shevardnadze asked in *Argumenty i fakty* in May 1989. "It is you and I who need them, our children, our future socialism. Without developed and guaranteed human rights, there is no—nor can there be any—democracy, and there can be no lawful state."[56]

The new state was going to conduct business in a morally superior manner as well. The ends, no matter how lofty, would no longer justify the

---

* In summer 1988 "over 100" top Soviet experts on international relations, diplomats, and "public figures" were asked to agree or disagree with this statement: "[A country's] human rights cannot be 'a zone outside criticism,' including criticism by other countries." Of the polled, 92 percent agreed. (Andrei Mel'vil' and Alexander Nikitin, "Edino myslit' vse ne mogut" [Everyone cannot think in the same way], *Moskovskie novosti*, August 8, 1988.)

means because the means were but "the ends in progress": they shaped the goals.[57] A truly powerful, "strong" state did not have to deploy "a wide repressive system": it secured order without massive violence and coercion. Such a state would not be afraid of its people.[58]

Just as it necessitated a new concept of the state, "putting man in the center" caused a rethinking of the country's economic system. First to be overhauled were the very criteria of success: national wealth was no longer to be measured in the growth of "industries" ("heavy" or "light"), in the tons of pig iron and chemical fertilizer, the miles of rolled steel or fabrics, or the billions of watts of electricity. Instead, the national economy's sole goal was the prosperity it brought to the people. "A powerful and rich state is not the same as a powerful and rich people," wrote *Literaturnaya gazeta*'s editor, Fyodor Burlatsky. "The state could be wealthy but the people are doomed to bare store shelves, shortage of housing, and pensions as low as thirty rubles a month! Just as the freedom of a nation is based only on the freedom of each individual, so is the wealth of a nation derived solely from the wealth of each family."[59] A state with 40 million people in poverty, he continued, can no longer be considered advanced and prosperous![60]

No longer a mere "factor" or a "resource," man was to become the ultimate goal of economic production, the sun around which the economy would revolve.[61] The "utmost satisfaction of the material and spiritual needs" of the people, as the striking Kuzbass miners proclaimed in November 1989, should be the top national priority.[62] Instead of the overall GDP (*valovoy produkt*) figures, the miners continued, economic achievement should be defined by "the physical and moral health of individuals, their leisure, and their spiritual development."[63] Reaching, in two to three decades, the "world standard" of prosperity—a house or an apartment of one's own, a car, kitchen appliances, a "freely chosen" job, and "access to education, healthcare, culture"[64]—this is how economic success was to be defined from now on.

Society would be shaping the direction of the economy because goods and services would cost not what a bureaucrat said but what a consumer would be ready to pay.[65] By giving people choice, the market would give them "the power of the consumer" and thus a say in how the economy developed, which enterprises ought to prosper, and which, "punished by customer derision," leave the scene.

To let this happen, the economy needed to be "de-ideologized." Every kind of property and every kind of economic activity was acceptable so long as it helped to "feed the country," to "cloth and shod man," to provide him with the "articles of daily necessity" (*predmety pervoy neobkhodimosti*).[66] The economy had to stop being "political" and start being "effective."

In the modern world, so seemed to be the gathering consensus, such an economy could not exist without the "freedom factor."[67*] For Burlatsky, Leonid Brezhnev's eighteen years in power (universally decried as the "period of stagnation") were at least useful in proving beyond any doubt that state socialism as practiced in the Soviet Union was an economic "dead end."[68] Instead, the key conditions of the "modern technological revolution" were "free labor, personal initiative and personal interest, and competition."[69] Tabooed for seven decades, "private property" and "market"[†] had to be revived as the means to secure these conditions.

This meant the abandonment of the state's economic monopoly. Perhaps one day, Vasily Selyunin wrote, "a courageous man" would stand in front of the national television cameras and say something like this:

> Brothers and sisters, my friends.[‡] The state obviously has failed you in the task of feeding and clothing you. But, truth be told,

---

[*] "We must return to freedom," a liberal economist quoted from a 1921 letter of a prominent Russian writer Vladimir Korolenko to Maxim Gorky. "Much has been despoiled already, but if there is anything that can return us to some approximation of our former well-being, it is only liberty. First off, freedom of trade. Then, freedom of the press and of opinion. . . . We must unite and with combined efforts find the way out of the dead end into which we stumbled." (Tatyana Karyagina, "Ya i my" [I and we], *Literaturnaya gazeta*, May 24, 1989: 12.)

[†] The 1921–29 NEP interlude notwithstanding, the fundamental economic principle of the Soviet state was derived from Marx's 1848 *Communist Manifesto:* "the theory of the Communists may be summed up in the single sentence: abolition of private property."

[‡] Most Russians over fifty years of age were likely to recognize in this oration the beginning of Stalin's July 3, 1941, radio address to the nation after the Nazi invasion.

this is not really its job. There is, however, one thing that the
state can promise you: it will not interfere with your work and
it will protect a peasant from his aggressive neighbor, it will
save an entrepreneur from a bandit and shield a plant worker
from "plans" and "valuable instructions" from above.[70]

Most of all, however, private property was a political tool, a battering ram
with which to destroy the economic foundation of totalitarianism and
forge the "material base" of democracy.[71] Understood as the return of
property from the state to the people,[72] the end of the state's economic
monopoly was viewed as liberation from modern serfdom.[73] A lawful
state was impossible without "independent citizens," Alexander Solzhenitsyn insisted in his 1990 manifesto "How We Should Make Russia Good
for Living" ("Kak nam obustroit' Rossiyu"), and such a citizen cannot be
without private property.[74]

People's "economic independence" was to become the foundation of
democracy.[75] For "democratization" could unfold under any combination
of ownership—private, cooperative, shareholding—except under the state's
unchallenged control of the economy.[76] Private property is the basis
without which "free individuality cannot be formed," a teacher from the
Volgograd province wrote *Komsomol'skaya pravda* in November 1990.
"This property is the backbone of man's independence and his protection."[77]

To the authors of the September 1990 blueprint of an economic
revolution, "economic self-determination" and the freedom of economic
choice guaranteed personal freedom and responsibility, which promoted
modern citizenship and, with it, political stability.[78] Along with political
rights and liberties, "economic independence" would remake "people"
into "individuals"—thinking, active, and responsible.[79] They titled their
manifesto "Man. Liberty. Market."

Just as this "free-and-enterprising" (*svobodno-predprinimatel'skiy*) labor was hoped to be capable of working "economic miracles,"* it would

---

* There is only one way for the state to become rich—through the enrichment of
  its citizens, a columnist concluded. Thus the state had no other choice than to
  "untie" its people's hands. (Boris Vishnevskiy, "Voyna bogateyushchim?" [A war
  on those who are becoming richer?], *Komsomol'skaya pravda*, July 29, 1989: 1.)

also spawn the institutions of a free society.[80] "We want to introduce market economy as a precondition for the forging of liberal democracy," essayist Andranik Migranyan said to eighty-nine-year-old Karl Popper, when Migranyan came to consult the renowned advocate of liberalism in 1990 in Bristol on the ways and means of establishing and maintaining an "open society" in the Soviet Union.[81] A leading member of the democratic opposition and chairman of the Leningrad City Council, Anatoly Sobchak, too, believed that only if the country managed to overcome the "system's" resistance and successfully to "break through to market," would the "powerful forces of democracy" prevent a return to the past.[82]

Similarly, but even more so, the "de-nationalization" of land[83] was not merely an economic necessity.* To be sure, as a group of collective farmers wrote to a popular magazine,[84] if the land was "returned" to peasants to own and to work, they would fill the country "to the brim" with food. Yet the adoption of a law permitting family farms, based on the private ownership of land and equipment, was not more than just a matter of tactical necessity. It was viewed as a key "strategy of the state's self-renewal" central to the revival of human dignity—an act akin to the abolition of serfdom by Alexander II in 1861.[85]

The moral imperative of land privatization was made stronger still by the hope that it would begin to make up for the huge "moral losses" wrought by the trauma of collectivization, which had left behind indifference, apathy, mistrust,[86] pandemic alcoholism, and near-universal sloth.† The countryside's moral revival would be much helped also by the posthumous "rehabilitation" (acquittal) of the kulak families in each and

---

* "I am convinced," wrote a leading Soviet agricultural expert and member of the Academy of Agricultural Sciences Vladimir Tikhonov, "that we will not overcome the permanent agricultural crisis until we re-create a system of land ownership, until we revive the peasant-land owner." ("Vladet' zemlyoy" [To own the land], *Moskovskie novosti*, June 25, 1989: 12.)

† "Go to the kolkhoz 'Lenin's behests' (*Zavety Lenina*) in the Nizhnedevitsky district of some of Russia's most fertile, black earth region of Voronezh," a reader wrote a popular magazine. "A dying village, a kolkhoz with millions of rubles in losses, with impassable mud, . . . drunkenness, and the absence of young people." The only way out, the reader continues, is to give back all the land to those who work on it—"although each year there are fewer and fewer people who can." (V. Novichikhin, letter to the editor, "Narodnaya publitsistika" [People's political journalism] *Oktyabr'*, August 1989: 183.)

every district of Russia where the collectivization proscription lists could still be found.[87]

Oh, what a wonderful life we would be able to live if only we were given freedom, a peasant family in Crimea believed.[88] "To be the master of my land has been a hope of my entire life," wrote a reader from the Krasnoyarsk countryside. "For if a man could feel himself the master of the land, he would be spiritually richer, and there would be less alcoholism without any government anti-drinking decrees."[89] It is not true that we don't have real peasants, who are willing to become masters on the land, wrote a collective farmer from the Altai region.

> They do exist but they have neither land nor freedom. . . . But I am writing not for myself. I have done my life's work, and illness has at last claimed me. I am writing for my children. Life has been taken from three generations of peasants: my grandfather's, my father's, and mine. Will my children and grandchildren, too, be doomed to being someone's lab animals? This is why I cannot sleep at night. That is why I am writing this.[90]

With the urgency of the transformation from "the totalitarian regime to civil society" and from "subjects" to "citizens"[91] agreed upon, bringing about "material and legal conditions" for the realization of political and economic liberties[92] became the order of the day. Freeing society from the giant "combine" of the Soviet state (*gosudarstvo-kombinat*) was declared the "essential political issue."[93] A new political order was to force the state to abandon the "commanding heights" it had seized and held for seventy years. The state would have to "self-limit"[94] and the governance devolve to civil society, its institutions, and its political representatives.

First, what Boris Yeltsin, a leader of the Supreme Soviet's radical wing, the Interregional Group of Deputies, called the "commanding bureaucratic apparatus of a totalitarian regime, founded on hypocrisy, lies and mistrust," would have to be "dismantled."[95] An article in Andrei Sakharov's draft constitution prohibited any domestic secret services.[96] A former KGB counterintelligence chief called for an immediate 50 percent cut in the agency's personnel and for bans on paid informers, telephone eavesdropping, perlustration, and the spreading of disinformation inside and outside the country.[97] At a nationally televised session of the newly elected Congress of People's Deputies in June 1989, the former world champion weight lifter Yuri Vlasov commenced the first public attack on the secret police in Soviet history. The KGB was not an "agency," Vlasov declared; it was a "veritable underground empire," and its control over society as a whole and over each citizen was "comprehensive" (*vseokhvatyvayushchiy*).[98]* Having existed outside society's supervision or even knowledge, the KGB finally had to be forced to give an account of all the violations of laws it had committed. The time had come, Vlasov concluded, to remove the KGB from its headquarters:

> Too unforgettable is the bloody history of this building. It is from here that for decades orders were issued for the hounding or extermination of millions of people. Grief, groans, agony— that's what this service has sown in the Motherland's soil. It is in the bowels of this building that people were tormented—as a rule the finest people, the pride and flower of the Soviet peoples. This building—so inexplicably huge, as if a testament to whom the real power in the land belongs—is out of place in the center of Moscow.[99]

Domestic passports and the resident permits (*propiskas*) stamped in their pages were decried as the "means of super-control" (*sverkhkontrol'*) by the state, the instruments of a permanent "psychological attack" and "state blackmail."[100] Instead of the birthright of all those born in the country, citizenship was something that only the state bureaucracy could grant and take away.[101] Without passports, "we are not shoppers, hotel guests, or hospital patients—nobody," fulminated a leading legal scholar.[102] And why, he demanded to know, in his own country did he have to ask for permission from the police to live where he wanted?[103] It was necessary to abolish all limitations on the movement of the citizens of the USSR

---

* When a year later, a draft law on the KGB was made public, it was criticized for continuing to treat the secret police and counterintelligence agency as the "subjects" of the law, while the citizens remained the law's "objects": the law allotted them only duties, not rights. (Alexander Larin, "Bezopasnost' ot gozbeso-pasnosti" [Security from state security], *Moskovskie novosti*, September 9, 1990: 6.)

throughout the country, read the resolution adopted by the "Democratic perestroika" club in Moscow on June 5, 1988.[104]

Until now only "a shameful cover of tyranny," the legal system had to be remade to regulate relationships between the state, society, and the individual "in the spirit of equality and justice."[105] A re-moralized state would have to be, above all, a "lawful" state (*pravovoe gosudarstvo*).[106] Laws must be "laid down between man and state"—laws that for the first time would protect individuals from the state, not the other way around. They would do so by defending individuals from violence by local authorities and police, by upholding the "inalienable rights" of the people and thus guaranteeing their personal dignity.[107]

The ability to contest in a court of law any "acts of state" was to become the "main lever" of societal control over the state.[108] Only a fully sovereign court—independent of and able to resist "any orders and demands" from the government[109]—could measure up to such an enormously important mission.[110] Calls for securing the "real independence of judges at every level" were heard already in summer 1988.[111] A year and a half later, among the first pieces of legislation passed by the Supreme Soviet, elected by the First Congress of People's Deputies, was a packet of laws that spelled out the procedures for contesting actions of state bodies and individual functionaries in court. The same legislation spelled out the penalties for the "disrespect of courts."[112]

The presumption of innocence, too, had to be resurrected. In Imperial Russia, acquittals constituted 40 percent of the verdicts; in the Soviet Union a mere 10 percent.[113] Legal scholars argued for the "maximum extension" of the right of the accused to legal representation, and for the recovery of another pre-1917 tradition: a trial by jury, without which the courts could never be truly autonomous.[114]

Like the state's ownership of justice, the state's unchallenged control of the media, first and foremost the press, was to become a thing of the past. The "marketplace of ideas" (*rynok idey*) was as essential to spiritual autonomy, dignity, and self-governance as the market of goods and services.[115] State control over information and thought, and with it censorship of and outright bans on topics and authors, could not be allowed to exist in a "civilized society." The only counterargument to a book was to be another book.[116]

Freedom of information was deemed "extraordinarily important"[117]— a key measure of the state's responsibility before society, without which people would again become malleable and leaders unaccountable.[118] Protected only by good faith, by the declarations of a liberalizing Party leadership, and the resolutions of its conferences, glasnost lacked permanence. It had to be replaced with freedom of speech grounded in law that would forever "paralyze the habitual instinct to prohibit" so deeply ingrained in state functionaries from top to bottom.[119] The press was to be transformed from an "instrument of power" to an independent enterprise with no obligations "whatsoever" to "any government."[120]

Most important, politics would have to stop being the state's monopoly. Already by June 1988, the readers of *Komsomol'skaya pravda* insisted on people's right to belong to any political or civic organization if its aims did not contradict the constitution.[121] A year and a half later, essayist Vasily Selyunin argued that like-minded citizens should be able to unite in a party or a movement "without asking anyone's permission."[122]

There should be no obstacles to the self-organization of this new civil society. Its developing institutions ought to be "fully autonomous": "partial pluralism" would no longer do.[123] By January 1990, the electoral platform of one of the first "voters' blocs," "Democratic Russia," called for the "unconditional right" of the citizens of the Russian Soviet Socialist Federated Republic to "organize into parties, organizations, and unions."[124]

Political power was to be divided between three independent branches: executive, legislative, and judicial.[125] Joining the chorus of essayists and legislators, the Kuzbass miners demanded direct, multi-candidate elections of the executives, from town mayors to the heads of the republics, by secret ballot.[126] To dislodge the present "command-and-administer" political regime, a nurse from Moscow wrote *Moskovskie novosti* in January 1989, the "entire power" would have to be handed over to deputies elected in free competition with one another.[127] By the time Mikhail Gorbachev was elected president by the Congress of People's Deputies in March 1990, 84 percent of those surveyed by the brand-new, "nongovernmental" public opinion firm *Mnenie* (Opinion) thought he should have been elected directly by the people, not by two thousand or so deputies.[128]

Standing in the way of all these plans was the cornerstone of the Soviet state: the Communist Party, with its unchallenged dominance and its "leading and guiding" function, enshrined in Article 6 of the constitution. The cause of all our misfortunes is the same: a one-party system, a pensioner and a war veteran from the Kalinin region told public opinion pollsters in early 1989.[129] There were many calamities in Russia's history, Boris Yelstin said to an interviewer a year later, but the main one was the Party's monopoly on power.[130] Radical essayists and political philosophers were convinced: a one-party regime was the "source" of authoritarianism; it inevitably reproduced a pyramid with a "leader or führer at the top."[131] Without a multi-party system, a lawful state would be impossible to construct.[132]

The abolition of Article 6 was first publicly broached by Andrei Sakharov as the lead item of his "Decree on Power"—in essence, a draft of a new constitution—which he outlined on the last day of the First Congress of People's Deputies, June 9, 1989.[133] Three months later, the Union of the Laborers of Kuzbass passed a resolution calling on the Second Congress of People's Deputies to "exclude" Article 6 from the constitution.[134] The "annulment" of the article was third on the list of demands that the striking miners of the Vorkuta basin sent to the Supreme Soviet on November 1, 1989.[135] The Confederation of Labor, another independent union of Kuzbass, declared the "liquidation of the diktat of the CPSU and its apparatus" the most important task of the workers' movement "and of all working people." The Confederation went on to "affirm its solidarity with those who advocated a multi-party system.[136] Critical to the creation of such a system was "de-politicization," that is, removing from the Party's control the key instruments of the Party's dictatorship: the police, the KGB, the armed forces, the courts, and the prosecutors' offices.[137]

A few weeks before the Second Congress of People's Deputies convened in December 1989, Sakharov and five other leaders of the Interregional Group of Deputies called for a two-hour general strike in support of the abolition of Article 6, the creation of private farms, and the relaxation of state planning in the economy. The number of deputies who sided with this agenda had grown exponentially since the previous summer: on December 12, 839 of them (or over one-third of the Congress) voted with Sakharov.

Sakharov devoted the last five days of his life, between December 10 and the evening of December 14, almost entirely to speaking and writing in support of the strike.[138] Five hours before his death he said at an Inter-regional Group meeting:

> I want to give a formula of the opposition. What is the opposi-
> tion? We cannot accept responsibility for what the leadership [of
> the USSR] is doing. It is leading the country to a catastrophe,
> dragging out perestroika for many years . . . while the disap-
> pointment in the country is growing. And this disappointment
> is making impossible the evolutionary path of development in
> our country. The only way, the only opportunity for an evolu-
> tionary path is the radicalization of perestroika. . . . The aboli-
> tion of Article 6 of the constitution and other related articles
> [would be] the most important political action, which is needed
> by the country now, not in a year. . . . Then it will be too late.[139]

Seven weeks later between 200,000 and 300,000 people demon-strated in Moscow, demanding the abolition of Article 6.

By then democracy was accepted by the radical reformers as the most important condition of the country's "normalization"—not just of a political renewal but of an economic revival as well. Democracy, Yuri Vlasov told the First Congress, "feeds and clothes" just as the economy does: it "expands life" and "untangles economic relations."[140] For us to become free and end the poverty, we must, first and foremost, restore people's power in our state, concluded the cosmonaut Feoktistov.[141] No single individual, no group of individuals, no single organization or a party has the right to appropriate all the power in the state, turning its citizens into "subjects, into the 'led,'" into a community that, like a herd, is 'shepherded' by bosses, large and small."[142]

"Only democracy" could clear away the dead wood in the economy, politics, and ideology, wrote Gavriil Popov, a leading economic reformer, who two years later would become Moscow's first elected mayor. Even with the inevitable difficulties and "costs," Popov continued, democracy would secure normal economic development.[143]

Democracy's effects were said to be far from uniformly benign.[144] Yet its "social value" was so enormous that it more than made up for its drawbacks.[145] It was simply the most important instrument of progress: part and parcel of the "organic progress of life," of the "unstoppable course of world history."[146] Without it the country had "no future."[147] To resist it was "death."[148]

CHAPTER EIGHTEEN

In Man's Image, II

THE EMPIRE, THE "GARRISON STATE," AND THE WORLD

A severe choice [is] before us: between the empire, which is destroying us—and the spiritual and physical salvation of our people. . . . To maintain a great empire is to exterminate our own people. . . . The spiritual life of a people is more important than [the empire's] territorial expanse or even its economic wealth; the [moral] recovery and well-being of a people is incomparably more valuable than any external aims.
—Alexander Solzhenitsyn, "Kak nam obustroit' Rossiyu" (How we should make Russia good for living), a supplement to *Komsomol'skaya pravda*, September 18, 1990

In the problem of the military-industrial complex perestroika is confronting the old and painful question of the entire Russian history: how does our country see itself in the world?
—Vladlen Sirotkin, "Voenno-promyshlennyi kompleks: gde vykhod is tupika" (The military-industrial complex: Where is the way out of the dead end?), *Stolitsa*, no. 13, 1991: 1

We have to become humble, to reconcile ourselves to the fact that we may not be first, or second, or even third [in the world]. We must stop trying to catch up! We must simply live—like human beings, if possible, and live already today.
—Alexey Kiva, "Krizis 'zhanra'" (The crisis of the "genre"), *Novy mir*, March 1990: 211

IT WAS ONLY A MATTER of time before the effort at "privatization," or humanization, of national priorities reached the wall of silence and se-crecy surrounding the Soviet state's most exclusive and jealously guarded prerogative: foreign policy and defense.

Proceeding in the by now well-established pattern from the bitter truth of the "what" to the value-bound "why," glasnost thinkers found that the crushing military burden was not an "objective necessity." Rather, it was the price paid for "totalitarianism" combined with "great power ambitions and ideological messianism" (ideologicheskoe messianstvo).[1] Just as the Russian empire, proclaimed by Peter the Great in 1721, was rooted in "serfdom, militarization, and bureaucratization,"[2] so was the "totali-tarian, anti-democratic character" of Stalinism responsible for "pushing" violence further and further both inside and outside the country.[3] After the victory over Nazi Germany, the Soviet Union was said to return to the "great power expansionist" (velikoderzhavniy ekspansionistskiy), "imperial" policies started by the August 23, 1939, pact with Hitler and the invasion of Poland that followed.[4] It was the Soviet Union's "overlordship" (gos-podstvo) over Eastern Europe that the new Soviet historians saw as the "main cause of the cold war" and the "exhausting confrontation" with the "entire West."[5]

After Stalin's death, the first timid attempts at de-Stalinization in foreign policy were said to be snuffed out by the "bloody repression" of the 1956 revolution of the Hungarian people "against the tyrannical rule of Rákosi," who was forced on them by the Soviet Union.[6] The "Brezhnev Doctrine"—which postulated the permanence of the USSR's ownership of east-central Europe and Moscow's duty (and right) to sup-press any movement toward the region's independence[7]—was traced to the Soviet Union's "anti-democratic system, alien to the people and com-pletely outside their control."[8]

It was this domestic political "system" that was viewed as "100 per-cent" responsible for the Soviet Union's foreign policy, especially vis-à-vis the countries of the "socialist camp."[9] Its "internal logic of violence and repression" was to blame for the invasion of Czechoslovakia in 1968[10]—as it was for the Molotov-Ribbentrop Pact before and the "inter-national assistance" to Afghanistan later. They were now seen as the "links of the same chain."[11]

"Stalinism" in the Soviet Union's foreign policy also explained the emergence of what Soviet propaganda for decades called the "hostile forces of the West."[12] In the vicious circle the regime itself drew, the need to defend against these "forces" by strengthening and guarding the Eastern European empire led to the "extraordinary militarization" of Soviet society.[13] A "garrison state" had been created—armed to the teeth and yet relentlessly insatiable in arming itself.

Gradually widened, the breach of one of the last "zones of secrecy" that concerned the military-industrial complex (or VPK, the acronym for *voenno-promyshlennyi kompleks*) caused first astonishment, then despondency, then fury.

Never before challenged, the official myth of the "peaceful Soviet state" that spent "only 20 billion rubles" on its military was dismissed by Mikhail Gorbachev in a speech to the First Congress of People's Deputies in May 1989: defense was said to consume 77 billion, or about 9 percent of the country's GDP of 875 billion rubles.[14] Less than a year later, a Committee on Science of the Supreme Soviet "rejected" the 77 billion figure. Its experts estimated defense spending at 200 billion, or 23 percent of the economy.[15] Gorbachev, too, raised the figure to 18–20 percent of GDP.[16] A few months later Foreign Minister Eduard Shevardnadze put the expenditures at a "quarter" of the Soviet economy—compared to average military spending of 4 percent in Europe and 6 percent in the United States.[17*] According to a Soviet expert, of the more than one hundred countries for which reliable defense expenditure data existed, only in five or six Middle Eastern states was the share of GDP devoted to defense higher than in the Soviet Union.[18]

Three-quarters of all the science funding went to "military research."[19] In Moscow, the Soviet Union's best-educated city by far, one-third of the total industrial output was defense related and half of all

* Seven years later, then–foreign minister Evgeniy Primakov would claim that as much as 70 percent of the Soviet GDP was spent "on defense and defense-related projects." (Evgeniy Primakov, "Russia Must Be a Star Player in the World Arena," speech at a conference of the Council on Foreign and Defense Policy, Moscow, March 14, 1998, distributed by the Information Department of the Embassy of the Russian Federation in Washington, DC.)

research institutes and construction bureaus worked for defense; that is, every fourth Muscovite.[20] In a major industrial city like Ryazan, 72 percent of all industrial enterprises was engaged in military production, "directly or indirectly."[21]

In the "capital of the VPK," the Soviet Union's second largest city, Leningrad, three-quarters of all plants and factories were part of the defense industry.[22] Unmarked on the Soviet maps were dozens of "closed" (secret) cities and towns, entirely devoted to defense. With names like Arzamas-16 and Chelyabinsk-40, they were a veritable military "archipelago," as a Soviet expert put it.[23]

A *Komsomol'skaya pravda* columnist called the VPK a "state within the state."[24] Or, perhaps, like eighteenth-century Prussia (in the words of Georg Heinrich Berenhorst, adjutant to Friedrich the Great), the Soviet Union of the late 1980s was not "a country that had an army but an army which had a country."[25] As liberal Russian experts put it in an open letter to President Gorbachev, theirs was "a military economy forced to function in peacetime."[26]

When in early 1989 the size of the country's armed forces was truthfully stated for the first time, the Soviet Union turned out to have 4,258,000 men under arms—more than the United States, China, and the Federal Republic of Germany together.[27] There were sixteen soldiers per one thousand citizens in the Soviet Union, compared to ten in France and in the United States, eight in the Federal Republic of Germany, six in Great Britain, and four in China.[28]

The country was said to "bristle" with its missiles and tanks,[29] with more of the latter made in the Soviet Union every year than in the rest of the world. The Warsaw Pact turned out to have almost twice as many tanks as NATO (59,470 versus 30,690) and the Soviet Union alone had amassed almost as many armored vehicles (46,900) as the entire Western alliance (45,000).[30]

The Soviet Union, concluded a *Moskovskie novosti* commentator, armed itself as if it were going to "fight almost the entire world."[31] It was as if the war did not end in 1945, said the chairman of the Supreme Soviet's Committee on Science, Academician Yuri Ryzhov, and the Soviet Union continued to "fight on many fronts."[32] The country's life was "shot through by militarism," and the "monstrous abnormality" of the

militarization was the country's scourge, wrote the veteran foreign affairs reporter and columnist Kondrashov.[33] The "besieged-barrack"
(*osadno-kazarmennoe*) mentality, other essayists agreed, "penetrated into
every pore" and threatened to completely "paralyze" the "creative potential" of the people.[34]

The VPK claimed not only the single largest piece of the national pie
but also the choicest one: the finest scientists and engineers, the best
workers—what Prime Minister Ryzhkov called the "elite, most modern
enterprises."[35] For "decades," high officials in charge of the defense production now admitted, the Soviet economy had been divided into two
"realms" that rarely intersected: the military and the civilian, with the latter receiving what was left after the needs of the former were "sated."[36]

The "domestic" economy had had to "settle for" what "remained
after the [spending on] foreign policy and defense," Foreign Minister
Eduard Shevardnadze said in May 1989.[37] But now, he continued, the
postulate that there was "nothing" that the country "could not afford"
in foreign policy or defense would no longer do.[38] The cost of the pervasive militarization suddenly seemed unbearable. "We are suffocating
under the press of military spending," wrote economist Nikolai Shmelyov.[39]

With the country's entire economy now said to be the "material
foundation of militarism," like other formerly sacrosanct arrangements,
the militarization of the economy and society was perceived as far from
being "in the people's interests."[40] Indeed, the satisfaction of these "interests" was now deemed unfeasible without reducing a budget deficit of
12 percent of the GDP, which, in turn, was "impossible" without a "radical diminution" of defense spending.[41]

"It is hard for me to delve into the details [of defense spending],"
popular writer Daniil Granin noted in August 1988, "as there is no opportunity for us, the citizens, to learn how our money is spent on defense, space, and some other things. Still, I know that there are four
most urgent problems: food, housing, healthcare, and environment.
To solve them, all other things must be economized on."[42] When four
months later the Soviet government announced that it would unilaterally cut defense expenditures by 14.2 percent, experts calculated that the

savings of 15–20 billion rubles would equal the annual costs of the national healthcare system or the entire kindergarten-to-high-school education system.[43] To maintain the largest army in the world and, at the
same time, raise the standard of living in a poor country was "economic
adventurism," concluded Academician Stanislav Shataling, a leading
economist and a top advisor to Gorbachev.[44]

The addiction to the empire, what Solzhenitsyn called the "imperial nar-
cotic" and the pride in the "great Soviet power with which everyone reck-
ons" were the most damaging distortion of the national conscience, the
Nobel Prize winner wrote in *Komsomol'skaya pravda* in September 1990.
Not only did they gnaw the national economy down to the bone by manu-
facturing weapons that nobody needed but, Solzhenitsyn continued,
these obsessions "shamed us before an entire planet," which viewed Soviet
Russia as a "brutal, greedy, and uncontrollable invader."[45]

Prescriptions for bringing the country's behavior in the world in
line with the new domestic priorities multiplied quickly in number and
urgency. Perhaps the country should stop playing benefactor when it
was so poor itself, the writer Granin suggested in summer 1988.[46] Discard imperial ambitions, adventurism, and dogmatism in foreign policy,
Sakharov told the First Congress of People's Deputies in June 1989.[47]
Should we not stop "tiring other peoples with our tender cares," a reader
asked in a letter to *Komsomol'skaya pravda,* and, instead, take care, finally,
of our own people?[48] Solzhenitsyn urged an immediate end to "supplying and maintaining" the "tyrannical regimes" in Cuba, Vietnam, Ethiopia, Angola, and North Korea, which the Soviet Union had "planted in all
the ends of the Earth."[49*] Andrei Sakharov added, ban "political subver-
sion and disinformation" carried out worldwide by the country's secret
services and let them concern themselves only with intelligence and
counterintelligence.[50]

---

* "How much is our war in Afghanistan?" a popular writer Vasily Belov asked
at the First Congress of People's Deputies. "And [the support of] Cuba, and
Nicaragua, and Ethiopia? . . . And how much do our grandiose festivals,
Olympiads, and international forums cost?" (*Izvestia,* June 2, 1989: 9.)
"Kuba—si, pomoshch—no!" (Cuba—yes, aid—no!) read the headline in a
spring 1991 issue of *Argumenti i fakty* (no. 12, 1991: 2).

Most important, ridding Russia of its empire became a moral imperative—a central condition to reviving the country and its people. No people that repressed other peoples could be free, noted a Soviet historian, recalling Marx.[51] Overcoming the "imperial syndrome"—regardless of its supposed justifications and disguises—was a key to restoring the "moral health" of the society.[52]

"De-imperialization" was to start with the Soviet Union itself. Sakharov branded it an "imperial structure," bequeathed by Stalinism, a product of a "violent imperial unification" and a "divide-and-rule" policy.[53] A "unitary" (that is, rigidly centralized) Soviet Union could be maintained only by a totalitarian state, "founded on violence," decided leading *Komsomol'skaya pravda* columnist Leonid Nikitinsky.[54] With such a state rejected as morally repugnant, the Soviet Union in its present form, too, was doomed.

The only hope of saving the Union, Sakharov warned in the summer of 1989, was in remaking it into a democratic voluntary confederation of "sovereign peoples," each of whom would be able to "chart its fate" according to the principles of international law.[55] A year later, Solzhenitsyn saw the only solution as shedding the non-Slavic "republics" altogether in order for Russia "to free itself for its *internal* development."[56]

Outside its borders, glasnost essayists prescribed "de-ideologization":[57] ridding the Soviet foreign policy of a "defective leftist-sectarian approach" (*ushcherbnyi levo-sektantskiy podkhod*)[58] and freeing it from "revolutionary messianism."[59] Just as it was poised to do domestically, the Soviet Union had to forswear violence as a "tool of progress" and respect other peoples' "freedom of political choice."[60] Arbitrariness had to be supplanted with deference to international law, and the Brezhnev Doctrine with noninterference.[61] Both the East and the West must understand that the Brezhnev Doctrine and the "adventurist gambles" like a war in Afghanistan were dead and buried.[62]

Not just the means but the ends had to change. The Soviet Union's new foreign policy was "deeply moral," Foreign Minister Shevardnadze told an interviewer in summer 1989. "Look at the principles we have declared and are defending on the world stage: the priority of universal [*obshchechelovecheskie*] values, the rule of law and the defense of human rights, the overcoming of confrontation and the consolidation of the world community in order to preserve civilization. Is there anything more ethical?!"[63]*

There was only one guarantee of keeping the country's behavior in the world to so high a standard: a moral overhaul. Soviet history proved with "absolute clarity" that a foreign policy could never be more just and more moral than the domestic political order, two leading young political scientists argued in an article titled "Diplomacy and Morality at the Time of Perestroika."[64] A foreign policy that put the creation of an "international order" before restoring a moral order in one's own country would never gain lasting international trust and domestic support.[65] Therefore, the sine qua non of domestic moral cleansing—remembrance and repentance— must have "an international dimension" as well.[66] The country must admit past transgressions and ask for forgiveness from those peoples and countries that had been wronged. Without such an atonement, the break with the past would not be "sincere" and, therefore, durable.[67]

The country's foreign policy also must be "open and public."[68] It had to emerge from the "darkness of secrecy" and into "full view of the people," argued Stanislav Kondrashov.[69] Like other facets of the state, the entire "diplomatic service" had to move "into the glasnost zone": exposed to public debate and subjected to "control from below."[70] The shame and horror felt by Kondrashov and a handful of Soviet experts and journalists during the 1962 Cuban missile crisis—when the entire world except for the Soviet people, kept ignorant by their government, knew it was on the brink of a nuclear war[71]—must never be repeated!† (In autumn 1990, the world was still "astounded," fulminated *Moskovskie novosti* columnist

---

* In spring and summer 1989, Shevardnadze was taken to task by leading foreign policy commentators for failing to live up to these ideals after he had failed to protest publicly the death sentence meted out to the novelist Salman Rushdie by Ayatollah Ruhollah Khomeini in February 1989, and a few months later for keeping silent about the killing of unarmed protestors in Tiananmen Square. (Alexander Bovin, "Politika i moral'" [Politics and morals], *Moskovskie novosti*, March 19, 1989: 3; and Alexei Izyumov and Andrei Kortunov, "Diplomatiya i nravstvennost' vremyon perestroiki" [Diplomacy and morality at the time of perestroika], *Moskovskie novosti*, August 6, 1989: 6.)

† The same "absence of a law-bound duty by the authorities to give account to citizens" was responsible, according to Kondrashov, for the fact that the number of Soviet troops (100,000) and casualties (13,310 killed, 35,478 wounded) in Afghanistan was first disclosed in May 1988—eight and a half years after the

Sergei Volovets, to find that in a "severe economic crisis," the USSR still continued to spend financial, material, and intellectual resources without the "slightest attempt at a public debate about what its defense really needs.")[72]

The Soviet state was doomed to brinksmanship with the West, punctuated by brief and "superficial" détentes, until the "full restoration of universal values" inside the country: honor, dignity, humanitarianism (*chelovechnost*), tolerance. Only then would it find genuine acceptance by and lasting peace and friendship with other states. Only thus would the Soviet Union permanently "open the door" to Europe,"[73] into which some leading experts hoped it would be integrated—not only economically but also politically and eventually "militarily."[74]

Just as the militarization was a product of a dictatorship married to a bureaucratic "command-and-administer" system that defined national priorities without people's "advice," only "democratization" would bring de-militarization.[75] The "garrison state" would not be needed when the world learned to trust and not be afraid of the Soviet Union. But to change others' opinion of us, wrote a *Komsomol'skaya pravda* columnist, we must first change ourselves.[76]

Soviet troops entered that country. Stanislav Kondrashov, "Iz mraka secretnosti" (From the darkness of secrecy), *Novy mir*, August 1989: 187.

Epilogue

THE IMPACT OF IDEAS on social action can never be measured with any precision. Still, the record compiled in this book at least furnishes plausible approaches to explaining the remarkably swift, mostly nonviolent, and just as surprisingly unforeseen disintegration of the Soviet state.

The foregoing seems to establish that preceding and inspiring the radical reforms (and then unfolding alongside them) was a powerful quest for self-knowledge, dignity, and moral renewal. The spiritual engine of all great modern revolutions, this quest was very much in evidence in Soviet Russia as well. The revelation of appalling moral failings in the regime's past and present led to the questioning and then rejection of some of the key legitimizing myths and public values. Alternative concepts of what constituted a dignified and honorable life, public or private, were articulated. There followed attempts to devise and implement political and economic arrangements in accord with these new ideals in the hope of forging a morally superior order.

Stemming from these ideals and enjoying consistent support by millions of Russians,* the ensuing revolutionary "reforms" resulted in a four-

---

* Tracked by the Levada Center monthly in national representative public opinion surveys from March 1992 to July 2004, the "evaluation of the reform course"

pronged political, economic, and social overhaul. "De-Bolshevization," for want of a better term, has ended civil society's complete subjugation to the state, along with utopia as an ultimate societal goal and totalitarian dictatorship as a means of reaching it. "Privatization," second, was designed not only as a sharp curtailment of the state's ownership of the economy and, with it, the diminution of the state's control over the livelihood of every citizen. It marked the end of the state's ownership of national culture and, most critically, morality. A morally autonomous individual began to emerge, able to make his or her own ethical choices—the ability that from Milton to Kant to Kierkegaard was considered the essence of a fully human existence. Third, "de-imperialization" brought about a voluntary surrender of the domestic and east-central European empires. Finally, de-militarization resulted in a de facto disarmament on a scale likely unprecedented for a great military power undefeated in a war and unoccupied by the victors.

No great revolution has ever fully lived up to the ideals on its banners. The outbreak of moral fastidiousness that almost always precedes such upheavals, inspiring and shaping it, cannot last long. The white heat of moral indignation is impossible to sustain, even for those who did the most to fan the flames. People have to make a living, to care for families, and so they leave the public square to the political class, which at this early stage cannot be but a moral centaur: half forward-looking human and half beast of the past.

Russia's was hardly the first revolution to be followed by a restoration. De Tocqueville wrote about "events, mistakes, [and] misjudgments,"

---

yields a diagram in which, save for a few months here and there, the line charting the percentages of those wishing that reforms would continue is above the one reflecting the opinions of those wishing for the reforms to stop. Support for reforms was the greatest during the economically hardest and politically most contentious period of March 1992–January 1993. ("Otsenka kursa na reform" [The evaluation of the reform course], *Vestnik obshchestvennogo mneniya,* no. 4, [72], July–August 2004, table 8, p. 5.) In the April 1993 referendum, with inflation reaching 19 percent *monthly,* a majority of Russians voted to support "the social and economic policy" of the Yeltsin administration. In the first fully democratic elections in December 1993, Egor Gaidar's pro-reform Demokraticheskiy vybor Rossii (Russia's democratic choice) party ended up with the most deputies in the Duma.

which led the French to "abandon their original ideal," turn "their backs on freedom," and "acquiesce in an equality of servitude."[1] America's second revolution—the Civil War—remained mired in the racism of Jim Crow for almost a century. The glorious Mandela-led South African liberation is threatened by violent crime, corruption, and the conceit of the ruling elite. Across Eastern and Central Europe, the moral cleansing and thirst for virtuous politics of the 1980s seem all but choked by cynicism and mistrust. Ukraine's Orange Revolution seems extinct today.

If Russia's regress has been among the severest, it is, first of all, because it had so much more to overcome. Writing about the aftermath of the reign of Ivan the Terrible, the great Ukrainian-Russian historian Nikolai Kostomarov concluded that "serious illnesses of human societies, like physical illnesses, cannot be cured quickly. . . . Those spoiled juices which had built up during the frightful epoch of Ivan's atrocities finally rose to the surface."[2] Ivan ruled for thirty-seven years; the Bolsheviks, for seventy-four. The stores of "spoiled juices" resulting from the daily offenses to human dignity and the encouragement of the worst human instincts by the totalitarian state and its offensively irrational economy were perhaps unrivaled in modern history in volume and toxicity. And when the terror was gone, a veritable geyser of these "juices" spilled over an already disfigured moral landscape, where the young, crude, and very hungry capitalism of the "oligarchs" (what Marx called "primeval accumulation") met the greedy, venal, and badly underpaid bureaucrats still in charge of the choicest chunks of the rapidly disintegrating state-owned economy.

But the privatization shenanigans were only a symptom of a far larger moral devastation, which the glasnost essayists had foreseen and outlined with the customary passion, eloquence, and perspicacity. One could, with greater or lesser precision, assess the damage to Russian culture from everything that was blown up, burnt, lost, thrown out, and spoiled under the Soviet regime, the writer Boris Vasiliev wrote in January 1989. From the starved-to-death great poet Alexander Blok to those who were lost to Russia because of forced emigration: Bunin and Rakhmaninov, Repin and Chaliapin, Shagal and Kandinsky. But who, Vasiliev asked, could ever calculate the moral loss inflicted by the regime?[3] Those who led the moral revolution were well aware of the vastness of the distance that must be traveled before their work was completed. As the sociologist Vladimir Shubkin wrote in April 1989 in the leading liberal magazine *Novy mir:* "We have miles to go before the public morality is restored . . . before we even approach what might be called the moral Renaissance." He was right, of course. Sixteen years later Vladimir Putin—then a mere president, soon the "National Leader"—called the demise of the Soviet Union the greatest geopolitical catastrophe of the twentieth century.

Even after most of the spoiled-juices flood receded by the end of the 1990s, two infernal sources continued to poison Russian public mores and, thus, its politics. One was the empire; the other, Stalinism.

That empire was incompatible with Russia's liberty and sustained prosperity and progress was something the finest of the Russian liberal thinkers, from Herzen to Sakharov, have emphasized again and again. Throughout history, over and over again, the efforts to re-moralize and "normalize" the country by making the regime more humane and rational were subverted by the need to preserve and extend the empire: from Russia's greatest pre-Gorbachev liberator, Alexander II, who crushed the Polish rebellion in 1863–64, to Khrushchev's "thaw," badly set back by the 1956 Hungarian revolution, to the Kosygyn economic liberalization, ended by the Soviet tanks killing the Prague Spring in 1968.

By dint of enormous moral courage, Gorbachev and Yeltsin became the first Russian rulers who decisively and self-consciously chose domestic liberalization over the preservation of empire: the east-central European one and the one inside the Soviet Union's borders. Yet as in every post-imperial society, the lost lands, like severed limbs, gave off phantom pains. Riven by almost incessant crises, Yeltsin's tenure was not enough to impress on the Russians both the finality of the loss and the moral imperative of leaving the empire behind. Instead of alleviating these pains, by example and patient education, after succeeding Yeltsin, the Putin restoration made imperial nostalgia a key source of the regime's legitimacy.

The recovery of the geo-political assets lost in the Soviet collapse became the alpha and omega of post-Yeltsin foreign policy, complete with the desperate, at times almost grotesque, striving for global parity with the United States. There followed attempts to restart the old Soviet zero-sum strategic game with Washington—from Venezuela to Georgia and from Iran to Ukraine—amid the deafening and soon unchallenged official propaganda of Russia's "rising off its knees" amid mortal enemies, relentlessly plotting to dismember it and take possession of its natural riches.

Yet the most powerful cause of the moral and therefore political retardation by far has been the still largely unexpurgated and unatoned national sin of Stalinism. Though among its most ruthlessly decimated victims, Russia was also the foundation of the Soviet totalitarianism—and thus morally its most damaged product. "Not one religion, not one religious order left a future generation such a spiritual desert as has Stalin's 'church' [left Russia]," wrote Igor Klyamkin.[4] The brilliant Polish poet, philosopher, and essayist Zbigniew Herbert, who knew about such things, wrote that a nation subject to "whispers, informing, a fear of one's neighbor" crumbles from within. Even the "most ruthless hand-to-hand combat is less disastrous" for its soul.[5]

Glasnost extended the responsibility for enabling and perpetrating the horrors far beyond Osip Mandelstam's "Kremlin mountaineer." The literary critic Lazar' Lazarev, who first dared to admire and interpret Grossman's *Zhizn' i sud'ba* (Life and fate), noted the skill with which the novelist showed convincingly that fear alone could not have sustained Stalinism. It was helped by a society "corroded, poisoned, demoralized."[6] Where did the Gulag come from? asked the contributors to the 1989 collection of essays *Osmyslit' kul't Stalina* (To comprehend the Stalin cult), still far and away the best volume in Russian on the subject. Stalin thought it up?[7] No. Did the various NKVD functionaries—Frenkel, Berman, Yagoda, and Firin—invent it, while Stalin "only approved"?[8] But how many more were needed to guard millions who passed through camps in almost a quarter of a century? To "service" and "maintain"[9] the "giant man-grinder" (*chelovekorubka*)?[10] Millions. Where did *they* come from? Did they "fall from the sky"?[11] "Stalin," noted the writer Vyacheslav Kondratiev, "made the entire people his accomplice."[12] As Mandelstam's widow, Nadezhda, said in the early 1960s: *Delo ne v nyom. Delo v nas.* "He [Stalin] is not the issue. We are."[13]

Stalin embodied and Stalinism epitomized the glorification of violence in pursuit of the state's goals; the penchants for shortcuts and seemingly simple solutions; the absolution of personal guilt in return for blind faith, complicity in, or silent condonation of state-perpetrated terror and lies; servility and xenophobia; and the belief that a glorious future justifies the indignities of the present. Stalinism parasitized on the worst elements in the Russian political and moral traditions, nourished and honed them, while relentlessly subverting, disfiguring, or extirpating the best of the Russian character: generosity, courage, self-sacrifice, kindness, ecumenism, and patriotism.

Yet just as the authoritarian political tradition helped the rise of Stalinism, every instance of de-Stalinization is a blow to that culture. That is why, during the almost six decades since Stalin's death, the national debate about his place in history has been not so much about the past as about Russia's present and, even more so, her future. For without national contrition, without the excision of the monstrous malignancy of Stalinism—political, civic, and, most of all, ethical—it is impossible to forge and sustain the rise of a moral and free individual— the master of his own life, and thus a responsible citizen-steward of his country and Russia's best hope for membership in the community of "civilized nations.

In this prediction the troubadours of glasnost were as correct as they were in most of their diagnoses and proposed cures. Reclaiming a detailed and daily-sustained memory of the atrocities and their victims was inextricably bound with repentance and moral rebirth. Unexpiated, Stalinism was like "an open bleeding wound," or an "abscess" that needed to be "lanced" and reckoned with, honestly and unflinchingly, before it burst again and poisoned the entire body.[14] Only when the people "knew the entire, whole truth about our past" would the country be ready for a "spiritual cleansing"—and only then would it feel a "true, deep need" for it, wrote Igor Vinogradov.[15]

From the span of over a century and a half, the brilliant Petr Chaadaev was summoned to illuminate the essence of the connection between memory, repentance, and rebirth. We must, Chaadaev insisted,

> understand fully the path we have traveled [so that] almost
> despite ourselves, a confession of all our delusions, all the
> errors of our past escapes our lips [and] the cry of repentance
> and grief springs from our depth and its echo fills the world.
> Only then will we naturally take a place among the peoples

who are fated to act in the world not only as battering rams and
cudgels but as [creators of] ideas.[16]

Defying the prescription of repentance as a prerequisite for Russia's
moral rebirth has cost post–Soviet Russia grievously. As they do in humans, willful amnesia, hiding, minimizing, distorting, or rationalizing
away their crimes make countries and states insecure and aggressive;
furtive and blustery; indulgent of solemn but sterile dreams of the glory
they imagine to have been cheated of; reveling in victimhood; and blaming all but themselves for their faults, blunders and misfortunes.

The "horrible" lesson of Stalinism was to teach Russia wariness of
those who tempt Russia with easy solutions and the promise of quick
results, as the philosopher Alexander Tsypko warned in early 1989.[17] In
the absence of sustained de-Stalinization, this lesson, too, remains unlearned. Hence, the political culture of Putinism (and the foreign policy
it gave rise to): of alleged loss and wounded pride; frustrated hopes; nostalgia for the world that never was and never could have been; and perennial
vigilance against imaginary enemies, domestic and foreign. Hence, too,
the resurrection of a state's image as, in the words of a top independent
Russian pollster, "the wise power standing over society . . . and does not
permit for any mechanisms of control" by the society.[18] Cynicism and corruption, remarkable even among the notoriously knavish restorationist
regimes, followed logically.

Just as the glasnost authors suspected, the "giant voids" in Russia's
historic memory are inseparable from the "giant voids in the country's
moral framework."[19] These voids grow larger every time a high school
textbook, among other blasphemies, extols Stalin's managerial skills and
justifies the occupation of east-central Europe.[20] Or when the Russian
president honors in plaques, street names, and monuments the heads of
the Cheka and the KGB, Felix Dzerzhinsky and Yuri Andropov. Or when,
on the seventieth anniversary the Molotov-Ribbentrop Pact, Russian state-
controlled television attempts to justify the deal[21] and the Foreign Ministry's spokesman denounces as "the distortion of history" a resolution by
the parliamentary assembly of the Organization for Security and Cooperation in Europe, which equated Stalinism and Nazism as "the two powerful
totalitarian regimes . . . that brought about genocide, violations of human
rights, and liberties, war crimes and crimes against humanity."[22]

A decade and a half after the exposés of the Katyn murders in *Komsomol'skaya pravda, Moskovskie novosti,* and *Novy mir;* after Mikhail Gorbachev, in 1990, handed over to the Polish government the lists with the names of the executed Polish officers; after the Office of the Chief Prosecutor of the Armed Forces started a criminal investigation of "Katyn case"; and after Boris Yeltsin ordered the publication of some key documents in 1992,* the "Katyn case" was closed in 2004 and its materials declared a state secret. In 2009, the Supreme Court upheld the decision of a lower court to throw out a lawsuit by relatives of the murdered Polish officers to force the Russian government to open the Katyn archive.†

Swallowed without a trace in this swamp of organized distortion and oblivion have been both President Dmitry Medvedev's condemnation of Stalinism on his videoblog[23] and human rights groups' statement that "the successful future of Russia would be impossible without an honest assessment of its totalitarian past"[24] What moral renewal, essential to Russia's economic and political progress, can there be if in a television poll at the end of 2009 Stalin was recognized as the third greatest Russian in history (ahead of Pushkin and Dostoevsky)?[25] How can moral immunity to authoritarianism take root when Russia's top independent public opinion expert reports "quiet rehabilitation of Stalin as a great government and national leader"?[26] Just as the glasnost crusaders warned, the proverbial "dead seize the living"—a past that has been not "overcome," but only bypassed, silenced, or willfully misrepresented—will not let Russia "live normally."[27]

---

* The most graphic of these was the March 5, 1940, Politburo resolution, authorizing the execution and signed by Stalin, Voroshilov, Molotov, Mikoyan, Kalinin, and Kaganovich.

† Possible movement away from hiding Stalin's crimes may have been signaled by Prime Minister Putin's speech in Katyn on April 7, 2010. He admitted that the Polish officers were murdered by a "secret order" and deplored the "evil deeds of a totalitarian regime." Yet Stalin was not mentioned by name. Nor, although Russia has long declared itself a legal successor to the Soviet Union in every regard, was there an admittance of guilt and an apology. It has taken Serbia fifteen years to apologize for the 1995 massacre of Bosnian Muslims. It has taken fifteen years for Croatia to apologize for its part in the Bosnian war. At this writing, it has been seventy-one years since the Soviet Union executed thousands of Poles in Katyn. Still, no apology.

Glasnost authors were correct about yet something else: even under the best of circumstances, the "re-norming" of Russia would be long and painful. It would take "eras" and "generations" to put the country "in order," Gorbachev's advisor Viktor Kuvaldin wrote in 1990; to bring it "back to civilization" after the traumas and depredation of Stalinism.[28] It would be a very long road to a moral renaissance, not to mention a "moral revolution," warned the brilliant Vladimir Shubkin. For such moral revolutions are "so much more complicated than a seizure of power and so much rarer."[29] Thirty years are enough to spoil a people," says a hero of Solzhenitsyn's *In the First Circle*. "Three hundred years may not suffice to mend it."[30]

Amid the intellectual myopia, vulgarity, and, above all, utter cynicism of Putinism, it is occasionally hard to believe that the luminous explosion of moral courage and intellectual incandescence, which this book has attempted to outline, ever took place. Still, already permanently among the most glorious episodes of Russian history, the "noble disquiet"[31] of the moral revolution of 1987–91 will forever remain an unimpeachable proof of Russia's capacity for self-betterment. The two conditions, which the glasnost troubadours have identified as central to Russia's becoming a free, just, and prosperous county at peace with itself and the world—truth and liberty—continue to hold. Their splendid moral quest will continue to inspire and guide the country's search for individual and collective dignity. This search is bound to be recovered and revisited like the rivers in de Tocqueville's metaphor, which go underground only to reemerge later, "in new surroundings."[32]

For those brave and brilliant men and women who began this moral crusade a quarter of a century ago the coda of Zbigniew Herbert's poem is a eulogy. It is also a battle cry for those who will rise to finish what they started:

Yes blackthorn
a few measures
in an empty hall
and then torn musical notes
lie among puddles and rusty weeds
so no one remembers

someone however must have courage
someone must begin

yes blackthorn
a few clear measures
it is a lot
it is everything.[33]

GLASNOST'S SIGNPOSTS
The Themes and the Texts

To convey glasnost's dynamics, the texts are arranged chronologically from earlier to later. Essays and articles that were central to several themes appear in each relevant thematic section.

THE "MORAL DEGRADATION OF THE SOCIETY" AND THE URGENCY OF A MORAL OVERHAUL

Mikhail Bulgakov, Sobach'e serdtse (Dog's heart), *Znamya*, June 1987

Alexander Yakovlev, "Perestroika i nravstevnnost'" (Perestroika and morality), *Sovetskaya kul'tura*, July 21, 1987: 2

Mikhail Antonov, "Tak chto zhe s nami proiskhodit?" (What really is happening to us?), *Oktyabr'*, August 1987

Igor Klyamkin, "Kakaya ulitsa vedyot k khramu?" (Which street leads to the temple?), *Novy mir*, November 1987

Pavel Bunich, *Novye tsennosti* (New values), *Oktyabr'* 12, December 1987

Andrei Sakharov, "Neizbezhnost' perestroiki" (The inevitability of perestroika), in Yuri Afanasiev, ed., *Inogo ne dano* (There is no other way), Moscow: Progress, 1988

Maya Ganina, "Bez obol'shcheniy prezhnikh dney" (Without the delusions of bygone days), *Literaturnaya gazeta*, January 13, 1988

Igor Klyamkin, "Pochemu tak trudno govorit' pravdu" (Why it is so difficult to speak the truth?), *Novy mir*, February 1988

A. Karpychev, "Krizis doveriya?" (The crisis of trust?), *Pravda*, June 24, 1988

N. Loginova, "Unyat' strakhi" (To overcome fear), *Literaturnaya gazeta*, October 5, 1988

Georgiy Zhzhyonov, "Sud'ba naroda i cheloveka" (The fate of the people and of an individual), *Komsomol'skaya pravda*, November 7, 1988: 4

Maya Ganina, "Tsena El'dorado" (The price of El Dorado), *Literaturnaya gazeta*, February 22, 1989

Vladimir Shubkin, "Trudnoe proshchanie" (The difficult farewell), *Novy mir*, April 1989

Marat Baglay, "Moral' i politika" (Morality and politics), *Sovetskaya kul'tura*, July 27, 1989

Stanislav Govorukhin, "Voyna s prestupnost'yu" (The war on crime), *Sovetskaya kul'tura*, July 29, 1989

No Moral Recovery without "Unflinching Self-Discovery"

Alexander Tvardovsky, *Po pravu pamyati* (In memory's name), *Znamya*, February 1987

Boris Vasiliev, "Prozrenie" (The recovery of sight), *Sovetskiy ekran* 6 (March), 1987

Vladimir Kantor, "Trudnyi put' k tsivilizatsii" (A difficult road to civilization), *Novy mir*, June 1987

V. Svirskiy, "Istoriya umalchivaet" (History omits), *Izvestia*, July 21, 1987

Igor Vinogradov, "Mozhet li pravda byt' poeatpnoy?" (Can the truth be doled out in stages?), in Yuri Afanasiev, ed., *Inogo ne dano* (There is no other way), Moscow: Progress, 1988

Vitaly Korotich, "Uchimsya nazyvat' veshchi svoimi imenami" (We learn to call things by their right names), *Moskovskie novosti*, July 3, 1988: 15

Gennady Lisichkin, "Mify i real'nost'" (Myths and reality), in Kh. Kobo, ed., *Osmyslit' kul't Stalina* (To comprehend Stalin's cult), Moscow: Progress, 1989

Yuri Afanasiev, "Perestroika i istoricheskoe znanie" (Perestroika and historical knowledge) in Afanasiev, ed., *Inogo ne dano* (There is no other way), Moscow: Progress, 1988

Andrei Sakharov, "Neizbezhnost' perestroiki" (The inevitability of perestroika), in Afanasiev, ed., *Inogo ne dano* (There is no other way), Moscow: Progress, 1988

Len Karpinskiy, "Pochemu stalinizm ne skhodit so stseny?" (Why won't Stalinism leave the stage?), in Afanasiev, ed., *Inogo ne dano* (There is no other way), Moscow: Progress, 1988

Vasily Selyunin, "Istoki" (The sources), *Novy mir*, May 1988

Igor Zolotusskiy, "Krushenie abstraktsiy" (The downfall of abstractions), *Novy mir*, January, 1989

Yuri Vlasov, speech at the First Congress of People's Deputies of the USSR, in "S'ezd Narodnykh Deputatov SSSR," *Izvestia*, June 2, 1989

Stanislav Kondrashov, "Iz mraka secretnosti" (From the darkness of secrecy), *Novy mir*, August 1989

A. Bocharov, "Mchatsya mify, b'yutsya mify" (Myths are whirling, myths are stirring), *Oktyabr'*, January 1990

Alexey Kiva, "Krizis 'zhanra'" (The crisis of the "genre"), *Novy mir*, March 1990

STALIN AND STALINISM

Alexander Bek. *Novoe naznachenie* (A new appointment), *Znamya*, November–December 1986

Tengiz Abuladze, *Pokoyanie* (Repentance), January 1987

Daniil Granin, *Zubr* (Bison), *Novy mir*, January–February 1987

Vladimir Dudintsev, *Belye odezhdy* (White garments), *Neva*, January–April 1987

Alexander Tvardovsky, *Po pravu pamyati* (In memory's name), *Znamya*, February 1987

Anna Akhmatova, *Requiem*, Oktyabr', March 1987

Anatoly Pristavkin, *Nochevala tuchka zolotaya* (A little golden cloud spent a night), *Znamya*, March and April, 1987

Anatoly Rybakov, *Deti Arbata* (The children of Arbat) *Druzhba narodov*, April 1987

Andrei Platonov's *Kotlovan* (The foundation pit), *Novy mir*, June 1987

Igor Klyamkin, "Kakaya ulitsa vedyot k khramu?" (Which street leads to the temple?), *Novy mir*, November 1987

Vasily Grossman, *Zhizn' i sud'ba* (Life and fate), *Znamya*, January–April 1988

Igor Klyamkin, "Pochemu tak trudno govorit' pravdu" (Why is it so difficult to speak the truth?), *Novy mir*, February 1988

Vasily Seluynin, "Istoki" (The sources), *Novy mir*, May 1988

Varlam Shalamov, *Proza, stikhi* (Fiction, poetry), *Novy mir*, June 1988

Evgeniya Al'bats, "Proshcheniyu ne podlezhat" (No forgiveness for them), *Moskovskie novosti*, May 8, 1988

Zenon Poznyak, "Kuropaty: narodnaya tragediya, o kotoroy dolzhny znat' vse" (Kuropaty: a national tragedy about which everyone must know), *Moskovskie novosti*, October 9, 1988

Lev Razgon, "Privodyashchiy v ispolnenie" (The one who carried out the sentence), *Moskovskie novosti*, November 27, 1988: 11

Irina Shcherbakova, "Nado li pomnit' proshloe?" (Should the past be remembered?), *Moskovskie novosti*, November 27, 1988: 12

Roy Medvedev, "Nash isk Stalinu" (Our case against Stalin), *Moskovskie novosti*, November 27, 1988: 8

Yuri Dombrovsky, *Fakul'tet nenuzhnykh veshchey* (The department of unnecessary things), Moscow: Sovetskiy pisatel', 1989

Kh. Kobo, ed., *Osmyslit' kul't Stalina* (To comprehend Stalin's cult), Moscow: Progress, 1989

Roy Medvedev, "Tragicheskaya statistika" (Tragic statistics), *Argumenty i fakty*, February 4–10, 1989: 5–6

Zamira Ibragimova and Ilya Kartushin, "Matryonin grekh" (Matryona's sin), *Ogonyok*, 5, 1989

Timur Pulatov, "Krymskie tatary zhazhdut iskhoda" (The Crimean Tatars are thirsting for the resolution), *Moskovskie novosti*, April 9, 1989

Vladimir Shubkin, "Trudnoe proshchanie" (The difficult farewell), *Novy mir*, April 1989

Vasily Grossman, *Vsyo techoyt* (Forever flowing), *Oktyabr'*, June 1989

Varlam Shalamov, *Iz "Kolymskikh rasskazov"* (From "Kolyma tales"), *Znamya*, June 1989

Alexander Solzhenitsyn, *Gulag Archipelago*, *Novy mir*, August, September, October 1989

Sergey Kiselyov, "Eshcho raz o Bykovne" (Once more about Bykovnya), *Literaturnaya gazeta*, October 10, 1990

Nikolai Bugay, "V bessrochnuyu ssylku" (Into indefinite exile), *Moskovskie novosti*, October 14, 1990

THE PEASANT HECATOMB: 1930–33

V. Danilov, N. Teptsov, and L. Smirnov, "Kollektivizatsiya: kak eto bylo" (Collectivization: how it all happened), *Pravda*, September 16, 1988

Roy Medvedev, "Nash isk Stalinu" (Our case against Stalin), *Moskovskie novosti*, November 27, 1988: 8

V. Popov and N. Shmelyov, "Na razvilke dorog" (At a crossroad), in Kh. Kobo, ed., *Osmyslit' kul't Stalina* (To comprehend Stalin's cult), Moscow: Progress, 1989

Yuri Chernichenko, "Zemlya, ekologiya, perestroika" (Land, ecology, perestroika), *Literaturnaya gazeta*, January 29, 1989

Yuri Chernichenko. "O khlebe nasushchnom" (Of our daily bread), *Komsomol'skaya pravda*, March 12, 1989

Pavel Voshchanov, "Zloba i zavist' obrekayut nas na bednost'" (Spite and envy doom us to penury), *Komsomol'skaya pravda*, December 2, 1989

Vasil' Bykov, "Oblava" (Man-hunt), *Novy mir*, January 1990

Sergey Zavorotnyi and Petr Polozhevets, "Operatsiya GOLOD" (Operation HUNGER), *Komsomol'skaya pravda*, February 3, 1990

THE KATYN MASSACRE

V. Shutkevich, "Molchit katyn'skiy les" (The Katyn' forest is silent), *Komsomol'skaya pravda*, January 20, 1990

Gennady Zhavoronkov, "Posle rasstrela myli ruki spirtom . . ." (After an execution [they] washed their hands with strong alcohol), *Moskovskie novosti*, September 16, 1990

N. Lebedeva, *Katynskie golosa* (The voices of Katyn'), *Novy mir*, February 1991: 211

THE "IMMORAL ECONOMY"

Anatoly Strelyaniy, "Prikhod i raskhod" (Profit and expense), *Znamya*, June 1986

Vasily Selyunin and Grigory Khanin, "Lukavaya tsifra" (The cunning figure), *Novy mir*, February 1987

Nikolai Shmelyov "Avansy i dolgi" (Advances and debts), *Novy mir*, June 1987

Vladimir Popov and Nikolai Shmelyov, "Anatomiya defitsita" (The anatomy of shortages), *Znamya*, May 1988

Abel Aganbegyan, "Chelovek i ekonomika" (Man and economy), interview with *Ogonyok* 29, 1987

V. Rusakova, "Telefonnye istorii, kotorye tyanutsya 22 goda" (Telephone stories that have dragged for 22 years), *Pravda,* December 2, 1987

Andrei Sakharov, "Neizbezhnost' perestroiki" (The inevitability of perestroika), in Yuri Afanasiev, ed., *Inogo ne dano* (There is no other way), Moscow: Progress, 1988

Nikolai Shmelyov, "Ne smet' komandovat'!" (Stop giving orders!), *Oktyabr',* February 1988

V. Popov and N. Shmelyov, "Na razvilke dorog" (At a crossroad), in Kh. Kobo, ed., *Osmyslit' kul't Stalina* (To comprehend Stalin's cult), Moscow: Progress, 1989

Vasily Belov, Speech at the First Congress of People's Deputies of the USSR, June 1, 1989, *Izvestia,* June 2, 1989

Alexander Zaychenko, "Kak delit' pirog" (How to divide the pie), *Moskovskie novosti,* June 11, 1989

Anatoly Anan'ev. "Po techeniyu ili naperkor" (Going with the flow or against it), *Oktyabr',* October 1989

Vasily Selyunin, "Chyornye dyry ekonimki" (The black holes of the economy), *Novy mir,* October 1989

V. Radaev and O. Shkaratan, "Vozvrashchenie k istokam" (The return to the sources), *Izvestia,* February 16, 1990

Vasily Selyunin, "Rynok: khimery i real'nost" (Market: chimeras and reality), *Znamya,* June 1990

Larisa Piyasheva, "V pogone za Siney ptitsey" (Chasing the blue bird [of happiness]), *Oktyabr',* September 1990

Food Shortages and Rationing

Alexander Bekker, "Myaso na vyvoz" (Meat for export), *Moskovskie novosti,* July 10, 1988

Daniil Granin, "Doroga k zdravomu smyslu" (A road to common sense), *Pravda,* August 5, 1988

A. Chernyak, "Edoki po statistike i v zhizni" ("Food consumers in statistics and in real life"), *Pravda,* September 1, 1988

Alexander Zaychenko, "SShA—SSSR: lichnoe potreblenie (nekotorye sopostavleniya)" (USA-USSR: personal consumption [some juxtapositions]), *SShA,* December 1988

Yuri Chernichenko, "Zemlya, ekologiya, perestroika" (Land, ecology, perestroika), *Literaturnaya gazeta,* January 29, 1989

Yuri Chernichenko, "O khlebe nasushchnom" (Of our daily bread), *Komsomol'skaya pravda,* March 12, 1989

"Semeyniy byudzhet: dokhod i raskhod" (Family budget: income and expenses), *Pravda,* May 19, 1989

A. Zaychenko, "Imushchestvennoe neravenstvo" (Material inequality), *Argumenty i fakty,* July 8–14, 1989

Boris Bolotin, "Debyut Vadima Kirichenko" (Vadim Kirichenko's debut), *Moskovskie novosti,* August 13, 1989

Rimashevskaya, "Prozhitochniy minimum" (The minimum subsistence level), *Argumenty i fakty,* April 7–13, 1990

THE HEALTHCARE CRISIS
Evgeny Chazov, "Kogda bolezn' obgonyaet lekarstva" (When disease outpaces remedies), *Literaturnaya gazeta,* February 3, 1988

Svyatoslav Fedorov, "Voinstvo so strelami" (An army with arrows), *Pravda,* September 28, 1987

V. Korneev and S. Tutorskaya, "Lekarstva, kotorykh zhdut" (The drugs people are waiting for), *Izvestia,* January 1988

P. Sergeev, "Defitsit lekarstv: ch'ya vina?" (The shortage of drugs: whose fault?), *Pravda,* July 13, 1989

S. Leskov, "Zarazilis v bol'nitse" (Infected in a hospital), *Izvestia,* May 12, 1989

INFANT MORTALITY, SCHOOLS, PEDIATRICS, MATERNITY WARDS
V. I. Kulakov. "Rebyonok bez prismotra?" (An unattended child?), *Pravda,* August 10, 1987

O. Yarunina, "K chemu privodit bezdushie" (What callousness leads to), *Trud,* January 19, 1988

Evgeny Chazov, Minister of Healthcare of the Soviet Union, Speech at the Nineteenth All-Union Party Conference, *Pravda,* June 30

G. A. Yagodin (Chairman of the USSR State Committee on Education), Speech at the Nineteenth All-Union Party Conference, *Pravda.* July 2, 1988

"Durnoy son?" (A nightmare?) *Rabotnitsa,* November 1988

"Poterpite, zhenshina!" (Hang in there, woman!), Letters to *Rabotnitsa,* February 1989

POVERTY
A. Lemyatskikh, "Ni slova dobrogo, ni drov . . ." (Neither a kind word nor wood), *Pravda,* August 17, 1987: 1

Vasily Ostanchuk, "Ya trudilsya, skol'ko mog . . ." (I have worked as long as I could . . .), *Izvestia,* September 3, 1987: 3

Mikhail Berger, "Skol'ko stoit odet' rebyonka?" (How much does it cost to dress a child?), *Izvestia,* September 23, 1987

Marina Mozhina, "Kto tam, za chertoy bednosti?" (Who is there behind the poverty line?), *Sotsialisticheskaya industriya,* June 1, 1988: 3

Yu Rytov, "Kak zhivyotsya pensioneru?" (How is the pensioner faring?), *Izvestia,* August 20, 1988

Z. Voronina, "Nuzhna pomoshch" (Help is needed), *Izvestia,* September 21, 1988

Ruslan Khazbulatov, "Bednye lyudi otechestva" (The poor people of the Fatherland), *Komsomol'skaya pravda,* July 6, 1989

Evgeny Starikov, "Marginaly" (The marginal people). *Znamya,* October 1989

Stanislav Govorukhin, "Zhut'!" (Dread!), *Sovetskaya kul'tura,* October 7, 1989

THE HOUSING CRISIS
"Zhivyom pasynkami" (We live like unwanted stepchildren), *Pravda,* September 18, 1987

A. Simurov, P. Studenikin, "Net v dushe blagodarnosti . . ." (There is no gratitude in my soul . . .), *Pravda,* November 25, 1987

S. Nikolaev "Kazhdoy sem'e—zdorovuyu kvartiru" (For every family—a healthy apartment), *Literaturnaya gazeta,* August 31, 1988

V. Tolstov, "Kak obespecheny zhil'yom krupneyshie goroda strany" (How well are the largest cities of the country provided with housing), *Izvestia,* September 4, 1988

Alexander Zaychenko, "SShA–SSSR: lichnoe potreblenie (nekotorye sopostav-leniya)" (USA–USSR: personal consumption [some juxtapositions]), *SShA,* December 12, 1988

"THE STATE OF WORKERS AND PEASANTS"
Alexander Zaychenko, "SShA–SSSR: lichnoe potreblenie (nekotorye sopostav-leniya)" (USA–USSR: personal consumption [some juxtapositions]), *SShA,* December 1988

Yuri Vlasov, Speech at the First Congress of People's Deputies of the USSR, *Izvestia,* June 2, 1989

Yuri Bespalov and Valery Konovalov, "Novocherkassk, 1962," *Komsomol'skaya pravda,* June 2, 1989

Vladimir Fomin and Yuri Shchekochikhin, "Togda, v Novocherkasske" (Then, in Novocherassk), *Literaturnaya gazeta,* June 21, 1989

Yuri Apenchenko, "Kuzbass: zharkoe leto" (Kuzbass: a hot summer), *Znamya,* October 1989

Oleg Kalugin, "KGB bez grima" (The KGB without makeup), *Argumenty i fakty,* June 30–July 6, 1990

O. Volkov, "Novocherkassk, 2 iyunya 1962" (Novocherkassk, June 2, 1962), *Komsomol'skaya pravda,* April 27, 1991

THE GREAT PATRIOTIC WAR :"I HAVE FOUGHT IN A DIFFERENT WAR"
Viktor Astaf'ev, Speech at the Conference "Istoriya i literature" (History and literature), *Literaturnaya gazeta,* May 18, 1988

Vasily Kulish, "U poroga voyny" (On the war's threshold), *Komsomol'skaya pravda,* August 24, 1988: 3

Mikhail Semiryaga, "23 avgusta 1939 goda" (August 23, 1939), *Literaturnaya gazeta,* October 5, 1988

Nikolai Pavlenko, Lieutenant General, Professor, "Tragediya i triumph Krasnoy armii" (The Red Army's tragedy and triumph), *Moskovskie novosti,* May 7, 1989

Yu. Fel'shtinskiy and N. Eydel'man, "Za nedelyu do nachala vtoroy mirovoy voyny," *Moskovskie novosti,* August 20, 1989

Vyacheslav Dashichev, "Stalin v nachale 39-go" (Stalin in the beginning of 1939), *Moskovskie novosti,* August 27, 1989

Yuri Geller, "Nevernoe ekho bylogo" (A wrong echo of the past), *Druzhba narodov,* September 1989

Vyacheslav Kondrat'ev, "Parii voyny" (The pariahs of the war), *Literaturnaya gazeta,* January 31, 1990

Yuri Teplyakov, "Po tu storonu fronta" (On the other side of the front line), *Moskovskie novosti*, May 13, 1990

THE "NATIONALIZATION OF CONSCIENCE," THE STATE'S
ECONOMIC MONOPOLY, AND THE "POLITICAL" ECONOMY
Yulia Latynina, "V ozhidanii Zolotogo veka" (Waiting for the Golden Age), *Oktyabr'*, June 1987
Alexander Shindel', "Svidetel'" (Witness), *Znamya*, September 1987
Vladimir Kantor, "Trudnyi put' k tsivilizatsii" (A difficult road to civilization), *Novy mir*, June 1987
Lev Anninskiy, "Monolog byvshego stalintsa" (A monologue of a former Stalinist), in Yuri Afanasiev, ed. *Inogo ne dano* (There is no other way), Moscow: Progress, 1988
Len Karpinsky, "Pochemu stalinizm ne skhodit so stseny?" (Why won't Stalinism leave the stage?), in Afanasiev, ed., *Inogo ne dano* (There is no other way), Moscow: Progress, 1988
Vladimir Kantor, "Imya rokovoe" (The fateful name), *Voprosy literatury*, March 1988
Alexander M. Yakovlev, "Otverzhenie i utverzhdenie" (Rejection and affirmation), *Ogonyok* 43, 1988
Yuri Karyakin, "Zhdanovskaya zhidkost'" (Zhdanov's liquid), in Afanasiev, ed., *Inogo ne dano* (There is no other way), Moscow: Progress, 1988
Nikolai Shmelyov, "Ne smet' komandovat'!" (Stop giving orders!), *Oktyabr'*, February 1988
Igor Klyamkin, "Pochemu tak trudno govorit' pravdu" (Why it is so difficult to speak the truth), *Novy mir*, February 1988
Vasily Seluynin, "Istoki" (The sources), *Novy mir*, May 1988
Gennady Lisichkin, "Mify i real'nost'" (Myths and reality), in Kh. Kobo, ed., *Osmyslit' kul't Stalina* (To comprehend Stalin's cult), Moscow: Progress, 1989
L. Gozman and A. Etkind, "Kul't vlasti: Struktura totalitarnogo soznaniya" (The cult of power: The structure of totalitarian conscience), in Kobo, ed., *Osmyslit' kul't Stalina* (To comprehend Stalin's cult), Moscow: Progress, 1989
Vladimir Lakshin, "Nravstvennost', spravedlivost', gumanizm" (Morality, justice, humanism), *Kommunist* 10, 1989
Vladimir Shubkin, "Trudnoe proshchanie" (The difficult farewell), *Novy mir*, April 1989
Andranik Migranyan, "Dolgiy put' k evropeyskomu domu" (A long road to the European home), *Novy mir*, July 1989
V. Popov and N. Shmelyov, "Na razvilke dorog" (At a crossroad), in Kobo, ed., *Osmyslit' kul't Stalina* (To comprehend Stalin's cult), Moscow: Progress, 1989
Igor Zolotusskiy, "Krushenie abstraktsiy" (The downfall of abstractions), *Novy mir*, January 1989
Alexander Tsypko, "Istoki stalinizma" (The sources of Stalinism), *Nauka i zhizn'*, January and February 1989

Yuri Chernichenko, "Zemlya, ekologiya, perestroika" (Land, ecology, perestroika), *Literaturnaya gazeta,* January 29, 1989

Yuri Chernichenko. "O khlebe nasushchnom" (Of our daily bread), *Komsomol'skaya pravda,* March 12, 1989

Vasily Grossman, *Vsyo techoyt* (Forever flowing), *Oktyabr',* June 1989

Andranik Migranyan, "Dolgiy put' k evropeyskomu domu" (A long road to the European home), *Novy mir,* July 1989

Stanislav Kondrashov, "Iz mraka secretnosti" (From the darkness of secrecy), *Novy mir,* August 1989

Vasily Selyunin, "Planovaya anarkhiya ili balans interesov?" (Planned anarchy or a balance of interests?), *Znamya,* November 1989

Boris Pinsker and Larisa Piyasheva, "Sobstvennost' i svoboda" (Property and liberty), *Novy mir,* November 1989

A. Lapin, "Korruptsiya" (Corruption), *Komsomol'skaya pravda,* December 21, 1989

A. Bocharov, "Mchatsya mify, b'yutsya mify" (Myths are whirling, myths are stirring), *Oktyabr',* January 1990

Alexey Kiva, "Krizis "zhanra" (The crisis of the "genre"), *Novy mir,* March 1990

Viktor Yaroshenko, "Partii interesov" (The parties of issues), *Novy mir,* February 1990

Alexander Tsypko, "Khoroshi li nashi printsipy?" (How good are our principles?), *Novy mir,* April 1990

V. Radaev and O. Shkaratan, "Vozvrashchenie k istokam" (The return to the sources), *Izvestia,* February 16, 1990

Alexander Yakovlev, Speech at Moscow State University on February 12, 1990, in Alexander Yakovlev, *Muki prochteniya bytiya* (The torments of reading life), Moscow: Novosti, 1991

Vasily Selyunin, "Rynok: khimery i real'nost" (Market: chimeras and reality), *Znamya,* June 1990

Larisa Piyasheva, "V pogone za Siney ptitsey" (Chasing the blue bird[of happiness]), *Oktyabr',* September 1990

STALIN, MEMORY, REPENTANCE, ATONEMENT

Dmitry Likhachev, "Trevogi sovesti" (Troubles of conscience), *Literaturnaya gazeta,* January 1, 1987

N. Zorkaya, "Dorogoy, kotoraya vedyot k khramu (On a road that leads to the temple), *Iskusstvo kino* 5, 1987

Igor Klyamkin, "Kakaya ulitsa vedyot k khramu?" (Which street leads to the temple?), *Novy mir,* November 1987

Ludmila Saraskina, "Smotret' pravde v glaza" (To look the truth in the eye), *Moskovskie novosti,* April 10, 1988: 12

Evgeniya Al'bats, "Proshcheniyu ne podlezhat" (No forgiveness for them), *Moskovskie novosti,* May 8, 1988: 13

Yuri Afanasiev, "Perestroika i istoricheskoe znanie" (Perestroika and historical knowledge), *Literaturnaya Rossiya,* June 17, 1988. Reprinted in Yu. Afanasiev, ed., *Inogo ne dano* (There is no other way), Moscow: Progress, 1988

Evgeny Evtushenko, "Sud'ba Platonova" (Platonov's fate), *Sovetskaya kul'tura,*
August 20, 1988

Anatoly Rybakov, "Rana, kotoraya krovotochit" (The wound that is bleeding),
Moskovskie novosti, November 27, 1988

Ol'ga Nemirovskaya, "Nedelya sovesti" (The week of conscience), *Ogonyok,* 48, 1988

Irina Shcherbakova, "Nado li pomnit' proshloe?" (Should the past be remembered?), *Moskovskie novosti,* November 27, 1988

Andrey Vasilevsky, "Stradanie pamyati" (The anguish of memory), *Oktyabr',* April
1989

Yuri Vlasov, Speech at the First Congress of People's Deputies of the USSR, in
"S'ezd Narodnykh Deputatov SSSR," transcript, *Izvestia,* June 2, 1989

Alexander Yakovlev, "Akty spravedlivosti i pokoyaniya" (The acts of justice and
repentance), a television address, August 20, 1990, in Alexander Yakovlev,
Muki prochteniya bytiya (The torments of reading life), Moscow: Novosti, 1991

Stanislav Kondrashov, "Iz mraka secretnosti" (From the darkness of secrecy),
Novy mir, August 1989

Alexander Tsypko, "Khoroshi li nashi printsipy?" (How good are our principles?),
Novy mir,

The "Spirit of Freedom" and the Power of *Nyet*

Vladimir Dudintsev, *Belye odezhdy* (White garments), *Neva,* January–April 1987

Vasily Grossman, *Zhizn' i sud'ba* (Life and fate), *Znamya,* January–April 1988

Lev Razgon, "Nakonetz!" (Finally!), *Moskovskie novosti,* June 26, 1988: 11

Anatoly Zhigulin, Chyornye kamni (Black rocks), *Znamya,* July and August 1988

Anatoly Zhigulin, "Vina! Ona byla, konechno . . ." (The guilt! Of course it was
there . . .), interview with *Moskovskie novosti,* July 31, 1988: 12

Lazar' Lazarev, "Dukh svobody" (The spirit of freedom), *Znamya,* September 1988

Martimyan Ryutin, "Ko vsem chlenam VKP (b)," in Kh. Kobo, ed., *Osmyslit' kul't
Stalina* (To comprehend Stalin's cult), Moscow: Progress, 1989

Yuri Dombrovsky, *Fakul'tet nenuzhnykh veshchey* (The department of unnecessary
things), Moscow: Sovetskiy pisatel', 1989

Andrey Vasilevsky, "Stradanie pamyati" (The anguish of memory), *Oktyabr',* April
1989

Varlam Shalamov, Iz "Kolymskikh rasskazov" (From "The Kolyma tales"),
Znamya, June 1989

Varlam Shalamov, "Mayor Pugachev" (Major Pugachev), in Varlam Shalamov,
Proza, stikhi (Prose, poetry), *Novy mir,* June 1988

Vladimir Fomin and Yuri Shchekochikhin, "Togda, v Novocherkasske" (Then, in
Novocherassk), *Literaturnaya gazeta,* June 21, 1989

Yuri Rost, "Ushol Chelovek" (Gone is Man), An obituary for Andrei Sakharov,
Literaturnaya gazeta, December 20, 1989

Yuri Burtin, "Velikiy russkiy intelligent: Pamyati Andreya Dmitrievicha Sakharova" (The great man of the Russian intelligentsia: In memory of Andrei
Dmitrievich Sakharov), *Oktyabr',* January 1990

Yu. Bespalov, "Novocherkassk. 1962," *Komsomol'skaya pravda*, June 3, 1990

THE FREEDOM CANON

Anatoly Bocharov, "Pravoe delo Vasiliya Grossmana" (Vasily Grossman's just
cause), *Oktyabr'*, January 1988

Vladimir Kantor, "Imya rokovoe" (The fateful name), *Voprosy literatury*, March
1988

Vladimir Lakshin, "Narod i lyudi: O romane Vasiliya Grossmana" (People and
men: About Vasily Grossman's novel) *Izvestia*, June 25, 1988.

Evgeny Evtushenko, "Sud'ba Platonova" (Platonov's fate), *Sovetskaya kul'tura*,
August 20, 1988

Benedikt Sarnov, "Zalozhnik vechnosti (Sluchay Mandel'shtama)" (The hostage of
eternity: The case of Mandelstam), *Ogonyok* 47, 1988

Grigory Anisimov and Mikhail Emtsev, "Etot khranitel' drevnostey. (O pisatele
Yurii Dombrovskom i ego knigakh)" (This keeper of antiques: About the writer
Yuri Dombrovsky and his books), afterword to Dombrovsky, *Fakul'tet nenuzh-
nykh veshchey*, Moscow: Sovetskiy pisatel', 1989

Alexander Solzhenitsyn, "Nobelevskaya lektsiya" (The Nobel lecture), *Novy mir*,
July 1989

Igor Zolotusskiy, "Solzhenitsyn: krug pervyi" (Solzhenitsyn: the first circle),
Moskovskie novosti, August 26, 1990

Alla Latynina, "Solzhenitsyn i my" (Solzhenitsyn and we), *Novy mir*, January 1990

MORAL AUTONOMY, LIBERTY, DEMOCRACY, PRIVATE PROPERTY: "NOT
AN INDIVIDUAL FOR THE STATE BUT THE STATE FOR AN INDIVIDUAL"

Nikolai Popov, "Kto vyshe vlasti?" (Who is above the state's power?), *Sovetskaya
kul'tura*, April 26, 1988

Ernest Ametistov, "Lichnnost' i zakon" (An individual and law), *Moskovskie
novosti*, December 11, 1988

Yuri Feofanov, "Vozvrashchenie k istokam" (The return to the sources), *Znamya*,
February 1989

Alexander Yakovlev, "Rabotat' po sovesti, zhit' chestno" (To work conscientiously,
to live honorably), *Pravda*, February 28, 1989

Yuri Burtin, "Vozmozhnost' vozrazit' " (The opportunity to object), in Yuri
Afanasiev, ed., *Inogo ne dano* (There is no other way), Moscow: Progress, 1988

Vladimir Shubkin, "Trudnoe proshchanie" (The difficult farewell), *Novy mir*, April
1989

Eduard Shevardnadze, "Novy oblik diplomatii" (A new image of diplomacy),
Argumenty i fakty, May 6–12, 1989

Yuri Vlasov, Speech at the First Congress of People's Deputies of the USSR, in
"S'ezd Narodnykh Deputatov SSSR," transcript, *Izvestia*, June 2, 1989

Andrei Sakharov, Speech at the First Congress of People's Deputies on June 7, 1989

Andranik Migranyan, "Dolgiy put' k evropeyskomu domu" (A long road to the
European home), *Novy mir*, July 1989

Nikolai Travkin, "Put' k narodovlastiyu lezhit cherez samoupravlenie" (The road to government by the people runs through self-rule), *Sovetskaya kul'tura*, July 8, 1989

B. Nazarov, "Formula svobody" (The formula of freedom), *Sovietskaya kul'tura*, July 11, 1989

Marat Baglay, "Moral' i politika" (Morality and politics), *Sovetskaya kul'tura*, July 27, 1989: 4

L. Gol'din, "Nado snova nauchit'sya zhit' " (We must relearn to live), *Sovetskaya kul'tura*, August 29, 1989

Andrei Sakharov, "Stepen' svobody" (The degree of freedom), *Ogonyok* 31, 1989

Rayr Simonyan and Anatoly Druzenko, "Kuda my idyom?" (Where are we going?), *Ogonyok* 37, 1989: 3

Anatoly Anan'ev, "Po techeniyu ili naperkor" (Going with the flow or against it), *Oktyabr'*, October 1989

Vasily Selyunin, "Chyornye dyry ekonimki" (The black holes of the economy), *Novy mir*, October 1989

Vasily Selyunin, "Planovaya anarkhiya ili balans interesov?" (Planned anarchy or a balance of interests?), *Znamya*, November 1989

Alexander Yakovlev, "Only Moral Democracy," *Moskovskie novosti*, January 1, 1990

V. Radaev and O. Shkaratan, "Vozvrashchenie k istokam" (The return to the sources), *Izvestia*, February 16, 1990

Pavel Voshchanov, "Zemlya i volya" (Land and freedom), *Komsomol'skaya pravda*, February 28, 1990

Viktor Malukhin, "Pole pod svobodnym nebom" (A field under a free sky), *Izvestia*, March 7, 1990

Alexey Kiva, "Krizis 'zhanra' " (The crisis of a "genre"), *Novy mir*, March 1990

Vyacheslav Dashichev, "Evropa otkrytykh dverey" (A Europe of open doors), *Komsomol'skaya pravda*, February 20, 1990

Pavel Gurevich, "Kakaya ideologiya nam nuzhna?" (What ideology do we need?), *Literaturnaya gazeta*, March 14, 1990

Alexander Tsypko, "Vozmozhno li chudo?" (Is a miracle possible?), *Sovetskaya kul'tura*, May 26, 1990

Larisa Piyasheva, "V pogone za Siney ptitsey" (Chasing the blue bird [of happiness]), *Oktyabr'*, September 1990

S. Shatalin, N. Petrakov, G. Yavlisnky, S. Aleksashenko, A. Vavilov, L. Grigor'ev, M. Zadornov, V. Martynov, V. Mashits, D. Mikhaylov, V. Fedorov, T. Yarygina, E. Yasin, "Chelovek. Svododa. Rynok." (Man. Liberty. Market.), *Komsomol'skaya pravda*, September 5, 1990

Andrei Sakharov, "Konstitutsiya Soyuza Sovetskikh Respublik Evropy i Azii" (Constitution of the Union of Soviet Republic of Europe and Asia), December 1989, in "Konstitutsionnye idei Andreya Sakharova" (Constitutional ideas of Andrei Sakharov), *Oktyabr'*, May 1990

Alexander Solzhenitsyn, "Kak nam obustroit' Rossiyu" (How we can make Russia good for living), a supplement to *Komsomol'skaya pravda*, September 18, 1990

THE EMPIRE AND THE "GARRISON STATE"

Andrei Sakharov, Speech at the First Congress of People's Deputies on June 7, 1989

Stanislav Kondrashov, "Iz mraka secretnosti" (From the darkness of secrecy), *Novy mir*, August 1989

Alexei Izyumov and Andrei Kortunov, "Diplomatiya i nravstvennost' vremyon perestroiki" (Diplomacy and morality at the time of perestroika), *Moskovskie novosti*, August 6, 1989

Viktor Sheynis, "Avgustovskaya zhatva" (The August harvest), *Izvestia*, October 13, 1989

Andrei Sakharov, "Stepen' svobody" (The degree of freedom), *Ogonyok* 31, 1989

V. Dashichev, "Evropa otkrytykh dverey" (A Europe of open doors), *Komsomol'skaya pravda*, February 20, 1990: 2

Yuri Ryzhov, "Bezopasnost', kotoraya nam nuzhna" (Security that we need), *Novoe vermya*, no. 10, 1990

Sergei Blagovolin, "Otkrytyi mir ili osazhdyonnyi lager'? (An open world or a besieged camp?), *Moskovskie novosti*, August 12, 1990

Igor Birman, "Nosha ne po plechu" (Too heavy a burden), interview with *Izvestia*, November 29, 1990

GLASNOST'S TROUBADOURS

TENGIZ ABULADZE (1924–94)
A Soviet Georgian film director. His anti-Stalinist allegory *Repentance* (finished in 1984 and released in 1987) was one of the very first cultural expressions of glasnost, became its enduring symbol, and supplied one of its key tropes: "the roads to the temple." The film won the Special Jury Prize at the 1987 Cannes Film Festival. The next year, *Ablaze* received a Lenin Prize, the Soviet Union's most prestigious award.

ALES ADAMOVICH (1927–94)
A Soviet Belarusian writer and a critic. As a teenager, he fought the Nazis in one of many guerrilla (*partisan*) detachments in Belarus and is best known for *The Khatyn Story* (*Khatynskaya istoriya*), based on his experience as a fighter and a messenger. In collaboration with Daniil Granin (see below) he wrote *The Blockade Book* (*Blokadnaya kniga*, 1977–81) about the Nazi siege of Leningrad.

YURI AFANASIEV (B. 1934)
In his youth, chairman of the Young Pioneers Organization and a member of the Komsomol leadership. Graduated from the History Department of Moscow University, with a Ph.D. in history. Rector (dean) of the Moscow Institute of History and Archives. In 1989 was elected to the Congress of People's Deputies of the Soviet Union from a Moscow district and became one of the co-chairmen of the radical Interregional Group of Deputies. One of the founders and co-chairs of the "Democratic Russia" movement. Dean, Moscow State University for Humanities, which he founded.

ANATOLY ANAN'EV (1925–2001)
A writer known mostly for his novels about the Great Patriotic War. From 1973 and
until his death was editor of the *Oktyabr'* "thick" literary journal, which published
some of the key texts of glasnost, including Anna Akhamtova's *Requiem;* Vasily
Grossman's *Vsyo techyot* (Forever flowing); Andrei Sakharov's Nobel lecture; and
essays by Anatoly Bocharov (see below), Yuri Burtin (see below), Alexei Kiva (see
below), and Nikolai Shmelyov (see below).

MARAT BAGLAY (B. 1931)
Professor of constitutional law at the Moscow State Institute of International Relations (1977–95), the head of a department at the Institute of International Workers'
Movement, and deputy dean of the Highest School of the Trade Union Movement
(later, the Academy of Labor and Social Relations, 1977–95). Chairman of the Constitutional Court of the Russian Federation, 1997–2003.

GRIGORY BAKLANOV (1923–2009)
A war veteran and a popular Soviet Russian writer known for his novels about the
Great Patriotic War. Between 1986 and 1993, editor of *Znamya,* one of the main
literary magazines of glasnost, which published, among other key works of fiction
and essays, Vasily Grossman's *Life and Fate* (*Zhizn' i sud'ba*) in its January–April
1988 issues.

ANATOLY BOCHAROV (B. 1922–97)
A literary critic, professor of philology, Moscow State University. A major explica-
tor of the art of Vasily Grossman and the author of essays about the ethical, existential, and political themes in Grossman's *Life and Fate.*

ALEXANDER BOVIN (1930–2004)
From 1963 to 1972 political consultant to the Central Committee of the Communist
Party of the Soviet Union. Speechwriter for General Secretary Leonid Brezhnev and
a member of Yuri Andropov's "brain trust." In 1972–91, international affairs columnist for *Izvestia* and a popular television commentator. After the reestablishment of
diplomatic relations with Israel, became the Soviet Union's first ambassador to Israel, 1991–97.

FEDOR BURLATSKY (B. 1927)
Deputy editor of the International Department of the Central Committee's main
theoretical journal, *Kommunist,* in 1953–60, and head of the Department of Socialist Countries of the Central Committee's Group of Consultants. A top advisor
and speechwriter to First Secretary Nikita Khrushchev, 1960–65. Deputy director
of the Institute of Sociological Research of the Academy of Sciences, 1969–72.
Editor in chief of *Literaturnaya gazeta,* 1987–91. People's Deputy of the Soviet
Union, 1989–91.

YURI BURTIN (1932–2000)

A *Novy mir* author from 1959. In 1967–70, an editor of *Novy mir*. A close colleague of Andrei Sakharov and a founder of the "Moscow Tribune" Club in 1987. People's Deputy (1989) and a member of the Interregional Group of Deputies. After August 1991, a member of the leadership of Democratic Russia and co-editor of the *Demokraticheskaya Rossiya* newspaper.

YURI CHERNICHENKO (1929–2000)

Before 1987, an agricultural columnist for *Znamya, Sovetskya Rossiya,* and *Pravda.* In 1987–91, a key essayist of glasnost and the main critic of collectivized agriculture and of the environmental degradation of the Russian countryside. A co-chairman of the liberal writers' association "April." In the 1990s, the founder and leader of the Peasant Party of Russia.

LYDIA CHUKOVSKAYA (1907–96)

Daughter of Russia's most beloved children's poet, Korney Chukovsky, and a close friend of Anna Akhmatova. An editor of the cultural monthly *Literaturnaya moskva.* Her novel about the Great Purge of 1937–38, *Sofia Petrovna,* was based on her ordeal after the arrest and execution of her husband. An active supporter of Joseph Brodsky, Alexander Solzhenitsyn, Alexander Ginzburg, and other ostracized writers and dissidents. Expelled from the Writer's Union in 1974 and not published until 1987.

VLADIMIR DUDINTSEV (1918–98)

A writer whose 1956 novel *Not by Bread Alone (Ne khlebom edinym)* became perhaps the most celebrated literary work of Khrushchev's "thaw." Thirty years later, his *While Robes (Belye odezhdy),* about Lysenkovism's assault on Soviet genetics, became one of the first instances of glasnost in literature.

NATAN EIDELMAN (1930–89)

A literary historian and biographer, a key authority on the Decembrist movement and its leaders, the author of books about Alexander Pushkin and Russia's first great historian Nikolai Karamzin.

EVGENY EVTUSHENKO (B. 1933)

One of the most popular Soviet Russian poets, an ardent supporter of Khrushchev's "thaw," the author of poems "Baby Yar" (1961), about the murder of Kiev's Jews in September 1941, and "To Stalin's Heirs" ("Nasledniki Stalina") (1961), in which he described the removal of Stalin's body from the Red Square Mausoleum. Protested Solzhenitsyn's expulsion from the Soviet Union in 1974. In 1989 was elected a People's Deputy of the Soviet Union. Left Russia in the 1990s and lives in New York.

SVYATOSLAV FEDOROV (1927–2000)

The leading Russian ophthalmologist and eye surgeon. In 1960 performed the first intraocular lens replacement operation in the Soviet Union. From 1980, director of Moscow Research Institute of Eye Microsurgery. A People's Deputy of the USSR in 1989–91. Resigned from the Communist Party in 1990 and joined the Democratic Party of Russia. Member of the First Duma, 1993–95, re-elected in 1995. Ran for president in 1996. Died in a helicopter crash on the outskirts of Moscow.

STANISLAV GOVORUKHIN (B. 1936)

Since the 1960s, one of the most popular Soviet and Russian film directors. Directed such Soviet cult classics as *Vertical* and *A Meeting Place Cannot Be Changed* (*Mesto vstrechi izmenit' nel'zya*), starring the popular bard and actor Vladimir Vysotsky. In 1990 became a leader of the Democratic Party of Russia. The same year, produced and directed one of the most devastating works of glasnost, the documentary *We Can't Live Like This* (*Tak zhit' nel'zya*). Was elected to the First Duma in 1993. After the 1993 crisis, sided with the Left nationalist opposition.

DANIIL GRANIN (B. 1919)

One of the most popular Soviet Russian writers, specializing in stories and novels about scientists. His 1987 novel *Bison* (*Zubr*) was a key text of early glasnost. The book recounts the life and work of a leading Soviet geneticist, Nikolay Timofeev-Resovsky, who decided not to return to the Soviet Union from Germany, where he was sent to conduct research. The scientist was captured by the Soviet troops at the end of World War II, sent to the Gulag, and then headed a Gulag research facility (*sharashka*). Granin was People's Deputy of the Soviet Union, 1989–91.

LEN KARPINSKIY (1929–95)

A son of an "Old Bolshevik" and Lenin's comrade in arms. A Komsomol leader in 1957–62 and a senior editor of *Pravda* in 1962–67. Fired from *Pravda* for an article opposing censorship in the theater and became a freelance book and art agent. In 1989 was invited by the editor of *Moskovskie novosti*, Egor Yakovlev (see below), to join the paper as the chief political columnist. Was the paper's editor in chief in 1991–93, when he retired because of illness.

YURI KARYAKIN (B. 1930)

Philologist, critic, writer, and essayist, an expert on Dostoevsky. Graduated from the Department of Philosophy of the Moscow University and worked in the Central Committee's journal, *Problems of the World and Socialism*. Expelled from the Party in 1968 for an anti-Stalinist speech at an event commemorating Andrei Platonov. In 1987–89, a founder of the pro-reform Club Moscow Tribune (*Moskovskaya tribuna*) and anti-Stalinist "Memorial." A People's Deputy of the Soviet Union, 1989–91, and member of the Presidential Council, 1992–99.

ALEXEY KIVA (B. 1931)
Graduated from the Department of Philology (Romance and German Languages) of Moscow State University and the Academy of Social Sciences of the Central Committee of the Communist Party. Worked in the International Department of the Trade Union's Central Committee, in the State Committee for Radio and Television, for the journals *International Life* and *Asia and Africa Today*. Earned a Ph.D. in history in 1980 and joined the Institute of Oriental Studies. A board member of the Gorbachev Foundation (1991) and a member of the president's Human Rights Commission in 1996–2000.

IGOR KLYAMKIN (B. 1941)
A graduate of the Department of Journalism (by correspondence) of the Moscow State University, holds a doctorate in philosophy. During perestroika was a senior fellow (*starshiy nauchnyy sotrudnik*) at the Institute of the World Socialist System and a senior researcher of the Institute of Economic and Political Studies of the Academy of Sciences. Since 2000, the head of the analytical center of the "Public Opinion Foundation," director of the Institute of Sociological Analysis, and the vice president of the "Liberal Mission" Foundation.

STANISLAV KONDRASHOV (1928–2007)
Joined *Izvestia* in 1951. Between 1961 and 1976 was *Izvestia*'s correspondent in New York and Washington—the most prestigious assignments in Soviet journalism. In 1977 became a world affairs columnist and the host of the popular television talk show "International Panorama." Retired from *Izvestia* in 2000.

VITALY KOROTICH (B. 1936)
A Soviet Ukrainian and Russian writer and journalist. Trained as a physician, he worked as a doctor in Ukraine in 1959–66, then became a full-time writer and an officer of the Writers' Union. In the late 1970s, editor of the Kiev-based Ukrainian-language literary magazine *Vsesvit*. In 1984 worked in New York as a member of the Ukrainian SSR's delegation at the United Nations. In 1985 traveled in Canada as part of the official Soviet campaign for world peace and nuclear disarmament. In 1986 became editor of the illustrated weekly *Ogonyok*, which he fashioned into one of the most radical "megaphones of glasnost."

OTTO LATSIS (1934–2005)
A Soviet Russian journalist of Latvian descent. A graduate of Moscow State University (1956), he worked for *Ekonomicheskaya gazeta*, the Soviet Union's main economic newspaper. Moved to *Izvestia* at the end of Khrushchev's "thaw" (1963–64), where he advocated the loosening of censorship and making *Izvestia* into a popular liberal publication. Fired from *Izvestia* in 1971 after the KGB found a manuscript of his book about the end of NEP and Stalin's "revolution from above," titled *The Turning Point* (*Perelom*). Sent to Prague to work for the magazine *Problems of*

the World and Communism, which at the time was a place of "honorary exile" for a number of dissenting liberals from the Party *nomenklatura.* In 1986 appointed first deputy editor of the Central Committee's main theoretical journal, *Kommunist,* which became a key pro-reform publication. (In 1990–91 its Economics Department was headed by Yegor Gaidar.) Was elected to the Central Committee in 1990, where he advocated further liberalization.

GENNADY LISICHKIN (B. 1929)

Graduated from Moscow State Institute of International Relations (MGIMO) in 1953. Ph.D in economics. Joined the Communist Party in 1956. In 1963–66 deputy editor of the Department of Industry at *Izvestia,* later editor of the Department of Agriculture. Fired from *Izvestia* for an article criticizing collectivized agriculture and state planning but continued to write pro-reform books and pamphlets about "market and plan."

ANDREI NUYKIN (B. 1931)

Essayist, literary critic, ethicist. A Ph.D. in art history, a member of the Writers' Union (1976). In 1964–89, the author of nine books about literature, ethics, "art, and morality."

GAVRIIL POPOV (B. 1936)

Graduate of the Department of Economics of Moscow State University. Joined the Party upon graduation in 1959. A Komsomol leader. Ph.D. in political economy from the Moscow State University. In 1978 was appointed dean of the university's Economics Department, where Yegor Gaidar was one of his students. In the 1987 review of Daniil Granin's *Zubr* (see Granin, above), coined the term "command-and-administer system" (*komandno-administrativnaya sistema*), which became one of the most popular shorthands of perestroika for describing the Soviet economic regime. In 1988–91, editor of the main theoretical economic journal *Voporsy Ekonomiki* (The problems of economy). People's Deputy of the Soviet Union, 1989, a co-chairman of the Interregional Group of Deputies. Resigned from the Party in 1990. In April 1990 became the first elected mayor of Moscow.

VLADIMIR POPOV (B. 1954)

Graduated from the Department of Economics of the Moscow State University in 1976. A Ph.D. in economics and a senior scholar at the Institute of the United States and Canada. With Nikolai Shmelyov (see below), co-authored some of the key pro-reform essays about Soviet economy.

ANATOLY PRISTAVKIN (1931–2008)

A Soviet Russian novelist, the author of the 1987 autobiographical novel *Nochevala tuchka zolotaya* (A little golden cloud spent a night), about the horrific conditions in Soviet orphanages during World War II and the deportations of the Chechen people in 1944. The book was translated into over thirty languages and was awarded the Lenin Prize in 1988. A member of the pro-reform writers' organization "April" (1988). In 1991 supported Latvian independence movement, stood on the barricades in Riga, and appealed to Soviet soldiers on television not to shoot at civilians. In 1995 and 1996 traveled to Chechnya and criticized Moscow's Chechnya policies in Russian media. In 1990s, headed the President's Commission on Pardons.

ANATOLY RYBAKOV (1911–98)

A Soviet Russian writer. Until glasnost, mostly the author of children's books. In 1987 published a widely popular autobiographical novel *Deti Arbata* (Children of Arbat), written in the early 1960s. The novel was published in fifty-two countries with a total press run of over 20 million. President of the Soviet PEN Russian Center in 1989–91.

ANDREI SAKHAROV (1921–89)

A world-renowned physicist and astrophysicist, the "father" of the Soviet hydrogen bomb. Graduate of the Department of Physics of Moscow State University. A dissident leader and a Nobel Peace Prize laureate (1975). Exiled to Gorky (now Nizhny Novgorod) in 1980–86. Allowed to return to Moscow, after Gorbachev's phone call in December 1986. People's Deputy of the Soviet Union and a co-chairman of the Interregional Group of Deputies (1989).

VASILY SELYUNIN (1927–94)

A graduate of the Journalism Department of the Moscow State University (1954) and of the Highest Economic School of Gosplan (the Soviet top economic planning agency). In 1965–85, a columnist for a major national economics daily *Sovetskaya industriya* (Socialist industry). Deputy of the First Duma (1993–95).

NIKOLAI SHMELYOV (B. 1936)

Graduated from the Moscow State University with a degree in economics (1958). A Ph.D. in economics. Khrushchev's son-in-law divorced Yula Khrushcheva in 1962 after a short marriage. In 1961–68, a senior researcher at the Institute of the Economy of the World Socialist System. A lecturer of the Propaganda Department of the Central Committee (1968–70). A department head at the Institute of the Economy of the World Socialist System (1970–83) and at the Institute of the United States and Canada (1983–92). Author of a novel, *Pashkov dom* (The Pashkov house), about professional and ethical dilemmas of a Soviet Sinologist. People's Deputy of the Soviet Union in 1989–91 and a member of the Presidential Council in 1991–93. Since 1999, director of the Institute of Europe of the Russian Academy of Sciences.

VLADIMIR SHUBKIN (1923–2010)

One of the founders of Soviet sociology, the author of over 200 scholarly publications. A son of an "enemy of the people," who was executed in the late 1930s.

A Ph.D. in economics and philosophy, specializing in sociology of labor, education, and youth. An author of a survey methodology widely adopted for the study
of youth in the Soviet Union and the socialist countries in the 1970s and 1980s.
Beginning in 1991 and until retirement, a senior researcher at the Institute of
Sociology of the Russian Academy of Sciences.

VLADISLAV STARKOV (1940–2004)

A professional journalist and editor. In 1973–80 worked in Moscow radio; a senior
staffer of the main propaganda publishing house *Znanie* and then director of the
Mezhdunarodnye otnosheniya (International Relations) publishers. In 1980 was
appointed editor of *Argumenty i fakty,* then a "thin" bulletin for party propagandists,
and by 1989 remade it into one of the most sought-after publications of glasnost—a
hard-hitting, factual, multi-page tabloid distributed weekly to over 20 million subscribers and with at least twice as many readers. In 1989, Starkov was nearly dismissed after the publication of the first popularity rating of top Soviet politicians, in
which Gorbachev was second after Sakharov. In 1990 the paper's press run reached
30 million. In 1990–93, People's Deputy of Russia.

ANATOLY STRELYANIY (B. 1939)

Graduate of the Journalism Department of the Moscow State University. For many
years, a special correspondent of *Komsomol'skaya pravda,* specializing in economics and agriculture. The author of twelve books of essays and fiction. In 1987, a
member of the *Novy mir* editorial board and a key critic of planned economy and
collectivized agriculture. The author of a popular documentary "A Peasant from
Arkhangel'sk" (*Arkhangel'skiy muzhik,* 1989) sharply critical of the kolkhoz system.
In 1989 elected editor in chief of the most prestigious Soviet publishing house,
Sovetskiy pisatel' (Soviet Writer).

YURI VLASOV (B. 1935)

A son of a prominent Soviet diplomat. Graduated from the Suvorov military school
and then the Moscow Air Force Academy. A champion weight lifter at the 1960
Olympics in Rome, where he broke three world records and was proclaimed the
"strongest man on the planet." Between 1968 and 1976, published several books of
essays and fiction. In 1989, elected to the Congress of People's Deputies from the
Lyublinsky district of Moscow and joined the radical Interregional Group of Deputies. Later moved closer to the nationalists and Christian Democrats. Elected to the
First Duma in 1993. Ran as a candidate in the 1996 presidential election and came
in second-to-last among the ten participants, with 0.02 percent of the vote.

ALEXANDER YAKOVLEV (1923–2005)

Born to a peasant family in the Yaroslavl region. A World War II veteran, a marine.
He was badly wounded in 1942 and discharged as an invalid. In 1946 graduated
from the Department of History of the Yaroslavl Pedagogical Institute. In 1950–53,
deputy head of the Propaganda Department of the Yaroslavl Regional Party Commit-

tee and the head of the Department of Schools and Colleges. Transferred to Moscow and worked as an instructor in the Department of Schools, Science, and Colleges of the Central Committee. In 1956–59, studied in the Academy of Social Sciences of the Central Committee and graduated with a Ph.D. in history. In 1958–59 studied at Columbia University in New York. In 1965, at thirty-two, became the youngest-ever first deputy head of the Propaganda Department of the Central Committee. In 1969–73, acting head of the Propaganda Department. In November 1972 published an article in which he criticized Russian nationalism and chauvinism. The following year, removed from the Central Committee apparatus and appointed ambassador to Canada (1973–83). Met with a Politburo member and Central Committee Secretary, Mikhail Gorbachev, during the latter's visit to Canada in May 1983.

Returned to Moscow in 1983 to head the Institute of World Economy and International Relations. In 1985 became head of the Propaganda Department of the Central Committee. Secretary of the Central Committee (1986) and a Politburo member (1987) with responsibility for ideology, information, and culture. Persuaded the Politburo to approve the release of Abuladze's *Repentance;* and appointed liberal editors to several key newspapers and journals. Became known as the "godfather of glasnost." At the Nineteenth Party Conference in 1988 headed the commission that drafted the resolution "On Glasnost." In September 1988 was given additional responsibility for foreign policy and accompanied Gorbachev to all summits with President George H. W. Bush.

In March 1990, appointed a member of the Presidential Council and immediately resigned from the Politburo and the Central Committee Secretariat. In July 1991 resigned his position as president's senior advisor and founded, with former Foreign Minister Eduard Shevardnadze, the Movement for Democratic Reforms. On August 16, 1991, he resigned from the Party.

In 1992, appointed chairman of the Commission for the Rehabilitation of the Victims of Political Repression by President Yeltsin. Chairman of the Federal Agency for Television and Radio and head of the Ostankino state television network (1993–95). Founded and headed the international foundation "Democracy" (also known as the Alexander N. Yakovlev Foundation), which prepared for publication materials from the formerly secret Party and state archives. One of the compilations was *History of Violence in the Soviet Union.* Published articles, collections of essays, and his memoirs *Omut pamyati* (The whirlpool of memory) and *Sumerki* (Dusk). In February 2005 signed a letter calling on the world human rights community to consider Mikhail Khodorkovsky a political prisoner.

EGOR YAKOVLEV (1930–2005)

A graduate of the Moscow Institute of History and Archives (1954). In 1966, was appointed editor of *Sovietskaya pechat* (Soviet press), which later became *Zhurnalist,* the magazine of the Union of Journalists. In 1968–72 was *Izvestia's* special correspondent in Czechoslovakia. In August 1986, was appointed editor in chief of a propaganda sheet, *Moskovskie novosti* (Moscow news), distributed mostly abroad, and turned it into one of the most daring and sought-after media outlets and a flagship of glasnost. In 1991–92, chairman of the State Television Company. In 1993, became the publisher of *Obschaya gazeta* (Common newspaper), which he sold in 2002.

SERGEI ZALYGIN (1913–2000)

A prominent Soviet Russian writer. In 1986 was appointed editor of *Novy mir*, where he published some of the most significant essays and fiction of glasnost, including Valily Selyunin's *Istoki*, Andrei Platonov's *Kotlovan*, and Alexander Solzhenitsyn's *Arkhipelag Gulag*.

ALEXANDER ZAYCHENKO (B. 1938)

Earned a Ph.D. in economics from the graduate school of the Scientific Research Institute of the Gosplan with a Ph.D. in economics. Senior research fellow, Institute of the United States and Canada, 1980–89. In 1986, advisor to the Council of Ministers of the USSR. In 1989–91, a consultant of the commission on economic reform of the Council of Ministers. In December 1988, published an article in the journal of the Institute of the United States and Canada comparing the standard of living in the USSR with that of the United States (and with Russia in 1913). The article's findings, especially the cost of food, consumer goods, and housing in both countries in relation to salaries, became an instant sensation. Several more articles on similar subjects appeared in *Argumenty i fakty* and *Moskovksie novosti*. In 1991–94, Zaychenko was director of the International Center for the Support of Private Enterprise. Co-founder and professor of the Russian-American Christian University (2001).

IGOR ZOLOTUSSKIY (B. 1930)

A son of a military officer, arrested in 1937, and a nurse, arrested in 1941. Grew up in an orphanage. Graduated from the Department of Philology of Kazan State University. Worked as a radio and print journalist in Khabarovsk in the Far East. A correspondent of *Literaturnaya gazeta* in 1967–71 and a commentator for *Literaturnoe obozrenie* (Literary review) in 1978–90. A member of the Writers' Union since 1963. In 1990–94, editor of the department of Russian literature of *Literaturnaya gazeta*. Co-chair and first secretary of the Union of Russian Writers (1991–96).

NOTES

INTRODUCTION

1. This list has been drawn from repeated mentions in the Soviet press of the time, public opinion polls, and articles by Western experts. See, for example, "Chto my dumaem?" (What do we think?), *Literaturnaya gazeta*, March 29, 1989: 12; Yuri Levada, ed., *Est'mnenie!* (There is an opinion!), Moscow: Progress, 1990: 125; Riitta H. Pittman, "Perestroika and Soviet Cultural Politics: The Case of the Major Literary Journals," *Soviet Studies* 42, no. 1, January 1990: 111–32; and Josephine Woll, "Glasnost: A Cultural Kaleidoscope," in Harley Balzer, ed., *Five Years That Shook the World*, Boulder: Westview Press, 1991: 114.

2. Yuri Chernichenko, "Zemlya, ekologiya, perestroika" (Land, ecology, perestroika), *Literaturnaya gazeta*, January 29, 1989: 3.

3. This list of glasnost's most "subversive" books was culled from the mentions in the contemporary newspapers and magazines and public opinion polls, and was validated by experts' articles and the witnesses' memoirs. See, for example, Yuri Karyakin, "Stoit li nasupat' na grabli?" (Is it necessary to step on the rake?), *Znamya*, no. 9, September 1987: 207; Julia Wishnevsky, "A Guide to Some Major Soviet Journals," RL Supplement 2/88, *Radio Liberty Research Bulletin*, July 20, 1988; Yuri Chernichenko, "Trava iz pod stoga" (The grass from under a haystack), in Yuri N. Afanasiev, ed., *Inogo ne dano* (There is no other way), Moscow: Progress, 1988: 592; Levada, ed., op. cit., 131 ("the leaders of the readers' interests"); Pittman, op. cit.; Helena Goscilo, "Alternative Prose and Glasnost Literature," in Balzer, op. cit., 120–21; Alexander Yakovlev, *Sumerki* (Twilight), Moscow: Materik, 2003: 394.

4. Bernard Bailyn, *The Ideological Origins of the American Revolution*, Cambridge: Belknap Press of Harvard University Press, 1992: xiv.

5. A. F. Bourreau-Deslandres, *Histoire critique*: iii. As quoted in Donald R. Kelley, "What Is Happening to the History of Ideas?" *Journal of the History of Ideas* 51, no. 1, January–March 1990: 7.

1. The years are those of the Central Committee meeting where Mikhail Gorbachev declared openness and democratization to be *the* goals of the reform (January 1987) and the end of the party state and the dissolution of the Soviet Union (August–December 1991).

2. The two most notable exceptions are the Soviet dissident Andrei Amalrik and British journalist Bernard Levin. Amalrik predicted in the 1960s that "this great Eastern Slav empire, created by Germans, Byzantines and Mongols, has entered the last decades of its existence," but he thought the cause of the collapse would be a protracted war with China. (Andrei Amalrik, *Will the Soviet Union Survive until 1984*, New York: Harper and Row, 1970: 57.) Levin's 1977 article was unique in its unhedged confidence in the coming of a "new Russian revolution" in the near future, because the "thirst for freedom and decency" within the Soviet empire had eroded its foundation to the point at which either increase in repression or substantive reforms would lead to cataclysmic changes. (Bernard Levin, *Times of London*, August 1977, as quoted in the *National Interest*, Special Issue, Spring 1993: 64.)

3. As quoted in Paul Hollander, *Personal Will and Political Belief*, New Haven: Yale University Press, 1999: 1.

4. Richard Pipes, a back cover endorsement of Paul Hollander's *Political Will and Personal Belief*.

5. Martin Malia, "A Fatal Logic," in Owen Harries, ed., *The Strange Death of Soviet Communism*, Special issue, *National Interest*, Spring 1993: 80.

6. François Furet, *The Passing of an Illusion*, Chicago: University of Chicago Press, 1999: 500–501.

7. Harries, op. cit.

8. "Devastated by war with more than twenty-five million dead, the collective farm system in tatters, needing to absorb a huge military, and come to grips with a new capitalist 'foe' possessing atomic weapons and the most powerful economy in world history, the Soviet Union did not collapse," Ken Jowitt noted. "Stalin did not have second thoughts about Nikolai Bukharin or start reading Eduard Bernstein. Stalin approached his task in the Leninist spirit of what is to be re-done. In contrast, Mikhail Gorbachev approached his task in the spirit of what is to be un-done, in spite of having the world's third largest economy. Something more important than the economy was involved." (Ken Jowitt, "Really Imaginary Socialism," *East European Constitutional Review* 6 [2 & 3], Spring/Summer 1997: 43.) Archie Brown, similarly, suggested that had it not

been for Gorbachev, "the Soviet Union would have postponed facing up to the fundamental problems of the system. The regime had, after all, been politically repressive and economically inefficient for the greater part of seven decades." (Archie Brown, *The Gorbachev Factor,* Oxford: Oxford University Press, 1997: 90.)

9. Leon Aron, *Yeltsin: A Revolutionary Life,* New York: St. Martin's Press, 2000: 177–81.
10. Irina Starodubrovskaya and Vladimir Mau, *Velikie revolutsii ot Kromvelya do Putina* (Great revolutions from Cromwell to Putin), Moscow: Vagrius, 2004: 109.
11. Ibid. The economy grew 3–5 percent in 1986, 2.5 percent in 1987, 3.7 percent in 1988, and 1.4 percent in 1989.
12. Egor Gaidar, *Dologoe vremya,* Moscow: Delo, 2005: table 8.30, p. 344; Starodubrovskaya and Mau, op. cit., table 8.5, p. 313; and Anders Åslund, *How Russia Became a Market Economy,* Washington, DC: Brookings Institution, 1995, table 2-5, p. 47.
13. Gaidar, op. cit., table 8.25, p. 342. The figures are in the year 2000 constant prices.
14. Ibid.
15. Gaidar, op. cit., table 8.31, p. 345; Starodubrovskaya and Mau, op. cit., table 8.5, p. 313; and Åslund, op. cit., 49.
16. Gaidar, op. cit., 339, and Åslund, op. cit., 48.
17. Anders Åslund, *Building Capitalism,* New York: Cambridge University Press, 2002: 47.
18. Starodubrovskaya and Mau, op. cit., 312.
19. Peter Rutland, "Sovietology: Notes for a Post-Mortem," in Harries, op. cit., 121.
20. Åslund, *How Russia,* 47. Vladmir Kontorovich points out that the "business as usual" was all the more feasible because the Soviet economy was likely to rebound as the slowdown in growth was caused at least in part by a series of poor harvests. (Vladimir Kontorovich, "The Economic Fallacy," in Harries, op. cit., 9.)
21. Åslund, op. cit., 51.
22. Ibid., 50–51. Rutland, op. cit., 121.
23. For a good summary of the Soviet Union's festering "nationality problem" and the regime's repressive responses see Bohdan Nahaylo and Victor Swoboda, *Soviet Disunion,* New York: Free Press, 1989, esp. chaps. 13 and 14 (pp. 199–230).
24. Stephen Sestanovich, "Did the West Undo the East?" in Harries, ed., op. cit., 1993: 31.
25. In the end, the Soviet Union lost around 15,000 soldiers in Afghanistan: a tragic waste of young lives, yet, as Walter Laqueur points out, fewer than the number of casualties in one hour of the 1943 battle of Kursk in World War II. (Walter Laqueur, "The Origins of the Russian Crisis," *Journal of Contemporary History* 28, 1993: 405.)

26. Ibid. and Anders Åslund, "How Small Is Soviet National Income?" in Henry S. Rowen and Charles Wolf, eds., *The Impoverished Superpower,* San Francisco: Institute for Contemporary Studies, 1990: 37. This estimate lends credibility to the suggestion that the decision to withdraw Soviet troops from Afghanistan in 1988 was "political," with the cost playing only a secondary role (Laqueur, op. cit., 396–97).

27. As quoted in Paul Hollander, *Political Will and Personal Belief,* New Haven: Yale University Press, 1999: 87. Another apposite summary recalls a country that had a relatively small foreign debt and excellent credit rating and suffered no serious civil disorders until it began to reform. The Soviet Union, indeed, was "falling behind" but could have attempted "a retrenchment" without the "upheaval" of perestroika; Stephen Kotkin, *Armageddon Averted,* New York: Cambridge University Press, 2001: 173. Cf. Vladimir Kontorovich: "There were no political challenges to the 'business as usual' strategy pursued by Chernenko in 1984–85. The country was at the height of its military power, enjoying newly acquired 'strategic parity.' Dissidents were suppressed and the population subdued." ("The Economic Fallacy," in Harries, ed., op. cit., 9.)

28. Karl Marx, Preface to "A Contribution to the Critique of Political Economy" and "Manifesto of the Communist Party" in Robert C. Tucker, ed., *The Marx-Engels Reader,* New York: W. W. Norton, 1978: 4–5, 474–77.

29. See, for example, H. H. Gerth and C. Wright Mills, *From Max Weber: Essays in Sociology,* New York: Oxford University Press, 1978: 47.

30. The term "structuralist," rather than "structural," is used here deliberately to underscore the reductionism of the former. The structural approach, of course, is an indispensable analytical method that seeks explanations for social phenomena in the relatively stable, recurring patterns of interaction that are generally unaffected by variations among individual components. Thus, for instance, an economic system remains the same regardless of whether Worker A retires and is replaced by Worker B, just as the Catholic Church remains unaffected by the comings and goings of individual priests or even by most popes. Similarly, cultural structures of a particular society include status, roles, norms, and expectations, as well as goals, purposes, and interests and the acceptable modes of reaching such goals. (See, for instance, Lewis A. Coser, ed., *Masters of Sociological Thought,* New York: Harcourt Brace Jovanovich, 1971: 181, and Robert Merton, *Social Theory and Social Structure,* New York: Free Press, 1968: 186–87.) As we shall see shortly, structural analysis may very profitably include ideas and other "metaphysical" factors. (William H. Sewell, Jr., "Ideologies and Social Revolutions: Reflections on the French Case," in Theda Skocpol, ed., *Social Revolutions in the Modern World,* Cambridge: Cambridge University Press, 1994: 169–98.)

31. As quoted in Eric Selbin, "Agency and Culture in Revolutions," in Jack A. Goldstone, *Revolutions,* Belmont, CA: Thomson, 2003: 77.

32. Among these elements are the urgent necessity of raising taxes and the resistance to increased taxation; high expectations caused by pre-revolutionary

economic growth and thus "hopes" that are frustrated; the economic imperatives of transition to capitalist agriculture; population growth that impedes
upward mobility, causes prices to rise, and produces a "sharp increase" in
the "competitiveness and insecurity" of the lower classes and elites alike and
declining living standards; or military defeats and "geopolitical pressure"
from "competitor states" that exacerbate disparate domestic economic, social,
and political discontents. (Charles Tilly, *European Revolutions:* 163–67, and
Charles Tilly, "Does Modernization Breed Revolution?" in Jack Goldstone,
Revolutions: Theoretical, Comparative and Historical Studies. Belmont, CA:
Wadsworth/Thomson, 2003: 45–54; Crane Brinton, *The Anatomy of Revolution,* New York: Vintage Books, 1965: 250–52; Barrington Moore, *Social Origins of Dictatorship and Democracy,* Boston: Beacon Press, 1966; Jack A.
Goldstone, "The English Revolution: A Structural-Demographic Approach,"
in Jack A. Goldstone, ed., op. cit., 159, 168, 169–70, and, by the same author in
the same collection, "Revolution in the U.S.S.R., 1989–1991": 262; and Theda
Skocpol, *Social Revolutions in the Modern World,* New York: Cambridge University Press, 1997: 7.)

33. Charles Tilly, *European Revolutions, 1492–1992,* Cambridge, MA: Blackwell,
    1995: 14, 17, 49, 184, 234–35, 239–41.

34. As usual in social science, where so much is adumbrated, Charles A. Ellwood
    and Chalmers Johnson have anticipated me by more than thirty years in
    pointing out that "the objective explanations of revolutions . . . have failed to
    reveal the universal mechanism through which all revolutions must take
    place." Even with the "sufficient background disfunctions," they continued,
    what actually "triggers" revolution? (Charles A. Ellwood, "A Psychological
    Theory of Revolutions," in Clifford T. Payton and Robert Blackey, eds., *Why
    Revolution? Theories and Analyses.* Cambridge, MA: Schenkman, 1971: 151–52,
    and Chalmers Johnson, "Revolution and the Social System," in Payton and
    Blackey, op. cit., 205–6.)

35. A creative and potentially fruitful attempt to enable structuralism at least to
    begin to address these questions is made by Michael McFaul in a "contin-
    gent structural theory" of revolution. While accepting structural contradic-
    tions and the state's inability to resolve them as necessary conditions of a
    revolution, McFaul does not consider them sufficient because structural vari-
    ables only "define the menu of options." For a revolutionary situation to
    evolve into a revolution, McFaul continues, "voluntaristic choices" must be
    made by individuals. (Michael McFaul, "Revolutionary Transformation in
    Comparative Perspective: Defining a Post-Communist Research Agenda," in
    David Holloway and Norman Naimark, eds., *Reexamining the Soviet Experi-
    ence: Essays in Honor of Alexander Dallin,* Boulder, CO: Westview Press, 1996:
    173–75.)

    Apart from McFaul's theoretical venture, structuralist explanations con-
    tinue to dominate accounts of the latest Russian revolution. The literature is
    too large to describe in any detail, so several books and articles will have to

suffice by way of example. Gordon Hahn traces what he considers to be a "revolution from above" to the "macrostructural" crisis engendered by "fundamental contradictions between the global scientific-technological revolution that emerged in the 1970s led by . . . the United States, and increasingly stagnant and obsolete Soviet regime-type." He goes on to provide an exhaustive (and often exhausting) record of the "institutional constraints" that led to the failure of the reforms and collapse of the Soviet political and economic system—an analysis which, because of its preoccupation solely with the pinnacle of the Soviet political hierarchy, at times reads like a Kremlinological exegesis par excellence. (Gordon M. Hahn, *Russia's Revolution from Above,* New Brunswick, NJ: Transaction Publishers, 2002: 16–17.)

By contrast, Jack Goldstone is convinced that what happened in the Soviet republics *was* "major revolutions and that behind them lay a causal pattern similar to that of great revolutions in history," including the collapse of the political regime, and the disintegration of all major institutions, and the ideology that supported them. He points to the demonstrations in Moscow in February 1990, January 1991, and August 1991 as undeniable instances of mass participation "from below." Still, he, too, feels that the causes of the revolution can be best addressed within the demographic version of a structuralist paradigm: the "clogged arteries" of social mobility ("occupational stagnation" and the surplus of increasingly "frustrated" young, college-educated urban dwellers"); the "heightened competition and frustration" among the aspirants for elite positions; and the declining living standards, including worsening medical care, increased mortality, and urbanization. (Jack A. Goldstone, "Revolution in the U.S.S.R., 1989–1991," in Jack A. Goldstone, ed., *Revolutions. Theoretical, Comparative and Historical Studies,* Belmont, CA: Wadsworth/ Thomson, 2003: 261–71.)

Similarly, despite providing an excellent record of the mass political mobilization in the "popular democratic revolution" in the Soviet Union, Steven Fish chooses to "deemphasize" the role of ideology and "belief systems." Instead, he opts for a "statist, institutional" approach, in which state power ("rather than beliefs, ideals and policy orientations") determines both the scope of popular mobilization and the content of popular movements by shaping "political opportunity structures" available to the opposition. (M. Steven Fish, *Democracy from Scratch,* Princeton: Princeton University Press, 1995: 27, 189, 200.)

Vladimir Mau and Irina Starodubrovskaya make an intriguing and sophisticated case for a pre-revolutionary crisis triggered by the sharp diminution in oil revenues in the mid-1980s. In their explanation, the impact went far beyond the economic loss, however, since the oil profits had allowed the Soviet Union to spend at least a quarter of the GDP on defense, to subsidize the Soviet bloc nations, and to support "anti-imperialist" regimes and movements throughout the world, on the one hand, and to fund the massive imports of grain, food, and consumer goods to ensure a minimally acceptable, or even growing, standard of living, on the other. After over a decade of oil wealth, the many institutions that shared in the oil-revenue pie expected the oil subsidy to continue indefinitely. The dashing of such expectations became a "catalyst" for the social and political destabilization that precipitated the revolution. (Irina Starodubrovskaya and Vladimir Mau, *Velikie revolutsii ot Kromvelya do Putina* [Great revolutions from Cromwell to Putin], Moscow: Vagrius, 2004: 429. The reference to the share of Soviet GDP devoted to defense is from Åslund, op. cit., 1995, 43. Similarly, Egor Gaidar has singled out the collapse of world oil prices in the mid-1980s as the key cause of the Soviet Union's collapse. (Egor Gaidar, *Gibel' imperi, The Death of an Empire*, Moscow: Rosspen, 2006.)

36. William H. Sewell, Jr., "Ideologies and Social Revolutions: Reflections on the French Case," in Skocpol, ed., 1994: 181–82, 191, and 171. That the structuralists miss this "variable" is hardly surprising since they virtually define their method (which they label "impersonal and non-subjective," "nonintentionalist and nonvoluntarist") by its contrast with what they call "voluntarist," "purposive," "intentionalist," or even "moralistic" ways of explaining revolutions. (Skocpol, op. cit., 1994: 9, 112, 199, 106, 100, 9, 104–5.) "Are revolutions really made by ideological movements, consisting of elites and masses committed to alternative societal values?" Skocpol asks. And she answers: "In no sense did . . . vanguards with large, ideologically imbued mass followings, ever create the essentially politico-military revolutionary crisis they exploited" (ibid., 107).

37. Isaiah Berlin, *The Crooked Timber of Humanity*, New York: Knopf, 1991: 1–2.

38. David C. Schwartz, "Political Alienation: The Psychology of Revolution's First Stage," in Ivo K. Feierabend, Rosalind L. Feierabend, and Ted Robert Gurr, eds., *Anger, Violence, and Politics*, Englewood Cliffs, NJ: Prentice-Hall, 1972: 58.

39. Selbin, op. cit., 77.

40. Alexis de Tocqueville, *The Old Regime and the French Revolution*, trans. Stuart Gilbert, New York: Anchor Books, 1983: 176–77.

41. Tocqueville's insight about the central role of ruling elites in initiating liberalization has since been confirmed by leading "transitologists" who studied the change from authoritarian regimes to democracies in the twentieth century. See, for example, Samuel Huntington, "Will More Countries Become Democratic?" *Political Science Quarterly* 99 (1984): 193–218; Guillermo O'Donnel and Phillipe C. Schmitter, "Tentative Conclusions about Uncertain Democracies," in O'Donnel, Schmitter, and Whitehead, eds., *Transitions from Authoritarian Rule: Prospects for Democracy*, Part 4, Baltimore: Johns Hopkins University Press, 1986: 1–72; and Dankwart A. Rostow, "Transitions to Democracy: Toward a Dynamic Model," *Comparative Politics* 2, no. 3, April 1970: 337–63.

42. Ibid., 174.

43. Ibid., 174–76. The "Tocquevillian paradox" has been echoed, for instance, in Crane Brinton's classic comparison of English, American, French, and Russian

(1917) revolutions. It would not be "easy to argue," Brinton wrote, "that early Stuart England was less prosperous than [pre-revolutionary] Tudor England had been" and, just as in France almost a century and a half later, it was precisely the more prosperous who were "the loudest against the government." Thus, Brinton concluded, the [English] revolution was "certainly not due to economic distress." Even in the 1917 Russia, wracked by three years of war, "the productive capacity of society as a whole was certainly greater than in any other time in Russian history . . . and the progress in trade in production since the abortive revolution of 1905 had been notable." (Crane Brinton, *The Anatomy of Revolution*, New York: Vintage Books, 1965: 30–31.)

44. Tocqueville, op. cit., 177.
45. George Pettee, "Revolution—Typology and Process," in Carl J. Friedrich, ed., *Revolution*, New York: Atherton Press, 1966: 20; Sewell, op. cit., 179.
46. Brinton, op. cit., 49.
47. Ibid., 99.
48. Charles Tilly, "Revolutions and Collective Violence," in Fred. I. Greenstein and Nelson W. Polsby, eds., *Handbook of Political Science*, vol. 3, Reading, MA: Addison-Wesley, 1975; Richter, op. cit., 91, 93. Perhaps the most celebrated hypothesis, to which this role of ideas was central, was Weber's standing Marx on his head by tracing the origins of the world's greatest economic revolution, the birth of capitalism, to "the Protestant ethic," which supplied a powerful "positive ethical sanction" to the pursuit of riches through hard labor, investment, and postponed gratification. (Max Weber, *The Protestant Ethic and the Spirit of Capitalism*, New York: Scribner, 1958.) See also Lewis Coser, *Masters of Sociological Thought: Ideas in Historical and Social Context*, New York: Harcourt Brace Jovanovich, 1971: 227.
49. Selbin, op. cit., 81, 77.
50. Furet, op. cit., 22, 25.
51. Harry Eckstein, "On the Etiology of Internal Wars," in Clifford T. Payton and Robert Blackey, eds., *Why Revolution? Theories and Analyses*, Cambridge, MA: Schenkman, 1976: 136; Sewell, op. cit., 181.
52. H. H. Gerth and C. Wright Mills, eds., *From Max Weber: Essays in Sociology*, New York: Oxford University Press, 1978: 62–63.
53. Tocqueville ascribed much of the dynamic of the French Revolution (as well as the instability of post-revolutionary regimes) to a decidedly "metaphysical" cause: the contradiction between the ideals of equality and centralization, on the one hand, and liberty, on the other. (Richter, op. cit., 99–100.)

Sewell, too, argued that the abolition of privileges by the National Assembly on the night of August 4, 1789, was an example of the autonomous, self-perpetuating "ideological component" of the revolution, which resulted in the "ideological process of conceptual transformation," and "ideological redefinitions" of the revolution's agenda. It was this "redefined" agenda that, together with international war and peasant revolts (the two key factors of the structuralist causal scheme), shaped the revolution's course. Although the impending bankruptcy of the ancien régime was the precursor to the revolutionary crisis, once the crisis began to unfold, it was propelled by the "development of a radical Enlightment program," which culminated in the August 4, 1798, denunciation of the privileges of the nobility and the clergy and, shortly thereafter, by the Declaration of the Rights of Man and Citizen, which set forth the "metaphysical principles" of the new order.

Indeed, the very revival of the Estates General after over a century and a half was an ideological necessity, Sewell contends. The arguments about the privileges were an "immense and unprecedented ideological debate," which cut the French state loose from its "decaying moral and metaphysical moorings." (Sewell, op. cit., 178–82, 191.) In the same vein, both Furet and Sewell see the Terror as a product of "internal ideological dynamic," rooted in Rousseau's notion of the unity of the general will and thus implicit in the revolutionary ideology from the beginning, far more than of any "objective" factor of "class interests," aristocratic plots, or foreign intervention. The revolution was "an ideological event of the first magnitude" shaped by "unanticipated ideological outcomes." (François Furet, *Interpreting the French Revolution*, New York: Cambridge University Press, 1981: 61–62; and Sewell, op. cit., 183–84, 194.)

In a classic study of the revolutionizing power of ideas, which was an inspiration for this book, Bernard Bailyn shows how attitudes, which imparted "meaning" to the American colonists' perception of post-1763 events, had coalesced decades before "any of the famous political events of the struggle with Britain" took place. In the pamphlets circulated in the Colonies he found "not merely positions taken but the reasons why positions were taken; . . . the assumptions, beliefs, and ideas—the articulated world view—that lay behind the manifest events of the time." Bailyn concludes that "the American Revolution was above all else an ideological, constitutional, political struggle and not primarily a controversy between social groups undertaken to force changes in the organization of the society or the economy." (Bernard Bailyn, *The Ideological Origins of the American Revolution*, Cambridge: Harvard University Press/Belknap, 1992: 94, 95, x.)

54. Theda Skocpol, *Social Revolutions in the Modern World*, New York: Cambridge University Press, 1997: 106.
55. Brinton, op. cit., 42; Pettee (1966), op. cit., 47; Eckstein, op. cit., 136–37.
56. Richter, op. cit., 93.
57. Tocqueville, op. cit., 145, 146–47. In a characteristically fine piece of cultural archeology, Robert Darnton dwells on two aspects of the crucial contribution made by underground publishing in the French ancien régime. First, the works of the *philosophes* "articulated and propagated a value system, or an ideology, that undermined the traditional values Frenchmen inherited from their Catholic and royalist past." Despite its having "no coherent political program or even any distinctive ideas of its own," the often scandalously salacious anti-aristocratic Grub Street literature (especially the *libelles*, or

pamphlets) portrayed the "social rot . . . consuming French society." The decades of Enlightenment had undercut the "elite's faith" in the legitimacy of
the social order, and the libelles spread dissatisfaction "deeper and more
widely" among the general reading public. The result, according to Darnton,
was "ideological discontent" that, welling up with other currents, produced
the first great revolution of modern times." (Robert Darnton, *The Literary
Underground of the Old Regime,* Cambridge: Harvard University Press, 1982:
ix, 35, 37.)

58. Brinton, op. cit., 251; Pettee (1966), op. cit., 19.
59. Brinton, op. cit., 251.
60. Brinton, op. cit., 68, 45.
61. David C. Schwartz, "Political Alienation: The Psychology of Revolution's
    First Stage," in Ivo K Feierabend, Rosalind L. Feierabend, and Ted Robert
    Gurr, eds., *Anger, Violence and Politics,* Englewood Cliffs, NJ: Prentice-Hall,
    1972: 64.
62. Furet, op. cit., 48.
63. As quoted in Richter, op. cit., 89, 117.
64. Alexis de Tocqueville, *Souvenirs* (Paris: 1942), as quoted in Richter, op. cit., 117.
65. Brinton, op. cit., 54.
66. Ibid., 251.
67. If only the "objective" threats to the regime were to be taken into consideration,
    Myron Rush contended, "there was no compelling reason for the Soviet Union
    to enter on the dangerous path of systemic reform." (Myron Rush, "Fortune
    and Fate," *National Interest,* Spring 1993: 21.) The leading economic historian
    of the latest Russian revolution, Vladimir Mau, concurs, concluding that Gor-
    bachev's attempts at reforming the Soviet system were "not rooted in the real-
    ization that an economic or a systemic crisis had begun. . . . The crisis did not
    influence everyday life; it did not impinge on the mood of the elite or the pub-
    lic and it was not a decisive factor in economic decision-making." (Vladimir
    Mau, "Economic Reforms and Revolution," in Egor Gaidar, ed., *The Economics
    of Transition,* Cambridge: MIT Press, 2003: 36.)

    The sociologist Tatiana Zaslavskaya, who became famous for her unusu-
    ally frank description of the enormous structural problems of Soviet agricul-
    ture (the so-called Novosibirsk Report of 1983) told an interviewer in 2005
    that "if Gorbachev had not come to head the Politburo in 1985, that half-
    existence, half-life we had in Russia would continue still for several decades."
    (Tatiana I. Zaslavskaya, "The Correlation between Healthy and Ill Forces Is
    Not in Our Favor," interview with Fredo Ariesking, *Demokratizatsiya,* Spring
    2005: 297.)

    The centrality of Gorbachev "would hardly need restating," wrote Walter
    Connor, "were it not for a tendency of retrospective commentary to slight the
    'human factor' and assert that, had Gorbachev not pushed radical change,
    another general secretary would have been compelled to do so by internal
    factors and, perhaps, pressures imposed by the United States." By all

evidence, Connor continued, no one else on the 1985 Politburo would have behaved in the office of the General Secretary in the way Gorbachev did. "They would not have started out that way. Nor would they have been convinced, had they been engaged in moderate adjustment that fell short of the desired results, that the problems and solutions ran deeper than initially understood." (Walter D. Connor, "Builder and Destroyer: Thoughts on Gorbachev's Soviet Revolutions, 1985–1991," *Demokratizatsiya* 13 [2], Spring 2005: 177.) Analyzing a key facet of Gorbachev's revolution-from-above, the Soviet Union's new foreign policy, George Breslauer hypothesized that the profound transformation was rooted less in "objective necessity"—Would Chernenko have effected a similar change? Would Andropov?—than "in the evolution in the values of the Soviet leadership, followed by the loss of self-confidence." (George W. Breslauer, "How Gorbachev Sold His Concessionary Foreign Policy," in David Holloway and Norman Naimark, eds., *Reexamining the Soviet Experience: Essays in Honor of Alexander Dallin,* Boulder, CO: Westview Press, 1996: 122, 124.)

Paul Hollander, the author of the only book-length inquiry into the elite "intentionalism" in the 1987–91 revolutions in the Soviet Union and Eastern Europe and the ideological change among the Soviet and Eastern European Communist elites, advances the proposition that it was "not only the political and economic forces [that] undermined [the communist states in Eastern and Central Europe] but also the part played by particular human beings and their beliefs in [the states'] decline and fall." Hollander concludes that the "changed attitude of those who presided" over Soviet communism was central to its "unraveling." (Hollander, op. cit., 1, 278.)

68. Walter Connor pointed to the same feature in perestroika's public articulation, noting, "There is the continuing thread of discrepancy between the language Gorbachev used, including its ideological tint, and the content and tendency of his actions. To a degree, this was tactical—he could not show his hand to the Party. But it also highlights the deficiency of the political vocabulary available to him in the mid-1980s, which made it difficult for him to express how far he was willing to go, or perhaps even to understand it, before the fact, himself." (Connor, op. cit., 174.)

69. Mikhail Gorbachev, *Perestroika and the Party's Personnel Policy,* Moscow: 1987: 19.

70. Mikhail Gorbachev, interview with ITAR-TASS, October 13, 1992.

71. Nikolai Ryzhkov, *Perestroika: Istoriya predatel'stv* (Perestroika: The History of Betrayals), Moscow: Novosti, 1992: 33.

72. Eduard Shevardnadze, *The Future Belongs to Freedom,* London: Sinclair and Stevenson, 1991: 27–28.

73. Ibid.

74. Ibid., 37. Gorbachev also recalled Shevardnadze telling him: "It's all gone rotten." (*Pravda,* December 1, 1990, as quoted in Gooding [1992], 47, n33.)

75. Gooding (1990), op. cit., 207.

76. Starodubrovskaya and Mau, op. cit., 238, 245.

77. Vladmir Treml, "Gorbachev's Anti-Drinking Campaign: A Noble Experiment or a Costly Exercise in Futility," *RL Supplement* (RL 2/87), March 18, 1987: 6.

78. Mikhail Gorbachev, "Krepit' klyuchevoe zveno ekonomiki" (To strengthen the key link of the economy), *Pravda*, December 10, 1990.

79. Ryzhkov, op. cit., 94.

80. Ibid., 243.

81. The GNP figure is from Anders Åslund, "How Small Is Soviet National Income?" in Henry S. Rowen and Charles Wolf, Jr., *The Impoverished Superpower*, San Francisco: Institute for Contemporary Studies, 1990: 37. The size of the Soviet budget is from Judy Shelton, *The Coming Soviet Crash*, New York: Free Press, 1989: 9, and of the healthcare expenditures, from Treml, op. cit., 12.

82. Ryzhkov, op. cit., 95.

83. According to the sociologist Tatiana Zaslavskaya, who also served as Gorbachev's advisor, Gorbachev's "dream" was "to build socialism with a human face" (Zaslavskaya, "The Correlation," 298).

   For a good description of the concept of "socialism with a human face" as articulated by Gorbachev, see Dmitry Mikheyev, *The Rise and Fall of Gorbachev*, Indianapolis: Hudson Institute, 1992: 48–49. For an analysis of the official version of the doctrine, see also Leon Aron, "The Search for Socialist Pluralism," *Global Affairs*, Winter 1989: 104–17.

84. Kotkin, op. cit., 9.

85. Marietta Chudakova, "Itogi and perspektivy sovremennoy rossiyskoy revolutsii" (krugliy stol uchyonykh) (Results and prospects of the modern Russian revolution. A roundtable discussion by scholars), *Obshestvennye nauki i sovremennost'*, no. 2, 2002: 24. Later Gorbachev wrote: "Human lives are the main value. Someone may say that it is the fate of a Russian ruler to be ready to put people under the knife. I don't agree. I have a different credo. To the extent possible one must rule without blood. . . . I personally have given up the chair of the leader of a state in order to live up to the moral principles I declared." (*Nezavisimaya gazeta*, January 16, 1997, as quoted in Roy Medvedev, "Pochemu raspal'sya Sovetskiy Soyuz?" [Why did the Soviet Union fall apart?], *Otechestennaya istoriya*, October 31, 2003: 122.)

86. Alexander Yakovlev, *Muki prochteniya bytiya* (The torments of reading life), Moscow: Novosti, 1991: 31, 7–8.

87. Alexander Yakovlev, "Reformatsiya v Rossii," *Obshshestvennye nauki i sovremennost'*, no. 2, April 2005: 5. In April 1987, in a speech titled "Perestroika and social conscience," Yakovlev told the party and cultural elite of the Tajik Soviet Socialist Republic that the purpose of the reforms was not "only and not so much" economic development as a "search for ways" to make the Soviet Union "an embodiment of all that is . . . humane in the world" and a "paragon of . . . spiritual abundance." He called on the creative intelligentsia to undertake the "work of . . . moral progress and spiritual cleansing." (Alexander

Yakovlev, "Perestroika i obshchestvennoe soznanie" [Perestroika and social conscience], *Pravda,* April 10, 1987: 3.)

88. Alexander Yakovlev, *Sumerki* (Twilight), Moscow: Materik, 2003: 380.

89. Ibid., 382.

90. "Dossier," *Moskovskie Novosti,* October 21–27, 2005: 6.

91. Yakovlev, *Muki* . . . : 7–8.

92. Robert Darnton, *The Literary Underground of the Old Regime,* Cambridge: Harvard University Press, 1982: viii.

93. Tatiana Koryagina, "Ya i my" (I and we), *Literaturnaya gazeta,* May 24, 1989: 12.

94. Alexander Bovin, "Perestroika: pravda o sotsializme i sud'ba sotsializma" (The truth about socialism and the fate of socialism), in Yuri Afanasiev, ed., *Inogo ne dano* (There is no other way), Moscow: Progress, 1988: 539. See also, Vladimir Shlapentokh, chap. 3 ("Soviet Society in the Early 1980s"), pp. 61–74, in his *Soviet Ideologies in the Period of Glasnost. Responses to Brezhnev's Stagnation,* New York: Praeger, 1988; and Ellen Carnaghan, "A Revolution in Mind: Russian Political Attitudes and the Origins of Democratization under Gorbachev," Ph.D. diss., New York University, 1992. Cf. John Bushnell, "The 'New Soviet Man' Turns Pessimist," *Survey* 24, no. 2, 1980: 1–18, and Gail W. Lapidus, "Society under Strain," *Washington Quarterly* 6, Spring 1983: 29–47.

95. Mikhail Krasnov, "My prosnulis' v drugoy strane" (We woke up in a different country), *Rossiyskaya gazeta,* August 18, 2001: 4. See also John Bushnell, "The 'New Soviet Man' Turns Pessimist," *Survey* 24, no. 2 (1980): 1–18, and Gail W. Lapidus, "Society under Strain," *Washington Quarterly* 6 (Spring 1983): 29–46.

96. Mikhail Krasnov, op. cit., 4, and Donna Bahry, "Society Transformed? Rethinking the Social Roots of Perestroika," *Slavic Review,* no. 3, Fall 1993: 512; and John Gooding, "Gorbachev and Democracy," *Soviet Studies* 42, No. 2, April 1990: 218.

In a widely accepted theory of social and political change, growing urbanization and higher levels of education contribute to the dissemination of new values and expectations, which are increasingly in conflict with the archaic political institutions that stifled political participation. The result is frustration and then anger. (Samuel P. Huntington, *Political Order in Changing Societies,* New Haven: Yale University Press, 1968.)

Building on Emil Durkheim's insight about the changing nature of social "integration" ("solidarity") as a result of the growing complexity in the division of labor in modern societies, scholars have suggested that the "critical" expectations engendered by "modernization" in the Soviet urban middle class had "outpaced" the regime's performance. (I draw here on Steven Fish's very useful summary of the "socioeconomic" approach to democratic transition in "Russia's Crisis and the Crisis of Russology" in David Holloway and Norman Naimark, eds., *Reexamining the Soviet Experience. Essays in Honor of Alexander Dallin,* Boulder, CO: Westview Press, 1996: 142–44.) From this perspective, the emergence of an industrial economy in the Soviet Union and the resulting

doubling in size of the Soviet professional class between 1960 and 1980 created "social differentiation" and "recast" a multitude of "social, political, military, and economic" relationships, precipitating a greater independence from
paternalistic institutional ties and undercutting the legitimacy of institutional
structures—a "quiet revolution of the mind." (Blair A. Ruble, "The Soviet
Union's Quiet Revolution," in George W. Breslauer, ed., *Can Gorbachev's Reforms Succeed?* Berkeley: University of California Press, 1990: 83, 84, 86.) Urbanization, progress in education, wider availability of information about the
outside world and the expansion of middle class patterns of consumption were
seen as causes of the regime's erosion. After the first "timid liberalization"
steps taken by Gorbachev in the early period of perestroika, 1985–87, these factors accounted for a powerful democratic "wave," which quickly outpaced the
reforms from above and broke out of the government's control. The coinciden-
tal economic crisis, brought by a fall in oil revenues and the failure of the economic strategy of the past two decades, imparted "an added impetus to this
wave." (Egor Gaidar, "The Inevitability of Collapse of the Socialist Economy," in
Egor Gaidar, ed., *The Economics of Transition,* Cambridge: MIT Press, 2003: 30.)

By the early 1980s, the new urban middle class is said to be grappling with
"growing pessimism," "disillusionment," alienation from "official norms,"
and the "erosion of faith." (S. Frederick Starr, "Soviet Union: A Civil Society,"
Foreign Policy, no. 70, Spring 1988: 26–41; Donna Bahry, "Politics, Generations, and Change in the USSR," in James R. Millar, ed., *Politics, Work and
Daily Life in the USSR,* Cambridge: Cambridge University Press, 1987: 95;
Gail Warshofsky Lapidus, "Social Trends," in Robert F. Byrnes, ed., *After
Brezhnev: Sources of Soviet Conduct in the 1980s,* Bloomington: Indiana University Press, 1983: 233, and, also by Lapidus, "State and Society: Toward the
Emergence of Civil Society in the Soviet Union," in Seweryn Bialer, ed., *Politics, Soviety, and Nationality Inside Gorbachev's Russia,* Boulder, CO: Westview
Press, 1989: 127–28.) The "long-held dreams for a better, more just world" became the "main chemical agent" in the system's unexpected dissolution (Stephen Kotkin, *Armageddon Averted,* New York: Cambridge University Press,
2001: 174, 180) as the people began to "see linkages" between disparate areas of
dissatisfaction (Donna Bahry, "Society Transformed? Rethinking the Social
Roots of Perestroika," *Slavic Review* 52, no. 3, Fall 1993: 549). Cf. Lucian Pye's
argument that the emergence of a middle class and the growth of an educated
population lead to "drastically altered" attitudes toward authority in authoritarian regimes in general. He saw the urbanized and educated Soviet middle
class in particular as "demanding greater intellectual and cultural freedoms"
and contemptuous of the poorly educated party apparatchiks. (Lucian Pye, "Political Science and the Crisis of Authoritarianism," *American Political Science
Review* 84 [1990]: 3–19.) For good summaries of the pre-1992 theorizing, which
focused on modernization-induced value changes, their impact on the structure of expectations, and the formation of the new intelligentsia as an equiva-

lent of an urban middle class beholden to the newly crystallized "values, priorities and aspirations," see Thomas F. Remington, "Sovietology and System Stability," *Post-Soviet Affairs* 8, no. 3 (1992): 250–53; and Alexander Dallin, "Causes of the Collapse of the USSR," *Post-Soviet Affairs* 8, no. 4: 290–91.

In keeping with her earlier insights into the impact of generational changes on the Soviet collapse, Bahry compared the results of the surveys of Soviet refugees in the 1940s and 1970s with those of Soviet citizens in the early 1990s to conclude, as did Fukuyama, that the attitudes of the Soviet people had shifted significantly in the previous forty years to produce, by 1985, a new set of values and expectations and "generational and educational cleavages [that] . . . widened into major fault lines." (Donna Bahry, "Society Transformed? Rethinking the Social Roots of Perestroika," *Slavic Review*, no. 3 (Fall 1993): 527, 549.) Similarly, Gooding found perestroika distinguished by "middle-class values and emphases" and "predicated" on the support of intelligentsia, whereas Hough saw the revolution stemming from a systemic disequilibrium brought about by the emergence of a middle class as a product of Soviet modernization. Embodying competing values, the modernization is said to have supplied both the foot soldiers and the leaders of the revolution, whose goals corresponded to their aspirations. (Gooding, op. cit., 1992: 56; Jerry Hough, *Democratization and Revolution in the USSR, 1985–1991*, Washington, DC: Brookings Institution Press, 1997: 4, 63–64, 92.)

97. Starodubrovskaya and Mau, op. cit., 181–82.
98. Yakovlev, *Sumerki*, 503. The primacy of ideas and ideology in the emergence and maintenance of the Soviet regime was extraordinary—thus making it especially vulnerable to any weakening in the resolve to defend the official mythology. Even among the great revolutions of modernity, the Russian transformation that began in 1917 stands out as an instance in which ideas and the relentless will of relatively few men convinced of these ideas' final and eternal correctness shaped a nation's destiny so decisively and for so long, molding the economic and social structures to fit the founding credo. As Martin Malia put it, without "the millenarian intoxication" and the "utopian ambition" of the ideologues who seized power in October 1917, the Soviet regime could hardly have achieved "the prodigies of social transformation and mass violence to which it immediately proceeded." (Martin Malia, "The Archives of Evil," *New Republic*, November 29 and December 6, 2004: 36, 41.) One need only recall Stalin's 1929–34 "revolution from above" (collectivization and industrialization), which was nothing if not the implementation of an ideological agenda. Although couched in economic terms, its costs would have been found prohibitive by any rational economic analysis. Thus both the belief in the Soviet system and its ideology were "quasi-religious" and both collapsed, concluded a witness, because the Soviet power no longer looked "as something sacred."(Marietta Chudakova, "Itogi and perspektivy . . . :25.)

"Bolshevism was compatible with nationalism, as Stalin had shown all along, even with some autonomy restored to the market—as a temporary expedient, of course—as Lenin had thought to do with the NEP," wrote François Furet. "But Bolshevism had no flexibility whatsoever in matters of ideology. . . . Even Khrushchev had to kill Nagy. Brezhnev put up with Ceauşescu and Kádár, but not with Dubcek. . . . [Once] the Communist regimes were forced to make way for ideas that the October Revolution had believed it was destroying and replacing— private property, the market, individual rights, 'formal' constitutionalism, the separation of powers— . . . the failure was total, for it wiped out the original aspiration." (François Furet, op. cit., 1999: 500–501.)

99. Gooding, op. cit., 1992: 56.

100. Lapidus, "State and Society," 125, 127. Searching for causes of "the decline and loss of the sense of legitimacy" of the Soviet regime, Hollander hypothesizes that although economic problems may have fatally undermined it, the regime's actual end "had more to do with the ways economic weakness was perceived and registered by the political elite and, less importantly, by the population at large." (Hollander, op. cit., 276.)

101. Robert K. Merton, *Social Theory and Social Structure*, New York: Free Press, 1968: 475.

102. Vadim Bakatin in *Nedelya*, no. 12, 1989, as quoted in Dmitry Mikheyev, *The Rise and Fall of Gorbachev*, Indianapolis: Hudson Institute, 1992: 136.

103. Tatiana Zaslavskaya in Andrew Rosenthal, "A Soviet Voice of Innovation Comes to Force," interview with the *New York Times*, August 28, 1987: A6.

104. Already in the first semi-free national election (to the Congress of People's Deputies in March 1989), thirty-eight regional party bosses (obkom first secretaries) were defeated. A year later, in the spring 1990 elections to Moscow City Council, the radical Democratic Russia took fifty-seven of sixty-five seats. Forty-five million people voted for Boris Yeltsin in the Russian presidential election in June 1991, giving him 57 percent of the vote in a field of six candidates.

105. Vladmir Sorgin, "Tri prevrashcheniya sovremennoy Rossii" (The three metamorphoses of the contemporary Russia), *Otechestvennaya Istoriya*, no. 3, 2005: 7. See also Fish, op. cit., 35, 42–43, 189. Cf. Blair Ruble: "At each stage, and despite significant variations in the pace of political change across regional and ethnic boundaries, Soviet citizens pursued demonstrations, strikes, protest actions, and electoral politics to push the political system to new frontiers of liberalization and democratization." (Blair Ruble, "The Soviet Union's Quiet Revolution," in George Breslauer, ed., *Can Gorbachev's Reforms Succeed?* Berkeley: University of California, 1990: 92.)

106. Alexander Rahr, "Inside the Interregional Group," *RL/RFE Report on the USSR* 2, no. 43, October 26, 1990: 1. For details of the political mobilization and electoral revolution "from below," see Vladimir Brovkin, "Revolution

from Below: Informal Political Associations in Russia, 1988–89," *Soviet Studies* 42 (2), 1990; Brendan Kiernan and Joseph Aistrup, "The 1989 Elections to the Congress of People's Deputies in Moscow, *Soviet Studies* 43 (6), 1991; and Geoffrey A Hosking, Jonathan Aves, and Peter J. S. Duncan, *The Road to Post-Communism: Independent Political Movements in the Soviet Union, 1985–1991*, London and New York: Pinter Publishers, 1992.

107. Sorgin, op. cit., 7.
108. Ibid.
109. Ibid.
110. Ibid., 8.
111. On February 4, 1990, 250,000 people demonstrated in Moscow for the abolition of Article 6 of the constitution, which mandated the "leading" role of the Communist Party. On January 20, 1991, 200,000 protested the military intervention in the Baltic republics, which had declared their independence. In February and March of the same year, there were "vast" demonstrations in Moscow, Leningrad, Yaroslavl, and Volgograd, as well as other cities in support of Yeltsin and Russia's sovereignty. (Jack A. Goldstone "Revolution in the U.S.S.R., 1989–1991," in Jack A. Goldstone, ed., *Revolutions: Theoretical, Comparative, and Historical Studies,* Belmont, CA: Wadsworth/Thomson, 2003: 270. See also Fish, op. cit., 47–48.)
112. Harley Balzer, "Ordinary Russians? Rethinking August 1991," *Demokratizatsiya* 13 (2), Spring 2005: 200–204.
113. Ibid., 198.
114. Gavriil Popov, "Igry patriotov. Chetvyortaya revolutsiya" (Patriots' games: The fourth revolution), *Moskovskiy Komsomoletz,* May 25, 2004: 4.
115. As quoted in Len Karpinsky, "Pochemu stalinizm ne skhodit so stzeny?" (Why won't Stalinism leave the stage?), in Yuri N. Afanasiev, ed., *Inogo ne dano* (There is no other way), Moscow: Progress, 1988: 662.
116. Hedrick Smith, *The New Russians,* New York: Random House, 1990: 88.
117. G. Valyuzhenich, "Nashe sotsial'noe samochustvie" (Our social well-being), an interview with Vilen Ivanov, director, the Institute for Sociological Research, Moscow, *Argumenty i fakty,* no. 1, January 1–January 8, 1988: 2. A "center for the study of public opinion" was created within the Institute for Sociological Research in 1985 and by the end of 1987 it had conducted over fifty surveys "on very different matters." (G. Valyuzhenich, op. cit.) In 1989, the All-Union Center for the Study of Public Opinion (VTzIOM) unveiled a regional network of field offices and began national surveys. In the first year, VTzIOM conducted 24 such polls and interviewed 41,325 respondents. (Valyuzhenich, op. cit., and Vera Nikitina, "God za godom: 1989" [Year after year: 1989], *Informatsionnyi bulleten' monitoringa* [The public opinion monitoring information bulletin], no. 4 (30), July–August 1997: 38.)
118. An article published on July 29, 1990, on the front page of one of the most popular Soviet newspapers, *Izvestia,* reported the results of the May 1990

survey by VTzIOM: 66 percent of the Soviet citizens polled now supported a market economy and 19 percent opposed. ("Kto za rynok?" *Izvestia,* July 29, 1990: 1.)

119. Ada M. Finifter and Ellen Mickiewicz, "Redefining the Political System of the USSR: Mass Support for Political Change," *American Political Science Review* 86, no. 4, December 1992: table 1, p. 859. Competitive elections were supported by 95 percent of the respondents. The study included seven of the Soviet Union's fifteen republics: Estonia, Belarus, Georgia, Kazakhstan, Russia (RSFSR), Ukraine, and Uzbekistan.

In the Moscow region, surveyed in February–March 1990, 77 percent were in favor of legalizing political parties; 85 percent disagreed with the proposition that "it is necessary to ban elections and allow the CPSU to rule the country (without elections)"; and multi-candidate local elections, again, were supported by 95 percent of the sample (Gibson et al., op. cit., table 8, p. 351). Of course, one must be cautious in extrapolating to the rest of Russia the opinions of the Moscow region residents: although considerably more conservative than the Muscovites, they still were likely more liberal than most Russians outside big cities. Yet when a few months later largely analogous questions were posed to a sample in the "European portion of the USSR (Russia, Lithuania, and Ukraine)," the same authors found the results "remarkably similar" (ibid., 361).

The results of the two surveys appear side by side in James L. Gibson and Raymond M. Duch, "Emerging Democratic Values in Soviet Political Culture," in Arthur H. Miller, William M. Reisinger, and Vicki L. Hesli, *Public Opinion and Regime Change: The New Politics of Post-Soviet Societies,* Boulder, CO: Westview Press, 1993.

120. Polled after the first-ever nationally broadcast parliamentary debates at the First Congress of People's Deputies in May–June 1989, which most Russians watched live (as did between 70–90 percent of adults in the Soviet Union's largest cities), 84 percent of a sample of the citizens of the Russian Republic (RSFSR) thought that the disagreements were "natural," that they did not hinder the adoption of necessary decisions, and helped to arrive at "well thought-out" or "considered" decisions (Nikitina, op. cit.).

121. James L. Gibson, Raymond M. Duch, and Kent L. Tedin, "Democratic Values and the Transformation of the Soviet Union," *Journal of Politics* 54, no. 2, May 1992: table 3, p. 342, and table 4, p. 344.

122. Ibid. While in 1989 almost two-thirds of the citizens of the seven Soviet republics, including Russia, preferred "traditional methods of political process," over one-third thought that "strikes, protests and demonstration" were legitimate political actions—a degree of radicalism that the interpreters of the survey found "remarkable." (Ibid. See also Ada M. Finifter and Ellen Mickiewicz, "Redefining the Political System of the USSR: Mass Support for Political Change," *American Political Science Review* 86, no. 4, December 1992: 860.)

123. Gibson et al., op. cit., table 3, p. 342. The corresponding numbers were 56 percent and 28 percent. In addition, half of the sample was opposed to denying "radical and extremist" political groups' right to demonstrate, even if their demonstrations were "disorderly and disruptive."

124. Nikitina, "God za godom: 1989": 38. One-fourth of the sample thought the Russians needed a "strong hand," and 15 percent would allow personal dictatorship "under some circumstances."

125. Gregory J. Embree, "RSFSR Election Results and Roll Call Votes," *Soviet Studies* 43, no. 6, 1991: 1069–71.

126. Gibson et al., op. cit., 343.

127. Ibid., table 4, p. 344. The number was 94 percent.

128. Ibid., 345, and table 5, p. 346. Nine in ten respondents in the Moscow region thought that the press ought to be legally protected from government persecution. (Gibson et al., op. cit., table 7, p. 349.) After decades of the state's complete control over print, radio, and television (and with no private newspapers, let alone radio or television, yet existing), over half of the same sample felt that privately owned media "should exist alongside" state-owned ones (ibid.).

129. Finifter and Mickiewicz, op. cit., 857.

130. Ibid., table 1, p. 859, and pp. 860, 861, and 872. Asked in the same year what their country should rely on, less than one-fifth mentioned "the working class" (18 percent), the government (16 percent), or the still officially "ruling" Communist Party (4 percent), and 54 percent thought that the most reliable source of success was "honest daily labor by individuals." (Nikitina, "God za godom: 1989": 38.)

131. Gibson et al., op. cit., table 6, p. 348. Reinterpretation of the results of 1990–92 surveys confirmed a shift of attitudes among the Russians from the state's responsibility for jobs and standard of living to "strong preferences for individualism." Arthur H. Miller, Vicki L. Hesli, and William M. Reisinger, "Reassessing Mass Support for Political and Economic Change in the Former USSR," *American Political Science Review* 88, no. 2, June 1994: 401, 410.

132. L. A. Sedov, "Peremeny v strane i otnoshenie k peremenam" (Changes in the country and the attitude toward the changes), *Informatsionnyi byulleten' monitoringa*, January–February 1995: 24.

133. Ibid. In the USSR as a whole, by the fall of 1990, a 36 percent plurality approved of a program of rapid transition to a market economy, leading Tatiana Zaslavskaya to conclude that "in people's consciousness there could be no way back [to Soviet socialism]." (Tatiana Zaslavskaya, "Eto kakoe-to nervnoe istoshchenie" [It is something like a nervous exhaustion]," *Komsomol'skaya Pravda*, October 30, 1990: 2 [interviewed by I. Savvateeva].) Less than a year later, in July 1991, almost two-thirds of the Soviet urban population supported the transition to a market economy, with one-fourth opposed and one in ten undecided. (Nikitina, "God za godom: 1991": 49.)

(The exact breakdown was 45 percent for it and 20 percent "more for than against"; 13 percent opposed and 10 percent "more against than for." Twelve percent were undecided.)

134. Incomes that would be dependent solely on individual effort were preferred by 87 percent, while greater income equality was supported by 13 percent. Sixty-five percent of the respondents thought that enterprises are best run by private entrepreneurs, and 31 percent favored state ownership. A well-paying job and the risk of unemployment were chosen by 58 percent, as compared with 40 percent who opted for a secure job, even if it did not "pay much." The sale of state enterprises to private owners was thought by 58 percent to leave their families better off, and 23 percent expected a worsening of their situation as a result. Three-quarters welcomed "most farming done by private owners of land," and only 11 percent opposed. (At the same time, however, the respondents were almost evenly divided between the 50 percent who chose personal responsibility for oneself and the 48 percent who favored the state's duty of providing for every family. Most respondents also thought they would be worse off if prices were freed from state control: 73 percent vs. 13 percent [Boeva and Shironin, op. cit., 6–7].)

135. Finifter and Mickiewicz, table 1, p. 859. The corresponding numbers were 45 percent and 38 percent, with 17 percent undecided.

136. Gibson et al., table 6, p. 348.

137. Finifter and Mickiewicz, op. cit., 864–66, 868, and Gibson et al., 356–57, 359.

138. William Zimmerman, "Intergenerational Differences in Attitudes toward Foreign Policy," in Arthur H. Miller, William M. Reisinger, and Vicki L. Hesli, *Public Opinion and Regime Change: The New Politics of Post-Soviet Societies*, Boulder, CO: Westview Press, 1993: 259–60; and Gibson et al., 356–57.

139. Zimmerman, op. cit., 259.

140. Yuri Levada and Leonid Gudkov, "The People's Voices," *Moscow News*, April 22, 1990: 7.

141. Tatiana Zaslavskaya, "Eto kakoe-to nervnoe istoshchenie" (It is something like a nervous exhaustion), *Komsomol'skaya pravda*, October 30, 1990: 2 (interviewed by I. Savvateeva).

142. Ibid. More Russians reported leaving the Communist Party between 1985 and 1990 (26 percent of the Party members) than after the collapse of the Soviet regime in August 1991 (21 percent). (Irina Boeva and Vyacheslav Shironin, "Russians between State and Market," *Studies in Public Policy*, no. 205, 1992: 38.)

143. Vera Tolz, "Informal Groups and Soviet Politics in 1989," *Report on the USSR*, November 24, 1989: 4.

144. Lev Gudkov and Boris Dubin, "Konets kharizmaticheskoy epokhi" (The end of the charismatic era), *Svobodnaya mysl'*, no. 5, 1993: 39.

145. Krasonv, op. cit., 4.

146. Andrei Mel'vil', "Politicheskie tsennosti i orientatsii i politicheskie instituty (Political values and orientations and political institutions), in Liliya

Shevtsova, ed., *Rossiya politicheskaya* (Russian political), Moscow: Carnegie Center, 1998: 157. The survey results cited are compiled by Mel'vil' from half a dozen surveys by major Russian polling organizations (see op. cit., 185, n16).

147. Ibid., 157.

148. Ibid.

149. Nikitina, "God za godom: 1991," 50. The disappearance of the CPSU "made happy" 29 percent of the respondents; the rejection of communist ideology, 20 percent. Thirty-three percent of the respondents did not answer the question.

An elaborate analysis of attitudes of the Moscow elite in summer 1991 showed the evolution of ideological perestroika from "a radical reformulation of orthodox Marxism-Leninism" to "distinct, internally consistent and coherent worldviews" that included at least a "partial embrace of central tenets of Western liberal philosophy," human rights, and the importance of checks on state power. Moscow intellectuals, Party functionaries, leaders of new political parties, and military officers in the sample evinced "almost no support" for the "political hegemony" of the Communist Party and "very little support for the basic features of Soviet-style socialism." Correlated with almost every other preference, the support for individual rights was especially widespread and strong. It was seen by the majority of the respondents as a "very desirable" destination or even the "central" goal. The survey's designer hypothesizes that the formation of this new "dominant ideology" was "an integral part of the political and social upheaval that began in 1985" and that Boris Yeltsin's subsequent dismantling of the CPSU and his pursuit of rapid economic reform could have been "made possible by the almost total de-legitimation of the old order among elites." (Judith S. Kullberg, "The Ideological Roots of Elite Political Conflict in Post-Soviet Russia," *Europe-Asia Studies* 46 [6], 1994: 946, 947, 931, 951, and n22.)

Interpreting the results of far larger surveys in Russia, Lithuania, and Ukraine in 1990–92, Miller, Hesli, and Reisinger (op cit., 410) also concluded that to the extent that perestroika promoted political democracy and decentralization, "it reflected public preferences."

150. Zimmerman, op. cit., 260–61. The surveys are those of the residents of Moscow in May 1988, December 1988, and October 1990, and the "New Soviet Citizens" poll, in which a representative sample of 1,800 Soviet citizens in Lithuania, Ukraine, and the RSFSR was interviewed in May 1990 by the Institute of Sociology (Moscow) "in conjunction with" researchers from the University of Iowa.

151. Ibid., 265. Asked to identify what was "the most dangerous and [leading] toward destabilization in our country," 72 percent of those interviewed in May 1990 in Lithuania, Ukraine, and the RSFSR saw foreign threats to be only of "no or some danger."

152. In May 1989, the 14 percent reduction in the Soviet military budget proposed by Gorbachev seemed insufficient to between one-fourth and one-third of respondents in Russia's two largest cities (Moscow and Leningrad) and the

two cities with a very substantial ethnic Russian presence, Kiev and Alma-Ata. A year later, 72 percent of the Lithuanians, Russians, and Ukrainians surveyed thought that the military spending should be "cut back." In October 1990, almost two-thirds of the Muscovites interviewed thought that the appropriations should be reduced further, with one-third considering the defense expenditures just right, and less than 5 percent thinking them too low (ibid., 266).

153. Ibid., 264.

154. Ibid. The corresponding numbers were 71 percent, 68 percent, and 40 percent.

155. "The policy is correct but change should be faster," *Moscow News*, January 21, 1990: 9.

156. Ibid., 268. The data are from the May 1990 "New Soviet Citizen" Survey.

157. Ibid.

158. Vera Nikitina, "God za godom: 1990" (Year after year: 1990), *Informatsionnyi bulleten' monitoringa* (The public opinion monitoring information bulletin), no. 5 (31), September–October 1997: 43. Another ideological underpinning of Soviet foreign policy, the "world anti-imperialist struggle" and its corollary, "socialist internationalism" (that is, assistance to pro-Soviet regimes and movements), were succumbing to the iconoclasm as well. After watching Andrei Sakharov's speech at the First Congress of People's Deputies in June 1989, 55 percent of the national sample agreed with Sakharov that the war in Afghanistan was "criminal" (Nikitina, "God za godom: 1989," 38). In 1988, seven in ten Muscovites surveyed thought the Soviet Union should send military aid when asked; in 1990, the same proposition was endorsed by one in ten respondents. In the same year, three-fourths of those interviewed in a territorially larger sample thought that the Soviet Union should reduce its foreign aid (Zimmerman, ibid., 266).

159. Vera Nikitina, "God za godom: 1991" (Year after year: 1991), *Informatsionnyi bulleten' monitoringa* (The public opinion monitoring information bulletin), no. 6 (32), November–December 1997: 47.

160. Ibid.

161. Boeva and Shironin, op. cit., 33. Fewer than one in five Russians wished for the "USSR as it formerly was," and 22 percent wanted a reformed Soviet Union with stronger republics (ibid.).

Of course the revolution in values did not end in 1991; in many respects the forging of the post-Soviet political, social, and moral consensus began only then. Those wishing to follow the continuing transformation of Russia's goals and values can begin by consulting the following studies, listed alphabetically by the authors' names or titles of publications:

E. I. Bashkirova, "Transformatsiya tsennostei rossiyskogo obshchestva," *Polis*, no. 6, 2002: 53–62; L. N. Belyaeva, *Sotsial'naya modernizatsiya v Rossii v kontse XX veka* (Social modernization in Russia at the end of XX century), Moscow: Institute of Philosophy, Russian Academy of Sciences, 1997; Timo-

thy J. Colton and Michael McFaul, "Are Russians Undemocratic?" Working
Paper No. 20, 2001, Washington: Carnegie Endowment for International
Peace; Ludmila Khokhulina, "Sub'ektivnyi sredniiy klass: dokhody,
material'noe polozhenie, tsennostnye orientatsii" (A subjective middle class:
income, material status, value orientations), *Informatsionnyi bulleten' monitoringa*, February 1999: 24–34; L. A. Khokhulina, B. V. Golovachev, "Pyat' let
ekonomicheskikh reform: izmeneniya v otsenkakh I mneniyakh naseleniya"
(Five years of economic reforms: changes in the evaluations and opinions of
the population), *Informatsionnyi bulleten' monitoringa*, February 1995: 33–36;
T. Koval', chaps. 23 and 24 (pp. 931–1003) in E. T. Gaidar, ed., *Ekonomika perekhodnogo perioda. Ocherki ekonomicheskoy politiki post kommunisticheskoy
Rossii, 1991–1997* (Economy of the transitional period: Essays on economic
policy in post-communist Russia, 1991–1997), Moscow: IEPP, 1998; V. V.
Lapkin, "Izmenenie tsennostnykh orientatsiy rossiyan," *Polis*, no. 1, 2000:
47–50; Nikolai I. Lapin, ed., *Kak chuvstvyut sebya, k chemu stremyatsya grazhdane Rossii. Osnovnye fakty i vyvody analitcheskogo doklada po rezul'tatam
monitoringa "Nashi tsennosti i interesy segodnya: 1990–1994–1998–2002"* (How
the citizens of Russia feel and what they strive for: The main facts and conclusions of an analysis of the data collected by the longitudinal study "Our
values and interests today: 1990–1994–1998–2002"), Moscow: Center for
the Study of Social and Cultural Changes of the Institute of Philosophy of
the Russian Academy of Sciences, 2002; N. I. Lapin and L. A. Belyaeva, *Dinamika tsennostey naseleniya reformiruemoy Rossii* (The dynamics of the values
of the population of the reformed Russia), Moscow: URSS, 1996; Yuri
Levada, " 'Chelovek sovetskiy': chetvyortaya volna. Funktsii i dinamika obshchestvennykh nastroeniy" (The "soviet man": fourth wave. Functions and
dynamics of public moods), *Vestnik obshchestvennogo meninya*, July–August
2004: 8–18. See also Levada's "Vremya peremen glazami obshchestvennogo
mneniya (The time of change in the eyes of public opinion), *Vestnik*,
January–February, 2003: 8–16; and "Chelovek 'osobennyi' " (A "special"
man), *Vestnik*, March–April, 2003: 7–14; *Ot mneniy k ponimaniyu: Sotsiologicheskie ocherki, 1993–2000* (From opinions to understanding: Sociological
essays, 1993–2000), Moscow: Moscow School of Political Research, 2000;
" 'Chelovek sovetskiy' pyat' let spustya, 1989–1994: Predvaritel'nye itogi
sravnitel'nogo issledovaniya" ("The Soviet man" five years later, 1989–1994:
Preliminary results of a comparative study), *Informatsionnyi byulleten' monitoringa*, January–February 1995: 9–13; Yuri Levada, ed., *Sovetskiy prostoy chelovek: Opyt sotsial'nogo portreta na rubezhe 90-ykh* (A regular Soviet man: An
attempt at a sociological portrait at the beginning of the 1990s), Moscow:
1993; "Otsenka kursa na reformy, 1992–2004" (The evaluation of the policy
of reforms), *Vestnik obshshesvennogo mneniya*, July–August, 2004: 5; Richard Rose, William Mishler, and Neil Munro, *How Russians Have Responded
to Political Transformation*, Cambridge: Cambridge University Press, 2006;
Sotsiologicheskie nablyudeniya, 2002–2004 (Sociological observations, 2002–4),

Moscow: Public Opinion Foundation's Institute, 2005; William Zimmerman, *The Russian People and Foreign Policy: Russian Elite and Mass Perspectives, 1993–2000*, Princeton: Princeton University Press, 2002.

162. That the political and economic agendas of the "radical democrats" were guided by a radical ideology was quite obvious to the witnesses. "The political 'pedigree' of those around the Supreme Soviet chairman [Boris Yeltsin] predetermined the contents of his agenda," noted a moderately conservative, Party journal in spring 1991. "It is in the ideology of the democratic orientation that one is to find the sources of those ideas with which Yeltsin returned to national politics after the election campaigns of 1989 and 1990: the radical versions of the transition to market economy, privatization, political pluralism, the law-based state and civil society, and the sovereignty of Russia [within the Soviet Union]. The priorities [of this agenda] have the same origin." (Vladimir V'yunitskiy, "Gorbachev i El'tsin: algoritmy vlasti" [Gorbachev and Yeltsin: The algorithms of power], *Dialog,* March 1991: 48.)

CHAPTER 2. FOR TRUTH AND GOODNESS

1. Alexander Yakovlev, *Sumerki* (Twilight), Moscow: Materik, 2003: 464.
2. Boris Vasiliev, "Prozrenie," *Sovetskiy ekran* 6, March 1987: 5.
3. Yuri Chernichenko, "Zemlya, ekologiya, perestroika" (Land, ecology, perestroika), *Literaturnaya gazeta*, January 29, 1989: 3.
4. Andrei Nuykin, "Idealy ili interesy?" (Ideals or interests?), *Novy mir* 1, January 1988: 190; and Vasiliev, "Prozrenie," 5.
5. Yakovlev, *Sumerki*, 373.
6. Ibid., 471; A. Zotikov, "Vozvrashchenie s prodolzheniem" (Return with continuation), *Znamya* 5, May 1990: 220.
7. Igor Vinogradov, "Mozhet li pravda byt' poeatpnoy?" (Can the truth be doled out in stages?), in Yuri Afanasiev, ed., *Inogo ne dano* (There is no other way), Moscow: Progress, 1988: 279.
8. Leonid Batkin, "Vozobnovlenie istorii" (The resumption of history), in Afanasiev, ed., *Inogo ne dano.* 155.
9. Ibid.
10. Alexander Gel'man, "Chto snachala, chto potom . . ." (What comes first, what comes later), *Literaturnaya gazeta*, September 10, 1986: 10.
11. A. N. Yakovlev, "Perestroika i nravstevnnost'" (Perestroika and morality), *Sovetskaya Kul'tura*, July 21, 1987: 2.
12. Fyodor Burlatsky, "Sud'ba reformatorov strany" (The fate of the country's reformers), *Literaturnaya gazeta*, June 27, 1990: 1.
13. Alexander Bovin, "Perestroika: Pravda o sotsializme i sud'be sotsializma (Perestroika: The truth about socialism and the fate of socialism), in Afanasiev, ed., *Inogo ne dano*, 520.
14. Geoffrey A. Hosking, "At Last an Exorcism," *Times Literary Supplement*, October 9–15, 1987: 1111, and Philip Taubman, "Soviet Party Conference Delegates Turn Anger on Press and Economy," *New York Times*, June 30, 1988: A1.

15. Igor Klyamkin, "Pochemu tak trudno govorit' pravdu" (Why it is so difficult to speak truth), *Novy mir* 2, February 1988: 238.

16. L. Lazarev, "Dukh svobody" (The spirit of freedom), *Znamya* 9, 1988: 218.

17. See, for example, Lev Gudkov and Boris Dubin, "Literaturnaya kul'tura: protsess i ratsion" (The literary culture: the process and the allotment), *Druzhba narodov* 2, February 1988: 182; Dmitry Kazutin, "Simvoly vmesto tseley" (Symbols instead of goals), *Moskovskie novosti*, June 5, 1988: 10; Marina Pavlova-Sil'vanskaya, "Neterpenie" (Impatience), *Literaturnaya gazeta*, April 29, 1987: 10; and A. E. Tugaev, "Spiritual Food Shortage," a letter to *Ogonyok*, April 1988, reprinted in Christopher Cerf and Marina Albee, eds., *Small Fires: Letters from the Soviet People to Ogonyok Magazine, 1987–1990*, New York: Summit Books, 1990: 61.

18. Nikolai Bykov, "Pryamaya rech" (Direct speech), *Ogonyok* 33, 1987: 19.

19. Gudkov and Dubin, "Literaturnaya kul'tura . . . ," 179.

20. Bykov, op. cit.

21. Marina Pavlova Sil'vanskaya, "Neterpenie" (Impatience), *Literaturnaya gazeta*, April 29, 1987: 10.

22. "Tirazhi ryada tsentral'nykh gazet i zhurnalov v 1985–1989," (The pressruns of the central newspapers and magazines in 1985–1989), *Izvestiya TsK KPSS*, no. 1, 1989: 139. (See also the reprint in *Argumenty i fakty*, May 6–12, 1989: 3.)

23. *Le Monde*, November 4, 1987, reprinted in FBIS-SOV, November 10, 1987: 7.

24. See, for example, Andrei Romanov, "The Press We Choose," *Moscow News*, February 21, 1988: 2; Boris Nazarenko, "Pravdu i tol'ko pravdu!" (Truth and only truth!), a letter to the editor, *Moskovskie novosti*, December 4, 1988: 9, and Hedrick Smith, *The New Russians*, New York: Random House, 1990: 107.

25. Alain Jacob, "Democracy, Openness, and Patriotism," *Le Monde*, November 4, 1987: 4, reprinted in English translation in FBIS-SOV-87–217, November 10, 1987: 71.

26. Christopher Cerf and Marina Albee, Acknowledgments, in Cerf and Albee, eds., *Small Fires*, 7.

27. "Slovo chitatelya" (A word from the reader), *Ogonyok* 1, 1989: 6.

28. Cerf and Albee, *Small Fires*, 69. (The letter was published in *Ogonyok* in September 1988.)

29. Lev Gudkov and Boris Dubin, "Chto my chitaem" (What we read), interviewed by Mikhail Gurevich, *Literaturnoe obozrenie* 1, 1988: 93–94.

30. *Izvestiya TsK KPSS* (Herald of the Central Committee of the CPSU), no. 1, 1981: 139.

31. Gudkov and Dubin, "Chto . . . ": 93.

32. David Remnick, "Soviets Publish Shalamov Tales of the Gulag," *Washington Post*, June 22, 1988: C9.

33. V. Stel'makh, "Novye starye knigi" (New old books), *Izvestia*, February 1, 1989: 2.

34. S. Bobkova, "Avtor b'yot pryamo v tsel' " (The author hits the bull's eye), *Novy mir*, January 1987: 267.

35. Alexander Arkhangel'skiy, "Mezhdu svobodoy i ravenstvom: Obshchesvennoe soznanite v zerkale 'Ogon'ka' i 'Nashego sovremennika' (Between freedom and equality: Public conscience as reflected in *Ogonyok* and *Nash sovremennik*, 1986–1990), *Novy mir* 2, February 1991: 230.

36. Yuriy Afanasiev, Len Karpinskiy, Marina Ogorodnikova, "Myshlenie bez 'pogon' " (Thought that knows no rank distinctions), *Moskovskie novosti*, September 25, 1988: 8.

37. Ibid.

38. V. Arseniev, "S'ezd v televizionnom izmerenii" (The television dimension of the Congress), *Izvestia*, June 16, 1989: 7. The proceedings of the Congress were "regularly" watched by between 70 and 90 percent of adults in Moscow, Leningrad, Kiev, Tallin, and Alma-Ata. (Vera Nikitina, "God za godom: 1989" [Year after year: 1989], *Informatsionnyi bulleten' monitoringa* [The public opinion monitoring information bulletin] 4, no. 30, July–August 1997: 38.)

39. N. Bondaruk, "Den' vtoroy" (Day two), *Izvestia*, May 27, 1989: 1.

40. Vera Nikitina, "God za godom: 1989" (Year after year: 1989), *Informatsionnyi bulleten' monitoringa* (The public opinion monitoring information bulletin) 4, no. 30 (July–August 1997): 38.

41. Igor Klyamikin, *Trudniy spusk s ziyayushchikh vysot* (The difficult descent from the yawning heights), Moscow: Pravda/Biblioteka Ogon'ka, 1990: 3.

42. Grigoriy Tsitrinyak, "Stepen' svobody" (The degree of freedom), an interview with Andrei D. Sakharov, *Ogonyok* 31, 1989: 29.

43. Ibid.

44. A. D. Sakharov, "S'ezd ne mozhet sdelat' vsyo srazu . . ." (The Congress cannot do everything right away), *Literaturnaya gazeta*, June 21, 1989: 11.

45. Ibid.

46. Alexander Bovin, "Perestroika: Pravda o sotsializme i sud'be sotsializma (Perestroika: The truth about socialism and the fate of socialism), in Yuri Afanasiev, ed., *Inogo ne dano* (There is no other way), Moscow: Progress, 1988: 519.

47. Alexei Kiva, "Krizis 'zhanra' " (The crisis of the "genre"), *Novy mir* 3, March 1990: 206.

48. Klyamkin, "Pochemu . . . ": 229 and 219.

49. Ibid., 220.

50. Leonid Lazarev, "Dukh svobody," (The spirit of liberty), postscript to Vasily Grossman, *Zhizn' i sud'ba* (Life and fate), Moscow: Knizhnaya palata, 1989: 661, and Alexander Tsypko, "Istoki Stalinizma" (The sources of Stalinism), *Nauka i zhizn'* 2, February 1989: 56.

51. Alexander Tsypko, "Khoroshi li nashi printsipy?" (How good are our principles?), *Novy mir* 4, April 1990: 201.

52. Igor Zolotusskiy, "Krushenie abstraktsiy" (The downfall of abstractions), *Novy mir* 1, January 1989: 236.

53. Tsypko, "Khoroshi li," 192.

54. Ibid.

55. Ibid.

56. Klyamkin, "Pochemu . . . ," 215, and Viktor Krivorotov, Sergei Chernyshov, and Georgiy Tselms, "Mify nashey revolyutsii" (The myths of our revolution), *Literaturnaya gazeta,* March 7, 1990: 5.

57. A. Bocharov, "Mchatsya mify, b'yutsya mify" (Myths are whirling, myths are stirring), *Oktyabr'* 1, January 1990: 191.

58. Kiva, "Krizis 'zhanra,'" 215.

59. Klyamkin, "Pochemu . . . ," 230.

60. Ibid.

61. Andrei Sakharov, Neizbezhnost' perestroiki" (The inevitability of perestroika), in Afanasiev, ed., *Inogo ne dano,* 123.

62. Yuri Burtin, "Vam, iz drugogo pokolen'ya . . ." (To you, from a different generation), *Oktyabr'* 8, August 1987: 202.

63. Ibid.

64. Klyamkin, "Pochemu . . . ," 205.

65. Georgiy Zhzhyonov, "Sud'ba naroda i cheloveka" (The fate of the people and of an individual), *Komsomol'skaya pravda,* November 7, 1988.

66. Ibid.

67. A. Kozhevnikov, "Proigran li nami etot vek?" (Have we lost this century?), letter to the editor, *Komsomol'skaya pravda,* December 28, 1990: 2.

68. Andrei Sakharov, "Neizbezhnost' perestroiki" (The inevitability of perestroika), in Afanasiev, ed., *Inogo ne dano,* 123; Zhzhyonov, "Sud'ba naroda," 4.

69. Igor Vinogradov, "Mozhet li pravda byt' poetapnoy?" (Can the truth be doled out in stages?), in Yuri Afanasiev, ed., *Inogo ne dano* (There is no other way), Moscow: Progress, 1988: 277.

70. Ibid.

71. L. Lazarev, "Dukh svobody," postscript to Vassily Grossman, *Zhizn' i sud'ba* (Life and fate), Moscow: Knizhnaya palata, 1989: 661.

72. Anatoly Pristavkin, "Otvetsvennost'" (Responsibility), *Ogonyok* 32, 1987: 7; Chingiz Aytmatov, "Tsena prozreniya" (The price of regaining one's sight), *Ogonyok* 28, 1987: 6.

73. Pristavkin, "Otvetstvennost'."

74. Vladimir Shubkin, "Trudnoe proshchanie" (The difficult farewell), *Novy mir,* April 1989: 175.

75. Ibid.

76. Mikhail Antonov, "Tak chto zhe s nami proiskhodit?" (What really is happening to us?), *Oktyabr'* 8, August 1987: 44.

77. Ibid., and Mikhail Shatrov, "Neobratimost' peremen" (The irreversibility of the changes), *Ogonyok* 4, January 1987: 4.

78. *Ogonyok* 5, 1989: 23.

79. Boris Vasiliev, "Prozrenie" (The recovery of sight), *Sovetskiy ekran* 6, March 1987: 5.

80. Yakovlev, "Perestroika."

81. Ibid.

82. Ibid.

83. Ibid.

84. Ibid.

85. Andrei Nuykin, "Otkrytoe pis'mo" (An open letter), *Ogonyok* 40, 1989: 6; Alexander M. Yakovlev, "Otverzhenie i utverzhdenie" (Rejection and affirmation). *Ogonyok* 43, 1988: 14.

86. Shubkin, "Trudnoe proshchanie," 184.

87. Oleg Poptsov, "Kak stat' realistom" (How to become a realist), in V. G. Kazakov, ed., *Razvedka slovom* (Reconnaissance by word), Moscow: Moskovskiy rabochiy, 1988: 70, and Antatoly Rybakov, "Deti Arbata v 1937 godu" (The children of Arbat in 1937), interview with *Moskovskie novosti*, September 2, 1990: 16.

88. Shubkin, "Trudnoe proshchanie," 183.

89. Zhzhyonov, "Sud'ba naroda."

90. Shubkin, "Trudnoe proshchanie, 174, 176.

91. "Andrey Dmitrievich Sakharov," an obituary, *Novy mir* 2, February 1990: 271.

92. Sakharov, "Neizbezhnost'," 127.

93. As quoted in Svyatoslav Fyodorov, "Chtoby nikogda ne povtorilos'!" (So as this does not happen again!), *Ogonyok* 8, 1987: 1.

94. Pavel Bunich, "Novye tsennosti" (New values), *Oktyabr'* 12, December 1987: 149.

95. Marat Baglay, "Moral' i politika" (Morality and politics), *Sovetskaya kul'tura*, July 27, 1989: 4.

96. Francis Fukuyama, *The Great Disruption: Human Nature and the Reconstitution of Social Order,* New York: Free Press, 1990: 250.

97. Klyamkin, "Pochemu . . . ," 205, 237.

98. Zhzhyonov, "Sud'ba naroda."

99. Mikhail Kapustin, "Kamo gryadeshi?" (Whither art thou?), *Oktyabr'*, August 1987: 175.

100. Yuri Karyakin, "Eto nash posledniy shans," in "Chto budet, esli i eta perestroika pogibnet?" (What will happen if this restructuring, too, perishes?), a roundtable discussion, *Moskovskie novosti*, June 5, 1988: 9.

101. Dmitry Furman, "Nash put' k normal'noy kul'ture" (Our road to a normal culture), in Afanasiev, ed., *Inogo ne dano,* 570.

102. Ibid.

103. Vladimir Kantor, "Imya rokovoe" (The fateful name), *Voprosy literatury* 3, March 1988: 85.

104. Ibid., 69.

105. William Shakespeare, *Henry the Fourth,* part 1, act 3, scene 1, 58.

106. K. Anisova, a letter to the editor, in "Chitateli o poeme A. T. Tvardovskogo 'Po pravy pamayati'" (Readers on A. T. Tvardvoskiy's poem "In memory's name"), *Znamya* 8, August 1987: 233.

107. Alexander Gel'man, "Chto snachala, chto potom . . ." (What comes first and what comes later), *Literaturnaya gazeta,* September 10, 1986: 10.

108. Len Karpinsky, "Pochemu stalinizm ne skhodit so stseny?" (Why won't Stalinism leave the stage?), in Afanasiev, ed., *Inogo ne dano,* 660.

109. Alexey Kiva, "Krizis 'zhanra'" (The crisis of the "genre"), *Novy mir* 3, March 1990: 207.

110. Michael Gerson, *Heroic Conservatism,* New York: HarperOne, 2007, as quoted in John Podhoretz, "Activist," *Commentary,* January 2008: 54.

111. Samuel Johnson, *Rasselas, Poems, and Selected Prose,* ed. Bertrand H. Bronson, New York: Holt, Rinehart and Winston, 1971: 259.

112. Burlatsky, "Sud'ba reformatorov . . ."

113. Yakovlev, *Sumerki,* 2003: 587.

114. Yuri Burtin, "Vam," 194.

115. Alexander Tsypko, "Do We Need Yet Another Experiment? Ideological Paradoxes of Reform," *Rodina,* no. 1, January 1990.

116. Yuri Chernichenko, "Trava iz-pod stoga" (Grass from under a haystack), in Afanasiev, ed., *Inogo ne dano,* 591–620.

117. Yakovlev, *Sumerki,* 2003: 587.

118. Yuri Chernichenko, "Trava iz-pod stoga" (Grass from under a haystack), in Afanasiev, ed., *Inogo ne dano,* 601.

119. Arkhangel'skiy, "Mezhdu svobodoy," 230.

120. Zolotusskiy, "Krushenie abstraktsiy," 241.

121. Ibid., 241.

122. Ibid., 394–95.

123. Lord Macaulay, *The History of England,* New York: Penguin Classics, 1968: 273.

124. Shubkin," Trudnoe proshchanie," 168.

125. Zolotusskiy, "Krushenie abstraktsiy," 240.

126. Ibid.

127. Andrei Sakharov, "Neizbezhnost' perestroiki" (The inevitability of perestroika), in Afanasiev, ed., *Inogo ne dano,* 122–23; and Alexei Kiva, "Krizis 'zhanra'" (The crisis of the "genre"), *Novy mir* 3, March 1990: 213.

128. Kiva, "Krizis 'zhanra,'" 216, and Karyakin, "Eto nash."

129. Georgiy Zhzhyonov, "Sud'ba naroda i cheloveka" (The fate of the people and of an individual), *Komsomol'skaya pravda,* November 7, 1988: 4.

130. Ales' Adamovich, "Vospominanie o budushchem, kotorogo ne dolzhno byt'" (Remembrance of a future that must not be allowed to be), in "Chto budet, esli . . ."

131. Leonid Batkin, "Vozobnovlenie istorii" (The resumption of history), in Afanasiev, ed., *Inogo ne dano,* 154.

132. Ibid.

133. Karyakin, "Stoit li," 220, and Vasily Selyunin, "Istoki," *Novy mir* 5, May 1988: 189.

134. Selyunin, "Istoki," 163.

135. Karyakin, "Eto nash," and Karyakin, "Stoit li," 220.

136. Karyakin, "Eto nash," 8.

137. Ales' Adamovich, "Optimizm delaniya" (The optimism of doing something), *Moskovskie novosti,* September 11, 1988: 13.

138. Chingiz Aytmatov, "Tsena prozreniya" (The price of recovering sight), interview with Felix Medvedev, *Ogonyok* 28, 1987: 7.

139. Dmitry S. Likhachev, Speech at the First Congress of People's Deputies, a transcript, *Izvestia,* June 1, 1989: 4.

140. As quoted in James M. McPherson, *Battle Cry of Freedom,* New York: Oxford University Press, 1988: 63–64.

141. Chernichenko, "Trava . . . ," 601.

142. Jonathan Yardley, "Reexamining a neglected era of invention and expansion," *Washington Post Book World,* November 25, 2007: 15.

143. Alexander Vasinskiy, "Terpimost' k inakomysliyu" (The tolerance toward dissent), *Moskovskie novosti,* September 11, 1988: 13.

144. Leonid Gozman, in "Bol'she sotsializma!" (More socialism!), a roundtable discussion, *Ogonyok* 14, 1988: 7.

145. Lev Voskresenskiy, "Obresti dostoinsvo v bor'be" (To find dignity in a struggle), *Moskovskie novosti,* January 17, 1988: 13.

146. Yuri Karyakin, in "Bol'she sotsializma!" (More socialism!), a roundtable discussion. *Ogonyok* 14, 1988: 7, and Karyakin, "Nastupat' li," 219.

147. Karyakin, "Nastupat' li," 219.

148. Ibid.

149. Louis Menand, *The Metaphysical Club,* New York: Farrar, Straus and Giroux, 2001: 14.

150. Boris Vasiliev, "Prozrenie" (Recovery of sight), *Sovetskiy ekran* 6, March 1987: 5.

151. Igor Kon, "Psikhologiya sotsial'noy inertsii" (The psychology of social inertia), *Kommunist* 1, January 1988: 64.

152. Sergey Zalygin, "God Solzhenitsyna" (The year of Solzhenitsyn), *Novy mir* 1, January 1990: 240.

153. Ibid.

154. Ibid.

155. Zolotusskiy, "Krushenie abstraktsiy," 243.

156. Kiva, "Krizis 'zhanra,'" 208.

157. Ibid.

158. Alexander Vasinskiy, "Terpimost' k inakomysliyu" (The tolerance toward dissent), *Moskovskie novosti,* September 11, 1988: 13.

159. Zolotusskiy, "Krushenie abstraktsiy," 243.

160. Igor' Dedkov, "Vozmozhnost' novogo myshleniya" (The possibility of new thinking), *Novy mir* 10, October 1986: 229.

161. Ibid.

162. N. Zorkaya, "Dorogoy, kotoraya vedyot k khramu" (By the road which leads to the temple), *Iskusstvo kino* 5, 1987: 53, and Anatoly Pristavkin, "Otvetsven-nost' " (Responsibility), *Ogonyok* 32, 1987: 7.

163. Evgeniy Starikov, "Marginaly" (The marginal people), *Znamya* 10, October 1989: 158.

164. Zalygin, "God Solzhenitsyna," 237.

165. Viktor Erofeev, "Pominki po sovetskoy literature" (A wake for Soviet litera-ture), *Literaturnaya gazeta*, July 4, 1990: 8.

166. Zalygin, "God Solzhenitsyna," 237.

167. Grigoriy Baklanov, "Vystuplenie . . . ," speech at the Plenum of the Presidium of the Writers' Union, April 27–28, 1987, *Literaturnaya gazeta*, May 6, 1987: 2.

168. Zolotusskiy, "Krushenie abstraktsiy," 239.

169. Ibid., 238.

170. Andrei Voznesensky, "A Poet's View of Glasnost," *The Nation*, June 13, 1987; and Maya Ganina, "Bez obol'shcheniy prezhnikh dney" (Without the delu-sions of bygone days), *Literaturnaya gazeta*, January 13, 1988: 11.

171. Bocharov, "Mchatsya myfy," 190.

172. Anatoly Rybakov, "Rana, kotoraya krovotochit" (The wound that is bleeding), *Moskovskie novosti*, November 27, 1988.

173. Vitaliy Korotich, foreword to Korotich and Cathy Porter, eds., *The New Soviet Journalism: The Best of the Soviet Weekly Ogonyok*, Boston: Beacon Press, 1990: vii.

174. Vitaliy Korotich, introduction to Christopher Cerf and Marina Albee, eds., *Small Fires: Letters from the Soviet People to Ogonyok Magazine, 1987–1990*, New York: Summit Books, 1990: 15.

175. Yuri Chernichenko, "Zemlya, ekologiya, perestroika" (Land, ecology, pere-stroika), *Literaturnaya gazeta*, January 29, 1989: 3.

176. Arkhangel'skiy, "Mezhdu svobodoy," 230; Egor Yakovlev, "Chetyre dnya: Kak eto bylo" (Four days: This is how it was), *Moskovskie novosti*, July 10, 1988: 3; and Anatoliy Vengerov, "Zaslon vozhdizmu" (The hedge against a leader's cult), *Ogonyok* 23, 1988: 14.

177. "Andrey Dmitrievich Sakharov," an obituary, *Novy mir* 2, February 1990: 271.

178. Ibid.

179. Yakovlev, "Chetyre dnya."

180. V. Starkov, N. Zyat'kov, A. Meshcherskiy, and L. Novikova, "Za chto kriti-kuyut 'AiF' " (What do they criticize AiF for), *Argukmenty i fakty*, November 18–24, 1989: 2.

181. Korotich, introduction: 14.

182. Ibid., 13.

183. K. Anisova, letter to the editor.

184. Alexander Gasparishvili, Alexander Kolokol'tsev, and Sergey Tumanov, "Por-tret kandidata v Narodnye Deputaty SSSR" (The portrait of a candidate for a People's Deputy), *Moskovskie novosti*, March 19, 1989: 7.

185. Pavlova-Sil'vanskaya, "Neterpenie."

CHAPTER 3. INSIDE THE "DEAFENED ZONE"

1. Mikhail Fedotov, "Bol'she svobody—vyshe otvetstvennost' " (More freedom [means] greater responsibility), *Moskovskie novosti*, October 23, 1988: 12.

2. Alexander Bovin, "Dva soobrazheniya" (Two thoughts), *Sovetskaya kul'tura*, June 23, 1988: 3.

3. Pavel Vorobuev, "Drama samopoznaniya" (The drama of self-discovery), *Sovetskaya kul'tura*, July 18, 1989: 3.

4. Yu. Sorokin, "Eto sladkoe slovo svoboda!" (This sweet word: liberty!), *Komsomol'skaya pravda*, May 5, 1990: 1.

5. Igor Vinogradov, "Mozhet li pravda byt' poeatpnoy?" (Can the truth be doled out in stages?), in Yuri Afanasiev, ed., *Inogo ne dano* (There is no other way), Moscow: Progress, 1988: 287; Tatyana Zaslavskaya, "Perestroika i sotsologiya" (Perestroika and sociology), *Pravda*, February 6, 1987: 3; Bovin, "Dva soobrazheniya."

6. Alexei Izyumov, "Glasnost v ekonomike" (Glasnost in economy), *Moskovskie novosti*, July 10, 1988: 13.

7. F. Ivanov, "O prestupnosti—glasno" (To talk openly about deviance), *Izvestia*, September 10, 1988: 2.

8. Yuri Chernichenko, "Zhurnalist" (Journalist), *Znamya*, July 1987: 223; Yuri Burtin, "Vam, iz drugogo pokolen'ya . . ." (To you, from a different generation . . .), *Oktyabr'* 8, August 1987: 194.

9. "Po pravu pamyati," or "In the name of memory," *Znamya*, February 1987: 11.

10. Burtin, "Vam," 191–202.

11. P. Gal'tseva and I. Rodnyanskaya, "Pomekha—chelovek" (Man is the problem), *Novy mir* 12, December 1988: 227.

12. Ibid.

13. V. Svirskiy, "Istoriya umalchivaet" (History omits), *Izvestia*, July 21, 1987: 3.

14. Yu. Polyakov, "Dorozhit' kazhdym godom nashey istorii" (To treasure every year of our history), an interview with *Literaturnaya gazeta*, July 29, 1987: 10.

15. Yuri Karyakin in "Bol'she sotsializma!" (More socialism!), a roundtable discussion, *Ogonyok* 12, 1988: 10.

16. Grigory Vodolazov, in "Bol'she sotsializma!" (More socialism!), a roundtable discussion, *Ogonyok* 14, 1988: 5.

17. Yu. Polyakov, "Istoriya i istoriki" (History and historians), a roundtable discussion, *Kommunist* 12, August 1987: 74.

18. Grigory Vodolazov, in "Bol'she sotsializma!"

19. M. Shur, op. cit.

20. Stanislav Kondrashov, "Iz mraka secretnosti" (From the darkness of secrecy), *Novy mir* 8, August 1989: 182.

21. Ibid.

22. Ibid., 194.

23. Pavel Gutionov, "Boi mestnogo nazancheniya" (Combat of local significance), *Ogonyok* 39, 1987: 30.

24. Arlen Blyum, "Svobodno ot evreev" (Free from Jews), *Novoe vremya*, no. 20, 2005: 37.

25. Ibid., 37–38, and Vladimir Novikov, "Vozvrashchenie k zdravomu smyslu" (The return to common sense), *Znamya*, no. 7, 1989: 216.

26. Blyum, "Svobodno ot evreev," 38.

27. Ibid., 36.

28. A. Bocharov, "Sud'ba narodnaya" (People's fate), *Oktyabr'*, no. 3, March 1988: 156, and Blyum, "Svobodno ot evreev," 36.

   Grossman's first published work, "V gorode Berchive" (In the town of Berdichev) appeared in 1934 to praise by Babel, Bulgakov, and Gorky. It told a story of a female Red Army commissar who gave birth and left the baby in the care of a Jewish couple. In the final scene, added by Askol'dov, the adopted boy, now a young man, walks with his family and other Jews to be shot in 1941. As if Grossman's authorship were not enough, with Jews and the Holocaust included in the plot, the film hadn't a prayer in the Soviet Union of the 1960s. What was Askol'dov thinking?

29. Blyum, "Svobodno ot evreev," 37.

30. Alexander Solzhenitsyn, "Nobelevskay lektsiya" (The Nobel lecture), *Novy mir* 7, July 1989: 140.

31. See, for example, L. Lazarev, "Dukh svobody" (The spirit of freedom), *Znamya*, September 1988: 218.

32. See, for instance, Marietta Chudakova, "V zashitu zhizni chelovecheskoy" (In defense of human life), *Moskovskie novosti*, January 31, 1988: 11.

33. See, for example, Evgeniy Barabanov, "Predskazanie ili preduprezhdenie?" (A prediction or a warning?), *Moskovskie novosti*, February 28, 1988: 11, and Vsevolod Revich, "Preduprezhdenie vsem" (A warning to everyone), *Literaturnoe obozrenie*, no. 7, 1987: 44–46.

34. See, for instance, Alexander Shindel', "Svidetel'" (A witness), *Znamya*, September 1987: 207–17; Inna Rostovtseva, "U chelovecheskogo serdtsa" (Next to a human heart), in "Platonov segodnya" (Platonov today), *Oktyabr'*, November 1987: 158–62; Vladimir Gusev, "Minutu molchaniya" (In a moment of silence), ibid., 162–65; and Viktor Malukhin, "Rekviem po utopii" (A requiem for utopia), *Znamya*, October 1987: 219–21.

35. Shindel', "Svidetel'," 208.

36. See, for example, G. Belaya, "Tret'ya zhizn' Isaaka Babelya" (The third life of Isaak Babel), *Oktyabr'*, no. 10, October 1989: 185–97.

37. Lionel Trilling, *Liberal Imagination*, New York: Doubleday, 1953: 22.

38. Viktor Erofeev, "Pominki po sovetskoy literatre" (The wake for Soviet literature), *Literaturnaya gazeta*, April 7, 1990: 8.

39. Yuri Burtin, "Zhivoe i myortvoe" (The living and the dead), *Literaturnaya gazeta*, no. 34, 1990: 7.

40. Igor Zolotusskiy, "Krushenie abstraktsiy" (The downfall of abstractions), *Novy mir* 1, January 1989: 245.

41. Ibid.

42. Ibid.

43. Nikolai Bykov, "Pryamaya rech" (Direct speech), *Ogonyok* 33, 1987: 19.

44. A. Malysheva, "Samizdat," *Komsomol'skaya pravda,* February 9, 1989: 2.
45. E. Chernykh, "Reabilitatsiya" (Acquittal), *Komsomol'skaya pravda,* March 19, 1989: 2.
46. Karyakin, "Bol'she sotsializma!" 6.
47. Leonid Gordon in "Bol'she sotsializma!" *Ogonyok* 14, 1988: 6.
48. Vinogradov, "Mozhet li pravda," 289.
49. Alexander Bovin, "Perestroika: Pravda o sotsializme i sud'ba sotsializma" (Perestroika: The truth about socialism and the fate of socialism), in Yuri Afanasiev, ed., *Inogo ne dano* (There is no other way), Moscow: Progress, 1988: 519.
50. Alexander Solzhenitsyn, "Nobelevskaya lektsiya" (The Nobel lecture), *Novy mir,* July 1989: 142 and 140, and *Gulag Archipelago,* New York: Harper and Row, 1978: vol. 3, part 7, chap. 1, p. 475.
51. Alexander Solzhenitsyn, *Cancer Ward,* chap. 32.
52. Osip Mandel'shtam, "My zhivyom pod soboya ne chuya strany . . ." (We live not feeling the country's soul under us . . .) (op. 286), in O. E. Mandel'shtam, *Collected Works,* Moscow: Terra, 1991: 1: 202.

CHAPTER 4. IN SEARCH OF HISTORY

1. Arkady Sakhnin, "Ne brosat'sya slovami" (Not to waste words), *Moskovskie novosti,* April 24, 1988: 15.
2. Ibid.
3. N. I. Krasnoborodko, "Write the Truth!" a letter to *Ogonyok,* January 1988. In Christopher Cerf and Marina Albee, eds., *Small Fires: Letters from the Soviet People to Ogonyok Magazine, 1987–1990,* New York: Summit Books, 1990: 240.
4. Yuri Afanasiev, "Perestroika i istoricheskoe znanie" (Perestroika and historical knowledge), in Afanasiev, ed., *Inogo ne dano* (There is no other way), Moscow: Progress, 1988: 498.
5. Yu. Afanasiev, "Perestroika i istoricheskoe znanie" (Perestroika and historical knowledge), *Literaturnaya Rossiya,* June 17, 1988: 8.
6. I. Ovchinnikova, "Ekzamen otmenyon: Istoriya ostayotsya!" (The examination is abolished: History remains!), *Izvestia,* June 10, 1988: 1.
7. M. Belaya, "Ekzamen budet, no uchebnikov poka net" (There will be the exam, but so far there are no textbooks), *Izvestia,* February 8, 1989: 3. See also, Vera Tolz, "New History Textbook for Secondary Schools," *Radio Liberty Report on the USSR,* September 1, 1989 (RL 396/89): 5–7.
8. Len Karpinsky, "S 'sotsializmom napereves'" (Attacking with socialism), *Moskovskie novosti,* May 27, 1990: 7.
9. Natan Eydel'man, "Optimizm istoricheskogo soznaniya" (The optimism of historical knowledge), interview with *Ogonyok* 44, 1988: 2.
10. Alexander Tsypko, "Istoki Stalinisma" (The origins of Stalinism), *Nauka i zhizn'* 2, February 1989: 61.
11. V. Svirskiy, "Istoriya umalchivaet" (History omits), *Izvestia,* July 21, 1987: 3.
12. Ibid.
13. Ibid.

14. Ibid.

15. Ibid.

16. Ibid.

17. Yuri Karyakin, "Stoit li nastupat' na grabli? (Do we really want to step on a rake?): 219.

18. Svirskiy, "Istoriya umalchivaet" (History omits), *Izvestia*, July 21, 1987: 3.

19. Svyatoslav Fyodorov, "Chtoby nikogda ne povtorilos'!" (So as not to let it not happen again!), *Ogonyok* 8, 1987: an insert between pp. 5 and 6.

20. Abel Aganbegyan, "Chelovek i ekonomika" (Man and economy), *Ogonyok* 30, 1987: 15.

21. E. S. Kochetkov, letter to the editor, *Znamya*, August 1987: 228. The quoted phrase is in Alexander Tvardovsky, "Po pravu pamyati" (In the name of memory), *Znamya* 2, February 1987: 12.

22. Nikolar Sennikov, letter to the editor, *Znamya*, August 1987: 223.

23. Igor Klyamkin, "Pochemu tak trudno govorit' pravdu?" (Why is it so difficult to speak the truth?), *Novy mir* 2, February 1988: 229 and 219.

24. Ibid., 219, and Nikolai Shmelyov, "Libo sila, libo rubl'" (Either brute force or the ruble), *Znamya* 1, January 1989: 129.

25. A. Bocharov, "Mchatsya mify, b'yutsya mify" (Myths are whirling, myths are stirring), *Oktyabr'*, January 1990: 183.

26. Alexander Tsypko, "Istoki Stalinisma" (The origins of Stalinism), *Nauka i zhizn'* 2, February 1989: 61.

27. Igor Klyamkin, "Kakaya ulitsa vedyot k khramu?" (Which street leads to the temple?), *Novy mir*, November 1987: 150.

28. Ibid.

29. Shubkin, "Trudnoe proshchanie," 18.

30. Vinogradov, "Mozhet li pravda," 283.

31. Marietta Chudakova, "V zashchitu zhizni chelovecheskoy: Roman Borisa Pasternaka 'Doktor Zhivago' na stranitsakh 'Novogo mira'" (In defense of human life: Boris Pasternak's novel *Doctor Zhivago* in the pages of *Novy mir*), *Moskovskie novosti*, January 31, 1988: 11.

32. Evgeny Evtushenko, Introduction to Natliya Rapoport, "Pamyat'—tozhe meditsina" (Memory is medicine, too), *Yunost'*, no. 4, 1988: 76.

33. Boleslav Vol'ter, "Prozrenie idyot slishkom medlenno" (The recovery of sight is proceeding too slowly), *Moskovskie novosti* 45, November 6, 1988: 2.

34. Yuri Karyakin, "Chto budet, esli i eta perestroika pogibnet?" (What will happen if this perestroika, too, perishes?), *Moskovskie novosti* 23, June 5, 1988: 9.

35. Alexander Tsypko "Khoroshi li nashi printsipy?" (How good are our principles?), *Novy mir*, April 1990: 202.

36. Kantor, "Imya rokovoe," 84.

37. Mikhail Shatrov, "Neobratimost' peremen" (The irreversibility of the changes), *Ogonyok* 4, January 1987: 4. First published in 1906, Tolstoy's article, "Nikolay Palkin" (Nikolas the Stick) is to be found in *L. N. Tolstoy: Polnoe*

sobranie sochineniy (L. N. Tolstoy, Collected Works), Moscow: Khudozhestven-naya literatura, 1936, vol. 26: 555–62.

38. Tolstoy, "Nikolai Palkin," 558.

CHAPTER 5. "THE INNOCENT, THE SLANDERED,
THE EXTERMINATED"

1. Sergey Muratov, "Esli eto i revolutsiya, to podpol'naya" (If this indeed is a revolution, it is an underground one), *Moskovskie novosti,* July 10, 1988: 10.

2. L. Gozman and A. Etkind, "Kul't vlasti. Struktura totalitarnogo soznaniya" (The cult of power: The structure of totalitarian consciousness), in Kh. Kobo, ed., *Osmyslit' kul't Stalina* (To comprehend Stalin's cult), Moscow: Progress, 1989: 338.

3. Zenon Poznyak, "Kuropaty: narodnaya tragediya, o kotoroy dolzhny znat' vse" (Kuropaty: a national tragedy about which everyone must know), *Moskovskie novosti,* October 9, 1988: 16.

4. Ibid.

5. Sergey Kiselyov, "Eshcho raz o Bykovne" (Once more about Bykovnya), *Literaturnaya gazeta,* October 10, 1990: 13.

6. Ibid.

7. Ibid.

8. Roy Medvedev, "Nash isk Stalinu" (Our case against Stalin), *Moskovskie novosti,* November 27, 1988: 8; and Roy Medvedev, "Tragicheskaya statistika" (Tragic statistics), *Argumenty i fakty,* February 4–10, 1989: 5–6.

9. Roy Medvedev, Tragicheskaya statistika" (Tragic statistics), *Argumenty i fakty,* February 4–10, 1989: 6.

10. Vladimir Shubkin, "Trudnoe proshchanie" (The difficult farewell), *Novy mir,* April 1989: 172.

11. V. Popov and N. Shmelyov, "Na razvilke dorog" (At a crossroad), in Kh. Kobo, ed., *Osmyslit' kul't Stalina* (To think through Stalin's cult), Moscow: Progress, 1989: 301.

12. Ales' Adamovich, "Oglyanis' okrest!" (Look around you!), *Ogonyok* 39, 1988: 29.

13. L. P. Bueva, F. M. Burlatsky, O. P. Tyomushkin, "Osvobodit'sya ot deformatsii sotsializma" (To free ourselves from the deformation of socialism), *Argumenty i fakty,* April 23–29, 1988: 3.

14. Zamira Ibragimova and Ilya Kartushin, "Matryonin grekh" (Matryona's sin), *Ogonyok* 5, 1989: 21, 23.

15. M. Kytmanova, letter to *Znamya,* August 1987: 230.

16. Vasily Grossman, *Zhizn' i sud'ba* (Life and fate), Moscow: Knizhnaya palata, 1989: 477.

17. Alexander Yakovlev, *Sumerki* (Twilight), Moscow: Materik, 2005: 148.

18. Ibid. and Oleg. V. Khlevnyuk, *The History of Gulag: From Collectivization to the Great Terror,* New Haven: Yale University Press, 2004: 127.

19. Varlam Shalamov, "*Novaya proza* (New fiction), *Novy mir*, December 1989: 12.

20. Varlam Shalamov, *Iz "Kolymskikh rasskazov"* (From "The Kolyma tales"), *Znamya*, June 1989: 27.

21. Shalamov, *Novaya proza*, 12, and *Iz "Kolymskikh,"* 27.

22. Alexander Solzhenitsyn, *Arkhipelag Gulag, Novy mir*, August, September, October 1989.

23. Anatoly Rybakov, *Deti Arbata: Kniga vtoraya: Strakh* (The children of Arbat: Book two: Fear), St. Petersburg: Amphora: 2004: 276–77.

24. Alexander Yakovlev, *Sumerki* (Twilight), 2d ed., Moscow: Materik, 2005.

25. Alexander Tvardovsky, *Po pravu pamyati* (In memory's name), *Znamya* 2, February 1987: 9.

26. Anatoly Rybakov, *Deti Arbata: Kniga Trety'a: Prakh i pepel* (Dust and ashes), St. Petersburg: Amphora, 2004: 295.

27. Ibid.

28. Irina Shcherbakova, "Nado li pomnit' proshloe?" (Should we remember the past?), *Moskovskie novosti*, November 27, 1988: 12.

29. Ibid.

30. Ibid.

31. Irina Shcherbakova, "Odin iz sta, iz pyatisot, iz tysyachi . . ." (One out of a hundred, five hundred, thousand . . .), *Moskovskie novosti*, October 30, 1988: 16.

32. Grossman, *Zhizn' i sud'ba*, 476.

33. Ibid.

34. Irina Shcherbakova, "Odin iz sta, iz pyatisot, iz tysyachi . . ." (One out of a hundred, five hundred, thousand . . .), *Moskovskie novosti*, October 30, 1988: 16.

35. Evgeniya Al'bats, "Proshcheniyu ne podlezhat" (No forgiveness for them), *Moskovskie novosti*, May 8, 1988: 13.

36. Ibid.

37. Poznyak, "Kuropaty."

38. Grigory Anisimov and Mikhail Emtsev, "Etot khranitel' drevnostey" (O pisatele Yurii Dombrovskom I ego knigakh), the postscript to Yuri Dombrovsky, *Fakul'tet nenuzhnykh veshchey* (The department of unnecessary things), Moscow: Sovetskiy pisatel', 1989: 696.

39. Yuri Dombrovsky, *Fakul'tet nenuzhnykh veshchey*, Moscow: Sovetskiy pisatel', 1989: 555.

40. Mikhail Shreyder, "Ivanovo, 1937," *Moskovskie novosti*, November 27, 1988: 7.

41. Ibid.

42. Ibid.

43. Medvedev, "Nash isk" and "Tragicheskaya statistika," 6.

44. Dombrovsky, *Fakul'tet*, 289.

45. Varlam Shalamov, *Novaya proza* (New fiction), *Novy mir*, December 1989: 51.

46. Medvedev, "Nash isk."

47. Iosif Gerasimov, "Stuk v dver'" (A knock on the door), *Oktyabr'*, February 1987.

48. Ibid., 150.
49. Ibid., 132.
50. Timur Pulatov, "Krymskie tatary zhazhdut iskhoda" (The Crimean Tatars are thirsting for the resolution), *Moskovskie novosti*, April 9, 1989: 13.
51. Iibd.
52. Ibid.
53. Ibid.
54. B. E. Aksakova ("neé Bekirova"), a letter to the editor, *Ogonyok* 4, 1989: 3.
55. Ibid.
56. Nikolai Bugay, "V bessrochnuyu ssylku" (Into indefinite exile), *Moskovskie novosti*, October 14, 1990: 11.
57. Bugay, "V bessrochnuyu ssylku."
58. Medvedev, "Nash isk," 9.
59. V. Shutkevich, "Molchit katyn'skiy les" (The Katyn forest is silent), *Komsomol'skaya Pravda*, January 20, 1990: 3, and N. Lebedeva, *Katynskie golosa* (The voices of Katyn'), *Novy mir*, February 1991: 211.
60. Ibid. Lebedeva, op. cit., 211.
61. Ibid.
62. Ibid.
63. Gennady Zhavoronkov, "Posle rasstrela myli ruki spirtom . . ." (After an execution [they] washed the hands with strong alcohol), *Moskovskie novosti*, September 16, 1990: 15.
64. Ibid.
65. Lebedeva. *Katyn'skie golosa*, 212–16.
66. Ibid., 216.
67. Kiselyov, "Eshcho raz . . ."
68. Ibid.
69. Zhavoronkov, "Posle rasstrela . . ."
70. Ibid.
71. Ibid.
72. Ibid.
73. Ibid.
74. Gennady Zhavoronkov, "Tayny katynskogo lesa" (The secrets of the Katyn' forest), *Moskovskie novosti*, August 6, 1989: 15.
75. Ibid.
76. Lev Razgon, "Privodyashchiy v ispolnenie" (The one who carried out the sentence), *Moskovskie novosti*, November 27, 1988: 11.
77. Natalya Izyumova, "Ston" (Groan), *Moskovskie novosti*, October 23, 1988: 16.
78. Ibid.
79. Dombrovsky, *Fakul'tet*, 353.
80. Varlam Shalamov, *Novaya proza* (New fiction), *Novy mir*, December 1989: 4.
81. Ibid.
82. Dombrovsky, *Fakul'tet*, 353.
83. Andrey Vasilevsky, "Stradanie pamyati," *Oktyabr'*, April 1989: 182.

84. Ibid.
85. Dombrovsky, *Fakul'tet*, 583.
86. Lidya Chukovskaya, *Spusk pod vodu* (Descent underwater), Moscow: Moskovsky Rabochiy, 1988: 158.
87. A. Kosinova (Podboronova), letter to *Ogonyok*, October 1989, in Christopher Cerf and Marina Albee, eds., *Small Fires: Letters from the Soviet People to Ogonyok Magazine, 1987–1990*, New York: Summit Books, 1990: 245–46.
88. Shalamov, *Novaya proza*, 11, 13.
89. Shalamov, *Iz Kolymskikh rasskazov*, 20.
90. Ibid.
91. Dombrovsky, *Fakul'tet*, 523; Shalamov *Iz Kolymskikh rasskazov*, 9.
92. Shalamov, ibid.
93. Dombrovsky, *Fakul'tet*, 583.
94. Shalamov, *Novaya proza*, 52.
95. Shalamov, *Iz Kolymskikh rasskazov*, 27, 28, 9; Chukovskaya, *Spusk pod vodu*, 136.
96. Shalamov, *Iz Kolymskikh rasskazov*, 17.
97. Shalamov, *Novaya proza*.
98. Shalamov, *Iz Kolymskikh rasskazov*, 16–17.
99. *Novaya Proza*, 43.
100. Varlam Tikhonovich Shalamov was imprisoned in the north Ural camps in 1929–32 and in Kolyma in 1937–51. (A biographical note to *Varlam Shalamov: Proza, Stikhi* in *Novy mir*, June 1988: 106.)
101. Varlam Shalamov, "O moey proze" (About my fiction), in *Novaya proza*, 59, 63.
102. Shalamov, *Iz Kolymskikh rasskazov*, 10.
103. Shalamov, *Novaya proza*, 42.
104. Vasily Selyunin, "Istoki" (The sources), *Novy mir*, May 1988: 177.
105. Shalamov, *Iz Kolymskikh rasskazov*, 11; and *Novaya proza*, 9.
106. Shalamov, *Novaya proza*, 12.
107. Shalamov, *Proza, Stikhi*, 133; *Novaya proza*, 20.
108. Shalamov, *Iz Kolymskikh rasskazov*, 11.
109. Ibid., 17.
110. Shalamov, *Novaya proza*, 43, and *Iz Kolymskikh rasskazov*, 31.
111. Shalamov, *Novaya proza*, 52–53.
112. Shalamov, *Iz Kolymskikh rasskazov*, 8; *Proza, Stikhi*, 113; *Novaya proza*, 6.
113. Shalamov, *Iz Kolymskikh rasskazov*, 8.
114. Ibid.
115. Muratov, 'Eto i est' . . ."
116. Ibid.
117. Shalamov, *Iz Kolymskikh rasskazov*, 12.

CHAPTER 6. THE PEASANT HECATOMB
1. V. Danilov, N. Teptsov, and L. Smirnov, "Kollektivizatsiya: kak eto bylo" (Collectivization: how it all happened), *Pravda*, September 16, 1988: 3.

2. V. Oskotskiy, "Za chto?" (What for?), *Znamya*, April 1990: 223–24.

3. Georgy Zhzhyonov, "Sud'ba naroda i cheloveka" (The fate of the people and of an individual), *Komsomol'skaya pravda*, November 7, 1988: 4; Vladimir Shubkin, "Trudnoe proshchanie" (The difficult farewell), *Novy mir*, April 1989: 170.

4. See, for example, Alexander Yakovlev, *Sumerki* (Twilight), Moscow: Materik, 2005: 163–64.

5. V. Danilov, N. Teptsov, and L. Smirnov, "Kollektivizatsiya: kak eto bylo" (Collectivization: how it all happened), *Pravda*, September 16, 1988: 3; and Pavel Voshchanov, "Zloba i zavist' obrekayut nas na bednost'" (Spite and envy doom us to penury), *Komsomol'skaya pravda*, December 2, 1989: 3.

6. Danilov, Teptsov, and Smirnov, "Kollektivizatsiya," 3.

7. Medvedev, "Nash isk."

8. Nikolai Shmelyov, "Ne smet' komandovat'!" (Stop giving orders!), *Oktyabr'*, February 1988: 13.

9. Vasily Grossman, *Vsyo techoyt* (Forever flowing), *Oktyabr'*, June 1989: 76.

10. Medvedev, "Nash isk." A leading historian of the Soviet agriculture, Academician Tikhonov, estimated that no less than 3 million families were "repressed" (or 10–11 percent of all Soviet peasants) and "significantly more" than 10 million people. (See V. Popov and N. Shmelyov, "Na razvilke dorog" [At a crossroad], in Kh. Kobo, ed., *Osmyslit' kul't Stalina* [To think through Stalin's cult], Moscow: Progress, 1989: 296.)

11. Sergey Zavorotnyi and Petr Polozhevets, "Operatsiya GOLOD" (Operation HUNGER), *Komsomol'skaya pravda*, February 3, 1990: 2; and Medvedev, "Nash isk." "It was a terrible struggle," Stalin told Churchill. "I thought you would have found it bad," Churchill replied, "because you were not dealing with a few score thousands of aristocrats or big landowners, but with millions of small men." "Ten million," Stalin said. "These were what you call Kulaks?" Churchill asked. "Yes." "What happened?" "Oh, well," Stalin replied. "Many of them agreed to join us. Some of them were given land of their own to cultivate in the province of Tomsk or the province of Irkutsk or father north, but a great bulk were very unpopular and were wiped out by their laborers." (Winston S. Churchill, *The Second World War*, vol. 4, *The Hinge of Fate*, London: Penguin Books, 1985: 447–48.)

12. A decade and a half later, Donald Rayfield would report that of the 1,518,524 deported in 1932, 90,000 died. Of the 1,153,846 exiled the following year, 150,000, or 13 percent, perished. (*Stalin and His Hangmen: The Tyrant and Those Who Killed for Him*, New York: Random House, 2004: 191.) This still leaves the years of heaviest deportations, 1930 and 1931, unaccounted for.

13. Medvedev, "Nash isk."

14. Alexander Tsypko, "Istoki Stalinisma" (The origins of Stalinism), *Nauka i zhizn'*, February 1989: 56.

15. Rayfield, *Stalin*, 189.

16. Ibid. Rayfield's estimate ranges from the "very conservative" 7 million to 11 million (*Stalin*, 191).

17. Pavel Voshchanov, "Zloba i zavist' obrekayut nas na bednost.'" (Spite and envy doom us to penury), *Komsomol'skaya pravda*, December 2, 1989: 3.

18. Vladimir Shubkin, "Trudnoe proshchanie" (The difficult farewell), *Novy mir* 4, April 1989: 171.

19. V. Danilov, N. Teptsov, and L. Smirnov, "Kollektivizatsiya: kak eto bylo" (Collectivization: how it all happened), *Pravda*, September 16, 1988: 3.

20. Ibid.

21. Ibid.

22. Grossman, *Vsyo techyot*, 75.

23. Voshchanov, "Zloba."

24. Ibid.

25. Ibid.

26. Natl'ya Kirilovna Mochalova, letter to *Komsomol'skaya pravda*, January 25, 1989: 2.

27. Grossman, *Vsyo techyot*, 76.

28. Vasil' Bykov, "Oblava" (Man-hunt), *Novy mir*, January 1990: 132, 139.

29. V. J. Bulgakov, "Songs of 'Our Happy Childhood,'" a letter to *Ogonyok*, Spring 1989, in Christopher Cerf and Marina Albee, eds., *Small Fires: Letters from the Soviet People to Ogonyok Magazine, 1987–1990*. New York: Summit Books, 1990: 244.

30. Natl'ya Kirilovna Mochalova, letter to *Komsomol'skaya pravda*, January 25, 1989: 2. Bulgakov, "Songs," 244; Andrey Vasilevsky, "Stradanie pamyati," (The anguish of memory), *Oktyabr'*, April 1989: 185; and Voshchanov, "Zloba . . . ," 3.

31. Grossman, *Vsyo techyot*, 76.

32. Bulgakov, "Songs," 244.

33. Ibid.

34. Mochalova, op. cit.

35. Ibid.

36. Grossman, *Vsyo techyot*, 76.

37. Bulgakov, "Songs," 244.

38. Ibid.

39. Mochalova, op. cit.

40. Ibid.

41. Ibid.

42. Danilov, Teptsov, and Smirnov, "Kollektivizatsiya."

43. Yuri Chernichenko, "Podnyavshiysya pervym" (The first to rise), *Novy mir*, September 1989: 188; Danilov, Teptsov, and Smirnov, "Kollektivizatsiya"; Zavorotnyi and Polozhevets, "Operatsiya"; Vasiliy Selyunin, "Istoki" (The sources), *Novy mir* 5, May 1988: 178. See also Alexander Yakovlev, *Sumerki* (Twilight), Moscow: Materik, 2005: 165.

44. Zavorotnyi and Polozhevets, op. cit.

45. Yakovlev, *Sumerki*, 165.

46. Danilov, Teptsov, and Smirnov, op. cit.

47. Zavorotnyi and Polovezhets, op. cit.

48. Danilov, Teptsov, and Smirnov, op. cit.

49. Ibid.

50. Vasily Grossman, *Vsyo techoyt* (Forever flowing), *Oktyabr'*, June 1989: 77.

51. Zavorotnyi and Polozhevets, op. cit.

52. Ludmila Saraskina, "Smotret' pravde v glaza" (To look the truth in the eye), *Moskovskie novosti*, April 10, 1988: 12.

53. Ibid.

54. Zavorotnyi and Polozhevets, op. cit.

55. Yuri Chernichenko, "Podnyavshiysya pervym" (He was the first to stand up), *Novy mir*, September 1989: 189.

56. Medvedev, "Nash isk," Danilov, Teptsov, and Smirnov, op. cit; Yuri Chernichenko, "Zemlya, ekologiya, perestroika" (Land, ecology, perestroika), *Literaturnaya gazeta*, January 29, 1989: 3; Zavorotnyi and Polozhevets, op. cit.

57. Medvedev, "Nash isk."

58. Yuri Chernichenko. "O khlebe nasushchnom" (Of our daily bread), *Komsomol'skaya Pravda*, March 12, 1989: 2; and Zavorotnyi and Polozhevets, op. cit.

59. Zavorotnyi and Polozhevets, op. cit.

60. Ibid.

61. Grossman, *Vsyo techoyt*, 77.

62. Ibid., 78.

63. P. Penezhko, "Poezdka v Zagor'e" (A trip to Zagor'e), *Novy mir*, June 1990: 194–95.

64. Grossman, *Vsyo techoyt*, 79.

65. Ibid.

66. M. E. Galushko, "The Famine of 1933," in Christopher Cerf and Marina Albee, eds., *Small Fires: Letters from the Soviet People to Ogonyok Magazine, 1987–1990*, New York: Summit Books, 1990: 242.

67. Zavorotnyi and Polozhevets, op. cit.; Grossman, *Vsyo techyot*, 79, 80.

68. Grossman, *Vsyo techoyt*, 79, and *Zhizn' i sud'ba* (Life and fate), Moscow: Knizhnaya palata, 1989: 425.

69. Selyunin, "Istoki" (The sources), *Novy mir*, May 1988: 162; and Grossman *Vsyo techoyt*, 79.

70. Selyunin, "Istoki," 162.

71. Grossman, *Vsyo techoyt*, 80.

72. Ibid.

73. Zavorotniy, Polozhevets "Operatsiya," and Grossman, *Vsyo techoyt*, 80.

74. Grossman, *Vsyo techoyt*, 82.

75. Zavorotnyi, Polozhevets "Operatsiya."

76. Yuri Chernichenko, "Trava iz-pod stoga" (Grass from under a haystack), in Yuri Afanasiev, ed., *Inogo ne dano* (There is no other way), Moscow: Progress, 1988: 609.

77. Ibid.

78. Zavorotniy, Polozhevets "Operatsiya."
79. Ibid.
80. Ibid.
81. Grossman, *Vsyo techoyt,* 81.
82. Ibid.
83. Ibid.
84. Zavorotnyi and Polozhevets, op. cit.
85. Ibid.

CHAPTER 7. THE UNRAVELING OF THE LEGITIMIZING MYTHS, I

1. Robert K. Merton, *Social Theory and Social Structure,* New York: Free Press, 1968: 475.
2. A. Karpychev, "Krizis doveriya?" (The crisis of trust?), *Pravda,* June 24, 1988: 3.
3. Viktor Loshak, "Strana kvartirnogo ucheta" (The country of apartment record-keeping), *Moskovskie novosti,* June 3, 1990: 3.
4. Alexander Bekker, "Myaso na vyvoz" (Meat for export), *Moskovskie novosti,* July 10, 1988: 13.
5. Yuri Chernichenko, "Trava iz-pod stoga" (Grass from under a haystack), in Yuri Afanasiev, ed., *Inogo ne dano* (There is no other way), Moscow: Progress, 1988: 616.
6. Leonid Batkin, "Vozobnovlenie istorii" (The resumption of history), in Afanasiev, ed., *Inogo ne dano,* 155.
7. Abel Aganbegyan, "Chelovek i ekonomika" (Man and economy), interview with *Ogonyok* 29, 1987: 4.
8. Petr Aleshkovsky, "Pro kolbasu" (About sausage), *Ogonyok* 33, 1988: 28.
9. Larissa Vasilieva, "A glimpse of diplomacy from the sideline," *International Affairs,* February 1989: 93.
10. See, for example, Stanislav Govorukhin, "Zhut'!" (Dread!), *Sovetskaya kul'tura,* October 7, 1989: 11; and V. Tsamalaidze, "Chuzhaya sredi svoikh" (A stranger among her own), *Pravda,* November 30, 1989: 2.
11. Tsamalaidze, "Chuzhaya sredi svoikh," 2.
12. Yuri Chernichenko, "Zemlya, ekologiya, perestroika" (Land, ecology, perestroika), *Literaturnaya gazeta,* January 29, 1989: 3.
13. P. Voroshilov and A. Solovyov, "Konstruktivniy dialog s shakhterami" (A constructive dialogue with the miners), *Izvestia,* July 18, 1989: 1.
14. Viktor Loshak, "Strana kvartirnogo ucheta" (The country of apartment record-keeping), *Moskovskie novosti,* June 3, 1990: 3.
15. Loshak, "Strana"; and L. Velikanova and S. Nikolaev, director, the Central Scientific Research Institute of Housing, "Kazhdoy sem'e—zdorovuyu kvartiru" (To every family—a "healthy apartment"), *Literaturnaya gazeta,* August 31, 1988: 4. Abel Aganbegyan (a leading Russian economist and advisor to Mikhail Gorbachev), "Chelovek i ekonomika" (Man and economy), interview with *Ogonyok,* part 2: *Ogonyok* 30, 1987: 12.

16. Aaron Trehub, "Social Issues on the Eve of the Twenty-Seventh Party Congress," *Radio Liberty Research* (RL 84/86), February 19, 1986: 1.

17. Velikanova and Nikolaev, "Kazhdoy."

18. Mikhail Antonov, "Tak chto zhe s nami proiskhodit?" (What really is happening to us?), *Oktyabr'*, August 1987: 5.

19. A. Karpychev, "Krizis doveriya?" (The crisis of trust?), *Pravda*, June 24, 1988: 3.

20. A. Simurov, P. Studenikin, "Net v dushe blagodarnosti . . ." (There is no gratitude in my soul . . .), *Pravda*, November 25, 1987: 2.

21. Valentina Pokhodnya, "Doesn't anybody need our family?" (September 16, 1989), in Christopher Cerf and Marina Albee, eds., *Small Fires: Letters from the Soviet People to Ogonyok Magazine, 1987–1990*, New York: Summit Books, 1990: 127.

22. Ibid.

23. Yuri Levada, ed., *Est' mnenie!* (I have an opinion!), Moscow: Progress, 1990: 253 (Comment No. 6989).

24. Ibid., 265.

25. M. Ovcharov, "100 zapisok iz zala" (100 notes from the audience), *Izvestia*, September 6, 1988: 3.

26. Ibid.

27. Ibid.

28. I. Voytko, "Negde zhit'" (Without a home), *Pravda*, July 2, 1989: 3.

29. Simurov, Studenikin, "Net v dushe," 2.

30. "Zhivyom pasynkami" (We live like unwanted stepchildren), *Pravda*, September 18, 1987: 3.

31. Karpychev, "Krizis doveriya?"

32. V. Kozin, "Tayna kvadratnykh metrov" (The secret of square meters). *Komsomol'skaya pravda*, February 3, 1987: 2.

33. A. Krivoruchko, "Chto stoit za problemami" (What is behind the problems?), *Argumenty i fakty*, January 6–12, 1989: 4.

34. Abel Aganbegyan, "Chelovek i ekonomika" (Man and economy), interview with *Ogonyok* 30, 1987: 13; and Evgeny Chazov, minister of Healthcare of the Soviet Union, Speech at the Nineteenth All-Union Party Conference, *Pravda*, June 30, 1988: 4.

35. Svyatoslav Fedorov, "Voinstvo so strelami" (An army with arrows), *Pravda*, September 28, 1987: 3.

36. Ibid.

37. Evgeny Chazov, "Kogda bolezn' obgonyaet lekarstva" (When disease outpaces remedies), interview with *Literaturnaya gazeta*, February 3, 1988: 11; and Evgeny Chazov, "Sotni voiteley stoit odin vrachevatel' iskusnyi" (One skillful physician is worth a hundred warriors), interview with *Ogonyok* 42, 1988: 2.

38. I. A. Egorova, department head, the Altai regional hospital in Barnaul, speech at the First Congress of People's Deputies on June 8, 1989, in *Pervyi S'ezd*

Narodnykh Deputatov SSSR. Stenographicheskiy otchyot. Tom III (The First Congress of People's Deputies of the USSR. Official Transcript, vol. 3), Moscow: Publishing House of the Supreme Soviet, 1989: 72.

39. Chazov, the speech at the Nineteenth Party Conference.

40. I. A. Egorova, op. cit., 73.

41. N. Trofimov, "Tsifry vmesto bol'nykh." (Numbers instead of patients), *Pravda*, September 2, 1987: 2.

42. Ibid.

43. Dmitry Shevarov, "SPID. Sotsial'nyi portret yavleniya" (AIDS: A social portrait of a phenomenon), *Komsomol'skaya pravda*, May 24, 1990: 2.

44. Yuri Chernichenko, "Zhurnalist" (The journalist), *Znamya*, July 1987: 220.

45. V. Korneev and S. Tutorskaya, "Lekarstva, kotorykh zhdut" (The drugs people are waiting for), *Izvestia*, January 1988: 2.

46. Egorova, op. cit., 73.

47. P. Sergeev, "Defitsit lekarstv. Ch'ya vina?" (The shortage of drugs: Whose fault?), interview with *Pravda*, July 13, 1989: 3. (The author was chairman of the Department of Molecular Pharmacology and Radiobiology of the Second Moscow Medical Institute, corresponding member of the Academy of Medical Sciences.)

48. Sergeev, "Defitsit lekarstv."

49. Nikolai Ryzhkov, "Sluzhit' intersam naroda" (To serve the people's interests), speech at the First Congress of People's Deputies on June 7, 1989, *Izvestia*, June 8, 1989: 2.

50. V. Kurasov, "Izlechima li lekarstvennaya problema?" (Can the problem of medicines be cured?), "Notes from the joint meeting of the Committee for the Preservation of People's Health of the Supreme Soviet of the USSR and the Committee of People's Control of the USSR," *Izvestia*, October 21, 1989: 3.

51. Egorova, op. cit., 74.

52. Chazov, the speech at the Nineteenth All-Union Party Conference.

53. Mark Tol'tz, "Vdovy" (Widows). *Ogonyok* 18, 1987: 18.

54. Fedorov, "Voinstvo so strelami."

55. Chazov, "Kogda."

56. Esther Fine, "10 AIDS Babies Baffling Moscow Hospital Team," *New York Times*, February 12, 1989.

57. S. Leskov, "Zarazilis v bol'nitse" (Infected in a hospital), *Izvestia*, May 12, 1989: 7, and Shevarov, "SPID."

58. S. Tutorskaya, "Potryasenie" (Shock), *Izvestia*, March 7, 1989: 3, and Alla All-ova, "Luchshe ne dumat'?" (Better not to think?), *Ogonyok* 26, 1989: 28.

59. Leskov, op. cit.

60. Shevarov, "SPID."

61. Ibid.

62. Ibid.

63. See, for example, Rolan Bykov, Speech at the First Congress of People's Deputies on June 9, 1989. In *Pervyi S'ezd Narodnykh Deputatov SSSR. Stenographicheskiy otchyot. Tom III* (The First Congress of People's Deputies of the USSR. Official Transcript, vol. 3), Moscow: Publishing House of the Supreme Soviet, 1989: 230; and Natal'ya Davydova, "Dolgi nashi" (Our debts), *Moskovskie novosti*, September 10, 1989: 5.

64. G. A. Yagodin (chairman of the USSR State Committee on Education), speech at the Nineteenth All-Union Party Conference, *Pravda*, July 2, 1988: 9.

65. Yagodin, op. cit., and Bykov, op. cit., 230.

66. Vadim Churbanov, ". . . Prinadlezhit narodu" ([Culture] belongs to the people), *Ogonyok* 37, 1988: 19.

67. O. Yarunina, "K chemu privodit bezdushie" (What callousness leads to), *Trud*, January 19, 1988: 2.

68. Ibid.

69. Ibid.

70. Evgeny Chazov, minister of Healthcare of the Soviet Union, speech at the Nineteenth All-Union Party Conference, *Pravda*, June 30, 1988: 4.

71. Evgeny Chazov, "Zdorov'e kazhdogo—dostoyanie obshchestva" (The health of every individual [is] society's achievement), speech at the All-Union Congress of Physicians, *Pravda*, October 18, 1988: 3.

72. Profession V. I. Kulakov, director of the All-Union Center for the Health and Safety of Mother and Child (Moscow), "Rebyonok bez prismotra?" (An unattended child?). *Pravda*, August 10, 1987: 4.

73. Ibid.

74. Ibid.

75. "Poterpite, zhenshina!" (Hang in there, woman!), letters to *Rabotnitsa*, February 1989: 23.

76. Shevarov, "SPID."

77. Storozhenko, Starodubova, Koryakina et al., letter to *Ogonyok* 42: 5.

78. "Durnoy son?" (A nightmare?), *Rabotnitsa*, November 1988: 36.

79. "Poterpite, zhenshina!" (Hang in there, woman!), letters to *Rabotnitsa*, February 1989: 24.

80. Ibid.

81. Ibid., 22.

82. Ibid., 23.

83. As quoted in Nikolai Petrakov, "Dokhody i raskhody" (Incomes and expenses), interview with *Sovetskaya kul'tura*, July 6, 1989: 6.

84. A. Chernyak, "Edoki po statistike i v zhizni" (The food consumers in statistics and in real life), *Pravda*, September 1, 1988: 3; Nikolai Petrakov, "Dokhody i raskhody" (Incomes and expenses), interview with *Sovetskaya kul'tura*, July 6, 1989: 6.

85. Marina Mozhina, "Kto tam, za chertoy bednosti?" (Who is there behind the poverty line?), interview with *Sotsialisticheskaya industriya*, June 1, 1988: 3.

86. Ibid.

87. I. Rimashevskaya, "Prozhitochniy minimum" (The minimum subsistence level), *Argumenty i fakty*, April 7–13, 1990: 2. A year before, these people, "almost 80 million, almost a third of the Soviet population," were classified "barely made ends meet" (*edva svodili kontsy s kontsami*). (Boris Bolotin, "Debyut Vadima Kirichenko" [Vadim Kirichenko's debut], *Moskovskie novosti*, August 13, 1989: 12.)

88. Rimashevskaya, op. cit.

89. Yuri Levada, ed., *Est' mnenie!* (I have an opinion!), Moscow: Progress, 1990: 262.

90. Ruslan Khazbulatov, "Bednye lyudi otechestva" (The poor people of the Fatherland), *Komsomol'skaya pravda*, July 6, 1989: 2.

91. Marina Mozhina, "Kto tam, za chertoy bednosti?" (Who is there behind the poverty line?), interview with *Sotsialisticheskaya industriya*, June 1, 1988: 3.

92. Mikhail Berger, "Skol'ko stoit odet' rebyonka?" (How much does it cost to dress a child?), *Izvestia*, September 23, 1987: 2.

93. Levada, op. cit., 254.

94. L. Gordon and E. Klopov, "Stalinizm i poststalinizm: neobkhodimost' preodoleniya" (Stalinism and post-Stalinism: the necessity of overcoming), in Kh. Kobo, ed., *Osmyslit' kul't Stalina* (To comprehend Stalin's cult), Moscow: Progress, 1989: 483.

95. "Semeyniy byudzhet: dokhod i raskhod" (Family budget: income and expenses), *Pravda*, May 19, 1989: 5.

96. Ibid.

97. V. D. Zhulyov, "A Solution for Single Mothers," in Christopher Cerf and Marina Albee, eds., *Small Fires: Letters from the Soviet People to Ogonyok Magazine, 1987–1990*, New York: Summit Books, 1990: 119.

98. "Semeyniy byudzhet: dokhod i raskhod" (Family budget: income and expenses), *Pravda*, May 19, 1989: 5.

99. Andrei Sakharov, "Neizbezhnost' perestroiki" (The inevitability of perestroika), in Yuri Afanasiev, ed., *Inogo ne dano* (There is no other way), Moscow: Progress, 1988: 124.

100. V. Morozov, "Starikam vezde u nas pochyot?" (The elderly are honored everywhere in our country?), *Ogonyok* 14, 1989: 26.

101. Yu Rytov, "Kak zhivyotsya pensioneru?" (How is the pensioner faring?), *Izvestia*, August 20, 1988: 1.

102. Mozhina, op. cit.

103. Stanislav Govorukhin, "Zhut'!" (Dread!), *Sovetskaya kul'tura*, October 7, 1989: 11.

104. A. Lemyatskikh, "Ni slova dobrogo, ni drov . . ." (Neither a kind word nor wood). *Pravda*, August 17, 1987: 1.

105. Vasily Ostanchuk, "Ya trudilsya, skol'ko mog . . ." (I have worked as long as I could . . .), *Izvestia*, September 3, 1987: 3.

106. Andrey Nuykin. "O tsene slova i tsenakh na produkty" (About the value of word and food prices), *Ogonyok* 22, 1988: 7.

107. A. Likhanov, speech at the First Congress of People's Deputies of the USSR on June 1, 1989, *Izvestia,* June 2, 1989: 8.

108. Z. Voronina, "Nuzhna pomoshch" (Help is needed), *Izvestia,* September 21, 1988: 6.

109. Ibid.

CHAPTER 8. THE UNRAVELING OF THE LEGITIMIZING MYTHS, II

1. L. Gol'din. "Nado snova nauchit'sya zhit' "(We have to relearn to live), *Sovetskaya kul'tura,* August 29, 1989: 3.

2. Vasily Selyunin and and Grigory Khanin, "Lukavaya tsifra" (The cunning figure), *Novy mir,* February 1987: 192.

3. Ibid., 176–77, and Vladimir Popov and Nikolai Shmelyov, "Na razvilke dorog" (At a crossroad), in Kh. Kobo, ed., *Osmyslit' kul't Stalina* (To think through Stalin's cult), Moscow: Progress, 1989: 288.

4. Selyunin and Khanin, "Lukavaya tsifra," 193.

5. Ibid.

6. Popov and Shmelyov, "Na razvilke dorog," 298.

7. Ibid., 296, 298.

8. Ibid., 295.

9. Alexey Kiva, "Oktyabr' v zerkale utopiy i antiutopiy" (The October Revolution in the mirror of utopias and anti-utopias), *Izvestia,* November 5, 1990: 3.

10. Abel Aganbegyan, "Chelovek i ekonomika" (Man and economy), interview with *Ogonyok* 30, 1987: 14, 13. Tatiana Zaslavskaya's breakdown for the Soviet workers "engaged in a simple manual labor" was 30 percent in industry and 70 percent in agriculture. (T. Zaslavskaya, "Chelovecheskiy faktor razvitiya ekonomiki i sotsial'naya spravedlivost' " [The human factor in the development of economy and social justice], *Kommunist* 13, 1986: 68.)

11. Evgeny Chazov, "Sotni voiteley stoit odin vrachevatel' iskusnyi" (One skillful physician is worth a hundred warriors), interview with *Ogonyok* 42, 1988: 2.

12. Ibid.

13. Vladimir Volin, "Okhrana ot bezopasnosti" (Protection from security), *Moskovskie novosti,* August 27, 1989: 10.

14. F. T. Morgun, speech at the Nineteenth Party Conference on July 1, 1988, *Pravda,* July 2, 1988: 6.

15. A. V. Yablokov, head of a laboratory in the Institute of Evolutionary Biology of the USSR Academy of Sciences, speech at the First Congress of People's Deputies on June 8, 1989. In *Pervyi S'ezd Narodnykh Deputatov SSSR. Stenographicheskiy otchyot. Tom III* (The First Congress of People's Deputies of the USSR. Official Transcript, vol. 3), Moscow: Publishing House of the Supreme Soviet, 1989: 98.

16. Andrei Sakharov, "Neizbezhnost' perestroiki" (The inevitability of perestroika), in Yuri Afanasiev, ed., *Inogo ne dano* (There is no other way), Moscow: Progress, 1988, 123.

17. Nikolai Ryzhkov. *Perestroika: Istoriya predatel'stv* (Perestroika: The history of betrayals), Moscow: Novosti, 1992: 236.
18. Ibid.
19. V. Popov and N. Shmelyov, "Na razvilke dorog" (At a crossroad), in Kh. Kobo, ed., *Osmyslit' kul't Stalina* (To think through Stalin's cult), Moscow: Progress, 1989: 299.
20. A. Sizov, "Sverim tsyfry" (Let's compare the numbers), *Kommunist*, 15, 1989: 63.
21. N. Dmitriev, "O chyom grustyat tkachi" (What are weavers sad about?), *Sovetskaya kul'tura*, April 5, 1989: 2.
22. Alexander Shumskiy, "Pakhat' poka nechem" (So far, there is nothing to plow with), *Moskovskie novosti*, July 31, 1988: 9.
23. Vasily Belov, speech at the First Congress of People's Deputies of the USSR, June 1, 1989, *Izvestia*, June 2, 1989: 9.
24. Yuri Apenchenko, "Kuzbass. Zharkoe leto" (Kuzbass: A hot summer), *Znamya*, October 1989: 166.
25. Stanislav Govorukhin, "Zhut'!" (Dread!), *Sovetskaya kul'tura*, October 7, 1989: 11.
26. G. Dankov, "Zashchitnik zhdyot zashchity" (The protector is waiting for protection), *Sovetskaya kul'tura*, October 5, 1989: 3.
27. V. Rusakova, "Telefonnye istorii, kotorye tyanutsya 22 goda" (Telephone stories that have dragged for 22 years), *Pravda*, December 2, 1987: 4.
28. Yu. K. Sharipov, speech at the First Congress of People's Deputies of the USSR on June 1, 1989. *Izvestia*, June 2, 1989: 8.
29. Ibid.
30. Ibid.
31. Rusakova, "Telefonnye istorii."
32. V. Radaev and O. Shkaratan, "Vozvrashchenie k istokam" (The return to the sources), *Izvestia*, February 16, 1990: 3.
33. Viktor Yaroshenko. "Partii interesov" (The parties of issues), *Novy mir*, February 1990: 129.
34. Ibid.
35. Alexander Zaychenko, "SShA–SSSR: lichnoe potreblenie (nekotorye sopostavleniya)" (USA–USSR: personal consumption [some juxtapositions]), *SShA*, December 12, 1988: 17–18.
36. Ibid., 15, 18.
37. Ibid., table 1, p. 16. See also by the same author, "Kak delit' pirog" (How to divide the pie), *Moskovskie novosti*, June 11, 1989: 12.
38. Ibid., 17.
39. Ibid.
40. Zaychenko, "SShA–SSSR," 19, and Zaychenko, "Kak delit' pirog."
41. Zaychenko, "SShA–SSSR," 19.
42. Ibid., 20.
43. Ibid., 20, 22.

44. Vadim Churbanov, ". . . Prinadlezhit narodu" ([Culture] belongs to the people), *Ogonyok* 37, 1988: 19.

45. Ibid.

46. Lev Gudkov and Boris Dubin, "Literaturnaya kul'tura: Protsess i ratsion" (The literary culture: the process and the rationing), *Druzhba narodov* 2, February 1988: 178.

47. Ibid.

48. Vadim Churbanov, ". . . Prinadlezhit narodu" ([Culture] belongs to the people), *Ogonyok* 37, 1988: 19.

49. Ibid.

50. Alexander Vasinskiy, "Ne dat' zadut' svechu" (Not to let the candle be blown out), *Izvestia,* March 3 1989: 3.

51. Zaychenko, "SShA–SSSR," 22.

52. Yuri Apenchenko, "Kuzbass: zharkoe leto" (Kuzbass: a hot summer), *Znamya,* October 1989: 175.

53. V. M. Gvozdev, speech at the First Congress of People's Deputies of the USSR on June 9, 1989, *Pravda,* June 10, 1989: 5.

54. Zamira Ibragimova, "Ploshchadi boli" (The town squares of pain), *Ogonyok* 32, 1989: 2.

55. A. V. Kasyanov, chairman of the Voroshilovgrad Regional Executive Committee, speech at a conference of the Central Committee of the Communist Party of Ukraine, Radyan'ska, Ukraina, August 10, 1989: 2.

56. Ibragimova, "Ploshchadi boli," 2.

57. Larisa Piyasheva, "V pogone za Siney ptitsey" (Chasing the blue bird [of happiness]), *Oktyabr',* September 1990: 154.

58. Pavel Volin, "Tayna, izvestnaya vsem" (A secret known to everyone). *Ogonyok* 35, 1989: 6.

59. Ibid.

60. Ibid., 7.

61. Ibid.

62. Ibid.

63. A. Zaychenko, "Imushchestvennoe neravenstvo" (The property inequality), *Argumenty i fakty,* July 8–14, 1989: 5; Andrey Nuykin, "Otkrytoe pis'mo" (An open letter), *Ogonyok* 40, 1989: 6.

64. Volin, "Tayna," 7.

65. Ibragimova, "Ploshchadi boli," 2.

66. Apenchenko, "Kuzbass," 176.

67. A. Nikolaeva, "Recipe for Change," letter to *Ogonyok,* published in November 1987, in Christopher Cerf and Marina Albee, eds., *Small Fires: Letters from the Soviet People to Ogonyok Magazine, 1987–1990,* New York: Summit Books, 1990: 137.

68. Nuykin, "Otkrytoe pis'mo," 5.

69. Vitaly Tret'yakov, "Sotsial'naya spravedlivost' i privilegii: kak sovmeshcha-yutsya eti ponyatiya" (Social justice and privileges: how these notions are combined), *Moskovskie novosti,* July 3, 1988: 11.

70. Ibid., 10.

71. Zaychenko, "Imushchestvennoe," 6.

72. Ruslan Khazbulatov, "Bednye lyudi otechestva" (The poor people of the Fatherland), *Komsomol'skaya pravda*, July 6, 1989: 2; Alexander Zaychenko, "Kak delit' pirog" (How to divide the pie), *Moskovskie novosti*, June 11, 1989: 12; Nikolai Shmelyov, speech at the First Congress of People's Deputies on June 8, 1989, in *Pervyi S'ezd Narodnykh Deputatov SSSR. Stenographicheskiy otchyot. Tom III* (The First Congress of People's Deputies of the USSR. Official Transcript, vol. 3), Moscow: Publishing House of the Supreme Soviet, 1989: 50; Nikolai Petrakov, "Dokhody i raskhody" (Incomes and expenses), interview with *Sovetskaya kul'tura*, July 6, 1989: 6.

73. Zaychenko, "Imushchestvennoe."

74. Zaychenko, "Kak delit' pirog."

75. Oleg Bogomolov, "Sotsializm, 90-e gody" (Socialism, the 1990s), *Komsomol'skaya pravda*, October 3, 1990: 2; Alexander Lapin, "Bednost'" (Poverty), *Komsomol'skaya pravda*, April 19, 1990: 2.

76. Vasily Selyunin, "Chyornye dyry ekonimki" (The black holes of the economy), *Novy mir*, October 1989: 157, and Lapin, "Bednost'."

77. Vitaly Tret'aykov, "Vash punkt v predvybornoy programme" (Your plank in the electoral platform), *Moskovskie novosti*, January 29, 1989: 8.

78. "Programnoe zayavlenie "Soyuza trudyashchikhsya Kuzbassa," prinyatoe na IV konferentsii rabochikh komitetov Kuzbassa, 18–19 noyablrya 1989, g. Novokuznetsk (The statement of a program of the "Union of the laborers of Kuzbass," adopted at the Fourth Conference of the Workers' Committees of Kuzbass, on November 18–19 in the city of Novokuznetsk), in L. Lopatin, ed., *Rabochee dvizhenie Kuzbassa. Sbornik documentov i materialov. Aprel' 1989– Mart 1992* (The workers' movement of Kuzbass: A collection of documents and materials, April 1989–March 1992), Kemerovo: Sovremennaya otechestvennaya kniga, 1993: 158.

79. Andranik Migranyan, "Dolgiy put' k evropeyskomu domu" (A long road to the European home), *Novy mir*, July 1989: 175.

80. Oleg Kalugin, "KGB bez grima" (The KGB without makeup), *Argumenty i fakty*, June 30–July 6, 1990: 6–7.

81. Ibid., 6.

82. Popov and Shmelyov, "Na razvilke dorog," 318.

83. Boris Vasiliev, "Lyubi Rossiyu v nepogodu . . ." (Love Russia in bad weather), *Izvestia*, January 18, 1989: 3.

84. Ibid.

85. See, for example, Vladimir Popov and Nikolai Shmelyov, "Na razvilke dorog" (At a crossroad), in Kh. Kobo, ed., *Osmyslit' kul't Stalina* (To think through Stalin's cult), Moscow: Progress, 1989: 297; Boris Vasiliev, "Lyubi Rossiyu v nepogodu . . ." (Love Russia in bad weather), *Izvestia*, January 17, 1989: 3; Alla Latynina, "Solzhenitsyn i my" (Solzhenitsyn and we), *Novy mir*, January 1990: 242; and Viktor Krivorotov, "Russkiy put'" (The Russian path), *Znamya*,

September, 1990: 149; Yuri Chernichenko, "Podnyavshiysya pervym" (The first to have risen), *Novy mir,* September 1989: 185; and Boris Vasiliev, "Na oborotnoy storone" (On the reverse side), *Moskovskie novosti,* May 13, 1990: 3.

86. Yuri Chernichenko, "Zhurnalist" (Journalist), *Znamya,* July 1987: 223, and Popov and Shmelyov, "Na razvilke dorog," 287.

87. Anatoly Strelyaniy, "Prikhod i raskhod" (Profit and expense), *Znamya,* June 1986: 179.

88. Yuri Chernichenko, "Podnyavshiysya pervym" (The first to have risen), *Novy mir,* September 1989: 184.

89. Anatoly Strelyaniy, "Prikhod i raskhod" (Profit and expense), *Znamya,* June 1986: 178.

90. Popov and Shmelyov, "Na razvilke dorog," 296.

91. Boris Nazarenko, a letter to the editor, in "Pravdu i tol'ko pravdu! (Truth and only truth!), *Moskovskie novosti,* December 4, 1988: 9.

92. "Istoki" (The sources), *Novy mir,* May 1988: 162.

93. Yuri Chernichenko, "Podnyavshiysya pervym" (The first to have risen), *Novy mir,* September 1989: 178.

94. Popov and Shmelyov, "Na razvilke dorog," 297.

95. Ibid., 298.

96. N. Shmelev, "Ne smet' komandovat'!" (Stop giving orders!), *Oktyabr',* February 1988: 11.

97. M. A. Kytmanova, letter to *Znamya,* in "Iz pochty 'Znameni,'" August 1987: 230.

98. Yuri Chernichenko, "Zhurnalist" (Journalist), *Znamya,* July 1987: 223.

99. P. Penezhko, "Poezdka v Zagor'e" (A trip to Zagor'e), *Novy mir,* June 1990: 202.

100. A. Bystrov, "Prostye lyudi" (The ordinary people), *Komsomol'skaya pravda,* January 29, 1989: 4.

101. Anatoly Anan'ev, "Po techeniyu ili naperkor" (Going with the flow or against it), *Oktyabr',* October 1989: 10.

102. N. Shmelev, "Ne smet' komandovat'!" (Stop giving orders!), *Oktyabr',* February 1988: 23.

103. Dmitry Motornyi, "Vernut' krest'yaninu dolgi" (To repay our debts to the peasant), *Ogonyok* 33, 1988: 2.

104. Ibid.

105. Maya Ganina, "Tsena El'dorado" (The price of El Dorado), *Literaturnaya gazeta,* February 22, 1989: 11.

106. Ibid., Motroniy, "Vernut'," 2.

107. G. A. Shmakov, letter to the editor, in "Narodnaya publitsistika" (People's political journalism), *Oktyabr',* August 1989: 181–82.

108. Yuri Bespalov and Valery Konovalov, "Novocherkassk, 1962," *Komsomol'skaya Pravda,* June 2, 1989: 4.

109. Vladimir Fomin and Yuri Shchekochikhin, "Togda, v Novocherkasske" (Then, in Novocherassk), *Literaturnaya gazeta,* June 21, 1989: 13.

110. Ibid.; Yu. Bespalov and Valery Konovalov, "Novocherkassk, 1962," *Komsomol'skaya pravda,* June 2, 1989: 4.

111. Bespalov and Konovalov, op. cit.

112. Fomin and Shchekochikhin, op. cit.; Bespalov and Konovalov, op. cit.

113. O. Volkov, "Novocherkassk, 2 iyunya 1962" (Novocherkassk, June 2, 1962), *Komsomol'skaya pravda,* April 27, 1991: 3.

114. Fomin and Shchekochikhin, op. cit.

115. Fomin and Shchekochikhin, op. cit.; Bespalov and Konovalov, op. cit.

116. O. Volkov, "Novocherkassk, 2 iyunya 1962" (Novocherassk, June 2, 1962,) *Komsomol'skaya pravda,* April 27, 1991: 3.

117. Fomin and Shchekochikin, op. cit.

118. Ibid.

119. Ibid.

120. Fomin and Shchekochikin, op. cit.; Yu. Bespalov, "Novocherkass. 1962," *Komsomol'skaya pravda,* June 3, 1990: 2; and Bespalov and Konovalov, op. cit.

121. Bespalov, op. cit.

122. Bespalov, op. cit.

123. Volkov, op. cit.

124. Volkov, op. cit.

125. Ibid.

126. Ibid.

127. Fomin and Shchekochikhin, op. cit.

128. Bespalov and Konovalov, op. cit.

129. Bespalov and Konovalov, op. cit.

130. O. Volkov, op. cit.

131. Ibid.

132. Ibid.

133. Fomin and Shchekochikin, op. cit.

134. Bespalov and Konovalov, op. cit.

135. Bespalov, op. cit.

136. Bespalov, op. cit.

137. Volkov, op. cit.

138. Bespalov, op. cit.

CHAPTER 9. THE UNRAVELING OF THE LEGITIMIZING MYTHS, III

1. For aspects of this myth, as summarized by the critics, see, for example, Yuri Geller, "Nevernoe echo bylogo" (A wrong echo of the past), *Druzhba narodov,* September 1989: 229–44; Mikhail Semiryaga, "23 avgusta 1939 goda" (August 23, 1939), *Literaturnaya gazeta,* October 5, 1988: 14; Vyacheslav Dashichev, "Stalin v nachale 39-go" (Stalin in the beginning of 1939), *Moskovskie novosti,* August 27, 1989: 16.

2. Dashichev, "Stalin v nachale"; Vasily Kulish, "U poroga voyny" (On the war's threshold), interview with *Komsomol'skaya pravda,* August 24, 1988: 3.

3. Dashichev, "Stalin v nachale."

4. Ibid.

5. Dashichev, "Stalin v nachale"; Vasily Kulish, "Byl li vybor?" (Was there a choice?), *Moskovskie novosti*, September 3, 1989: 12.

6. Nikolai Popov, "Vse my v odnoy lodke" (We are all in the same boat), *Literaturnaya gazeta*, March 1, 1989: 14.

7. Popov, op. cit.; Vyacheslav Dashichev, "Vostok-Zapad: poisk novykh otnosheniy" (East-West: a search for new relations), *Literaturnaya gazeta*, May 18, 1988: 14.

8. Popov, op. cit., and A. Chubar'yan, "Avgust 1939 goda" (August 1939), *Izvestia*, July 1, 1989: 3.

9. Kulish, "Byl li vybor?" and Nina Smirnova, "Neobkhodimye utochneniya" (Some necessary clarifications), *Moskovskie novosti*, September 3, 1989: 12.

10. Kulish, "U poroga voyny."

11. Yu. Fel'shtinskiy and N. Eydel'man, "Za nedelyu do nachala vtoroy mirovoy voyny," *Moskovskie novosti*, August 20, 1989: 8.

12. Popov, op. cit.

13. Mikhail Semiryaga, "23 avgusta 1939 goda" (August 23, 1939), *Literaturnaya gazeta*, October 5, 1988: 14. See also Fel'shtinskiy and Eydel'man, op. cit., 8.

14. Kulish, "Byl li vybor?"

15. Ibid.

16. Dashichev, "Stalin v nachale."

17. Alexander Yakovlev, "Sobytiya 1939 goda—vzglyad s poluvekovoy distantsii" (The events of 1939: a view from a distance of half a century), interview with *Pravda*, August 18, 1989: 2.

18. Alexander Yakovlev, "An amended version of the Molotov-Ribbentrop resolution adopted on the 24th of December, 1989," the BBC, Summary of World Broadcasts, December 30, 1989, the USSR; Special Supplement; USSR Congress of People's Deputies, Soviet television 1350 gmt 24 Dec 89, p. SU/0650/C/1: p. 3.

19. Alexander Yakovlev, *Sumerki* (Twilight), Moscow: Materik, 2003: 419.

20. Yakovlev, "Amended version," 5.

21. "Dossier," *Moskovskie Novosti* Oct. 21–27, 2005: 6.

22. Fel'shtinsky and Eydel'man, "Za nedlyu . . . ," 9.

23. Smirnova, op. cit.

24. V. Kulish, "U poroga voyny," and I. Rishina and A. Egorov, "Lish tot dostoin zhizni i svobody . . . (Vasily Grossman. *Zhizn' i sud'ba*)." Chitatel'skay konferentsiya "LG" (Only he deserves life and liberty [who every day goes to battle for them] [Vasily Grossman, *Life and Fate*]. A readers' conference at *Literaturnaya gazeta*), *Literaturnaya gazeta*, August 24, 1988: 5; and Avdevich and Vlasova, op. cit., part 1: 3.

25. Kulish, "U poroga voyny"; Chubar'yan, "Avgust."

26. Kulish, "U poroga voyny"; Chubar'yan, "Avgust."

27. Kulish, "U poroga voyny."

28. A. Chubar'yan, "Avgust 1939 goda" (August 1939), *Izvestia*, July 1, 1989: 3.

29. Kulish, "U poroga voyny."
30. Ibid.; Vladimir Amlinsky, "Ten'" (Shadow), *Literaturnaya gazeta*, September 7, 1988: 12.
31. Kulish, "U poroga voyny"; Nikolai Pavlenko, Lieutenant General, Professor, "Tragediya i triumph Krasnoy armii" (The Red Army's tragedy and triumph), *Moskovskie novosti*, May 7, 1989: 9.
32. Kulis, "U poroga voyny."
33. Vikenty Matveev, "V Berline pyat'desyat let nazad" (Berlin, fifty years ago), *Moskovskie novosti*, November 16, 1990: 14.
34. Chubar'yan, "Avgust."
35. Ibid. and Semiryaga, "23 avgusta."
36. Kulish, "U poroga voyny."
37. Ibid.
38. Geller, "Nevernoe," 238–39.
39. Ibid., 238.
40. Ibid.
41. Ibid., Pavlenko, op. cit., and Dashichev, "Vostok-Zapad . . ."
42. Semiryaga, "23 avgusta"; Kulish, "U poroga voyny."
43. Kulish, "U poroga voyny"; and Avdevich and Vlasova, op. cit., part 1, p. 3; Pavelenko, "Tragediya."
44. Semiryaga, "23 avgusta."
45. Kulish, "U poroga voyny."
46. Ibid.
47. Geller, op. cit., 240.
48. Kulish, "U poroga voyny."
49. Ibid.
50. Geller, op. cit., 239.
51. Kulish, "U poroga voyny."
52. Ibid.; Pavlenko, "Tragediya."
53. Kulish, "U poroga voyny."
54. Konstantin Simonov, "Uroki istorii i dolg pisatelya" (Lessons of history and a writer's duty), *Nauka i zhizn'*, June 1987: 45.
55. Geller, op. cit., 240.
56. Nikolai Pavlenko, Lieutenant General, Professor, "Tragediya i triumph Krasnoy armii" (The Red Army's tragedy and triumph), *Moskovskie novosti*, May 7, 1989: 9.
57. Ales' Adamovich, "Voynu vyigral narod" (The people have won the war), *Moskovskie novosti*, February 28, 1988: 2.
58. Ibid.
59. Geller, op. cit., 240.
60. Ibid., 241.
61. Ibid.
62. Viktor Astaf'ev, speech at the Conference "Istoriya i literature" (History and literature), *Literaturnaya gazeta*, May 18, 1988: 4.

63. V. Kulish, comments at a reader's conference, in I. Rishina and A. Egorov, "Lish tot dostoin zhizni i svobody . . . (Vasily Grossman. *Zhizn' i sud'ba*)." Chitatel'skay konferentsiya "LG" (Only he deserves life and liberty [who every day goes to battle for them] [Vasily Grossman, *Life and Fate*]. A readers' conference at *Literaturnaya gazeta*), *Literaturnaya gazeta*, August 24, 1988: 5.

64. Yuri Geller, "Nevernoe echo bylogo" (A wrong echo of the past), *Druzhba narodov*, September 1989: 242.

65. Ibid.

66. Alexander Bovin, "Perestroika: pravda o sotsializme i sud'ba sotsializma" (Perestroika: The truth about socialism and the fate of socialism), in Yuri Afanasiev, ed., *Inogo ne dano* (There is no other way), Moscow: Progress, 1988: 529; Grigory Baklanov, "Vysota dikha" (The spiritual height), *Znamya*, May 1990: 6.

67. Pavlenko, op. cit.

68. Ibid.; Alexander Bovin, "Perestroika: pravda o sotsializme i sud'ba sotsializma" (Perestroika: The truth about socialism and the fate of socialism), in Yuri Afanasiev, ed., *Inogo ne dano* (There is no other way), Moscow: Progress, 1988: 529; Igor Sergeev, Deputy Chief Commander of the Strategic Missile Forces, Lieutenant General. "My otvykli razoruzhat'sya" (We are not used to disarm), *Moskovskie novosti*, February 25, 1990: 7; Geller, "Nevernoe," 238.

69. Geller, op. cit., 238.

70. Kulish, op. cit.

71. Pavlenko, op. cit.

72. Ibid.

73. Konstantin Simonov, "Uroki istorii i dolg pisatelya" (Lessons of history and a writer's duty), *Nauka i zhizn'*, June 1987: 45; Baklanov, "Vysota dikha," 6; Pavlenko, op. cit.

74. Baklanov, op. cit.

75. *Ogonyok* 50, 1989: 30, an unsigned editorial.

76. Vyacheslav Kondrat'ev, "Parii voyny" (The pariahs of the war), *Literaturnaya gazeta*, January 31, 1990: 8.

77. Vyacheslav Kondrat'ev, "Net, zhizn' prozhita ne zrya," *Sovetskaya kul'tura*, November 7, 1989: 3.

78. Ibid.

79. Yuri Chernichenko, "Podnyavshiysya pervym" (The first to rise), *Novy mir*, September 1989: 190–91; Ales' Adamovich, "Voynu vyigral narod" (The people have won the war), *Moskovskie novosti*, February 28, 1988: 2; Yuri Teplyakov, "Po tu storonu fronta" (On the other side of the front line), *Moskovskie novosti*, May 13, 1990: 8.

80. Astaf'ev, op. cit.

81. Evgeny Evtushenko, "Stalinizm po Platonovu" (Stalinism according to Platonov), in Kh. Kobo, ed., *Osmyslit' kul't Stalina* (To comprehend Stalin's cult), Moscow: Progress, 1989: 199.

82. Ibid.

83. Kontrat'ev, "Parii voyny."

84. Ibid.

85. Ibid.

86. Evgeny Evtushenko, "Stalinizm po Platonovu" (Stalinism according to Platonov), in Kh. Kobo, ed., *Osmyslit' kul't Stalina* (To comprehend Stalin's cult), Moscow: Progress, 1989: 199.

87. http://www.stalingrad-info.com/order227.htm. Accessed on March 28, 2010.

88. Kontrat'ev, "Parii voyny."

89. Ibid. For another instance of the "military march wife" term, see, for example, Valentina Chudaeva, "Zhivu i pomnyu" (I live and I remember), *Moskovskie novosti*, May 7, 1989: 9.

90. Kondrat'ev, "Parii voyny." The emphasis is in the original.

91. Teplyakov, "Po tu storonu."

92. Ibid.

93. Ibid.

94. Ales' Adamovich, "Voynu vyigral narod" (The people have won the war), *Moskovskie novosti*, February 28, 1988: 2; Teplyakov, op. cit.

95. Teplyakov, "Po tu storonu."

96. Teplyakov, op. cit. See also Alexander Solzhenitsyn, *V kruge pervom* (In the first circle), Moscow: Act, 2006: 608.

97. Solzhenitsyn, *V kruge . . .*, 211.

98. Teplyakov, op. cit.

99. Ibid.

100. Ibid.

101. Ibid.

102. Ibid.

103. Ibid.

104. Evtushenko, "Stalinizm," 199.

105. Alexander Solzhenitsyn, *Odin den' Ivana Denisovicha* (One day in the life of Ivan Denisovich), St. Petersburg: Azbuka-klassika, 2001: 56–57.

106. Teplyakov, "Po tu storonu."

107. Ibid.

108. Solzhenitsyn, *V kruge . . .*, 409.

109. Baklanov, "Vysota dikha," 9.

110. Solzhenitsyn, *V kruge . . .*, 405.

111. Baklanov, op. cit., 9.

112. Teplyakov, op. cit.

113. Ibid.

114. Ibid.

115. Ibid.

116. Philosopher V. Mezhuev's comments at a readers' conference, in I. Rishina and A. Egorov, "Lish tot dostoin zhizni i svobody . . . (Vasily Grossman. *Zhizn' i sud'ba*)." Chitatel'skaya konferentsiya "LG" (Only he deserves life and liberty [who every day goes to battle for them] [Vasily Grossman. *Life*

and Fate]. A readers' conference at Literaturnaya gazeta), Literaturnaya gazeta, August 24, 1988: 5.

117. Evgeny Evtushenko, "Sud'ba Platonova" (Platonov's fate), Sovetskaya kul'tura, August 20, 1988: 5.

118. Boris Vasiliev, "Na oborotnoy storone" (On the reverse side), Moskovskie novosti, May 13, 1990: 3.

119. Alexander Solzhenitsyn, V kruge pervom (In the first circle), Moscow: Act, 2006: 465.

120. Grossman, Zhizn' i sud'ba, 494.

CHAPTER 10. THE "IMMORAL" ECONOMY

1. Nikolai Shmelyov, "Libo sila, libo rubl'" (Either brute force or the ruble), Znamya, January 1989: 134.

2. Vasily Selyunin, "Radi konechnoy tseli" (For the final goal), in V. G. Kazakov, ed., Razvedka slovom, Moscow: Moskovskiy rabochiy, 1988: 38; and Vasily Selyunin, "Rynok: khimery i real'nost" (Market: chimeras and reality), Znamya, June 1990: 201.

3. Selyunin, "Radi . . . ," 41; Selyunin, "Rynok . . . ," 201; and Tatyana Koryagina, "Ya i my" (I and we), Literaturnaya gazeta, May 24, 1989: 12.

4. Gennady Lisichkin, "Mify i real'nost'" (Myths and reality), in Kh. Kobo, ed., Osmyslit' kul't Stalina (To think through Stalin's cult), Moscow: Progress, 1989: 264–65.

5. Ibid., 265.

6. Vasily Slyunin, "Planovaya anarkhiya ili balans interesov?" (Planned anarchy or a balance of interests?), Znamya, November 1989. See also Vasily Selyunin, "Revansh burokratii" (Bureaucracy's revanche), in Yuri Afanasiev, ed., Inogo ne dano (There is no other way), Moscow: Progress, 1988: 205.

7. Anatoly Strelyaniy, "Prikhod i raskhod" (Profit and expense), Znamya, June 1986: 181.

8. V. Andryushchyuk, "Samorazorenie" (Self-ruination), Komsomol'skaya pravda, April 11, 1989: 2.

9. Vasily Selyunin, "Istoki" (The sources), Novy mir, May 1988: 179.

10. Nikolai Shmelyov, "Libo sila, libo rubl'" (Either brute force or the ruble), Znamya, January 1989: 131.

11. Mikhail Kapustin, "Kamo gryadeshi?" (Whither art thou?), Oktyabr', August 1987: 162.

12. Mikhail Antonov, "Tak chto zhe s nami proiskhodit?" (What really is happening to us?), Oktyabr', August 1987: 48. The author cites a Pravda article as the source.

13. Vasily Selyunin, "Chyornye dyry ekonimki" (The black holes of the economy), Novy mir, October 1989: 168, and S. T. Melekhin, speech at the First Congress of People's Deputies, Izvestia, May 31, 1989: 6.

14. Boris Fyodorov, "Nash vnutrenniy dolg" (Our domestic debt), Moskovskie novosti, April 30, 1989: 10.

15. Shmelyov, "Libo sila . . . ," 137.
16. Nikolai Shmelyov, "Novye trevogi" (New concerns), *Novy mir,* April 1988: 172.
17. Ibid., and Andryushchyuk, "Samorazorenie," 2.
18. Anatoly Strelyaniy, "Prikhod i raskhod" (Profit and expense), *Znamya,* June 1986: 183.
19. See, for example, Antonov, "Tak chto zhe," 12; and Nikolai Popov and Nikolai Shmelyov, "Anatomiya defitsita" (The anatomy of shortages), *Znamya,* May 1988: 163.
20. Sergei Zalygin, "Nastupaem ili otstupaem?" (Advancing or retreating?), in Yuri Afanasiev, ed., *Inogo ne dano* (There is no other way), Moscow: Progress, 1988: 230.
21. Ibid.
22. Gennady Lisichkin, "Put' k rynku" (The road to market economy), *Moskovskie novosti,* July 31, 1988: 8.
23. Vasily Selyunin, "Chyornye dyry ekonimki" (The black holes of the economy), *Novy mir,* October 1989: 165, and Shmelyov, "Novye trevogi," 171.
24. Yuri Chernichenko, "O khlebe nasushchnom" (Of our daily bread), *Komsomol'skaya pravda,* March 12, 1989: 2.
25. Ibid.
26. Ibid.
27. Antonov, "Tak chto zhe . . . ," 9.
28. Ibid.
29. Oleg Volkov, "Iz redaktsionnoy pochty" (From the mail to the editorial offices), a letter to *Novy mir,* June 6, 1986: 262.
30. Ibid.
31. Ibid.
32. Ion Chobanu, "Garantiya—pravovoe gosudarstvo" (A state of laws is the guarantee), *Literaturnaya gazeta,* February 8, 1982: 3.
33. Anatoly Strelyaniy, "Prikhod i raskhod" (Profit and expense), *Znamya,* June 1986: 190.
34. Ibid.
35. Antonov, "Tak chto zhe . . . ," 44.
36. Nikolai Shmelyov, "Novye trevogi" (New concerns), *Novy mir,* April 1988: 167.
37. Nikolai Petrakov, "Dokhody i raskhody" (Incomes and expenses), *Sovetskaya kul'tura,* July 6, 1989: 6.
38. Yuri Chernichenko, "Zemlya, ekologiya, perestroika" (Land, ecology, perestroika), *Literaturnaya gazeta,* January 29, 1989: 3, and Yuri Chernichenko, "O khlebe nasushchnom" (Of our daily bread), *Komsomol'skaya pravda,* March 12, 1989: 2.
39. Nikolai Popov and Nikolai Shmelyov, "Anatomiya defitsita" (The anatomy of shortages), *Znamya,* May 1988: 159.
40. Ibid.
41. Ibid.

42. V. Yaroshenko. "'Printsy' i 'nishchie'" (The "princes" and the "paupers"), *Pravda,* October 12, 1988: 2.

43. Alexander Bovin, "Bol'she posledovatel'nosti!" (More consistency!), *Moskovskie novosti,* January 1, 1989: 2; Andrei Nuykin, "Idealy ili interesy?" (Ideals or interests?), *Novy mir* 1, January 1988: 215.

44. Yaroshenko, op. cit.

45. Yaroshenko, op. cit., Bovin, op. cit.

46. Leonid Abalkin, "Kuda my idyom" (Where we are going), interview with *Novoe vremya,* no. 28, 1987: 3, and Strelyaniy, "Prikhod . . . ," 201.

47. Vasily Selyunin, "Chyornye dyry ekonimki" (The black holes of the economy), *Novy mir,* October 1989: 165; and Anatoly Strelyaniy, "Prikhod i raskhod" (Profit and expense), *Znamya,* June 1986: 183.

48. Valery Vyzhutovich, "Vlast' rublya" (The power of the ruble), *Ogonyok* 44, 1987: 6, and Antonov, "Tak chto zhe . . . ," 43.

49. Vasily Selyunin and Grigory Khanin, "Lukavaya tsifra" (The cunning figure), *Novy mir,* February 1987: 199; and Ivan S. Silaev (deputy chairman, Council of Ministers of the USSR, and chairman, Machine Building Bureau, Council of Ministers) "Trebuyutsya idei" (Ideas are needed), interview in *Ogonyok* 48, 1987: 2.

50. Andryushchyuk, "Samorazorenie," 2.

51. Ibid.

52. Evgeny Starikov, "Marginaly" (The marginal people), *Znamya,* October 1989: 149; Nikolai Popov and Nikolai Shmelyov, "Anatomiya defitsita" (The anatomy of shortages), *Znamya,* May 1988: 169; and Silaev, "Trebuyutsya . . . ," 2.

53. Selyunin and Khanin, "Lukavaya tsifra," 199.

54. Vasily Selyunin, "Chyornye dyry ekonimki" (The black holes of the economy), *Novy mir,* October 1989: 164; and Nikolai Popov and Nikolai Shmelyov, "Anatomiya defitsita" (The anatomy of shortages), *Znamya,* May 1988: 169.

55. Yuri Chernichenko, "Kombayn prosit i kolotit" (A harvester begs and beats), *Novy mir,* December 1986: 193; Popov and Shmelyov, "Anatomiya . . . ," 164; Chernichenko, "Zemlya, ekologiya . . . ," Selyunin, "Chyornye dyry . . . ," 161; and Chernichenko, "O khlebe . . ."

56. Selyunin, "Istoki," 179.

57. Ibid.

58. Cherninchenko, "Kombayn . . . ," 193, Selyunin "Revansh burokratii" (Bureaucracy's revanche), in Yuri Afanasiev, ed., *Inogo ne dano* (There is no other way), Moscow: Progress, 1988: 198; Selyunin, "Chyornye dyry . . . ," 173.

59. Popov and Shmelyov, "Anatomiya . . . ," 164.

60. Ibid.

61. Selyunin, "Revansh burokratii," 198.

62. S. Men'shikov, "Ekonomicheskaya struktura sotsializma: chto vperedi?" (The economic structure of socialism: what is ahead?), *Novy mir,* March 1989: 196.

63. Nikolay Shmelyov, "Ostorozhno, tseny!" (Careful: Prices!), interviewed by Viktor Loshak, *Moskovskie novosti*, December 11, 1988: 10; Chernichenko, "O khlebe . . ."

64. Shmelyov, "Novye trevogi," 172.

65. Tatiana Zaslavskaya, "Chelovecheskiy faktor razvitiya ekonomiki i sotsial'naya spravedlivost' " (The human factor in the development of economy and social justice), *Kommunist* 13, 1986: 63.

66. Petrakov, "Dokhody . . ."

67. Abel Aganbegyan, "Chelovek i ekonomika" (Man and economy), *Ogonyok* 30, 1987: 15.

68. Ibid. and Igor Klyamkin, "Pochemu trudno govorit' pravdu" (Why it is difficult to speak truth), *Novy mir*, February, 1989: 235.

69. Zaslavskaya, op. cit., 64.

70. Shmelyov, "Novye trevogi," 173; and Nikolay Shmelyov in Nikolay Shmelyov and Fyodor Burlatsky, "Chto zhe dal'she?" (What next?), a dialogue in *Literaturnaya gazeta*, July 18, 1990: 3.

71. The "Total of Economically Active Population" of the Soviet Union in 1987 was estimated to be 142,027 million by the Statistics Division of the UN Food and Agriculture Organization. (http://faostat.fao.org/site/550/DesktopDfault .aspz?PageID=550. Accessed on December 18, 2008.)

72. Vasily Selyunin: "Istoki" (The sources), *Novy mir*, May 1988: 188, and Shmelyov, "Libo sila . . . ," 134.

73. Gennady Lisichkin, "S toskoy o 'ravenstve' " (With the dream of equality), iIn V. G. Kazakov, ed., *Razvedka slovom*, Moscow: Moskovskiy rabochiy, 1988: 10.

74. Ibid., 9.

75. Ibid.

76. Ibid.

77. Ibid., 10.

78. Larisa Piyasheva, "V pogone za Siney ptitsey" (Chasing the blue bird [of happiness]), *Oktyabr'*, September 1990: 153.

79. Mikhail Antonov, "Tak chto zhe s nami proiskhodit?" (What really is happening to us?), *Oktyabr'*, August 1987: 44.

80. Ibid., 57.

81. Ibid., and the Statistics Division of the UN Food and Agriculture Organization. (http://faostat.fao.org/site/550/DesktopDfault.aspz?PageID=550. Accessed on December 18, 2008.)

82. Andrey Nuykin, "O tsene slova i tsenakh na produkty" (On the value of word and food prices), *Ogonyok* 22, 1988: 8.

83. Mikhail Antonov, "Tak chto zhe s nami proiskhodit?" (What really is happening to us?), *Oktyabr'*, August 1987: 32.

84. Abel Aganbegyan, "Chelovek i ekonomika" (Man and economy), part 1: *Ogonyok* 29, 1987: 4, and Nuykin, "O tsene . . . ," 6.

85. Shmelyov, "Novye trevogi," 171.

86. Nuykin, op. cit., 7, and Abel Aganbegyan, "Chelovek i ekonomika" (Man and economy), part 1: *Ogonyok* 29, 1987: 4.

87. Shmelyov, "Libo sila . . . ," 138.

88. Lisichkin, "Put' . . ."

89. Shmelyov, "Libo sila . . . ," 132, and Nikolai Petrakov, "Tovar i rynok" (Goods and market), *Ogonyok* 34, 1988: 7.

90. Vyzhutovich, "Vlast' . . . ," 6.

91. Ibid.

92. Ibid.

93. Ibid.

94. Strelyaniy, "Dokhod . . . ," 193.

95. Ibid.

96. Ibid. and Aganbegyan, "Chelovek i ekonomika" (Man and economy), part 1: *Ogonyok* 29, 1987: 5.

97. Ibid.

98. "Vremya vybora" (A time of choice), *Sovetskaya kul'tura*, November 11, 1989: 3.

99. Pavel Bunich, "Novye tsennosti" (New values), *Oktyabr'*, December 1987: 145.

100. Ibid.

101. Men'shikov, "Ekonomicheskaya structura," 198.

102. Petrakov, "Goods . . . ," 34.

103. Nikolai Popov and Nikolai Shmelyov, "Anatomiya defitsita" (The anatomy of shortages), *Znamya*, May 1988: 172.

104. Ibid.

105. Ibid., 166.

106. Yuri Chernicheko, "Zhdat' uzhe pozdno" (It is already too late to wait), *Ogonyok* 23, 1989: 4.

107. Ibid.

108. Ibid., 172.

109. Ibid.

110. Ibid.

CHAPTER 11. THE "DISINTEGRATION OF SOULS"

1. Anatoly Strelyaniy, "Prikhod i raskhod" (Profit and expense): 185.

2. See, for example, Max Weber, *From Max Weber: Essays in Sociology*, H. H. Gerth and C. Wright Mills, eds., New York: Oxford University Press: 1978: 59–60, and Max Weber, *Max Weber: The Theory of Social and Economic Organization*, Talcott Parsons, ed., New York: Free Press, 1964: 89, 92, 110.

3. Alexander Zinoviev, *Homo Sovieticus*, New York: Atlantic Monthly Press, 1985.

4. V. Andryushchyuk, "Samorazorenie" (Self-ruination), *Komsomol'skaya Pravda*, April 11, 1989: 2.

5. Shemlyov, "Libo sila . . . ," 135, Nikolai Shmelyov, "Novye trevogi" (New concerns), *Novy mir*, April 1988: 175; and Nikolai Shmelyov, "Vyiti iz tumana predrassudkov" (To exit from the fog of superstitions), *Literaturnaya gazeta*, July 8, 1987: 3.

6. Yuri Ryzhov, "Vremya vybora" (A time of choice), *Sovetskaya kul'tura*, November 11, 1989: 3.

7. Stanislav Kalinichev, "Vsegda odna" (Always one), *Ogonyok* 52, 1987: 2.

8. Nikolai Shmelyov, Novye trevogi" (New concerns), *Novy mir*, April 1988: 164.

9. Len Karpinsky, "Pochemu stalinizm ne skhodit so stseny?" (Why won't Stalinism leave the stage?), in Yuri N. Afanasiev, ed., *Inogo ne dano* (There is no other way), Moscow: Progress, 1988: 650, and Leonid Nikitinskiy, "Rozhdaetsya pravo" (Legality is being born), *Komsomol'skaya pravda*, June 27, 1989: 1.

10. L. Gol'din, "Nado snova nauchit'sya zhit' "(We have to relearn to live), *Sovetskaya kul'tura*, August 29, 1989: 3.

11. Stanislav Govorukhin, "Voyna s prestupnost'yu" (The war on crime), *Sovetskaya kul'tura*, July 29, 1989: 6.

12. Shmelyov, "Vyiti iz tumana . . ."

13. Ibid.

14. Vasiliy Selyunin, "Planovaya anarkhiya ili balans interesov?" (Planned anarchy or a balance of interests?), *Znamya*, November 1989: 213.

15. Pavel Bunich, "Novye tsennosti" (New values), *Oktyabr'*, December 1987: 145, and L. V. Skvortsov, "Kul'tura samosoznaniya i formirovanie novogo gumanizma" (The culture of self-consciousness and the formation of a new humanism), in M. I. Melkumyan, ed., *Drama obnovleniya* (The drama of renewal), Moscow: Progress: 1990: 532, and Maya Ganina, "Tsena El'dorado" (The price of El Dorado), *Literaturnaya gazeta*, February 22, 1989: 11, and, also by Ganina, "Bez obol'shcheniy prezhnikh dney" (Without the delusions of bygone days), *Literaturnaya gazeta*, January 13, 1988: 11.

16. Selyunin, "Planovaya anarkhiya . . . ," 213.

17. Leonid Zhukhovitskiy, "Chto pochyom?" (What is the price of this and that?), *Ogonyok* 39, 1988: 5.

18. Bunich, "Novye tsennosti," 144.

19. Inna Kosheleva, "Nachal'niki moi i ne moi" (My bosses and not mine), *Novy mir*, September 1987: 195.

20. Nikolai Shmelyov: "Libo sila, libo rubl'" (Either brute force or the ruble), *Znamya*, January 1989: 135.

21. Kirill Lavrov, "U kul'tury net zameny" (There is no substitute for culture), *Izvestia*, June 29, 1989: 4.

22. "Bunich, "Novye . . . ," 145, Alexander Tsypko "Istoki Stalinisma" (The origins of Stalinism) *Nauka i zhizn'*, part 3, February 1989: 59, and Igor Kon, "Psikhologiya sotsial'noy inertsii" (The psychology of social inertia), *Kommunist* 1, January 1988: 71.

23. Nikolai Shmelyov, "Libo sila, libo rubl'" (Either brute force or the ruble), *Znamya*, January 1989: 128.

24. Alexander Tsypko, "Istoki Stalinisma" (The origins of Stalinism), part 4, *Nauka i zhizn'*, February 1989: 56.

25. Leonid Abalkin, "Lunniy landshaft" (A Moon-like landscape), interview with *Komsomol'skaya pravda*, February 8, 1989: 2.

26. "Poryadok i poryadochnost'" (Order and decency), *Ogonyok* 3, 1987: 3.

27. Ibid.

28. Nikolai Shmelyov, "Ne smet' komandovat'!" (Stop giving orders!), *Oktyabr'*, February 1988: 25.

29. Anatoly Anan'ev, "Po techeniyu ili naperkor" (Going with the flow or against it), *Oktyabr'*, October 1989: 6.

30. Lavrov, "U kul'tury . . ." and Alexei Kiva, "Krizis 'zhanra'" (The crisis of the "genre"), *Novy mir*, March 1990: 213.

31. A. Terekhov, "Strakh pered morozom" (The fear of frost), *Ogonyok* 19, 1988: 8.

32. Kon, "Psikhologiya . . . ," 71.

33. "Velikiy russkiy intelligent: Pamyati Andreya Dmitrievicha Sakharova" (The great man of the Russian intelligentsia: In memory of Andrei Dmitrievich Sakharov), *Oktyabr'*, January 1990: 3.

34. Terekhov, op. cit., 8.

35. Daniil Granin, "Doroga k zdravomu smyslu" (A road to common sense), *Pravda*, August 5, 1988: 3.

36. Ganina, "Bez obol'shcheniy . . ." and "Tsena . . ."

37. Ibid.

38. Yuri Nagibin, "O tom, chto trevozhit—v literature i zhizni" (About that which troubles—in literature and in life), *Oktyabr'*, February 1988: 194.

39. Alexander Tsypko, "Khoroshi li nashi printsipy?" (How good are our principles?), *Novy mir*, April, 1990: 184.

40. Nikolai Ryzhkov, *Perestroika: Istoriya predatel'stv* (Perestroika: the history of betrayals). Moscow: Novosti, 1992: 94.

41. Oksana Dmitrieva, "Ekspertiza" (Expertise), *Moskovskie novosti*, February 15, 2000. http://dlib.eastview.com/sources/article.jsp?id=137994. Accessed on July 17, 2007.

42. Nagibin, op. cit.

43. Evgeny Starikov, "Marginaly" (The marginal people), *Znamya*, October 1989: 156.

44. Yuri Levada, ed., *Est' mnenie!* (I have an opinion!), Moscow: Progress, 1990: 258.

45. Levada, *Est'* . . . , 281.

46. Andrei Popov, "Kogda vybora net" (When there is no choice), *Ogonyok* 33, 1988: 19.

47. Ibid.

48. Ibid.

49. Ibid.

50. Vasily Grossman, *Zhizn' i sud'ba* (Life and fate), Moscow: Knizhnaya palata, 1989: 474. Translated by Leon Aron.

51. Yuri Karyakin, "Stoit li nastupat' na grabli? (Do we really want to step on a rake?), *Znamya* 9, September 1987: 220, and Govorukhin, "Voyna . . ."

52. N. Loginova, "Unyat' strakhi" (To overcome fear), *Literaturnaya gazeta*, October 5, 1988: 12.

53. Ganina, "Tsena . . ."
54. Karpinsky, "Pochemu . . . ," 650.
55. Robert Rozhdestvensky, "Short Poems," *Literaturnaya gazeta*, March 1, 1989: 5.
56. Ganina, "Tsena . . ."
57. Ibid.
58. Levada, op. cit., 261.
59. M. Mel'nik, "Sluchay v spetsvagone" (An incident in a special car), *Komsomol'skaya pravda*, July 29, 1988: 2.
60. G. Matyukhina, G. Grazhdankin, A. Levinson, and L. Sedov, "Rekord uk-hodyashchego goda?" (The expiring year's record?), *Komsomol'skaya pravda*, December 29, 1988: 2. For yet another tale of abuse and humiliation, see Terekhov, "Strakh . . . ," 8.
61. Anatoly Anan'ev, "Po techeniyu ili naperkor" (Going with the flow or against it), *Oktyabr'*, October 1989: 3.
62. Stepan Filippovich Yakubov in "O vremeni, kotoroe vypalo na nashu dolyu . . ." (About the times we have been destined to live in . . .), a collection of readers' letters, *Komsomol'skaya pravda*, January 25, 1989: 2.

CHAPTER 12. THE HOUSE THAT STALIN BUILT

1. Evgeny Starikov, "Marginaly" (The marginal people), *Znamya*, October 1989: 136; Len Karpinsky, "Pochemu stalinizm ne skhodit so stseny?" (Why won't Stalinism leave the stage?), in Yuri N. Afanasiev, ed., *Inogo ne dano* (There is no other way), Moscow: Progress, 1988: 649; Mikhail Kapustin, "Kamo gryadeshi?" (Whither art thou?), *Oktyabr'*, August 1987: 155; Shubkin, "Trudnoe proshchanie," 176; Migranyan, "Dolgiy . . . ," 174.
2. A. Kovalenko, "My vse shli k Chernobylyu" (We all were approaching Chernobyl), *Argumenty i fakty*, July 15–21, 1989: 6 (the "administrative-bureaucratic system"); Alexei Kiva, "Bezotvetsvennost'" (Irresponsibility), *Sovetskaya kul'tura*, October 12, 1989: 3, and Alexander Bovin, "Kak communist, schitayu . . ." (As a Communist, I think . . .), *Moskovskie novosti*, April 30, 1989: 6 (the "barrack socialism"); Fyodor Burlatsky, "Pervyi, no vazhnyi shag" (The first, but important step), *Literaturnaya gazeta*, June 14, 1989: 1; A. Butenko, "O revolyutsionnoy perestroike gosudarstvenno-administrativnogo sotsializma" (On the revolutionary restructuring of the state-administrative socialism), in Yuri Afanasiev, ed., *Inogo ne dano* (There is no other way), Moscow: Progress, 1988: 553 (the "state-bureaucratic socialism"); Fyodor Burlatsky, "Kakoy sotsializm narodu nuzhen" (Socialism that people want), *Literaturnaya gazeta*, April 26, 1988: 2 ("state socialism"); Klyamkin, "Pochemu . . . ," 208, A. Blyudin, "Kommunizm: mezhdu proshlym i budyshchim" (Communism: between past and future), *Komsomol'skaya pravda*, March 27, 1989: 3, and L. Gozman and A. Etkind, "Kul't vlasti: Struktura totalitarnogo soznaniya (The cult of power: The structure of totalitarian consciousness," in Kh. Kobo, ed., *Osmyslit' kul't Stalina* (To comprehend Stalin's cult), Moscow: Progress, 1989:

338 (the "totalitarian regime" and "totalitarian, anti-democratic regime"); and Andranik Migranyan, "Dolgiy put' k evropeyskomu domu" (A long road to the European home), *Novy mir,* July 1989: 170.

3. Grossman, *Vsyo techyot,* 91.

4. V. Radaev and O. Shkaratan, "Vozvrashchenie k istokam" (The return to the sources), *Izvestia,* February 16, 1990: 3.

5. Batkin, "Vozobnovlenie . . . ," 160, and Evgeny Evtushenko, "Stalinizm po Platonovu" (Stalinism according to Platonov), in Kh. Kobo, ed., *Osmyslit'* . . . , 200.

6. Gozman and Etkind, "Kul't vlasti," 338.

7. Kh. Kobo, ed., *Osmyslit' kul't Stalina,* "Ot izdatel'stva" ("From the publisher" Introduction): 6.

8. O. Shkaratan, "Vremya vybora puti" (The time to choose the way), *Sovetskaya kul'tura,* September 19, 1989: 3.

9. Gozman and Etkind, "Kul't vlasti," 342.

10. Ibid., 338.

11. Kondrashov, "Iz mraka . . . ," 183, and Batkin, "Vozobnovlenie . . . , 160.

12. Batkin, "Vozobnovlenie . . . ," 160, and Karpinsky, "Pochemu . . . ," 649.

13. Karpinsky, "Pochemu . . . ," 649.

14. Vinogradov, "Mozhet li pravda," 248.

15. Blyudin, "Kommunizm."

16. Nikoloi Shmelyov, "Libo sila, libo rubl' " (Either brute force or the ruble), *Znamya,* January 1989: 132.

17. Vinogradov, "Mozhet li pravda," 277; Yuri Burtin, "Chto takoe KPSS" (What is CPSU), *Oktyabr',* May 1991: 170–71; Blyudin, "Kommunizm."

18. G. Vodolazov, "Lenin i Stalin" (Lenin and Stalin), *Oktyabr',* June 1989: 23; Andranik Migranyan, "Mekhanizm tormozheniya v politicheskoy systeme i puti ego preodoleniya" (The breaking mechanism in the political system and the ways to overcome it), in Yuri. Afanasiev, ed., *Inogo ne dano* (There is no other way), Moscow: Progress, 1988: 107.

19. Shubkin, "Trudnoe proshchanie, 170.

20. Ibid.

21. Ibid.

22. Burtin, "Chto takoe . . . ," 171; Blyudin, "Kommunizm"; Shubkin, "Trudnoe proshchanie," 169.

23. Gozman and Etkind, "Kul't vlasti," 339.

24. Blyudin, "Kommunizm."

25. Shubkin, "Trudnoe proshchanie," 169 and 165; G. Vodolazov, "Lenin i Stalin: Filosofsko-sotsiologicheskiy kommentariy k povesti V. Grossmana 'Vsyo techyot' (Lenin and Stalin: Philosophical and sociological commentary to V. Grossman's novella "Forever flowing"), in Yuri Afanasiev, ed., *Inogo ne dano* (There is no other way), Moscow: Progress, 1988: 142.

26. Shubkin, "Trudnoe proshchanie," 170.

27. Yuri Vlasov, speech at the First Congress of People's Deputies of the USSR, in "S'ezd Narodnykh Deputatov SSSR," transcript, *Izvestia,* June 2, 1989: 4.

28. Grossman, *Zhizn' i sud'ba*, 304–5, 301.

29. Fyodor Burlatsky, "K sovremennoy tsivilizatsii" (Toward the modern civiliza-tion), *Literaturnaya gazeta*, September 5, 1990: 2.

30. B. Nazarov, "Chelovek—eto zvuchit . . ." (Man—[a word] that resonates [proudly]), *Komsomol'skaya pravda*, March 23, 1990: 2; Vasily Selyunin, "Plano-vaya anarkhiya ili balans interesov?" (Planned anarchy or a balance of inter-ests?), *Znamya*, November 1989: 19; Gavriil Popov, speech at the First Congress of People's Deputies, *Izvestia*, June 11, 1989: 3; Bovin, "Pravda . . . ," 524; Klyamkin, "Pochemu . . . ," 231.

31. Len Karpinsky, "Pochemu stalinizm ne skhodit so stseny?" (Why won't Stalin-ism leave the stage?), in Yuri N. Afanasiev, ed., *Inogo ne dano* (There is no other way), Moscow: Progress, 1988: 648.

32. Starikov, "Marginaly," 136; V. Radaev and O. Shkaratan, "Vozvrashchenie k is-tokam" (The return to the sources), *Izvestia*, February 16, 1990: 3; Nazarov, "Chelovek . . ."

33. See, for example, Alexander Bovin, "Perestroika: pravda o sotsializme i sud'ba sotsializma" (The truth about socialism and the fate of socialism), in Yuri Afa-nasiev, ed., *Inogo ne dano* (There is no other way), Moscow: Progress, 1988: 532.

34. Selyunin, "Planovaya anarkhiya . . . ," 206; Klyamkin, "Pochemu . . . ," 232.

35. Radaev and Shkaratan, "Vozvrashchenie . . ."; Burlatskiy, "Kakoy sotsial-izm . . ."; and Larisa Piyasheva, "Kontury sotsial'noy reformy" (The outlines of the social reform"), in F. M. Borodkin, L. Ya. Kosals and P. V. Ryvkina, *Postizhenie*, (Attainment of truth), Moscow: Progress, 1989: 278.

36. Selyunin, "Revansh burokratii" (Bureaucracy's *revanche*), in Yuri Afanasiev, ed., *Inogo ne dano*, 206.

37. Ibid.

38. V. Popov and N. Shmelyov, "Anatomiya defitsita" (The anatomy of shortages), *Znamya*, May 1988: 159; Andrei Nuykin: "Idealy ili interesy?" (Ideals or inter-ests?), *Novy Mir* 1, January 1988: 198.

39. A. Nekipelov, "Est' li svet v kontse tunnelya? (O sovremennom krizise eko-nomicheskoy teorii sotsializma) (Is there the light at the end of the tunnel? On the current crisis in the economic theory of socialism), in M. I. Melku-myan, ed., *Drama obnovleniya* (The drama of renewal), Moscow: Progress, 1990: 602; Alexey Kiva, "Krizis 'zhanra' " (The crisis of the "genre"), *Novy Mir*, March 1990: 210.

40. Nikolai Shmelyov, "Iz dokladnykh zapisok ekonomista" (From economist's memoranda), *Znamya*, December 1989: 173; V. Popov and N. Shmelyov, "Na razvilke dorog" (At a crossroad), in Kh. Kobo, ed., *Osmyslit' kul't Stalina* (To think through Stalin's cult), Moscow: Progress, 1989: 290.

41. Popov and Shmelyov, "Na razvilke dorog," 290.

42. Ibid., 295.

43. Boris Pinsker and Larisa Piyasheva, "Sobstvennost' i svoboda" (Property and liberty), *Novy mir*, November 1989: 190.

44. Nuykin, "Idealy ili . . . ," 198.

45. A. Kovalenko, "My vse shli k Chernobylyu" (We all were approaching Chernobyl), *Argumenty i fakty*, July 15–21, 1989: 6; "Zemlya, ekologiya, perestroika" (Land, ecology, perestroika), *Literaturnaya gazeta*, January 29, 1989: 3; Selyunin, "Planovaya anarkhiya . . . ," 216, 218.
46. A. Lapin, "Korruptsiya" (Corruption), *Komsomol'skaya pravda*, December 21, 1989: 4.
47. Nikolai Shmelyov, "Novye trevogi" (New concerns), *Novy mir*, April 1988: 168.
48. A. Matlin, "Patologiya defitsita: gosudarstvo i naselenie" (The deficit pathology: the state and the people), in M. I. Melkumian, *Drama obnoveleniya* (The drama of renewal), Moscow: Progress, 1990: 620.
49. Yuri Chernichenko, "Zhurnalist" (Journalist), *Znamya*, July 1987: 218.
50. Vladimir Kantor, "Trudnyi put' k tsivilizatsii" (A difficult road to civilization), *Novy mir*, June 1987: 255. Yet another version of the Chernyshevsky adage read: "How could you wish to find energy at work in the very same man who has been trained not to show it in defending himself against oppression?" (Sergei Yakovlev, "Osobaya prichina" [A special reason], *Novy mir*, September 1989: 263.)
51. Vyacheslav Kostikov, "Vremay ottayavshikh slov" (A time of thawed-out words), *Ogonyok* 22, 1989: 5.
52. Evgeny Evtushenko, "Stalinizm po Platonovu" (Stalinism according to Platonov), in Kh. Kobo, ed., *Osmyslit' kul't Stalina* (To comprehend Stalin's cult), Moscow: Progress, 1989: 204.
53. Klyamkin, "Pochemu . . . ," 224.
54. Ibid.
55. Ibid.
56. Alexander Tsypko, "Khoroshi li nashi printsipy?" (How good are our principles?), *Novy mir*, April, 1990: 202.
57. Blyudin, "Kommunizm," and Alexander M. Yakovlev, "Otverzhenie i utverzhdenie" (Rejection and affirmation), *Ogonyok* 43, 1988: 15.
58. Vasily Selyunin, "Chyornye dyry ekonimki" (The black holes of the economy), *Novy mir*, October 1989: 176.
59. Starikov, "Marginaly," 150.
60. Matlin, "Patologiya . . . ," 620.
61. Kiva, "Bezotvetsvennost'" (Irresponsibility), *Sovetskaya kul'tura*, October 12, 1989: 3; Blyudin, "Kommunizm."
62. Nuykin, "Idealy ili . . . ," 218.
63. Shmelyov, "Novye . . . ," 164.
64. S. Men'shikov, "Ekonomicheskaya struktura sotsializma: chto vperedi?" (The economic structure of socialism: what is ahead?), *Novy mir*, March 1989: 195; Selyunin, "Rynok . . . ," 204.
65. Pavel Bunich. "Tsar', kotoriy pravit" (The czar who rules), *Literaturnaya gazeta*, November 7, 1990: 10.
66. Selyunin, "Rynok . . . ," 204.
67. Ibid

68. Burtin, "Chto takoe . . . ," 171.
69. Blyudin, "Kommunizm"; Mikhail Kapustin, "Kamo gryadeshi?" (Whither art thou?), *Oktyabr'*, August 1987: 163, 162; Selyunin, "Rynok . . . ," 204.
70. Kaputsin, "Kamo . . . ," 163; Nuykin, "Idealy . . . ," 209.
71. Selyunin, "Chyornye . . . ," 171.
72. Starikov, "Marginaly," 137.
73. Men'shikov, "Ekonomicheskaya struktura . . . ," 195.
74. V. Popov and N. Shmelyov, "Na razvilke dorog" (At a crossroad), in Kh. Kobo, ed., *Osmyslit' kul't Stalina* (To think through Stalin's cult), Moscow: Progress, 1989: 319.
75. Shmelyov, "Libo sila . . . ," 130–31.
76. Gennady Lisichkin, "Mify i real'nost'" (Myths and reality), in Kh. Kobo, ed., *Osmyslit' kul't Stalina* (To think through Stalin's cult), Moscow: Progress, 1989: 268.
77. Grossman, *Vsyo techoyt*, 87 and Grossman, *Zhizn'*, 211.
78. Grossman, *Zhizn' i sud'ba*, 211.
79. Kondrashov, "Iz mraka . . . ," 185.
80. Shmelyov, "Libo sila . . . ," 130.
81. Selyunin, "Planovaya anarkhiya . . . ," 212.
82. M. I. Melkumyan, "Sotsial'nye utopii and deystvitel'nost'," (The social utopias and reality), in M. I. Melkumyan, ed., *Drama obnovleniya* (The drama of renewal), Moscow: Progress, 1990: 255.
83. Igor Klyamikin, *Trudniy spusk s ziyayushchikh vysot* (The difficult descent from the yawning heights), Moscow: Pravda/Biblioteka Ogon'ka, 1990: 4; Alexander Tsypko, "Khoroshi li nashi printsipy?" (How good are our principles?), *Novy mir*, April 1990: 174; Sergei Alexeev, "Ploshchad' pered parlamentom" (The square in front of the parliament), *Komsomol'skaya pravda*, July 11, 1989: 2.
84. A. Butenko, "Kakim byt' sotsializmu" (What socialism should be), *Pravda*, August 8, 1989: 3; Klyamkin, 'Kakaya ulitsa . . . ," 154; Vladimir Rubanov, "Demokratiya i besopasnost' strany" (Democracy and the country's security), *Kommunist*, 11 (July), 1989: 50.
85. Viktor Krivorotov, "Russkiy put'" (The Russian path), *Znamya*, September, 1990: 149.
86. Stanislav Kondrashov, "Yasnovidenie gumanista" (One humanist's clairvoyance), *Moskovskie novosti*, August 27, 1989: 11.
87. Ibid., 150.
88. Alexander M. Yakovlev, "Otverzhenie i utverzhdenie" (Rejection and affirmation), *Ogonyok* 43, 1988: 15. The author, interviewed by the magazine, was a professor at the Institute of State and Law in Moscow.
89. Ibid.
90. Ibid., 14.
91. Selyunin, "Planovaya anarkhiya . . . ," 206.
92. Ibid.

93. Butenko, op. cit.

94. Pinsker and Piyasheva, "Sobstvennost' . . . ," 197; Tsypko, "Khoroshi li . . . ," 174.

95. Tsypko, "Khoroshi li . . . ," 174.

96. Starikov, "Marginaly," 137.

97. Burtin, "Cho takoe . . . ," 177.

98. Ibid.

CHAPTER 13. "DE-INDIVIDUALIZATION," THE "ORIGINAL SIN,"
AND THE NATIONALIZATION OF CONSCIENCE

1. Igor Kon, "Psikhologiya sotsial'noy inertsii" (The psychology of social inertia), *Kommunist*, January, 1988: 65, 66.

2. Alexei Kiva, "Bezotvetsvennost' " (Irresponsibility), *Sovetskaya kul'tura*, October 12, 1989: 3.

3. Vladimir Shubkin, "Trudnoe proshchanie" (The difficult farewell), *Novy mir*, April 1989: 181.

4. Ibid., 173.

5. A. M. Yakovlev, "Otverzhenie . . . ," 15.

6. Daniil Granin, "Doroga k zdravomu smyslu" (A road to common sense), *Pravda*, August 5, 1988: 3.

7. Yuri Chernichenko, "Delo zavmaga Siddikova" (The case of the store manager Siddikov). *Druzhba narodov*, August 1986: 182.

8. Chernichenko, "Delo . . . ," 181.

9. S. Inozemtsev, a letter to the editor, in "Prostye lyudi" (The ordinary people), *Komsomol'skaya pravda*, March 25, 1989: 2.

10. Yuri Feofanov, "Vozvrashchenie k istokam" (The return to the sources), *Znamya*, February 1989: 150.

11. Zh. T. Toshchenko, "Zastoy dukha i ego preodolenie" (The stagnation of spirit and how to overcome it), in M. I. Melkumian, *Drama obnoveleniya* (The drama of renewal), Moscow: Progress, 1990: 575.

12. Starikov, "Marginaly," 225; Toshchenko, "Zastoy . . . ," 575.

13. Migranyan, "Dolgiy . . . ," 168.

14. Shubkin, "Trudnoe proshchanie," 177; Mikhail Kapustin, "Kamo gryadeshi?" (Whither art thou?), *Oktyabr'*, August 1987: 155.

15. Larisa Piyasheva, "V pogone za Siney Ptitsey" (Chasing the blue bird [of happiness]), *Oktyabr'*, September 1990: 150.

16. Ibid.

17. Alexander Tsypko, "Istoki Stalinisma" (The origins of Stalinism), part 3, *Nauka i zhizn'*, January 1989: 53.

18. Anatoly Bocharov, "Mchatsya mify, b'yutsya mify" (Myths are whirling, myths are stirring), *Oktyabr'*, January 1990: 187; E. Starikova, "Kniga o dobre i zle, ili smert' Ivana Il'icha" (A book about good and evil, or the death of Ivan Il'ich), *Novy mir*, December, 1987: 223. Alexander Tsypko, "Khoroshi li nashi printsipy?" (How good are our principles?), *Novy mir*, April, 1990: 201.

19. Yulia Latynina, V ozhidanii Zolotogo veka" (Waiting for the Golden Age), *Oktyabr'*, June 1987: 180, 181.

20. Ibid.

21. Alexander Tsypko, "Istoki Stalinisma" (The origins of Stalinism), part 3, *Nauka i zhizn'*, January 1989: 49.

22. Sergey Zalygin, "God Solzhenitsyna" (The year of Solzhenitsyn), *Novy mir* 1, January 1990: 238.

23. Klyamkin, "Pochemu . . . ," 229, 230.

24. Ibid., 229.

25. Anatoly Bocharov, "Chast' pravdy—eto ne pravda . . ." (Partial truth is not truth), *Oktyabr'*, April 1988: 147.

26. Lazar' Lazarev, "Dukh svobody" (The spirit of freedom), *Znamya*, September 1988: 224.

27. Grossman, *Zhizn' i sud'ba*, 399.

28. Lazarev, "Dukh svobody," 226; Pavel Voshchanov, "Zloba i zavist' obrekayut nas na bednost' " (Spite and envy doom us to penury), *Komsomol'skaya pravda*, December 2, 1989: 2.

29. Burtin, "Chto takoe," 177; Grossman, *Vsyo techoyt*, 94.

30. Grossman, *Vsyo techoyt*, 94.

31. Ibid., 90, 109.

32. *Zhizn' i sud'ba*, 144.

33. Ibid., 105.

34. Ibid., 62.

35. Piyashva, "V pogone . . . ," 157.

36. P. Gal'tseva and I. Rodnyanskaya, "Pomekha—chelovek" (Man is the problem), *Novy mir* 12 (December), 1988: 219.

37. Bovin, "Kak communist . . ."

38. Grossman, *Vsyo techoyt*, 98.

39. Viktor Krivorotov, "Russkiy put' " (The Russian path), *Znamya*, September, 1990: 189.

40. Feofanov, "Vozvrashchenie . . ."; Shubkin, "Trudnoe proshchanie," 197.

41. As quoted in Nikolai Bykov, "Pryamaya rech" (Direct speech), *Ogonyok* 33, 1987: 19.

42. Klyamkin, "Pochemu . . . ," 210.

43. Ibid.

44. Kiva, "Bezotvetsvennost' "; L. Gozman and A. Etkind, "Kul't vlasti: Struktura totalitarnogo soznaniya" (The cult of power: The structure of totalitarian consciousness), in Kh. Kobo, ed., *Osmyslit' kul't Stalina* (To comprehend Stalin's cult), Moscow: Progress, 1989: 352.

45. Gozman and Etkind, "Kul't vlasti."

46. Evgeny Starikov, "Pered vyoborom" (Forced to choose), *Znamya*, May 1991: 227; Georgy Gachev, Arsenal dobroy voli (The stockpile of goodwill), *Oktyabr'*, August 1987: 190.

47. Starikov, "Pered . . . ," 226.

48. Yuri Karyakin, "Zhdanovskaya zhidkost'" (Zhdanov's liquid), in Yuri N. Afanasiev, ed., *Inogo ne dano* (There is no other way), Moscow: Progress, 1988: 417; Grossman, *Zhizn' i sud'ba*, 159.

49. G. Vodolozov, "Lenin i Stalin. Filosfsko-sotsiologicheskiy kommentariy k povesti V. Grossmana "Vsyo techyot" (Lenin and Stalin. A philosophical and sociological commentary on V. Grossman's novella *Forever Flowing*), in Kh. Kobo, ed., *Osmyslit' kul't Stalina* (To comprehend Stalin's cult), Moscow: Progress, 1989: 142; Igor Zolotusskiy, "Krushenie abstraktsiy" (The downfall of abstractions), *Novy mir*, January 1989: 246; Natal'ya Ivanova, "Proshchanie s utopiey" (A farewell to utopia), *Literaturnaya gazeta*, July 18, 1990: 4.

50. Alexei Zverev, "Bez starshego brata" (Without the Big Brother), *Novoe vremya*, 37, 1989: 40.

51. Selyunin, "Istoki," 170.

52. N. Zorkaya, "Dorogoy, kotoraya vedyot k khramu" (By the road that leads to the temple), *Iskusstvo kino* 5, 1987: 44.

53. Ibid., 48.

54. Benedikt Sarnov, "Skol'ko vesit nashe gosudarstvo?" in Kh. Kobo, ed., *Osmyslit' kul't Stalina* (To comprehend Stalin's cult), Moscow: Progress, 1989: 187; Vyacheslav Kostikov, "O 'Fenomene Lokhankina' i russkoy intelligentsii" (About the 'Lokhankin phenomenon' and the Russian intelligentsia), *Ogonyok* 49, 1988: 7.

55. Tsypko, "Khoroshi li . . . ," 203, 201; Shubkin, "Trudnoe proshchanie," 179; Vladimir Rubanov, "Demokratiya i besopasnost' strany" (Democracy and the country's security), *Kommunist* 11, July 1989: 47.

56. Tsypko, "Khoroshi li . . . ," 170, 180; P. Gurevich, "Kakaya ideologiya nam nuzhna?" (What ideology do we need?), *Literaturnaya gazeta*, March 14, 1990: 10; Tsypko, "Istoki stalinizma," part 4: 61; "Lyubi Rossiyu v nepogodu" (Love Russia in bad weather), *Izvestia*, January 17, 1989: 3.

57. As quoted in Shubkin, "Trudnoe proshchanie," 178–79, and Selyunin, "Planovaya anarkhiya ili balans interesov?" (Planned anarchy or a balance of interests?), *Znamya*, November 1989: 213. Central to the understanding of the moral underpinnings of Soviet state, this speech, "Zadachi soyuzov molodyozhi" (The tasks of the youth unions), at the Third All-Union Congress of the Russian Communist Union of Youth, October 2, 1920, is to be found in V. I. Lenin, *Polnoe sobranie sochineniy* (Collected Works), 5th ed., Moscow: Politicheskaya literatura, 1963: 309, 313.

58. Selyunin, "Planovaya anarkhiya . . . ," 213.

59. Stanislav Kondrashov, "Yasnovidenie gumanista" (One humanist's clairvoyance), *Moskovskie novosti*, August 27, 1989: 11.

60. Tsypko, "Khoroshi li . . . ," 178.

61. Klyamkin, "Pochemu . . . ," 230.

62. Alexander Shindel', "Svidetel'" (Witness), *Znamya*, September 1987: 211; Selyunin, "Planovaya anarkhiya . . . ," 214; Vladimir Lakshin, "Nravstvennost',

spravedlivost', gumanizm" (Morality, justice, humanism), *Kommunist* 10, 1989: 34.

63. Selyunin, "Planovaya anarkhiya . . . ," 214.

64. Shubkin, "Trudnoe proshchanie," 166, 170; Leonid Radzikhovsky, "1 dekabrya" (December 1), *Moskovskie novosti*, November 27 1988: 6.

65. Kondrashov, "Yasnovidenie . . ."

66. Inna Rudenko, "S voynoy pokonchili my schyoty?" (Have we settled our scores with the [Afghan] war?), *Komsomol'skaya pravda*, February 15, 1989: 1.

67. Yuri Karyakin, "Zhdanovskaya zhidkost'" (Zhdanov's liquid), in Yuri N. Afanasiev, ed., *Inogo ne dano* (There is no other way), Moscow: Progress, 1988: 417.

68. Ibid.

69. Alexander Tvardovsky, *Po pravu pamyati* (In memory's name), *Znamya*, February, 1987: 10.

70. Vasiliev, "Lyubi . . ."

71. Latynina, "V ozhidanii . . . ," 182.

72. Vasiliev, "Lyubi . . ."; Shubkin, "Trudnoe proshchanie," 178.

73. Shubkin, "Trudnoe proshchanie," 178.

74. Ibid., 176.

75. Ibid., 176–77.

76. Latynina, "V ozhidanii . . . ," 182.

77. Starikov, "Pered vyborom," 227.

78. Kostikov, "O fenomene . . . ," 7; Selyunin, "Planovaya anarkhiya . . . ," 213.

79. Grossman, *Vsyo techyot*, 40; Selyunin, "Planovaya anarkhiya . . . ," 213.

80. Alexander Yakovlev, "Pervaya barkhatnaya revolutsiya" (The first velvet revolution), *Novoe vremya* 11, 2005: 19.

81. Ibid.

CHAPTER 14. STALIN, MEMORY, REPENTANCE, ATONEMENT

1. Vitaly Korotich, "Uchimsya nazyvat' veshchi svoimi imenami" (We learn to call things by their right names), *Moskovskie novosti*, July 3, 1988: 15.

2. "Nedelya sovesti," (The week of conscience), no author, *Ogonyok* 49, 1988: 32.

3. Anatoly Rybakov, "Rana, kotoraya krovotochit" (The wound that is bleeding), *Moskovskie novosti*, November 27, 1988: 7.

4. Otto Latsis, "Stalin protiv Lenina" (Stalin against Lenin), in Kh. Kobo, ed., *Osmyslit' kul't Stalina* (To comprehend Stalin's cult), Moscow: Progress, 1989: 215.

5. Ibid.

6. Leonid Gozman, in "Bol'she sotsializma!" (More socialism!), a roundtable discussion, *Ogonyok* 14, 1988: 10.

7. Ludmila Saraskina, "Smotret' pravde v glaza" (To look the truth in the eye), *Moskovskie novosti*, April 10, 1988: 12.

8. Alexander Yakovlev, "Akty spravedlivosti i pokayaniya" (The acts of justice and repentance), a television address, August 20, 1990, in Alexander Yakovlev,

Muki prochteniya bytiya (The torments of reading life), Moscow: Novosti, 1991: 261.

9. Dmitry Kazutin, "Zhertvoyu pali" (Fallen a victim), *Moskovskie novosti*, November 27, 1988: 5; and Korotich, "Uchimsya . . ."

10. Alexander Tsypko, "Khoroshi li nashi printsipy?" (How good are our principles?), *Novy mir*, April 1990: 201.

11. Ibid.

12. Svyatoslav Fyodorov, "Chtoby nikogda ne povtorilos'!" (So as not to let it happen again!), *Ogonyok* 8, 1987: an insert between pp. 5 and 6.

13. Tatyana Ivanova, "Kto chem riskuet" (Who risks what), *Ogonyok* 24, 1988: 12.

14. Rybakov, "Rana, kotoraya krovotochit," 7; Ol'ga Nemirovskaya, "Nedelya sovesti" (The week of conscience), *Ogonyok* 49, 1888: 1.

15. Nemirovskaya, op. cit.

16. Rybakov, "Rana, kotoraya krovotochit," 7, and Tamara Sevko, a letter to the editor, published in *Pravdu i tol'ko pravdu* (Truth and only the truth), *Moskovskie novosti*, December 4, 1988: 9.

17. Anatoliy Rybakov, "S proshlym nado rasstavat'sya dostoyno" (Bidding farewell to the past must be done with dignity), *Moskovskie novosti*, July 1988: 11.

18. Vinogradov, "Mozhet li pravda," 283, 288.

19. Rybakov, "Rana, kotoraya krovotochit."

20. Fyodorov, "Chtoby . . . ," 1.

21. Rybakov, "Rana, kotoraya krovotochit," 7.

22. Nikolai Shmelyov, *Paskhov dom* (Pashkov's house), *Znamya*, March 1987: 99, 135.

23. Rybakov, "Rana, kotoraya krovotochit," and Shmelyov, *Pashkov dom*, 99, 135.

24. Shmelyov, *Pashkov dom*, 98.

25. Vinogradov, "Mozhet li pravda," 282.

26. Rybakov, "Rana, kotoraya krovotochit," and Yakovlev, "Akty . . . ," 261.

27. Evgeniya Al'bats, "Proshcheniyu ne podlezhat" (No forgiveness for them), *Moskovskie novosti*, May 8, 1988: 13; Evgeniya Al'bats, "Anatomiya merzosti" (The anatomy of villainy). *Moskovskie novosti*, October 16, 1988: 13; and Alexander Yakovlev, "Akty . . . ," 261.

28. "Memorial sovesti" (The memorial of conscience), *Ogonyok* 47, 1988: 7.

29. Alexander Yakovlev, "Only moral democracy can overcome our tragic past," *Moskovskie novosti*, 1, 1990: 6.

30. Ibid.

31. Kazutin, "Zhertvoyu . . ."

32. Zhzhyonov, "Sud'ba naroda."

33. Fodorov, "Chtoby . . . ," 1.

34. "Ot redaktsii" (From the Editorial Board), no author, *Ogonyok* 32, 1988: 5.

35. Ales' Adamovich, "Optimism delaniya," *Moskovskie novosti*, September 11, 1988: 13; and "Memorial sovesti" (The memorial of conscience), *Ogonyok* 37, 1988, no author: 29.

36. *Moskovskie novosti,* November 27, 1988: 12; and Yuri Afanasiev, "Memorial—v dialoge s proshlym i nastoyashchim" (Memorial—in a dialogue with the past and the present), *Moskovskie novosti,* February 5, 1989: 4.

37. Afanasiev, "Memorial . . ."

38. Ibid.

39. Vladimir Zapetskiy, "I snova: 'Egor, ty ne prav?' " (Again: "Egor, you are wrong"?), *Literaturnaya gazeta,* November 7, 1990: 11.

40. Ibid.

41. Ibid.

42. Ibid.

43. Ibid.

44. Ibid.

45. Ibid.

46. Grant Gukasov, "Za sem'yu pechatyami" (Behind seven seals), *Moskovskie novosti,* July 16, 1989: 16.

47. Ibid.

48. Grant Gukasov, "Za sem'yu pechatyami."

49. "Nuzhna Belaya kniga" (A "White Book" is needed), *Moskovskie novosti,* November 27, 1988: 11.

50. A. Babiy, V. Sirotin, "Mnogoe nado vyasnit' " (Much remains to be found out), *Moskovskie novosti,* November 27, 1988: 7.

51. Viktor Kurochkin, "Nazvat' vsekh poimyonno" (To recall all by their names), *Moskovskie novosti,* November 27, 1988: 11.

52. Ibid.

53. Alexander Kabakov, "Nedelya sovesti: prodolzhenie neobkhodimo" (The week of conscience: Continuation is necessary), *Moskovskie novosti,* December 4, 1998: 14.

54. Ol'ga Nemirovskaya, "Nedelya sovesti" (The week of conscience), *Ogonyok* 48, 1988: 1.

55. "Nedelya sovesti" (The week of conscience), no author, *Ogonyok* 49, 1988: 32, and Nemirovskaya, "Nedelya sovesti," 1.

56. "Ot redaktsii" (From the Editorial Board), no author, *Ogonyok* 37, 1988: 29.

57. "Vnimanie: konkurs!" (Attention: competition!), no author, *Ogonyok* 42, 1988: 5.

58. Kabakov, "Nedelya . . ."

59. Ibid.

60. Ibid.

61. Nemirovskaya, "Nedelya sovesti," 1.

62. Ibid.

63. "Moskva. Nedelya sovesti" (Moscow: The week of conscience), no author, *Moskovskie novosti,* November 27, 1988: 9.

64. Ibid.

65. Kabakov, "Nedelya . . ." and "Moskva. Nedelya sovesti" (Moscow: The week of conscience), no author, *Moskovskie novosti,* November 27, 1988: 9.

66. Ibid.

CHAPTER 15. THE "SPIRIT OF FREEDOM" AND THE POWER OF
NYET

1. Lazar' Lazarev, "Dukh svobody" (The spirit of freedom), *Znamya*, September 1988: 218–29. The actual phrase "the spirit of freedom" is in a later version of the essay in "Dukh svobody" (The spirit of freedom), postscript to Vasily Grossman, *Zhizn' i sud'ba* (Life and fate), Moscow: Knizhnaya palata, 1989: 667.

2. Vasily Grossman, *Zhizn' i sud'ba* (Life and fate), Moscow: Knizhnaya palata, 1989: 323.

3. Lazarev, "Dukh svobody," 228.

4. Ibid.

5. Ibid., 387.

6. Ibid., 369.

7. Ibid., 599.

8. Grossman, *Zhizn' i sud'ba*, 369; Lazarev, "Dukh svobody," 222.

9. As quoted from Grossman's wartime novel *Za pravoe delo* (For the right cause) by Lazar' Lazarev in "Dukh svobody" (The spirit of freedom), postscript to Vasily Grossman, *Zhizn' i sud'ba* (Life and fate), Moscow: Knizhnaya palata, 1989: 659.

10. Ibid., 323–24.

11. Lazarev, "Dukh svobody," 667; Bocharov, "Sud'ba narodnaya" (People's fate), *Oktyabr'*, March 1988: 151.

12. Ibid., 238–39.

13. Ibid., 239–40.

14. Yuri Dombrovsky, *Fakul'tet nenuzhnykh veshchey* (The department of unnecessary things), Moscow: Sovetskiy pisatel', 1989: 509.

15. Isaiah Berlin, *Four Essays on Liberty*, New York: Oxford University Press, 1969: 122–23.

16. *Zhizn' i sud'ba*, 406, 404.

17. Ibid., 408, 411.

18. Ibid., 231.

19. Varlam Shalamov, *Iz "Kolymskikh rasskazov"* (From "The Kolyma tales"), *Znamya*, June 1989: 12.

20. Alla Latynina, "Solzhenitsyn i my" (Solzhenitsyn and we), *Novy mir*, January 1990: 256.

21. Varlam Shalamov, "Mayor Pugachev" (Major Pugachev), in Varlam Shalamov, *Proza, stikhi* (Prose, poetry), *Novy mir*, June 1988: 116, 122–23.

22. Alexander Solzhenitsyn, *V kruge pervom* (In the first circle), Moscow: Act, 2006: 452.

23. Andrey Vasilevsky, "Stradanie pamyati" (The anguish of memory), *Oktyabr'*, April 1989: 186–87.

24. Lev Razgon, "Nakonetz!" (Finally!), *Moskovskie novosti*, June 26, 1988: 11; and Martimyan Ryutin, "Ko vsem chlenam VKP (b)" in Kh. Kobo, ed., *Osmyslit' kul't Stalina* (To comprehend Stalin's cult). Moscow: Progress, 1989: 621.

25. Ryutin, "Ko vsem . . . ," 618–19.

26. Ibid., 619–20, 623.

27. Razgon, op. cit.

28. Ibid.

29. Ibid.

30. Anatoly Zhigulin, *Chyornye kamni* (Black rocks), *Znamya*, part 1, July 1988: 10–75, and part 2, August 1988: 48–119.

31. Anatoly Zhigulin, "Vina! Ona byla, konechno . . ." (The guilt! Of course it was there . . .), interview with *Moskovskie novosti*, July 31, 1988: 12.

32. Ibid.

33. Andrey Vasilevsky, "Stradanie pamyati" (The anguish' of memory), *Oktyabr'*, April 1989: 184.

34. Ibid., and Zhigulin, *Chyornye kamni*, part 2.

35. Daniil Granin, *Zubr* (Bison), *Novy mir*, February 1987: 67.

36. Vladimir Dudintsev, *Belye odezhdy* (White garments), Moscow: Sovetskiy pisatel', 1988: 105.

37. Starikova, "Kniga . . . ," 227, 226.

38. Georgy Gachev, "Arsenal dobroy voli. O romane V. Dudintseva 'Belye odezhdy' i v svyazi s nim" (The arsenal of good will. About Vladimir Dudint-sev's novel, "White garments" and in connection with it), *Novy mir*, August 1987: 184, 188.

39. Dudintsev, *Belye odezhdy*, 90.

40. Ibid., 91.

41. Ibid., 107.

42. Ibid., 142.

43. Peter Pringle, *The Murder of Nikolai Vavilov*, New York: Simon and Schuster, 2008: 297.

44. E. Starikova, "Kniga o dobre i zle, ili smert' Ivana Il'icha" (A book about good and evil, or the death of Ivan Il'ich), *Novy mir*, December, 1987: 227, and Pringle, 297.

45. Daniil Granin, *Zubr*, *Novy mir*, February1 1987: 60, 61.

46. Starikova, "Kniga . . . ," 221, and Granin, *Zubr*, 69.

47. Granin, *Zubr*, 69.

48. See, for example, Yuri Dombrovsky, *Fakul'tet nenuzhnykh veshchey* (The department of unnecessary things), Moscow: Sovetskiy pisatel', 1989: 509.

49. Varlam Shalamov, *Novaya proza* (New fiction), *Novy mir*, December 1989: 67.

50. Dombrovsky, *Fakul'tet*, 271.

51. Grossman, *Zhizn' i sud'ba*, 218.

52. Ibid.

53. Ibid., 209.

54. Ibid., 219.

55. Alla Bossart, "V Moskvu za pravdoy" (To Moscow to find truth), *Ogonyok* 45, 1988: 3.

56. A. Kalinin, letter to Alexei Tolstoy, in "Oni ne mogli molchat'" (They could not remain silent), *Moskovskie novosti,* November 27, 1988: 10.

57. Ibid., Georgy Solovyov's letter to Alexei Tolstoy.

58. Natliya Rapoport, "Pamyat'—tozhe meditsina" (Memory is medicine, too), *Yunost',* no. 4, 1988: 80.

59. Sofya Kalistratova, "Takoe bylo vremya" (Such was that time), *Moskovskie novosti,* August 6, 1989: 13.

60. A. Vasiliev, "Nedogovarivaem" (We are not telling the whole story), *Komsomol'skaya pravda,* August 7, 1990: 4.

61. Ibid.

62. Ibid.

63. Ibid.

64. Vasiliev, "Nedogovarivaem."

65. Vladimir Fomin and Yuri Shchekochikhin, "Togda, v Novocherkasske" (Then, in Novocherassk), *Literaturnaya gazeta,* June 21, 1989: 13.

66. Yu. Bespalov, "Novocherkassk. 1962," *Komsomol'skaya pravda,* June 3, 1990: 2.

67. Fomin and Shchekochikhin, op. cit.

68. Yu. Bespalov, "Novocherkassk. 1962," *Komsomol'skaya pravda,* June 3, 1990: 2.

69. Fomin and Shchekochikhin, op. cit., 13; Yu. Bespalov and Valery Konovalov, "Novocherkassk, 1962" *Komsomol'skaya pravda,* June 2, 1989: 4.

70. Fomin and Shekochikhin, op. cit.

71. Ibid.

72. Ibid.

73. Ibid.

74. Ibid.

75. Fomin and Shchekochikhin, op. cit.

76. Yuri Burtin, "Velikiy russkiy intelligent. Pamyati Andreya Dmitrievicha Sakharova" (The great man of the Russian intelligentsia: In memory of Andrei Dmitrievich Sakharov), *Oktyabr',* January 1990: 3.

77. Alexander Yakovlev, "Sud'ba i sovest'" (Fate and conscience), *Ogonyok* 52, 1989: 2.

78. Evgeny Evtushenko, "Pechal'no, no tverdo" (With sadness but firmly). *Ogonyok* 52: 2.

79. Yakovlev, "Sud'ba . . ."

80. Andrei Sakharov, the Nobel Peace Prize speech, December 1, 1975, *Oktyabr',* January 1990: 14.

81. Yuri Rost, "Ushol Chelovek" (Gone is [a great] Man), *Literaturnaya gazeta,* December 20, 1989: 1.

82. Boris Yeltsin, speech at the Second Congress of People's Deputies on December 17, 1989. *Izvestia,* December 18, 1989: 4; Yakovlev, "Sud'ba . . ."

83. Burtin, op. cit., and Lev Timofeev, "S trevogoy i nadezhdoy" (With anxiety and hope), *Oktyabr',* January 1990: 7.

CHAPTER 16. THE FREEDOM CANON

1. Vladimir Kantor, "Imya rokovoe" (The fateful name), *Voprosy literatury* 3 March 1988: 85.
2. Osip Mandel'shtam, "My zhivyom pod soboya ne chuya strany . . ." (We live not feeling the country's soil under us . . .), in O. E. Mandel'shtam, *Sobranie sochineniy v chetyryokh tomakh* (Collected works in four volumes), ed. G. P. Struve and B. A. Filippov, Moscow: Terra, 1991, vol. 1: 202.
3. Benedikt Sarnov, "Zalozhnik vechnosti (Sluchay Mandel'shtama)" (The hostage of eternity: The case of Mandelstam), *Ogonyok* 47, 1988: 26.
4. Ibid.
5. Ibid., 29.
6. Nikita Struve, "Sud'ba Mandel'shtama" (Mandelstam's fate), in O. E. Mandel'shtam, *Sobranie sochineniy v chetyryokh tomakh* (Collected works in four volumes), ed. G. P. Struve and B. A. Filippov, Moscow: Terra, 1991, vols. 3–4: xxxi.
7. Ibid.
8. Sarnov, op. cit., 28.
9. Ibid.
10. Ibid.
11. Ibid., 26.
12. Gleb Struve, "O. E. Mandel'shtam. Opyt biografii i kriticheskogo kommentariya" (O. E. Mandelstam: An experiment in biography and critical commentary), in O. E. Mandel'shtam, *Sobranie sochineniy v chetyryokh tomakh* (Collected works in four volumes), ed. G. P. Struve and B. A. Filippov, Moscow: Terra, 1991, vol. 1: l–li.
13. Dombrovsky, *Fakul'tet*, 368.
14. Grigory Anisimov and Mikhail Emtsev, "Etot khranitel' drevnostey. (O pisatele Yurii Dombrovskom i ego knigakh)" (This keeper of antiques: About the writer Yuri Dombrovsky and his books), afterword to Dombrovsky, *Fakul'tet nenuzhnykh veshchey*, 697.
15. Dombrovsky, *Fakul'tet*, 577.
16. Anisimov and Emtsev, "Etot khranitel' drevnostey. (O pisatele Yurii Dombrovskom i ego knigakh)," 697.
17. Ibid.
18. Ibid., 694.
19. Ibid., 700.
20. Ibid., 696.
21. Ibid.
22. Ibid.
23. Dombrovsky, *Fakul'tet*, 256.
24. Ibid., 597.
25. Alla Latynina, "Solzhenitsyn i my" (Solzhenitsyn and we), *Novy mir*, January 1990: 258. The author refers to the title of one of Solzhenitsyn's famous *samizdat* essays.

26. Ibid.

27. Ibid., 242, 251, 253–54.

28. Ibid., 255.

29. Alexander Solzhenitsyn, "Nobelevskaya lektsiya" (The Nobel lecture), *Novy mir,* July 1989: 137.

30. Ibid., 144.

31. Viktor Chalmaev, " 'Zhil chelovek na pravakh pozhara.' ('Nechayannoe' i vechnoe sovershenstvo Andreya Platonova)" (There once was a man who lived like a fire: The "accidental" and eternal perfection of Andrei Platonov), in Andrei Platonov, *Sobranie sochineniy v pyati tomakh* (Collected works in five volumes), vol. 23, Moscow: Informpechat', 1998.

32. Alexander Shindel', "Svidetel' " (A witness), *Znamya,* September 1987: 207.

33. Andrei Platonov, "Usomnivshiysya Makar" (Makar who has doubted), in Platonov, *Sobranie sochineniy v pyati tomakh,* vol. 1: 530.

34. Chalmaev, "Zhil . . . ," 20, and Viktor Malukhin, "Sovremennik vsem vremenam. K vykhodu v svet trilogii Andreya Platonova" (A contemporary for all times: On the publication of Andrei Platonov's trilogy), *Izvestia,* August 6, 1988: 3.

35. V. A. Chalmaev and Yu. V. Tikhonov, "Istoriko-literaturnyi kommentariy" (A historical and literary commentary), in Platonov, *Sobranie sochineniy v pyati tomakh,* vol. 1: 525, 527, 538; and Malukhin, "Sovremennik . . ."

36. Evgeny Evtushenko, "Stalinizm po Platonovu" (Stalinism according to Platonov), in Kh. Kobo, ed., *Osmyslit' kul't Stalina* (To comprehend Stalin's cult), Moscow: Progress, 1989: 195.

37. Evgeny Evtushenko, "Sud'ba Platonova" (Platonov's fate), *Sovetskaya kul'tura,* August 20, 1988: 5, and "Stalinizm po Platonovu" (Stalinism according to Platonov), in Kh. Kobo, ed., *Osmyslit' kul't Stalina,* 201.

38. Chalmaev and Yakovlev, "Istorichesko . . . ," 598, and Evtushenko, "Stalinizm . . . ," 196.

39. Chalmaev, "Zhil chelovek . . . ," 19; Evtushenko, "Stalinizm . . . ," 196; and Chalmaev and Yakovlev, "Istoriko . . . ," 540.

40. Chalmaev, "Zhil chelovek," 19; Benedikt Sarnov, "Skol'ko vesit nashe gosudarstvo?" in Kh. Kobo, ed., *Osmyslit' kul't Stalina* (To comprehend Stalin's cult), Moscow: Progress, 1989: 165.

41. Chalmaev and Yakovlev, "Istorichesko . . . ," 526; Chalmaev, "Zhil chelovek," 23; Evtushenko, "Stalinizm . . . ," 196.

42. Evtushenko, "Stalinizm . . . ," 209.

43. Chalmaev, 20; Malukhin, op. cit.

44. Shindel', "Svidetel'," 214.

45. Andrei Platonov, *Chevengur,* in Andrei Platonov, *Sobranie sochineniy v pyati tomakh,* vol. 2: 5–307, and Kotlovan, ibid., 308–97.

46. Platonov, "Usomnivshiysya Makar," 530.

47. Chalmaev, 5.

48. Chalmaev and Yakovlev, 525.

49. Chalmaev, 6.

50. Chalmaev and Yakovlev, 525.

51. Chalmaev, 5.

52. Ibid.

53. Ibid., 24.

54. Lazar' Lazarev, "Dukh svobody" (The spirit of freedom), postscript to Vasily Grossman, *Zhizn' i sud'ba* (Life and fate), Moscow: Knizhnaya palata, 1989: 218.

55. Vladimir Lakshin, "Narod i lyudi. O romane Vasiliya Grossmana" (People and men: About Vasily Grossman's novel), *Izvestia,* June 25, 1988: 3.

56. Igor Zolotussky, "Krushenie abstraktsiy" (The downfall of abstractions), *Novy mir,* January 1989: 239.

57. Lazarev, "Dukh svovody," 654, 655.

58. Lakshin, "Narod i lyudi."

59. "Ot izdatel'stva" (From the Publisher), Introduction to Vasily Grossman, *Zhizn' i sud'ba* (Life and fate), Moscow: Knizhnaya palata, 1989: 13.

60. Lazarev, "Dukh svobody," 219.

61. Ibid.

62. Lakshin, "Narod i lyudi," 3.

63. Stephen Greenblatt, "How It Must Have Been," *New York Review of Books,* November 5, 2009: 24.

64. Ibid.

65. Grossman, *Zhizn' i sud'ba,* 213.

66. Ibid., 214.

67. Lakshin, "Narod i lyudi."

68. Anatoly Bocharov, "Pravoe delo Vasiliya Grossmana" (Vasily Grossman's just cause), *Oktyabr',* January 1988: 134.

69. Grossman, *Zhizn' i sud'ba,* 308.

70. Lev Anninskiy, "Monolog byvshego stalintsa" (A monologue of a former Stalinist), in Kh. Kobo, ed., *Osmyslit' kul't Stalina* (To comprehend Stalin's cult), Moscow: Progress, 1989: 71.

71. I. Rishina and A. Egorov, "Lish tot dostoin zhizni i svobody . . . (Vasily Grossman. *Zhizn' i sud'ba*)." Chitatel'skay konferentsiya "LG" (Only he deserves life and liberty [who every day goes to battle for them] [Vasily Grossman. *Life and Fate*]. A readers' conference at Literaturnaya gazeta), *Literaturnaya gazeta,* August 24, 1988: 5.

72. Grossman, *Zhizn' i sud'ba,* 170.

73. Ibid.

74. Ibid.

75. Ibid., 231.

76. Ibid., 519, and Lakshin, "Narod i lyudi."

77. Grossman, *Zhizn' i sud'ba,* 419 and Bocharov, "Pravoe delo . . . ," 132.

78. Grossman, *Zhizn' i sud'ba*, 160.

79. Ibid., 160–61.

80. Grossman, *Vsyo techyot*, 105.

81. Grossman, *Zhizn' i sud'ba*, 505.

82. Ibid., 505, 565.

83. Ibid., 573, 622.

84. Ibid., 577.

85. Ibid., 630, 615.

86. Ibid., 630.

87. Ibid., 524–35.

88. Lazarev, "Dukh svobody," 670.

89. Grossman, *Zhizn' i sud'ba*, 631.

CHAPTER 17. IN MAN'S IMAGE, I

1. S. Men'shikov, "Ekonomicheskaya struktura sotsializma: chto vperedi?" (The economic structure of socialism: what is ahead?), *Novy mir*, March 1989: 202. The author quoted Mikhail Gorbachev's speech at the July 29, 1988, session (Plenum) of the Central Committee.

2. As quoted in Mikhail Antonov, "Tak chto zhe s nami proiskhodit?" (What really is happening to us?), *Oktyabr'*, August 1987: 55.

3. Alexander Tsypko, "Istoki Stalinisma" (The origins of Stalinism), part 3, *Nauka i zhizn'*, January 1989: 58.

4. V. Radaev and O. Shkaratan, "Vozvrashchenie k istokam" (The return to the sources), *Izvestia*, February 16, 1990: 3.

5. Alexander Bovin, "Kitay i my" (China and we), *Moskovskie novosti*, April 8, 1990: 3.

6. B. Nazarov, "Chelovek—eto zvuchit . . . " (Man—[a word] that resonates [proudly] . . .), *Komsomol'skaya pravda*, March 23, 1990: 2.

7. Evgeny Ambartsumov, "O putyakh sovershenstvovaniya politicheskoy sistemy sotsializma" (On the ways to perfect the political system of socialism), in Yuri Afanasiev, ed., *Inogo ne dano* (There is no other way), Moscow: Progress, 1988: 86.

8. Vladimir Shubkin, "Trudnoe proshchanie" (The difficult farewell), *Novy mir*, April 1989: 183; Alexander Arkhangel'skiy, "Mezhdu svobodoy i ravenstvom. Obshchesvennoe soznanite v zerkale 'Ogon'ka' i 'Nashego sovremennika' " (Between freedom and equality: Public conscience as reflected in *Ogonyok* and *Nash sovremennik*, 1986–1990), *Novy mir*, February 1991: 231.

9. Dmitry Kazutin and Vladimir Loshak, "Na kakom etape nakhoditsya perestroika?" (At what stage is perestroika?), *Moskovskie novosti*, July 9, 1989: 10; Yuri Feofanov, "Vozvrashchenie k istokam" (The return to the sources), *Znamya*, February 1989: 149.

10. Shubkin, "Trudnoe proshchanie," 184.

11. Larisa Piyasheva, "V pogone za Siney ptitsey" (Chasing the blue bird [of happiness]), *Oktyabr'*, September 1990: 153.

12. A. Klimov, "Tsel': puti i sredstva realizatsii" (The goal: the ways and means of achieving it), in M. I. Melkumyan, ed., *Drama obnovleniya* (The drama of renewal), Moscow: Progress: 1990: 433.

13. Alexander Yakovlev, "Rabotat' po sovesti, zhit' chestno" (To work conscientiously, to live honorably). *Pravda*, February 28, 1989: 2.

14. Feofanov, "Vozvrashchenie . . . ," 138.

15. D. Ivans, "Kakimi my byli, kakimi my stanem?" (What have we been and what will we be?), *Komsomol'skaya pravda,* June 28, 1988: 1.

16. Ibid.

17. "Sozdan izbiratelnly blok 'Demokraticheskaya Rossiya' " (A voters' bloc 'Democratic Russia' has been organized), *Ogonyok* 6, February 1990: 17.

18. Evgeny Starikov, "Marginaly" (The marginal people), *Znamya*, October 1989: 144; Andranik Migranyan, "Mekhanizm tormozheniya v politicheskoy systeme i puti ego preodoleniya" (The breaking mechanism in the political system and the ways to overcome it), in Yuri Afanasiev, ed., *Inogo ne dano* (There is no other way), Moscow: Progress, 1988: 108; V. Kiselev, "Skol'ko modeley sotsializma bylo v SSSR?" (How many models of socialism were there in the USSR?), in Yuri Afanasiev, ed., *Inogo . . .* : 369; A. Zhuravlev, "K sotsial'noy garmonii" (Toward social harmony), *Argumenty i fakty,* November 4–10, 1989: 2; Shubkin, "Trudnoe proshchanie," 184; Marat Baglay, "Moral' i politika" (Morality and politics), *Sovetskaya kul'tura,* July 27, 1989: 4.

19. Evgeny Evtushenko, "Stalinizm po Platonovu" (Stalinism according to Platonov), in Kh. Kobo, ed., *Osmyslit' kul't Stalina* (To comprehend Stalin's cult), Moscow: Progress, 1989: 206.

20. Len Karpinsky, "Instinkt demokratii" (The instinct of democracy), *Moskovskie novosti,* January 29, 1989: 8.

21. S. Sokolov, letter to the editor, in "Prostye lyudi" (The ordinary people), *Komsomol'skaya pravda,* March 25, 1989: 2.

22. Yu. F. Karyakin, speech at the First Congress of People's Deputies, *Pravda,* June 5, 1989: 4.

23. Konstantin Feoktistov, "Skazhem drug drugu pravdu" (Let us tell each other the truth), *Literaturnaya gazeta,* November 7, 1990: 11.

24. Zhuravlev, "K sotsial'noy garmonii," 2.

25. Ernest Ametistov, "Lichnnost' i zakon" (An individual and law), *Moskovskie novosti,* December 11, 1988: 5.

26. Fyodor Burlatsky, "Pervyi no vazhnyi shag" (The first, but important step), *Literaturnaya gazeta,* June 14, 1989: 1.

27. Ibid.

28. Ibid.

29. Leonid Gozman and A. Etkind, "Kul't vlasti. Struktura totalitarnogo soznaniya (The cult of power: The structure of totalitarian consciousness," in Kh. Kobo, ed., *Osmyslit' kul't Stalina* (To comprehend Stalin's cult), Moscow: Progress, 1989: 370.

30. Nikolai Popov, "Kto vyshe vlasti?" (Who is above the state's power?), *Sovetskaya kul'tura*, April 26, 1988: 3.

31. Nikolai Travkin, "Put' k narodovlastiyu lezhit cherez samoupravlenie" (The road to government by the people runs through self-rule), *Sovetskaya kul'tura*, July 8, 1989: 2.

32. Alexander Tsypko, "Khoroshi li nashi printsipy?" (How good are our principles?), *Novy mir*, April, 1990: 204.

33. Vasily Selyunin, "Planovaya anarkhiya ili balans interesov?" (Planned anarchy or a balance of interests?), *Znamya*, November 1989: 215.

34. Ibid.

35. Piyasheva, "V pogone . . . ," 153.

36. Liliya Shevtsova, "Privyknut' zhit' bez povodka" (To get used to live without the leash), *Literaturnaya gazeta*, April 19, 1989: 11.

37. L. Gol'din, "Nado snova nauchit'sya zhit' " (We must relearn to live), *Sovetskaya kul'tura*, August 29, 1989: 3.

38. Igor Kon, "Psikhologiya sotsial'noy inertsii" (The psychology of social inertia), *Kommunist*, January 1988: 72.

39. Pavel Gurevich, "Kakaya ideologiya nam nuzhna?" (What ideology do we need?), *Literaturnaya gazeta*, March 14, 1990: 10; Alexander Tsypko, "Vozmozhno li chudo?" (Is a miracle possible?), *Sovetskaya kul'tura*, May 26, 1990: 4.

40. Tsypko, "Vozmozhno li . . ."; Shubkin, "Trudnoe proshchanie," 180.

41. Alexander Nezhnyi, "Nikto ne vprave posyagat' na sovest' drugogo . . ." (No one has the right to interfere with anyone's conscience), *Moskovskie novosti*, October 29, 1989: 13.

42. Ibid.

43. Gurevich, op. cit.

44. M. Gostev, in "O vremeni, kotoroe vypalo na nashu dolyu . . ." (About the times we have been destined to live in . . .), a collection of readers' letters, *Komsomol'skaya pravda*, January 25, 1989: 2.

45. Ibid.

46. Vyacheslav Dashichev, "Evropa otkrytykh dverey" (A Europe of open doors), *Komsomol'skaya pravda*, February 20, 1990: 2.

47. Alexander Yakovlev, "Only Moral Democracy," *Moscow News*, January 1, 1990: 6.

48. Marat Baglay, "Moral' i politika" (Morality and politics), *Sovetskaya kul'tura*, July 27, 1989: 4.

49. Ales' Adamovich, in "Proshchanie s Andreem Dmitrievichem Sakharovym" (Farewell to Andrei Dmitrievich Sakharov), *Literaturnaya gazeta*, December 20, 1989: 10.

50. Yuri Burtin, "Vozmozhnost' vozrazit' " (The opportunity to object), in Yuri Afanasiev, ed., *Inogo ne dano* (There is no other way), Moscow: Progress, 1988: 490.

51. B. Nazarov, "Formula svobody" (The formula of freedom), *Sovetskaya kul'tura*, July 1989: 3.

52. Ibid.

53. Ibid.

54. Ibid.

55. Yuri Kashlev, "Venskiy proryv: prava cheloveka v SSSR" (The Vienna break-through: human rights in the USSR), *Moskovskie novosti,* March 26, 1989: 10.

56. Eduard Shevardnadze, "Novy oblik diplomatii" (A new image of diplomacy), *Argumenty i fakty,* May 6–12, 1989: 2.

57. Yuir Karyakin, "Stoit li nastupat' na grabli? (Do we really want to step on a rake?), *Znamya,* September 1987: 207.

58. Piyasheva, "V pogone . . . ," 152.

59. Burlatsky, "Perviy, no vazhnyi . . . ," 2.

60. Nazarov, "Chelovek . . ."

61. Vasily Selyunin, "Revansh burokratii" (Bureaucracy's revanche), in Yuri Afa-nasiev, ed., *Inogo ne dano* (There is no other way), Moscow: Progress, 1988: 198.

62. Programnoe zayavlenie Soyuza trudyashchikhsya Kuzbassa, prinyatoe na IV konferentsii rabochikh komitetov Kuzbassa, 18–19 noyabrya 1989, g. No-vokuznetsk (A program statement of the Union of the Laborers of Kuzbass, adopted at the 4th conference of the workers' committees of Kuzbass on November 18–19, 1989 in the city of Novokuznetsk), Document No. 111, in L. Lopatin, ed., *Rabochee dvizhenie Kuzbassa. Sbornik documentov i materialov. Aprel' 1989–Mart 1992* (The workers' movement of Kuzbass: A collection of documents and materials, April 1989–March 1992), Kemerovo: Sovremen-naya otechestvennaya kniga, 1993: 159.

63. Ibid.

64. Fyodor Burlatsky, Sud'ba reformatorov strany," (The fate of our country's re-formers), *Literaturnaya gazeta,* June 27, 1990: 1.

65. Anatoly Strelyaniy, "Prikhod i raskhod" (Profit and expense), *Znamya,* June 1986: 203; Vasily Selyunin, "Chyornye dyry ekonimki" (The black holes of the economy), *Novy mir,* October 1989: 169.

66. Boris Yeltsin, speech at the Second Congress of People's Deputies of the USSR, December 17, 1989, *Izvestia,* December 18, 1989: 4; and Kirill Lavrov, People's Actor of the Soviet Union, speech at the Second Congress of People's Deputies of the USSR on December 17, 1989, *Izvestia,* December 18, 1989: 4.

67. Chingiz Aytmatov, "Tsena prozreniya" (The price of recovering sight), inter-view with Felix Medvedev, *Ogonyok* 28, 1987: 6.

68. Fyodor Burlatsky, "Brezhnev i krushenie ottepeli" (Brezhnev and the collapse of the thaw), *Literaturnaya gazeta,* September 14, 1988: 13.

69. Ibid.

70. Vasily Selyunin, Chyornye dyry ekonimki" (The black holes of the economy), *Novy mir,* October 1989: 177.

71. Selyunin, "Planovaya anarkhiya . . . ," 212.

72. S. Shatalin, N. Petrakov, G. Yavlisnky, S. Aleksashenko, A. Vavilov, L. Grigor'ev, M. Zadornov, V. Martynov, V. Mashits, D. Mikhaylov, V. Fedorov, T.

Yarygina, E. Yasin, "Chelovek. Svoboda. Rynok." (Man. Liberty. Market.), *Komsomol'skaya pravda*, September 5, 1990: 2.

73. Shubkin, "Trudnoe proshchanie," 183.

74. Kak nam obustroit' Rossiyu" (How we can make Russia good for living), a supplement to *Komsomol'skaya pravda*, September 18, 1990.

75. Shubkin, "Trudnoe proshchanie," 183.

76. Selyunin, "Planovaya anarkhiya . . . ," 219.

77. Vladmir Polyakov, letter to the editor, in "Tak kak zhe nam obustroiti' Rossiyu?" (So how do we better Russia?), *Komsomol'skaya pravda*, November 23, 1990: 2.

78. S. Shatalin et al., "Chelovek . . . ".

79. Shubkin, "Trudnoe proshchanie," 182; and Tsypko, "Khoroshi li . . . ," 204.

80. Anatoly Anan'ev, "Po techeniyu ili naperkor" (Going with the flow or against it), *Oktyabr'*, October 1989: 3; and Alexander Lapin, "Bednost'" (Poverty), *Komsomol'skaya pravda*, April 19, 1990: 2.

81. Andranik Migranyan, "Karl Popper: 'Ya byl marksistom do 17 let'" (I was a Marxist until I was seventeen), *Moskovskie novosti*, November 18, 1990: 16.

82. Anatoly Sobchak, "Khozhdenie vo vlast'" (The journey into power), *Moskovskie novosti*, November 25, 1990: 14.

83. Dmitry Kazutin and Viktor Loshak, "Na kakom etape nakhoditsya perestroika?" (At what stage is perestroika?), *Moskovskie novosti*, July 9, 1989: 10.

84. The Mazun family, letter to the editor, in "Narodnaya publitsistika" (People's political journalism), *Oktyabr'*, August 1989: 180.

85. Vladimir Bashmachnikov, "O zemle i vole" (On land and freedom), *Moskovskie novosti*, December 2, 1990: 3.

86. Anatoly Anan'ev, "Po techeniyu ili naperkor" (Going with the flow or against it), *Oktyabr'*, October 1989: 3.

87. Anan'ev, "Po techeniyu . . . ," 3.

88. The Mazun family, letter to the editor, in "Narodnaya publitsistika" (People's political journalism), *Oktyabr'*, August 1989: 180.

89. V. A. Arangol'd, letter to the editor, in "Narodnaya publitsistika" (People's political journalism), *Oktyabr'*, August 1989: 180.

90. G. A. Shmakov, letter to the editor, in "Narodnaya publitsistika" (People's political journalism), *Oktyabr'*, August 1989: 182.

91. S. Kiselev, "Poka schtayut golosa . . ." (While they are counting the votes . . .), *Komsomol'skaya pravda*, March 6, 1990: 1.

92. "Nasha pozitsiya" (Our view), suggestions by the readers of *Komsomol'skaya pravda* in connection with the Theses of the Central Committee of the CPSU for Nineteenth Party Conference, *Komsomol'skaya pravda*, June 28, 1988: 3.

93. Viktor Yaroshenko, "Partii interesov" (The parties of issues), *Novy mir*, February 1990: 140.

94. Yuri Feofanov, "Vozvrashchenie k istokam" (The return to the sources), *Znamya*, February 1989: 153.

95. Boris Yeltsin, speech at the Second Congress of People's Deputies of the USSR, December 17, 1989, *Izvestia*, December 18, 1989: 4.

96. Andrei D. Sakharov, "Konstitutsiya Soyuza Sovetskikh Respublik Evropy i Azii" (Constitution of the Union of Soviet Republic of Europe and Asia), in "Konstitutsionnye idei Andreya Sakharova" (Constitutional ideas of Andrei Sakharov), *Oktyabr'*, May 1990: 146.

97. Oleg Kalugin, "KGB bez grima" (The KGB without makeup), *Argumenty i fakty*, June 30–July 6, 1990: 7.

98. Yuri Vlasov, speech at the First Congress of People's Deputies of the USSR, in "S'ezd Narodnykh Deputatov SSSR," transcript, *Izvestia*, June 2, 1989: 4.

99. Ibid.

100. Alexander M. Yakovlev, "Otverzhenie i utverzhdenie" (Rejection and affirmation), *Ogonyok* 43, 1988: 16; Vitaly Vitaliev, "Chelovek bez pasporta?" (A man without a passport), *Ogonyok* 40, 1988: 25.

101. Ibid.

102. Alexander M. Yakovlev, "Otverzhenie . . . ," 16.

103. Ibid.

104. "Vasha pozitsiya?" (Your view?), *Komsomol'skaya pravda*, June 7, 1988: 1.

105. Feofanov, "Vozvrashchenie . . . ," 157.

106. Alexander M. Yakovlev, "Otverzhenie i utverzhdenie" (Rejection and affirmation), *Ogonyok* 43, 1988: 14; Vasily Selyunin, "Planovaya anarkhiya ili balans interesov?" (Planned anarchy or a balance of interests?), *Znamya*, November 1989: 216.

107. Feofanov, "Vozvrashchenie . . . ," 138 and 150; Larisa Piyasheva, "Obeshchaniyami svetlogo budushchego syt ne budesh" (Hunger cannot be sated by the promises of a bright future), *Komsomol'skaya pravda*, May 25, 1989: 2; Shubkin, "Trudnoe proshchanie," 184; V. Frolov, "Chtoby eto ne povtorilos'" (So that this does not happen again), in Yuri Afanasiev, ed., *Inogo ne dano* (There is no other way), Moscow: Progress, 1988: 398.

108. Alexander M. Yakovlev, "Sud-mesto sostyazatel'noe" (Court is a place of competition), *Moskovskie novosti*, November 19, 1989: 12.

109. Feofanov, "Vozvrashchenie . . . ," 152.

110. Fedor Burlatsky, "Sudebnaya reforma" (The court reform), *Literaturnaya gazeta*, November 15, 1989: 1; Yakovlev, "Sud . . ."

111. "Vasha pozitsiya?" (Your view?), *Komsomol'skaya pravda*, June 7, 1988: 1.

112. Yakovlev, "Sud . . ."

113. S. Petrov, "Presumptsiya nevinovnosti?" (The presumption of innocence?), *Komsomolskaya pravda*, November 25, 1988: 4.

114. Frolov, "Chtoby eto ne povtorilos'," 398; Burlatsky, "Sudebnaya . . . ," and Yakovlev, "Sud . . . ," 30.

115. Alexei Izyumov, "Idei dolzhny sostyazat'sya" (Ideas must compete), *Komsomol'skaya Pravda*, January 9, 1990: 1.

116. Viktor Malukhin, "Pole pod svobodnym nebom" (A field under a free sky), *Izvestia*, March 7, 1990.

117. Boris Nikolaevsky, deputy chairman of the Committee on Glasnost and the Rights and Petitions of Citizens of the Supreme Soviet of the USSR, "Bez bumagi net *Chizha*" (Without paper, there is no *Chizh* [magazine]), *Sovetskaya kul'tura*, November 4, 1989: 2.

118. T. Men'shikova, "Chto znaet narod . . ." (What people know . . .), *Sovetskaya kul'tura*, July 27, 1989: 2.

119. Vladimir Lakshin, "Ot glasnosti k svodobe slova" (From glasnost to freedom of speech), *Moskovskie novosti*, April 9, 1989.

120. Yu. Sorokin, "Eto sladkoe slovo—svoboda!" (This sweet word—freedom!), *Komsomol'skaya pravda*, May 5, 1990: 1.

121. "Vasha pozitsiya?" (Your view?), *Komsomol'skaya pravda*, June 7, 1988: 1.

122. Selyunin, "Planovaya anarkhiya . . . ," 212.

123. Shevtsova, "Privyknut' . . ."

124. "Sozdan izbiratel'nyi blok 'Demokraticheskaya Rossiya'" (A voters' bloc, "Democratic Russia," has been organized), *Ogonyok* 6, February 1990: 17.

125. Leonid Gordon, in "Bol'she sotsializma!" *Ogonyok* 14, 1988: 7; Feofanov, "Vozrashchenie . . . ," 147, 156; Evgeny Ambartsumov, "Grani vlasti" (The facets of power), *Moskovskie novosti*, August 6, 1989: 3; Anatoly Vengerov, "Zaslon vozhdizmu," *Ogonyok* 23, 1988: 15; Andranik Migranyan, "Dolgiy put' k evropeyskomu domu" (A long road to the European home), *Novy mir*, July 1989: 178; Burlatsky, "Sudebnaya . . ."; Nikolai Amosov, "Real'nosti, idealy i modeli" (Realities, ideals and models), *Literaturnaya gazeta*, October 5, 1988: 13.

126. Vlasov, speech . . . , 5; Andranik Migranyan, "Mekhanizm tormozheniya v politicheskoy systeme i puti ego preodoleniya" (The breaking mechanism in the political system and the ways to overcome it), in Yuri. Afanasiev, ed., *Inogo ne dano* (There is no other way), Moscow: Progress, 1988: 112; Amosov, "Real'nosti . . ."; A. M. Emel'yanov, speech at the First Congress of People's Deputies on June 7, 1989, in *Pervyi S'ezd Narodnykh Deputatov SSSR. Stenographicheskiy otchyot. Tom III* (The First Congress of People's Deputies of the USSR: Official Transcript, vol. 3), Moscow: Publishing House of the Supreme Soviet, 1989: 82; "Programnoe zayavlenie . . . ," in L. Lopatin, ed., *Rabochee dvizhenie . . .* , 163.

127. Vitaly Tret'yakov, "Vash punkt v predvybornoy platforme" (Your plank in the electoral platform), *Moskovskie novosti*, January 29, 1989: 8.

128. G. Pashkov, "Prezident . . . Vashe mnenie?" (Prezident . . . Your opinion?), *Komsomol'skaya pravda*, March 18, 1990: 1.

129. Yuri Levada, ed., *Est' mnenie!* (I have an opinion!), Moscow: Progress, 1990: 277.

130. Boris Yeltsin, "V poiskakh soglasiya" (In search of accord), interview with *Moskovskie novosti*, January 14, 1990: 4.

131. Fyodor Burlatsky, "Bezopasnost' i smelye reformy" (Security and bold reforms), *Literaturnaya gazeta*, March 7, 1990: 1.

132. Alexander Tsypko, "Vozmozhno li chudo?" (Is a miracle possible?), *Sovetskaya kul'tura*, May 26, 1990: 4.

133. A. D. Sakharov, speech at the First Congress of People's Deputies on June 7, 1989, in *Pervyi S'ezd Narodnykh Deputatov SSSR. Stenographicheskiy otchyot. Tom III* (The First Congress of People's Deputies of the USSR. Official Transcript, vol. 3), Moscow: Publishing House of the Supreme Soviet, 1989: 326. For Sakharov's draft of a constitution, see "Konstitutsiya Soyuza Sovetskikh Respublik Evropy i Azii" (Constitution of the Union of Soviet Republic of Europe and Asia), in "Konstitutsionnye idei Andreya Sakharova" (Constitutional ideas of Andrei Sakharov), *Oktyabr'*, May 1990: 145–68.

134. "Rezolyutsiya III konferentsii Soyuza trudyashchikhsya Kuzbassa o polnoy peredache gosudartsvennoy vlasti v tsentre i na mestakh Sovetam narodnykh deputatov" (The resolution of the 3rd conference of the Union of the laborers of Kuzbass on the complete transfer of state power in the center and locally to the Soviets of people's deputies), Document No. 65, in L. Lopatin, ed., "Rabochee dvizhenie . . . ," 121.

135. "Iz trebovaniy gorodskogo stachechnogo komiteta g. Vorkuty, napravlennykh v Verkhovniy Sovet SSSR" (From the demands of the city striking committee of the city of Vorkuta, sent to the Supreme Soviet of the USSR), in V. V. Zhuravlev, L. N. Dobrokhotov, and V. N. Kolodezhnyi, eds., *Istoriya sovremennoy Rossii, 1985–1994* (History of modern Russia, 1985–1994), Moscow: Terra, 1995: 47.

136. "Programnoe zayavlenie . . ." in L. Lopatin, ed., *Rabochee dvizhenie . . . ,* 164, and "Deklaratsiya osnovnykh printsipov Konfederatsii truda. 1 maya 1990 g., g. Novokuznetsk" (Declaration of the main principles of the Confederation of labor. May 1, 1990, the city of Novokuznetsk), Document No. 210, in L. Lopatin, ed., *Rabochee dvizhenie . . . ,* 284.

137. "Deklaratsiya . . . ," 284.

138. Elena Bonner, "Polupravda ne luchshe lzhi" (A half-truth is no better than a lie), *Literaturnaya gazeta*, November 11, 1992: 11.

139. Ibid.

140. Yuri Vlasov, speech at the First Congress of People's Deputies of the USSR, in "S'ezd Narodnykh Deputatov SSSR," transcript, *Izvestia*, June 2, 1989: 4.

141. Feoktistov, "Skazhem drug drugu pravdu."

142. Ibid.

143. Gavriil Popov, in "Kto protiv" (Who is against?), a roundtable discussion in *Ogonyok* 18, 1988: 6.

144. L. Nikitinskiy, "Zakon o pechati—prinyat!" (The law on the press has been adopted!), *Komsomol'skya pravda*, June 9, 1990: 1.

145. Ibid.

146. Alexey Kiva, "Krizis 'zhanra' " (The crisis of the "genre"), *Novy mir*, March 1990: 208, and Yuri Burtin, "Chto takoe KPSS" (What is CPSU), *Oktyabr'*, May 1991: 181.

147. P. Volobuyev, "Vlast' sovetov: raschyoty i proschyoty" (The power of the soviets: hopes and miscalculations), *Kommunist*, 11, 1991: 82.
148. Yuri Burtin, "Chto takoe KPSS" (What is CPSU), *Oktyabr'*, May 1991: 181.

CHAPTER 18. IN MAN'S IMAGE, II

1. V. Dashichev, "Evropa otkrytykh dverey" (A Europe of open doors), *Komsomol'skaya pravda*, February 20, 1990: 2.
2. Evgeny Anisimov, "Oskolki imperii" *Moskovskie novosti*, December 17, 1989: 10.
3. V. Dashichev, "Evropa otkrytykh dverey" (A Europe of open doors), *Komsomol'skaya pravda*, February 20, 1990: 2.
4. Dashichev, op. cit., and Anisimov, op. cit.
5. Dashichev, op. cit.
6. Ibid.
7. Ibid.
8. Yu. Novopashin, "Proshchay, oruzhie!" (Farewell to arms!), interview with *Komsomol'skaya pravda*, December 6, 1989: 2.
9. Ibid.
10. Ibid.
11. Viktor Sheynis, "Avgustovskaya zhatva" (The August harvest), *Izvestia*, October 13, 1989: 6.
12. Dashichev, op. cit.
13. Viktor Sheynis, "Avgustovskaya zhatva" (The August harvest), *Izvestia*, October 13, 1989: 6.
14. Igor Birman, "Sovetskie voennye raskhody" (Soviet military expenditures), *Oktyabr'*, September 1991: 135, 149. See also Igor Birman, "Nosha ne po plechu" (Too heavy a burden), interview with *Izvestia*, November 29, 1990: 5.
15. Yuri Ryzhov, "Bezopasnost', kotoraya nam nuzhna" (Security that we need), *Novoe vermya*, no. 10, 1990: 27.
16. Birman, "Sovetskie voennye raskhody," 136, and Sergei Blagovolin, "Otkrytyi mir ili osazhdyonnyi lager'? (An open world or a besieged camp?), *Moskovskie novosti*, August 12, 1990: 3.
17. Sergei Volovets, "Bol'she pushek—men'she myasa" (More cannons—less meat), *Moskovskie novosti*, October 28, 1990: 3; Vladlen Sirotkin, "Voenno-promyshlennyi kompleks: Gde vykhod iz tupika?" (The military-industrial complex: Where is a way out of the dead-end?), *Stolitsa*, no. 13, 1991: 4.
18. Alexander Zaychenko, "Kak delit' pirog" (How to divide the pie), *Moskovskie novosti*, June 11, 1989: 12.
19. V. Yashchenko, "Vol'no-nayomnaya?" (Voluntary and for hire), a roundtable discussion in *Komsomol'skaya pravda*, November 15, 1989: 2.
20. Birman, op. cit., 145.
21. Ibid.

22. Sirotkin, op. cit., 4.
23. "Krizis vlasti ili vlast' v usloviyakh krizisa?" (A crisis of power or power in crisis?), interview with the chairman of Leningrad City Soviet, Anatoly Sobchak, *Argumenty i fakty,* no. 12, 1991: 2.
24. Pavel Voshchanov, "Zemlya i volya" (Land and freedom), *Komsomol'skaya pravda,* February 28, 1990: 2.
25. István Deak, "Discipline and Decline," *New Republic,* March 12, 2008: 44.
26. Sirotkin, op. cit., 3.
27. Alexei Kireev, "Sekretnaya stat'ya" (The secret article), *Literaturnaya gazeta,* October 18, 1989: 11; Andrei Sakharov, speech at the First Congress of People's Deputies on June 7, 1989, in *Pervyi S'ezd Narodnykh Deputatov SSSR. Stenographicheskiy otchyot. Tom III* (The First Congress of People's Deputies of the USSR. Official Transcript, vol. 3), Moscow: Publishing House of the Supreme Soviet, 1989: 327; and Yashchenko, op. cit.
28. Stanislav Kondrashov, "Iz mraka secretnosti" (From the darkness of secrecy), *Novy mir,* August 1989: 198.
29. Fyodor Burlatsky, "Sud'ba reformatorov strany" (The fate of our country's reformers), *Literaturnaya gazeta,* June 27, 1990: 2.
30. Kondrashov, "Iz mraka . . . : 202–3.
31. Sergei Blagovolin, "Otkrytyi mir ili osazhdyonnyi lager'?" (An open world or a besieged camp?), *Moskovskie novosti,* August 12, 1990: 3.
32. As quoted by Sirotkin, op. cit., 4.
33. Kondrashov, op. cit., 196.
34. Evgeny Ambartsumov, "Sotsializm ili Stalinizm" (Socialism or Stalinism), *Sovetskaya kul'tura,* September 19, 1989: 2; and Sirotkin, op. cit., 3.
35. Sirotkin, op. cit., 1; Birman, "Sovetskie voennye raskhody," 147–48.
36. Birman, op. cit., 147.
37. Eduard Shevardnadze, "Novy oblik diplomatii" (A new image of diplomacy), *Argumenty i fakty,* May 6–12, 1989: 2.
38. Ibid.
39. Shmelyov, "Libo sila, libo rubl'" (Either brute force or the ruble), *Znamya,* January 1989: 130.
40. R. A. Faramazyan, "Izderzhki sverkhvooruzhennosti" (The costs of superarmament), in M. I. Melkumyan, ed., *Drama obnovleniya* (The drama of renewal), Moscow: Progress, 1990: 205–6.
41. Kireev, "Sekretnaya"; and Alexei Kireev, "Skol'ko tratit' na oboronu?" (How much [should we] spend on defense?), *Ogonyok* 17, 1989: 6.
42. Daniil Granin, "Doroga k zdravomu smyslu" (A road to common sense), *Pravda,* August 5, 1988: 3.
43. Kireev, "Skol'ko . . . ," 7.
44. Stanislav Shatalin, "Risk perekhoda k rynku men'she, chem toptanie na meste" (The risk of the transition to market is less than that of marching in place), *Izvestia,* April 21, 1990: 3.

45. Alexander Solzhenitsyn, "Kak nam obustroit' Rossiyu" (How we can make Russia good for living), a supplement to *Komsomol'skaya pravda*, September 18, 1990.

46. Daniil Granin, "Doroga k zdravomu smyslu" (A road to common sense), *Pravda*, August 5, 1988: 3.

47. Andrei Sakharov, speech at the First Congress of People's Deputies on June 7, 1989, in *Pervyi S'ezd Narodnykh Deputatov SSSR. Stenographicheskiy otchyot. Tom III* (The First Congress of People's Deputies of the USSR. Official Transcript, vol. 3), Moscow: Publishing House of the Supreme Soviet, 1989: 328.

48. Yakimova, letter to the editor, in "Tak kak zhe nam obustroit' Rossiyu?" (So how can we make Russia good for living?), *Komsomol'skaya pravda*, November 23, 1990: 2.

49. Solzhenitsyn, "Kak nam . . ."

50. Andrei D. Sakharov, "Konstitutsiya Soyuza Sovetskikh Respublik Evropy i Azii" (Constitution of the Union of Soviet Republic of Europe and Asia), in "Konstitutsionnye idei Andreya Sakharova" (Constitutional ideas of Andrei Sakharov), *Oktyabr'*, May 1990: 146.

51. V. Dashichev, "Evropa otkrytykh dverey" (A Europe of open doors), *Komsomol'skaya pravda*, February 20, 1990: 2.

52. Viktor Sheynis, "Avgustovskaya zhatva" (The August harvest), *Izvestia*, October 13, 1989: 6.

53. Andrei Sakharov, "Stepen' svobody" (The degree of freedom), interview with *Ogonyok* 31, 1989: 26.

54. Leonid Nikitinskiy, "Do vstrechi v moratorii?" (Until we meet in the moratorium?), *Komsomol'skaya pravda*, November 21, 1990: 1.

55. Sakharov, "Stepen' . . . ," 26. See also Igor Klyamkin, *Trudniy spusk s ziyayushchikh vysot* (The difficult descent from the yawning heights), Moscow: Pravda/Biblioteka Ogon'ka, 1990: 21.

56. Solzhenitsyn, "Kak nam . . ."

57. Georgy Shakhnazarov, "Vostok-Zapad. K voprosu o deideologizatsii mezhgosudarstvennykh otnosheniy" (East-West. On the question of the de-ideologization of international relations), *Kommunist*, 3, 1989: 67.

58. Dashichev, op. cit.

59. Viktor Sheynis, "Perestroika na novom etape: opasnosti i problemy" (A new phase of perestroika: dangers and problems), in F. M. Borodkin, L. Ya. Kosals, and P. V. Ryvkina, *Postizhenie* (Attainment of truth), Moscow: Progress, 1989: 375.

60. Vladimir Chernyak, "My—na odnom korable" (We [are] in the same boat), *Komsomol'skaya pravda*, October 15, 1988: 3.

61. Asked at the end of 1989 by the Center for Political and Sociological Studies if the Soviet Union should "actively oppose" a decision by an Eastern European country to "adopt a Western model of economic development," 80 percent of the sampled Muscovites said "no." By a 64-to-23 ratio they also rejected inter-

vention if any of the former satellites decided to leave the Warsaw Pact. ("Politika pravil'naya no izmeneniya nado provodit' bystrey" [The policy is correct but changes have to be implemented faster], *Moskovskie novosti,* January 14, 1990: 9.)

62. Evgeny Ambartsumov, "Ne agoniya, a povorot k zhizni" (Not an agony but a turn to life), *Moskovskie novosti,* November 5, 1989: 7, and Sheynis, "Avgustovskaya . . ."

63. Alexei Izyumov and Andrei Kortunov, "Diplomatiya i nravstvennost' vremyon perestroiki" (Diplomacy and morality at the time of perestroika), *Moskovskie novosti,* August 6, 1989: 6.

64. Ibid.

65. Ibid.

66. Ibid.

67. Ibid.

68. Yu. Novopashin, "Proshchay, oruzhie!" (Farewell to arms!), interview with *Komsomol'skaya pravda,* December 6, 1989: 2.

69. Stanislav Kondrashov, "Iz mraka secretnosti" (From the darkness of secrecy), *Novy mir,* August, 1989: 183.

70. Alexander Bovin, "Perestroika i vneshnyaya politika" (Perestroika and foreign policy), *Izvestia,* June 16, 1988: 5.

71. Stanislav Kondrashov, "Iz mraka secretnosti" (From the darkness of secrecy), *Novy mir,* August 1989: 178–206.

72. Sergei Volovets, "Bol'she pushek—men'she myasa" (More cannons—less meat), *Moskovskie novosti,* October 28, 1990: 3.

73. Dashichev, op. cit.

74. Sergei Karaganov, "Arkhitektura dlya Evropy" (Architecture for Europe), *Moskovskie novosti,* May 13, 1990: 12.

75. Kondrashov, "Iz mraka . . . : 198.

76. Vladimir Chernyak, "My—na odnom korable" (We [are] in the same boat), *Komsomol'skaya pravda,* October 15, 1988: 3.

EPILOGUE

1. Alexis de Tocqueville, *The Old Regime and the French Revolution,* trans. Stuart Gilbert, New York: Anchor Books, 1983: x.

2. Nikolai Kostomarov, *Russkaya instoriya v zhizneopisaniyakh eyo glavnykh deyateley* (Russian history in biographies of its main figures), Moscow: Kniga, 1991, vol. 1: 565.

3. Boris Vasiliev, "Lyubi Rossiyu v nepogodu . . ." (Love Russia in bad weather), *Izvestia,* January 17, 1989: 3.

4. Igor Klyamkin, "Pochemu trudno govorit' pravdu" (Why it is difficult to speak truth), *Novy mir,* February, 1989: 233.

5. Zbigniew Herbert. *Barbarians in the Garden.* New York: Harvest/Harcourt, 1985: 120.

6. Lazar' Lazarev, "Dukh svobody" (The spirit of freedom), *Znamya*, September 1988: 225.

7. L. Gozman and and A. Etkind, "Kul't vlasti. Struktura totalitarnogo soz-naniya" (The cult of power: The structure of totalitarian consciousness), in Kh. Kobo, ed., *Osmyslit' kul't Stalina* (To comprehend Stalin's cult), Moscow: Progress, 1989: 78–79.

8. Ibid.

9. Ibid.

10. Igor Vinogradov, "Mozhet li pravda byt' poeatpnoy?" (Can the truth be doled out in stages?), in Yuri Afanasiev, ed., *Inogo ne dano* (There is no other way), Moscow: Progress, 1988: 281.

11. Gozman and Etkind, "Kul't vlasti," 79.

12. In L. Gol'din, "Nado snova nauchit'sya zhit'" (We must again learn to live), *Sovetskaya kul'tura*, August 29, 1989: 3.

13. As quoted in Lev Annenskiy, "Monolog byvshego stalintsa" (A monologue of a former Stalinist), in Kh. Khobo, ed., *Osmyslit' kul't Stalina* (To comprehend Stalin's cult), Moscow: Progress, 1989: 59.

14. Anatoly Rybakov, "Rana, kotoraya krovotochit" (The wound that is bleeding), *Moskovskie novosti*, November 27, 1988: 7, and Tamara Sevko, a letter to the editor, published in *Pravdu i tol'ko pravdu* (Truth and only the truth), *Moskovskie novosti*, December 4, 1988: 9.

15. Vinogradov, "Mozhet li pravda," 283.

16. Vladimir Kantor, "Imya rokovoe" (The fateful name), *Voprosy literatury* 3, 1988: 83.

17. Alexander Tsypko, "Istoki Stalinisma" (The origins of Stalinism), part 4, *Nauka i zhizn'*, February 1989: 53. See also Leon Aron, "After the Leviathan," *Journal of Democracy* 18(2), April 2007: 121.

18. Lev Gudkov, the director of the Levada Center, quoted in Paul Goble "Putin Ideological Effort Promotes Political Passivity, Russian Pollster Says," *Window on Eurasia*, September 30, 2009.

19. Marietta Chudakova, "V zashchitu zhizni chelovecheskoy. Roman Borisa Pasternaka 'Doktor Zhivago' na stranitsakh 'Novogo mira'" (In defense of human life: Boris Pasternak's novel *Doctor Zhivago* in the pages of *Novy mir*), *Moskovskie novosti*, January 31, 1988: 11.

20. For a discussion of the textbook in question, see my "The Problematic Pages," *New Republic*, September 24, 2008: 35–41.

21. Paul Goble, "Russia Must Face Up to the Tragic Reality of the Hitler-Stalin Alliance, Memorial Says," *Window on Eurasia*, September 17, 2009.

22. "Russia Replies to OSCE." *Moscow Top News, July 9, 2009.* http://www.moscowtopnews.com/?area=listByTag&id=693. Accessed on November 1, 2011.

23. Dmitri Medvedev, "Pamyat' o natsional'nykh tragediyakh tak zhe svyashchenna, kak pamyat' o pobedakh" (The Memory of National Tragedies Is as Sacred as the Memory of Triumphs), Dmitri Medvedev's videoblog, October 30, 2009, available at http://blog. kremlin.ru/post/35/transcript (accessed December 2, 2009).

24. Paul Goble, "Memorial Calls on Medvedev to Denounce Katyn as Crime against Humanity," *Window on Eurasia,* March 5, 2010.

25. http://www.nameofrussia.ru. Accessed on June 23, 2010.

26. Gudkov in Goble, "Putin Ideological Effort . . ."

27. See, for example, Viktor Sheynis, "Avgustovskaya zhatva" (The August harvest), *Izvestia,* October 13, 1989: 6.

28. See, for example Viktor Kuvaldin, "Nazad—v tsivilizatsiyu" (Back—to civilization), *Moskovskie novosti,* August 5, 1990: 3.

29. Vladimir Shubkin, "Trudnoe proshchanie" (The difficult farewell), *Novy mir,* April 1989: 183.

30. Alexander Solzhenitsyn, *V kruge pervom* (In the first circle), Moscow: Act, 2006: 687.

31. Darrin McMahon, *Happiness: A History,* New York: Atlantic Monthly Press, 2006, as quoted by Harvey C. Mansfield, "Good and Happy," *New Republic,* July 3, 2006.

32. Alexis de Tocqueville, *The Old Regime and the French Revolution,* trans. Stuart Gilbert, New York: Anchor Books, 1983: x.

33. Zbigniew Herbert, "Blackthorn," in *Elegy for the Departure and Other Poems.* Hopewell: Ecco Press, 1999: 93.

Leonid Abalkin. "Lunniy landshaft" (A moon-like landscape). Interview with
   Komsomol'skaya pravda, February 8, 1989: 2.
———. "Kuda my idyom" (Where we are going). Interview with *Novoe vremya*, no.
   28, 1987: 3–5.
Fyodor Abramov. "And people are waiting and waiting for changes. From diaries
   and working notes." *Izvestia*, February 3, 1990: 3.
Ales' Adamovich. In "Proshchanie s Andreem Dmitrievichem Sakharovym"
   (Farewell to Andrei Dmitrievich Sakharov). *Literaturnaya gazeta*, December 20,
   1989: 10.
———. "Oglyanis' okrest!" (Look around you!). *Ogonyok* 39, 1988: 28–30.
———. "Vospominanie o budushchem, kotorogo ne dolzhno byt'" (Remembrance
   of a future that must not be allowed to be). In "Chto budet, esli i eta perestroika
   pogibnet?" (What will happen if this perestroika, too, perishes?), a roundtable
   discussion. *Moskovskie novosti*, June 5, 1988: 8.
———. "Optimizm delaniya" (The optimism of doing something). *Moskovskie
   novosti*, September 11, 1988: 13.
———. "Voynu vyigral narod" (The people have won the war). *Moskovskie novosti*,
   February 28, 1988: 2.
Yuri Afanasiev. Interview with *Sovetskaya molodyozh*, July 7, 1989: 3. In Ol'ga
   Avdevich and Elena Vlasova, "Sdelka" (A deal), part 2.
———. "Memorial–v dialoge s proshlym i nastoyashchim" (Memorial–in a dialogue
   with the past and the present). *Moskovskie novosti*, February 5, 1989: 4.
———. "Perestroika i istoricheskoe znanie" (Perestroika and historical knowledge).
   Literaturnaya Rossiya, June 17, 1988: 2–3, 8–9.
———, ed. *Inogo ne dano* (There is no other way). Moscow: Progress, 1988.

——. "Perestroika i istoricheskoe znanie" (Perestroika and historical knowledge). In Afanasiev, ed., *Inogo ne dano:* 491–508.

——. "Otvety istorika" (The historian's answers). *Pravda,* July 26, 1988: 2.

——. "Afisha nedeli" (The playbill of the week). *Ogonyok* 46, 1988: 31.

Yuri Afanasiev, Len Karpinskiy, and Marina Ogorodnikova, "Myshlenie bez 'pogon'" (Thought that knows no rank distinctions). *Moskovskie novosti,* September 25, 1988: 8.

Abel Aganbegyan, "Chelovek i ekonomika" (Man and economy). Interview with *Ogonyok.* Part 1: *Ogonyok* 29, 1987: 2–5.

——. Part 2: *Ogonyok* 30, 1987: 12–18.

T. Aglyamova. "Bosye po nasledstvu?" (Hereditarily barefoot?). *Pravda,* December 19, 1989: 2.

Anna Akhmatova. *Requiem. Oktyabr',* March 1987.

B. E. Aksakova ("neé Bekirova"). Letter to the editor. *Ogonyok* 4, 1989: 3.

Petr Aleshkovsky. "Pro kolbasu" (About sausage). *Ogonyok* 33, 1988: 28–30.

Sergei Alexeev. "Ploshchad' pered parlamentom" (The square in front of the parliament). *Komsomol'skaya pravda,* July 11, 1989: 2.

Evgeniya Al'bats. "Anatomiya merzosti" (The anatomy of villainy). *Moskovskie novosti,* October 16, 1988: 13.

——. "Proshcheniyu ne podlezhat" (No forgiveness for them). *Moskovskie novosti,* May 8, 1988: 13.

Alla Allova. "Luchshe ne dumat'?" (Better not to think?). *Ogonyok* 26, 1989: 28–31.

Evgeny Ambartsumov. "Ne agoniya, a povorot k zhizni" (Not an agony but a turn to life). *Moskovskie novosti,* November 5, 1989: 7.

——. "Sotsializm ili Stalinizm" (Socialism or Stalinism). *Sovetskaya kul'tura,* September 19, 1989: 2.

——. "Grani vlasti" (The facets of power). *Moskovskie novosti,* August 6, 1989: 3.

——. "O putyakh sovershenstvovaniya politicheskoy sistemy sotsializma" (On the ways to perfect the political system of socialism). In Afanasiev, ed., *Inogo ne dano:* 77–96.

Ernest Ametistov. "Lichnnost' i zakon" (An individual and law). *Moskovskie novosti,* December 11, 1988: 5.

Vladimir Amlinsky. "Ten'" (Shadow). *Literaturnaya gazeta,* September 7, 1988: 12.

Nikolai Amosov. "Real'nosti, idealy i modeli" (Realities, ideals, and models). *Literaturnaya gazeta,* October 5, 1988: 13.

Anatoly Anan'ev. "Po techeniyu ili naperkor" (Going with the flow or against it). *Oktyabr',* October 1989: 3–10.

V. Andryushchyuk. "Samorazorenie" (Self-ruination). *Komsomol'skaya pravda,* April 11, 1989: 1–2.

Evgeny Anisimov. "Oskolki imperii." *Moskovskie novosti,* December 17, 1989: 10.

Grigory Anisimov and Mikhail Emtsev. "Etot khranitel' drevnostey (O pisatele Yurii Dombrovskom I ego knigakh). Postscript to Yuri Dombrovsky, *Fakul'tet nenuzhnykh veshchey* (The department of unnecessary things). Moscow: Sovetskiy pisatel', 1989.

K. Anisova. Letter to the editor, in "Chitateli o poeme A. T. Tvardovskogo 'Po pravy pamayati'" ("Readers on A. T. Tvardvoskiy's poem 'In Memory's Name'"). *Znamya*, August 1987: 233.

Lev Anninskiy. "Monolog byvshego stalintsa" (A monologue of a former Stalinist). In Kh. Kobo, ed., *Osmyslit' kul't Stalina* (To comprehend Stalin's cult). Moscow: Progress, 1989: 54–80.

Mikhail Antonov. "Tak chto zhe s nami proiskhodit?" (What really is happening to us?). *Oktyabr'*, August 1987: 3–66.

——. "Poryadok i poryadochnost'" (Order and decency). *Ogonyok* 3, 1987: 3–4.

Yuri Apenchenko. "Kuzbass: zharkoe leto" (Kuzbass: a hot summer). *Znamya*, October 1989: 163–86.

V. A. Arangol'd. Letter to the editor. In "Narodnaya publitsistika" (People's political journalism). *Oktyabr'*, August 1989: 180.

Alexander Arkhangel'skiy. "Mezhdu svobodoy i ravenstvom. Obshchesvennoe soznanite v zerkale *Ogon'ka* i *Nashego sovremennika*" (Between freedom and equality. Public conscience in the mirror of *Ogonyok* and *Nash sovremennik*, 1986–1990). *Novy mir*, February 1991: 225–41.

Leon Aron. "The Problematic Pages." *New Republic*, September 24, 2008: 35–41.

——. "After the Leviathan." *Journal of Democracy* 18 (2), April 2007: 120–21.

——. *Yeltsin: A Revolutionary Life*. New York: St. Martin's, 2000.

——. "The Search for 'Socialist Pluralism,'" *Global Affairs*, Winter 1989: 104–17.

Anders Åslund. *How Russia Became a Market Economy*. Washington, DC: Brookings Institution, 1995.

Viktor Astaf'ev. Speech at the conference "Istoriya i literature" (History and literature). *Literaturnaya gazeta*, May 18, 1988: 4.

Ol'ga Avdevich and Elena Vlasova. "Sdelka" (A deal). Part 1. *Sovetskaya molodezh*, July 5, 1989: 1, 3.

Chingiz Aytmatov. "Tsena prozreniya" (The price of recovering sight). Interview with Felix Medvedev. *Ogonyok* 28, 1987: 4–7.

L. Ayzerman, "Trevozhit'sya i dumat'" (To worry and to think). *Novy mir* 10, October 1987: 180–93.

A. Babiy and V. Sirotin, "Mnogoe nado vyasnit'" (Much remains to be found out). *Moskovskie novosti*, November 27, 1988: 7.

Marat Baglay. "Moral' i politika" (Morality and politics). *Sovetskaya kul'tura*, July 27, 1989: 4.

Donna Bahry. "Society Transformed? Rethinking the Social Roots of Perestroika." *Slavic Review*, no. 3, Fall 1993: 527–54.

——. "Politics, Generations, and Change in the USSR." In James R. Millar, ed., *Politics, Work and Daily Life in the USSR*. Cambridge: Cambridge University Press, 1987, 61–99.

Bernard Bailyn. *The Ideological Origins of the American Revolution*. Cambridge: Harvard University Press/Belknap, 1992.

Grigory Baklanov. "Vysota dikha" (The spirtual height). *Znamya*, May 1990: 3–10.

———. "Vystuplenie na plenume pravleneniya soyuza pisateley." Speech at the Plenum of the Presidium of the Writers' Union, April 27–28, 1987. *Literaturnaya gazeta*, May 6, 1987: 2.

Evgeniy Barabanov. "Predskazanie ili preduprezhdenie?" (A prediction or a warning). *Moskovskie novosti*, February 28, 1988: 11.

E. I. Bashkirova. "Transformatsiya tsennostei rossiyskogo obshchestva." *Polis* 6, 2002: 53–62.

Vladimir Bashmachnikov. "O zemle i vole" (On land and freedom). *Moskovskie novosti*, December 2, 1990: 3.

Leonid Batkin. "O konstitutsionnom proekte Andreya Sakharova" (On Andrei Sakharov's constitutional project). In "Konstitutsionnye idei Andreya Sakharova" (Constitutional ideas of Andrei Sakharov). *Oktyabr'*, May 1990: 150–64.

———. "Vozobnovlenie istorii" (The resumption of history). In Afanasiev, ed., *Inogo ne dano:* 154–91.

Alexander Bek. *Novoe naznachenie* (A new appointment). *Znamya*, November–December 1986.

Alexander Bekker. "Myaso na vyvoz" (Meat for export). *Moskovskie novosti*, July 10, 1988: 13.

G. Belaya. "Tret'ya zhizn' Isaaka Babelya" (The third life of Isaak Babel). *Oktyabr'*, October 1989: 185–97.

M. Belaya. "Ekzamen budet, no uchebnikov poka net" (There will be the exam, but so far there are no textbooks). *Izvestia*, February 8, 1989: 3.

T. Belaya. "Moya ital'yanskaya mechta . . ." (My Italian dream). *Komsomol'skaya pravda*, February 13, 1990: 2.

Vasily Belov. Speech at the First Congress of People's Deputies of the USSR, June 1, 1989. *Izvestia*, June 2, 1989: 9.

L. N. Belyaeva. *Sotsial'naya modernizatsiya v Rossii v kontse XX veka* (Social modernization in Russia at the end of XX century). Moscow: Institute of Philosophy, Russian Academy of Sciences, 1997.

Isaiah Berlin. *The Crooked Timber of Humanity*. New York: Knopf, 1991.

———. *Four Essays on Liberty*. New York: Oxford University Press, 1969.

Yuri Bespalov. "Novocherkass. 1962." *Komsomol'skaya pravda*, June 3, 1990: 2.

Yuri Bespalov and Valery Konovalov. "Novocherkassk, 1962." *Komsomol'skaya pravda*, June 2, 1989: 4.

Igor Birman. "Sovetskie voennye raskhody" (Soviet military expenditures). *Oktyabr'*, September 1991: 132–53.

———. "Nosha ne po plechu" (Too heavy a burden). Interview with *Izvestia*, November 29, 1990: 5.

Sergei Blagovolin. "Otkrytyi mir ili osazhdyonnyi lager'?" (An open world or a besieged camp?). *Moskovskie novosti*, August 12, 1990: 3.

A. Blyudin. "Kommunizm: mezhdu proshlym i budyshchim" (Communism: between past and future). *Komsomol'skaya pravda*, March 27, 1989: 3.

Arlen Blyum. "Svobodno ot evreev" (Free from Jews). *Novoe vremya*, no. 20, 2005: 36–38.

S. Bobkova. "Avtor b'yot pryamo v tsel' " (The author hits the bull's eye). *Novy mir*, January 1987: 267.

Anatoly Bocharov. "Mchatsya mify, b'yutsya mify" (Myths are whirling, myths are stirring). *Oktyabr'*, January 1990: 181–91.

——. "Chast' pravdy–eto ne pravda . . ." (Partial truth is not truth). *Oktyabr'*, April, 1988: 143–48.

——. "Sud'ba narodnaya" (People's fate). *Oktyabr'*, March 1988: 150–56.

——. "Bolevye zony" (The zones of pain). *Oktyabr'*, February 1988: 104–9.

——. "Pravoe delo Vasiliya Grossmana" (Vasily Grossman's just cause). *Oktyabr'*, January 1988: 128–34.

Irina Boeva and Vyacheslav Shironin. "Russians between State and Market." *Studies in Public Policy*, no. 205, 1992.

Oksana Bogdanova, Alexander Stanislavsky, and Evgeny Starostin. "Soprotivele-nie" (Resistance). *Ogonyok* 23, 1989: 10–11.

Oleg Bogomolov. "Sotsializm, 90-e gody" (Socialism, the 1990s). *Komsomol'skaya pravda*, October 3, 1990: 2.

N. Bondaruk. "Den' vtoroy" (Day two). *Izvestia*, May 27, 1989: 1.

Elena Bonner. "Polupravda ne luchshe lzhi" (A half-truth is no better than a lie). *Literaturnaya gazeta*, November 11, 1992: 11.

——. "Iz vospominaniy" (From the memoirs). In "Konstitutsionnye idei Andreya Sakharova" (Constitutional ideas of Andrei Sakharov). *Oktyabr'*, May 1990: 165–68.

Alexander Borshchagovsky, ed. "Prislushaemsya k golosu Ryutina. Otryvki iz rukopisi tak i ne stavshey knigoy" (Let's listen to Ryutin's voice: Passages from a manuscript that has never become a book). *Moskovskie novosti*, May 27, 1990: 16.

Alla Bossart. "V Moskvu za pravdoy" (To Moscow to find truth). *Ogonyok* 45, 1988: 1–3.

A. F. Bourreau-Deslandres. *Histoire critique: iii.* As quoted in Donald R. Kelley. "What Is Happening to the History of Ideas?" *Journal of the History of Ideas* 51, no. 1, January–March 1990: 7.

Alexander Bovin. "Kitay i my" (China and we). *Moskovskie novosti*, April 8, 1990: 3.

——. "Kak kommunist, schitayu . . ." (As a Communist, I think . . .). *Moskovskie novosti*, April 30, 1989: 6.

——. "Politika i moral' " (Politics and morals). *Moskovskie novosti*, March 19, 1989: 3.

——. "Bol'she posledovatel'nosti!" (More consistency!). *Moskovskie novosti*, January 1, 1989: 2.

——. "Perestroika: Pravda o sotsializme i sud'ba sotsializma" (Perestroika: The truth about socialism and the fate of socialism). In Afanasiev, ed., *Inogo ne dano*: 519–50.

——. "Dva soobrazheniya" (Two thoughts). *Sovetskaya kul'tura*, June 23, 1988: 3.

——. "Perestroika i vneshnyaya politika" (Perestroika and foreign policy). *Izvestia*, June 16, 1988: 5.

Crane Brinton. *The Anatomy of Revolution*. New York: Vintage Books, 1965.

Vladimir Brovkin. "Revolution from Below: Informal Political Associations in Russia 1988–89." *Soviet Studies* 42 (2), 1990: 233–57.

L. P. Bueva, F. M. Burlatsky, and O. P. Tyomushkin. "Osvobodit'sya ot deformatsii sotsializma" (To free ourselves from the deformation of socialism). *Argumenty i fakty,* April 23–29, 1988: 3.

Nikolai Bugay. "V bessrochnuyu ssylku" (Into indefinite exile). *Moskovskie novosti,* October 14, 1990: 11.

V. J. Bulgakov. "Songs of 'Our Happy Childhood.'" Letter to *Ogonyok,* Spring 1989. In Christopher Cerf and Marina Albee, eds., *Small Fires: Letters from the Soviet People to Ogonyok Magazine, 1987–1990.* New York: Summit Books, 1990: 243–44.

Pavel Bunich. "Tsar', kotoriy pravit" (The czar who rules). *Literaturnaya gazeta,* November 7, 1990: 10.

——. "Novye tsennosti" (New values). *Oktyabr',* December 1987: 144–57.

Fyodor Burlatsky. "K sovremennoy tsivilizatsii" (Toward the modern civilization). *Literaturnaya gazeta,* September 5, 1990: 1, 2, 3.

——. "Sud'ba reformatorov strany" (The fate of our country's reformers). *Literaturnaya gazeta,* June 27, 1990: 1–2.

——. "Bezopasnost' i smelye reformy" (Security and bold reforms). *Literaturnaya gazeta,* March 7, 1990: 1.

——. "Sudebnaya reforma" (The court reform). *Literaturnaya gazeta,* November 15, 1989: 1.

——. "Faktor vremeni" (The factor of our time). *Literaturnaya gazeta,* March 15, 1989: 6.

——. "Pervyi no vazhnyi shag" (The first, but important step). *Literaturnaya gazeta,* June 14, 1989: 1–3.

——. "Brezhnev i krushenie ottepeli" (Brezhnev and the collapse of the thaw). *Literaturnaya gazeta,* September 14, 1988: 13.

——. "Kakoy sotsializm narodu nuzhen" (Socialism that people want). *Literaturnaya gazeta,* April 26, 1988: 2.

Yuri Burtin. "Chto takoe KPSS" (What is CPSU). *Oktyabr',* May 1991: 168–81.

——. "Zhivoe i myortvoe" (The living and the dead). *Literaturnaya gazeta,* no. 34, 1990: 7.

——. "Velikiy russkiy intelligent. Pamyati Andreya Dmitrievicha Sakharova" (The great man of the Russian intelligentsia: In memory of Andrei Dmitrievich Sakharov). *Oktyabr',* January 1990: 3–4.

——. "Vozmozhnost' vozrazit'" (The opportunity to object). In Afanasiev, ed., *Inogo ne dano:* 468–90.

——. "Vam, iz drugogo pokolen'ya ..." (To you, from a different generation ...). *Oktyabr',* August 1987: 191–202.

John Bushnell. "The 'New Soviet Man' Turns Pessimist." *Survey* 24, no. 2, 1980: 1–18.

A. Butenko. "Kakim byt' sotsializmu" (What socialism should be). *Pravda,* August 8, 1989: 3.

——. "O revolyutsionnoy perestroike gosudarstvenno-administrativnogo sotsializma" (On the revolutionary restructuring of the state-administrative socialism"). In Afanasiev, ed., *Inogo ne dano:* 551–68.

Nikolai Bykov. "Pryamaya rech" (Direct speech). *Ogonyok* 33, 1987: 19.

Rolan Bykov. Speech at the First Congress of People's Deputies on June 9, 1989. In *Pervyi S'ezd Narodnykh Deputatov SSSR. Stenographicheskiy otchyot. Tom III* (The First Congress of People's Deputies of the USSR. Official Transcript. Vol. 3). Moscow: Publishing House of the Supreme Soviet, 1989: 227–31.

Vasil' Bykov. *Oblava* (Man-hunt). *Novy mir,* January 1990: 87–140.

A. Bystrov. "Prostye lyudi" (The ordinary people). *Komsomol'skaya pravda,* January 29, 1989: 4.

Ellen Carnaghan. "A Revolution in Mind: Russian Political Attitudes and the Origins of Democratization under Gorbachev." Ph.D. diss., New York University, 1992.

Christopher Cerf and Marina Albee, eds. *Small Fires: Letters from the Soviet People to Ogonyok Magazine, 1987–1990.* New York: Summit Books, 1990.

Viktor Chalmaev. " 'Zhil chelovek na pravakh pozhara.' ('Nechayannoe' i vechnoe sovershenstvo Andreya Platonova)" (There once was a man who lived like a fire: The 'accidental' and eternal perfection of Andrei Platonov). In Andrei Platonov, *Sobranie sochineniy v pyati tomakh* (Collected Works in Five Volumes), vol. 1: 5–24. Moscow: Informpechat', 1998.

V. A. Chalmaev and Yu. V. Tikhonov. Comments on "Usomnivshiysya Makar" (Makar who has doubted). In Andrei Platonov, *Sobranie sochineniy v pyati tomakh* (Collected Works in Five Volumes), vol. 1: 596–98. Moscow: Informpechat', 1998.

——. "Istoriko-literaturnyi kommentariy" (A historical and literary commentary). In Andrei Platonov, *Sobranie sochineniy v pyati tomakh* (Collected Works in Five Volumes), vol. 2: 524–42. Moscow: Informpechat', 1998.

Evgeny Chazov, Minister of Healthcare of the Soviet Union. "Zdorov'e kazhdogo–dostoyanie obshchestva" (The health of every individual [is] society's achievement). Speech at the All-Union Congress of Physicians. *Pravda,* October 18, 1988: 2–3.

——. "Sotni voiteley stoit odin vrachevatel' iskusnyi" (One skillful physician is worth a hundred warriors). Interview with *Ogonyok* 42, 1988: 1–3.

——. Speech at the Nineteenth All-Union Party Conference. *Pravda,* June 30, 1988: 4.

——. "Kogda bolezn' obgonyaet lekarstva" (When disease outpaces remedies). Interview with *Literaturnaya gazeta,* February 3, 1988: 11.

Yuri Chernichenko. "Podnyavshiysya pervym" (He was the first to stand up). *Novy mir,* September 1989: 178–92.

——. "Zhdat' uzhe pozdno" (It is already too late to wait). *Ogonyok* 23, 1989: 4–5.

——. "O khlebe nasushchnom" (Of our daily bread). *Komsomol'skaya pravda,* March 12, 1989: 2.

——. "Zemlya, ekologiya, perestroika" (Land, ecology, perestroika). *Literaturnaya gazeta,* January 29, 1989: 3.

——. "Trava iz-pod stoga" (Grass from under a haystack). In Afanasiev, ed., *Inogo ne dano:* 591–620.

——. "Zhurnalist" (Journalist). *Znamya,* July 1987: 217–28.

——. "Kombayn prosit i kolotit" (A harvester begs and beats). *Novy mir,* December 1986: 190–211.

——. "Delo zavmaga Siddikova" (The case of the store manager Siddikov). *Druzhba narodov,* August 1986: 180–98.

A. Chernyak. "Edoki po statistike i v zhizni" (The food consumers in statistics and in real life). *Pravda,* September 1, 1988: 3.

Vladimir Chernyak. "My–na odnom korable" (We [are] in the same boat). *Komsomol'skaya pravda,* October 15, 1988: 3.

E. Chernykh. "Reabilitatsiya" (Acquittal). *Komsomol'skaya pravda,* March 19, 1989: 2.

Ion Chobanu. "Garantiya–pravovoe gosudarstvo" (A state of laws is the guarantee). *Literaturnaya gazeta,* February 8, 1982: 3.

A. Chubar'yan. "Avgust 1939 goda" (August 1939). *Izvestia,* July 1, 1989: 3.

Valentina Chudaeva. "Zhivu i pomnyu" (I live and I remember). *Moskovskie novosti,* May 7, 1989: 9.

Marietta Chudakova. "V zashitu zhizni chelovecheskoy. Roman Borisa Pasternaka 'Doktor Zhivago' na stranitsakh 'Novogo mira'" (In defense of human life: Boris Pasternak's novel *Doctor Zhivago* in the pages of *Novy mir*). *Moskovskie novosti,* January 31, 1988: 11.

Lidiya Chukovskaya. *Sof'ya Petrovna* and *Spusk pod vodu* (Descent underwater). Moscow: Moskovsky Rabochiy, 1988.

Vadim Churbanov. ". . . Prinadlezhit narodu" ([Culture] belongs to the people). *Ogonyok* 37, 1988: 18–21.

Winston S. Churchill. *The Second World War.* Vol. 4, *The Hinge of Fate.* London: Penguin Books, 1985.

Cicero, *Second Phillipic* 2.116. As quoted in Luciano Canfora, *Julius Caesar.* Berkeley: University of California Press, 2007: 347.

Timothy J. Colton and Michael McFaul, "Are Russians Undemocratic?" Working Paper No. 20, 2001. Washington: Carnegie Endowment for International Peace.

Walter D. Connor, "Builder and Destroyer: Thoughts on Gorbachev's Soviet Revolutions, 1985–1991," *Demokratizatsiya* 13 (2), Spring 2005: 173–91.

Lewis A. Coser, ed. *Masters of Sociological Thought.* New York: Harcourt Brace Jovanovich, 1971.

Lewis A. Coser and Bernard Rosenberg. *Sociological Theory.* New York: Macmillan, 1969.

Alexander Dallin. "Causes of the Collapse of the USSR." *Post-Soviet Affairs* 8 (4): 279–302.

V. Danilov, N. Teptsov, and L. Smirnov. "Kollektivizatsiya: kak eto bylo" (Collectivization: how it all happened). *Pravda,* September 16, 1988: 3.

G. Dankov. "Zashchitnik zhdyot zashchity" (The protector is waiting for protection). *Sovetskaya kul'tura,* October 5, 1989: 3.

Robert Darnton. *The Literary Underground of the Old Regime.* Cambridge: Harvard University Press, 1982.

Vyacheslav Dashichev. "Evropa otkrytykh dverey" (A Europe of open doors). *Komsomol'skaya pravda*, February 20, 1990: 2.

———. "Stalin v nachale 39-go" (Stalin in the beginning of 1939). *Moskovskie novosti*, August 27, 1989: 16.

———. "Vostok-Zapad: poisk novykh otnosheniy." (East-West: a search for new relations). *Literaturnaya gazeta*, May 18, 1988: 14.

James C. Davies. "Toward a Theory of Revolution." In Clifford T. Payton and Robert Blackey, eds., *Why Revolution? Theories and Analyses*. Cambridge, MA: Schenkman, 1971: 177–98.

Natal'ya Davydova. "Dolgi nashi" (Our debts). *Moskovskie novosti*, September 10, 1989: 5.

István Deak, "Discipline and Decline." *New Republic*, March 12, 2008: 43–46.

"Deklaratsiya osnovnykh printsipov Konfederatsii truda. 1 maya 1990 g., g. Novokuznetsk" (Declaration of the main principles of the Confederation of labor. May 1, 1990, the city of Novokuznetsk). Document No. 210. In L. Lopatin, ed., *Rabochee dvizhenie Kuzbassa. Sbornkin documentov i materialov. Aprel' 1989–Mart 1992* (The workers' movement of Kuzbass: A collection of documents and materials, April 1989–March 1992). Kemerovo: Sovremennaya otechestvennaya kniga, 1993: 282–86.

N. Dmitriev. "O chyom grustyat tkachi" (What are weavers sad about?). *Sovetskaya kul'tura*, April 5, 1989: 3.

Oksana Dmitrieva. "Ekspertiza" (Expertise). *Moskovskie novosti*, February 15, 2000. Accessed at http://dlib.eastview.com/sources/article.jsp?id=137994 on July 17, 2007.

Yuri Dombrovsky. *Fakul'tet nenuzhnykh veshchey* (The department of unnecessary things). Moscow: Sovetskiy pisatel', 1989.

Maria Stepanovna Dranga. Letter to *Znamya*, August 1987: 234–35.

Vladimir Dudintsev. *Belye odezhdy* (White garments). Moscow: Sovetskiy pisatel', 1988.

"Durnoy son?" (A nightmare?). *Rabotnitsa*, 11 (November) 1988: 36.

Harry Eckstein. "On the Etiology of Internal Wars." In Clifford T. Payton and Robert Blackey, eds., *Why Revolution? Theories and Analyses*. Cambridge, MA: Schenkman, 1971: 124–50.

Editorial, *Ogonyok* 50, 1989: 30.

A. Egorova, department head, the Altai regional hospital in Barnaul. Speech at the First Congress of People's Deputies on June 8, 1989. In *Pervyi S'ezd Narodnykh Deputatov SSSR. Stenographicheskiy otchyot. Tom III* (The First Congress of People's Deputies of the USSR. Official Transcript. Vol. 3). Moscow: Publishing House of the Supreme Soviet, 1989: 70–77.

"18 grammov myl'nykh puzyrey" (18 grams of soap bubbles). Letter by miners from the Kiselev mine, the city of Torez. *Izvestia*, April 15, 1989: 2.

Charles A. Ellwood. "A Psychological Theory of Revolutions." In Clifford T. Payton and Robert Blackey, eds., *Why Revolution? Theories and Analyses*. Cambridge, MA: Schenkman, 1971: 151–59.

A. M. Emel'yanov. Speech at the First Congress of People's Deputies on June 7, 1989. In *Pervyi S'ezd Narodnykh Deputatov SSSR. Stenographicheskiy otchyot. Tom III* (The First Congress of People's Deputies of the USSR. Official Transcript. Vol. 3). Moscow: Publishing House of the Supreme Soviet, 1989: 77–84.

Viktor Erofeev. "Pominki po sovetskoy literature" (A wake for Soviet literature). *Literaturnaya gazeta,* July 4, 1990: 8.

Evgeny Evtushenko. "Stalinizm po Platonovu" (Stalinism according to Platonov). In Kh. Kobo, ed., *Osmyslit' kul't Stalina* (To comprehend Stalin's cult). Moscow: Progress, 1989: 195–213.

———. "Pechal'no, no tverdo" (With sadness but firmly). *Ogonyok* 52, 1989: 2.

———. "Sud'ba Platonova" (Platonov's fate). *Sovetskaya kul'tura,* August 20, 1988: 5.

———. Introduction to Natliya Rapoport, "Pamyat'–tozhe meditsina" (Memory is medicine, too). *Yunost',* no. 4, 1988: 76.

Natan Eydel'man. "Optimizm istoricheskogo soznaniya" (The optimism of historical knowledge). Interview with *Ogonyok* 44, 1988: 2–4.

Charles Fairbanks. "Introduction." Special issue, *National Interest,* Spring 1993: 5–9.

R. A. Faramazyan. "Izderzhki sverkhvooruzhennosti" (The costs of super-armament). In M. I. Melkumyan, ed., *Drama obnovleniya* (The drama of renewal). Moscow: Progress, 1990: 195–215.

Mikhail Fedotov. "Bol'she svobody–vyshe otvetstvennost" (More freedom [means] greater responsibility). *Moskovskie novosti,* October 23, 1988: 12.

Svyatoslav Fedorov. "Voinstvo so strelami" (An army with arrows). *Pravda:* September 28, 1987: 3.

———. "Chtoby nikogda ne povtorilos'!" (So as not to let it happen again!). *Ogonyok* 8, 1987: insert between pages 5 and 6.

Yu. Fel'shtinskiy and N. Eydel'man. "Za nedelyu do nachala vtoroy mirovoy voyny." *Moskovskie novosti,* August 20, 1989: 8–9.

Yuri Feofanov. "Vozvrashchenie k istokam" (The return to the sources). *Znamya,* February 1989: 138–57.

Konstantin Feoktistov. "Skazhem drug drugu pravdu" (Let us tell each other the truth). *Literaturnaya gazeta,* November 7, 1990: 11.

Esther Fine. "10 AIDS Babies Baffling Moscow Hospital Team." *New York Times,* February 12, 1989.

Ada M. Finifter and Ellen Mickiewicz. "Redefining the Political System of the USSR: Mass Support for Political Change." *American Political Science Review* 86, no. 4, December 1992: 857–74.

M. Steven Fish. "Russia's Crisis and the Crisis of Russology." In David Holloway and Norman Naimark, eds., *Reexamining the Soviet Experience: Essays in Honor of Alexander Dallin.* Boulder, CO: Westview Press, 1996.

———. *Democracy from Scratch.* Princeton: Princeton University Press, 1995.

Vladimir Fomin and Yuri Shchekochikhin, "Togda, v Novocherkasske" (Then, in Novocherassk). *Literaturnaya gazeta,* June 21, 1989: 13.

Fond Obshshesvennogo Mneniya (The Public Opinion Foundation), public opinion polls April 10–July 1, 1996. Unpublished, the author's archive.

V. Frolov. "Chtoby eto ne povtorilos'" (So that this does not happen again). In Yuri Afanansiev, ed., *Inogo ne dano* (There is no other way). Moscow: Progress, 1988: 392–411.

Francis Fukuyama. "The Modernizing Imperative." In Owen Harries, ed., *The Strange Death of Soviet Communism*. Special issue, *National Interest,* Spring 1993: 10–17.

———. *The Great Disruption: Human Nature and the Reconstitution of Social Order.* New York: Free Press, 1990.

François Furet. *The Passing of an Illusion*. Chicago: University of Chicago Press, 1999.

———. *Interpreting the French Revolution*. New York: Cambridge University Press, 1981.

Dmitry Furman. "Nash put' k normal'noy kul'ture" (Our road to a normal culture). In Yuri Afanansiev, ed., *Inogo ne dano* (There is no other way). Moscow: Progress, 1988: 569–80.

Georgy Gachev. "Arsenal dobroy voli. O romane V. Dudintseva 'Belye odezhdy' i v svyazi s nim" (The arsenal of good will. About Vladimir Dudintsev's novel "White garments" and in connection with it). *Novy mir,* August 1987: 183–90.

Egor Gaidar. *Dologoe vremya. Rossiya v mire* (Long time: Russia in the world). Moscow: Delo, 2005.

———. "The Inevitability of Collapse of Socialist Economy." In Egor Gaidar, ed., *The Economics of Transition*. Cambridge: MIT Press, 2003: 19–30.

P. Gal'tseva and I. Rodnyanskaya. "Pomekha–chelovek" (Man is the problem). *Novy mir* 12, December 1988: 217–30.

Maya Ganina. "Tsena El'dorado" (The price of El Dorado). *Literaturnaya gazeta,* February 22, 1989: 11.

———. "Bez obol'shcheniy prezhnikh dney" (Without the delusions of bygone days). *Literaturnaya gazeta,* January 13, 1988: 11.

Alexander Gasparishvili, Alexander Kolokol'tsev, and Sergey Tumanov. "Portret kandidata v Narodnye Deputaty SSSR" (The portrait of a candidate for a People's Deputy). *Moskovskie novosti,* March 19, 1989: 7.

Yuri Geller. "Nevernoe echo bylogo" (A wrong echo of the past). *Druzhba narodov,* September 1989: 229–44.

Alexander Gel'man. "Vozvrashchenie k nravstennym istokam" (A return to the moral sources). *Kommunist* 9, 1988: 17–21.

———. "Chto snachala, chto potom . . ." (What comes first, what comes later). *Literaturnaya gazeta,* September 10, 1986: 10.

Michael Gerson. *Heroic Conservatism*. New York: HarperOne, 2007. As quoted in John Podhoretz, "Activist," *Commentary,* January 2008: 54.

H. H. Gerth and C. Wright Mills. *From Max Weber: Essays in Sociology* (New York: Oxford University Press, 1978).

James L. Gibson and Raymond M. Duch. "Emerging Democratic Values in Soviet Political Culture." In Arthur H. Miller, William M. Reisinger, and Vicki L.

Hesli, *Public Opinion and Regime Change: The New Politics of Post-Soviet Societies.* Boulder, CO: Westview Press, 1993.

James L. Gibson, Raymond M. Duch, and Kent L. Tedin. "Democratic Values and the Transformation of the Soviet Union." *Journal of Politics* 54, no. 2, May 1992: 329–71.

Paul Goble. "Memorial Calls on Medvedev to Denounce Katyn as Crime Against Humanity." *Window on Eurasia,* March 5, 2010.

——. "Putin Ideological Effort Promotes Political Passivity, Russian Pollster Says." *Window on Eurasia,* September 30, 2009.

——. "Russia Must Face Up to the Tragic Reality of the Hitler-Stalin Alliance, Memorial Says." *Window on Eurasia,* September 17, 2009.

L. Gol'din. "Nado snova nauchit'sya zhit' "(We have to relearn to live). *Sovetskaya kul'tura,* August 29, 1989: 3.

Jack A. Goldstone. "The English Revolution: A Structural-Demographic Approach." In Jack A. Goldstone, ed., *Revolutions. Theoretical, Comparative and Historical Studies.* Belmont, CA: Wadsworth/Thomson, 2003: 157–70.

——. "Revolution in the U.S.S.R., 1989–1991." In Jack A. Goldstone, ed., *Revolutions. Theoretical, Comparative and Historical Studies.* Belmont, CA: Wadsworth/Thomson, 2003: 261–71.

——. *Revolution and Rebellion in the Early Modern World.* Berkeley, CA: University of California Press, 1991.

A. Golov, A. Grazhdankin, L. Gudkov, B. Dubinin, N. Zorkaya, Yu. Levada, A. Levinson, and L. Sedov "Chto my dumaem" (What we think). *Literaturnaya gazeta,* March 29, 1989: 12.

John Gooding. "Gorbachev and Democracy." *Soviet Studies* 42, no. 2, April 1990: 195–231.

——. "Perestroika as Revolution from Within: An Interpretation." *Russian Review* 51, no. 1, January 1992: 36–57.

Mikhail Gorbachev. *Memoirs.* New York: Doubleday, 1996.

——. Interview with ITAR-TASS, October 13, 1992.

——. "Krepit' klyuchevoe zveno ekonomiki" (Strengthen the key link of the economy). *Pravda,* December 10, 1990: 1.

——. *Perestroika: New Thinking for Our Country and the World.* New York: Harper and Row, 1988: 7–8.

Leonid Gordon. In "Bol'she sotsializma!" *Ogonyok* 14, 1988: 6.

Leonid Gordon and E. Klopov. "Stalinizm i poststalinizm: neobkhodimost' preodoleniya" (Stalinism and post-Stalinism: The necessity of overcoming). In Kh. Kobo, ed., *Osmyslit' kul't Stalina* (To comprehend Stalin's cult). Moscow: Progress, 1989: 460–96.

Stanislav Govorukhin. "Zhut'!" (Dread!). *Sovetskaya kul'tura,* October 7, 1989: 11.

——. "Voyna s prestupnost'yu" (The war on crime). *Sovetskaya kul'tura,* July 29, 1989: 6.

Leonid Gozman. In "Bol'she sotsializma!" (More socialism!), a roundtable discussion. *Ogonyok* 14, 1988: 7, 10.

Leonid Gozman and A. Etkind, "Kul't vlasti. Struktura totalitarnogo soznaniya" (The cult of power: The structure of totalitarian consciousness). In Kh. Kobo, ed., *Osmyslit' kul't Stalina* (To comprehend Stalin's cult). Moscow: Progress, 1989: 337–71.

Daniil Granin. "Doroga k zdravomu smyslu" (A road to common sense). *Pravda*, August 5, 1988: 3.

———. *Zubr* (Bison). *Novy mir*, January 1987: 19–95, and *Novy mir*, February 1987: 7–92.

Stephen Greenblatt. "How It Must Have Been." *New York Review of Books*, November 5, 2009: 22–25.

Vasily Grossman. *Zhizn' i sud'ba* (Life and fate). Moscow: Knizhnaya palata, 1989.

———. *Vsyo techoyt* (Forever flowing). *Oktyabr'*, June 1989: 30–108.

Lev Gudkov and Boris Dubin. "Chto my chitaem" (What we read). Interviewed by Mikhail Gurevich. *Literaturnoe obozrenie* 1, 1988: 93–97.

———. "Literaturnaya kul'tura: Protsess i ratsion" (The literary culture: the process and the rationing). *Druzhba narodov* 2, February 1988: 168–89.

Grant Gukasov. "Za sem'yu pechatyami" (Behind seven seals). *Moskovskie novosti*, July 16, 1989: 16.

P. Gurevich. "Kakaya ideologiya nam nuzhna?" (What ideology do we need?). *Literaturnaya gazeta*, March 14, 1990: 10.

Ted Robert Gurr. *Why Men Rebel*. Princeton: Princeton University Press, 1970.

Vladimir Gusev. "Minutu molchaniya" (In a moment of silence). In "Platonov segodnya" (Platonov today). *Oktyabr'*, November 1987: 162–65.

Pavel Gutionov. "Boi mestnogo nazancheniya" (Combat of local significance). *Ogonyok* 39, 1987: 30.

V. M. Gvozdev. Speech at the First Congress of People's Deputies of the USSR on June 9, 1989. *Pravda*, June 10, 1989: 5.

Owen Harries, ed. *The Strange Death of Soviet Communism*. Special issue, *National Interest*, Spring 1993.

Zbigniew Herbert. "Blackthorn," in *Elegy for the Departure and Other Poems*. Hopewell: Ecco Press, 1999: 92–93.

Paul Hollander. *Personal Will and Political Belief*. New Haven: Yale University Press, 1999.

Geoffrey A. Hosking. "At Last an Exorcism." *Times Literary Supplement*, October 9–15, 1987: 1111.

Samuel P. Huntington. "Will More Countries Become Democratic?" *Political Science Quarterly* 99, 1984: 193–218.

———. *Political Order in Changing Societies*. New Haven: Yale University Press, 1968.

Zamira Ibragimova. "Ploshchadi boli" (The town squares of pain). *Ogonyok* 32. 1989: 2–4.

Zamira Ibragimova and Ilya Kartushin. "Matryonin grekh" (Matryona's sin). *Ogonyok* 5, 1989: 21–23.

S. Inozemtsev. Letter to the editor. In "Prostye lyudi" (The ordinary people). *Komsomol'skaya pravda*, March 25, 1989: 2.

F. Ivanov. "O prestupnosti–glasno" (To talk openly about deviance). *Izvestia*, September 10, 1988: 2.

Natal'ya Ivanova. "Proshchanie s utopiey" (A farewell to utopia). *Literaturnaya gazeta*, July 18, 1990: 4.

——. "Perekhod cherez boloto" (Crossing a quagmire). *Ogonyok* 25, 1988: 13–14.

Tatyana Ivanova. "Kto chem riskuet" (Who risks what). *Ogonyok* 24, 1988: 10–12.

D. Ivans. "Kakimi my byli, kakimi my stanem?" (What have we been and what will we be?). *Komsomol'skaya pravda*, June 28, 1988: 1.

"Iz trebovaniy gorodskogo stachechnogo komiteta g. Vorkuty, napravlennykh v Verkhovniy Sovet SSSR" (From the demands of the city striking committee of the city of Vorkuta, sent to the Supreme Soviet of the USSR). In V. V. Zhuravlev, L. N. Dobrokhotov, and V. N. Kolodezhnyi, eds., *Istoriya sovremennoy Rossii, 1985–1994* (History of modern Russia, 1985–1994). Moscow: Terra, 1995: 47.

Alexei Izyumov. "Idei dolzhny sostyazat'sya" (Ideas must compete). *Komsomol'skaya pravda*, January 9, 1990: 1.

——. "Glasnost v ekonomike" (Glasnost in economy). *Moskovskie novosti*, July 10, 1988: 13.

Alexei Izyumov and Andrei Kortunov, "Diplomatiya i nravstvennost' vremyon perestroiki" (Diplomacy and morality at the time of perestroika). *Moskovskie novosti*, August 6, 1989: 6.

Natalya Izyumova. "Ston" (Groan). *Moskovskie novosti*, October 23, 1988: 16.

Alain Jacob. "Democracy, Openness, and Patriotism." *Le Monde*, November 4, 1987: 4 (reprinted in English translation in FBIS-SOV-87–217, November 10, 1987: 70–71).

Chalmers Johnson. "Revolution and the Social System." In Clifford T. Payton and Robert Blackey, eds., *Why Revolution? Theories and Analyses*. Cambridge, MA: Schenkman, 1971: 199–213.

Samuel Johnson. *Rasselas, Poems, and Selected Prose*, ed. Bertrand H. Bronson, New York: Holt, Rinehart and Winston, 1971: 259.

Ken Jowitt. "Really Imaginary Socialism." *East European Constitutional Review* 6 (2 & 3), Spring/Summer 1997: 43–49.

Alexander Kabakov. "Nedelya sovesti: prodolzhenie neobkhodimo" (The week of conscience: Continuation is necessary). *Moskovskie novosti*, December 4, 1998: 14.

D. Kabalevskiy (music) and A. Prishelets (lyrics). "Nash kray" (Our land). 1955.

Stanislav Kalinichev. "Vsegda odna" (Always only one). *Ogonyok* 52, 1987: 1–3.

A. Kalinin. Letter to Alexei Tolstoy. In "Oni ne mogli molchat' " (They could not remain silent). *Moskovskie novosti*, November 27, 1988: 10.

Sofya Kalistratova. "Takoe bylo vremya" (Such was that time). *Moskovskie novosti*, August 6, 1989: 13.

Oleg Kalugin, "KGB bez grima" (The KGB without makeup). *Argumenty i fakty*, June 30–July 6, 1990: 6–7.

Vladimir Kantor. "Imya rokovoe" (The fateful name). *Voprosy literatury*, March, 1988: 62–85.

——. "Trudnyi put' k tsivilizatsii" (A difficult road to civilization). *Novy mir*, June 1987: 253–58.

Mikhail Kapustin. "Kamo gryadeshi?" (Whither art thou?). *Oktyabr'*, August 1987: 151–75.

Sergei Karaganov. "Arkhitektura dlya Evropy" (Architecture for Europe). *Moskovskie novosti*, May 13, 1990: 12.

Len Karpinsky. "S 'sotsializmom napereves'" (Attacking with socialism). *Moskovskie novosti*, May 27, 1990: 7.

——. "Instinkt demokratii" (The instinct of democracy). *Moskovskie novosti*, January 29, 1989: 8.

——. "Pochemu stalinizm ne skhodit so stseny?" (Why won't Stalinism leave the stage?). In Yuri N. Afanasiev, ed., *Inogo ne dano* (There is no other way). Moscow: Progress, 1988: 648–70.

A. Karpychev. "Krizis doveriya?" (The crisis of trust?). *Pravda*, June 24, 1988: 3.

Tatyana Karyagina. "Ya i my" (I and we). *Literaturnaya gazeta*, May 24, 1989: 12.

Yuri Karyakin. Speech at the First Congress of People's Deputies. *Pravda*, June 5, 1989: 4.

——. "Eto nash posledniy shans" (This is our last chance). In "Chto budet, esli i eta perestroika pogibnet?" (What will happen if this perestroika, too, perishes?), a roundtable discussion. *Moskovskie novosti*, June 5, 1988: 8.

——. "Zhdanovskaya zhidkost'" (Zhdanov's liquid). In Yuri Afanasiev, ed., *Inogo ne dano* (There is no other way). Moscow: Progress, 1988: 412–23.

——. In "Bol'she sotsializma!" (More socialism!), a roundtable discussion. *Ogonyok* 14, 1988: 7.

——. In "Bol'she sotsializma!" (More socialism!), a roundtable discussion. *Ogonyok* 12, 1988: 10.

——. "Stoit li nastupat' na grabli?" (Do we really want to step on a rake?). *Znamya*, September 1987: 200–224.

Yuri Kashlev. "Venskiy proryv: prava cheloveka v SSSR" (The Vienna breakthrough: human rights in the USSR). *Moskovskie novosti*, March 26, 1989: 10.

A. V. Kas'yanov. Speech at a conference of the Central Committee of the Communist Party of Ukraine. *Radyan'ska Ukraina*, August 10, 1989: 2.

"Katyn. Trudnyi put' k istine" (A difficult path to the truth). *Moskovskie novosti*, April 22, 1990: 4.

V. G. Kazakov, ed. *Razvedka slovom* (Reconnaissance by word). Moscow: Moskovskiy rabochiy, 1988.

Dmitry Kazutin and Vladimir Loshak. "Na kakom etape nakhoditsya perestroika?" (At what stage is perestroika?). *Moskovskie novosti*, July 9, 1989: 10.

——. "Zhertvoyu pali" (Fallen a victim). *Moskovskie novosti*, November 27, 1988: 5.

——. "Simvoly vmesto tseley" (Symbols instead of goals). *Moskovskie novosti*, June 5, 1988: 10.

Ruslan Khazbulatov. "Bednye lyudi otechestva" (The poor people of the Fatherland). *Komsomol'skaya pravda,* July 6, 1989: 2.

Ludmila Khokhulina. "Sub'ektivnyi sredniiy klass: dokhody, material'noe polozhenie, tsennostnye orientatsii" (A subjective middle class: Income, material status, value orientations). *Informatsionnyi bulleten' monitoringa,* February 1999: 24–34.

Ludmila Khokhulina and B. V. Golovachev. "Pyat' let ekonomicheskikh reform: izmeneniya v otsenkakh i mneniyakh naseleniya" (Five years of economic reforms: Changes in the evaluations and opinions of the population). *Informatsionnyi bulleten' monitoringa,* February 1995: 33–36.

Brendan Kiernan and Joseph Aistrup. "The 1989 Elections to the Congress of People's Deputies in Moscow." *Soviet Studies* 43 (6), 1991: 1049–64.

Alexei Kireev. "Sekretnaya stat'ya" (The secret article). *Literaturnaya gazeta,* October 18, 1989: 11.

——. "Skol'ko tratit' na oboronu?" (How much [should we] spend on defense)? *Ogonyok* 17, 1989: 6–8.

S. Kiselev. "Poka schtayut golosa . . ." (While they are counting the votes . . .). *Komsomol'skaya pravda,* March 6, 1990: 1.

V. Kiselev. "Skol'ko modeley sotsializma bylo v SSSR?" (How many models of socialism were there in the USSR?). In Yuri Afanasiev, ed., *Inogo ne dano* (There is no other way). Moscow: Progress, 1988: 354–69.

Sergey Kiselyov. "Eshcho raz o Bykovne" (Once more about Bykovnya). *Literaturnaya gazeta,* October 10, 1990: 13.

Alexei Kiva. "Oktyabr' v zerkale utopiy i antiutopiy" (The October Revolution in the mirror of utopias and anti-utopias). *Izvestia,* November 5, 1990: 3.

——. "Krizis 'zhanra' " (The crisis of the "genre"). *Novy mir,* March 1990: 206–16.

——. "Bezotvetsvennost' " (Irresponsibility). *Sovetskaya kul'tura,* October 12, 1989: 3.

A. Klimov. "Tsel': Puti i sredstva realizatsii" (The goal: the ways and means of achieving it). In M. I. Melkumyan, ed., *Drama obnovleniya* (The drama of renewal). Moscow: Progress, 1990: 422–54.

Igor Klyamkin. *Trudniy spusk s ziyayushchikh vysot* (The difficult descent from the yawning heights). Moscow: Pravda/Biblioteka Ogon'ka, 1990.

——. "Pochemu tak trudno govorit' pravdu" (Why it is difficult to speak truth). *Novy mir,* February, 1989: 204–38.

——. "Kakaya ulitsa vedyot k khramu?" (Which street leads to the temple?). *Novy mir,* November 1987: 150–88.

Kh. Kobo, ed. *Osmyslit' kul't Stalina* (To comprehend Stalin's cult). Moscow: Progress, 1989.

E. S. Kochetkov. Letter to *Znamya,* August 1987: 228.

Vladimir Kolesnik. Letter to *Znamya,* August 1987: 235.

Igor Kon. "Psikhologiya sotsial'noy inertsii" (The psychology of social inertia). *Kommunist,* January, 1988: 64–75.

Stanislav Kondrashov. "Yasnovidenie gumanista" (One humanist's clairvoyance). *Moskovskie novosti,* August 27, 1989: 11.

——. "Iz mraka secretnosti" (From the darkness of secrecy). *Novy mir*, August 1989: 178–206.

Vyacheslav Kondrat'ev. "Parii voyny" (The pariahs of the war). *Literaturnaya gazeta*, January 31, 1990: 8.

——. "Net, zhizn' prozhita ne zrya" *Sovetskaya kul'tura*, November 7, 1989: 3.

Vladimir Kontorovich. "The Economic Fallacy." In Owen Harries, ed., *The Strange Death of Soviet Communism*. Special issue, *National Interest*, Spring 1993: 35–45.

V. Korneev and S. Tutorskaya. "Lekarstva, kotorykh zhdut" (The drugs people are waiting for). *Izvestia*, January 1988: 2.

Vitaliy Korotich and Cathy Porter, eds. *The New Soviet Journalism. The Best of the Soviet Weekly Ogonyok*. Boston: Beacon Press, 1990.

——. Introduction to Christopher Cerf and Marina Albee, eds., *Small Fires: Letters from the Soviet People to Ogonyok Magazine, 1987–1990*. New York: Summit Books, 1990: 13–16.

——. Foreword to Korotich and Cathy Porter, eds., *The New Soviet Journalism: The Best of the Soviet Weekly Ogonyok*. Boston: Beacon Press, 1990: vii–viii.

——. "Idyom k pravde" (Advancing toward truth). *Ogonyok* 47, 1988: 6.

——. "Uchimsya nazyvat' veshchi svoimi imenami" (We learn to call things by their right names). *Moskovskie novosti*, July 3, 1988: 15.

Tat'yana Koryagina. "Ya i my" (I and we). *Literaturnaya gazeta*, May 24, 1989: 12.

Inna Kosheleva. "Nachal'niki moi i ne moi" (My bosses and not mine). *Novy mir*, September 1987: 181–208.

Vyacheslav Kostikov. "Vremay ottayavshikh slov" (A time of thawed-out words). *Ogonyok* 22, 1989: 4–6.

——. "O 'Fenomene Lokhankina' i russkoy intelligentsii" (About the "Lokhankin phenomenon" and the Russian intelligentsia). *Ogonyok* 49, 1988: 6–8.

Stephen Kotkin. *Armageddon Averted: The Soviet Collapse, 1970–2000*. New York: Oxford University Press, 2001.

T. Koval'. Chapters 23 and 24 (pp. 931–1003) in E. T. Gaidar, ed., *Ekonomika perekhodnogo perioda. Ocherki ekonomicheskoy politiki post kommunisticheskoy Rossii 1991–1997* (Economy of the transitional period: Essays on economic policy in post-communist Russia, 1991–1997). Moscow: IEPP, 1998.

A. Kovalenko. "My vse shli k Chernobylyu" (We all were approaching Chernobyl). *Argumenty i fakty*, July 15–21, 1989: 6.

A. Kozhevnikov. Letter to *Komsomol'skaya pravda*, December 28, 1990: 2.

V. Kozin. "Tayna kvadratnykh metrov" (The secret of square meters). *Komsomol'skaya pravda*, February 3, 1987: 2.

N. I. Krasnoborodko. "Write the Truth!" A letter to *Ogonyok*, January 1988. In Christopher Cerf and Marina Albee, eds., *Small Fires: Letters from the Soviet People to Ogonyok Magazine, 1987–1990*. New York: Summit Books, 1990: 240.

Mikhail Krasnov. "My prosnulis' v drugoy strane" (We woke up in a different country). *Rossiyskaya gazeta*, August 18, 2001, p. 4.

Viktor Krivorotov. "Russkiy put'" (The Russian path). *Znamya,* September, 1990: 184–200.

——. "Kto za rynok?" *Izvestia,* July 29, 1990: 1.

——. "Chto stoit za problemami" (What is behind the problems?). *Argumenty i fakty,* January 6–12, 1989: 4.

Viktor Krivorotov, Sergei Chernyshov, and Georgiy Tselms. "Mify nashey revolyut-sii" (The myths of our revolution). *Literaturnaya gazeta,* March 7, 1990: 5.

Thomas S. Kuhn. *The Structure of Scientific Revolutions.* Chicago: University of Chicago Press, 1962.

V. I. Kulakov. "Rebyonok bez prismotra?" (An unattended child?). *Pravda,* August 10, 1987: 4.

Vasily Kulish. "Byl li vybor?" (Was there a choice?). *Moskovskie novosti,* September 3, 1989: 12.

——. "U poroga voyny" (On the war's threshold). Interview with *Komsomol'skaya pravda,* August 24, 1988: 3.

——. Comments at a readers' conference. In I. Rishina and A. Egorov, "Lish tot dostoin zhizni i svobody . . . (Vasily Grossman. *Zhizn' i sud'ba*)." Chitatel'skay konferentsiya "LG" (Only he deserves life and liberty [who every day goes to battle for them] [Vasily Grossman. *Life and Fate*]. A readers' conference at *Literaturnaya gazeta*). *Literaturnaya gazeta,* August 24, 1988: 5.

Vasily Kulish and Nina Smirnova, "Neobkhodimye utochneniya" (Some necessary clarifications). *Moskovskie novosti,* September 3, 1989: 12.

Judith S. Kullberg. "The Ideological Roots of Elite Political Conflict in Post-Soviet Russia." *Europe-Asia Studies* 46 (6), 1994: 929–53.

V. Kurasov. "Izlechima li lekarstvennaya problema?" (Can the problem of medicines be cured?). "Notes from the joint meeting of the Committee for the Preservation of People's Health of the Supreme Soviet of the USSR and the Committee of People's Control of the USSR." *Izvestia,* October 21, 1989: 3.

M. A. Kytmanova. Letter to *Znamya.* In "Iz pochty 'Znameni.'" August 1987: 230–31.

Vladimir Lakshin. "Ot glasnosti k svodobe slova" (From glasnost to freedom of speech). *Moskovskie novosti,* April 9, 1989.

——. "Nravstvennost', spravedlivost', gumanizm" (Morality, justice, humanism). *Kommunist* 10, 1989: 33–42.

——. "Narod i lyudi. O romane Vasiliya Grossmana" (People and men. About Vasily Grossman's novel). *Izvestia,* June 25, 1988: 3.

——. "Gresti vyshe" (Aim higher). *Moskovskie novosti,* December 20, 1987: 4.

Gail Warshofsky Lapidus. "State and Society: Toward the Emergence of Civil Society in the Soviet Union." In Seweryn Bialer, ed., *Politics, Society, and Nationality Inside Gorbachev's Russia.* Boulder, CO: Westview Press, 1989.

——. "Social Trends." In Robert F. Byrnes, ed., *After Brezhnev: Sources of Soviet Conduct in the 1980s.* Bloomington: Indiana University Press, 1983: 186–249.

——. "Society under Strain." *Washington Quarterly* 6, Spring 1983: 29–46.

Alexander Lapin. "Bednost'" (Poverty). *Komsomol'skaya pravda,* April 19, 1990: 2.

——. "Korruptsiya" (Corruption). *Komsomol'skaya pravda*, December 21, 1989: 4.

Nikolai I. Lapin, ed. *Kak chuvstvyut sebya, k chemu stremyatsya grazhdane Rossii. Osnovnye fakty i vyvody analitcheskogo doklada po rezul'tatam monitoringa "Nashi tsennosti i interesy segodnya: 1990–1994–1998–2002"* (How the citizens of Russia feel and what they strive for: The main facts and conclusions of an analysis of the data collected by the longitudinal study "Our values and interests today: 1990–1994–1998–2002"). Moscow: Center for the Study of Social and Cultural Changes of the Institute of Philosophy of the Russian Academy of Sciences, 2002.

Nikolai I. Lapin and L. A. Belyaeva. *Dinamika tsennostey naseleniya reformiruemoy Rossii* (The dynamics of the values of the population of the reformed Russia). Moscow: URSS, 1996.

V. V. Lapkin. "Izmenenie tsennostnykh orientatsiy rossiyan." *Polis* 1, 2000: 47–50.

Alexander Larin. "Bezopasnost' ot gozbesopasnosti" (Security from state security). *Moskovskie novosti*, September 9, 1990: 6.

Otto Latsis. "Stalin protiv Lenina" (Stalin against Lenin). In Kh. Kobo, ed., *Osmyslit' kul't Stalina* (To comprehend Stalin's cult). Moscow: Progress, 1989: 215–46.

Alla Latynina. "Solzhenitsyn i my" (Solzhenitsyn and we). *Novy mir*, January 1990: 241–58.

Yulia Latynina. "V ozhidanii Zolotogo veka" (Waiting for the Golden Age). *Oktyabr'*, June 1987: 177–87.

Kirill Lavrov. Speech at the Second Congress of People's Deputies of the USSR on December 17, 1989. *Izvestia*, December 18, 1989: 4.

Lazar' Lazarev. "'Pravda bezuslovnaya and chestnaya.' Vasily Grossman i traditsii russkoy klassiki" ("Truth unconditional and honest." Vasily Grossman and the traditions of the Russian classical literature). *Literatura*, no. 2, 2002. Accessed at http://lit.1september.ru/article.php?ID+200600215 on September 7, 2009.

——. "Dukh svobody" (The spirit of freedom). Postscript to Vasily Grossman, *Zhizn' i sud'ba* (Life and fate). Moscow: Knizhnaya palata, 1989: 654–63.

——. "Dukh svobody" (The spirit of freedom). *Znamya*, September 1988: 218–29.

N. Lebedeva. *Katyn'skie golosa* (The voices of Katyn'). *Novy mir*, February 1991: 208–21.

——. "I eshcho raz o Katyni" (Once more about Katyn). *Moskovskie novosti*, May 6, 1990: 6.

A. Lemyatskikh. "Ni slova dobrogo, ni drov . . ." (Neither a kind word nor wood). *Pravda*, August 17, 1987: 1.

V. I. Lenin, "Zadachi soyuzov molodyozhi" (The tasks of the youth unions). Speech at the III All-Union Congress of the Russian Communist Union of Youth, October 2, 1920. In V. I. Lenin, *Polnoe sobranie sochineniy* (Collected Works), 5th ed. Moscow: Politicheskaya literatura, 1963: 298–318.

S. Leskov. "Zarazilis v bol'nitse" (Infected in a hospital). *Izvestia*, May 12, 1989: 7.

Yuri Levada. "'Chelovek sovetskiy': chetvyortaya volna. Funktsii i dinamika obshchestvennykh nastroeniy" (The "Soviet man": fourth wave. Functions and dynamics of public moods). *Vestnik obshchestvennogo meninya*, July–August 2004: 8–18.

——. "Vremya peremen glazami obshchestvennogo mneniya" (The time of change in the eyes of public opinion). *Vestnik*, January–February, 2003: 8–16.

——. "Chelovek 'osobennyï'" (A "special" man). *Vestnik*, March–April, 2003: 7–14.

——. *Ot mneniy k ponimaniyu. Sotsiologicheskie ocherki. 1993–2000* (From opinions to understanding: Sociological essays, 1993–2000). Moscow: Moscow School of Political Research, 2000.

——. "'Chelovek sovetskiy' pyat' let spustya: 1989–1994. Predvaritel'nye itogi sravnitel'nogo issledovaniya" ("The Soviet man" five years later: 1989–1994. Preliminary results of a comparative study). *Informatsionnyi bulleten' monitoringa*, January–February 1995: 9–13.

——, ed. *Sovetskiy prostoy chelovek. Opyt sotsial'nogo portreta na rubezhe 90-ykh* (A regular Soviet man: An attempt at a sociological portrait at the beginning of the 1990s). Moscow: 1993.

——, ed. *Est' mnenie!* (I have an opinion!). Moscow: Progress, 1990.

——. "Poezd speshit i opazdyvaet" (The train hurries up and is being late). *Sovetskaya kul'tura*, October 14, 1989: 2.

Yuri Levada and Leonid Gudkov. "The People's Voices." *Moscow News,* April 22, 1990: 7.

Bernard Levin. "The One Who Got It Right." Special issue, *National Interest,* Spring 1993: 64.

Nora Levin. *The Jews in the Soviet Union Since 1917: Paradox of Survival.* New York: New York University Press, 1988.

Yuri Levitansky. "Iz raznykh desyatiletiy" (From different decades). *Ogonyok 26,* 1988: 16.

Dmitry Likhachev. Speech at the First Congress of People's Deputies, a transcript. *Izvestia,* June 1, 1989: 1–4.

——. "Trevogi sovesti" (Troubles of conscience). *Literaturnaya gazeta,* January 1, 1987: 7.

A. Likhanov. Speech at the First Congress of People's Deputies of the USSR on June 1, 1989. *Izvestia,* June 2, 1989: 8.

Gennady Lisichkin. "Mify i real'nost'" (Myths and reality). In Kh. Kobo, ed., *Osmyslit' kul't Stalina* (To comprehend Stalin's cult). Moscow: Progress, 1989: 247–83.

——. "Put' k rynku" (The road to market economy). *Moskovskie novosti,* July 31, 1988: 8.

——. "S toskoy o 'ravenstve'" (With the dream of equality). In V. G. Kazakov, ed., *Razvedka slovom.* (Reconnaissance by word). Moscow: Moskovskiy rabochiy, 1988: 4–13.

N. Loginova. "Unyat' strakhi" (To calm down the fears). *Literaturnaya gazeta,* October 5, 1988: 12.

L. Lopatin, ed. *Rabochee dvizhenie Kuzbassa. Sbornik documentov i materialov. Aprel' 1989–Mart 1992* (The workers' movement of Kuzbass: A collection of documents and materials, April 1989–March 1992). Kemerovo: Sovremennaya otechestvennaya kniga, 1993.

Viktor Loshak. "Strana kvartirnogo ucheta" (The country of apartment record-keeping). *Moskovskie novosti,* June 3, 1990: 3.

Lord Macaulay. *The History of England.* New York: Penguin Books, 1968.

Martin Malia. "The Archives of Evil." *New Republic,* November 29 and December 6, 2004: 34–41.

Viktor Malukhin. "Pole pod svobodnym nebom" (A field under a free sky). *Izvestia,* March 7, 1990.

———. "Sovremennik vsem vremenam. K vykhodu v svet trilogii Andreya Platonova" (A contemporary for all times. On the publication of Andrei Platonov's trilogy). *Izvestia,* August 6, 1988: 3.

———. "Rekviem po utopii" (A requiem for utopia). *Znamya,* October 1987: 219–21.

Osip Mandel'shtam. "My zhivyom pod soboya ne chuya strany . . ." (We live not feeling the country's soil under us . . .). In O. E. Mandel'shtam, *Sobranie sochineniy v chetyryokh tomakh* (Collected works in four volumes), ed. G. P. Struve and B. A. Filippov. Moscow: Terra, 1991, vol. 1, op. 286: 202.

Harvey C. Mansfield. "Good and Happy," *New Republic,* July 3, 2006.

Karl Marx. "Preface to 'A Contribution to the Critique of Political Economy'" and "Manifesto of the Communist Party." In Robert C. Tucker, ed., *The Marx-Engels Reader.* New York: W. W. Norton, 1978.

A. Matlin. "Patologiya defitsita: gosudarstvo i naselenie" (The deficit pathology: the state and the people). In M. I. Melkumian, *Drama obnovleniya* (The drama of renewal). Moscow: Progress, 1990: 615–52.

Vikenty Matveev. "V Berline pyat'desyat let nazad" (Berlin, fifty years ago). *Moskovskie novosti,* November 16, 1990: 14.

G. Matyukhina, G. Grazhdankin, A. Levinson, and L. Sedov. "Rekord ukhodyashchego goda?" (The expiring year's record?). *Komsomol'skaya pravda,* December 29, 1988: 2.

Vladimir Mau. "The Logic and Nature of the Soviet Economic Crisis." In Egor Gaidar, ed., *The Economics of Transition.* Cambridge: MIT Press, 2003.

The Mazun family. Letter to the editor. In "Narodnaya publitsistika" (People's political journalism). *Oktyabr',* August 1989: 179–80.

Michael McFaul. "Revolutionary Transformation in Comparative Perspective: Defining a Post-Communist Research Agenda." In David Holloway and Norman Naimark, eds., *Reexamining the Soviet Experience. Essays in Honor of Alexander Dallin.* Boulder, CO: Westview Press, 1996: 167–96.

———. "Revolutionary Ideas, State Interests, and Russian Foreign Policy." In Vladimir Tesmaneanu, ed., *Political Culture and Civil Society in Russia and the States of Eurasia.* New York: M. E. Sharpe, 1995: 27–52.

James M. McPherson. *Battle Cry of Freedom.* New York: Oxford University Press, 1988.

Dmitri Medvedev. "Pamyat' o natsional'nykh tragediyakh tak zhe svyashchenna, kak pamyat' o pobedakh" (The memory of national tragedies is as sacred as the memory of triumphs). Dmitri Medvedev's Videoblog, October 30, 2009. Available at http://blog. kremlin.ru/post/35/transcript (accessed December 2, 2009).

Roy Medvedev. "Pochemu raspal'sya Sovetskiy Soyuz?" (Why did the Soviet Union fall apart?). *Otechestennaya istoriya*, October 31, 2003: 119–29.

——. "Tragicheskaya statistika" (Tragic statistics). *Argumenty i fakty*, February 4–10, 1989: 5–6.

——. "Nash isk Stalinu" (Our case against Stalin). *Moskovskie novosti*, November 27, 1988: 8.

M. I. Melkumyan. "Sotsial'nye utopii and deystvitel'nost'" (The social utopias and reality). In M. I. Melkumyan, ed., *Drama obnovleniya* (The drama of renewal). Moscow: Progress: 1990: 244–79.

M. Mel'nik. "Sluchay v spetsvagone" (An incident in a special car). *Komsomol'skaya pravda*, July 29, 1988: 2.

Andrei Mel'vil' and Alexander Nikitin. "Edino myslit' vse ne mogut" (Everyone cannot think in the same way). *Moskovksie novosti*, August 8, 1988.

Memorial sovesti" (The memorial of conscience). *Ogonyok* 47, 1988: 7.

Louis Menand. "Regrets Only: Lionel Trilling and His Discontents," *New Yorker*, September 29, 2008: 80–90.

——. *The Metaphysical Club*. New York: Farrar, Straus and Giroux, 2001.

S. Men'shikov. "Ekonomicheskaya struktura sotsializma: chto vperedi?" (The economic structure of socialism: what is ahead?). *Novy mir*, March 1989: 190–212.

T. Men'shikova. "Chto znaet narod . . ." (What people know . . .). *Sovetskaya kul'tura*, July 27, 1989: 2.

Robert K. Merton. *Social Theory and Social Structure*. New York: Free Press, 1968.

Andranik Migranyan. "Karl Popper: 'Ya byl marksistom do 17 let'" (I was a Marxist until I was seventeen). *Moskovskie novosti*, November 18, 1990: 16.

——. "Dolgiy put' k evropeyskomu domu" (A long road to the European home). *Novy mir*, July 1989: 166–84.

——. "Mekhanizm tormozheniya v politicheskoy systeme i puti ego preodole-niya" (The breaking mechanism in the political system and the ways to overcome it). In Yuri Afanasiev, ed., *Inogo ne dano* (There is no other way). Moscow: Progress, 1988: 97–121.

Dmitry Mikheyev. *The Rise and Fall of Gorbachev*. Indianapolis: Hudson Institute, 1992.

Arthur H. Miller, Vicki L. Hesli, and William M. Reisinger. "Reassessing Mass Support for Political and Economic Change in the Former USSR." *American Political Science Review* 88, no. 2, June 1994: 399–411.

Natl'ya Kirilovna Mochalova. Letter to the editor. In "O vremeni, kotoroe vypalo na nashu dolyu . . ." (About the times we have been destined to live in . . .), a collection of readers' letters, *Komsomol'skaya pravda*, January 25, 1989: 2.

F. T. Morgun. Speech at the Nineteenth Party Conference on July 1, 1988. *Pravda*, July 2, 1988: 6.

V. Morozov. "Starikam vezde u nas pochyot?" (The elderly are honored every-where in our country?). *Ogonyok* 14, 1989: 26.

"Moskva. Nedelya sovesti" (Moscow. The week of conscience). *Moskovskie novosti*, November 27, 1988: 9.

Dmitry Motornyi. "Vernut' krest'yaninu dolgi" (To repay our debts to the peasant). *Ogonyok* 33, 1988: 1–2.

Marina Mozhina. "Kto tam, za chertoy bednosti?" (Who is there behind the poverty line?). Interview with *Sotsialisticheskaya industriya*, June 1, 1988: 3.

Sergey Muratov. "Esli eto i revolutsiya, to podpol'naya" (If this indeed is a revolution, it is an underground one). *Moskovskie novosti*, July 10, 1988: 10.

Vladimir Nabokov. *Lectures on Literature*. New York: Harcourt Brace, 1980.

Yuri Nagibin. "O tom, chto trevozhit–v literature i zhizni" (About that which troubles–in literature and in life). *Oktyabr'*, February 1988: 194–200.

"Nasha pozitsiya" (Our view). Suggestions by the readers of *Komsomol'skaya pravda* in connection with the Theses of the Central Committee of the CPSU for Nineteenth Party Conference. *Komsomol'skaya pravda*, June 28, 1988: 3.

Boris Nazarenko. Letter to the editor. In "Pravdu i tol'ko pravdu! (Truth and only truth!). *Moskovskie novosti*, December 4, 1988: 9.

B. Nazarov. "Chelovek–eto zvuchit . . ." (Man–[a word] that resonates [proudly] . . .). *Komsomol'skaya pravda*, March 23, 1990: 2.

——. "Formula svobody" (The formula of freedom). *Sovietskaya kul'tura*, July 11, 1989: 3.

"Nedelya sovesti." (The week of conscience). *Ogonyok* 49, 1988: 32.

A. Nekipelov. "Est' li svet v kontse tunnelya? (O sovremennom krizise ekonomi-cheskoy teorii sotsializma)" (Is there the light at the end of the tunnel? On the current crisis in the economic theory of socialism). In M. I. Melkumyan, ed., *Drama obnovleniya* (The drama of renewal). Moscow: Progress: 1990: 587–614.

Ol'ga Nemirovskaya. "Nedelya sovesti" (The week of conscience). *Ogonyok* 48, 1988: 1, 31–32.

Alexander Nezhnyi. "Nikto ne vprave posyagat' na sovest' drugogo . . ." (No one has the right to interfere with anyone's conscience). *Moskovskie novosti,* October 29, 1989: 13.

Alexander Nikishin. "Ne naverdi!" (Do no harm!). *Ogonyok* 28, 1989: 5–6.

Vera Nikitina. "God za godom: 1991" (Year after year: 1991). *Informatsionnyi bulleten' monitoringa* (The public opinion monitoring information bulletin), no. 6 (32), November–December 1997: 46–51.

——. "God za godom: 1990" (Year after year: 1990). *Informatsionnyi bulleten' monitoringa* (The public opinion monitoring information bulletin), no. 5 (31), September–October 1997: 42–46.

——. "God za godom: 1989" (Year after year: 1989). *Informatsionnyi bulleten' monitoringa* (The public opinion monitoring information bulletin), no. 4 (30), July–August 1997: 38–39.

Leonid Nikitinskiy. "Do vstrechi v moratorii?" (Until we meet in the morato-rium?). *Komsomol'skaya pravda*, November 21, 1990: 1.

——. "Zakon o pechati–prinyat!" (The law on the press has been adopted!). *Komsomol'skya pravda*, June 9, 1990: 1.

——. "Rozhdaetsya pravo" (Legality is being born). *Komsomol'skaya pravda*, June 27, 1989: 1.

Boris Nikolaevsky, deputy chairman of the Committee on Glasnost and the Rights and Petitions of Citizens of the Supreme Soviet of the USSR. "Bez bumagi net *Chizha*" (Without paper, there is no *Chizh* [magazine]). *Sovetskaya kul'tura*, November 4, 1989: 2.

V. Novichikhin. Letter to the editor. In "Narodnaya publitsistika" (People's political journalism). *Oktyabr'*, August 1989: 183.

Vladimir Novikov. "Vozvrashchenie k zdravomu smyslu" (The return to common sense). *Znamya*, July 1989: 214–20.

Yu. Novopashin. "Proshchay, oruzhie!" (Farewell to arms!). Interview with *Komsomol'skaya pravda*, December 6, 1989: 2.

Andrei Nuykin. "KPSS i zakony krasoty" (CPSU and the laws of beauty). *Moskovskie novosti*, August 12, 1990: 6.

——. "Otkrytoe pis'mo" (An open letter). *Ogonyok* 40, 1989: 4–7.

——. "O tsene slova i tsenakh na produkty" (About the value of word and food prices). *Ogonyok* 22, 1988: 6–8, 27.

——. "Idealy ili interesy?" (Ideals or interests?). *Novy mir* 1, January 1988: 190–211.

"Nuzhna Belaya kniga" (A "White Book" is needed). *Moskovskie novosti*, November 27, 1988: 11.

P. G. Oldak. "Sotsializm kak my ego vidim segodnya" (Socialism as we see it today). In F. M. Borodkin, L. Ya. Kosals, and P. V. Ryvkina, *Postizhenie* (Attainment of truth). Moscow: Progress, 1989: 279–88.

V. Oskotskiy. "Za chto?" (What for?). *Znamya*, April 1990: 223–26.

Vasily Ostanchuk. "Ya trudilsya, skol'ko mog . . ." (I have worked as long as I could . . .). *Izvestia*, September 3, 1987: 3.

"Ot izdatel'stva" (From the publisher). Introduction to Vasily Grossman. *Zhizn' i sud'ba* (Life and fate). Moscow: Knizhnaya palata, 1989: 12–14.

"Ot redaktsii" (From the editorial board). *Ogonyok* 37, 1988: 29.

"Ot redaktsii" (From the editorial board). *Ogonyok* 32, 1988: 5.

"Otsenka kursa na reformy (1992–2004)" (The evaluation of the policy of reforms). *Vestnik obshshesvennogo mneniya*, July–August, 2004: 5.

M. Ovcharov. "100 zapisok iz zala" (100 notes from the audience). *Izvestia*, September 6, 1988: 3.

I. Ovchinnikova. "Ekzamen otmenyon. Istoriya ostayotsya!" (The examination is abolished: History remains!). *Izvestia*, June 10, 1988: 1.

G. Pashkov. "Prezident . . . Vashe mnenie?" (President . . . Your opinion?). *Komsomol'skaya pravda*, March 18, 1990: 1.

Nikolai Pavlenko. "Tragediya i triumph Krasnoy armii" (The Red Army's tragedy and triumph). *Moskovskie novosti*, May 7, 1989: 9.

Marina Pavlova-Sil'vanskaya. "Neterpenie" (Impatience). *Literaturnaya gazeta*, April 29, 1987: 10.

Minxin Pei. *From Reform to Revolution: The Demise of Communism in China and the Soviet Union.* Cambridge: Harvard University Press, 1994.

P. Penezhko. "Poezdka v Zagor'e" (A trip to Zagor'e). *Novy mir,* June 1990: 194–204.

V. Perevedenstev, Ph.D. Letter to *Ogonyok* 4, 1989: 3.

Nikolai Petrakov. "Dokhody i raskhody" (Incomes and expenses). Interview with *Sovetskaya kul'tura,* July 6, 1989: 6.

——. "Tovar i rynok" (Goods and market). *Ogonyok* 34, 1988: 6–8, 23–24.

S. Petrov. "Presumptsiya nevinovnosti?" (The presumption of innocence?). *Komsomol'skaya pravda,* November 25, 1988: 4.

George Pettee. "Revolution–Typology and Process." In Carl J. Friedrich, ed., *Revolution.* New York: Atherton Press, 1966: 10–33.

——. "The Process of Revolution." In Clifford T. Payton and Robert Blackey, eds., *Why Revolution? Theories and Analyses.* Cambridge, MA: Schenkman, 1971: 31–56.

Boris Pinsker and Larisa Piyasheva. "Sobstvennost' i svoboda" (Property and liberty). *Novy mir,* November 1989: 184–98.

Riitta H. Pitman. "*Perestroika* and Soviet Cultural Politics: The Case of the Major Literary Journals." *Soviet Studies* 42, no. 1, January 1990: 111–32.

Larisa Piyasheva. "V pogone za Siney ptitsey" (Chasing the blue bird [of happiness]). *Oktyabr',* September 1990: 142–58.

——. "Obeshchaniyami svetlogo budushchego syt ne budesh" (Hunger cannot be sated by the promises of a bright future). *Komsomol'skaya pravda,* May 25, 1989: 2.

——. "Kontury sotsial'noy reformy" (The outlines of the social reform). In F. M. Borodkin, L. Ya. Kosals, and P. V. Ryvkina, *Postizhenie* (Attainment of truth). Moscow: Progress, 1989: 264–78.

Andrei Platonov. *Chevengur.* In Andrei Platonov, *Sobranie sochineniy v pyati tomakh* (Collected Works in Five Volumes), 2: 5–307. Moscow: Informpechat', 1998.

——. *Kotlovan,* In Andrei Platonov, *Sobranie sochineniy v pyati tomakh* (Collected Works in Five Volumes), 2: 308–97. Moscow: Informpechat', 1998.

——. "Usomnivshiysya Makar" (Makar who has doubted). In Andrei Platonov, *Sobranie sochineniy v pyati tomakh* (Collected Works in Five Volumes), 1: 521–34. Moscow: Informpechat', 1998.

Podpis' na karte" (The signature on a map). *Literaturnaya gazeta,* July 5, 1989: 9.

Valentina Pokhodnya. "Doesn't anybody need our family?" (September 16, 1989). In Christopher Cerf and Marina Albee, eds., *Small Fires: Letters from the Soviet People to Ogonyok Magazine, 1987–1990.* New York: Summit Books, 1990: 127–30.

"Politika pravil'naya no izmeneniya nado provodit' bystrey" (The policy is correct but changes have to be implemented faster). *Moskovskie novosti,* January 14, 1990: 9.

Vladmir Polyakov. Letter to the editor. In "Tak kak zhe nam obustroiti' Rossiyu?" (So how can we make Russia good for living?). *Komsomol'skaya pravda,* November 23, 1990: 2.

Lidiya Pol'skaya. "Televizionnaya provintsiya" (A television province). *Ogonyok* 10, 1989: 21–22.

Yu. Polyakov. "Istoriya i istoriki" (History and historians), a roundtable discussion. *Kommunist* 12, August 1987: 74.

——. "Dorozhit' kazhdym godom nashey istorii" (To treasure every year of our history). An interview with *Literaturnaya gazeta*, July 29, 1987: 10.

Andrei Popov. "Kogda vybora net" (When there is no choice). *Ogonyok* 33, 1988: 18–19.

Gavriil Popov. "Igry patriotov. Chetvyortaya revolutsiya" (The patriots' games: The fourth revolution). *Moskovskiy Komsomoletz*, May 25, 2004: 4.

——. Speech at the First Congress of People's Deputies. *Izvestia*, June 11, 1989: 3.

——. In "Kto protiv" (Who is against?). A roundtable discussion in *Ogonyok* 18, 1988: 6.

Nikolai Popov. "Vse my v odnoy lodke" (We are all in the same boat). *Literaturnaya gazeta*, March 1, 1989: 14.

——. "Kto vyshe vlasti?" (Who is above the state's power?). *Sovetskaya kul'tura*, April 26, 1988: 3.

Vladimir Popov and Nikolai Shmelyov. "Na razvilke dorog" (At a crossroad). In Kh. Kobo, ed., *Osmyslit' kul't Stalina* (To comprehend Stalin's cult). Moscow: Progress, 1989: 284–326.

——. "Anatomiya defitsita" (The anatomy of shortages). *Znamya*, May 1988: 158–83.

Oleg Poptsov. "Kak stat' realistom" (How to become a realist). In V. G. Kazakov, ed., *Razvedka slovom* (Reconnaissance by word). Moscow: Moskovskiy rabochiy, 1988: 70–91.

"Poterpite, zhenshina!" (Hang in there, woman!). Letters to *Rabotnitsa*, February 1989: 22–24.

Zenon Poznyak. "Kuropaty: narodnaya tragediya, o kotoroy dolzhny znat' vse" (Kuropaty: a national tragedy about which everyone must know). *Moskovskie novosti*, October 9, 1988: 16.

I. Prelovskaya. "Mif i sud'ba" (Myth and fate). *Izvestia*, July 15, 1989: 3.

Evgeniy Primakov. "Russia Must Be a Star Player on the World Arena." Speech at a conference of the Council on Foreign and Defense Policy, Moscow, March 14, 1998. Distributed by the Information Department of the Embassy of the Russian Federation in Washington, DC.

Peter Pringle. *The Murder of Nikolai Vavilov*. New York: Simon and Schuster, 2008.

Anatoly Pristavkin. "Otvetsvennost'" (Responsibility). *Ogonyok* 32, 1987: 7–8.

——. *Nochevala tuchka zolotaya* (A little golden cloud spent a night). *Znamya*, March 1987: 3–75 and April 1987: 25–79.

"Programnoe zayavlenie Soyuza trudyashchikhsya Kuzbassa, prinyatoe na IV konferentsii rabochikh komitetov Kuzbassa, 18–19 noyabrya 1989, g. Novokuznetsk" (A program statement of the Union of the laborers of Kuzbass, adopted at the 4th conference of the workers' committees of Kuzbass on

November 18–19, 1989, in the city of Novokuznetsk). Document no. 111. In
L. Lopatin, ed., *Rabochee dvizhenie Kuzbassa. Sbornkin documentov i materialov.
Aprel' 1989–Mart 1992* (The workers' movement of Kuzbass: A collection of
documents and materials, April 1989–March 1992). Kemerovo: Sovremennaya
otechestvennaya kniga, 1993: 158–65.

Timur Pulatov. "Krymskie tatary zhazhdut iskhoda" (The Crimean Tatars are
thirsting for the resolution). *Moskovskie novosti,* April 9, 1989: 13.

V. Radaev and O. Shkaratan. "Vozvrashchenie k istokam" (The return to the
sources). *Izvestia,* February 16, 1990: 3.

Leonid Radzikhovsky. "Ekonomika svyashchennykh korov" (An economy of holy
cows). *Moskovskie novosti,* June 4, 1989: 12.

———. "1 dekabrya" (December 1). *Moskovskie novosti,* November 27, 1988: 6.

Alexander Rahr. "Inside the Interregional Group," *RL/RFE Report on the USSR* 2,
no. 43, October 26, 1990: 1–4.

Natliya Rapoport. "Pamyat'–tozhe meditsina" (Memory is medicine, too). *Yunost',*
no. 4, 1988: 76–81.

Donald Rayfield. *Stalin and His Hangmen: The Tyrant and Those Who Killed for
Him.* New York: Random House, 2004.

Lev Razgon. "Nakonetz!" (Finally!). *Moskovskie novosti,* June 26, 1988: 11.

Peter Reddaway. "The Role of Popular Discontent." Special issue, *National
Interest,* Spring 1993: 57–63.

Thomas F. Remington. "Sovietology and System Stability," *Post-Soviet Affairs* 8 (3),
1992: 239–69.

David Remnick. "Soviets Publish Shalamov Tales of the Gulag," *Washington Post,*
June 22, 1988: C9.

Albert Resis. "The Fall of Litivinov." *Europe-Asia Studies* 52 (1), January 2000:
33–56.

Vsevolod Revich. "Preduprezhdenie vsem" (A warning to everyone). *Literaturnoe
obozrenie,* no. 7, 1987: 44–46.

"Rezolyutsiya III konferentsii Soyuza trudyashchikhsya Kuzbassa o polnoy
peredache gosudartsvennoy vlasit v tsentre in na mestakh Sovetam narodnykh
deputatov" (The resolution of the 3rd conference of the union of the laborers of
Kuzbass on the complete transfer of state power in the center and locally to the
Soviets of people's deputies). Document no. 65. In L. Lopatin, ed., *Rabochee
dvizhenie Kuzbassa. Sbornik documentov i materialov, Aprel' 1989–Mart 1992*
(The workers' movement of Kuzbass: A collection of documents and materials,
April 1989–March 1992). Kemerovo: Sovremennaya otechestvennaya kniga,
1993: 121.

Melvin Richter. "Tocqueville's Contribution to the Theory of Revolution." In Carl
J. Friedrich, ed., *Revolution.* New York: Atherton Press, 1966: 75–121.

Nancy Ries. *Russian Talk: Culture and Conversation during Perestroika.* Ithaca:
Cornell University Press, 1997.

I. Rimashevskaya. "Prozhitochniy minimum" (The minimum subsistence level).
Argumenty i fakty, April 7–13, 1990: 2.

I. Rishina and A. Egorov. "Lish tot dostoin zhizni i svobody . . . (Vasily Grossman. *Zhizn' i sud'ba*)." Chitatel'skay konferentsiya "LG" (Only he deserves life and liberty [who every day goes to battle for them] [Vasily Grossman. *Life and Fate*]. A readers' conference at *Literaturnaya gazeta*). *Literaturnaya gazeta*, August 24, 1988: 5.

Andrei Romanov. "The Press We Choose." *Moscow News,* February 21, 1988: 2.

Richard Rose, William Mishler, and Neil Munro. *How Russians Have Responded to Political Transformation.* Cambridge: Cambridge University Press, 2006.

Yuri Rost. "Ushol Chelovek" (Gone is Man). *Literaturnaya gazeta*, December 20, 1989: 1.

Inna Rostovtseva. "U chelovecheskogo serdtsa" (Next to a human heart). In "Platonov segodnya" (Platonov today). *Oktyabr'*, November 1987: 158–62.

Robert Rozhdestvensky. "Short Poems." *Literaturnaya gazeta*, March 1, 1989: 5.

Vladimir Rubanov. "Demokratiya i besopasnost' strany" (Democracy and the country's security). *Kommunist* 11, July 1989: 43–55.

Blair Ruble. "The Soviet Union's Quiet Revolution." In George Breslauer, ed., *Can Gorbachev's Reforms Succeed?* Berkeley: University of California Press, 1990.

Inna Rudenko. "S voynoy pokonchili my schyoty?" (Have we settled our scores with the [Afghan] war?). *Komsomol'skaya pravda*, February 15, 1989: 1.

V. Rusakova. "Telefonnye istorii, kotorye tyanutsya 22 goda" (Telephone stories that have dragged for 22 years). *Pravda*, December 2, 1987: 4.

Myron Rush. "Fortune and Fate." In Owen Harries, ed., *The Strange Death of Soviet Communism.* Special issue, *The National Interest,* Spring 1993: 19–25.

Peter Rutland. "Sovietology: Notes for a Post-Mortem." In Owen Harries, ed., *The Strange Death of Soviet Communism.* Special issue, *The National Interest,* Spring 1993: 109–22.

El'dar Ryazanov. "Pochemu v epokhu glasnosti ya ushyol s televideniya?" (Why have I left television in the era of glasnost?). *Ogonyok* 14, 1988: 26.

Anatoly Rybakov. *Deti Arbata. Kniga vtoraya: Strakh* (Book two: Fear). St. Petersburg: Amphora, 2004.

———. *Deti Arbata: Kniga Trety'a: Prakh i pepel* (Book three: Dust and ashes). St. Petersburg: Amphora, 2004.

———. "Deti Arbata v 1937 godu" (The children of Arbat in 1937). Interview with *Moskovskie novosti,* September 2, 1990: 16.

———. "Rana, kotoraya krovotochit" (The wound that is bleeding). *Moskovskie novosti,* November 27, 1988: 7.

———. "S proshlym nado rasstavat'sya dostoyno" (Bidding farewell to the past must be done with dignity). *Moskovskie novosti,* July 17, 1988: 11.

Yu Rytov. "Kak zhivyotsya pensioneru?" (How is the pensioner faring?). *Izvestia,* August 20, 1988: 1.

Martimyan Ryutin. "Ko vsem chlenam VKP (b)" (To all members of the VKP [b]). In Kh. Kobo, ed., *Osmyslit' kul't Stalina* (To comprehend Stalin's cult). Moscow: Progress, 1989: 618–23.

Nikolai Ryzhkov. *Perestroika: Istoriya predatel'stv* (Perestroika: the history of betrayals). Moscow: Novosti, 1992.

——. "Sluzhit' intersam naroda." (To serve the people's interests). Speech at the First Congress of People's Deputies on June 7, 1989. *Izvestia*, June 8, 1989: 1–3.

Yuri Ryzhov. "Bezopasnost', kotoraya nam nuzhna" (Security that we need). *Novoe vermya* 10, 1990: 26–28.

——. "Vremya vybora" (A time of choice). *Sovetskaya kul'tura*, November 11, 1989: 3.

Andrei D. Sakharov. "Konstitutsiya Soyuza Sovetskikh Respublik Evropy i Azii" (Constitution of the Union of Soviet Republic of Europe and Asia). In "Konstitutsionnye idei Andreya Sakharova" (Constitutional ideas of Andrei Sakharov). *Oktyabr'*, May 1990: 145–68.

——. The Nobel Peace Prize speech, December 1, 1975. *Oktyabr'*, January 1990: 8–15.

——. Speech at the First Congress of People's Deputies on June 7, 1989. In *Pervyi S'ezd Narodnykh Deputatov SSSR. Stenographicheskiy otchyot. Tom III* (The First Congress of People's Deputies of the USSR. Official Transcript. Vol. 3). Moscow: Publishing House of the Supreme Soviet, 1989: 325–28.

——. "Stepen' svobody" (The degree of freedom). Interview with *Ogonyok* 31, 1989: 26–28.

——. "S'ezd ne mozhet sdelat' vsyo srazu . . ." (The Congress cannot do everything right away). *Literaturnaya gazeta*, June 21, 1989: 11.

——. "Neizbezhnost' perestroiki" (The inevitability of perestroika). In Yuri Afanasiev, ed., *Inogo ne dano* (There is no other way). Moscow: Progress, 1988: 122–34.

Arkady Sakhnin. "Ne brosat'sya slovami" (Not to waste words). *Moskovskie novosti*, April 24, 1988: 15.

Ludmila Saraskina. "Smotret' pravde v glaza" (To look truth in the eye). *Moskovskie novosti*, April 10, 1988: 12.

Benedikt Sarnov. "Skol'ko vesit nashe gosudarstvo?" In Kh. Kobo, ed., *Osmyslit' kul't Stalina* (To comprehend Stalin's cult). Moscow: Progress, 1989: 160–94.

——. "Zalozhnik vechnosti (Sluchay Mandel'shtama)" (The hostage of eternity: The case of Mandelstam). *Ogonyok* 47, 1988: 26–30.

Matt Schudel. " 'No Easy Moments' for a Leader of the Warsaw Ghetto Uprising." *Washington Post*, October 5, 2009: B9.

David C. Schwartz. "Political Alienation: The Psychology of Revolution's First Stage." In Ivo. K Feierabend, Rosalind L. Feirebend, and Ted Robert Gurr, eds. *Anger, Violence and Politics*. Englewood Cliffs, NJ: Prentice-Hall, 1972: 58–66.

L. A. Sedov. "Peremeny v strane i otnoshenie k peremenam" (Changes in the country and the attitude toward the changes). *Informatsionnyi byulleten' monitoringa*, January–February 1995: 23–26.

Eric Selbin. "Agency and Culture in Revolutions." In Jack A. Goldstone, ed., *Revolutions*. Belmont, CA: Thomson, 2003: 76–84.

Vasily Selyunin. "U nas poluchitsya" (We shall succeed). *Ogonyok* 8, 1991: 12–14, 31.

———. "Rynok: khimery i real'nost" (Market: chimeras and reality). *Znamya*, June 1990: 193–205.

———. "Planovaya anarkhiya ili balans interesov?" (Planned anarchy or a balance of interests?). *Znamya*, November 1989: 203–20.

———. "Chyornye dyry ekonimki" (The black holes of the economy). *Novy mir*, October 1989: 153–78.

———. "Revansh burokratii" (Bureaucracy's *revanche*). In Yuri Afanasiev, ed., *Inogo ne dano* (There is no other way). Moscow: Progress, 1988: 192–209.

———. "Radi konechnoy tseli" (For the final goal). In V. G. Kazakov, ed., *Razvedka slovom* (Reconnaissance by word). Moscow: Moskovskiy rabochiy, 1988: 34–44.

———. "Istoki" (The sources). *Novy mir*, May 1988: 162–89.

Vasily Selyunin and Grigory Khanin. "Lukavaya tsifra" (The cunning figure). *Novy mir*, February 1987: 181–207.

"Semeyniy byudzhet: dokhod i raskhod" (Family budget: income and expenses). *Pravda*, May 19, 1989: 5.

Mikhail Semiryaga. "23 avgusta 1939 goda" (August 23, 1939). *Literaturnaya gazeta*, October 5, 1988: 14.

Nikolar Sennikov. Letter to the editor. *Znamya*, August 1987: 223.

Igor Sergeev. "My otvykli razoruzhat'sya" (We are not used to disarm). *Moskovskie novosti*, February 25, 1990: 7.

Tamara Sevko. Letter to the editor, published under "Pravdu i tol'ko pravdu" (Truth and only the truth) headline. *Moskovskie novosti*, December 4, 1988: 9.

William H. Sewell, Jr. "Ideologies and Social Revolutions: Reflections on the French Case." In Theda Skocpol, ed., *Social Revolutions in the Modern World*. Cambridge: Cambridge University Press, 1994: 169–96.

Georgy Shakhnazarov. "Vostok-Zapad. K voprosu o deideologizatsii mezhgosu-darstvennykh otnosheniy" (East-West. On the question of the de-ideologization of international relations). *Kommunist* 3, 1989: 67–78.

Varlam Shalamov. *Novaya proza* (New fiction). *Novy mir*, December 1989: 3–71.

———. Iz *"Kolymskikh rasskazov"* (From "The Kolyma tales"). *Znamya*, June 1989: 6–38.

———. *Proza, stikhi* (Prose, poetry). *Novy mir*, June 1988: 106–51.

V. Shamborant. Letter to *Ogonyok* 37, 1988: 29.

Yu. K. Sharipov. Speech at the First Congress of People's Deputies of the USSR on June 1, 1989. *Izvestia*, June 2, 1989: 8.

Stanislav Shatalin. "Risk perekhoda k rynku men'she, chem toptanie na meste" (The risk of the transition to market is less than that of marching in place). *Izvestia*, April 21, 1990: 3.

S. Shatalin, N. Petrakov, G. Yavlisnky, S. Aleksashenko, A. Vavilov, L. Grigor'ev, M. Zadornov, V. Martynov, V. Mashits, D. Mikhaylov, V. Fedorov, T. Yarygina, E. Yasin. "Chelovek. Svoboda. Rynok." (Man. Liberty. Market.). *Komsomol'skaya pravda*, September 5, 1990: 1–2.

Irina Shcherbakova. "Avgustovskaya zhatva" (The August harvest). *Izvestia,* October 13, 1989: 6.

———. "Nado li pomnit' proshloe?" (Should we remember the past?). *Moskovskie novosti,* November 27, 1988: 12.

———. "Odin iz sta, iz pyatisot, iz tysyachi . . ." (One out of a hundred, five hundred, thousand . . .). *Moskovskie novosti,* October 30, 1988: 16.

Eduard Shevardnadze. "Novy oblik diplomatii" (A new image of diplomacy). *Argumenty i fakty,* May 6–12, 1989: 1–2.

Dmitry Shevarov. "SPID. Sotsial'nyi portret yavleniya" (AIDS: A social portrait of a phenomenon). *Komsomol'skaya pravda,* May 24, 1990: 2.

Liliya Shevtsova. "Privyknut' zhit' bez povodka." *Literaturnaya gazeta,* April 19, 1989: 11.

Viktor Sheynis. "Perestroika na novom etape: opasnosti i problemy" (A new phase of perestroika: dangers and problems). In F. M. Borodkin, L. Ya. Kosals, and P. V. Ryvkina, *Postizhenie* (Attainment of truth). Moscow: Progress, 1989: 357–88.

Alexander Shindel'. "Svidetel'" (A witness). *Znamya,* September 1987: 207–17.

O. Shkaratan. "Vremya vybora puti" (The time to choose the way). *Sovetskaya kul'tura,* September 19, 1989: 3.

G. A. Shmakov. Letter to the editor. In "Narodnaya publitsistika" (People's political journalism). *Oktyabr',* August 1989: 181–83.

Nikolai Shmelyov. "Iz dokladnykh zapisok ekonomista" (From economists' memoranda). *Znamya,* December 1989: 173–86.

———. Speech at the First Congress of People's Deputies on June 8, 1989. In *Pervyi S'ezd Narodnykh Deputatov SSSR. Stenographicheskiy otchyot. Tom III* (The First Congress of People's Deputies of the USSR. Official Transcript. Vol. 3). Moscow: Publishing House of the Supreme Soviet, 1989: 48–57.

———. "Libo sila, libo rubl'" (Either brute force or the ruble). *Znamya,* January 1989: 128–47.

———. "Ostorozhno, tseny!" (Careful: Prices!), interviewed by Viktor Loshak. *Moskovskie novosti,* December 11, 1988: 10.

———. "Novye trevogi" (New concerns). *Novy mir,* April 1988: 160–75.

———. "Ne smet' komandovat'!" (Stop giving orders!). *Oktyabr',* February 1988: 3–26.

———. "Vyiti iz tumana predrassudkov" (To exit from the fog of superstitions). *Literaturnaya gazeta,* July 8, 1987: 3.

———. "Avansy i dolgi" (Advances and debts). *Novy mir,* June 1987.

———. *Paskhov dom* (The Pashkov house). *Znamya,* March 1987: 80–139.

Nikolai Shmelyov and Fyodor Burlatsky. "Chto zhe dal'she?" (What next?). A dialogue in *Literaturnaya gazeta,* July 18, 1990: 3.

Vladimir Shubkin. "Trudnoe proshchanie" (The difficult farewell). *Novy mir,* April 1989: 165–84.

Alexander Shumskiy, "Pakhat' poka nechem" (So far, there is nothing to plow with). *Moskovskie novosti,* July 31, 1988: 9.

M. Shur. "Secrets and Mysteries." In Christopher Cerf and Marina Albee, eds., *Small Fires: Letters from the Soviet People to Ogonyok Magazine, 1987–1990.* New York: Summit Books, 1990: 84.

V. Shutkevich. "Molchit katyn'skiy les" (The Katyn' forest is silent). *Komsomol'skaya pravda,* January 20, 1990: 3.

Ivan S. Silaev. "Trebuyutsya idei" (Ideas are needed). Interview in *Ogonyok* 48, 1987: 2–5.

Konstantin Simonov. "Uroki istorii i dolg pisatelya" (Lessons of history and a writer's duty). *Nauka i zhizn',* June 1987: 42–48.

Rayr Simonyan and Anatoly Druzenko. "Kuda my idyom?" (Where are we going?). *Ogonyok* 37, 1989: 1–3.

A. Simurov and P. Studenikin. "Net v dushe blagodarnosti . . ." (There is no gratitude in my soul . . .). *Pravda,* November 25, 1987: 2.

Vladlen Sirotkin. "Voenno-promyshlennyi kompleks: Gde vykhod iz tupika?" (The military-industrial complex. Where is a way out of the dead-end?). *Stolitsa,* no. 13, 1991: 1–4.

A. Sizov. "Sverim tsyfry" (Let's compare the numbers). *Kommunist* 15, 1989: 63–64.

Theda Skocpol. *Social Revolutions in the Modern World.* New York: Cambridge University Press, 1997.

L. V. Skvortsov. "Kul'tura samosoznaniya i formirovanie novogo gumanizma" (The culture of self-consciousness and the formation of a new humanism). In M. I. Melkumyan, ed., *Drama obnovleniya* (The drama of renewal). Moscow: Progress: 1990: 519–36.

"Slovo chitatelya" (A word from the reader). *Ogonyok* 1, 1989: 6.

Konstantin Smirnov. "Moment istiny i istina momenta" (The moment of truth and the truth of the moment). *Ogonyok* 36, 1988: 24.

Nina Smirnova. "Neobkhodimye utochneniya" (Some necessary clarifications). *Moskovskie novosti,* September 3, 1989: 12.

Hedrick Smith. *The New Russians.* New York: Random House, 1990.

Anatoly Sobchak. "Krizis vlasti ili vlast' v usloviyakh krizisa?" (A crisis of power or power in crisis?). *Argumenty i fakty,* no. 12, 1991: 2.

———. "Khozhdenie vo vlast' "(The journey into power). *Moskovskie novosti,* November 25, 1990: 14.

S. Sokolov. Letter to the editor. In "Prostye lyudi" (The ordinary people). *Komsomol'skaya pravda,* March 25, 1989: 2.

Alexander Solzhenitsyn. *V kruge pervom* (In the first circle). Moscow: Act, 2006.

———. *Odin den' Ivana Denisovicha* (One day in the life of Ivan Denisovich). St. Petersburg: Azbuka-klassika, 2001.

———. "Kak nam obustroit' Rossiyu" (How we can make Russia good for living). A supplement to *Komsomol'skaya pravda,* September 18, 1990.

———. *Arkhipelag Gulag. Novy mir,* August, September, October 1989.

———. "Nobelevskaya lektsiya" (The Nobel lecture). *Novy mir,* July 1989: 135–44.

———. *Gulag Archipelago.* New York: Harper and Row, 1978.

Vladmir Sorgin. "Tri prevrashcheniya sovremennoy Rossii" (The three meta-morphoses of the contemporary Russia). *Otechestvennaya istoriya*, no. 3, 2005: 3–24.

Yu. Sorokin. "Eto sladkoe slovo svoboda!" (This sweet word: liberty!). *Komsomol'skaya pravda*, May 5, 1990: 1.

Sotsiologicheskie nablyudeniya (2002–2004) (Sociological observations [2002–2004]). Moscow: Public Opinion Foundation's Institute, 2005.

"Sozdan izbiratelnly blok 'Demokraticheskaya Rossiya'" (A voters' bloc 'Demo-cratic Russia' has been organized). *Ogonyok* 6, February 1990: 17–18.

Evgeny Starikov. "Pered vyoborom" (Forced to choose). *Znamya*, May 1991: 225–32.

———. "Marginaly" (The marginal people). *Znamya*, October 1989: 133–62.

E. Starikova. "Kniga o dobre i zle, ili smert' Ivana Il'icha" (A book about good and evil, or the death of Ivan Il'ich). *Novy mir*, December 1987: 216–29.

V. Starkov, N. Zyat'kov, A. Meshcherskiy, and L. Novikova. "Za chto kritikuyut 'AiF'" (What do they criticize AiF for). *Argukmenty i fakty*, November 18–24, 1989: 2.

Irina Starodubrovskaya and Vladimir Mau. *Velikie revolutsii ot Kromvelya do Putina* (Great revolutions from Cromwell to Putin). Moscow: Vagrius, 2004.

S. Frederick Starr. "Soviet Union: A Civil Society." *Foreign Policy*, no. 70, Spring 1988: 26–41.

V. Stel'makh. "Novye starye knigi" (New old books). *Izvestia*, February 1, 1989: 2.

Storozhenko, Starodubova, Koryakina et al. Letter to *Ogonyok* 42: 5.

Anatoly Strelyaniy. "Prikhod i raskhod" (Profit and expense). *Znamya*, June 1986: 175–203.

Gleb Struve. "O. E. Mandel'shtam. Opyt biografii i kriticheskogo kommentariya" (O. E. Mandelstam: An experiment in biography and critical commentary). In O. E. Mandel'shtam, *Sobranie sochineniy v chetyryokh tomakh* (Collected works in four volumes), ed. G. P. Struve and B. A. Filippov. Moscow: Terra, 1991, vol. 1: v–xl.

Nikita Struve. "Sud'ba Mandel'shtama" (Mandelstam's fate). In O. E. Mandel'shtam, *Sobranie sochineniy v chetyryokh tomakh* (Collected works in four volumes), ed. G. P. Struve and B. A. Filippov. Moscow: Terra, 1991, vols. 3–4: xxii–xxxiv.

V. Svirskiy. "Istoriya umalchivaet" (History omits). *Izvestia*, July 21, 1987: 3.

Philip Taubman. "Soviet Party Conference Delegates Turn Anger on Press and Economy." *New York Times*, June 30, 1988: A1.

Yuri Teplyakov. "Po tu storonu fronta" (On the other side of the frontline). *Moskovskie novosti*, May 13, 1990: 8.

A. Terekhov. "Strakh pered morozom" (The fear of frost). *Ogonyok* 19, 1988: 7–8.

Vladimir Tikhonov. "Vladet' zemlyoy" (To own the land). *Moskovskie novosti*, June 25, 1989: 12.

Charles Tilly. *European Revolutions, 1492–1992*. Cambridge, MA: Blackwell, 1996.

———. "Revolutions and Collective Violence," in Fred. I. Greenstein and Nelson W. Polsby, eds., *Handbook of Political Science*, vol. 3. Reading MA: Addison-Wesley, 1975.

Lev Timofeev. "S trevogoy i nadezhdoy" (With anxiety and hope). *Oktyabr'*, January 1990: 7.

"Tirazhi ryada tsentral'nykh gazet i zhurnalov v 1985–1989" (The pressruns of the central newspapers and magazines in 1985–1989). *Izvestia TsK KPSS*, no. 1, 1989: 138, and in *Argumenty i fakty*, May 6–12, 1989: 3.

Alexis de Tocqueville. *The Old Regime and the French Revolution*. Translated by Stuart Gilbert. New York: Anchor Books, 1983.

Leo Tolstoy. "Nikolai Palkin" (Nikolas the Stick). In *L. N. Tolstoy, Polnoe sobranie sochineniy* (L. N. Tolstoy, Collected Works). Moscow: Khudozhestvennaya literatura, 1936, vol. 26: 555–62.

Mark Tol'tz. "Vdovy" (Widows). *Ogonyok* 18, 1987: 18.

Vera Tolz. "New History Textbook for Secondary Schools," *Radio Liberty Report on the USSR*, September 1, 1989 (RL 396/89): 5–7.

Zh. T. Toshchenko. "Zastoy dukha i ego preodolenie" (The stagnation of spirit and how to overcome it). In M. I. Melkumian, *Drama obnoveleniya* (The drama of renewal). Moscow: Progress, 1990: 560–86.

Nikolai Travkin. "Put' k narodovlastiyu lezhit cherez samoupravlenie" (The road to government by the people runs through self-rule). *Sovetskaya kul'tura*, July 8, 1989: 2.

Aaron Trehub. "Social Issues on the Eve of the Twenty-Seventh Party Congress." *Radio Liberty Research* (RL 84/86), February 19, 1986.

Vladmir Treml. "Gorbachev's Anti-Drinking Campaign: A Noble Experiment or a Costly Exercise in Futility." *RL Supplement* (RL 2/87), March 18, 1987.

Vitaly Tret'yakov. "Vash punkt v predvybornoy platforme" (Your plank in the electoral platform). *Moskovskie novosti*, January 29, 1989: 8.

———. "Spasyonnye perestroikoy" (Saved by perestroika). *Moskovskie novosti*, January 1, 1989: 3.

———. "Sotsial'naya spravedlivost' i privilegii: kak sovmeshchayutsya eti ponyatiya" (Social justice and privileges: how these notions are combined). *Moskovskie novosti*, July 3, 1988: 10–11.

Lionel Trilling. *Liberal Imagination*. New York: Doubleday, 1953.

N. Trofimov. "Tsifry vmesto bol'nykh" (Numbers instead of patients). *Pravda*, September 2, 1987: 2.

V. Tsamalaidze. "Chuzhaya sredi svoikh" (A stranger among her own). *Pravda*, November 30, 1989: 2.

Grigoriy Tsitrinyak. "Stepen' svobody" (The degree of freedom). Interview with Andrei D. Sakharov, *Ogonyok* 31, 1989: 29.

Alexander Tsypko. "Vozmozhno li chudo?" (Is a miracle possible?). *Sovetskaya kul'tura*, May 26, 1990: 4.

———. "Khoroshi li nashi printsipy?" (How good are our principles?). *Novy mir*, April, 1990: 173–204.

——. "Do We Need Yet Another Experiment? Ideological Paradoxes of Reform." *Rodina*, January, 1990.

——. "Istoki Stalinisma" (The origins of Stalinism). Part 3, *Nauka i zhizn'*, January 1989: 46–56; part 4, *Nauka i zhizn'*, February 1989: 53–61.

A. E. Tugaev. "Spiritual Food Shortage." Letter to *Ogonyok*, April 1988. In Christopher Cerf and Marina Albee, eds., *Small Fires: Letters from the Soviet People to Ogonyok Magazine, 1987–1990*. New York: Summit Books, 1990: 61.

S. Tutorskaya. "Potryasenie" (Shock). *Izvestia*, March 7, 1989: 3.

Alexander Tvardovsky. *Po pravu pamyati* (In memory's name). *Znamya*, February, 1987: 3–14.

G. Valyuzhenich. "Nashe sotsial'noe samochustvie" (Our social well-being). An interview with Vilen Ivanov, director, the Institute for Sociological Research, Moscow. *Argumenty i fakty*, no. 1, January 1–January 8, 1988: 2.

"Vasha pozitsiya?" (Your view?). *Komsomol'skaya pravda*, June 7, 1988: 1.

Andrey Vasilevsky. "Stradanie pamyati" (The torment of memory). *Oktyabr'*, April 1989: 180–91.

A. Vasiliev. "Nedogovarivaem" (We are not telling the whole story). *Komsomol'skaya pravda*, August 7, 1990: 4.

Boris Vasiliev. "Na oborotnoy storone" (On the reverse side). *Moskovskie novosti*, May 13, 1990: 3.

——. "Lyubi Rossiyu v nepogodu . . ." (Love Russia in bad weather). *Izvestia*, part 1, January 16, 1989: 3, part 2 *Izvestia*, January 17, 1989: 3, and part 3, January 18, 1989: 3.

——. "Prozrenie" (The recovery of sight). *Sovetskiy ekran* 6 (March) 1987: 4–5.

Larissa Vasilieva. "A glimpse of diplomacy from the sideline." *International Affairs*, February 1989: 85–94, 43.

Alexander Vasinskiy. "Ne dat' zadut' svechu" (Not to let the candle be blown out). *Izvestia*, March 3 1989: 3.

L. Velikanova and S. Nikolaev. "Kazhdoy sem'e–zdorovuyu kvartiru" (To every family—a "healthy apartment"). *Literaturnaya gazeta*, August 31, 1988: 4.

Anatoly Vengerov. "Zaslon vozhdizmu." *Ogonyok* 23, 1988: 11–15.

Igor Vinogradov. "Mozhet li pravda byt' poeatpnoy?" (Can the truth be doled out in stages?). In Afanasiev, ed., *Inogo ne dano* (There is no other way). Moscow: Progress, 1988: 277–96.

T. Vishnevskaya. "Raby-nemy" (The slaves are mute). *Komsomol'skaya pravda*, January 9, 1990: 2.

Vitaly Vitaliev. "Chelovek bez pasporta?" (A man without a passport). *Ogonyok* 40, 1988: 25.

Yuri Vlasov. Speech at the First Congress of People's Deputies of the USSR. In "S'ezd Narodnykh Deputatov SSSR," transcript, *Izvestia*, June 2, 1989: 4.

"Vnimanie: konkurs!" (Attention: competition!). *Ogonyok* 42, 1988: 5.

Grigory Vodolazov. "Lenin i Stalin" (Lenin and Stalin). *Oktyabr'*, June 1989: 3–29.

——. In "Bol'she sotsializma!" (More socialism!), a roundtable discussion. *Ogonyok* 14, 1988: 5.

———. "Lenin i Stalin. Filosfsko-sotsiologicheskiy kommentariy k povesti V. Grossmana 'Vsyo techyot'" (Lenin and Stalin: a philosophical and sociological commentary on V. Grossman's novella *Forever Flowing*). In Kh. Kobo, ed., *Osmyslit' kul't Stalina* (To comprehend Stalin's cult). Moscow: Progress, 1989: 126–59.

Pavel Volin. "Tayna, izvestnaya vsem" (A secret known to everyone). *Ogonyok* 35, 1989: 6–8.

Vladimir Volin. "Okhrana ot bezopasnosti" (Protection from security). *Moskovskie novosti,* August 27, 1989: 10.

D. Volkogonov, R. Medvedev, and L. Saraskina. "Triumf tirana, tragediya naroda." *Moskovskie novosti,* February 12, 1989: 8–9.

O. Volkov. "Novocherkassk, 2 iyunya 1962" (Novocherassk, June 2, 1962). *Komsomol'skaya pravda,* April 27, 1991: 3.

Oleg Volkov. "Iz redaktsionnoy pochty" (From the mail to the editorial offices). Letter to *Novy mir,* June 6, 1986: 261–64.

P. Volobuyev. "Vlast' sovetov: raschyoty i proschyoty" (The power of the soviets: hopes and miscalculations). *Kommunist* 11, 1991: 69–82.

Sergei Volovets. "Bol'she pushek–men'she myasa" (More cannons–less meat). *Moskovskie novosti,* October 28, 1990: 3.

———. "Kak vo vsekh tsivilizovannykh stranakh" (As in all civilized countries). *Moskovskie novosti,* February 4, 1990: 3.

Pavel Vorobuev. "Drama samopoznaniya" (The drama of self-discovery). *Sovetskaya kul'tura,* July 18, 1989: 3.

Z. Voronina. "Nuzhna pomoshch" (Help is needed). *Izvestia,* September 21, 1988: 6.

P. Voroshilov and A. Solovyov. "Konstruktivniy dialog s shakhterami" (A constructive dialogue with the miners). *Izvestia,* July 18, 1989: 1.

Pavel Voshchanov. "Zemlya i volya" (Land and freedom). *Komsomol'skaya pravda,* February 28, 1990: 2.

———. "Zloba i zavist' obrekayut nas na bednost'." (Spite and envy doom us to penury). *Komsomol'skaya pravda,* December 2, 1989: 2–3.

Lev Voskresensky. "Zdravstvuyte, Ivan Denisovich!" (Hello, Ivan Denisovich!). *Moskovskie novosti,* August 7, 1988: 11.

———. "Obresti dostoinsvo v bor'be" (To find dignity in a struggle). *Moskovskie novosti,* January 17, 1988: 13.

I. Voytko. "Negde zhit'" (Without a home). *Pravda,* July 2, 1989: 3.

Andrei Voznesensky. "V roddome" (In a maternity hospital). *Literaturnaya gazeta,* October 5, 1988: 6.

———. "A Poet's View of Glasnost," *The Nation,* June 13, 1987.

———. "My byli toshchiee, i uzhe togda nichego ne boyalis'" (We were thin as rails but already not afraid of anything). *Ogonyok* 9, 1987: 28.

Vladimir V'yunitskiy. "Gorbachev i El'tsin: algoritmy vlasti" (Gorbachev and Yeltsin: the algorithms of power). *Dialog,* March 1991: 48.

Valery Vyzhutovich. "Vlast' rublya" (The power of ruble). *Ogonyok* 44, 1987: 6–7.

Max Weber. *From Max Weber: Essays in Sociology*, ed. H. H. Gerth and C. Wright Mills. New York: Oxford University Press, 1978.

——. *Max Weber: The Theory of Social and Economic Organization*, ed. Talcott Parsons. New York: Free Press, 1964.

——. *The Protestant Ethic and the Spirit of Capitalism*. New York: Scribner, 1958.

Stephen Wheatcroft. "Unleashing the Energy of History, Mentioning the Unmentionable and Reconstructing Soviet Historical Awareness: Moscow 1987," *Australian Slavic and Eastern European Studies*, no. 1, 1987: 85–132.

Julia Wishnevsky. "A Guide to Some Major Soviet Journals." *RL Supplement* (RL 2/88), *Radio Liberty Research Bulletin*, July 20, 1988.

A. V. Yablokov. Speech at the First Congress of People's Deputies on June 8, 1989. In *Pervyi S'ezd Narodnykh Deputatov SSSR. Stenographicheskiy otchyot. Tom III* (The First Congress of People's Deputies of the USSR. Official Transcript. Vol. 3). Moscow: Publishing House of the Supreme Soviet, 1989: 97–105.

G. A. Yagodin (Chairman of the USSR State Committee on Education). Speech at the Nineteenth All-Union Party Conference. *Pravda*, July 2, 1988: 9.

Yakimova. Letter to the editor. In "Tak kak zhe nam obustroiti' Rossiyu?" (So how can we make Russia good for living?). *Komsomol'skaya pravda*, November 23, 1990: 2.

Alexander M. Yakovlev. "Sud-mesto sostyazatel'noe" (Court is a place of competition). *Moskovskie novosti*, November 19, 1989: 12.

——. "Otverzhenie i utverzhdenie" (Rejection and affirmation). *Ogonyok* 43, 1988: 14–16, 29–30.

Alexander N. Yakovlev. "Reformatsiya v Rossii" (Reformation in Russia). *Obshchestvennye nauki i sovremennost*, April 30, 2005: 5–15.

——. "Pervaya barkhatnaya revolutsiya" (The first velvet revolution). *Novoe vremya* 11, 2005: 19–20.

——. *Sumerki* (Dusk). 2nd ed. Moscow: Materik, 2005.

——. *Sumerki* (Dusk). Moscow: Materik, 2003.

——. *Omut Pamiati* (The whirlpool of memory). Moscow: Vagrius, 2001.

——. *Muki prochteniya bytiya* (The torments of reading life). Moscow: Novosti, 1991.

——. "Ob opasnosti revanshisma" Otkrytoe pis'mo kommunistam (On the danger of revanchism. An open letter to the communists), August 16, 1991. In *Muki prochteniya bytiya* (The torments of reading life). Moscow: Novosti, 1991: 341–46.

——. "Akty spravedlivosti i pokoyaniya" (The acts of justice and repentance). A television address, August 20, 1990. In Alexander Yakovlev, *Muki prochteniya bytiya* (The torments of reading life). Moscow: Novosti, 1991: 260–61.

——. "Only Moral Democracy." *Moscow News*, January 1, 1990: 6.

——. "An amended version of the Molotov-Ribbentrop resolution adopted on the 24th of December, 1989." Speech at the Second Congress of People's Deputies, December 24, 1989. The BBC, Summary of World Broadcasts, December 30, 1989, the USSR; Special Supplement; USSR Congress of People's Deputies, Soviet television 1350 gmt 24 Dec 89, p. SU/0650/C/1.

——. "Sud'ba i sovest'" (Fate and conscience). *Ogonyok* 52, 1989: 2.

——. "Sobytiya 1939 goda–vzglyad s poluvekovoy distantsii" (The events of 1939: a view from a distance of half a century). Interview with *Pravda*, August 18, 1989: 1–2.

——. "Rabotat' po sovesti, zhit' chestno" (To work conscientiously, to live honorably). *Pravda*, February 28, 1989: 2.

——. "Perestroika i nravstevnnost'" (Perestroika and morality). *Sovetskaya kul'tura*, July 21, 1987: 2.

——. "Perestroika i obshchestvennoe soznanie" (Perestroika and social conscience). *Pravda*, April 10, 1987: 3.

Egor Yakovlev. "S'ezd i politicheskaya reforma" (The Congress and the political reform). *Moskovskie novosti*, June 18, 1989: 3.

——. "Chetyre dnya. Kak eto bylo" (Four days. This is how it was). *Moskovskie novosti*, July 10, 1988: 3.

Sergei Yakovlev. "Osobaya prichina" (A special reason). *Novy mir,* September 1989: 263.

Stepan Filippovich Yakubov. In "O vremeni, kotoroe vypalo na nashu dolyu . . ." (About the times we have been destined to live in . . .), a collection of readers' letters. *Komsomol'skaya pravda*, January 25, 1989: 2.

Jonathan Yardley. "Reexamining a Neglected Era of Invention and Expansion." *Washington Post Book World*, November 25, 2007: 15.

V. Yaroshenko. "'Printsy' i 'nishchie'" (The "princes" and the "paupers"). *Pravda*, October 12, 1988: 2.

Viktor Yaroshenko. "Partii interesov" (The parties of issues). *Novy mir,* February 1990: 113–41.

O. Yarunina. "K chemu privodit bezdushie" (What callousness leads to). *Trud,* January 19, 1988: 2.

Boris Yeltsin. "V poiskakh soglasiya" (In search of accord). Interview with *Moskovskie novosti*, January 14, 1990: 4.

——. Speech at the Second Congress of People's Deputies, December 17, 1989. *Izvestia,* December 18, 1989: 4.

Sergey Zalygin. "God Solzhenitsyna" (The year of Solzhenitsyn). *Novy mir* 1, January 1990: 233–40.

——. "Nastupaem ili otstupaem?" (Advancing or retreating?). In Yuri Afanasiev, ed., *Inogo ne dano* (There is no other way). Moscow: Progress, 1988: 228–37.

Vladimir Zapetskiy. "I snova: 'Egor, ty ne prav?'" (Again: "Egor, you are wrong?"). *Literaturnaya gazeta*, November 7, 1990: 11.

Tatiana I. Zaslavskaya. "The Correlation between Healthy and Ill Forces Is Not in Our Favor." Interview with Fredo Ariesking, *Demokratizatsiya*, Spring 2005: 297–317.

——. "Eto kakoe-to nervnoe istoshchenie" (It is something like a nervous exhaustion). Interviewed by I. Savvateeva. *Komsomol'skaya pravda*, October 30, 1990: 2.

——. "A Soviet Voice of Innovation Comes to Force." Interview with *New York Times*, August 28, 1987: A6.

——. "Perestroika i sotsologiya" (Perestroika and sociology). *Pravda*, February 6, 1987: 3.

——. "Chelovecheskiy faktor razvitiya ekonomiki i sotsial'naya spravedlivost'" (The human factor in the development of economy and social justice). *Kommunist* 13, 1986: 61–73.

Sergey Zavorotnyi and Petr Polozhevets. "Operatsiya GOLOD" (Operation HUNGER). *Komsomol'skaya pravda*, February 3, 1990: 2.

Alexander Zaychenko. "Imushchestvennoe neravenstvo" (The property inequality). *Argumenty i fakty*, July 8–14, 1989: 5–6.

——. "Kak delit' pirog" (How to divide the pie). *Moskovskie novosti*, June 11, 1989: 12.

——. "SShA-SSSR: lichnoe potreblenie (nekotorye sopostavleniya)" (USA-USSR: personal consumption [some juxtapositions]). *SShA*, December 12, 1988: 12–22.

Mikhail Zhanetsky. "V Yaponiyu i nazad, k sebe" (To Japan and back home). *Izvestia*, September 8, 1989: 5.

Gennady Zhavoronkov. "Zapreshchyonnyi Sakahrov" (The forbidden Sakharov). *Moskovskie novosti*, December 9, 1990: 16.

——. "Posle rasstrela myli ruki spirtom . . ." (After an execution [they] washed the hands with strong alcohol). *Moskovskie novosti*, September 16, 1990: 15.

—— and Igor' Nekrasov. "Stranitsy katn'skoy tragedii" (Pages of the Katyn tragedy). *Moskovskie novosti*, May 13, 1990: 11.

——. "Tayny katynskogo lesa" (The secrets of the Katyn' forest). *Moskovskie novosti*, August 6, 1989: 15.

Anatoly Zhigulin. "Vina! Ona byla, konechno . . ." (The guilt! Of course it was there . . .). Interview with *Moskovskie novosti*, July 31, 1988: 12.

——. *Chyornye kamni* (Black rocks). Part 1, *Znamya*, July 1988: 10–75; part 2, *Znamaya*, August 1988: 48–119.

Leonid Zhukhovitskiy. "Chto pochyom?" (What is the price of this and that?). *Ogonyok* 39, 1988: 4–5.

V. D. Zhulyov. "A Solution for Single Mothers." In Christopher Cerf and Marina Albee, eds., *Small Fires: Letters from the Soviet People to Ogonyok Magazine, 1987–1990*. New York: Summit Books, 1990: 119.

A. Zhuravlev. "K sotsial'noy garmonii" (Toward social harmony). *Argumenty i fakty*, November 4–10, 1989: 1–2.

V. V. Zhuravlev, L. N. Dobrokhotov, and V. N. Kolodezhnyi, eds. *Istoriya sovremennoy Rossii, 1985–1994* (History of modern Russia, 1985–1994). Moscow: Terra, 1995.

Georgiy Zhzhyonov. "Sud'ba naroda i cheloveka" (The fate of the people and of an individual). *Komsomol'skaya pravda*, November 7, 1988: 4.

William Zimmerman. *The Russian People and Foreign Policy: Russian Elite and Mass Perspectives, 1993–2000*. Princeton: Princeton University Press, 2002.

——. "Intergenerational Differences in Attitudes toward Foreign Policy," in Arthur H. Miller, William M. Reisinger, and Vicki L. Hesli, eds., *Public Opinion and Regime Change: The New Politics of Post-Soviet Societies*. Boulder, CO: Westview Press, 1993: 259–70.

Alexander Zinoviev. *Homo Sovieticus*. New York: Atlantic Monthly Press, 1985.

Igor Zolotusskiy. "Solzhenitsyn: krug pervyi" (Solzhenitsyn: the first circle). *Moskovskie novosti*, August 26, 1990: 14.

——. "Krushenie abstraktsiy" (The downfall of abstractions). *Novy mir*, January 1989: 235–46.

N. Zorkaya. "Dorogoy, kotoraya vedyot k khramu" (On the road that leads to the temple). *Iskusstvo kino* 5, 1987: 33–53.

Alexei Zverev. "Bez starshego brata" (Without the Big Brother). *Novoe vremya* 37, 1989: 38–40.

N. Zyat'kov. "Laboratoriya perestroika" (The laboratory of perestroika). *Argumenty i fakty*, January 28–February 2, 1990: 7.

Abalkin, Leonid, 179
abolitionists, American, 55
abortions, 193, 193n
Abramov, Fyodor, 188
Abuladze, Tengiz, 321; *Pokayanie*
  (Repentance), 1–2, 1n, 53, 55
Academy of Agricultural Sciences
  Conference (August, 1948), 245
Academy of Science, Institute of Russian
  Literature, 67
Academy of Social Sciences, Central
  Committee, 65–66
Adamovich, Ales', 41n, 52n, 79, 131, 161,
  233, 275, 321
Afanasiev, Yuri, 41n, 52, 53n, 72, 224,
  229–30, 321
Afghanistan war, 14–15, 66, 251, 253, 288,
  293, 294n
Aganbegian, Abel, 73, 115, 181
age, political attitudes by, 32
agriculture: collectivization of, 105–11;
  excess equipment for, 180; inefficiency
  and waste in, 176–77; Lysenkovism and,
  245–46; non-agricultural enterprises
  involved in, 185–86
AIDS, 120–21

Akhmatova, Anna, 5, 40n, 76, 76n, 256,
  257, 261
Aksel'rod, Pavel, 66
Al'bats, Evgeniya, 85
alcohol, 330; anti-alcohol campaign, 24,
  120; economic significance of, 24, 192;
  as escape, 192; incidence of alcoholism,
  192–93; vodka production during
  1932–1933 famine, 111
Alexander II, 279, 299
alimentary dystrophy, 96
All-Union Center for the Health and
  Safety of Mother and Child, Moscow,
  124n
All-Union Council of Veterans, 170
All-Union Voluntary Historical and
  Educational Society, 229
Amalrik, Andrei, 332n2
Ambartsumov, Evgeny, 62
amenities, housing, 118, 137
American Revolution, 21, 339n53
Amlinsky, Vladimir, 158
Anan'ev, Anatoly, 191, 195, 265, 322
ancien régime, critique of, 21
Andropov, Yuri, 13, 302
Angaeva, Fatimat, 85

Angola, 15
Anninskiy, Lev, 197
anti-alcohol campaign, 24, 120
anti-communist sentiment, 28, 33
Antonescu, Ion, 87, 87n
Antonov, Mikhail, 36, 182, 187
Argumenty i fakty (periodical), 4, 39, 50n, 58, 275
arrests and imprisonments, 76–99; camp/prison conditions, 93–98; of children, 80–82; class as basis for, 86; deportations, 86–89; interrogations and torture, 83–85; of kulaks, 102–4; numbers of, 78–79; of Polish officers, 89; repatriates, 86; revelations of, 78–80; sentencing, 83, 86–87, 97; trials, 79, 84n, 86. *See also* camps, work/prison; violence and repression, state
art, 138
Article 6, Soviet constitution, 284–85
Article 58, Criminal Code of the Russian Federation, 94n, 168, 169
Article 70, Criminal Code of the Russian Federation, 69, 250, 252
Article 190, Criminal Code of the Russian Federation, 38, 69, 69n, 250
Askol'dov, Alexander, *Komissar*, 67, 363n28
Astaf'ev, Viktor, 151, 162
atonement, 52–54, 56, 225–35, 301
Aytmatov, Chingiz, 54

Babel, Isaak, 68
Babitskiy, Konstantin, 250
Baglay, Marat, 322
Bahry, Donna, 345n96
Baikal-Amur Railway (BAM), 173
Bailyn, Bernard, 3n, 5, 339n53
Baklanov, Grigory, 163, 170, 322
Balkars, 88
Baltics, 14
barter, 185–86
Basyubin, Vasily Grigorievich, 234
Basyubina, Svetlana Vasilievna, 234
Basyubina, Tatiana Efremovna, 234
Batkin, Leonid, 113

Beaumarchais, Pierre, *The Marriage of Figaro*, 21
Bek, Alexander, 5, 41n
Bekker, Anatoly, 82–83
Belarusian Railways, 182
Belaya, T., 178–79n
Belov, Vasily, 135, 292
Berenhorst, Georg Heinrich, 290
Berggol'ts, Olga, 238
Beria, Lavrenty, 80–81n, 82, 83, 162n
Berlin, Isaiah, vi, 18, 240
Bessarabia, 87–88
biology, and Lysenkovism, 245–46
black market, 179
Blank, Abel, 67
blocking units, 165–67, 167n
Blok, Alexander, 298
Blyukher, Vasily, 82
Bocharov, Anatoly, 112, 113, 221, 322
Bogoraz, Larisa, 250
Bolsheviks, 154, 214, 298
books, banned, 66–68
Border Guards, 107
Bosporus, 158
Bovin, Alexander, 27, 44, 52, 52n, 322
Boyarskiy, Vladimir, 85
Brauchitsch, Walter von, 154
Breslauer, George, 341n67
Brezhnev, Leonid, 46, 217, 251, 277
Brezhnev Doctrine, 288, 293
bribes, 177
Brinton, Crane, 20, 21, 337n43
Britain, 151, 153, 157
Bronshteyn, Matvey, 77n
Brown, Archie, 332n8
Buber, Martin, 67
Buber-Neumann, Margarete, 158
Bukharin, N. I., 43, 66, 242
Bukharin little school, 242
Bulgakov, Mikhail, 5, 41n, 261; *Sobach'e serdtse*, 42
Bunich, Paul, 221
burial sites and mass graves, 78–79, 85, 89–92, 147, 224–25, 230–31
Burlatsky, Fyodor, 41n, 52, 52n, 132, 276, 277, 322

Burtin, Yuri, 52n, 275, 323
Butenko, A., 208
Bykov, Rolan, 67
Bykov, Vasil', 103
Bykovnya (execution site), 78, 90
Bystrov, A., 198

camps, work/prison: conditions in,
  93–98, 104; deaths in, 94, 96–98, 104;
  doctors in, 95; food in, 95–96; schools
  in, 105. See also German prison camps
canal-digging, 174
cannibalism, 109–10, 168
catheters, 120–21
Catholic Church, 217
cattle cars, 86–87n, 90, 90n, 104, 170
Ceau'eşcu, Nicolae, 209
censorship: lifting of, 37–38, 282–83; of
  literature, 68–69, 255–69; and official
  representations of history, 64–68;
  organization overseeing, 63; topics
  subject to, 64
Center for the Study of Public Opinion,
  32
Central Committee, 106–8, 232
Central Historical Archive, 67
Chaadaev, Petr, 73, 213n, 256, 301
Chamberlain, Neville, 153
change, historical, 17
Chechens, 88
Chekhov, Anton, 56, 75, 264
Chernichenko, Yuri, 41n, 52, 57, 107,
  109–10, 116, 144, 175, 186, 227n, 233, 323
Chernyshevsky, Nikolai, 204, 398n50
child labor, 122, 122n, 123n
children: arrests and punishments of,
  80–82; cannibalizing of, 109–10; deaths
  of, 101, 121, 122, 123; of enemies of the
  state, 82–83; in famine of 1932–1933,
  109–10; healthcare for, 121–26; myths
  concerning, 121–26; scavenging of
  execution sites by, 91–92; working, 122,
  122n, 123n; in work/prison camps, 105
choice, moral, 240–42, 245–47, 274, 297
Chubar'yan, A., 158
Chuchalova, Matryona, 79

Chukovskaya, Lidya, 76–77n, 84n, 323
Churchill, Winston, 101, 152n, 370n11
citizenship, 273, 281
civil and political liberties, 207–8
Civil War, U.S., 298
Cold War, 288
collectivization: agriculture under, 105–11;
  atonement for, 279–80; effects of,
  133–34, 145; and famine of 1932–1933,
  107–11; peasant repression under,
  100–105
command-and-administer system, 133,
  203–5, 283, 295
Commission on Benefits and Privileges,
  141
Commission on the Political and Legal
  Evaluation of the Soviet-German
  Non-Aggression Treaty of 1939, 155
Commonwealth of Independent States, 34
communal apartments, 116–18
communism, tyrannical and despotic rule
  produced by, 208–9
Communist Party: Central Committee,
  40, 106–8, 232; one-party rule, 30–31,
  208, 284
complicity, 52, 300–301
computers, 135–36
Confederation of Labor, 284
conflict, societal, 273–74
Congo, 142
Congress of People's Deputies, 26, 30,
  43–44, 281–84, 289, 292
Connor, Walter, 340n67, 341n68
conscience, de-individualization/
  nationalization of, 217, 219–20
Constituent Assembly, 214, 214n
constitution, 31, 271, 271n, 280, 284
consumer goods, cost of, 128
consumption of goods, 136–38, 142
corruption, 176–77, 182, 204
Cossacks, 106–7
cost of living. See standard and cost of
  living
Council for Mutual Economic Assistance
  (Comecon), 138
Council of People's Commissars, 63, 80

Crimea, 88
Croatia, 303n
Cuba, 12, 66, 294
cult of personality, 200, 207, 213, 214
culture, consumption of, 138
currency, 183–85
Czechoslovakia, 1968 invasion of, 250, 253, 288, 299

daily life, difficulties of, 211. *See also* lines, for goods or services
Dal'story administration, Gulag in northeastern Siberia, 93
Dardanelles strait, 158
Darnton, Robert, 339n57
debating clubs, 43
de-Bolshevization, 297
defense. *See* military and national defense
de-individualization, 211–20
Delone, Vadim, 250
de-militarization, 297
democracy: economy and, 207–8, 278–79; necessity of, for political and economic progress, 285–86; private property and, 278; Russian Revolution (1917) and, 214; Russian Revolution (1987–1991) and, 274–75, 285–86; state control as incompatible with, 207
Democratic Russia, 283
democratization: importance of, 24; introduction of, 23; and morality, 48–49; perestroika and, 25–26; public perception of, 50n
demonstrations, 28–29, 347n111
de-mythologization, 45–46, 74, 114. *See also* legitimizing myths
deportation and exile, 86–89, 100–105, 107
de-Stalinization, 52–53, 146, 288, 301
dignity, 37, 191–92, 253, 258, 265
Dimitrov, Georgi, 154n
dissidents, 14, 15, 66, 69, 73, 253
Dombrovsky, Yuri, 5, 77, 223, 247, 257–58, 258n; *Fakul'tet nenuzhnykh veshchey* (The department of useless things), 57, 65n, 84n, 85, 201n, 240, 257–58

Dostoevsky, Fyodor, 56, 303
Dranga, Mariya Stepanovna, 77
Dremlyuga, Vladimir, 250
Drobko, A., 71
drugs, medical, 120
Druzenko, Anatoly, 132, 270
Druzhba narodov (journal), 4, 42
Dudinskaya, K. A., 234
Dudintsev, Vladimir, 5, 41n, 323; *Belye odezhdy*, 53, 218n, 245–47
Durkheim, Emile, 343n96
dysentery, 96
Dzerzhinsky, Felix, 302

east-central Europe, 2, 11, 12, 15, 30, 33–34, 155n, 288–89, 297, 298, 422n61
economy: barter in, 185–86; Communist foundation of, 277n; consumption as portion of, 142; corruption and, 176–77, 182, 204; criteria for measuring success of, 174, 276; democracy and, 207–8, 278–79; freedom and, 277–79, 277n; inefficiency and irrationality of, 172–86, 206–7; labor in, 179–82; market-driven, 31, 276–77, 279; Marxian theory of, 16; military vs. civilian sectors of, 291; money in, 183–85; morality and, 179, 181–82; myth of progress concerning, 133–36; NEP, 25, 133, 203; overproduction in, 179–81; plans and rules governing, 173–77, 203; political character of, 206–7, 277; prices in, 183; public opinion on, 31, 349n133; shortages in, 177–79, 183, 202–3; Soviet collapse and, 13–14; state ownership of, 202–9, 276–80; transformation of, 276–80; unnecessary work in, 179–82
Edelman, Marek, 240n
education: college attendance, 138; in prison camps, 105; spending on, 122
Efremov, Oleg, 270
Efroimson, Vladimir, 246
Eidelman, Natan, 41n, 72–73, 323
Eideman, R., 163n
elderly, financial situation of, 128–29

elections: first fully democratic, 297n; public opinion on, 283–84, 348n119; results of, 28, 346n104

Ellwood, Charles A., 335n34

employment, public opinion on, 350n134

environment, industrial degradation of, 134–35

equality: before the law, 208, 274, 282; myth of, 139–41

Esenin, Sergei, 231n

Estonia, 26, 48n, 86, 86–87n, 154

Ethiopia, 15

Etkind, A., 198

Evtushenko, Evgeny, 74, 171, 216, 223–24, 233, 237, 261, 323

executions: arbitrariness of, 85–86; descendants of victims of, 231; mass, 93; methods of, 90–93; of officials, 152, 159; of peasants, 105–7; of Polish officers, 89, 303, 303n; prisoner behavior leading to, 93–95; of Red Army officers, 162–63, 163n, 169; of soldiers, 165; under Stalin, 66, 78–79, 85; of writers, 68. See also burial sites and mass graves; violence and repression, state

exploitation, 141–46, 205–7

extermination camps, 93

Ezhov, Nikolai, 76n, 83, 85

Fadeev, Alexander, 262

families: attachment to state substituted for, 218–19, 218n; size of peasant, 101

famine (1932–1933), 101, 107–11

fascism, 152n

fear, 46, 193–94, 227

Fedorov, Svyatoslav, 324

Feinberg, Viktor, 250

Feldman, B., 163n

Feoktistov, Konstantin, 273, 285

fifty-eighths, 94, 94n

files. See secret files

Finland, 158

Fish, Steven, 336n35, 343n96

food: availability of, 114–16, 140; cost of, 137; inequalities concerning, 140–41;

peasants', 144; in prison camps, 95–96. See also famine (1932–1933)

food lines, 114, 115n, 212

food subsidies, 183

forces of production, 16

foreign policy, 288–89, 292–95, 299–300, 352n158, 422n61

forests, 175–76

France, 151, 153, 157

freedom: choice and, 240–42, 245–47; citizens' spirit of, 237–54, 406n1; destruction of, 214–16; and the economy, 277–79, 277n; literature and, 255–69; moral renaissance and, 56–58; negative, 240; Russian Revolution (1987–1991) and, 304

freedom of association, 283

freedom of expression. See freedom of speech

freedom of speech, 30, 43, 247, 283

freedom of the press, 53, 247–48, 283, 349n128

French Revolution, 19, 21, 297–98, 338n53

Frinovsky, Mikhail, 107

fruits, 176–77

Fukuyama, Francis, 49

Furet, François, 12, 339n53, 346n98

future, emphasis on, 213, 213n

Fyodorov, Svyatoslav, 41n, 229, 233

Gabon, 142

Gaidar, Egor, 297n, 337n35

Ganina, Maya, 188

garrison state, 289, 295

Gefter, Mikhail, 61

Geller, Yuri, 162n

Geneva Convention, 89, 168

Georgia, 14

German, Alexei, 255

German prison camps, 168. See also camps, work/prison

Germany, and Great Patriotic War, 151–71. See also Nazism

Ginzburg, Alexander, 250–51

Ginzburg, Arina, 251

glasnost, 36–59; beginnings of, 23, 53; history of term, 37n; history unveiled by, 72; literature and, 4–5, 245; and moral renaissance, 48–49, 211; *Pokayanie* and, 1, 53; political prose of, 4; significance of, 50n; troubadours of, 49–59, 301, 321–30; and truth, 37–38

Glavlit, 63, 67

Goebbels, Joseph, 220

Gogol, Nikolai, 213n; *Viy*, 53–54

golden childhood myth, 121–26

Goldstone, Jack, 17, 336n35

Gooding, John, 345n96

Gorbachev, Mikhail, 1n, 6, 11, 12, 22–25, 49, 50n, 54, 156, 340n67, 342n85; and democratization, 25, 48; elected president of the Soviet Union by the Congress of People's Deputies, 283; and freedom of the press, 42; and the morality of reform, 23, 24; and the nature of liberalization, 22, 50, 271; and the nature of Russia, 63; and the politics of reform, 24; popularity of, 28; pressures on, 27; and the Soviet defense budget, 289; and the "Soviet model," 24; and Stalinist repression, 25; and violence, 25; and Yeltsin, 299; and executed Polish officers, 303

Gorbanevskaya, Natalya, 250

Goskomstat, 64

Gossnab, 203

Govorukhin, Stanislav, 129, 130, 135, 187, 324

Gozman, L., 198

GPU/NKVD, 88

grain harvests and exports under collectivization, 105–11

grain imports, 135

Granin, Daniil, 5, 41n, 192, 247, 291, 292, 324

gray market, 185

Great Patriotic War, 151–71; de-mythologization of, 152–53, 170–71; German invasion in, 159–61, 163; German-Soviet relations in, 152–58; Grossman on, 265–66; inspirational and heroic actions in, 238–39; myth of, 151–52; Soviet casualties in, 162, 162n, 164–68, 164n; Soviet military strategy in, 158–62; Soviets taken prisoner in, 167–70

Great Purge (1937), 158, 257, 265

Greenblatt, Stephen, 264

Grossman, Vasiliy, 5, 41n, 67, 99, 100, 171, 199–200, 207, 214–16, 236, 238–41, 247, 263–70; *Forever Flowing*, 266–67; "V gorode Berchive," 363n28; *Vsyo techyot*, 109, 215; *Zhizn' i sud'ba* (Life and fate), 42, 53, 57, 65, 65n, 68, 79, 84, 193, 201, 215, 215n, 238–39, 247, 263–69, 268n, 300

Gudzenko, Semyon, 238

guilt, 227–28

Gukasov, Grant, 232n

Gumilyov, Lev, 76n

Gumilyov, Nikolay, 40n

Hahn, Gordon, 336n35

handicapped, financial situation of, 129–30

harvesters, 180

healthcare: for children, 121–26; short-comings of, 119–21

hecatomb, peasant, 100–105

Hegel, G.W.F., 133

Helsinki Accords, 275

Helsinki Group, 250

Herbert, Zbigniew, 300, 304–5

heroism. *See* inspirational and heroic actions

Herzen, Alexander, 299

Herzl, Theodore, 67

historical materialism, 16

history: inevitability and contingency in, 17; official representation of, 64–68, 303; recovery of, 71–75, 223–35; sources of change in, 17. *See also* memory

Hitler, Adolf, 153–54, 156, 158, 159, 160, 162, 163

Hollander, Paul, 346n100

Homo faber, 190, 205

Homo Sovieticus, 48, 188–91, 205

hospital conditions, 119–20, 124–26
Hough, Jerry, 345n96
housing: cost of, 137; legitimizing myth
of, 116–19; workers', 139, 147
Hoxha, Evner, 209
human rights, 26, 31, 251, 253, 275, 275n
humans and human life: de-
individualization, 211–20; dependence
of, on state, 207, 273–74; economic
transformation emphasizing, 276–80;
emphasis on, in Russian Revolution
(1987–1991), 270–86; responsibility,
216, 274; state in relation to, 272–76,
281–82; value of, 216, 218, 253–54.
See also individual rights and liberties;
moral degradation; values and
morality
Hungary, 288, 299
Huntington, Samuel P., 343n96
Hussein, Saddam, 12
Huxley, Aldous, Brave New World, 41n,
64–65

ideas: of American Revolution, 339n53; of
French Revolution, 338n53; revolutions
and social change predicated on, 18–22;
of Russian Revolution, 22–35, 340n67,
351n149; of Soviet regime, 345n98
ideology, 27, 30–32
imperialism, 288, 292–93, 299
imports, 135
income, 126–30, 136, 141–42, 181–82
individual rights and liberties: destruction
of, 214–16; private property and, 207–8;
Russian Revolution (1987–1991) and,
275; state usurpation of, 207–8. See also
de-individualization; human rights;
moral degradation
industrialization: and defense industry,
289–91; environmental degradation
from, 134; imports necessary for, 135;
inefficiency and irrationality in, 133–35,
172–86, 207; plans and rules governing, 173–77; unnecessary production in,
179–81
informers, 247

Ingush, 89
innocence, presumption of, 83–84, 208,
282
inspirational and heroic actions, 237–54
intelligentsia, 42, 165
international law, 293
interrogations and torture, 83–85
Iraq, 12
Ivanovo province, 86
Ivan the Terrible, 298
Izhevsk, 66
Izvestia (periodical), 4, 39, 65, 72, 73

James I, 21
The Jewish Question in the Communist
Movement, 68
Jews: control of information about,
67–68; persecution of, 249; in political
office, 152n
Johnson, Chalmers, 335n34
Johnson, Samuel, 51
journalists, servility of, 70
Jowitt, Ken, 332n8
judges, 282

Kafka, Franz, The Castle, 65n
Kaganovich, Lazar, 106
Kalinin, Mikhail, 244n
Kalistratova, Sofya, 250
Kalmyks, 88
KamAZ, 43
Kamenev, Lev, 81–82
Kamenev, Yuri, 81–82
Karachai, 88
Karaganda metallurgical plant, 173
Karamzin, Nikolai, 72–73
Karkach, Andrei, 149
Karpinsky, Len, 52, 52n, 72, 324
Karyakin, Yuri, 41n, 52n, 222, 233, 324
Katyn (execution site), 89–92, 303, 303n
Kennan, George, 11–12
KGB (national security agency), 89,
148–49, 231–32, 263, 280–81, 281n
Khandzhyan, Agasi, 80–81n
Khanin, Grigoriy, 41n
Khodasevich, Vladislav, 40n, 68

Khodorovich, Sergei, 251
Khodorovich, Tati'ana, 251
Khomeini, Ruhollah, 294n
Khrushchev, Nikita, 13, 24, 46, 51, 53, 54, 78, 136, 146–47, 200, 225, 264, 265, 299
Khudenko, Ivan, 182
Kirillov, Nikolai, 169
Kirov, Sergey, 86
Kistyakovsky, Andrei, 251
Kiva, Alexey, 112, 132, 197, 287, 325
Klimov, Petr, 91
Klyamkin, Igor, 1n, 43, 45, 49, 71, 74, 198, 221, 300, 325
Klyuchevsky, Vasily, 204
Klyuev, Nikolai, 231n
Kobulov (NKVD deputy chief), 87n
Kochetkov, E. S., 36
Kolesnik, Vladimir, 77, 224
kolkhoz activists, 102
Kolpashev, 231n
Kolyma, 96, 97, 224, 258
Kommunist (periodical), 4
Komsomol'skaya pravda (periodical), 4, 40, 46, 89, 124, 144, 150, 178n, 194–95, 208, 212, 251, 272, 274, 278, 283, 290, 292, 295, 303
Kondrashov, Stanislav, 66, 218, 294, 294n, 325
Kondrat'ev, Vycheslav, 164, 300; "Parii voyny," 167n
Konika, L., 83
Kontorovich, Vladimir, 333n20, 334n27
Kork, A., 163n
Korolenko, Vladimir, 277n
Korotich, Vitaly, 57, 61, 325
Koryakin, Yuri, 52
Kostomarov, Nikolai, 298
Kosygyn, Alexei, 299
Kotkin, Stephen, 334n27
Kotlas-Vorkuta railroad, 97
Kotlyar, Leonty, 160
Kozlov, Frol, 147
Krasnoyarks, 232
Krivorotov, Viktor, 61
Kryuchkov, Kolya, 144
Kulakov, V. I., 123n, 124

kulaks. See peasants
Kulish, Vasily, 163
Kurds, 88
Kuropaty (execution site), 78, 85, 91
Kuvaldin, Viktor, 304

labor: experiments concerning, 182; Homo Sovieticus and, 188–91; lack of skilled, 180; state control leading to degradation of, 204–5, 209; unnecessary and wasted, 179–82, 191
Lakshin, Vladimir, 37, 42n, 264
land, de-nationalization of, 279
Landa, Mal'va, 251
Laptev, Ivan, 52
Latsis, Otto, 41n, 325–26
Latvia, 26, 48n, 86, 154
Lavrov, Kirill, 190
law: citizens in relation to, 28n, 282; equality before, 208, 274, 282; international, 293; reform of, 282; state in relation to, 208, 28n, 282
law on five ears of wheat, 106
Lazarev, Lazar', 300, 406n1
legitimizing myths, 112–71; children, 121–26; de-mythologization and, 45–46; equality, 139–41; exploitation, 141–46; food, 114–16; Great Patriotic War, 151–71; healthcare, 119–21; housing, 116–19; impact of, 44–45; necessity of, 113–14; Novocherkaask massacre, 146–50; poverty, 126–30; progress, 133–36; standard and cost of living, 136–38; state of workers and peasants, 138–46
Lenin, Vladimir: ancestors of, 67; and de-individualization, 215; on ethics and morality, 217; highest value for, 219n; Marxist vision of, 207; NEP initiated by, 25; and October Revolution, 66, 154; saga about, 67
Leningrad, 28
letters from readers, 40, 58, 114, 150, 194–95
Levada, Yuri, 29, 43n
Levin, Bernard, 332n2
Levitansky, Yuri, 223

liberalism, 279
liberties. *See* civil and political liberties
life expectancy, 120
Likhachev, Dmitry, 54, 223
lines, for goods or services, 178–79, 178n, 184, 192, 212. *See also* food lines
Lisichkin, Gennady, 52, 52n, 61, 181–82, 326
literary ("thick") magazines, 40–42, 53
literature: arrests and murders of authors, 68; censorship of, 68–69; demand for, 40–42; freedom and, 255–69; glasnost and, 4–5, 245; political and social concerns of, 255–56; publishing of, 138; Russian tradition of, 57; state-sanctioned, 69. *See also* political prose
Literaturnaya gazeta (periodical), 4, 39, 117, 126n, 166, 233n, 252
Lithuania, 14, 26, 33, 48n, 86, 154
Litvinov, Maxim, 152, 152n
Litvinov, Pavel, 250
logging, 175–76
Louis XVI, 19, 21
Lysenko, Trofim, 245–46
Lysenkovism, 245–46

Macaulay, Thomas Babington, 53
magazines. *See* literary ("thick") magazines; periodicals
Makeev, Sergey Ivanovich, 234
Malia, Martin, 12, 345n98
man. *See* humans and human life
Mandela, Nelson, 298
Mandel'shtam, Nadezhda, 300
Mandel'shtam, Osip, 40n, 68, 70, 256–57, 257n, 261, 300
Mao Zedong, 12, 209
market economy, 31, 276–77, 279
Martem'yanov, Ivan Mikhailovich, 234
Martov, Yuli, 66
Marx, Karl, 16, 142, 202, 293; *Communist Manifesto*, 277n
Marxism: de-individualization grounded in, 212–13; eschatology and millenarianism of, 213; glasnost essayists and, 202; and progress, 133; state power grounded in, 207

mass graves. *See* burial sites and mass graves
maternity hospitals, 125–26
Mau, Vladimir, 336n35, 340n67
McFaul, Michael, 335n35
meat, availability of, 114–16
media, state in relation to, 282–83
medical equipment shortages, 119–21, 123–24
medications, 120
Medvedev, Dmitry, 303
Medvedev, Roy, 79, 101
Mekhlis, Lev, 164
Memorial, 229
memorials and monuments, 229, 233–35
memory, 224–35, 294, 301–2
Merton, Robert, 27, 113
Meskhetian Turks, 88
Migranyan, Andranik, 279
Mikoyan, Anastas, 106, 147
Mikutskaya, Krysya, 90
Mikutskiy, Eugeniush, 90
military and national defense: de-militarization, 297; distrust of, 165; equipping of, 159, 290; executions of officers of, 162–63, 163n; extent of, 290–91; people's volunteer corps and, 164–65; prisoners of war, 167–70; public opinion on, 33; reformers' view of, 288; revelations about, 289, 291; secrecy about, 288–90; spending on, 33, 289–92, 289n, 295, 351n152; surviving officers of, 163; treatment of soldiers in, 194–95
military march wives, 166
Milyukov, Pavel, 66
Ministry of Agriculture, 175
Ministry of Non-Ferrous Metals, 185
Ministry of Water Industry (*Minvodkhoz*), 174, 207
Minvodkhoz. See Ministry of Water Industry
Mochalova, Natal'ya Kirilovna, 99, 103
modernization, Peter the Great's, 204
Moldavia, 176
Molodya Gvardiya (periodical), 41n

Molotov, Vyacheslav, 102, 106, 152, 152n, 157, 158

Molotov-Ribbentrop Pact (Soviet-German treaty, 1939), 26, 48n, 86, 151, 153–56, 154–55n, 288, 302

money, 183–85

monuments. *See* memorials and monuments

Moore, Barrington, 17

moral degradation: abortion, 193; alcoholism, 192–93; bad work habits, 190–91; cruelty, 194–95; deception, 189–90; de-individualization, 211–20; deprivation of dignity leading to, 191–92; as effect of economy, 188–91; extent of, 46; fear, 193–94; *Homo Sovieticus*, 48, 188–91, 205; imperialism and, 293; as impetus to perestroika, 23; participation in Stalinism as source of, 228; perestroika as antidote to, 47; slave mentality, 194; state control resulting in, 187–95, 210–20, 281, 298–99; symptoms of, 46; theft, 189–90

morality. *See* values and morality

moral renaissance, 47–49, 299, 301–2, 304

Mordyukova, Nonna, 67

Moscow Institute of History and Archives, 232

Moskovksie novosti (periodical), 1n, 4, 38, 40, 58, 63, 74, 79, 85, 89n, 114, 141, 142, 158, 169, 170, 233n, 234n, 235, 254n, 283, 290, 303

museums, 138

music, 138

myth-making. *See* legitimizing myths

Nabokov, Vladimir, 41n, 68; *Priglashenie na kazn'*, 65n

Nagibin, Yuri, 192

Nash sovermennik (periodical), 41n

national defense. *See* military and national defense

National Interest (journal), 12

nationalists, Soviet repression of, 14

Nazism, 201, 239–40, 240n, 265, 302

Nazi-Soviet Non-Aggression Pact (1939), 26, 48n

needles, hypodermic, 120–21

Neer-Genschke, Karole, 82–83

NEP. *See* New Economic Policy

Neumann, Heinz, 158

NEVZ. *See* Novocherkassk Electric Locomotive Construction Plant

New Economic Policy (NEP), 25, 133, 203

newspapers. *See* periodicals

N. I. Bukharin Club, 43

Nicaragua, 15

Nicholas I, 75, 256

Nikitinsky, Leonid, 293

Nikulin, Yuri, 233

NKVD (People's Commissariat for Internal Affairs), 76–98, 80n, 87n, 107, 165, 169, 231, 232, 300

noninterference policy, 293

North Atlantic Treaty Organization (NATO), 290

North Caucasus, 106

North Korea, 12

Novikov, Vladimir, 221

Novocherkaask Electric Locomotive Construction Plant (NEVZ), 146, 149, 251–52

Novocherkaask massacre, 146–50, 251–53

Novoe vremya (periodical), 4

Novy mir (periodical), 4, 41, 42, 81, 214n, 299, 303

nuclear weapons, 33, 294

nurses, 119

nurse's aides, 119, 124

Nuykin, Andrei, 41n, 52n, 141, 326

objective factors in revolution and social change, 17

obstetrics, 121–26

October Revolution, 214

off-the-records, 86

Ogonyok (periodical), 4, 40, 47, 58, 66, 72, 78, 88, 94, 115, 117, 124, 140, 163, 191, 225, 226, 228, 229, 233–34, 233n

OGPU (political police), 107, 232, 244n

Oktyabr' (periodical), 4, 41, 57, 145, 263
one-party rule, 30–31, 208, 284
On Friendship and Borders (Soviet-German treaty, 1939), 157, 157n
Order 227, 165–66, 168n
Order 270, 168–69, 168n
Organization for Security and Cooperation in Europe, 302
orphanages: for children of imprisoned/executed enemies of the state, 82; conditions in, 122n
Orwell, George, 217; *Animal Farm*, 41n; *1984*, 53, 64–65
Oryol prison, 83
Osmyslit' kul't Stalina (essay collection), 300
Osoboe Soveshchanie (OSO), 84n, 97, 245
Ozerlag, Taishet, 258

paper-making, 176, 176n
parliamentarianism, 207–8
passports, 281
Pasternak, Boris, 40n, 41n, 257, 261; *Doktor Zhivago*, 42, 68
patriotism, 73
Paulus, Friedrich, 239
Pavlenko, Nikolai, 162, 162n
Pavolvskiy posad, 135
peasants: and agriculture under collectivization, 105–11, 144; arrests of, 102–4; casualties among, 101, 225, 370n12; executions of, 105–7; exploitation of, 143–45; and famine of 1932–1933, 101, 107–11; freedom for, 280; land ownership by, 279–80; living conditions of, 143–45; repression of, 100–105, 200–201, 225, 227n; size of families of, 101; status of, 138–46; taxes on, 144–45
pediatrics, 121–26
pellagra, 96
penal battalions, 80n, 166–67
pensions, 128–29
people's volunteer corps, 164–65
perestroika: democratization and, 25–26; foundation of, 23; and moral reform, 47; and personal responsibility, 274;

politics and morality joined in, 275; and symbolic politics, 24
periodicals, 4, 38–43, 72. *See also* literary ("thick") magazines
Peter the Great, 204
Petrakov, Nikolai, 183, 185
Pil'nyak, Boris, 68
Pincus, Steve, 3n
Pipes, Richard, 12
Piyasheva, Larisa, 182
Platform of the Ryutin Group, 242–43
Platonov, Andrei, 5, 41n, 260–63; *Chevengur*, 65n, 262; *Kotlovan*, 42, 68, 262
Plenum of the Central Committee, 1n
Pokayanie (film), 1–2, 1n, 53, 55
Poland, 15, 26, 48n, 86, 89–90, 154, 156–57, 303, 303n
police. *See* secret police
political participation, 43–44, 275, 283
political prisoners, 94, 94n
political prose: censorship of, 69–70; demand for, 38–43; of glasnost, 4. *See also* literature
political values, 30–33
Pol Pot, 209
Ponedelin, Pavel, 169
Popkova, Ludmila, 41n
Popov, Gavriil, 28, 29, 41n, 52n, 285, 326
Popov, Vladimir, 131, 134, 177, 178n, 326
Popper, Karl, 279
potatoes, 177
poverty, 126–30, 143–44
power: arbitrariness of, 142–43; privileges based on, 140–41, 183–84
Pravda (periodical), 4, 40n, 101, 102, 116, 129, 156
Prelovskaya, I., 237
Presidium, 147
Presidium of the Supreme Soviet, 185
prices, 183
Primakov, Evgeniy, 289n
Primakov, V., 163n
prison camps. *See* camps, work/prison; German prison camps
prisoners of war, 167–70

Pristavkin, Anatoly, 5, 41n, 123n, 326–27; *Nochevala tuchka zolotaya,* 53

Private property, 3, 191, 279; and democracy, 207, 208; and Marxism and Leninism, 207, 209, 213, 277n; and technological revolution, 277; and totalitarianism, 207, 209, 213, 278

privatization, 270–86, 297

privileges, based on political connections, 140–41, 183–84

production quotas, 174–75

progress, 133–36

property. *See* private property

public opinion: on defense spending, 351n152; on democracy, 50n; on the economy, 31, 349n133; on elections, 283, 348n119; emergence of, 29–34; on foreign policy, 352n158, 422n61; on freedom of the press, 349n128; on ideas behind reform, 351n149; on labor and employment issues, 350n134; on political process, 348n122; on reform, 296n; on Stalin, 303; study center for, 347n117

publishing, 138

Pugachev (major), 241–42

Pumpyansky, Alexander, 52

Pushkin, Alexander, 56, 86, 258, 303

Putin, Vladimir, 299, 302, 303n

Putna, V., 163n

Pyatakov, Georgy, 66

Pye, Lucian, 344n96

Rabotnitsa (periodical), 124, 125

Radek, Karl, 66

Rákosi, Mátyás, 209, 288

Rapoport, Natasha, 249–50

Rayfield, Donald, 80–81n

Razgon, Lev, 233

Reagan Doctrine, 15

reconnaissance-by-attack, 80n, 166–67, 167n

Red Army, 66, 78, 88, 107, 156, 158, 162, 238–39, 262

Red Cross, 168

Red Square Seven, 250

Red Star (periodical), 238, 262

reinstatement, 242

relations of production, 16

renorming, 49, 304

repatriates, 86

repentance, 229, 294, 301–2

resident permits, 281

responsibility, personal, 216, 274

retreat, prohibition of, 165–68

revolutionary crises, 17, 20

revolutions: from above, 3, 22; from below, 3, 27–29; crises precipitating, 17, 20; eschatological character of, 213n; ideals underpinning, 2, 271, 297–98; ideational factors in, 18–22; mechanics of change in, 21–22; metaphysical underpinnings of (*see* ideational factors in); modern, 3, 3n, 18; moral issues underlying, 23; motivations behind, 52; objective factors in, 17–18, 20; origins of, 3, 37; pace of, 53; restorations following, 297–98; shortfalls of, 297; theories of, 16–22; timing of, 19

Ribbentrop, Joachim von, 154

rights, public opinion on, 31. *See also* human rights; individual rights and liberties

"road to the temple," 1–3, 1n, 55,221,271

Rousseau, Jean-Jacques, 339n53

Rozhdestvensky, Robert, 194

Ruble, Blair, 346n105

Rudenko, Inna, 218

Rumania, 86, 158

Rush, Myron, 340n67

Rushdie, Salman, 294n

Russian Revolution (1987–1991): causes of, 18–19, 343n96; culmination of, 28–29; ideational factors in, 22–35, 340n67, 351n149; moral issues underlying, 2, 23–27, 55–56, 296; opposition to, 5; origins of, 3; pace of, 31–32; restoration following, 298–304; structural factors in, 18; unexpectedness of, 11–16; urgency of, 54, 57

Rutland, Peter, 14

Rybakov, Anatoly, 5, 327; *Deti Arbata*, 41n, 42n, 53, 81–82, 219n
Rychagov, Pavel, 163n
Rykov, Alexei, 242
Ryutin, Martimyan, 242–44
Ryzhkov, Nikolai, 23, 24, 120, 135, 192
Ryzhov, Yuri, 185, 290, 291

Sabinin, Dmitry, 246
sabotage, 94, 106
Sakharov, Andre,41n, 253–54, 254n, 255, 271n, 280–81, 284–85, 293, 299, 327; and the call for a national strike, 284; exile of, 14; and the First Congress of People's Deputies, 44; and foreign policy, 292; and glasnost, 49, 253; and the KGB, 292; and liberty, 253, 271; and morality in society, 5, 46, 49, 57, 253; patriotism of, 253; and pensions, 128; and perestroika, 41n; posthumous tributes to, 253; on science and technology, 135; and Stalinism, 198; and terror, 57
Sakhnin, Arkady, 72
salaries. *See* income
sanitary norm, 117
Saraskina, Ludmila, 106
schools, 105
scientists, resistance of, 245–47
scurvy, 96
secrecy: about foreign policy, 294; about military and defense, 288–90; about Russian/Soviet history and politics, 64–68, 303
secret files, 65, 231–32, 303
secret police, 143, 280–81
self-deception, 44–46, 50, 74
self-examination, 50–51, 57–58, 61–63, 68, 73, 225, 301–2
Selyunin, Vasiliy, 41n, 52, 62, 71–72, 131, 142n, 144, 205, 207, 208, 210, 218, 277, 283, 327
sentencing, 83, 86–87, 97
Serbia, 303n
Sewell, William, 18, 338n53

Shaginyan, Marietta, *The Ulyanov Family*, 67
Shalamov, Varlaam, 5, 41n, 96n, 197, 247; *Kolyma Tales*, 57, 65n, 96, 236; *Kolymskie rasskazy*, 53
Shaposhnikov, Matvey, 147, 252–53
Shataling, Stanislav, 292
Shatrov, Mikhail, 75, 233
Shchapov, Fedya, 80–81
shestidesyatniki (people of the 1960s), 51
Shevardnadze, Eduard, 23, 275, 289, 291, 293, 294n
Shilov, Kirill, 110
Shindel', Alexander, 188, 255
Shmelyov, Nikolai, 52, 52n, 127n, 131, 134, 172, 177, 178n, 203, 291, 327; "Avansy i dolgi," 41n
shortages of goods, 177–79, 183, 202–3
show trials, 244
Shtern, Grigory, 163n
Shubkin, Vladimir, 46–47, 48–49, 52n, 79, 201, 299, 304, 327–28
Shur, M., 63
Siberia, 258
Simiryaga, Mikhail, 159
Simonyan, Rayr, 132, 270
Sirotkin, Vladlen, 287
Siuda, Petr, 149, 251–52
Skocpol, Theda, 17, 337n36
slavery, as metaphor for Russian citizenry, 45, 47, 55–56, 194–95, 209, 216. *See also* workers: dependence of, on state
SMERSH military counterintelligence, 165, 169, 247
Smirnov, Konstantin, 36
Smolensk (execution site), 91
Smushkevich, Yakov, 163n
Sobchak, Anatoly, 28, 279
socialism, repudiation of, 28
Socialist realism, 69
Solidarity, 15
Solovki Islands, 93
Solovyov, Georgy, 248–49
Solzhenitsyn, Alexander, 68, 70, 146–50, 164n, 168, 171, 247, 258–60, 278, 287, 292, 293; *Arkhipelag Gulag*, 68, 81,

Solzhenitsyn, Alexander (continued)
250; *One Day in the Life of Ivan
Denisovich*, 146, 169, 200, 241, 247,
259; *Rakovyi korpus*, 68; *V kruge
pervom* (In the first circle), 68, 165n,
170, 214n, 242, 246n
Solzhenitsyn Fund, 250
Sorge, Richard, 159
souls. *See* humans and human life; moral
degradation; values and morality
South Africa, 298
Southern Bukovina, 158
Sovetskaya kul'tura (periodical), 4
Sovetskaya molodezh (periodical), 154n
Sovetskaya Rossiya (periodical), 40n
Soviet-German treaty (1939). *See* Molotov-
Ribbentrop Pact
Soviet Union: challenges and problems of,
12–15; collapse of, 11–16, 296; economy
of, 13–14; ideational factors in, 345n98;
mythology of, 113–14; political situation
in, 14; public opinion on, 33–34; the
state, its power and extent, 199–209, 217.
See also legitimizing myths; state
specially resettled peoples, 88–89
Speransky, Mikhail, 37n
spirit of freedom, 237–54
spirituality (*dukhovnost'*), 44n, 217
Stalin, Joseph, 12, 209, 277n; after
October Revolution, 214; burial place
of, 225; citizens' criticisms of, 242–43,
244n, 248–49; and collectivization, 105;
coming to terms with, 223–35; cult of
personality around, 200, 207, 213, 214;
executions under, 66, 78–79, 85, 152;
and Great Patriotic War, 151–70, 154n,
157n, 162n; highest value for, 219n; and
literature, 257, 261; NEP ended by, 25;
and peasants, 101, 370n11; popular
understanding of, 51–52; repression of
peasants by, 101; reputation of, 303; and
revolution from above, 345n98; on
workers, 202
Stalinism, 6; arrests, imprisonments, and
executions during, 76–98; collectivization under, 105–11; coming to terms with,

223–35, 300–304; complicity in,
300–301; essence of, 200, 218; in foreign
policy, 288–89; and Great Patriotic War,
151–71; hatred of, 51–52; and imperialism,
293; literature during, 256; moral
degradation resulting from, 46; Nazism
compared to, 201, 265, 302; peasants'
treatment under, 100–105; perpetrators
of, coming to terms with, 227–28, 228n
standard and cost of living, 136–38
Starikov, Evgeny, 126n
Starkov, Vladislav, 328
Starodubrovskaya, Irina, 336n35
state: "Asian" character of, 202,
209; conflict in, 273–74; and de-
individualization, 211–20; economy
owned and controlled by, 202–9, 217,
276–80; garrison state, 289, 295;
individuals in relation to, 272–76,
281–82; law as constraint on, 208;
media in relation to, 282–83; morality
and values determined by, 217–19, 274;
political transformation of, 280–81,
283–85; power and extent of, 199–209,
217; repressive measures of, 201; role
of, 31; workers in relation to, 204–9
State Committee for Prices, 183
state of workers and peasants, 138–46
stealing, 190
Stolitsa (periodical), 4
St. Petersburg, 28
Strategic Defense Initiative (SDI), 15
Strelyaniy, Anatoly, 41n, 52n, 174, 328
strikes, 28, 116, 138–39, 140, 146–47,
284–85
structural analysis, 334n30
structuralism, 16–20, 334n30, 335n35,
337n36
Struve, Petr, 66
subsidies, food, 183
Suleymenov, Olzhas, 101–2
Supreme Court, 148–49, 303; Traveling
Military Collegiums, 232n
Supreme Soviet, 248–49, 282, 284;
Committee on Science, 289; Interre-
gional Group of Deputies, 280, 284–85

survivors' stories, 226
Suslov, Mikhail, 264
Sverdlovsk, 115
Svetov, Felix, 251
Svirsky, V., 73
syringes, 120–21

Taishet, 258
TASS news agency, 160
Tatars, 88
taxes: on peasants, 144–45; turnover tax, 183
telephones, 136
Terent'eva, Zoya, 118
Terletsky, Gena, 148
textbooks, 65, 72, 73, 245
"thaw," under Khrushchev, 46, 54, 68, 200, 263, 265, 299
theft, 190
"thick" magazines. See literary ("thick") magazines
Thomas, W. I., 113
Thomas theorem, 27, 113
Tiananmen Square incident, 294n
Tikhonov, Vladimir, 279n
"till the first blood" rule, 166
Tilly, Charles, 17
Timofeev-Resovsky, Nikolai, 246–47, 246n
Tocqueville, Alexis de, vi, 19, 21–22, 213n, 297–98, 304, 337n41, 337n43, 338n53
Tolbukhin (general), 164
Tolstoy, Alexei, 248
Tolstoy, Leo, 56, 75, 242, 264
Tomilina, Natasha, 249–50
Tomsky, Mikhail, 242
torture. See interrogations and torture
totalitarianism, 199, 207, 226, 227, 240n, 261, 266, 278, 288, 293, 300
tractors, 180
traitor peoples, 86–88
transitologists, 337n41
Traveling Military Collegiums, Supreme Court, 232n
Treaty of Non-Aggression. See Molotov-Ribbentrop Pact
Tret'yakov, Vitaly, 55n

trials: reform of, 282; show, 244; under Stalinism, 79, 84n, 86
Trilling, Lionel, 68, 68n
Trotsky, Leon, 66
troubadours of glasnost, 49–59; biographies of, 51, 321–30; mission of, 50, 54–56, 301; as moralists, 49, 54–56; motivations of, 51–54; as "teachers of truth," 54–58; urgency of, 54–55, 57
Trud (periodical), 40n
truth, 36–39, 44, 50–51, 56–57, 74, 146, 247, 304
"Truth about Jews" (brochure), 68
Tsvetaeva, Marina, 41n
Tsypko, Alexander, 45, 74–75, 112, 190, 192, 270, 302
Tukhachevsky, M., 163n
turnover tax, 183
Tvardovsky, Alexander, 41n, 218–19; Po pravu pamyati, 53, 64, 73, 82
Twentieth Congress myth, 78–79
Tyutchev, Fyodor, 50

Uborevich, I., 163n
Ukraine, 14, 33, 106
Ulam, Adam, 16
Ul'yanov, Mikhail, 233
unemployment, 206
Union of Architects, 229
Union of Cinematographers, 229, 233n
Union of Composers of the Russian Federation, 233n
Union of Theater Workers of the Russian Federation, 229, 233n
Union of the Laborers of Kuzbass, 284
United States: abolition of slavery in, 55; Civil War, 298; revolution in, 21; Russian post-collapse foreign policy involving, 299–300
universal values, 274
urbanization, and social/political change, 343n96
Ustinov, 66
Uzbekistan, 88

values and morality: anti-imperialistic sentiments, 293; choice and, 240–42, 245–47, 274, 297; daily life struggles and degradation of, 211–12; democracy and, 274–75; and the economy, 179, 181–82; foreign policy and, 293–94, 294n; as foundation of society, 48; inspirational and heroic actions demonstrating, 237–54; loss of, 187–95; memory linked to, 302; political, 30–33; reform of, 36–37; renaissance in, 47–49, 299, 301–2, 304; and revolutionary change, 20–21; Russian Revolution (1987–1991) and, 2, 23–27, 54–56, 296; Stalinism's effect on, 300–301; state control leading to corruption of, 203–5; state determination of, 217–19, 274; traditional, 217–19, 274; universal, 274
Vasilevsky, Alexander, 163
Vasilevsky, Andrey, 224
Vasiliev, Boris, 47, 55, 71, 171, 298
Vavilov, Nikolai, 246
vegetables, 176–77
Vek XX i Mir (periodical), 4
Vienna Conference on Security and Cooperation in Europe (1989), 275
Vinogradov, Igor, 38, 74
violence and repression, state: and de-individualization, 216–17; extent of, 201, 212; and foreign policy, 288; Gorbachev's aversion to, 25; and imperialism, 293; peasants subject to, 100–105, 200–201; rejection of, 276; routine, 218; Stalin and, 101, 153. *See also* arrests and imprisonments; executions
Vladimir, Prince of Kiev, 45
Vlasov, Yuri, 201, 281, 285, 328
vodka, 111
Vodolazov, G., 197
Volga Germans, 88
Volovets, Sergei, 295
Vorkuta basin miners' strike, 284
Voronezh high school students, 244–45
Voroshilov, Klement, 81n, 153
Voschshanov, Pavel, 101

Voskresensky, Lev, 237
Voznesensky, Andrei, 69n; "In a maternity hospital," 124n
VPK (military-industrial complex), 289–91
Vysotksiy, Vladimir, 41n, 69n

Wall of Memory, 233–35
Warsaw Ghetto uprising (1942), 240n
Warsaw Pact, 33, 290, 422n61
water, in living quarters, 118, 139
Weber, Max, 16, 188, 338n48
Week of Conscience, 233–35, 233n, 234n
Wehrmacht, 156, 159–61, 163
welfare expenditures, 142
Western Belorussia, 154
Western Ukraine, 154
work. *See* labor
work camps. *See* camps, work/prison
work collectives, 179, 190
workers: dependence of, on state, 189, 204–7 (*see also* slavery, as metaphor for Russian citizenry); exploitation of, 141–43, 205–7; housing of, 139, 147; industrial vs. agricultural, 378n10; negligence and irresponsibility of, 188–91, 204–5; Novocherkaask massacre of, 146–50; place of, in Soviet state, 202; status of, 138–46; wages of, 142, 142n
working conditions, 139
World War II. *See* Great Patriotic War
Writers' Union, 262

Yakir, I., 163n
Yakovlev, Alexander, 52, 328–29; on democracy, 274; on Molotov-Ribbentrop treaty, 26, 48n, 155–56; on peasant repression, 225; on perestroika, 25–27, 271; on Sakharov, 253; on the state, 199; on state-citizen relationship, 272; on truth, 37–38; on values, 36, 48, 220, 342n87
Yakovlev, Egor, 44n, 52, 52n, 329–30
Yearbook of the Manuscript Section of the Pushkin House, 67
Yeltsin, Boris, 3, 28, 280, 284, 297n, 299, 303, 354n162

Young Pioneers, 8in
Yunost' (periodical), 233n
Yurasov, Dmitry, 233n

Zalygin, Sergei, 55, 56, 61, 330
Zamyatin, Evgeny, *My*, 41n, 64, 68
Zaslavskaya, Tatiana, 126n, 183n, 340n67,
    349n133
Zaychenko, Alexander, 137, 141, 330, 378n10
Zaytsev, Sergei Alexeevich, 234
Zhabotinsky, Vladimir, 67
Zhigulin, Anatoly, 228n, 245

Zhukov, Georgy, 162n
Zhvanetsky, Mikhail, 132–33
Zhzhyonov, Georgiy, 46, 229
Zinov'ev, Grigory, 66
Zinoviev, Alexander, 189
Zionism, 67
Znamya (periodical), 4, 41, 50, 58, 73, 79,
    144, 145, 263, 265
Zolotusskiy, Igor, 255, 330
Zolotya Gora goldmine (execution site),
    78–79
Zorkaya, N., 224